Holbrook

Little Colorado River

N E W
M E X I C O

FORT APACHE
INDIAN RESERVATION

WHITE
MOUNTAINS

Carrizo Creek

(North Fork)

(East Fork)

Fort
Apache

White
River

Black River

Fort
Bayard

WARM SPRINGS
INDIAN
RESERVATION

SAN CARLOS
INDIAN RESERVATION

Old
San Carlos

Gila River

STEIN'S
RANGE

Lordsburg

Deming

Fort
Bowie

CHIRICAHUA
INDIAN
RESERVATION

San Pedro River

M E X I C O

Scale in miles

0   50

George Skoch

EYEWITNESSES TO THE INDIAN WARS, 1865–1890

ALSO BY PETER COZZENS:

No Better Place to Die: The Battle of Stones River

This Terrible Sound: The Battle of Chickamauga

The Shipwreck of Their Hopes: The Battles for Chattanooga

The Civil War in the West, A Trilogy

The Darkest Days of the War: The Battles of Iuka and Corinth

The Military Memoirs of General John Pope

General John Pope: A Life for the Nation

EYEWITNESSES TO THE INDIAN WARS, 1865–1890

The Struggle for Apacheria

EDITED BY PETER COZZENS

STACKPOLE
BOOKS

Copyright © 2001 by Stackpole Books

Published by
STACKPOLE BOOKS
5067 Ritter Road
Mechanicsburg, PA 17055
www.stackpolebooks.com

Printed in the United States of America

10 9 8 7 6 5 4 3 2 1

FIRST EDITION

Library of Congress Cataloging-in-Publication Data

Eyewitnesses to the Indian Wars, 1865–1890 / edited by Peter Cozzens.— 1st ed.
    p. cm.
  Includes index.
  Contents: v. 1. The struggle for Apacheria
  ISBN: 0-8117-0572-2
  1. Western Apache Indians—Wars. 2. Chiricahua Indians—Wars.
3. Indians of North America—Wars—1866–1895. 4. Crook, George, 1829–1890.
5. Geronimo, 1829–1909. I. Cozzens, Peter, 1957–

E99.A6 E94 2001
973.8—dc21

                                      00-052270

To the memory of my father
JAMES WHITE COZZENS (1917–83)

CONTENTS

PART ONE:
Raids and Reprisals in Apacheria, 1865–72

PART TWO:
Crook's Tonto Basin Campaign and After, 1872–78

PART THREE:
Uprisings and Unrest, 1878–83

PART FOUR:
The Sierra Madre Campaign and After, 1883–85

PART FIVE:
Chasing Geronimo, 1885–86

PART SIX:
The End of the Apache Wars

ILLUSTRATIONS

Maps

PREFACE

Eyewitnesses to the Indian Wars, 1865–1890: The Struggle for Apacheria is the first volume in a planned five-volume series that will tell the saga of the military struggle for the American West in the words of the soldiers, noncombatants, and Native Americans who shaped it. Future volumes will be devoted to conflict in the Northwest and the Rockies, on the Southern Plains and in Texas, and on the Northern Plains. A fifth volume will include accounts of a general nature.

It is the purpose of this volume to present as complete a selection of outstanding original accounts pertaining to the struggle for that part of the Southwest once known as Apacheria as may be gathered under one cover. Most of the accounts presented here are taken from contemporaneous newspapers and magazines—a wealth of primary source material, much of which has remained unknown not only to the general reader, but also to serious students and historians of the Indian Wars.

In reviewing items for possible inclusion, I quickly found there to be no shortage of material from which to draw. Indian actions were front-page news nationwide. The Indian Wars in general, and the Apache wars in particular, were a source of constant fascination for eastern readers of the day. The desert Southwest was a new and strange land, with a native populace and a climate most Americans scarcely comprehended. Magazine editors were eager to run stories of army exploits, hostile depredations, Indian scouts, and the Apache way of life (as the white man understood it) that army officers submitted to supplement their meager pay and their wives penned to alleviate the tedium of life at godforsaken posts. Civilian Indian agents, prominent Arizonans and New Mexicans, and general officers like George Crook and Oliver O. Howard granted interviews and penned articles to explain their actions or to influence public opinion. In later years, a whole literature grew up around the pursuit and capture of Geronimo alone.

Several considerations have guided my choice of material for inclusion in this volume of *Eyewitnesses to the Indian Wars.* The events described must have taken place between the end of the Civil War and the tragedy at Wounded Knee. With but few exceptions, the articles were published during the authors' lifetimes. Articles published within the last fifty years have not been included, as they are for the most part readily available. Also excluded were many fine accounts that later appeared in book form, most notably a series of articles that Lt. John Bigelow, Jr., penned from the field during the Geronimo campaign for the March 1886 through April 1887 issues of *Outing* magazine, and which were reprinted as *On the Bloody Trail of Geronimo* (Los Angeles: Westernlore Press, 1958).

Besides articles of relatively recent vintage, I also rejected those that were of dubious reliability, regardless of how prominent their authors may have been. Notable in this category are six wildly inaccurate articles that former Indian agent and publisher of the famed *Tombstone Epitaph*, John P. Clum, penned for the *Arizona Historical Review* and the *New Mexico Historical Review* in his declining years. These are entitled "Victorio," "Eskiminzin," "Geronimo," "The Apaches," "The San Carlos Indian Police," and "Apache Misrule."

Manuscript sources account for a small but historically significant portion of the contents of this volume. I could not ignore the 124-volume diary of Capt. John G. Bourke, which arguably constitutes the greatest single primary source for the study of the post-Civil War American West. An able soldier, close observer, and accomplished scholar, Bourke faithfully recorded everything to which he was exposed during fifteen years of service on the frontier. First as an officer in the 3rd U.S. Cavalry, then as aide-de-camp to General Crook, Bourke participated in many of the crucial events of the Apache wars. Portions of his diary dealing with his ethnological work and related travels in the Southwest were reprinted in the *New Mexico Historical Review* in the 1930s. Annotated selections on his combat service and on General Crook's conferences with Indians in the field are presented here for the first time.

A third source of material was military reports, both official and unofficial, considered sufficiently important that their authors or the War Department had them published outside of normal channels. Among such documents are General Crook's *Resume of Operations against Apache Indians, 1882–1886*, which he had published as a rebuttal to the War Department's implied criticism of his handling of the Geronimo surrender; Lt. Col. John Green's report of a scout among the White Mountain Apaches that resulted in the establishment of Camp Apache; and Maj. William R. Price's report of a scout among the Havasupai and Hualapai Indians, which drew attention to their impoverished state and led to a relocating of the Havasupai reservation.

In the accounts presented in this volume, there is an unfortunate but unavoidable imbalance between white and Native American sources. Most of the few Apache narratives that exist were gathered in book form previously. Outstanding among them are the collected accounts of several Apache warriors and women in Keith H. Basso, ed., *Western Apache Raiding and Warfare, from the Notes of Grenville Goodwin* (Tucson: University of Arizona Press, 1971); engagingly written and reliable is Jason Betzinez's *I Fought with Geronimo* (Harrisburg, PA: The Stackpole Company, 1959). Invaluable for the Apache perspective are Eve Ball's *In the Days of Victorio* (Tucson: University of Arizona Press, 1970) and *Indeh, an Apache Odyssey* (Provo, UT: Brigham Young University Press, 1980). Despite the paucity of Native American sources, I am pleased to offer the compelling words of several prominent Apaches, recorded faithfully by John G. Bourke as they were uttered during conferences with General Crook after the Cibicue affair.

A few words about editorial practice in this first volume of *Eyewitnesses to the Indian Wars* are in order. My goal has been to present accurate and annotated texts of the articles, letters, and reports included in this work. I added notes to correct errors of fact, clarify obscure references, provide historical context where needed, and offer translations of Spanish terms. Editing of text has been light. Most nineteenth-century writers had a penchant for commas. I have eliminated them where their overuse clouded the meaning or impeded the rhythm of a sentence. I have regularized capitalization, punctuation, and the spelling of names and places; otherwise, I have left the writings largely as I found them.

ACKNOWLEDGMENTS

Being abroad on a diplomatic assignment with the Department of State, I found it particularly challenging to gather the articles and other primary accounts presented in this volume. Without the persons mentioned below, whose help I am pleased to acknowledge, it would have been impossible.

First, I thank my mother for her many trips to the Wheaton, Illinois, Public Library, submitting OCLC requests, and retrieving articles; my sincere thanks go also to the staff of the periodicals department of the Wheaton Public Library for their patience and diligence in filling these requests.

My good friend and collaborator on the *Military Memoirs of John Pope*, Robert I. Girardi, also obtained for me copies of several of the articles appearing in this volume.

I also thank Kim Frontz of the Arizona Historical Society, Tucson, who kindly provided me with manuscript material from the society's archives, as well as copies of newspaper and magazine articles from their holdings; Nan Card of the Rutherford B. Hayes Presidential Library, who provided me with microfilm copies of the John Bourke Diary made from that library's filmed set; Brian J. Kenny of the Denver Public Library, for copies of articles from the *Great Divide*; and Bonnie Hardwick of the Bancroft Library, University of California–Berkeley, for a copy of L. Y. Loring's "Report on Coyotero Apaches."

Much of the material presented here I obtained during several visits to the Newberry Library in Chicago. The reference staff of that institution was most helpful on every occasion.

I express my gratitude to the Arizona Historical Society, the Bancroft Library of the University of California–Berkeley, and the United States Military Academy Library for permission to reprint material from their manuscript collections.

I am indebted to Edwin Sweeney, the preeminent authority on the Indian Wars of the Southwest and on Apache-Anglo relations, and to Scott Forsythe of the National Archives for their penetrating and well-considered critique of the historical introduction. They saved me from several embarrassing errors of fact and of questionable interpretation. Any remaining errors are of course my own.

I am also grateful to my copyeditor, Joyce Bond, for her careful editing and constructive suggestions.

Finally, I thank my editor at Stackpole, Leigh Ann Berry, for her enthusiastic support of this project.

INTRODUCTION

Stretching from the Colorado River to the rugged mountains east of the Rio Grande, and from the great canyons of northern Arizona deep into the Mexican states of Chihuahua and Sonora, is the region once known as Apacheria. Its dominant Native American occupants first called themselves *Dine*, meaning "the people," and later, in the days of their demise, *Indeh*, or "the dead." History has labeled them Apache, perhaps from the Zuni word for "enemy." The Apaches were not a cohesive tribe, but rather a loose conglomeration of groups and bands. In addition to being of the same Athapascan language stock, all Apaches engaged in raiding as a means of subsistence and a cultural imperative. They were not, however, intrinsically warlike, as many nineteenth-century whites would have us believe, but were driven to prolonged conflict first by Spanish incursions and, later, by Mexican and Anglo treachery. Products of a harsh and cruel habitat, they were well adapted to resist encroachment on the lands they claimed.

Anthropologists have divided the Apaches into two great divisions, the Eastern and Western. Beyond that, designations have been the subject of exasperating differences of opinion. Among the Western Division were the two principal groups, or classifications, that composed the Apache population of Apacheria—the Western Apaches and the Chiricahuas.

The Western Apaches occupied much of eastern Arizona and are generally agreed to have consisted of the White Mountain, Cibicue, San Carlos, Southern Tonto, and Northern Tonto groups, each with its component bands.

The Chiricahuas are usually divided into three bands: the Central Chiricahuas (Chokonen), who inhabited the Chiricahua and Dragoon mountains of southeastern Arizona and of whom Cochise was the most famous chief; the Southern Chiricahuas (Nednhi), who roamed the northern reaches of Sonora and Chihuahua, Mexico, made the Sierra Madre their stronghold, and with whom were associated Geronimo and Juh; and the Eastern Chiricahuas (Chihenne), who occupied the country from the Arizona-New Mexico border to the Rio Grande. A fourth band, which Apache sources identify as the Bedonkohe and which looked to Mangas Coloradas for leadership, apparently was absorbed into the other three bands after his death.

The Eastern Chiricahua sometimes divided into the Mogollones, who dwelt near the mountains of the same name, and the Mimbres, also known as the Warm Springs or Ojo Caliente Apaches, whose dominant leader after the Civil War was Victorio. However Geronimo, Jason Betzinez, and the Chiricahua informants of Eve Ball regarded the Mogollones as Bedonkone peoples. East of the Rio Grande roamed the Mescalero Apaches, with whom the eastern band of Chiricahuas maintained friendly relations. The eminent historian of

Apacheria, Dan L. Thrapp, estimated the Western Apaches and Chiricahuas to have numbered approximately six thousand during the two decades following the Civil War.[1]

From Prescott, Arizona, westward to the Colorado River, the dominant hostile tribe was the Yavapai; the northwestern corner of Apacheria belonged principally to the Hualapai. Both were Yuman tribes linguistically unrelated to, but generally enjoying good relations with, their Western Apache neighbors. Hereditary enemies of the Apaches, and well disposed toward Europeans, were the Maricopas, the Papagos, and the Pimas, agricultural tribes of the Gila River region.

By the time the first Americans ventured into Apacheria in the 1820s, the Western and Chiricahua Apaches had been warring with interlopers—first Spaniards and later Mexicans—and their Indian allies for nearly two centuries. Confounding troops, laying waste to haciendas, and levying tribute on villages, the Apaches had rendered the European presence in Apacheria tenuous at best. In 1835, desperate Mexican authorities began offering bounties for Apache scalps. Two years later, American bounty hunters slaughtered a group of friendly Southern Chiricahuas under Juan Jose Compas, the first act in a gradual but unmistakable deterioration of what previously had been amicable Anglo–Apache relations.

General conflict became inevitable when the United States obtained much of Apacheria under the Gadsden Treaty, ratified in 1854, the conditions of which obligated Washington to prevent Apache raids into Mexico. This the Apaches could not comprehend: The Mexicans were their enemies and had been the enemies of the Americans; why, then, should they desist from raiding south of the border as long as they behaved themselves north of it? Tensions mounted. The discovery of gold, which the Apaches regarded as a metal sacred to their creator, Ussen, and not to be removed from the earth—first in southwestern New Mexico and later near Prescott, Arizona—brought whites in increasing numbers into Apacheria. Tragedy followed upon tragedy with brutal inevitability. Treaties were made and broken, reservations created and abandoned.

The discovery of gold at Pinos Altos, in the heart of the Eastern Chiricahua homeland, exacerbated tensions. Seeking to avoid hostilities Chief Mangas Coloradas spread stories of richer bonanzas to be found in Sonora. Belligerent and bullying, the miners stayed on. Already wary of the United States ascendancy in the region, and of increasing governmental interference with his bands, Mangas Coloradas went to war in 1861—a bloody rampage that claimed hundreds of American and Mexican lives.

Even more egregious was the treatment accorded the chief of the Central Chiricahuas, Cochise. His people had lived at peace with the whites; Cochise apparently had even secured a contract to supply wood for the Butterfield Stage Line station near Apache Pass. But a blundering second lieutenant named George H. Bascom changed all that when, in February 1861, he enticed

Cochise and several warriors to his camp, then arrested them on the mistaken impression the Chiricahua chief had stolen cattle and kidnapped a boy from a Sonoita Valley ranch. Cochise protested that marauding Pinal Apaches had perpetrated the outrages and offered to help Bascom find them. Bascom tried to hold the Apaches hostage for the boy's return, but Cochise escaped and took four hostages of his own. After several days of fruitless parleying, Cochise killed his hostages and Bascom hanged the Chiricahuas, among whom was Cochise's brother.

Whereupon Arizona exploded in a decadelong orgy of violence. Historian Thomas Farish calculated that Cochise's fury eventually cost "five thousand American lives and the destruction of hundreds of thousands of dollars worth of property." Indian agent John P. Clum asserted that the U.S. government spent $38 million between 1862 and 1871 in an effort to extirpate the Apaches. Fewer than one hundred Apaches were killed, however, at a cost of more than one thousand civilians and soldiers.[2] The calculations of Farish and Clum are disputable, but it is true that no traveler, settler, miner, small body of troops, or ranch was safe from the Chiricahuas.

The onset of the Civil War and consequent withdrawal of Federal troops from the territory convinced the Apaches and other hostile bands that the Americans had given up the fight, and their raiding escalated. Most settlements were abandoned, and Tucson sank to fewer than two hundred inhabitants. Conditions were equally chaotic in southern New Mexico, where Mangas Coloradas held sway.

To reassert its authority, the government sent a brigade of California volunteers under Brig. Gen. James H. Carleton into Apacheria. Cochise and Mangas Coloradas contested Carleton's march through Apache Pass in a bold but unsuccessful ambush on July 15, 1862. Erecting Fort Bowie to hold the pass, Carleton pressed on to Santa Fe. There he inaugurated a campaign to exterminate the Apaches, employing fast-moving columns of soldiers, miners, local partisans, and Indian allies to seek out the enemy. Under Carleton's auspices, Mangas Coloradas was lured in and murdered, a group of Pinal Apaches (a band of the San Carlos group of Western Apaches) were deceived into parleying and then slaughtered at Bloody Tanks, and a large Apache "rancheria," or village, was wiped out in the Tonto Basin by Prescott-based frontiersmen under King S. Woolsey. But the mustering out of the California volunteers in late 1864 created a power vacuum, and raiding resumed with greater fury throughout the territory.

As the Californians went home, local companies sprang up among the mostly Mexican residents of Tucson and nearby settlements. The Arizona volunteers made several good kills before they were disbanded in the autumn of 1866. A group of angry locals from the Prescott area called the Yavapai County Rangers also hunted Apaches and Yavapais for a few months before a lack of pay and supplies compelled them to disband.

Not only could civilian fighters not solve the Indian problem, but they also often exacerbated it. Indeed, many army officers not unreasonably accused the local populace of provoking war, often for purely monetary gain. Said one frustrated department commander, "Almost the only paying business the white inhabitants have is supplying the troops. . . . Hostilities are therefore kept up with a view to protecting inhabitants, most of whom are supported by the hostilities." A case in point were the Hualapais. Before 1866 there had been no Indian trouble of consequence in northwestern Apacheria. But the senseless murder at Beale's Springs that year of Wauba-Yuba, the most influential Hualapai chief, by a party of prospectors with whom he had expected to trade goods peaceably, touched off a two-year war. Prescott was besieged and the surrounding country overrun with war parties. Matters were little better elsewhere in the territory.

During the remainder of the decade (1866–69), army efforts to pacify Apacheria failed for several reasons. First, there were too few troops for both garrison duty and the endless scouts that seemed the only means of catching the elusive Apache raiders. Dozens of posts were created and abandoned in response to specific threats, the growth or demise of frontier communities, the ease or difficulty of supply, and considerations of health. Not until 1867 were volunteers wholly replaced with regulars, and two more years passed before the latter reached a paltry strength of two thousand men. Morale was low and desertion common.

A second problem was the military beaucracy itself. A general reorganization of the army on July 28, 1866, divided the United States into a confusing tapestry of divisions, departments, and districts. Responsibility for Apacheria fragmented: New Mexico became a district in the Department of the Missouri, and Arizona was carved into four separate districts of the Department of California.

Army doctrine posed a third problem. Nothing in their training or in their Civil War experience had prepared the officers or enlisted men who garrisoned the far-flung posts of Apacheria for guerrilla warfare over terrain as foreign and forbidding as a lunar landscape.

The inability of the army high command to settle on an Apache policy complicated affairs further. For instance, after a year of particularly brutal raids in northern Apacheria, in early 1867 Maj. Gen. Irvin McDowell, commander of the Department of California, promulgated a policy of vigorous warfare against the Yavapais and Tonto Apaches. No sooner did the commander of the District of Prescott, Brig. Gen. J. I. Gregg, move to comply, issuing orders that all Indians not found on reservations be treated as hostile, than McDowell relented. He concluded that wholesale war against Indians starving because of congressional and Indian Bureau negligence was inhuman. Later that year General Gregg himself became a proponent of pacific methods. In 1869 a new commander of the Department of California, Maj. Gen. E. O. C. Ord, first ordered his troops to hunt down the Apaches as they would wild animals; less than a week later, he reversed himself and suggested the Apaches be induced onto reservations. Maj. Gen. Henry Halleck, commander of the Military Division of the Pacific, had little constructive to offer his subordinates, arguing simply that nothing could be done without more troops.

In 1867 Maj. Roger Jones, inspector general of the Military Division of the Pacific, submitted a report sharply critical of the military administration in Arizona. He suggested that troops be concentrated at fewer posts, scouts be better coordinated, and infantry be mounted to help the overtaxed cavalry. Most importantly, he insisted that Arizona be elevated to the status of a separate department to eliminate the three months' time it took for orders to pass among the four territorial district headquarters and department headquarters in San Francisco. Not until April 15, 1870, however, did the War Department act on Jones's recommendation, creating the Department of Arizona under the command of Bvt. Maj. Gen. George Stoneman. By setting up headquarters on the coast of southern California, Stoneman promptly negated part of the organizational gain.

Despite a chaotic command structure, uncertain policies, and a shortage of troops, the army recorded some successes between 1866 and 1870, particularly in northern Apacheria. In November 1866 Capt. George B. Sanford and a troop of the 1st U.S. Cavalry smashed a rancheria deep in the Sierra Ancha. In April 1867 Capt. James M. Williams and eighty-five troopers of the 8th U.S. Cavalry destroyed a rancheria on the Verde River, killing fifty warriors in two fights. More impressive yet were the efforts of Maj. William R. Price, who in September 1867 started three columns of troops from Fort Mojave on an expedition to subdue the Hualapais. Eleven months of fighting followed before the Hualapais surrendered in August 1868 and agreed to remove to a reservation.

In Southern Apacheria, an impetuous young first lieutenant, Howard B. Cushing, punished Cochise's warriors and allied Aravaipa and Pinal bands in several sharp engagements—or slaughtered helpless women and children, as the Apaches told it—before blundering into an ambush in May 1871.[3] Across the territorial line in New Mexico, the army recorded only 33 engagements and 92 Apache casualties in the four years following the Civil War, compared with 137 combats and 647 Indians killed in Arizona.

As raids continued with unabated fury, General Stoneman announced his program in July 1870. Army camps were to be concentrated and civilian settlers were to organize for their own defense, thus freeing up troops to conduct aggressive field operations. However, little progress was made against the hostiles during the remainder of the year. In March 1871 Stoneman added a pacific element to his policy that had unintended tragic consequences. Rather than punish a number of hostile Pinals and Yavapais who had come to camps Verde and Grant to make tentative peace overtures, he elected to control them "through the medium of their bellies." Requisitioning huge stocks of meat, corn, and blankets, he announced that all who remained at peace would be rationed at "feeding stations." Several weeks earlier, the Aravaipa band of Eskiminzin had drifted into Camp Grant after securing a promise of kindly treatment from the commanding officer, Lt. Royal E. Whitman. By early March nearly five hundred Aravaipas had gathered under Whitman's protection. They cut hay and chopped wood for the army and hired themselves out to local ranches at harvest time.

Finding their chief means of livelihood endangered, army contractors made common cause with settlers, territorial press, the legislature, and the governor to discredit the system of Stoneman and Whitman. When depredations resumed near Camp Grant, subtle intriguers falsely proclaimed Eskiminzin's band responsible. At dawn on April 30, 1871, a group of Tucsonians and Papago Indians fell on the peaceable chief's sleeping rancheria, murdering scores of Apaches, mostly women and children.

The Camp Grant massacre had two fundamental consequences for Apacheria. First, at the insistence of Gov. Anson P. K. Safford, General Stoneman was replaced in May by George Crook, who brought with him a reputation as a no-nonsense Indian fighter of the first order. Crook conferred with his subordinates and leading civilians, toured the length of his command, and concluded that the Apaches must first be thrashed before a lasting peace could be secured. To do so, he would employ highly mobile commands consisting of cavalry units to fight the hostiles, mule trains to feed the troops, and friendly Indian scouts to locate the enemy. An expedition organized from Camp Apache under Capt. Guy V. Henry in July 1871 successfully tested Crook's methods, as the scouts not only proved loyal, but also were instrumental in locating a rancheria that the soldiers then cleaned out.

Crook planned five more such expeditions, to operate continuously until all hostiles were driven in or exterminated. Before he could outfit them, Crook was ordered to suspend military operations until a peace commission from the East first visited the Apaches.

The second great consequence of the Camp Grant massacre had been a decision to allow eastern humanitarians to try to conquer Apacheria through kindness—or "mesmerize the Apaches into peace," as frontier detractors put it. Two years earlier, Congress had authorized the president to organize a board of Indian commissioners to assume the duties of the corruption-plagued Office of Indian Affairs. President Ulysses S. Grant warmly supported efforts to correct past abuses, and he went Congress one further by accepting a recommendation of the executive committee of the Orthodox Friends that religious men be appointed as Indian agents and peace commissioners. Before the Camp Grant massacre, conditions in Apacheria had not been judged propitious for testing what had become known as the "Quaker Policy," or "Grant's Peace Policy." But in the wake of that outrage, Congress appropriated $70,000 "to collect the Apache Indians of Arizona and New Mexico upon reservations and to promote peace and civilization among them." The board of Indian commissioners gave the task to Vincent Colyer, a former Union colonel of impeccable humanitarian credentials.

Colyer worked swiftly. Arriving at Camp Apache on September 2, 1871,

he designated a vast surrounding area as a reservation and held a peace conference with the White Mountain Apaches. From Camp Apache, Colyer traveled
to Camp Grant, where he confirmed the existing reservation. At Camp Verde
on October 2 he acceded to Yavapai demands that they be permitted a reservation along the Verde River. After conferring with Crook, who characterized the
commissioner's peace with the Apaches as so much empty "humbug," Colyer
departed.

No sooner did Colyer reach Washington than a new wave of Indian depredations swept the territory, in part because Colyer's efforts had failed to extend
to Cochise. When the press reported the November 5, 1871 ambush of a stagecoach near Wickensburg, Arizona, in which six whites were killed, among
them Frederick W. Loring of Massachusetts, a promising young writer, eastern
public opinion swung against Colyer's peace plan. The war faction stepped
forward. From the commanding general of the army, William T. Sherman,
came official assurances that Crook would be "warmly supported in rigorous
aggressive operations." Pleased to learn of the "decapitation of Vincent the
Good," and anxious to act before others could "pop up in his place," Crook
prepared for a winter campaign. While he completed his plans, Crook gave all
Indians in the territory until February 15, 1872, to report to a reservation.

But the peace advocates were not finished, and before Crook could begin
his campaign, they induced the administration to restrain him. Grant appointed
Brig. Gen. Oliver O. Howard to travel to Apacheria as a special agent of the
Department of the Interior, with authority to "cooperate with the military" in
preserving peace.

Crook held his command in check while, during April and May 1872,
Howard retraced Colyer's steps. Howard made peace between the Aravaipa
Apaches and their Pima and Papago enemies and moved the Camp Grant
reservation to the Gila River, contiguous with the White Mountain agency,
renaming it San Carlos. But Howard failed, as had Colyer before him, to make
peace with Cochise. Consequently, President Grant asked him to make a second trip for that express purpose, which Howard did in the autumn of 1872.
Enlisting the help of Thomas J. Jeffords, a longtime friend of Cochise, Howard
entered the chief's Dragoon Mountains stronghold. Howard and Cochise concluded an agreement permitting the Chiricahuas a loosely administered reservation in the Chiricahua Mountains with Jeffords as their agent, thereby
ending a decade of warfare.

But elsewhere raiding and reprisals continued. Between September 1871
and September 1872, while the peripatetic Colyer and Howard had journeyed
from band to band with their overtures of peace, the Apaches and Yavapais conducted at least fifty raids, killing more than forty civilians and running off over
five hundred head of cattle. During the first eleven months of 1872, the army
engaged in thirty-three actions against the marauders, in which ten soldiers and
another twenty-six civilians lost their lives. That many of the raiding parties
came from the new reservations was indisputable. Before he left the territory,

Howard conceded to Crook that only force could bring lasting peace. Official Washington concurred, and Crook was at last free to unleash his offensive.

The plan Crook had spent sixteen months of forced inactivity perfecting called for a winter campaign, when food was scarce and the hostiles could more easily be starved or frozen—if not fought—into submission. The objective was to force them into the inner recesses of their preferred sanctuary, the Tonto Basin, by striking first at their outlying haunts. Nine troop-strength columns of the 1st and 5th Cavalry, each with a detachment of Indian scouts, would then penetrate the basin itself. Crook himself would ride from point to point around the narrowing perimeter. His instructions to column commanders were unequivocal and simple: accept the surrender of all Indians who wished to give up; hunt down and exterminate warriors who insisted on fighting, sparing women and children; enlist prisoners as scouts when possible; and under no circumstances abandon the trail—the campaign must be short, sharp, and decisive.

Which it proved to be. In the winter clashes that followed, nearly two hundred Indians perished. The most stunning reverse came on December 28, 1872, when the commands of Maj. William H. Brown and Capt. James Burns and their Indian auxiliaries joined forces to decimate a large band in a stronghold above the Salt River known as Skull, or Salt River, Cave. Seventy-six hostiles died; no soldiers were killed. Skull Cave weakened hostile morale; the destruction on March 27, 1873, of a rancheria atop Turret Peak, a site the Indians considered impregnable, broke their resistance. Hundreds streamed into the agencies and army camps to surrender.

On April 6, 1873, Crook met with Chalipun, a war chief of the Yavapais, to accept his surrender. Crook made Chalipun a pledge he repeated to every Native American leader who ever capitulated to him, and which he did his utmost to keep: that if Chalipun "would promise to live at peace and stop killing people, he [Crook] would be the best friend he ever had." By that autumn, more than six thousand Apaches and Yavapais had enrolled at Indian agencies throughout Apacheria.

But war parties under Chunz, Cochinay, Chan-deisi, and Delshay roamed free, and in the spring of 1874 Crook launched an offensive to eliminate them. The army enjoyed success nearly as complete as it had in the Tonto Basin campaign. The hostile bands were decimated in several sharp actions and their leaders killed.

For two years, Crook and his officers ruled the Camp Verde, Grant, and Apache reservations in fact, if not in form, feeding and protecting their wards and encouraging their efforts at farming and stock raising. Civilian officials complained of army usurpation of their prerogatives, but the prestige Crook enjoyed in Washington and his unique influence over his Native American charges kept the Indian Bureau at bay. Not until 1875, after Crook was transferred to the Department of the Platte and the Apaches and Yavapais were concentrated at the San Carlos Agency, did civilian agents reassert their authority.

In the meantime, civil-military wrangling served only to stir up trouble among the reservation Indians. As Crook put it, "As soon as the Indians became harmless the Indian agents, who had sought cover before, now came out as brave as sheep, and took charge of the agencies, and commenced their game of plunder." Not all the agents were dishonest, and at least one, twenty-three-year-old John P. Clum, was as brave and competent as anyone the military could muster.

Convinced military interference on the reservations was the greatest obstacle to peace, Clum appointed an Indian police force and an "Apache court" to administer discipline. The Indian Bureau complicated his work when, in March 1875, it closed the Camp Verde reservation and transferred fourteen hundred Yavapais to San Carlos, but Clum integrated them into his agency without incident. He fed his Indians well, made them work hard at agriculture, and won the grudging respect of the territorial government.

Less successful were Clum's efforts at bringing the White Mountain Apaches under his control. He relocated a portion of the band to San Carlos, but the military tightened its grip over those who chose to remain at Camp Apache. Unable to complete the removal of the White Mountain Apaches, and weary of his incessant quarrels with the commander of the Department of Arizona, Brig. Gen. August V. Kautz, Clum resigned as agent in February 1876. Hardly had he done so when he learned of unrest on the Chiricahua reservation. He elected to stay on as agent, if only to bring the Chiricahuas under his jurisdiction.

Trouble had been brewing since the death of Cochise in June 1874. His son proved a weak successor, and the Central Chiricahuas broke into factions. Agent Jeffords's control over the band slipped accordingly, and discontented warriors decamped in increasing numbers. A crisis was reached in March 1876, when a pair of drunken malcontents murdered two stagecoach station attendants and Skinya and fifty Chiricahuas fled to the mountains of southernmost Arizona. Peaceably inclined Chiricahuas feared indiscriminate military retribution, and the territorial government foresaw a general outbreak. Governor Safford convinced the Indian Bureau that the Chiricahua reserve should be abandoned and the Indians removed to San Carlos by Clum, the only man with the "nerve, ability, and confidence to do it."

The Chiricahuas feuded among themselves over whether to submit peacefully. Despite Clum's benevolent administration, San Carlos was a hellhole—"a place of death," said the Apache James Kaywaykla, with neither game nor edible plants, but only cactus, rattlesnakes, heat, and insects.[4] General Kautz concentrated the 6th Cavalry regiment near the Chiricahua reserve, and after an intraband skirmish that left eight dead, the peace faction prevailed—in a measure. Clum led 325 Chiricahuas off to San Carlos, but the remainder of the band, some four hundred strong, fled to New Mexico or melted into the Sierra Madre. Under the leadership of Juh, Nolgee, and Geronimo, they launched a bloody string of raids on both sides of the border. Kautz dismissed the threat as a hoax that nefarious contractors and crooked politicians—whom he, and later Crook, labeled the "Tucson Ring"—had concocted to have department headquarters relocated from Prescott to Tucson. An indignant Governor Safford demanded Kautz's removal. Not until his own officers assured him the threat was real did Kautz respond. Although the army failed to capture the renegades, scouting detachments did learn that much of the trouble in Arizona emanated from the Ojo Caliente reservation on the Rio Grande, to which Geronimo and the Chiricahuas from Mexico regularly repaired to rest, refit, and recruit for future raids.

A year earlier, Insp. E. C. Kemble of the Indian Bureau had uncovered widespread graft at Ojo Caliente, perpetrated by a timorous agent on behalf of Victorio and his Mimbres warriors. Conditions improved under a new agent, but the marauding continued. In February 1877 General Kautz sent Lt. Austin Henely to confirm reports of a Chiricahua sanctuary at Ojo Caliente. When Henely found Geronimo himself there, the Indian Bureau reacted with commendable swiftness. Clum was ordered to arrest the renegades with his police force and remove them and the Mimbres to San Carlos. Nine troops of cavalry under Col. Edward Hatch were ordered to the reservation to overawe the Indians.

Clum reached Ojo Caliente on April 20. With time at a premium and no sign of the promised cavalry, he and his police effected the arrests themselves. Placing Geronimo in shackles, Clum rounded up 343 Mimbres, including Victorio, and 110 Bedonkone Chiricahuas and marched them off to San Carlos. Clum returned to find that Kautz, with the approval of the secretary of the interior, had placed an army officer at San Carlos to watch Indian movements and inspect their supplies. A disgusted Clum resigned in July 1877.

Two months later, Victorio's Mimbres and Pionsenay's Chiricahuas decamped from San Carlos. While bloodlust and plunder motivated Pionsenay, Victorio wanted no more than to find a satisfactory home for his people.

Victorio's breakout was short-lived. Pursuing Apache police and soldiers inflicted fifty-six casualties on Victorio's band in less than a month, and the chief surrendered at Fort Wingate, New Mexico. Much to his relief, the army returned the Mimbres to their old home at Ojo Caliente. There they remained under army guardianship for nearly a year while the Indian Bureau considered their fate. Weary of providing for the Mimbres, General Sherman threatened to turn them loose. In response, the Department of the Interior asked the War Department to return the Mimbres to San Carlos, and, recorded an Arizona journalist, "in an evil hour the concentration policy was reaffirmed."

But Victorio refused to go. "You can take our squaws and children in your wagons," he shouted at Capt. F. T. Bennett, who had come with two companies of cavalry to escort the band, "but my men will not go!" With that, Victorio and ninety Mimbres fled into the mountains.

A particularly harsh winter in the southwestern New Mexico high country persuaded Victorio to again seek peace. He tried to settle at Ojo Caliente in

February 1879 but was frightened off by rumors that his band was to be taken to the Mescalero reservation at Tularosa. Victorio reconsidered and voluntarily settled on the Tularosa Agency in June, only to decamp three months later when word reached him that he was to be indicted for murder in nearby Silver City.

This time Victorio and his 150 Mimbre, Chiricahua, and Mescalero warriors stayed out for good. On September 6, 1879, Victorio declared war, wiping out an eight-man herd guard from the 9th U.S. Cavalry at Ojo Caliente. Twelve days later he ambushed a larger detachment twenty miles north of Hillsboro. Isolated ranches went up in flames, prospectors were shot down by the dozens, and the country fell into a panic. The army responded quickly but ineffectively. Eluding Apache scout companies under Lt. Charles B. Gatewood and Lt. Augustus P. Blocksom and nearly the entire 9th Cavalry regiment, Victorio slipped into the Candelaria Mountains of northern Chihuahua.

In January 1880 Victorio's band returned to New Mexico. They engaged the army in three sharp but inconclusive fights in the San Andres Mountains, then vanished. Unable to capture Victorio, the army instead went after his supposed base of supplies, arms, and recruits—the Mescalero reservation at Tularosa. Accordingly, plans were made to disarm and dismount the Mescaleros. Two large columns converged on the agency: from the west, Colonel Hatch with his own 9th Cavalry, two troops of the 6th Cavalry, and two companies of Indian scouts; from the east, five troops of the 10th U.S. Cavalry under Col. Benjamin H. Grierson.

Feeling his way through the San Andres Mountains in early April, Hatch missed a chance to destroy Victorio's warriors at Hembrillo Canyon when Lt. John Conline's Troop A, 9th U.S. Cavalry, scouting under orders from Capt. Henry Carroll, encountered the hostiles before Hatch could bring his entire command to bear. Hatch rendezvoused with Grierson at the Tularosa Agency on April 12, and after a brief skirmish, the Mescaleros were disarmed.

Deprived of his agency haven, Victorio withdrew into the Black and Mogollon mountain ranges, killing and pillaging as far west as San Carlos. Victorio's first setback came on May 23, when an Indian scout company under Capt. H. K. Parker ambushed his band in the canyon headwaters of the Palomas River. Wounded in the leg, Victorio retreated to Mexico. Anticipating Victorio's return, Colonel Grierson distributed his command along the Rio Grande west of Fort Davis, Texas, with strong parties guarding the available water holes.

Grierson's tactics proved effective. When Victorio crossed the Rio Grande in July, with Mexican troops in close pursuit, he fell prey to Grierson's chain of outposts. With a twenty-four man detachment that included his young son, Grierson held off Victorio and 150 warriors at the Tinaja de las Palmas water hole in Quitman Canyon on July 30. After a week of roaming the parched Texas landscape, encountering soldiers at every turn, Victorio withdrew to Mexico.

He was to enjoy no rest. In September, while Grierson realigned his Rio Grande defenses, strong columns under Col. George P. Buell and Col. Eugene A. Carr marched from New Mexico and Arizona to join Col. Joaquin Terrazas of the Mexican Army in a sweep of the Candelaria Mountains. Victorio withdrew deeper into Mexico. The American troops recrossed the international border at the behest of the Mexicans, but Terrazas trapped Victorio in a canyon of the Tres Castillos Mountains and slaughtered the Mimbres on October 15, 1880. Victorio was killed, and the handful of survivors gave allegiance to the septagenarian Nana. In a remarkable feat of endurance, the following summer Nana led fifteen warriors on a two-month-long raid through southwestern New Mexico. They rode a thousand miles; killed fifty Americans; captured hundreds of horses and mules; fought ten skirmishes with the army—winning most of them; eluded nearly one thousand pursuing soldiers and hundreds of civilian volunteers; and then vanished into Mexico.

As southern New Mexico at last settled down to comparative quiet, Apache troubles flared up where least expected, on the customarily tranquil White Mountain (Fort Apache) reservation. The very tranquility of the White Mountain Apaches had seemingly endangered their existence. Towns had sprung up around the reservation, and Mormon settlers had spilled into the country west of Fort Apache. Fearful of losing their lands, in the summer of 1881 many White Mountain and Cibicue Apaches fell under the sway of a medicine man and prophet, Noch-ay-del-klinne, who promised to resurrect dead chiefs before the autumn corn ripened—if the white intruders were expelled. Col. E. A. Carr, the commanding officer at Fort Apache, was not unduly alarmed by Noch-ay-del-klinne's prophecies, which also included pacific elements. However, Joseph C. Tiffany, the hopelessly inept successor to Clum as Indian agent for the San Carlos and White Mountain reservations, demanded that the military "arrest or kill the medicine man." Brig. Gen. Orlando B. Willcox, who had demonstrated a singular lack of understanding of Apache nature since replacing General Kautz as department commander three years earlier, ordered Carr to make the arrest "as soon as practicable." Tiffany followed with a telegram of his own, telling Carr he wanted the prophet "arrested or killed or both."

Carr obeyed reluctantly. Too many of his Apache scouts had fallen under the spell of the prophet to be relied upon, and he feared a violent confrontation with Noch-ay-del-klinne's followers. Nevertheless, on August 29, 1881, he started from Fort Apache for Noch-ay-del-klinne's village on the Cibicue Creek at the head of eighty-five troopers of the 6th U.S. Cavalry and twenty-three scouts. He arrested the prophet without incident the next day. But when Carr unwisely made camp near the village that evening, Noch-ay-del-klinne's warriors and his own scouts opened fire on the troopers, apparently without provocation, killing Capt. E. C. Hentig and four men. Noch-ay-del-klinne was cut down trying to escape. Carr repelled the assault and withdrew toward Fort Apache under the cover of darkness. Emboldened by their success, the warriors and mutinous scouts rushed Fort Apache on September 1 but, lacking strong leadership, were driven off.

The failure of the attack—and of Noch-ay-del-klinne himself to arise from the dead—disheartened most of the hostiles, who gradually drifted back onto the reservation or took refuge at the ranch of Corydon E. Cooley, a staunch friend of the Apaches. Only sixty of the most intractable remained out. Had Tiffany been replaced and agency police permitted to round up the ringleaders, the trouble most likely would have ended in a matter of weeks. But the War Department overreacted. "I want this annual Apache stampede to end right now," declared General Sherman, "and to effect that result will send every available man in the whole army if necessary." Reinforcements poured in from the departments of California and the Missouri, and the overawed renegades surrendered in droves. Five mutinous scouts were court-martialed. Two were sent to Alcatraz, and the remaining three were hung for killing Captain Hentig. Displaying commendable restraint, neither the army nor civil authorities punished the remaining Apache participants in the Cibicue affair.

In its zeal to suppress the Cibicue uprising, the army inadvertently touched off an outbreak among the Chiricahuas. Despite white encroachment, Indian Bureau graft, and factional intrigue among the San Carlos tribes, the Chiricahuas had remained quietly at their Camp Goodwin subagency for nearly five years. But the presence of so many troops on the reservation—which had been free of soldiers for nearly five years—threw them into a panic. Not understanding the reason for the military buildup, they feared they were to be punished for past transgressions. When Maj. James Biddle foolishly galloped into the subagency on September 30, 1881, with three troops of cavalry to arrest Bonito and George, two White Mountain chiefs who had retired there after having been paroled prematurely for their role in the Cibicue affair, seventy-four nervous Chiricahua warriors under Juh and Naiche bolted with their families. Among the 400 decamped Apaches were Chihuahua, Chatto, and Geronimo. After a skirmish with pursuing troops near Cedar Springs, the hostiles vanished into the Sierra Madre, where they joined the remnants of Victorio's band. In January 1882 messengers from Juh and Naiche infiltrated the camp of old Chief Loco of the Mimbres, who had refused to join the September breakout. They advised him that a raiding party would come in forty days to drag his band from San Carlos.

True to their word, on April 18, 1882, a war party under Chatto, Chihuahua, Naiche, and perhaps Geronimo cut the telegraph wires into San Carlos and coerced Loco and 300 Mimbres into breaking out. During their flight, agency police chief Albert D. Sterling was killed. Now outlaws anyway, the Mimbres perpetrated a string of brutal depredations. Military action was swift but inconclusive. Col. George A. Forsyth patrolled the Southern Pacific Railroad in southwestern New Mexico with six troops of the 4th U.S. Cavalry but succeeded simply in losing several scouts and six soldiers in a drawn battle at Horseshoe Canyon on April 23, 1882. While Forsyth drew off to the Gila River to regroup, the hostile warriors gathered their women and children and marched swiftly across the San Simon Valley and the Chiricahua Mountains, bound for Mexico.

Out of the mountains in pursuit came a column under Capt. William A. Rafferty and Capt. Tullius C. Tupper, with Al Sieber as chief of scouts. Crossing the border in violation of international law, they engaged the renegades at Sierra Enmedio. Seventeen warriors were killed before a lack of ammunition forced the soldiers to retire. Shortly after the fight, Colonel Forsyth arrived with seven cavalry troops and two scout companies, took command of Rafferty and Tupper's party, and decided to push deeper into Mexico. Fleeing the Americans, Loco's band stumbled into a Mexican ambush, losing 111 of their number. Forsyth called off his pursuit after the Mexican commander ordered him out of Mexico.

Although renegades from the Cibicue affair had precipitated the Chiricahua and Mimbre flights from San Carlos, they had not joined them. Instead, the sixty who had refused to surrender the previous autumn lingered about the reservation until early July 1882, when, under the leadership of a White Mountain warrior named Natiotish, they broke out to the west, hoping to spark a general uprising. Natiotish's warriors killed the new San Carlos police chief, J. L. "Cibicue Charlie" Colvig, and three of his scouts but found no support among the reservation Indians. Kidnapping some squaws, the disgruntled warriors raided northwest into the Tonto Basin.

Fourteen troops of cavalry took the field. On July 16 Al Sieber, guiding Capt. Adna Chaffee's troop of the 6th U.S. Cavalry, detected Natiotish's fugitives in an escarpment of the Mogollon Rim near General Springs, where they were waiting to ambush the cavalrymen. Unknown to the renegades, during the night four troops under Maj. A. W. Evans reinforced Chaffee. Instead of massacring a lone cavalry troop the next day, the hostiles found themselves overwhelmed in one of the few conventional battles of the Apache wars. Natiotish and at least sixteen warriors perished; many more were wounded. The survivors snuck back onto the reservations. As one historian observed of what was known as the Battle of the Big Dry Wash, "This fight was more than a victory; it was the end of an era in Apache affairs. Never again were the troops to fight the Apaches in Arizona; never again, with the exception of the Chiricahuas, were the Apaches violently to oppose governmental control."[5] It would, however, take four years and two changes of department commanders before the last of the Chiricahua recalcitrants were subdued.

The Loco and Natiotish outbreaks convinced Washington that a change of department commanders was imperative. On September 4, 1882, George Crook returned to Arizona to relieve the generally despised Orlando Willcox. He immediately concluded that "no military department could well have been in a more desperate plight." Continued instrusion on their land, cruel and corrupt agents, enigmatic army and civilian policies, and rumors that they were to be disarmed and removed had brought nearly all the reservation Indians in Apacheria to the brink of revolt. And across the Mexican border were some six hundred Chiricahuas, a magnet for the disaffected who could be counted on to renew their depredations in Arizona and New Mexico.

Crook acted quickly and tactfully. With the warm consent of the new agent at San Carlos, Philip P. Wilcox, Crook permitted the mountain Apaches whom Clum had forcibly relocated to San Carlos to return to their high-country homes near Fort Apache, removing a major source of disquiet. He met with the chiefs of the reservation bands, promising to correct abuses and preaching the benefits of peace. At the same time, he admonished his officers to deal justly, honestly, and impartially with the Indians. In his work of pacification Crook was greatly aided by Agent Wilcox, who allowed the army to manage and discipline the reservation Indians. Crook appointed four able officers to the task: Capt. Emmet Crawford and Lt. Britton Davis to deal with the Indians at San Carlos, and Lt. Charles B. Gatewood and Lt. Hamilton Roach to work with the White Mountain bands near Fort Apache. On September 27 Crook wired division headquarters that he had "arrived at a thorough understanding" with the disaffected Indians and that "there is now not a hostile Apache in Arizona."

But the Chiricahuas and Mimbres in the Sierra Madre loomed dangerously close. Reports came of widespread raiding in the states of Sonora and Chihuahua, and some said Juh was preparing to retrace Victorio's old path of destruction into Texas. Crook sent Apache emissaries into Mexico to treat with the renegades and blanketed the border with Indian scout companies. He also laid plans for an offensive campaign, reorganizing his commands and bringing the neglected pack-train service back up to field readiness.

Before Crook could secure either Mexican permission or Washington approval to operate in Mexico, two dozen warriors under Chatto, Bonito, and Naiche swept north out of the Sierra Madre. Crossing the border on March 21, 1883, in a six-day raid they spread terror from the Huachuca Mountains of Arizona to Lordsburg, New Mexico. Riding seventy-five miles a day, they killed twenty-six people, including Judge H. C. McComas and his wife, taking their young son, Charlie, captive; stole scores of horses; and then escaped into Mexico at the cost of one warrior dead—a son-in-law of Chihuahua—and one missing.

The missing warrior, whom the whites named Peaches for his light complexion, was to prove the recalcitrants' undoing. A Cibicue Apache who had married a Chiricahua, Peaches' loyalties were mixed. When Mexicans killed his wife and children, a heartsick and homesick Peaches not only surrendered willingly to Lieutenant Davis, but also volunteered to guide the army into the hostiles' Sierra Madre strongholds. Crook at once took advantage of this stroke of luck. After visiting civil and military authorities in Sonora and Chihuahua to explain his purpose and obtain their assent, he crossed the Mexican border at San Bernardino Springs on May 1, 1883, with Peaches, a handful of soldiers, and 193 Apache scouts under Captain Crawford. "The whole Sierra Madre is a natural fortress," marveled Crook, and into that fortress of towering ridges, bottomless canyons, and narrow, rocky trails, his command vanished for forty-two days.

While the nation speculated as to Crook's fate, Peaches led the command deep into the mountain recesses of the Sierra Madre. On May 15 Crawford's scouts attacked the camps of Chatto and Bonito, killing nine and burning the rancheria. Stunned by a defeat in their previously impregnable sanctuary, the hostiles sought peace. After several parleys, Crook agreed to forgive past offenses and allow the Chiricahuas to return with him to San Carlos. Geronimo and Naiche obtained Crook's leave to gather their scattered people and come in later. Short of supplies, Crook was forced to accept their terms. On May 30, 1883, he broke camp and started north with 52 warriors and 273 women and children, among them Nana, Loco, and Bonito.

The Interior and War Departments cooperated with rare dispatch. On July 7 the secretaries of war and the interior signed an agreement giving Crook exclusive authority over the recent hostiles and full police control on the San Carlos reservation. Crook delegated the duty to Captain Crawford.

Several months passed with no sign of the remaining renegades. Speculation grew that Crook had been betrayed. Finally, in December, Naiche reported to San Carlos with thirteen warriors and their families. Chatto came in two months later. And in early March, Geronimo and eighty of his people surrendered.

The army scattered the former renegades about the agency and set them to work farming and raising cattle. Geronimo, Naiche, and Chihuahua accepted reservation life grudgingly, but Chatto became a loyal army ally in preserving order. During 1884, the only serious Indian challenge came from Ka-ya-ten-nae, a restless survivor of Victorio's band suffering his first taste of reservation life. Wild as a wolf, Ka-ya-ten-nae skulked about, brutally beating his wives and secretly making the favorite Apache intoxicant, *tizwin*—actions prohibited under Crook's regime. Lieutenant Davis arrested Ka-ya-ten-nae and Crook shipped him off to Alcatraz. Ka-ya-ten-nae returned to San Carlos in 1886. Having seen the wonders and power of white civilization in San Francisco, he became one of the most persuasive Apache advocates of permanent peace.

Lieutenant Davis faced a far more explosive challenge in the spring of 1885. Discontent over the bans on wife beating and tizwin making had spread, and nearly all the principal Chiricahua leaders except Chatto conspired to test the limits of military indulgence. On the morning of May 15 Geronimo and several other headmen confessed to Davis that they had been on a tizwin drunk the night before and defied him to do something about it. Davis sent to Crook for instructions, but the telegram was pigeonholed en route on the advice of a less-than-sober Al Sieber. When two days passed without word from Crook, the agitated Apaches, fearing retribution, broke out. Forty-two warriors and ninety-two women and children, among them Geronimo, Naiche, Chihuahua, Nana, and Mangas, headed for Mexico. Along the way, part of the band attacked Capt. Henry W. Lawton's supply camp at Guadalupe Canyon.

A furious Crook set aside his benevolent policies in favor of "radical measures" to subdue or exterminate the renegades. Moving his headquarters from

Fort Whipple to Fort Bowie, near the border, Crook sent two mobile columns into Mexico to flush the Chiricahuas from their Sierra Madre strongholds. The first, consisting of one troop of the 6th Cavalry and ninety-two scouts under Captain Crawford and Lieutenant Davis, crossed the border on June 11. The second, composed of one troop of the 4th Cavalry and one hundred scouts under Capt. Wirt Davis, crossed on July 13. Behind them, Crook posted troops of cavalry and detachments of scouts at every watering hole from the Rio Grande to the Santa Cruz Valley and placed a line of reserves along the Southern Pacific Railroad. In all, nearly three thousand soldiers, mostly cavalry, patrolled the frontier.

Crook's measures failed. For three months Crawford and Davis struggled through the Sierra Madre with only four inconclusive skirmishes to show for their efforts. In October the two commands put in at Fort Bowie to refit and prepare for another campaign in Mexico.

Before Crook could reorganize his columns, ten warriors under Josanie, a hitherto obscure brother of Chihuahua, launched an audacious cross-border raid. Slipping through Crook's double cordon, the raiders traveled twelve hundred miles through southern Arizona and New Mexico, killing thirty-eight non-combatants, both white and western Apache, capturing 250 horses, and escaping to Mexico, having bested in battle several patrols from the eighty-three companies that dotted the region.

His official stock plummeting, Crook immediately sent a second expedition into the Sierra Madre. Wirt Davis entered Mexico with a mixed force of cavalry and Indian scouts from peaceable San Carlos tribes. Crawford, however, relied solely on scouts from the White Mountain Apaches and the very Chiricahua peoples he was hunting—two companies of fifty Indians each under Lt. Marion P. Maus and Lt. William E. Shipp. The only white men were the officers, interpreters, and mule packers.

Crawford's scouts found the main hostile rancheria on January 9, 1886, near the head of the Haros River. Crawford attacked the next morning. Most of the renegades escaped, but their herd and camp outfit were taken. Demoralized over the loss of their sanctuary, Geronimo and Naiche sent a squaw to Crawford's camp to ask for a parley. Before it could be arranged, a cruel twist of fate intervened. As Crawford and his scouts rested in the abandoned rancheria on the morning of January 11, confident that the campaign was all but over, they were attacked by a force of Mexican irregulars that also had been pursuing the hostiles. While Naiche and Geronimo watched from surrounding heights, the Mexicans and Crawford's scouts traded volleys for two hours. Crawford was mortally wounded while trying to persuade the Mexicans of their error. By the time the firing ceased, interpreter Tom Horn and three scouts had been wounded, and nine Mexicans, including their commanding officer, had fallen.

Assuming command, Lieutenant Maus made plans to leave Mexico at once. But the hostile leaders still wished to talk, and on January 13 Maus conferred with Geronimo, Naiche, Chihuahua, and Nana. They earnestly wanted to discuss surrender terms with General Crook and would meet him near San Bernardino in "two moons"; as an act of good faith, the renegades gave as hostages Nana and the favorite wives of Geronimo and Naiche.

Crook met the chiefs on March 25, 1886, at Cañon de los Embudos, twelve miles south of the Arizona line. Discussions were tense. Crook sought unconditional surrender; Geronimo, who did most of the talking for the hostiles, insisted on a return to the reservation with no punishment. Chihuahua, however, proved more tractable, as his family had been captured the year before, and at a second conference two days later, all agreed to surrender on the condition that they and such family members as wished to accompany them be sent east for just two years' confinement. Leaving Maus to bring in the prisoners, who remained armed and sullen, a prematurely elated Crook hurried to Fort Bowie to report the news to the commanding general of the army, Philip H. Sheridan. On the night of March 28, after becoming drunk on liquor bought from an unscrupulous trader, Naiche and Geronimo fled back into the Sierra Madre with twenty warriors and sixteen women and children.

In Washington, Crook's reputation plummeted. Even before news reached him of Geronimo's escape, President Grover Cleveland had repudiated Crook's terms, insisting on the unconditional surrender or extirpation of the Apaches. Now Sheridan added his voice, criticizing Crook's reliance on Indian scouts and demanding he change his methods. On April 1 Crook asked to be relieved.

Sheridan accepted his request with alacrity. Eleven days later, Brig. Gen. Nelson A. Miles assumed command at Fort Bowie from "a very much worried and disappointed" Crook. Under pressure from Sheridan to put a swift end to the Apache troubles, Miles planned a grand strategy that varied from Crook's methods more in appearance than substance. Gathering five thousand troops (nearly one-quarter of the entire Regular army), he divided southern Arizona and New Mexico into districts of observation. He posted infantry at every mountain pass and water hole and carpeted the country with cavalry patrols. Atop the twenty-seven highest peaks, he placed heliograph stations to scan the intervening plains. As a final measure, Miles organized an expeditionary force of infantry, cavalry, and Indian scouts under Capt. Henry W. Lawton, with Lt. Leonard Wood as surgeon, to run down the renegades in Mexico.

Before Miles had completed his preparations, the hostiles struck, sweeping into the Santa Cruz Valley on April 27, 1886, then scattering into small raiding parties to avoid detection. After several sharp clashes, the Apaches dropped back into Mexico. Lawton followed. For three months he chased the renegades ever deeper into Mexico. Horses gave out early on, officers and enlisted men had to be replaced on the march, and even the scouts grew exhausted. By mid-July Lawton had covered nearly fifteen hundred miles, with only a near miss at a hostile rancheria to his credit.

Learning that the hostiles had been dickering for peace with Mexican officials at Fronteras, a frustrated Miles resorted to one of Crook's favorite stratagems—employing as peace emissaries officers and friendly Apaches in whom the hostiles had confidence. On July 13 he sent Lieutenant Gatewood and two Chiricahuas, Ki-e-ta and Martine, to obtain the surrender of Geronimo and Naiche. Arriving at Lawton's camp on the Haros River in early August, Gatewood placed himself under the captain's command, and together they hastened north toward Fronteras. With Ki-e-ta, Martine, and an escort of scouts, Gatewood pushed ahead of Lawton's column and secured an audience with Geronimo on August 25. Gatewood delivered Miles's terms—that the hostiles and their families would be sent to Florida, there to await a presidential decision as to their fate. Geronimo dismissed the offer—that is, until Gatewood told him that family and friends back on the reservation already had been shipped off to Fort Marion, Florida. A crestfallen Geronimo agreed to give up, but only to General Miles in person. Gatewood concurred, and the final surrender took place at Skeleton Canyon, sixty-five miles southeast of Fort Bowie, on September 4, 1886. Three days later the entire band was marched out of the fort and put on a train to Florida.

It was not only Geronimo, Naiche, and their band who were bundled off into eastern captivity; all the Chiricahuas—hostile and loyal, including Ki-e-ta; Martine; and Chatto, who had been given a presidential medal while on a visit to Washington only a few weeks before; and most of the scouts who had served Crook faithfully—were sent to Florida. Unjust though it was, the exile of the Chiricahuas put an end to the Apache wars. As the historian Dan L. Thrapp concluded:

> The conquest [of Apacheria] now was all but a fact. The day of the Indian fighter was about gone. Now had arrived the day of the company miner, the banker, the merchant, the teachers and housewives, and all of the others. A few broncos would be left in the mountains of Mexico and Arizona. They would raid from time to time, and kill and steal and disappear. Troops would go after them, with the usual lack of success. But the Apache as a fighting force to be reckoned with militarily was but a memory in the ghostly peaks and endless deserts he had known so well and defended so bloodily.[6]

PART ONE

Raids and Reprisals in Apacheria, 1865–72

Indians in New Mexico

WILLIAM F. M. ARNY[1]

Army and Navy Journal 4, no. 19 (December 29, 1866)

A cting Governor Arny of New Mexico has issued a proclamation calling for volunteers against the Indians, in which he says:

The present condition of the territory of New Mexico, surrounded as it is by hostile tribes of Indians, whose constant incursions and depredations are the source of the greatest evil which afflicts our country, demands that our people should be prepared to protect their own lives and property, as the military force in this territory appears inadequate, and the militia inefficient and not in a condition to perform this work promptly. Our territory is in possession of a sufficient number of arms and a quantity of ammunition; and I do hereby recommend to all able-bodied male citizens of this territory to organize themselves into volunteer companies for home protection. Immediately upon the organization of any such company, they will report to the secretary of this territory, in conformity with the law, and the officers will be commissioned and furnished with the means of arming the company.

The Apaches in the south and southwest have been and are now on the warpath, killing and robbing wherever they can. The Utes in the north and northwest have made peace for the time being and consented to be quiet, which means simply a cessation of hostilities until they have exhausted the bounty of the government, which has just been paid to them, and which they expect to enjoy during the winter. When spring returns and circumstances are favorable, the state of things which has existed in New Mexico since it was acquired from Mexico will be renewed. We will never have peace until these wild Indians, who commit their murders and depredations almost in sight of the capital of our territory, are brought into proper subjection or extermination. Their daring is equalled only by their success in their butcheries and depredations. They must be conquered and placed upon reservations off the settlements and kept there. Humanity, with reference to our citizens and the Indians, demands this, and until it is accomplished we must protect ourselves. In the accomplishment of this work I ask the aid of every good citizen, so that this remedy for the sufferings and losses of our people may be put into successful operation and that life, property, and the firesides of the people may be rendered secure from the perils and dangers which now so constantly and daily threaten us.

The present appearance indicates that we are on the verge of an Indian war of great magnitude.

A Great Slaughter of Apaches

EDWARD PALMER[1]

Prescott *Arizona Miner*, February 28, 1866

We have to record a bold and highly successful movement on the part of Lieutenant Gallegos and forty men of Company E, Arizona Volunteers, Captain H. S. Washburn.[2] The lieutenant and men left Camp Lincoln,[3] on the Verde, fifty miles east from Prescott, on the eleventh instant—returned on the fifteenth. What they accomplished is told in the following letter:

> CAMP LINCOLN, Arizona, February 15, 1866
> EDITOR OF ARIZONA MINER—This has been a day of great rejoicing here. A party of our Company E, Arizona Volunteeers, under Lieutenant Gallegos, which left here on the eleventh instant at 7:00 A.M., returned reporting a great slaughter of Apaches. After traveling two nights and resting by day, they found Apache signs, and scouts were sent out from the main body to ascertain the exact position of the enemy. When found, they returned and the whole body moved in within sight of the Apache fires but occupied a secluded position until 2:00 A.M., when the command was formed into three divisions and moved in front of certain caves where the savages were sleeping. These were arranged one above another, and when the attack was begun at daybreak, the fight became desperate. The Apaches were taken by surprise, their dogs not even hearing the approach of the troops, so stealthy was the march. Some of the Indians declared that they would not surrender, and one who called himself a captain constantly defied the troops from an elevated and secure position, whence they could not dislodge him. All of the caves that were accessible were filled with dead and wounded. Some thirty are believed to have been killed outright. Thirteen scalps were brought to camp and twelve prisoners, two squaws and ten children; one of the latter has since died.
> Seven of the volunteers were wounded, but none dangerously. When it is remembered that these men had only rough rawhide san-

5

dals of their own make, packed their provisions on their backs, and traveled nearly one hundred miles in so short a time, the results are greatly to their credit. They are the men, in my judgment, to rid the country of the Apache. Give them a chance and they will make their mark every time. They are very happy over their victory and eager for another expedition. I have offered them a dollar's worth of tobacco for every Apache they kill in the future, that they may smoke the pipe of peace over the peaceable and harmless condition of those who fall under their guns.

Show this to the acting governor and say the Arizona Volunteers, Company E, have succeeded in the first movement they have had a chance to make.

Edward Palmer,
A.A. Surgeon, U.S.A.

Captain Washburn arrived at Fort Whipple on the twelfth instant with the prisoners and delivered them up to the post commandant. The captain was heartily congratulated by our citizens, and those who doubted the ability of our native troops to do good service are now convinced of their error. The captain was supplied with buckskins by Quartermaster Tuttle for new sandals for his company, and the following letter, accompanied by a number of pounds of tobacco for distribution among the men, was presented here by the acting governor:

TERRITORY OF ARIZONA, OFFICE OF THE GOVERNOR,
PRESCOTT, February 19, 1866

Captain H. S. Washburn, Company E,
Arizona Volunteers.

Captain—The plan, execution, and success of the recent raid of Lieutenant Gallegos and the men of your company upon the Apaches meet the hearty and general congratulation of our people. For myself, I wish formally to thank you, the lieutenant, and your men for the severe blow you have dealt our common and barbarous foe. It will be highly gratifying to the general commanding the district and to the friends of the territory everywhere as proving the capacity and spirit of our native troops. If vigorously followed up during the spring and summer, as I presume it will be, the Arizona Volunteers may do more than all who have preceded them in the subjugation of the Apaches in this part of the territory.[4] I am your obedient servant,

RICHARD C. McCORMICK,
Acting Governor

We will state for the information of our readers abroad that Company E, Arizona Volunteers is composed entirely of native-born Arizonians (Mexicans) and was recruited in the southern part of the territory by Captain Washburn. They recently arrived here from Tucson and were sent to Camp Lincoln to take the place of the California Volunteers, who have returned to California. The other officers are Lieutenant Ver Mehr, now upon General Mason's staff; Lieutenant Manuel Gallegos, who headed the present expedition and who was a captain in Pesqueira's army in Sonora, and has had much experience in Indian fighting. He has reason to be proud of his latest fight. A few more such will forever quiet the hellish Apache.

The Apache Race

JOHN C. CREMONY[1]

The Overland Monthly 1, no. 3 (September 1868): 201–9[2]

Since the foundation of our government, Indian wars have cost the American people nearly four hundred millions of dollars, and the stream of expenditure continues with unabated volume. When the whites were few and the savages many, the cost of keeping them in subjection was measurably less than it has been since the reversal of our respective numerical condition. Whence arises this anomaly? Simply because of our strange ignorance of Indian character as it really exists, and not as we have been taught to understand it by writers of attractive fiction, or the chroniclers of heroic deeds and romantic adventures.

Unfortunately, those who have been the best able from long and careful personal experience to give the requisite information have also been, for the most part, deficient in educational attainments and the capacity to impart their knowledge; while others have given no evidence of entertaining a just value of its public importance. Satisfied with their own acquirements, they have not sought to publish them for the benefit of others.

What has our government ever done in a concerted, intelligent, and liberal spirit to acquire a definite knowledge of Indian character as it exists among the tribes which wander over more than one-half the public domain?

The Indian Bureau, with its army of political camp followers bent upon improving their short and precarious official positions to "turn an honest penny," can scarcely be quoted as evidence of our search for the needed information. Tales of violence and wrong, of outrage and devilish malignity, committed by Indians are rife all along our frontiers; but who ever hears the other side? Who chronicles the inciting causes, the long, unbroken series of injuries perpetrated by the semi-civilized white savages who, like Cain, fled from the retributive justice of outraged humanity and sought refuge among the copper-colored savages of the woods and the plains?

Naturally ferocious, warlike, revengeful, and treacherous as were the aborigines of America, we have educated them to a pitch of refinement of cruelty, deceit, and villainy far beyond their normal standard.

If the white man has come to be regarded as his natural enemy, it may be set down as the result of long and murderous schooling. The inherent disposition of the American nomad inclined him to hospitality; but that inclination has been completely blotted out, and its opposite engrafted on his nature. Legends and traditions of white men's ingratitude have been handed down through so many generations, and the experiences of the living have been in such direct accordance with them, that they have become the prime articles of their creed.

Keenly alive to a sense of the inferiority of their armament, incapable of subsisting large bodies of men for any considerable period, and perpetually engaged in the work of exterminating each other, the several tribes have been reduced to the necessity of employing deceit against force, cunning against courage, artifice against honesty. When the Indian mutilates the dead body of his enemy, he knows as well as the most skilled anatomist that his victim is beyond all capacity of sensation; but it is done to terrify, if possible, all beholders, and as a caution to other invaders, as well as for the enjoyment of a savage gratification. Such deeds, while they horrify, also serve to excite the indignation and strengthen the resolve of civilized and enlightened men; but the aboriginal is incapable of such reflections.

Prominent among the tribes stands the Apache race. Occupying the largest regions of the public domain, holding possession of a belt which must soon become a grand national highway, wielding a sanguinary sway over two extensive and naturally rich territories, and filling the most important intervening space between the Atlantic and the Pacific states, we have as little real knowledge of them this day as we possessed when our acquaintance first commenced. Twenty-odd years of unremitted warfare have added comparatively nothing to our knowledge, but have cost thousands of lives and millions of treasure.

In point of intellect, in cunning and duplicity, in warlike skill and untiring energy, in tenacity of purpose and wondrous powers of endurance, the Apaches have no equals among the existing Indians of North America. In this widespread race are included the powerful Navajo and Lipan tribes, as they speak identically the same language and almost always remain friendly toward each other, while they war upon all other people.[3] The Apaches proper, or those specially known to us by that name, generally receive their distinctive appellations from some peculiar characteristic, or from the place which they mostly inhabit. The Coyoteros are so named from a fancied or real similitude to the coyote, or small prairie wolf; the Mescaleros derive their cognomen from the mescal plant, which abounds in their country and is with them a staple article of food. The Jicarillas are so called on account of their manufacture of a small water-tight basket, resembling a gourd, and named *jicara* in Spanish.[4] The Chiricahua, Rio Mimbres, El Pinal, and other branches of the tribe receive their nomenclatures from the localities in which they are generally met.

It is very common for a close observer to meet a group of Apaches one day on the Mimbres or in Apache Pass and encounter the same individuals at the head of the *Jornada del Muerto*,[5] or even on the Pecos River, several hundred miles distant.

It will be observed from this fact that the distinctive appellations given to them by the Mexican people are purely gratuitous and do not really exist, the tribe being one but ranging over an enormous extent of territory. Certain individuals affect particular localities, and when at home (if such a term can by any possibility apply to Apaches) they will resort there to enjoy their plunder, hold their feasts, and indulge in temporary rest from active campaigning. The various bands comprising these people number at least thirty-five thousand, of whom eight thousand can be made effective for warlike and plundering expeditions.[6] A lad of twelve years is expected to take his place among warriors of matured years and experience and is quite as deadly an enemy in their style of warfare. The Navajos are about as numerous but confine the bulk of their depredations to New Mexico, while the Apaches proper devastate portions of that territory, all Arizona, and nearly all parts of the Mexican states of Sonora, Chihuahua, and Durango. In 1850 the probable fighting force of the Apaches was ten thousand warriors, but they were not nearly as zealously active nor as hostile as now, neither were they so well armed. Their present condition renders them much more formidable than at that period.

A great and grievous mistake has been made in underrating the numerical strength and the armament of this tribe. This error has been attended with serious sacrifice of life, great additional cost, vexations and ineffective policy, and the continued retention by the Apaches of the richest mineral region in the Union—not to speak of it as the grand immigrant overland highway to the Pacific coast.

Their frequent and extensive massacres and robberies of immigrant trains have served to place them in possession of first-class rifles and Colt's revolvers. A force of seven hundred Apaches was encountered in Apache Pass by the first two companies of Carleton's column from California, and every individual was armed as above described. Although such large bodies are rarely met, yet it is not infrequent to find them in companies of from fifty to two hundred, and to underrate such a foe is simply to trifle with our own lives and interests.

On the northern borders of Chihuahua and Sonora are a number of small villages which are wholly under the control of these savages and are used by them for the purpose of obtaining arms and ammunition. After a successful raid into Sonora, the stolen animals are taken to one of these towns in Chihuahua, when certain men are selected to convey a number of the beasts to the more settled districts and to exchange them for the required articles, receiving a handsome gratuity for the service. During the absence of these factors, their families are retained as hostages for the fulfillment of their obligations. When the plunder is taken from Chihuahua, it is in like manner bartered off in Sonora. Portions of the race carrying on their operations in Arizona and New Mexico find little difficulty in having their wants supplied by unscrupulous New Mexican traders.

Apaches in ambush. NELSON A. MILES. *PERSONAL RECOLLECTIONS AND OBSERVATIONS.*

Within the past forty years, a belt of country comprising the northern frontier of the two Mexican states above named, and covering a space three hundred miles long, east and west, by forty miles wide, has been completely devastated by the Apaches. The once rich and magnificent ranches of the San Pedro, the Barbacomori, the San Bernardino, together with many towns and villages once flourishing, exist no longer. All is desolation, ruin, death.

The great hardihood, courage, and plucky determination of the American people, together with the superiority of their weapons, have saved Arizona from a similar fate so far, but the struggle has been desperate, unremitting, and sanguinary. Immense damages have been suffered. Settlers have been driven out time and again; mines of almost fabulous richness have been abandoned; from Tucson to El Paso, three hundred miles, is one continuous graveyard, marked throughout the whole distance with the grim and silent monuments of death from Apache animosity.

From the Pima villages to the Pecos River, eight hundred miles, and from Durango to Santa Fe, in New Mexico, the Apache is almost absolute "lord of all he surveys." To accomplish this argues the existence of numbers as well as of intense activity. Depredations by considerable bodies are frequently committed in widely separated districts at the same time, and with all his remarkable energy the Apache is not ubiquitous.

A close, personal acquaintance of over eight years, under peculiarly favorable circumstances, has given the writer such a knowledge of these Indians as to effectually dispel all his preconceived opinions.

Insensibly but surely the conclusions arrived at after a residence of one or two years in Arizona or New Mexico are rejected for fresher ones, and they in turn give place to still others as experiences and opportunities arise. But to meet the Apache upon his own ground, to descend to his level and interest ourselves in his pursuits; to converse with him in his own language, and gradually convince him of our indisposition to do him harm; to approach him without offensive arrogance and trust him as our equal; to be apparently under obligations to him for instruction in his modes of life and at the same time to let him quietly comprehend that we are not uneasy at his presence, nor afraid of his intentions, is to adopt the only method by which we can arrive at anything like a correct estimate of his inner nature. After all this has been done, and it is the work of labor, perseverance, and danger, one may reasonably indulge the conceit that he understands something of Apache character; but not until then.

He who has once or twice heard the war-whoop of the American savage, who has contended with them in the arena of battle, or who has listened to the tales of their exploits as related by persons who are supposed to be versed in the subject, is very apt to felicitate himself with the belief that he knows all about them. In no special instance is Pope's estimate of the danger of a "little learning" more applicable than to this asserted knowledge of Indian character so much boasted of by our frontier settlers and casual wayfarers through the regions inhabited by nomadic races.

Cautious, suspicious, treacherous, and crafty, the Apache meets all other races on the ground of distrust and doubt. An Ishmaelite himself, all other people are to his perverted senses objects to be shunned or destroyed. With him, the end justifies the means. Indebted to us for the refinement of his naturally savage instincts, it is but due to him to acknowledge that his schooling has not been thrown away. Excusable as this may appear to some, the fact remains that he is a viper, an untamable, ferocious, sanguinary monster, bent upon the destruction of all with whom he comes in contact and only restrained by fear. As the interests of the Apache race bear no appreciable proportion to those of civilized men, it becomes a duty to impose that condition of dread which only will ensure their discontinuance of revolting atrocities and the safety of our people.

The tribal organization of these savages has always been misunderstood. We have taken it for granted that they were similar to other tribes in this respect. But such is not the case. Under every aspect and at all times the Apache is a pure democrat. He acknowledges no chief, no ruler, no authority but his own will, nor does he ever delegate in another the right to act in his behalf.

When in camp, a temporary ruler is elected to preside over its affairs, and each person is free to remain or leave at his or her discretion. When on the warpath, a leader is chosen to direct proceedings, but he does not presume to exert control over individual proclivities. The warrior may submit to existing authority, but it is entirely optional, and his connection with the party may be sundered at any time he may see fit. The case is different among the Navajos, who in this respect, in their manufacture of superior blankets and in the construction of more durable homes, together with an inclination to pastoral life, exhibit much less of the nomadic tendencies.

This absolute personal license and freedom from all control, which are the highest prized rights of the Apache proper, form also the most insuperable bar to any permanent treaty relations between them and the American government. Our intercourse with other tribes led us to believe that a similar tribal organization obtained among Apaches; but it was a fatal error which has led to a false estimate of the adherence to treaty stipulations. If a hundred or more of them were gathered together to sign a treaty, that instrument would be binding upon none but the absolute signers. Every other individual present, although consenting by such presence, would hold himself entirely free from its conditions. What follows? Those who have not bound themselves continue their original course of depredations and massacres; we accuse them of want of faith and treachery and forthwith proceed to punish the offenders. Hostilities are again urged on either side, and those who did sign claim that we have violated our contract.

The tribe of which we treat is undoubtedly the most nomadic in existence. They build no houses and never remain longer than a week in any one place. Four or five slim and flexible branches of trees, with the butt ends sharpened and thrust into the ground, while the taper points are brought together and tied, constitutes the only residence of the Apache. Twenty minutes suffice to erect one, which is abandoned without regret. Even these ephemeral structures are never resorted to except in winter, or when the parties intend remaining for a few days. From eighty to ninety miles a day for several successive days are not considered long marches by these people when in a hurry. Their horses are ridden at a sharp pace throughout the journey. If one or more die under the fatigue, or from any other cause, they are immediately cut up for food, and the owners continue their march until opportunity serves to steal another horse.

It is indeed wonderful that with their intensely nomadic habits, their widely-scattered clans, the vast region which acknowledges their presence, and their perfect non-intercourse with all other races, except for war, their language should be so regular and full. Their verbs have the active and passive voices; the infinitive, indicative, subjunctive, and potential moods; the present, imperfect, perfect, and future tenses; the singular, dual, and plural numbers. Their nouns have the nominative, genitive, dative, accusative, and ablative cases, with three numbers corresponding to those of the verbs. Their numerals reach to the thousands and are very similar to our style of decimal enumeration.

Thus we say two, twelve, twenty, two hundred; three, thirteen, thirty, three hundred; four, fourteen, forty, four hundred. In a like manner the Apache says *nakee,* two, *nakesatah,* twelve, *natinyee,* twenty, *nat-too-oh,* two hundred; *kahyeh,* three, *kayesatah,* thirteen, *katinyee,* thirty, and *kat-too-oh,* three hundred; *tinyee,* four, *tinsatah,* fourteen, *tish-tinyee,* forty, and *tin-too-oh,* four hundred.

The word *to-dah* means no, and all their negative verbs are formed by splitting to-dah so as to place the first syllable at the commencement and the end of the positive verb. For example, the word *ink-tah* means sit down or sit, and to command do not sit, they say *to-ink-tah-dah*. *El-chin yashtee hashtee* means, I wish to speak with you, and *To-el-chin-yashtee-hashtee-dah* expresses, I do *not* wish to talk with you. Quite a number of words, having quite different meanings, are only distinguishable apart from the accent imparted to each; thus, the word *kah* means an arrow, and *kah* also means a rabbit, but the latter is distinguished from the former by a strong guttural accent on the first letter.

For all objects presented to their observation for the first time, they adopt the Spanish name, and then append the Apache aspirate, *hay.* *Pesh* means iron, and before they were acquainted with the relative values of gold, silver, brass, and iron, they called gold and brass *pesh-klitso,* which means yellow iron, and silver was termed *pesh-lick-oyee,* which means white iron; but since then they have adopted the Spanish terms and now call gold, *oro-hay,* and silver, *plata-hay,* while brass retains its original appellation of *pesh-klitso.*

The strange regularity of their language and the copiousness of their numerals indicate the possession of superior intelligence; but there is an abundance of other proof to this assumption. About fifteen hundred Apaches, including many of the most prominent warriors and councilmen of the Mescalero family, surrendered to the California troops in the winter of 1862. They had been the most formidable scourges of the country and had never before succumbed to any power. General Carleton located them on the extensive reservation at Fort Sumner, at a point called the *Bosque Redondo* on the Pecos River, nearly four hundred miles east of the Rio Grande. In the distance, 125 miles westward, could be seen the grand peak of the Capitan Mountain, towering among the clouds, while the intervening space was a rolling prairie, covered with fine grass, and the resort of thousands of antelope and deer. Among the more prominent of our Apache prisoners were Gianatah, which means "Always Ready"; Natch-in-ilk-isn, or the "Colored Beads"; Klosen, or the "Hair Rope"; Tooa-ah-yay-say, or the "Strong Swimmer"; Nah-Kah-yen, or "Keen Sight"; Nah-tank, or "Corn Flower," and many others unnecessary to name.

These men lost no opportunity to acquire all the information possible. Such officers as evinced any kindness toward them were besieged with questions, and of a character to excite the liveliest astonishment. On one occasion the writer was addressed as follows:

"*Tata* (you) *Inday-Pindah Lickoyee* (people with white eyes) say that the world is round. How can that be? I have traveled for many suns, and wherever I went, I found it flat. Tell me how it is."

Pointing to the sublime heights of *El Capitan,* the interrogated party said:"Do you see yonder mountain?"

"Yes; it is *El Capitan.*"

"What portion of it do you perceive?"

"The top."

"Why do you not see the bottom as well? It is broader and larger than the top."

"I do not know."

After this was duly explained the Apache was caused to look at the sun through a piece of smoked glass, in order that he might observe and note its round shape.

He then said: "But you also say that the world turns over and over; how can that be possible? If it did we would all fall off."

Having no means of explaining the attraction of gravitation, a strong magnet and a small piece of steel were used to convey the idea, which was received with marked approbation.

Questions as to what caused the drying up of the ponds and lakes, what formed the clouds, where does the rain come from, what was the nature of thunder and lightning, and many others of like character, were asked and answered.

From thirty to forty of their leading men came daily for two or three months to receive instruction on such points, until they comprehended them.

The delight which they evinced on acquiring information induced General Carleton to establish a school at the Bosque for the purpose of educating the young, but the Apaches regarded it with suspicion and loathing. They construed it into an attempt to enslave the mind and control personal freedom. They were over zealous to acquire knowledge orally imparted, but the idea of working to obtain it was horrible to them.

Quite a number of pictorials containing street views in some of our large cities, cuts of ships, steamers, carriages, etc., were received in camp and exhibited to the Apaches, who invariably looked at them upside-down, until they were properly placed before their vision, and the different objects carefully pointed out and explained.

After a pleasant discussion one day, Gianatah remarked:

> You desire our children to learn from books and say that, because you have done so, you are able to build all those big houses, and sail over the sea, and talk with each other at any distance, and do many wonderful things; now, let me tell you what we think. You begin when you are little to work hard, and work until you are men in order to begin fresh work. You say that you work hard in order to learn how to work well. After you get to be men, then you say, the labor of life commences; then, too, you build big houses, big ships, big towns, and everything else in proportion. Then, after you have got them all, you die and leave all behind. Now, we call that slavery. You are slaves from the time you begin to talk until you die; but we are free as air. We never work, but the Mexicans and others work for us. Our wants

are few and easily supplied. The river, the wood, and plain yield all we require, and we will not be slaves; nor will we send our children to your schools, where they will only learn to become like yourselves.

It was so utterly impossible to make them comprehend the other side of this specious argument that it was not attempted. It will, however, be seen how absurd it is to hope for any civilization of these savages by the employment of any means now known to us. Labor of all kinds is held to be so degrading that any effort to promote it among the Apaches will be resisted to the death.

Skill in hunting ranks high among them, being only second to dexterity and adroitness in stealing. The first award of merit is accorded to the individual who exhibits the greatest address in appropriating the property of another person. As he is deemed the best able to support wives and cater for their wants, he is the cynosure of their admiration. Personal prowess in battle takes the third rank in their estimation, and unless they have their enemy at the greatest possible disadvantage they refrain from attacking. "It is easier and safer to run than fight," is the maxim in vogue among them, especially when there is no plunder to tempt their cupidity and afford a field for the exercise of their cherished faculty.

Nah-tank, the "Corn Flower," and Nah-Kah-yen, the "Keen Sight," were hunting a very large cougar which had been feasting on some of their horses. Having discovered his lair, about five miles from camp down the Pecos, Nah-tank climbed a large cottonwood tree which flung some of its branches far over the stream, and from which he could survey the lair at his leisure. He had crawled out on a projecting branch and was intently peering into the covert when Nah-Kah-yen called his attention to a cougar crouched upon another branch some twelve feet and as fixedly gazing at Nah-tank, evidently with hostile intention. The wily savage turned his head and saw the beast, but made no other motion. On the other hand, the cougar was lashing its sides with its long tail and gripping the limb with spasmodic clutches of its powerful talons. Suddenly its outspread form dashed through the intervening space and alighted on the exact spot which had been occupied by the Indian; but the cool savage had let go his hold and had dropped into the stream at the very moment. The astonished and outwitted cougar gazed into the river below, while he tore great strips of bark from the limb and growled with intense rage. Nah-tank swam underwater until he reached the shelter of a projecting bank, and on regaining *terra firma,* the two warriors soon dispatched the cougar with their rifles.

This incident exhibits the surprising coolness and presence of mind possessed by the Apaches, for it was not regarded by them as worthy of special note.

As wampum was the standard of value among the Delawares, so are horses among the Apaches. Wives are purchased with horses, and their value is determined by the number of horses offered to the parents. Some fetch as high as six and seven horses, while others can be bought for one. The girl that brings six horses feels as much superior to the one who is sold for two, as a fine lady who sports a $1,500 cashmere affects to look down upon a neighbor who can only afford to pay $20 for a shawl.

But we have said enough to enable the reader to perceive that our policy in relation to these savages has been altogether erroneous. We have treated with them upon suppositious grounds, and all our efforts have failed in the past as they must in the future. We have entirely underrated their numbers, strength, mental capacity, and indomitable spirit. We have haughtily and offensively approached them with expressions of superiority and disdain. We have failed to inquire into their natural instincts, training, language, habits, or opinions. Everything has been done with the stiff formality of red tape, with an easy indifference to the result. We have already expended thirty million dollars in the futile attempt to reduce them by the ordinary means employed with other tribes and have only succeeded in rendering them vindictive, more alert and dangerous, and furnishing them with a very superior armament.

Considering the extent and value of the region over which these savages exercise almost unrestricted control, is it not almost time that the government should pay the subject that attention which its specialty indicates, and its importance demands?

The Days of the Empire—Arizona, 1866–1869

CAMILLO C. C. CARR[1]

Journal of the United States Cavalry Association 2, no. 4 (March 1889): 3–22

Twenty-three years ago, in 1866, the territory of Arizona, with an area of more than two-and-one-half times that of New York or Pennsylvania, was almost as little known and as inaccessible as the interior of Alaska is now.

The U.S. surveys which had been made were confined almost exclusively to the lines of the Thirty-second and Thirty-fifth parallels, along which ran the only roads traversing the territory from east to west. What lay in the vast extent of country between these lines may have formed the subject of many a conjecture, but no efforts to definitely determine the question had been made. The route principally used was that near the Thirty-second Parallel, extending from Fort Yuma to New Mexico, through Tucson and Fort Bowie, a dreary, sandy waste of quite four hundred miles; a vivid realization of the "abomination of desolation" spoken of by Jeremiah, the prophet. Between Yuma and Bowie there was but one settlement, Tucson, a dirty Mexican pueblo of a few hundred inhabitants. The stations, as they were called, were only brush shelters or adobe hovels, built near the watering places, at which all travelers were expected to stop to water and feed their stock and poison themselves with the beverage peculiar to the country, known as "Pickhandle Whiskey." This murderer's inspiration was said to be made of alcohol, water, cayenne pepper, and tobacco, in proportions varying with the stock of ingredients on hand. The whole having been thoroughly mixed with a pick handle, it was ready to be served to those desiring something stimulating but not hurtful to rouse their flagging energies, or soothe their excited brains.

During the War of the Rebellion the few posts existing in Arizona were occupied by California troops, and it was all they could do to keep possession of them and obtain rations enough to prevent starvation vanquishing the garrisons. Supplies were bought first from Los Angeles across the Colorado desert to Yuma, a distance of more than three hundred miles, and then began the tedious and uncertain journey to the Arizona posts. With such transportation as was furnished in those days, no dependence could be placed upon the arrival of supplies at any specified time, and each garrison was obliged to be as careful of the stores it had as though preparing to undergo a protracted siege.

There was but one sawmill in the territory, which was near Prescott, the territorial capital, where the pine forests of that region furnished ample material for it to work upon. In that vicinity lumber could be obtained for a little less than its weight in gold, but it was seldom shipped elsewhere on account of the increased expense of freighting over roads so infested by Apaches that it was considered an exceedingly fortunate thing to get from one station to another without the loss of some or all of the team mules.

There was not a stage line in the whole territory, and had not been since the Butterfield drew off in 1861. I believe the mail was carried on horseback from Los Angeles to Prescott once a week. The other posts received theirs when the quartermaster at Drum Barracks saw fit to send out a pack mule in charge of a civilian employee, carrying only the letter mail. As to newspapers and other printed matter, they came by bull train, or some other equally swift conveyance, or, more frequently, failed to come at all.

The territory formed a part of the Department of California, headquarters at San Francisco, and was under the command of General McDowell.[2] All the administrative business of the department was conducted there, and it may be imagined into what a muddle affairs in Arizona frequently fell when the difficulty of communications between the two places is considered. Each post commander was supreme on his own reservation and did exactly as he chose when he went off of it, provided he did not trespass upon that of his neighbor.

All business transactions were conducted on a gold basis, and during my first three years in Arizona, the pay we received from the government never exceeded in value seventy cents on the dollar, and for a great part of the time it was as low as sixty.

Excepting the Pimas and Maricopas, the Indians were all called Apaches. It might be truly said of them at any time, they have either just been hostile, are now, or soon will be. The Chiricahuas excepted, they were without horses, save those they stole for food. The fact that they were not mounted made it all the more difficult to capture them in the mountains. They wore no clothing except a breechcloth, and burdened only with their weapons, which were light, when they started to run up or down a mountainside, no soldier, burdened with his arms, clothing, and accoutrements, could hope to overtake them. The color of the rocks was such, too, that they were indistinguishable from them. Their numbers were estimated at about eighteen thousand. They were noted for their treachery and cruelty. Unlike the Indians of the Plains and the Northwest, they seemed to delight in lying and deception, and the truth was not in them—or if it was, never came out.

The First Cavalry landed in San Francisco in January 1866, or twenty-three years ago this month. After a stay of a few weeks at the Presidio, the regimental headquarters and five troops were sent to Drum Barracks, near Wilmington, the seaport of Los Angeles. Three of the troops had already been sent to Arizona, one by one, on account of the scarcity of transportation at the depot, and of water and forage on the road. The fourth, Colonel Sanford's,[3] was about to start, and being young and in the enjoyment of good health, and not knowing when I was well off, as young men seldom do, I resigned my office of regimental quartermaster and joined him as the first lieutenant of his troop.

Our horses we received from the Second California Cavalry, and better ones for the work required of them I have never seen. The only objection to them was their irresistible propensity for bucking when first mounted, and this they displayed to such an extent that the troop was seldom ordered to mount without the air being filled for a few minutes with flying men, carbines, and sabers in inextricable confusion. However, we had no one seriously injured and soon grew accustomed to this exhibition of the "high school" of riding, although not provided for in our drill book. Our carbines were the old Sharp's, using linen cartridges and percussion caps.

I do not propose to enter here upon a detailed description of the march across the Colorado desert and up the Gila River. The length of the marches was governed entirely by the supply of water and the presence or absence of sandstorms, which in that region make life a burden and traveling impossible. A part of our route lay over land lying below the level of the sea, and sometimes we wished the sea might return and reclaim its own, as it once did for Pharaoh and his hosts. So intense was the heat even at that early season, and so scarce and vile such water as we could get to drink, that to be engulfed and drowned by a tidal wave seemed to our heated minds and bodies a "consummation devoutly to be wished." For want of personal experience, the customs in vogue in regard to marching commands in that country were observed. Reveille sounded at about the only hour in the twenty-four when it was possible to sleep, and the march began at three or four o'clock in the morning. The result of this was that men and animals were deprived of absolutely necessary sleep, and, as the marches were generally short, the new camp was reached at so early an hour that the whole day was spent in fighting flies and other insects, and night came to find everyone more exhausted than if the journey had been made in the heat of the day after a night of refreshing sleep.

From the time we left Warner's Ranch, in California, until we reached Maricopa Wells, a distance of over three hundred miles, we never saw anything which, by a vigorous effort of our imagination, could be called a patch of grass.

As we came, in the early morning, down the slope leading to the wells after an all-night march across the forty-five mile desert between that place and Gila Bend, our eyes were gladdened by the sight of a verdant spot which, to our weary souls, promised a pleasant rest; but a nearer approach proved it to be an illusion as deceptive as the mirage of the desert. The green turf of our imagination was only a scanty growth of salt grass, each blade of which was strong enough to stand alone and so rank with alkali that even a hungry mule could not eat it and live.

Maricopa Wells, formerly a home station on the Overland Route, was the only place between Fort Yuma and Tucson where the table fare ever rose above the sodden, greasy level of bacon and beans. Owned by the only firm of any importance in the southern part of the territory and controlling nearly all the government contracts and freighting business, they had their trains always on the road and, in this way, could supply themselves and their friends with all the necessaries and some of the luxuries of life—including the best brands of whiskey and champagne to be obtained in San Francisco. It was a veritable oasis in the desert and was, in many respects, a reminder to weary travelers and sojourners in the land of that great world outside of Arizona, tenderly and tearfully designated by the name of "God's Country."

The wells themselves consisted of holes dug to a depth of three or four feet, in which the water from the Santa Cruz, a subterranean river, rose near to the surface. The water was so strongly impregnated with alkali that the porous earthen jars into which it was put when drawn were encrusted on the outside with a solid white deposit of soda and potash; but it was the best to be had in many miles and, bad as it was, was always a welcome beverage to thirsty souls choked with the impalpable dust of the traveled roads.

Near the wells were the reservations of the Pimas and Maricopas, two Indian tribes always friendly to the whites and hostile to the Apaches. The Maricopas were the remnant of a once large tribe which had been nearly annihilated in a battle with the Yumas and Cocapahs a mile or two west of the wells. The whitened bones of the slaughtered Maricopas and their opponents that lay piled upon the field when I visited it showed how desperate and destructive the struggle had been.

Since their disastrous defeat the remaining members of the tribe had virtually placed themselves under the protection of the Pimas, a tribe numbering nearly four thousand persons at the time of our entering the territory. According to their traditions, after the subsidence of the great flood which destroyed all the inhabitants of the earth except Montezuma and those with him in the ark, Montezuma made from the red earth the Pimas and from the black ooze and slime the Apaches, their hereditary enemies. It was the boast of the Pimas that they had always been the friends of the white man and that no member of their tribe had ever killed an American. As to the Mexicans, they were not so positive. They cultivated their lands by means of irrigation, and upon them the government depended for its supply of corn and wheat used for forage at Fort McDowell and the different stations along the Overland Road. They were the finest looking Indians I had ever seen and, all things considered, the most respectable. They were intelligent, hospitable, and ready to inconvenience themselves at any time to assist anyone wearing our uniform, and have always remained our firm and trusty friends.

At a point nearly opposite the center of the Pima reservation, upon a high rocky ridge, of which a view could be had by the whole tribe, were displayed two objects, the like of which, I venture to say, were never before exhibited in

The saguaro cactus. NELSON A. MILES. *PERSONAL RECOLLECTIONS AND OBSERVATIONS.*

any Christian land. Rising from the stones, between which cactus plants of different kinds lifted up their forbidding, thorny stems, were two rude Latin crosses, eight or ten feet high. Upon each was suspended the dried and shriveled body of a male Apache, with arms outstretched and feet placed one upon the other. The living Apaches had been secured to the crosses by green rawhide thongs, which, shrinking and drying in the sun, had cut through the flesh to the bones, thus increasing the tortures of the victims doomed to die a lingering death. Under the influence of the burning but drying sun the bodies had not decayed, but with their dried bones and parchment skins had assumed the appearance of Egyptian mummies. There they hung, a constant source of satisfaction to the Pimas and objects of astonishment and horror to the passersby. These Apaches, while making a raid into the Pima villages, had been captured alive, and the opportunity of wreaking vengeance upon their hated enemies was not one to be neglected by the Pimas. As torture was something seldom, if ever, practiced by their people, they were probably in a quandary as to what to do, when someone who had perhaps visited the old mission churches further south suggested the idea of crucifying them, and the proposal was accepted and put into practice, with the results I have described.

Nearer the wells two wooden headboards marked the spot where rested the remains of two men of the old First Dragoons who had fallen by the way on the terrible march made by a part of that regiment under its distinguished commander, Colonel Stephen W. Kearny in 1846, from Fort Leavenworth, Kansas, through New Mexico and Arizona, as it was afterwards named, to California, of which he took military possession after having defeated, with his worn and weary command, in three pitched battles the fresh Mexican forces opposed to him.

Turning off from the Overland Road we crossed the Gila and then traversed the thirty-five miles of dusty, waterless desert between that and the Salt River. We observed in passing that the southern edge of this vast plain was covered with a dense growth of mesquite trees; beyond that not one was to be seen, but in their stead only greasewood and cactus of many varieties, from the *Cereus giganteus* or "suwarro,"[4] towering to a height of thirty feet, with outstretched arms curving gracefully upwards, giving it the appearance of a great green candelabrum to the common prickly pear, sprawling raggedly over the ground. The land now covered with cactus had doubtlessly been highly cultivated while the mesquite was a part of the primeval forest of that region. Near the northern edge of the desert we saw for the first time the immense irrigating canals made by a prehistoric people occupying that section of the country, concerning whom the Indians of the present day have neither knowledge nor tradition.[5] These canals were of great size and length, branching out in various directions, and evidently had, at some long distant period of time, enabled the people who constructed them to cultivate thousands of acres of the land now justly characterized as desert. Ruins of what had been great adobe houses built on stone foundations could be seen in every direction. The wearing down of the superstructures by the action of the elements gave to the whole the appearance of immense monumental mounds or pyramids. In places, the ground was strewn with axes, hammers, and other implements made of green stone, hard enough to turn the edge of a steel chisel, and yet polished by their makers in some mysterious way until their surfaces were as smooth as satin. Pottery of various kinds, from the plain, half-baked, porous material to that having a brilliant glaze equal to some of the best modern styles and ornamented with intricate patterns, or adorned with the simple but effective fretwork employed upon the temples of Greece, were found scattered about in the greatest profusion. The colors, especially the yellows and blacks, were as fresh and brilliant as though the articles had been removed from the kiln only the day before.

In spite of its forbidding name the Salt River was found to be a large body of fresh, sweet water, without alkali or other perceptible impurity, and our camp upon its banks was a red-letter day in the calendar of our journey.

From the Salt River a march of fifteen miles brought us to our destination, Fort McDowell, the newest, largest, and best post in Arizona. It had been constructed during the previous winter by a regiment of California infantry whose time before being mustered out was thus employed. It was about half a mile back from the Verde River, from which all the water used by the garrison was hauled in a wagon. The parade ground, without grass or trees, was of granite gravel, closely packed, and as white and painful to the eyes in the blazing sun as though it had been whitewashed. It absorbed heat enough during the day to keep the air throughout the night nearly up to the temperature of the day, which for several months in the year averaged about 115 degrees in the shade, or would have done so if any shade could have been found.

The company officers' quarters were of adobe, built in one continuous line facing the parade ground, without any wings or rear extensions. Each officer was allowed one or two rooms, according to circumstances, and was permitted to use his quarters for drawing room, bedroom, or kitchen, as he might think best. The rooms were about twelve by fifteen feet, with one opening for a door but no windows except one facing away from the parade ground. The men's barracks were of the same style and material as those for the officers, but their windowless ends faced the parade. The floors of the officers' quarters were of common clay and were sprinkled with water as often as necessary to keep down the dust and moderate the temperature to such an extent as to render indoor life endurable. The principal objection to them was that they seemed to have some special attraction for a species of villainous and venomous red ant, which came up in swarms through them in one spot after another, overran the place, invaded the beds, and held possession of them to the exclusion of their rightful occupants.

The roofs were of mud put on to a depth of from nine to twelve inches with the expectation of keeping out the water during the rainy season. Unfortunately, in constructing the roofs to prevent the clay falling through, a deep layer of horse manure had been laid upon the small sticks spread over the rafters, and when the floods descended as they always did in January and February, and occasionally during July and August, the water that poured through the roofs into the rooms was at first of a dark brown color, then shaded off into a light yellow as the mud of the roof dissolved and made its way through the lower stratum. On such occasions the occupants of the quarters covered their bedding and other perishable articles with rubber blankets and passed their time outdoors, where, if there was more moisture, it was at least cleaner and less fragrant.

For more than a year after our arrival at Fort McDowell there was not a window or a door in any set of quarters occupied by bachelor officers. The commanding officer, by virtue of his rank and control over the quartermaster, indulged in the luxury of a wagon cover hung in graceful festoons before the hole in the wall where it was intended at some future time to put a door; the apertures for windows were covered with canvas or gunny sacks. With four crotches driven into the floor for a bedstead, a packing box for a table, a candle box for a chair, and a demijohn with its accompanying tin cup to represent the bric-a-brac of the establishment, the height of luxury was attained. Doors were not actually necessary for protection against the cold, but when we found our rooms, as we frequently did, invaded by rattlesnakes, centipedes of "monstrous size and mien," and whole families of scorpions with which the country was infested, there was a desire, almost a yearning, for something that might render their entrance a matter of greater difficulty. It was not altogether pleasant to wake at reveille and find one's boots and stockings gone to become the playthings of a litter of festive pups, having so little regard for the proprieties of life that they not infrequently distributed one's garments among two or three of the neighbors, whence they were recovered only after a prolonged search and general redistribution.

It even ceased, after a while, to be amusing to be aroused from slumber in the middle of the night by the yelping and snarling of a struggling pack of dogs and wolves fighting in front of one's doorway, with the chances of the battle-ground being transferred to within the contracted limits of the already crowded sleeping room. The liability to step on a coiled or crawling rattlesnake in the dark was so great that no one entered his room after dark without first striking a match with which to get a view of his surroundings.

The first centipede I ever saw, and it was nearly a foot in length, fell from the unceiled roof of the commanding officer's sitting room upon the center of a table around which was assembled a party of officers playing cards. An exploding bombshell would not have scattered the group more quickly or effectively, and there was great joy over the death of the intruder. At that time our information in regard to centipedes was limited to what we had acquired from our predecessors, and according to their accounts the reptile's feet were as venomous as the rattler's fangs.

Our wardrobes, which consisted of a few nails driven into the adobe walls, did not secure our clothing from invasion, as I discovered one morning on taking down my dress coat, when I found within its folds a whole family of about a dozen scorpions, looking like bleached prawns, except that each had ready in his upturned tail a sting, properly prepared for producing a lasting impression of warmth exceeding even that of the climate of the country.

The social life of the garrison may be described in very few words—there was none. The visits of the paymaster at intervals of from four to six months were the signal for the beginning of a saturnalia of drunkenness and gambling, which, we are happy to say, is so much a thing of the past in our army that even the recollection of it as it once existed were better not revived.

From the foregoing details it may be imagined that life within the post lacked some of the charms supposed to be essential to a happy existence, but relief was not to be attained outside. The surrounding country was interesting only from the novelty of its indigenous productions in the form of cactus plants of a dozen different varieties none of us had ever seen or heard of before; of trees like the palo verde that no fire could ever burn;[6] the mesquite, the dry parts of which were collected for fuel with a crowbar instead of being chopped with axes, whose edges it would break like glass; the useful but unlovely galleta grass, which was always mowed with a heavy hoe instead of a scythe; whose sharp thorns would have perforated the intestines of any animal less tough than the California horse or government mule. I have always believed that even they would have succumbed to its penetrating effects had it not always been fed in conjunction with corn and wheat mixed, which formed a glutinous mass that afforded a great degree of protection to the stomach. This grass, which was our only forage, cost about one hundred dollars per ton. The men filled their bed sacks with it, but after the experience of the first man who lay upon one of them just long enough to spring from it and call for the surgeon to bind up his bleeding wounds, they were beaten to something like smoothness, if not softness, before being used.

What part of the country was not occupied by the reptiles and cactus seemed to be so well held down by the ubiquitous and perniciously active Apache that no one was allowed to go half a mile away from the post in broad daylight without a suitable escort.

Their tracks could be found every morning in and around the post. They actually picked the bullets out of the target at which the old guard were accustomed to discharge their muzzle-loading muskets every morning and prowled about with a view of picking up old bottles or anything else of which arrowheads could be made. They occasionally shot men almost within the limits of the post, and yet no attempts were made to punish them. Why, it may be asked? The following will serve to explain. General McDowell had conceived and put into practical operation the idea of having a government farm which should either produce all the grain required by the troops for forage, or at least such an amount as would enable him to regulate the prices of that bought by the government. A piece of bottom land lying on the river near the post, containing about half a section, was selected, an irrigating ditch several miles in length and, in places, ten or twelve feet in depth, was dug; the land was cleared of its dense growth of mesquite trees, bull brush, and cactus—mainly by the labor of the three companies of the Fourteenth U.S. Infantry and one troop of the First U.S. Cavalry, constituting the garrison.

We had reveille about 3:00 A.M. The cavalry marched to stables, groomed their horses, and then returned to barracks for a sumptuous repast of bread and coffee, with sometimes a diminutive slice of salt pork. At 6:00 A.M. work on the farm began and continued without intermission until noon, when time was allowed for the consumption of the bean or rice soup and bread which constituted the dinner. The work was resumed at 1:00 P.M. and continued until 6:00 P.M. At that hour the command returned to the post, and the cavalry, after having groomed their horses, were permitted to close the day with a late supper so much like the early breakfast that a confusion in reckoning time was produced that rendered it difficult to distinguish reveille from retreat roll call.

Such labor on such food, a bare government ration of the poorest quality, without fresh vegetables of any kind, in a heat which any decent thermometer would have registered at 135 to 140 degrees in the sun, produced great suffering, of course. After an hour's work the men's garments were as wet as though they had swum a river with them on, and they dried only when, after the day's work, they lay down in the night air to rest and sleep. In their exhausted and half-famished condition the men were easily chilled, and the fruits of such treatment soon showed themselves in the appearance of a malignant type of dysentery which filled a great part of the space in the new post cemetery with the victims of insufficient food and overwork in a broiling sun.

I think some fifteen men died that summer and were buried either in their blankets or in rude coffins made of packing boxes from which the clothing had been emptied. More than once we assisted at the burial of soldiers who had done good service during the rebellion, whose coffins bore some such simple but eloquent inscription as "U.S. No. 20, 25 Pairs Gov't Boots," or "40 Pairs Cavalry Trousers," which had been placed there by the original packers of the boxes from which the coffins were made.

Requisitions for lumber to supply the demands for coffins were disapproved on the score of expense. It could be obtained in the vicinity only by whipsawing it from green cottonwood trees, a labor to be justly appreciated only by those who have had it to do.

Although the officers of the command did not work with the axe and shovel as did the men, yet they had no advantage in the quality of the food upon which they subsisted. They were allowed to purchase enough of it, such as it was. It was black coffee, dry bread, poor beef or poorer pork, with rice and beans, month after month for a year and a half. Vegetables were not to be had at any place within two hundred miles. Potatoes and onions would have brought fabulous prices could they have been obtained. The Subsistence Department kept no stores for sale to officers except crushed sugar and, occasionally, poor hams and dried apples. For the first half bushel of potatoes I was able to buy in Arizona I gladly paid sixteen dollars and would have given sixty had it been demanded. For once, money seemed to have lost its power. It could neither be eaten nor exchanged for that which the human system craved. When at last scurvy attacked the garrison, and the post surgeon demanded the purchase of anti-scorbutics, wagons were sent two hundred fifty miles and loaded with onions at forty-five dollars per bushel, and potatoes and cucumber pickles at corresponding prices. The remedy was expensive, but it was the natural result of the so-called economical measures originated by those in authority. The troops afterwards had fine gardens on a part of the farm land and might have had them the first year had work on both gone hand-in-hand; but, as work on the farm took precedence over everything else, it was too late to begin a garden after the completion of the farm.

Under such circumstances there may be some curiosity to know whether or not we lost many men by desertion. As a matter of fact it may be said that deserters were few and far between. It was not because men willingly submitted to exist as they did, but that there was no apparent way out of the difficulty. They were hardly a thousand white people in the whole territory outside of the military posts, and of them it is safe to say that about seventy percent were fugitives from justice in other lands; men who could not have looked in a mirror without immediately drawing a pistol and shooting at the reflection.[7] There were few settlements at which assistance or concealment could be obtained. If a deserter reached the Overland Road, no matter in which direction he followed it he must bring up against a military post. To go south was to invite murder at the hands of the Mexicans, and the interior was held exclusively by the Apaches. Had escape from the country been reasonably easy, I have no doubt that in a short time the officers would have been left with a small escort of a few old soldiers whose devotion to duty nothing could shake.

My first experience in command of a detachment of cavalry in Arizona may give some faint idea of the difficulties under which military operations were conducted. One day at 1:00 P.M., just after I had finished what by courtesy was called dinner, the commanding officer[8] said to me, "I want you to take thirty-five men of Colonel Sanford's troop, ten-days' rations, and plenty of ammunition and report to the commanding officer of Fort Grant for scouting duty. Your transportation will consist of ten pack mules, which your men will pack, and you will escort a wagon train to the Salt River crossing. You will be out of this post and on the road before 5:00 P.M. this afternoon."

As the commanding officer was one of the martinets of the old school who could give orders of any kind so long as obedience of them devolved upon someone else and had a habit of expecting prompt and exact compliance with them, I lost no time in setting out to make the preparations for which I was allowed four hours.

The detachment and wagon train I could have got away with easily in half an hour, but the pack train was something as novel to me as a steam engine would be to a Kamchatkan. The men, horses, rations, and ammunition were soon in a state of readiness. After that came the principal part of the procession—the ten bronco pack mules. By assigning one man to each mule and allowing a large space to each in which to give full play to his heels actual loss of life was prevented, but control over the animals was not gained for some time.

The second act consisted in the bringing into the vicinity of a wagonload of miscellaneous articles which but one man in the command had ever seen, and even he did not know the names of more than half of them. Strange sounds like aparejos, mantas, lash ropes, etc., were heard for the first time and were finally discovered to have some meaning as applied to the things before us; but it took several minutes to realize the fact that it was only with the assistance of all this apparatus that a band of mules could be converted into a pack train. Imagine a landsman put on board of an unrigged ship, the sails, cordage, etc., thrown down on deck before him, and being told to be ready to sail out of port in a given time, and some slight idea of the situation may be obtained.

An old sergeant who had served in A. J. Smith's troop of the First Dragoons during the Rogue River War and had seen things like these before, although he had never used them, came to the rescue with all the information and good will he possessed. The aparejos were finally placed upon the mules in spite of their vigorous protests, and then came the real tug of war—slinging the cargoes and securing them. Many here present have doubtless watched time and again a skillful packer handling his cargo, adjusting his lash ropes, making the diamond hitch, and finishing his work with the final indispensable kick and cry of "está bueno," and thought how easy it was to do, and discovered, only after repeated trials, that it was something to be learned only by taking hold of the ropes and conducting the operation to the finish—something which no amount of mere observation could teach—and may appreciate the difficulties under which I was laboring, working against time.

We put on the packs, bound them with the lash ropes and, of course, like any other tenderfoot, tied knots wherever it seemed they would do the most good, but for some mysterious reason, the mule was no sooner allowed to move off than the packs slipped and fell in all directions except the one in which they were finally fired by the bucking and kicking of the frightened animals.

Time was pressing; it was after 4:00 P.M. and not a pack had been induced to stay where it was put, but on the contrary, all were becoming rapidly pulverized and disintegrated by rough usage. We all knew we could learn the business if we only had time enough, but under existing orders that was not to be had in the post for learning even a simpler trade than that of packing mules. In this emergency my wagon train loomed up as the deliverer of the command. The cargoes, aparejos, and rigging were all thrown into the empty wagons, the vicious mules which I should have liked to throw in after them were safely secured, and the command sailed out of the post in true cavalry style, conscious of a literal compliance with orders and hoping to find time elsewhere for learning its new trade of running a pack train.

Knowing that the next day we had to cross a thirty-five mile desert, the command was aroused at midnight and the packing began at once. It continued in the same spot until 6:00 A.M. for the reasons already given in our first day's experience, and I thought we might as well have a change of scene, for the operations on the present one were growing monotonous, and moved out of camp. From 6:00 A.M. until 8:00 P.M. we were on that burning desert, beneath the blazing sun of midsummer, men and animals suffering from thirst which there was nothing to allay. The scanty supply of water in the canteens was exhausted early in the day.

Three days and nights more of similar worry and exhausting work and we arrived at Fort Grant, to the disgust of the commanding officer,[9] who regretted seeing cavalry coming to his post to consume his meager supply of forage. He had asked for infantry, he being one of those who thought mounted troops would never be able to pursue Apaches in the mountains. However, he made the best of a bad bargain, and the next evening, setting out from the post under cover of darkness with one half-breed guide, we started upon a scout into the Pinal Mountains. There was one Mexican with the command and, although not a professional packer, it was exasperating to see the ease and quickness with which, assisted by a few soldiers, he packed those mules, and packed the cargoes to stay. It was child's play to him, and under his instructions my men soon learned the art so well that we had little more trouble on that score with the light loads we carried.

For five or six nights we climbed the mountains on one side and slid down the other leading our horses, battered and bruised ourselves among the boulders, pricked our flesh with the cactus spines we ran against in the dark, dodged the rolling stones sent crashing down by those above us on the trail, and suffered for want of water which was hardly to be had at all. We marched all night and lay during the day in the red-hot canyons, their sides adding by reflected heat to the warmth of the sand on which we usually camped without shade and without having as much fire as would make a cup of coffee. It was understood we were going to attack a large rancheria of Apaches and the greatest secrecy was absolutely necessary.

One afternoon about an hour before sunset, we started from camp contrary to our custom of marching only by night and had not been half an hour on the trail before the mountainsides were swarming with Apaches fleeing to places of safety. We had undoubtedly been betrayed by our guide who, when we came near enough to the Apaches to make an early morning attack possible, had become alarmed for his own safety perhaps, having been for years a captive among the Apaches and, not having much confidence in the strange soldiers, had persuaded the commanding officer, much against his will, to make the move he did. The game had flown, and as with foot troops it was not thought possible to follow the Apaches rapidly enough to bring them to a stand, and as the mounted force was not considered sufficiently large to operate alone against them, we returned to Fort Grant, a weary and disgusted command.

Soon after my return to McDowell permission to make a scout against the Apaches living in that vicinity was obtained, and the troop, under command of Colonel Sanford, started by the light of the new moon, having with it one civilian guide and one Pima Indian as a trailer.[10] In the dimness of night, illumined only by the light of a young moon, we broke a new trail over the Mazatzal Mountain range and descended into the valley of Tonto Creek. The next night we crossed the Sierra Ancha and camped in Meadow Valley.

We were astonished at the character of the country in which we found ourselves. The desert wastes of the Verde and Gila were replaced by high plateau and deep valleys well supplied with water, forests of oak, pine and walnut trees, and a luxuriant growth of grass. Everywhere was to be seen the ruins of the buildings of an ancient civilization—one so far advanced that the stone walls were laid with mortar made from the gypsum beds in the vicinity, and as white and hard as Parian marble. We felt all the excitement of explorers of an unknown land and enjoyed in anticipation the surprises in store for us whenever we moved from one place to another.

While the main body of the command was examining the surrounding country a small party of Apaches attacked the guard left in camp but were quickly driven off. Hastily returning to the camp, we started on the back trail of these Indians, our Pima trailer never delaying for a moment to hunt for a lost track, and about 4:00 P.M., on rounding a mountain spur, we came in full view of quite a large rancheria of Apaches, utterly unconscious of our proximity.

The women and children were engaged in gathering grass and sunflower seeds, of which they made almost the only bread they ever had. Making the most of the surprise, with a whoop and a hurrah, the whole troop charged, mounted, down the mountainside into the seething crowd of Indians, and the fight was on, our men using their pistols and carbines, the Apaches relying for defense principally upon their bows and arrows, although a few of them had firearms.

Surprise of an Apache village. OUTING MAGAZINE, NOVEMBER 1886.

When the mounted charge had spent its force the men dismounted, turned their horses loose, and used their carbines so well that in about fifteen minutes the affair was ended and we counted as the results of it fifteen dead bucks and a number of women and children prisoners.

Another result was that in a day or two after our return to Fort McDowell, Delshay, the chief of the Coyoteros, to which tribe the Indians we had killed belonged, came to the post to make peace, bringing with him several hundred of his people.[11] He made the most liberal promises as to future good behavior, and as an unquestionable guarantee of his good faith offered to bring all his warriors, about three hundred, and join the troops of our garrison for the purpose of attacking and capturing Fort Grant. This offer was declined with thanks, but it showed that the Apaches had no idea that the troops of different posts belonged to the same army, but were regarded as independent bodies hostile to each other and simply holding places in the country for their own profit and advantage. In spite of his promises Delshay, with his band, stole away from the post within a week and was engaged in his regular employment, murdering travelers on the roads and stealing stock whenever it could be done. There was no reservation to which the Apaches could be sent when they came in and it was impossible to hold and guard them as prisoners, so the game of see-saw, fight and palaver, was indefinitely continued.

With our one troop of cavalry we overran and routed the Apaches, temporarily at least, from nearly every part of the country bounded by the Mogollon, the Verde, Salt River, and the East Fork. As the Indians had no permanent homes, when the pursuit of those who escaped from an attack made upon a rancheria stopped, fresh wickiups or brush shelters were put up, and the Apaches were again as much settled as before.

All our applications for civilians to handle a pack train for us so that we could continue in the field longer were refused by General Halleck, who thought soldiers should do that kind of work themselves.[12] As our men were needed for fighting purposes we carried on our horses nearly all the food we expected to subsist on for twelve or fifteen days. This consisted sometimes of jerked beef, with the addition of pinole, a meal made of parched Indian corn coarsely ground and prepared for us by mixing it with water and sugar to make a gruel. It quenched thirst and appeased hunger, if it did not satisfy it, but in a short time became tiresome. Its long continued use produced intestinal troubles, and in other respects it was objectionable as a steady article of diet. When possible we carried salt pork and hard bread, which were made to last without reference to the number of days or rations. That trick we had learned well in the Army of the Potomac.

All our scouting had to be done by night. Apaches were always on the lookout around the post during the day, and if a command attempted to start before sunset it would hardly get across the Verde River before signal smokes would shoot up from a dozen mountain peaks to alarm and warn the Apaches of the threatened danger. As there were no mounted Indians in our vicinity, any dust raised during the day would produce the same effect.

There were no other cavalry troops to cooperate with us. Until late in 1867 the four troops of the First Cavalry were the only ones in all southern Arizona, and they were stationed at McDowell, Bowie, Buchanan, and Calabasas. Those at the three last-named posts had all they could do to hold Cochise and the Chiricahuas in check and escort trains and paymasters along the roads from post to post. The Chiricahuas were then at their best. Well mounted and using Mexico as a depot from which to draw supplies, they were a terror to all who traversed, or attempted to reside in, the country between Bowie and Tucson. As there were no other troops to cooperate with us and the game must be played, we had to go it alone. There was no one in the territory who had the authority to order the troops from different posts to execute any combined movements against the common enemy. Scouting was done or not according to the caprice or judgment of the different post commanders. Indians driven from the field of operations of one command took refuge in another where the troops were inactive.

In addition to our continued scouting, we were obliged to furnish escorts for all paymasters coming into the territory, a duty which deprived the troop of a number of its men for a month or two at a time and reduced its effective strength by just that number.

A superstitious belief peculiar to the Pimas, upon whom we depended for our trailers, was a constant impediment to steady work. The moment a Pima touched an Apache, dead or alive, or even killed one in a fight, it was bad medicine to go a step further. The Pima who thus contaminated himself was at once taken in charge by older men whose duty it was to see that he drank water until vomiting and purging were produced; that he was provided with a stick with which alone he was to touch his body, so that his fingers would not be employed; that he tasted nothing containing salt; and that, upon his return to the reservation, he was taken to a solitary place and provided with drinking water and pinole. After forty days of fasting and isolation, the whole tribe went out in procession to greet and bring home the slayer of the hated Apache and celebrate the prowess of the hero with general feasting and rejoicing. As a superstitious practice it was harmless enough, and probably originated in the quarantine of someone who had encountered the Apaches during the prevalence among them of small pox or some other contagious disease; but it seriously interfered with continuous operations against the Apaches and compelled the command to return to its post almost always after a single fight instead of keeping on with the good work.

In 1867, I Troop of the Eighth Cavalry, just organized, joined us at McDowell, and thenceforth we had more men for scouting purposes but no greater facilities than before. It was still the same hard work, scanty food, and lack of cooperation.

Until General Crook was placed in command of the department there was never any organized or systematic plan of campaign.[13]

Under his regime in 1872 the seventeen troops of cavalry, two companies of the Twenty-third U.S. Infantry, with a sufficient number of Indian scouts, comprising the active forces, took the field with everything necessary in the way of supplies, and pack trains handled by civilian packers to carry them, necessary for continuous and comfortable campaigning. So large a command, operating in any single district covered the face of the country with trails until it looked like a great cobweb. Fleeing Indians could not run away from one command without rushing into the arms of another. Captured Apaches were placed on reservations and kept there as much as possible, instead of being allowed to come and go at will on their own worthless promises of good behavior. Much hard fighting and scouting had yet to be done, but ample means with which to do it were supplied, and there was a feeling that although inevitably delayed, final success and comparative rest must crown the work. Before that time campaigning was unnecessarily severe, performed under every disadvantage and in a desultory way. The only hope of ultimate peace seemed to depend upon the utter annihilation of the hostile Apache tribes—an apparently endless task for the number of troops engaged.

It may not be uninteresting to relate here a singular experience I once had while in command of the troop and searching for a wagon route from Fort

McDowell to Fort Lincoln, now Verde, through an unexplored region. Having been sent out in the rainy season, the *malpais*[14] over which I had to travel was of the consistency of fresh mush. The animals, which we hardly ever mounted, mired to such an extent that to make a distance of nine miles in a day's journey was considered good work. Quite a number of the animals had already died of hunger and exhaustion when the Verde River was reached at a point where it must be crossed, but could not be forded. A raft of large size was made of dried cottonwood poles, and when put into the water floated as lightly as cork. The raft was partly laden with canvas pack covers and other buoyant articles, and two men started with it for the further bank. The water was as smooth as glass, not a ripple disturbing its surface, and the current apparently sluggish. When about the middle of the stream there was a cry from the men, an opening in the surface of the water, and the raft went down bow foremost, never to be seen again. The men swam to shore, but neither the freight nor a stick of the raft ever came to the surface, or was seen again, although the stream was carefully examined for some distance below the scene of the wreck. The disappearance of that raft is a mystery for which no rational explanation has ever been offered. Another was built, launched at a different place, and started upon its journey, but secured this time by guys made of lash ropes, which were carried to the farther bank by men who stripped to the buff, notwithstanding the falling snow, and waited, naked, on the other side until their clothing was brought over to them.

In December 1868 I was the lucky recipient of a recruiting detail ordering me to New York City. No persuasion was necessary to obtain my prompt acceptance of it, and preparations for the journey of seven thousand miles were quickly completed.

At Maricopa Wells, as suggested by the agent, I climbed very quietly into a buckboard, before which two partially hitched mules were held by the stable men. The driver, with lines in hand, followed as gently as though treading on eggs. The outer traces were hooked, the blinds removed from the eyes of the mules, when with a bound into the air which made every buckle and strap crack like a whip and nearly broke my neck, they started, and "lit" again upon solid ground about six miles from the point where they made their rise. When they came down they were still going at full speed, and it was some time before they were sufficiently blown to take an ordinary gait. The driver's only object in life seemed to be to keep them in or near the road and prevent them wandering off into the trackless desert.

We passed the Maricopa Mountain, and I bade farewell forever, as I hoped, to the colossal reclining figure of Montezuma, one of the grandest pieces of natural sculpture in the world.[15] The bold Aztec head thrown back upon the mountain pillow, the rays of the setting sun projecting in high relief the clearly outlined features composed in sleep, presented a picture of dignified repose bordering upon the sublime. There he lay, waiting the coming of the time appointed for his shaking off his deathlike slumber and, according to the Pima belief, commanding the Aztec Gabriel to sound the signal for the general resurrection of all those who had perished since the great flood from which only Montezuma and his family had been saved.

Three days and two nights of torture on the narrow seat of a buckboard, without support of any kind for the back, the monotony broken only by occasional halts at the station for the necessary supply of bacon and beans to support life, and Fort Yuma was reached.

The quartermaster at Yuma having no other conveyance, hired a civilian wagon for the transportation of myself and two other officers to the seacoast. In this trap, which had no springs and whose seats were rough boards laid across the top of the wagon bed, we journeyed for five or six days across the Colorado Desert. Finally, after a disastrous wreck on the Jacumba Range, where we nearly perished of cold, we came down to the shores of the beautiful bay of San Diego and, with a few days' rest, the long nightmare of three years' service in Arizona was partially dispelled, if not entirely removed.

An Incident of the Hualapais War

JAMES DEINE

Prescott *Arizona Miner*, April 4, 1868

A gain we are called upon to record another inhuman butchery of white men by Indian murderers which took place on the morning of Saturday, March 21, 1868, at a point on the Prescott and Hardyville road between Camp Willows and the Cottonwoods, eighty miles west from Prescott. We are indebted to Private James Deine of Company E, Fourteenth U.S. Infantry, for the following account of the affair, as given him by the wounded mailrider, Charles Spencer:[1]

CAMP WILLOW GROVE, Arizona
March 23, 1868

I am extremely sorry to inform you that Charles Spencer has been severely wounded by the Indians, but, I am happy to state, not mortally. He is now in the hospital at this post and is doing as well as could be expected. He and the escort started from this post with the mail for Hardyville and California on the morning of the twenty-first instant at the usual time, 9:00 A.M. Before they got to the Cottonwoods, four miles from here, they were fired into by a party of Hualapais Indians, and the escort, consisting of Corporal Troy and Private Flood, were killed at the first fire, as was also the mule which the mail carrier was riding. Spencer as quick as possible disengaged himself from the saddle, grabbed his seven-shooting rifle, and ran behind a greasewood bush, the only protection close at hand.

Soon he saw a party of the savages go up to the dead body of the corporal, strip, and mutilate it. While they were engaged in this brutal work, Spencer kept up a steady fire on them and had the satisfaction of killing two of the red devils. The others then ran for shelter; Spencer did the same thing, and on reaching a safe retreat, and just as he was about to get securely covered, he was fired upon by about a dozen Indians, who were hid behind some rocks. One of their shots hit him in the thigh, passing through the fleshy part, causing him to fall. They then rushed towards him, thinking they had him

36

Stripping the murdered soldiers. OUTING MAGAZINE, MARCH 1887.

sure. In this they were mistaken. For Charlie had not yet commenced to fight. He soon gathered himself up and made the savages hunt their holes. He then crawled into a cavity between some rocks and took a rest, which he needed.

During all this time, a party of Indians were stripping the bodies of the murdered soldiers and cutting up the carcasses of the horses and mules, which occupied about twenty minutes. They then surrounded Spencer and tried to shoot him out, but he could shoot and hit too, and they found that that was no go. Then they tried to scare him out with yells, but he yelled back defiance at them and, whenever an opportunity offered, sent a bullet after them. Changing their tactics, they tried to blarney him by telling him to go home, that they did not want to kill him and would not shoot any more. But he would not be blarneyed by them. At length, about 4:00 P.M., they got up and dusted. The cause of their leaving was the appearance of a squad of soldiers sent from this post to ascertain the cause of the firing, which had been heard at the camp. The men came upon the dead body of the corporal, hastened to camp, and reported, when a wagon and twenty men under Lieutenant Robinson[2] started to bring in the bodies. Spencer heard the rumbling of the wagon, but being unable to go to it, he yelled and discharged his pistol, by which means he attracted the attention of the lieutenant to his situation. He was immediately placed in the wagon and brought to camp, where all the care and attention necessary was, and will be, rendered him by officers and men. He says there were all of seventy-five Indians, more than half of whom were armed with guns.

Johnny O'Donnell and the station keeper at the Willows, who arrived here with the mail Saturday last, called upon us, and in their account of the above affair blamed the officer in command at the Willows for not sending troops to the scene of conflict earlier in the day. They said that, upon hearing the firing in the forenoon, he was asked to send out men but did not then do so. In explanation of his conduct, he says he looked for the arrival of Major Price[3] and command and took it for granted that the command was encamped at the Cottonwoods, and that it was they that did the firing. Be this as it may, our humble opinion is that troops should have been sent out upon hearing the continuous firing. We have been told also that Major Price was expected from the east, instead of from the west, and if this be the case, we cannot, for the life of us, account for the officer's apathy. We do know that if citizens were placed in a similar position to that of the troops, they would have gone out and seen what the matter was.

Up to this time, we have not learned anything in regard to the mail but suppose that it and the mule upon which it was packed fell into the hands of the Indians. This mail left Prescott Thursday morning, March 19. Those of our citizens who sent letters by it need not, of course, expect answers to them. Serum[4] and his warriors will probably destroy them all.

The details of the fight and struggle for life made by Spencer against seventy-five or one hundred infuriated savages, as related by O'Donnell, put us in mind of the heroic deeds of some of the pioneers of the "Dark and Bloody Ground." Luckily for him, on starting in the morning he provided himself with plenty of rifle and pistol cartridges, which enabled him to keep his enemies at bay for so long a time. Once, during the afternoon, a single Indian approached Spencer's "fortification," telling him in broken English to come out and go home, as they did not intend to kill any more soldier men; said he and the other Indians were going home, and then walked off over a hill. Spencer soon after placed his hat upon the rammer of his gun, raised it above the rocks, when in an instant it was riddled with bullets fired by Indians who were secreted in the vicinity and who, no doubt, supposed his head was in the hat. As soon as night would come, if previous thereto succor did not arrive, it was his intention to crawl (for he could not walk) to the creek, wash and bathe his wound, and endeavor to reach the Willows.

This is the second time Spencer has been jumped by Indians in this territory, and in both instances he has proven himself to be a man of undoubted bravery and great presence of mind. The first time they attacked him was while he was herding a band of horses and cattle at Banghart's Ranch in Chino Valley about a year ago, when by his coolness and bravery he saved most of the stock from falling into their hands. He has carried the mail over the Hardyville road for some time past and has had many hair-breadth escapes.

In connection with this affair, a military gentleman says: "It has been asserted that one man could travel over this road in safety; that the Indians were tired of war and longed for peace. This looks like it with a vengeance. Now, I do not believe they want peace; the only peace they deserve is the peace that has no waking; I mean the peace of death. Let there be a war of extermination inaugurated against all hostile tribes, and not let up until they are swept from the earth or lay down their arms and beg for peace." Our sentiments exactly.

Interesting Scout among White Mountain Apaches Some of Whom Sue for Peace and a Reservation

JOHN GREEN[1]

Headquarters Camp Grant, A.T.,
August 20, 1869

ASSISTANT ADJUTANT GENERAL,
Department of California,

SIR:

I have the honor to report that, in compliance with Special Orders No. 73, dated Headquarters Sub-District of Tucson, July 5, 1869, I left this camp on the evening of July 13, 1869, on a scouting expedition with a command composed as follows: Brevet Lieutenant Colonel John Green, major, First Cavalry, commanding; Lieutenant James Calhoun, Thirty-second Infantry, and twenty-five men of Company I, Thirty-second Infantry; thirty enlisted men of Troop K, First Cavalry; Acting Assistant Surgeon L. L. Dorr, U.S.A.; guides, scouts, etc.

For general direction and camps I would respectfully refer to the map herewith enclosed.[2]

I scouted carefully between this and Camp Goodwin, with a hope of finding Indians, for seven days but found nothing to guarantee further delay. I arrived at Camp Goodwin July 19.

July 20: Remained at Camp Goodwin to prepare the command which was to accompany me from that post.

July 21: Left Camp Goodwin with the following additional command: Captain John Barry, First Cavalry; Lieutenant F. K. Upham, First Cavalry; Lieutenant James Bassel, Second Artillery; forty-five enlisted men of Troop L, First Cavalry; Captain J. H. Gallager and Lieutenant E. B. Rheem, Thirty-second Infantry; and forty enlisted men of companies B and F, Thirty-second Infantry. I gave orders the evening previous that the packing of the mules should commence at 7:00 A.M. and move out as soon as packed, escorted by the infantry detachments of the respective commands (as I had not yet organized

A mounted infantryman. CENTURY MAGAZINE, MARCH 1891.

the command, intending to do so in the first camp where it would be together). I left my camp near Camp Goodwin with the Camp Grant detachment of cavalry at 9:00 A.M. The Camp Goodwin cavalry, under command of Captain Barry, soon followed; marched twelve miles and went in camp on the Gila River at 1:00 P.M., the Camp Grant pack train arriving an hour afterwards. The Camp Goodwin pack train was left in charge of Captain Gallager, who had one officer and forty men to guard it, but from some unaccountable mismanagement on his part did not get into camp till the next day, when five mules were missing which have not yet been found. I sent him back to his post in arrest and ordered Captain Barry to find out particulars and prefer charges against him on his return.[3] Owing to the loss of these mules with their packs, I had also to send back fifteen men of the infantry.

July 22: Whilst waiting for the Camp Grant pack train, I sent my chief scout, Manuel, with Jose Maria (a guide) and six scouts to see if they could find any fresh Indian signs. After crossing the river and going down three-and-one-half miles, they suddenly met eighteen wild Apaches going south, evidently on a marauding expedition, as they were well provisioned. A fight at once ensued in which two wild Indians were killed on the spot. Another dead body was found next morning in the vicinity, and I learned afterwards from captives that a fourth died the same day, both from their wounds, and that three others were mortally wounded if not already dead. As soon as the firing was heard in camp, I sent Lieutenant Calhoun with ten men of Troop K in its direction, but as he had to go round some distance, the fight was over and scouts returning before he reached the scene of action.

July 23: I placed Lieutenant Bassel in command of the infantry detachments and Lieutenant Calhoun of the detachment of Troop K, First Cavalry, and left camp at 9:00 A.M. Nothing occurred of note till July 25. On this day I took twenty mounted men and the scouts and moved in advance of the command to look for Indian signs. After marching fifteen miles fresh ones were seen in an oak grove, where some Indians had been gathering acorns. Believing that a rancheria was close by, we moved cautiously up a small stream and soon captured an old squaw. We endeavored to ascertain from her where the rancheria was, but she was very reluctant to give information and inclined to mislead us. Soon after a younger squaw was captured who told us it was on a hill to our left. We at once charged up this hill and found it as she had said, but other squaws having discovered us meantime from near the rancheria had given the alarm, and the occupants had fled up the rugged mountains, where it was impossible to follow. All their provisions and camp equipage were captured and destroyed; one child and two donkeys were also captured. I then moved down the creek, met the command, and went into camp. The prisoners informed me that there was a white woman captive somewhere among the Apaches, and they believed an exchange might be effected. The next day I sent the old squaw (who was of no value to the Indians and only an encumbrance) to endeavor to find the white woman and to say I would exchange the young squaw and boy for her, but I did not hear of her afterwards.

July 27: Whilst on the march, the captive squaw informed me that there was a cornfield about three miles from the trail, on one of the small tributaries of the San Carlos. I sent Corporal Miles and twelve men of the Thirty-second Infantry with the scouts to destroy it. On his return he reported he had found and destroyed about four acres of corn.

July 28: The trail ran through a very deep canyon with high rocky bluffs on each side. I sent the infantry in advance on this day, so that in case of attack they would not be encumbered with horses in this narrow place. Captain Barry with the detachment of his troop was left to escort the pack train. After passing through the canyon and whilst making a halt, two mounted Indians were discovered some distance off. I ordered some of the scouts and Lieutenant Calhoun with ten men of Troop K, First Cavalry, to pursue, thinking there might be more nearby. The Indians were so closely pushed that they killed one of their horses but escaped in the mountains. I then moved on and at 3:30 P.M. arrived at the Rio Prieto and went into camp. On arriving at this stream we found some eight or ten Indians on the opposite side looking for us. I learned afterwards they had been notified that we were coming in that direction by other Indians.

July 29: Owing to the roughness of the trail of yesterday, and many of the horses and mules having lost their shoes, I had to remain in camp in order to have the animals reshod. I had learned that there was a large amount of corn planted on the White Mountain River, for which point I started on the morning of July 30; marched about eighteen miles and went into camp on that stream. I sent Lieutenant Upham with twenty mounted men and some scouts to look for the cornfields. They returned in the evening and reported that they had found some very large ones and that the farther up they went the larger they seemed to get, but they had not time that evening to explore farther.

About sunset a party was discovered approaching the camp which proved to be two white men (a Mr. Cooley[4] and Mr. Dodd[5]), an Apache chief (Pin-dah-kiss, or Miguel[6]), another Indian, and a Mexican who lives with them and acts as their interpreter. The white men stated they were prospecting for gold and had come with Miguel from Fort Wingate, New Mexico, from the commanding officer of which post (Colonel Evans) Miguel had a letter of recommendation. He had also letters from General Carleton, former commander of the District of New Mexico, and General Getty,[7] present commander. I placed the party under guard that night and on the following morning had a talk with them.

Miguel stated that his village was thirty miles distant, on the Rio Cariga;[8] that he had never been at war with the whites and always wanted to be at peace; and that he now saw, since the troops had found their way into that country, it was necessary he should get on a reservation where he could be protected. He also stated he had been several times to the posts in New Mexico and had always been well treated. I then informed him he did not belong to New Mexico but to Arizona and that if he wanted to make any arrangements with the military authorities he must go to Camp McDowell and see the district commander. I then told him I had nothing more to say but would send some officers and men with him to his village to see if the white men were trading arms and ammunition with them, as I had previously understood; but that if everything was found right, the officer in command would have a further talk with him. I then detailed Captain Barry; lieutenants Upham and Calhoun, and fifty mounted men; chief scout Manuel with eight of his men; Gallegos, a guide; and Mr. George Coller, interpreter, for this purpose.

They left my camp at 8:00 A.M. (this July 31). Believing that many of these Indians, if not all, had been guilty of marauding, I instructed Captain Barry, if possible, to exterminate the whole village but gave no positive order; he was to be governed by circumstances. Soon after Captain Barry left I broke up camp and moved up White Mountain River about five miles to where I supposed was the central point of the cornfields and went into camp, then detailed all the men, except a small guard for camp, and commenced to destroy the corn. At least one hundred acres of fine corn, just in silk, were destroyed, and it took the command nearly three days to do it. I was astonished and could hardly believe that the Apache Indians could and would cultivate the soil to such an extent; and when we consider their very rude implements and the great labor it requires to dig the *aceguias*[9] for irrigation, one cannot help but wonder at their success. Their fields compare very favorably with those of their more civilized brethren.

On the night of August 1 Captain Barry returned with his command and reported that when he approached Miguel's village there was a white flag flying from every hut and every prominent point; that the men, women, and children came out to meet them and went to work at once to cut corn for their horses and showed such a spirit of delight at meeting them that the officers united in saying if they had fired on them, they would have been guilty of cold-blooded murder. Even my chief scout, Manuel, who has no scruples in such matters and whose mind was filled with taking scalps when he left camp, said he could not have fired on them after what he saw. Captain Barry also found that the white men had nothing but some provisions and implements—being what they represented themselves: prospecting miners.

Miguel reiterated that he wanted to go on a reservation where he could be protected, and Captain Barry repeated what I had previously told him—that he must go to Camp McDowell and see the district commander. He also gave him a letter for that purpose. Miguel promised to start on the following day and commenced to make preparations at once. The white men also were to accompany him.

The Apaches have but few friends and, I believe, no agent. Even the officers, when applied to by them for information, cannot tell them what to do. There seems no settled policy but a general idea to kill them wherever found. I also am a believer in that if we go for extermination, but I think—and I am sustained in my opinion by most of the officers accompanying the expedition—that if Miguel and his band were placed on a reservation properly managed and had a military post to protect them, they would form a nucleus for the civilization of the Apaches, as they seem more susceptible of it than any tribe I have ever seen. I even believe the Apache, if properly managed, could be used against the Apache and so end the war in a short time. Miguel said he had soldiers and would place them at my disposal whenever I wanted them. The reservation, with a military post, should be in the White Mountain country, where they could raise their crops and sustain themselves with but little cost to the government—the climate and soil being excellent for such a purpose. The only difficulty would be to make a wagon road into that country, but by proper exploration it might be accomplished. If this scheme should fail, a post in that country would be invaluable service in suppressing the Indian war in Arizona.[10]

August 2: The destruction of corn was completed. On the morning of the second we left the beautiful valley of the White Mountain River and moved in a southeast direction through a beautiful, rolling, grassy country interspersed with pine forests. Nothing occurred till August 6, when, after descending the Natanes Mountain[11] into the grassy plain, the scouts captured a squaw who was gathering acorns. She informed them there was a rancheria to the left and one to the right. Lieutenant Calhoun with his detachment; Mr. Hutton, post guide; and some scouts were ordered to the right. After going some distance they found one which had been abandoned several days. I took Captain Barry with his detachment and the balance of the scouts and went to the left. After galloping at full speed for about a mile and a half, several more squaws and children were captured and the rancheria was discovered to be on a high point, back of which was a high rugged peak, up which the Indians had made their escape, abandoning all their property, which was a very large amount of provisions, skins, baskets, ollas, hatchets, knives, powder and lead, ropes, moccasins, saddles, etc., all of which were destroyed or brought away. One Indian was killed; seven ponies, one mule, and one colt captured. During the destruction of the property the Indians shot arrows from their heights but did no damage. I then crossed the grassy plain and went into camp.

August 7: I left camp at 9:00 A.M. and arrived at Camp Goodwin at 3:00 P.M.

Having reason to believe that there were Indians in the Aravaipa Mountains,[12] I determined to scout them thoroughly, and for the purpose of doing so I took the following command from Camp Goodwin: Captain Barry, Lieutenant Upham, and thirty enlisted men of Troop L, First Cavalry; Lieutenant Sheldon, Guthrie, and twenty-five enlisted men of Companies B and F, Thirty-second Infantry—intending to divide the command at or near Eureka Springs.[13]

I left Camp Goodwin on the night of August 9 with the cavalry and moved fifteen miles to Black Rock that night. I left orders for the pack train, which was escorted by the infantry, to move out on the Tucson road the following morning and join me at Cottonwood, or Eureka Springs. As soon as it was light enough on August 10 I left Black Rock and moved in a southeast direction, arriving at Cottonwood at 11:30 A.M., where I camped and awaited the pack train, which arrived at 1:30 P.M. Mr. Hutton discovered some Indian tracks, apparently several days old, and I sent Manuel and several of his scouts to ascertain what direction they had taken. He returned in the evening and reported that he had found the trail of four or five Indians and one mule, going up the Cottonwood. He also found their camping place of a night or two previous.

On April 11, left camp at 7:30 A.M. and moved up Cottonwood to follow their trail. After marching six or eight miles to the southeast, I took Manuel and some of his scouts, Lieutenant Calhoun and his detachment of cavalry, and continued to follow the trail, leaving orders for Captain Barry and the balance of the command to march to the Aravaipa[14] and go into camp at the first water. When I had gone about two miles (keeping the scouts in front as trailers, and who followed the trail like bloodhounds), they discovered a party of Indians about three-fourths of a mile distant. A charge was at once ordered, and notwithstanding the roughness of the country (being near some deep canyons and ravines) three out of the five Indians were killed, and two children, one mule, and all their provisions captured. Captain Barry, hearing the firing, followed my trail and joined me after the charge. I then moved to the Aravaipa and went into camp.

August 12: I moved camp about ten miles to Eureka Springs. At this point I had intended to divide the command, one half to move on the north side, the other on the south side of the Aravaipa Mountains, but I was informed by the guides it would be impossible to get animals through on the north side. On the morning of the thirteenth, I detailed Lieutenant Upham (Lieutenant Guthrie being sick), thirty-eight men of the infantry command, Mr. Hutton and Gallegos, guides, and three scouts with orders to carry four days rations and scout through the northern side of the Aravaipa Mountains and join me on the San Pedro. I marched with the cavalry, balance of the infantry, and pack trains in a direction a little west of south over a grassy plain for fifteen miles and camped at the foot of the mountains.

August 14: Marched through a pass in the mountains in a southwest direction. On this day the march was very difficult owing to the roughness of the country and the heavy rains which raised the streams and made the traveling very muddy.

August 15: Had to remain in camp until 2:00 P.M., not being able to cross the stream on account of high water. I then moved six miles, crossing several different streams. That night the three Indian scouts accompanying Lieutenant Upham arrive in camp and reported that the command could not pass through the northern side of the mountain but had turned back, crossed the mountain, and struck my trail. They also reported that many of the men were sick, but that the command would join me on the following day.

August 16: I sent Captain Barry back with twenty led horses to meet and bring up Lieutenant Upham's command; they reached my camp at 2:00 P.M. At 3:00 P.M. I moved camp about seven miles to the San Pedro river.

August 17: I moved down the San Pedro towards Camp Grant, where I arrived on the afternoon of August 19.

The result of the expedition is eight Indians killed (all warriors except one grown boy), three mortally wounded, thirteen women and children captured, seven ponies, one colt, two mules, and two donkeys captured. Two rancherias with the property of the Indians, such as provisions and camp equipage, captured and destroyed, and at least one hundred acres of fine corn just in silk destroyed (on White Mountain River).

In conclusion, I must speak in the highest terms of Captain John Barry, First Cavalry, and Lieutenant James Calhoun, Thirty-second Infantry, commanders of the cavalry detachments, for the eagerness and zeal they evinced on all occasions toward the success of the expedition.

Owing to the sickly season, the services of Acting Assistant Surgeon L. L. Dorr were invaluable. Manuel and his scouts are entitled to great credit for the gallant fight they made on the Gila. In regard to the enlisted men, where all (with a very few exceptions) are so eager to distinguish themselves it is hard to make a selection for mention, but Corporal John H. Ward, Troop K, First Cavalry, has on several occasions come under my own observation for perseverance and gallantry, killing one Indian himself in the last encounter.

Lieutenant Calhoun also mentions Private William Williams, Troop K, First Cavalry, for particular gallantry.

I would also respectfully state that I was informed by some of the Indian captives that in my attack on the rancheria in Mount Turnbull of April last, thirty Indians were killed and a great many had died afterwards from their wounds.[15]

I am, sir, very respectfully,
Your obedient servant,

(Signed) JOHN GREEN,

Major, First Cavalry,
Bvt. Lieut. Col.,
U.S.A., Commanding post.

The department commander regards this expedition as of great importance and commends the zeal, bravery, and perseverance of the officers and men who composed it. He has forwarded a copy of it to the adjutant general for the information of the commissioner of Indian affairs, asking that steps be taken to protect and provide for the friendly Apaches in their own country, and he renews a previous recommendation that an additional brevet be conferred on Colonel Green and that Captain Barry and Lieutenant Calhoun be breveted one grade; that Corporal John W. Ward, Troop K, First Cavalry, and Private William Williams, Troop K, First Cavalry, have some mark of commendation conferred upon them for special gallantry in the field.

FURNISHED BY COMMAND OF BREVET MAJOR GENERAL ORD:

JOHN P SHERBURNE,
Assistant Adjutant General

Military Surgery among the Apache Indians

E. ANDREWS[1]

The Chicago Medical Examiner 16 (October 1869): 599–601

The Apaches of New Mexico and Arizona are the most inveterate nomads, perhaps, in the world. They not only have no agriculture, but they despise even the chase. The only occupations they deem worthy of a man are stealing and fighting, the first being the most honorable. Like other Indians, they have their medicine men, and, from the necessities of their position, they have developed a set of ideas and system of practice in military surgery.

Incantations and other modes of appeasing the unseen powers constitute a large portion of the resources of the Apache military surgeons, but they are by no means altogether negligent of material appliances. Their prime idea is that the chief danger of a wound is from the loss of blood, a notion which must have been very near the truth in the days when they only received wounds from knives and arrows. They have no idea of a circulation of the blood, but suppose that each part of the body has its own permanent stock of that fluid; but they recognize that hemorrhage from the head, neck, and breast is more dangerous than that from the extremities. From this prime pathological idea, they have naturally made the deduction that the chief surgical aim should be to plug the wound and thus put a stop to the hemorrhage. This pathology and treatment they doubtless established centuries ago from observations upon the incised wounds made by arrows and knives, and being eminently conservative, they naturally apply the same notions and treatment to the gunshot wounds which they receive from the U.S. troops and white settlers.

The first care of the Apache medicine man is to have on the field of battle some fresh boughs of the ash, whose leaves are used in the dressings. Quite as important also is a quantity of the mescal root. The latter is a nutritious root, which is roasted and carried with them as food. When it is chewed and the nutritive part extracted, there remains in the mouth a wad of woody fibers, like a plug of coarse tow. The doctor first lays in the wound a fresh ash leaf; he then places on it a plug of the chewed mescal fibers and thrusts the whole into the wound, a plan which in arrow wounds must often be very successful, but rarely of any benefit in gunshot injuries, as the latter seldom bleed. It would seem that they are not content to leave the tampon quietly in its place, but deem it important to change it frequently. After one of the battles in New Mexico,[2] where some twenty or thirty savages were wounded, the U.S. surgeons found the Apache field hospital and discovered in it about a bushel of the bloody mescal plugs, which had accumulated from their constant change of dressings. After this process has been continued until they deem the danger of hemorrhage entirely over, the next step is to go deeper, for the first plugs were only pushed into the orifices of the wounds. They now fill the entire track of the arrow or bullet to its extremity with a tampon, which they allow to remain a short time. Finally, they remove it and complete the cure by the application of herbs externally. All this treatment is accompanied with a suitable amount of superstitious mummery.

During the past year Mr. S. D. Phelps, a citizen of Chicago, accompanied the U.S. troops to an attack on one of the Apache villages, which was taken by surprise. In the rush, Mr. Phelps came in contact with the medicine man and shot him, and as a matter of course, captured his set of surgical instruments. They consisted of five stones and a sea shell. The stones were carbonate of lime and were cut out of pieces of beautiful stalagmite from some cave or spring, the stone being handsomely striped with black and fawn-colored veins. Four of the stones apparently constituted a set of tampons. The largest was about five inches long, cylindrical and slightly tapering, and was just about the right size to enter a wound made by an army-musket ball. The others were of successive sizes smaller and probably used in the same way on the wounds made by the very small stone arrowheads of the Apaches and other tribes of that region. The fifth stone is supposed to be a charm only. It represents in form the Texan armadillo, and the stone is ingeniously cut in such a way that the bands of color show stripes across the back like the rows of scales on the armor of the armadillo. The eyes of the animal are represented by pieces of mother of pearl, set into stone. The sixth object was a sea shell, perforated and suspended to the neck by a string. It was probably a charm. When the stones were shown to the squaws captured in the assault, the latter exhibited great emotion and begged that they might be thrown away, otherwise they said not a single soldier would live to return to his camp.

Mr. Phelps presented these relics to the Chicago Academy of Science, where they may be seen, with other ethnological curiosities, by those desirous to investigate such subjects.

An Arizona Adventure: An Incident of Army Life on the Frontier

MARY W. ADAMS[1]

The Midland Monthly 1 (March 1894): 284–86

In the month of February, in the year 1871,[2] a gay little party started from Tucson, Arizona, to make the long overland trip to San Diego. It was in the days when the savage Apaches, led by their still more savage chief Cochise, were filling with terror the hearts of the people in all that region by their depredations and wanton murders. Captain B. was going on sick leave with his wife and little daughter;[3] Lieutenant R.[4] was also on leave. He was going to meet his wife[5] and little ones after many months of separation. My husband had received his first promotion, and we were on our way to his new troop in Oregon.

Lieutenant Russell and my husband on horseback took the lead. Captain Bernard, his wife, and [son], myself and baby, with the driver, filled the ambulance which followed. Six mounted and armed soldiers, our escort, were close behind the ambulance. At a little distance four army wagons containing baggage and two or three discharged soldiers, with the driver, brought up the rear.

Our minds were filled with pleasant anticipations as we waved a merry goodbye to friends gathered to bid us Godspeed.

After the first long, weary day's ride, we were gathered around the campfire; our joy had not diminished, for Arizona was a good place to emigrate from in those days. Happy talk and laughter passed the time till we were admonished by the lateness of the hour that we must separate for the night. We went to our cozy tents for sleep and rest preparatory to the morrow's long ride. We did not dream how hard and full of peril it would be!

The early morning found us with refreshed minds and bodies, and we again started in the same order of march, with song and jest. The morning hours were fast passing when we were suddenly startled into silence by the sound of shouts and of firearms in the direction of the wagons. We could see nothing, for they were hidden from view by a slight bend in the road. We breathed again when someone said, "It is only the men firing at coyotes."

But the relief was only momentary. A soldier came running to us, exclaiming, "The Indians are surrounding us!"

While speaking, he was endeavoring to extract an Indian arrow which had pierced his shoulder.

The officers held a hurried consultation.

Mrs. Bernard and I bound the poor fellow's bleeding wound as well as possible with the meager materials at hand and, making a pillow of shawls and wraps, we laid him upon the bottom of the ambulance. Before this was accomplished other men came and reported the rest of their comrades killed.

But our danger was not yet over. Several miles farther on, at the foot of the Picacho Mountains[6] was a narrow pass. Our hearts stood still when we realized the possibility that the Indians, mounting the mules they had taken from the wagons and riding through a shortcut, might intercept us at the pass.

We hastily prepared to start. Lieutenant Russell and my husband took the lead, but now the soldiers were distributed about the ambulance, two at each side and two at the back, each soldier with one of the men from the wagons on the horse behind him, and in the ambulance the fainting, dying soldier at our feet. Thus we began our mad race for life.

How the ambulance swayed and rocked as the driver urged the horses into a gallop! And how bloodless was every man's face as he leaned forward in the saddle, with revolver ready in hand, peering behind each rock and bush for a hidden foe! The brave, steady eyes assured us that every one of them would die to defend the women and children. Only God heard the agonizing prayers uttered as we sped along that dreary Arizona road—prayers for deliverance from a horrible death, or, if captured, from a more horrible life.

As we neared the pass, every eye was strained to catch sight of the dread forms, but we passed on and into the open plains unmolested, and our peril was over.

That night our little company, gathered around the fire in the stage station, was very quiet. I thought sorrowfully of the three brave men whose bodies lay out in the moonlight, alone and uncared for, but my heart also overflowed with a joy too solemn for words for, though we had lost every worldly possession except the clothing we wore, what cared I for such loss! Was not my husband sitting there beside me? And was not a dear little sunny-haired baby sleeping peacefully upon my bosom?

On the March to Fort Yuma

"GASHUNTZ"[1]

Army and Navy Journal 8, no. 34 (April 8, 1871)

To the Editor of the Army and Navy Journal

SIR: If you will accept what strikes an individual, in the most humble and lowly capacity of a dismounted cavalryman, in a march of several hundred miles over a dreary, desert waste, and so strikes us as to leave impressions, here they are.

First, then, the party consisted of Lieutenant George R. Bacon, commanding; Assistant Surgeon John D. Hall, U.S. Army; Troop K, First Cavalry (sixty-seven aggregate); Lieutenant W. W. Robinson, Third Cavalry, commanding a detachment of recruits destined for "infantry camp" who left the command at Florence. Six baggage wagons and one ambulance constituted our transportation.

After the usual adieus, "Don't forget to write," "Will you write?" etc., the start was made on the morning of February 17, 1871, and the confusion which attended it, without being seen, cannot well be imagined.

As I turned to take a farewell look at sombrous Grant, with its dilapidated buildings, where I had for more than two years been constantly engaged in soldiering and working—mostly the latter, to confess the truth—I could not feel otherwise than sad notwithstanding the change, which, happy to note, fairly promised to be for the better.

The party were all on foot except the officers, laundresses, and a happy favored few, to which class, unfortunately, your correspondent does not belong. Yet I felt contented, if not happy, in the change, which necessarily brings me to the golden city of the Far West, San Francisco, California, where, as it might be inferred, I anticipate a jolly time in company with friends—that is, if I be so fortunate as to get a pass.

Our march for the first day was over a dry sandy road of a gentle inclination, leading through a narrow canyon, whose rocky walls or sides maintain a perpendicular front, or nearly so, and justly exhibit the denuding effects of water on a grand and extensive scale. The rocks are of an igneous origin and, judging from the manner in which they jut out and [from] the graves of some of Arizona's best men, particularly adapted to the strange and usually successful manner in which the Apaches fight.

After a dry, severe, and fatiguing day's march we encamped at Cottonwood Springs, where we found, much to the discomfort of all, wood and water scarce, the latter to be had only by digging in the sand.

I soon found a comfortable place between blankets and would have slept the few hours allowed me were it not that a few of my buoyant associates kept up a continual clatter till the time arrived for the second start, which was made after we had eaten what in Arizona would be called an early breakfast for a soldier; yet I felt inclined to call it supper, so barely did the time escape being twelve o'clock midnight.

When the much looked-for "haymaker" made his effulgent appearance,[2] we were several miles on the road, struggling through sand which relentlessly gave way at each would-be long step.

Sixteen miles of our dry sandy road being left behind, we reached Round Valley, where a lunch was partaken of with avidity. Should any of your readers not possess a good appetite, I heartily recommend them a dose of Arizona's sand, in the humble capacity of a dismounted cavalryman, as the manner in which government rations "disappear" on this march defies competition elsewhere.

Our party, much like a piece of India rubber, was inclined to lengthen as we neared Florence settlement, which is situated on the Gila River and probably contains five hundred inhabitants.

The following day, Sunday, we were allowed a day to recuperate, after a march of fifty miles, with three hours' rest.

At daylight on the following day we were on the move, the early part of which was cloudy and cool, and one among the finest for marching; but later in the day the sun made his appearance, which, together with a dusty road, had a tendency to render us generally uncomfortable.

I did not fail to see the famous Casa Grande,[3] situated between White's Ranch and Blackwater Station. It probably contained nine rooms in all. The walls are of immense thickness compared to other ruins I have seen on Salt River, Tonto Creek, and other places in Arizona and seems to have been indurated to such a degree that the elements have had but little effect upon them. It stands alone with legends, not history, and when I turned away, footsore and weary, from the grand old edifice, curious questions concerning the hands that built and the people that inhabited it naturally forced themselves upon me.

A march of fourteen miles brought us to Agua Prieto, where we encamped at midday.

An Indian village of some forty curious-shaped huts is situated there. I failed to discover any stock, and judging from this fact, they possessed none. A quantity of dried pumpkins were all I discovered in the culinary department, yet they appear more happy with their scarcity than we do with our plenty; our superior artificial wants will easily account for this. After supper we were visited by a number of Pimas, in honor of whom, I presume, the banjo was brought out and our little party for awhile apparently forgot their sufferings.

The next day, as usual, made an early start. Such a sameness exists along the road from Agua Prieto to Sacaton that it renders it generally dull and uninteresting. We were in high hopes that we could encamp at Sacaton, but alas! no such good luck was ours, and accordingly pushed forward to Sweetwater. More huts, more Indians, and more pumpkins.

Two days' march through Pima villages brought us to Maricopa Wells where, during the night we remained there, we were visited by anything but a pleasant shower. As very few were fortunate enough to possess a tent, nearly all received a good ducking.

The following morning opened cool and clear, and as we were to remain there until midday, preparatory to crossing the Maricopa desert, a drying of blankets [and] a hunting of hats which were carried away by the wind the night previous began quite earnestly.

I cannot say that anyone suffered from the want of water in crossing the desert, but the mere fact of there being a scarcity of water makes one uncommonly thirsty.

After leaving Gila Bend, a mail station, the water at the stations was so impregnated with alkali as to render it totally unfit for use "even by soldiers," as I heard a human being in the form of a man remark.

As the Gila is near, we found good water at Antelope Peak but were equally bad off for wood. Here Lieutenant Bacon indulged the troop in a little target practice, and it seemed a matter of astonishment to the pioneers residing there that a soldier could shoot at all. But nevertheless they did shoot, and with such especial accuracy that the citizens voluntarily acknowledged the practice to be first-class.

After a march of 268 miles we reached this corner of the human garden, Fort Yuma, California, upon which, I can safely say, "the eyes of Heaven shed but few tears." Yes, here we are, shirtless, shoeless, and I might with propriety add brainless. This misfortune—so far as the clothing is concerned—will, however, soon be remedied, as the lieutenant issues today.

Captain Bernard, with and commanding Troop G, First Cavalry, and Lieutenant Kyle, First Cavalry, we found here, apparently awaiting the arrival of Troop K, First Cavalry. But they did not wait long, having shuffled off at an early hour this morning. I failed to discover any wet handkerchiefs and judged from this fact that Jones's "palace" in Arizona City had no visible effect on them, but time works wonders.

We leave here tomorrow for San Diego, California.

GASHUNTZ

FORT YUMA, CALIFORNIA, March 6, 1871

Historical Truth: The So-called "Camp Grant Massacre" of 1871

WILLIAM S. OURY[1]

Tucson *Arizona Daily Star*, June 29 and July 1, 1879

As General Stoneman in a recent lecture has traveled out of his road to refer to the so-called Camp Grant massacre, characterizing it as a dastardly outrage, the writer, who was a participant in that (to southern Arizona) important enterprise, deems it but simple justice to himself and the brave and long-suffering men who were his companions in that pregnant campaign to lay before the public a truthful account of all the causes which drove a patient people to the degree of desperation which culminated in that sad affair. In order to [gain] a proper understanding of the matter, it will be necessary to go back nearly a year before this memorable occurrence to the period of the collecting of the Apaches on a reservation near Camp Grant, where they remained for some six or eight months, comparatively quiet and under the management of two or three rather feeble specimens of "Dutch Reform Indian agents," each of whom, becoming soon convinced of their inability to control their savage wards, returned in fear and disgust, and in an evil hour for the peace and welfare of the patient and quiet people of Pima County these cruel fiends were placed under the charge of the notorious Royal E. Whitman, a lieutenant of the Third Cavalry, U.S.A. He, being a shrewd fellow with an eye to the main chance, discovered that there was money in the business and lost no time in putting into practice "those ways which are dark and tricks that are vain," by which the average Indian agent with a salary of $1,500 becomes rich in two or three years.

From January 1, 1871, to April 30, of the same year, the day on which the so-called Camp Grant massacre took place, every page of the history of southern Arizona is written in the blood of her people, as the following facts fully attest: James Pennington, whilst in pursuit of his oxen stolen by the Apaches, was ambushed and killed by those who had stolen them (this within three miles of Tucson); the Tubac mail rider murdered, and horse and saddle taken, near Lee's mill, not more than two miles from Tucson; Simms and Sam Brown, murdered near Tres Alamos whilst hauling a load of timber for farm use. All these murders occurred in the month of January 1871.

The record of the month of February is so replete with robbery and murder that to particularize would be an endless undertaking. During all these dark days the people of Tucson, who better than anyone else knew the nature of the Apaches, had charged time and again that the depredations and murders were committed by the Indians of the Camp Grant reservation. These charges were denied by Whitman, supported by the affidavits of the whole crew of his strikers and understrappers, and the people of Tucson were thus compelled in their desperation to take matters in their own hands, finding that remonstrance was of no avail. However, before resorting to measures of violence our people, with the extremity of forbearance, determined in council to send a deputation to General Stoneman, the commander of the department, who it was known could be found at or near Florence on the Gila River. The committee chosen for the mission consisted of the writer of this article, S. R. DeLong, J. W. Hopkins, and another gentleman whose name is not at present recollected.[2]

The result of our mission is so much more ably given by our friend P. W. Dooner[3] in the Los Angeles *Express* that the writer considers it necessary to say no more than that it was a complete failure, and we were to given to understand that Tucson contained a population large enough to take care of itself. In the meantime, the scenes of blood and plunder were continued with greater frequency, as is sadly attested by the murders in the month of March of Wooster[4] and his wife at his ranch on the Santa Cruz above Tubac; Cook[5] on the Sonoita; Saunders and Blanchard at Calabasas; Long, McKenzie, and Chapin near their farms on the San Pedro; Ainsa's train attacked between Florence and Picket Post, three men killed and a large amount of property carried away;[6] John T. Smith's ranch attacked on the Santa Cruz River above Tubac, and although the brave ranchmen succeeded in driving the Indians away without loss of life, yet the poor farmers lost all stock, even to their plow horses, and as Shakespeare makes Shylock so aptly say, "You do take my life when you do take the means by which I live."

Meanwhile, these scenes of blood and devastation were occurring in such rapid succession that the excitement in Tucson had grown to a red heat. Frequent excited and angry meetings were held at the courthouse, many valiant but frothy speeches were pronounced, and many determined resolves were resoluted, but nothing definite was done beyond a list being gotten up and signed by some eighty-odd valiant and doughty knights, resolved to do or die; but in a few days, with sorrow it must be said, the valor of all these plumed knights seemed to have oozed out at their finger ends, and everything was at a standstill. But the scenes of carnage and pillage did not stand still. We have now reached the middle of that eventful month of April 1871. About 10:00 P.M., as the writer was wending his way wearily and sadly to his domicile, just before reaching it he was met by one of his old and tried neighbors,[7] and the following dialogue took place.

"Don Guillermo, what are we to do? The Camp Grant Indians are slowly but surely murdering our people and carrying away our means of subsistence. I have just returned from following a party of them who stole stock from San Xavier night before last. We succeeded in killing one of them, and I pledge you my solemn word that I know him to be a Camp Grant Indian; have seen him there frequently and know him by his having a front tooth out."

My reply was, "Well, Don Jesus, let us call our people together at the courthouse tomorrow and lay all of this before them, collect together our eighty-odd doughty knights, and immediately take the warpath."

"Don Guillermo, all your speechifying and resoluting amounts to nothing, and no good can come of it. In the meantime the slaughter of our people goes on."

"Well, Don Jesus, what do you propose to do to remedy the evil? I will assist you to the utmost of my ability in any plan you may propose."

"Don Guillermo, you know that the Papagos have always been our faithful allies against the murderous Apaches; you also know that they place implicit confidence in yourself and me. Now I propose that we go together tomorrow to San Xavier; have a talk with our trusty friend Francisco[8] and get him to send runners at once to all the Papago villages to collect their youngest and bravest warriors and bring them to San Xavier by the morning of April 28, and in the meantime we will talk privately with old and tried neighbors and get as many of them to embark in the campaign as can mount and arm themselves, and when all are ready we will get out of town by ones and twos without creating excitement or attracting the attention of the Indian lovers, who will surely betray us if they learn our purpose. We will also direct our Papago friend Francisco that as soon as the warriors from the villages arrive at San Xavier to send them across the country to the Rillito without one of them showing himself in Tucson, and when we have all assembled at the Rillito we will take the same trail made by the Indians who stole the stock at San Xavier and follow it until we overtake the Indians, wherever they may go, and kill all we can; and I tell you candidly, Don Guillermo, that I am sure the trail will lead us to the Camp Grant reservation, so that if you are afraid to take the responsibility of fighting the reservation Indians, we had better give up the expedition."

"Don Jesus, I am not afraid of any such responsibility; nor do I believe that any of our people will be frightened by any such bugbear. These Indians are stripping us of all our means of subsistence. They are robbing us from two to three times a week regularly, and in self-preservation we must kill them wherever found, and we must go in sufficient force to overcome every obstacle to our purpose that may present itself, whether it may be white men or Indians."

Here ended our conversation, and the next morning at six we mounted our horses and went to San Xavier to meet our friend Francisco. Our arrangements were soon made, and before we left we had the satisfaction of seeing a mounted runner dispatched to each of the Papago villages westward of San Xavier. We then returned to Tucson to complete our arrangements with our neighbors there.

The intervening days were spent in gathering arms, horses, and provisions for the campaign, in which undertaking (much to their praise be it said) we were fully assisted by all the old people of Tucson of every nationality.

We have now reached the memorable morning of April 28, 1871. At 7:00 A.M., a Papago drove furiously up to my door with the welcome news from Francisco that our auxiliary force of Papagos had arrived at San Xavier and would leave for the place of rendezvous at the Rillito as soon as they had taken their breakfast. I lost no time in communicating the fact to Jesus Elias and others of the faithful and at once dispatched the wagon, already loaded with arms, ammunition, and provisions, to the point agreed upon; and soon after quietly mounted my horse and started out, leaving directions for all others to go out in the same way. By 1:00 P.M. all the party were quietly assembled and resting on the shady bank of the Rillito. The whole command numbered 140 men, divided as to nationality as follows: 92 Papago Indians, 42 Mexicans, and six Americans. About 4:00 P.M., arms, ammunition, and provisions having been distributed and all preparations completed, the command took up the line of march up the Rillito, and just before dusk, in the canyon going over the divide between the Rillito and the San Pedro, we struck the trail made some days before by the Indians returning from their raid on San Xavier, which was the one we had previously arranged to follow, and after a few miles' travel arrived at the place where the Indian heretofore spoken of had been killed. After a short detention in examining the ground where the fight had taken place and the carcass of the dead Indian, the line of march was resumed, and after passing the summit of the divide, and being on the down slope towards the San Pedro, about 1:00 A.M. we halted for a rest and sleep, resuming our line of march at the dawn of day, so as to reach the San Pedro bottom before we would be likely to be discovered by any roving party of Indians that might happen to be out on a plundering excursion. The command lay concealed in the shady bottom of the San Pedro River until just before dark on the evening of April 29, when our organization, having been completed by the unanimous election as commander of the expedition of the gallant little Mexican, Jesus Maria Elias, who had been its most active promoter. Again taking the trail which we had thus far persistently followed and under cover of the night, to prevent discovery by our wily foes, our last march was resumed. To our great surprise and mortification, however, those of us most intimate with the country were mistaken in the distance which yet remained to be overcome before arriving at the Indian camp, and this fact came very near rendering all our labor fruitless, for instead of fifteen miles, as we had all reckoned, we found the distance nearly double that, so instead of arriving near the ground in time to halt and send out a scout to ascertain the exact locality of the Indian rancheria, the day was breaking when we arrived at a point which we supposed to be near the Indian camp, and no time for anything but a haphazard dash and kill all we could, remained.

Just here an amusing episode occurred when the writer, who during the long night march had been continually in front encouraging the Papagos, most of whom were on foot, as were also several Mexicans, lost his canteen from the horn of his saddle, and dismounting to hunt for it whilst it was not yet light enough to see clearly, necessarily got behind, as the column was in motion, and being delayed some time in finding the canteen was considerably astonished, on reaching the rear of the command, to find it halted and word passed back that he was wanted immediately at the front. He pushed forward at once, and overtaking the commander, upon inquiry of him learned that he had ordered the Papagos to form in skirmish line and advance rapidly, and that they had halted and refused to advance because they could not see the writer and were afraid to move forward on account of his not being with them, and they in close proximity to the military post, and were afraid of the interference of the soldiers. Galloping rapidly to the front with a few words of encouragement, the Papagos bounded forward like deer, notwithstanding their night march of nearly thirty miles, and we never witnessed a prettier skirmish [line] in all our military life than was made by those hard-marched foot Papago soldiers for about two miles before we struck the rancheria, nor quicker or more effective work after it was struck, for in less than a half an hour not a living Apache was to be seen, save the children taken prisoners and some seven Indians who escaped by being up and ahead of our skirmish line, so they could not be overtaken without breaking it.

Thus ended the so-called Camp Grant massacre, denounced as a dastardly outrage by General Stoneman in the killing of about 144 of the most bloodthirsty devils that ever disgraced mother earth.[9]

Now a few lines in the way of summing up, and we will leave this page of veritable history to the impartial judgment of the American people. Just before leaving Tucson on this expedition so vital to the weal or woe of our people, the writer had met in the streets one of the oldest settlers of the San Pedro River, John Montgomery,[10] who gave him the sad information that himself and the few other settlers of the San Pedro, who had escaped the scalping knife of the red-handed Apaches,[11] had determined to abandon their homes and bring their families for safety to Tucson, leaving their crops, the result of their sweat and toil, at the mercy of the pitiless savages.

Without daring to state to him what had already been determined upon, for fear of its reaching unfriendly ears, we simply advised him to wait a few days before carrying their resolution into effect—that something might turn up to obviate the necessity of an absolute abandonment of their little all—and turned away from him with a heart brim full. With a few mere words by way of correction of an error into which friend Dooner in the Los Angeles *Express* unwittingly falls, we will close this already too lengthy narrative. He says in that article that the parties engaged in the Camp Grant affair procured their own indictment as a means to their full vindication. In this he is very much mistaken; not one of those interested failed to characterize the act of indictment by a grand jury of our neighbors as a cowardly yielding of honest convictions to the blandishments and sophistries of a United States district attorney prompted by no higher ambition than a desire to filch from the government, which it was his sworn duty to protect, every dollar which the solemn farce could be made to yield. Many of those who were indicted had friends and relatives in California and the Eastern states who would never learn more about the affair than the fact that their friends or relations had been put on trial for an infamous crime, which certainly would not be a pleasant picture to look upon. However, this trial for our lives developed the following facts: That we had followed the trail of the party of Indians who had recently stolen property from San Xavier; that one Indian killed was on the back of a horse belonging to one of our party; the moccasins of poor Wooster were stripped from the feet of another dead Indian, with his name written by his own hand in the inside of one of them; many articles of clothing belonging to Wooster's murdered wife were found in the Indian camp and fully identified, as also was the saddle of the mail rider murdered near Lee's mill, as well as various articles too numerous to detail, taken from parties killed on the Sonoita, Santa Cruz, and San Pedro. Here ends the chapter, and with the single statement that in all we have written we have told the simple, plain truth.

The Camp Grant Massacre

ANDREW H. CARGILL

Arizona Historical Review 7, no. 3 (July 1936): 73–79

Camp Grant, Arizona, located at the junction of the San Pedro River and Aravaipa Creek, seventy miles from Tucson, was a post of some importance in the early Apache warfare and at times was garrisoned by four or five companies of troops. It was there I first met John G. Bourke, Ross,[1] and Brodie,[2] lieutenants fresh from West Point. Early in 1870, Brigadier General George Crook, then commanding in Arizona,[3] had withdrawn all but fourteen men from Camp Grant for his campaign. He left Lieutenant Colonel Royal E. Whitman, lieutenant of Company H, Third Cavalry, in command with the fourteen men.

In November 1870 I was again at the post on one of my trips to audit the books of the sutler's store, which belonged to Lord and Williams; Fred Austin, Dr. Lord's brother-in-law, was in charge. While there I roomed with Colonel Whitman. One morning when Colonel Whitman and myself were taking our smoke after breakfast Merejildo Grivalja, the scout and interpreter,[4] came and said that the Indians were sending up smoke in the mountains indicating that they wanted to come in and talk.[5] The colonel told him to answer it and tell them to come. About noon, Eskiminzin,[6] Delshay, and three other chiefs arrived and were taken into a large room,[7] and after seating themselves around the room, they were given tobacco and paper, and all began to smoke. After this had continued for some fifteen minutes, Eskiminzin rose and, turning to Colonel Whitman, spoke somewhat as follows (Merejildo Grijalva interpreting from time to time):

I am a chief and have command of fifteen hundred warriors belonging to the Pinal and Aravaipa Apaches.[8] For many years we have lived here and roamed over these hills and valleys, hunting and gathering mesquite beans, mescal, and saguaro, and raising a little corn and melons. When the white men first came here, we received them as friends and for a long time our people attended to the stock of the express line and lived with them at peace. Then soldiers came and

63

one time they unjustly hung some of our Indians whom they had asked to come into their camp and eat. Among them was the brother of our head chief, Cochise. Up to that time we had no enemies but the Papagos and the Mexicans. Cochise then declared war against all white men, and we have been fighting ever since. The White Father who lives at Washington has sent thousands of soldiers against us and chased us all over this country until now we have no safe place in the land.

I and my people are tired of war, and we want to come in and make peace. And we want to raise cattle and corn and live like your people do. Our women and children are worn out, roaming from one place to another. This is what we came to talk about.

He was the finest specimen of an Indian I have ever seen, and I have met a good many.

The other chiefs spoke to the same effect.

Colonel Whitman told them he was glad that they came in, that the White Father could send many more soldiers against them and that it was foolish to try to fight with him, that he had no authority to make a peace treaty with them, as he was only an officer of the army, but if they were sincere in wanting to live at peace hereafter and would bring in their people to the post and surrender as prisoners of war, giving up all their arms, he would locate them on the military reservation about three miles below them where there was plenty of shade and water and would issue them one-half a ration every day. He would also write to the White Father, telling him what they had said, and he would send out someone to make peace with them.

After more talk they agreed to the terms, and Eskiminzin went outside and returned with a stone and said: "I and my chiefs have faith in you; you have spoken to us like men and not like dogs," and laying down the stone in front of the colonel, he continued, "I will bring my people in here to you, and so long as this stone shall last, so long will I keep the peace with you and your people."

The next day they came in, men, women, and children, and as they filed by the colonel at the quartermaster's storehouse, each one deposited his rifles, guns, bows and arrows, war clubs, etc. Colonel Whitman and myself stood there and saw that they retained only their knives. They were then taken down three miles below the post, still on the reservation, counted and enrolled by families, and one-half ration was issued as follows:

The head of the family with his wives and children were called forward, counted, and the head man received the rations for all. Then the next, and so on. No one was allowed to leave the line until all were counted and rations issued, so that we knew every day just how many were present.

Colonel Whitman wrote to Washington through the regular channels and in due course received orders relieving him from military duty and appointing him special Indian agent, instructing him to continue the issue of rations until a commissioner could be sent to arrange a peace and a reservation for them.

To show that they had laws of their own among them, I would here relate an incident that took place in December. We were down issuing rations and counting them, when suddenly there was a commotion in the line, and then the two tribes separated like a flash and took up positions opposite each other. The chiefs were talking. So the colonel rode between them and called the chiefs to him and asked what was the matter. He was told that they had just heard that one of the Aravaipas had killed a Pinal and fled. And the Pinals wanted to fight and take reparation. The colonel told Eskiminzin there could be no fighting and to tell them to wait and talk to him.

When quiet was somewhat restored, Eskiminzin explained the law of the tribes: "An eye for an eye and a tooth for a tooth." And as the murderer had escaped, the Pinals were entitled to kill one of his family or fight his tribe. The colonel found that the only relative of the murdered man was an old Indian about sixty, and he offered to buy a whole beef for him. The relative was willing, but Eskiminzin said that it would only postpone the trouble, that the Aravaipas themselves must make reparations in order to satisfy the Pinals.

Finally we found that there was another way to settle it—namely, that the Aravaipas agree to give the old man everything they had in the world and go forth naked. After a good deal of talk, they agreed. So all the Aravaipa men, women, and children marched by and stripped themselves to their breech cloths, giving up all their clothes, baskets, etc.

It was quite cold and seemed almost inhuman to turn them out without even a blanket to sleep with. But they stuck it out. So the colonel evolved a plan. Fred Austin had the hay contract for the post, the hay being brought in by Mexicans. It was arranged to let the Aravaipa women cut and bring in the hay, for which they were given tickets to trade for anything at the sutler's store except arms, ammunition, or liquor. Thus in a month or so they were able to buy clothes and blankets.

Matters went on very smoothly until the first day of May 1871. One morning we had not finished our coffee when Merejildo Grijalva came and said he thought there was something wrong, as he had not seen an Indian nor any smoke from their camp. We mounted at once and rode down to find eighty-six women and children and one very old man killed. No live Indians were about, so we buried the bodies before leaving the scene.[9] We knew at once that it had been done by parties from Tucson. The Indians sent up another smoke that afternoon, saying they would come and talk. We answered it, and the same five chiefs came in. After the usual smoke, Eskiminzin spoke:

Last fall we came in and surrendered to you, giving up all our arms, as you said we must, and made a peace with you, giving you a stone to show we would keep it. Last night, white men, Mexicans, and Papago

Indians came and attacked us; we had no arms. The men ran to the hills, taking such women and children that they could. I have lost two wives and two children.[10] The others have also lost their people. You said you would protect us. I know you had nothing to do with this for we saw you bury our dead. We have come in now to ask you what we shall do.

The colonel told them he knew nothing about it, but that as they had surrendered to the government and were on a government reserve, it was murder and a violation of the White Father, that he would write and see that the offenders were punished. He asked them to come back and camp at the post on the river, saying that he had only fourteen men but plenty of guns and ammunition and that they should put out guards, and if it was ever attempted again he would arm and lead them himself in defense.

Eskiminzin said, "I do not expect ever to see any of them punished, for they will never punish a white man for killing an Indian, but I do ask you to get back fourteen of our children that they have taken captive."

They came in again and camped on the river. The colonel wrote a letter to the department at Washington, and the district attorney was ordered from California to take proceedings to punish the perpetrators.

In the meantime the people in Tucson, with the help of Governor A. P. K. Safford, trumped up a charge against Colonel Whitman of having been under the influence of liquor three years before, at the time he entered the territory. He was relieved and brought before a court martial; inside of two months the new agent had driven the Indians out on the warpath again. Whitman was acquitted and ordered back to the post, for he could and did get the Indians in again.

I was back in Tucson when the United States district attorney came out.[11] I had known him before and asked him to share our quarters, which he did. When the grand jury was drawn, I was on it and was made secretary, and Charles Hayden was made foreman. The district attorney tried every way to get an indictment, but it was no use, so he telegraphed to Attorney General Ackerman. One evening, when we came back from supper, he said to me: "There was once a district attorney who was staying with a friend. He went out, left a secret telegram from the attorney general on the table." With that, he placed the telegram on the table and left. I took it for granted that I was to read it and did so. It said, "If you cannot indict in three days, telegraph—we will declare martial law and trial by court martial." I knew that meant sure conviction, as the feeling was very strong among the army people, and the evidence was perfect. We knew who the five white men and the twenty Mexicans were, but we had to guess concerning the Papagos.

So the next day, after the attorney had failed to get any action, I asked him to leave the room, and I addressed the jury. I told them that if they indicted the parties, they knew there was no jury that would convict them, but if they did not, martial law would probably be proclaimed, and they would be tried by court martial. I finally got them to agree to indict them, and the district attorney and myself sat up most of the night drawing up the papers—five white men and twenty Mexicans whose names we knew, and seventy-five Papagos by fictitious names. The next day the grand jury adjourned, and in an hour it was known that I was the cause of the indictment.

The district attorney and myself were burned in effigy that night, and I was compelled to resign my position with Lord and Williams, as they said the feeling was so strong they would lose business by keeping me. So then I became clerk for the district attorney.

One day he came to me and said: "Cargill, I guess I must change my quarters, I don't want to get you into any trouble, but I have got a notice to quit town in twenty-four hours."

I told him he need not change, for I had received the same notice. So I said to leave it to me. I went that night and called on Colonel Mizner,[12] the commander of the post at Camp Lowell (Tucson) and told him, or rather showed him, the notices. Of course he was furious at the idea of the United States district attorney being ordered to leave. I had a Mexican boy that took care of my rooms and ran errands for me and the colonel knew it. He said, "Any time anyone interferes with the district attorney or yourself, send me word by Alijemoro, and I will wipe Tucson off the map." In the meantime he detailed a number of soldiers to mingle among the people and keep an eye on us.

Grant Oury[13] and Hiram Stevens[14] were elected delegates to Congress; Sidney De Long was made registrar of the land office. I could get no employment so finally had to go back to California. But before I left, Vincent Colyer was sent out. He called the Indians into his prayer meetings but did nothing but go back to Washington and make a report. Then General O. O. Howard was sent out, who sent for me at Camp Crittenden. I came to Tucson, met him, and had a long interview. Then he asked me to bring the Papagos, Maricopas, and Pima Indians into the peace congress at Grant. Captain Jeffords was to get the Apaches and Cochise's band.

The congress was held and peace made with them all. Apaches were given the reservation which they now occupy, and Eskiminzin was made head chief.

The last time I saw Sidney DeLong in 1909, he told me the only thing he regretted in his life was that he took part in the Camp Grant affair.

It afterwards came out that the governor and his adjutant general were parties to the massacre, as the adjutant general furnished a wagonload of arms and ammunition for the Papago Indians.

The Arizona Indians

SYLVESTER MOWRY[1]

Army and Navy Journal 8, no. 41 (May 27, 1871)

M r. Sylvester Mowry, a gentleman well known in the far west territories, sends to the New York *Herald* the subjoined letter apropos of the Apache fight in Arizona. It is a sufficient answer to the plea for the Apaches which we copied last week:

To the Editor of the Herald.
SIR: The following appears in today's Associated Press telegrams:

THE INDIAN WAR IN ARIZONA—LIEUTENANT
H. B. CUSHING[2]
ONE SOLDIER KILLED

SAN FRANCISCO, May 14,1871
On the fifth instant Lieutenant W. B. Cushing, with twenty men of the Third Cavalry, were routed by Cochise, a noted Apache chief, with 150 warriors, at Whitestone Mountain southeast of Tucson. Cushing and one soldier were killed. Captains Lanwood and Moore, with forty men each, gave pursuit to the savages, who are committing numerous murders.

By this time the people of the United States must have had a surfeit of Apache atrocities in Arizona, while English, French, and Russian officers and people have come to regard these unwhipped horrors as evidence of the inability of this government to protect its frontiers. The English whip into submission their recalcitrant East Indian population, the French the Algerian hordes, the Russians the mountaineers of Caucasus and the tribes bordering on India. The United States permits its most important territory to be overrun by a small tribe of Indians who have rejected kindness, religion, and civilization for three hundred years. It permits the people to be slaugh-

Apache atrocities in Arizona. OUTING MAGAZINE, JUNE 1886.

tered, burned at the stake; women to be violated; the territory to be depopulated; and its mails to be scattered from the Rio Grande to the Colorado. More than that, it establishes a reservation where every Indian can go, stay as long as he pleases in safety, sally forth on his errand of rapine and murder, and return to enjoy his booty in safety under the flag of the Union.

This all-powerful and beneficent government sends a young man like my dear friend Cushing—poor, dear fellow, a man the army could not afford to lose—with twenty men to fight the bravest, wildest Indian chief on the continent, Cochise, with 150 warriors entrenched in a mountain range, every foot of which is as familiar to the Apache as your own doorstep is to you.[3]

It is not simply the killing of an officer. It is an officer's duty and expectation every time he goes out to be killed, for in Arizona the troops always fight at a disadvantage in numbers and position. I spent a night in the field with Cushing a few months ago and he was in great hopes and determination of capturing Cochise and his band, and he would have done so had he been properly supported. But no. Cochise, who has been on the warpath fourteen years; who numbers his white slain by hundreds and counts his destruction of property by millions, sought the protection of Major [Whitman], United States army, said he "was tired, wanted to sleep, and to live on the reservation." Major [Whitman] then threw over him the aegis of the United States. General [Stoneman] opposed it. The War Department records will show this atrocious fact, against which I protested in person and in writing.[4] Now we have the result. There is not a hostile tribe in Arizona or New Mexico that will not celebrate the killing of Cushing as a great triumph. He was a *beau sabreur,* an unrelenting fighter, and although the Indians have "got him" at last, he sent before him a long procession of them to open his path to that "undiscovered country." To his brother, "Albemarle" Cushing of the navy and his other relatives, it will be consoling to know that he has left behind him in Arizona a name that will not die in this generation.

I have no apology to make for my own indignation, or that of the people of Arizona, against the psuedo-philanthropists—the senators or members of Congress who from a maudlin sympathy cry out for religion and blankets for the Indians, or vote the troops to put an end to their bloody orgies. If it was in my power to call down on them some curse as potent for evil as that we of the frontier have suffered and are suffering under so that their eyes might be opened, not only would I do it, but my prayer would be echoed by ten thousand people in Arizona.

The president has just assigned a most gallant and effective Indian fighter, General Crook, to the Arizona command. Let him do more. Give Crook all the force he asks for—he will not ask too much—and give him the support of every able-bodied man in the territory. We have asked long enough for justice, now we demand vengeance. Your obedient servant.

SYLVESTER MOWRY.

UNION CLUB, NEW YORK, May 16, 1871.

Indians and Indigo

CHARLES B. GENUNG[1]

Los Angeles Mining Review 8, no. 8 (May 13, 1911): 9–10; no. 9
(May 20, 1911): 13–15; and no. 10 (May 27, 1911): 12–13

In June 1871 I was farming in Peeples Valley, Arizona. Having occasion to go to Prescott, and my wife not feeling safe at the ranch with the small force of men that I could leave behind, she concluded to go with me as far as Ed Bowers's[2] ranch and station and visit Mrs. Bowers until I returned. The Bowers family were our nearest family neighbors at that time, and they were twelve miles away on the road to Prescott in Skull Valley. I took with me W. H. Smith, my wife's brother, and a young man named Boyce for escort. We all stayed at Bowers's ranch the first night, and the next morning my wife called after me: "Don't forget the indigo!" She had sent by me for indigo before and I had forgotten it.

I had told my wife that I would remain in Prescott but one day and return the third day. I had some business with the quartermaster which took me to Whipple, where Herbert Bowers was keeping the sutler store. I found Herbert a very sick man, and as he was a dear friend of mine I spent a good deal of time with him trying to cheer him up. He had a bad case of yellow jaundice and was in bed all the time that I stayed with him.

I got settled up with the quartermaster and got my voucher for what he owed me, and was back in Prescott late in the evening and had everything ready to start home in the morning. At 9:30 P.M. I started from the Diana Saloon, across the plaza to where I slept. Right out on the plaza I came upon Herbert Bowers standing there like a statue! My first impression was that he was out of his head. I asked him what in the world he was doing there. He said, "Charlie, the Indians killed one of the herders[3] and have gone with 137 head of horses, mules, and cattle from my Agua Fria ranch. Nathan, my brother, sent a courier in to me, also one to Camp Verde. I have applied at Whipple for help, but there are no men nor animals there to go; all I can get there is one old pack mule."

I said to him: "You go to Brook and Lind's stable and get all the saddle horses they have and have them brought down and tied here at the Diana Saloon, then go to C. C. Bean and tell him that I want his buckskin team—one for me and the other for my Smith, my brother-in-law."

71

I walked into the saloon and told the people what had happened and called for volunteers to go out and get the stock back. The Diana Saloon stood on the corner where the St. Michael Hotel now stands, and there were several more saloons right along side by side. The news spread like a flash, and there were plenty of men to go but they had no horses. Just two men who were willing to go had horses, Tom Roddick[4] of Kirkland Valley and Jeff Davis of Davis ranch on the head of the Hassayampa. I saw John McDerwin in the crowd and called him to one side and asked him if he would tell my wife the next day that I had gone after Indians and not to expect me back until she saw me, which he agreed to do. By this time the horses began to come to the hitching rack. I singled out the men that I wanted, and we all got some lunch of whatever kind we could scrape together and at 11:00 P.M.—just an hour and a half from the time I left the saloon to go to bed—there were eleven of us armed and mounted and ready to make the most successful raid against the Apaches that ever started from northern Arizona.

I had met John Townsend[5] and been introduced the day that I stayed in Prescott, and as he was an Indian fighter I made inquiry for him before we got started and learned that he had started for his ranch on the lower Agua Fria, which was about twenty miles below Bowers's ranch; that he had gone via the Vickers's ranch, which was on the then only wagon road from Prescott to the Agua Fria. I wished to take the short trail; so sent two men via Vickers's ranch to ask Townsend to join us, which he did, and we were all at the Bowers's ranch before daylight. As several of our horses needed shoeing we got the Negro blacksmith who was working for Bowers and had a good shop to fit the shoes, while the men drove them on as fast as three hammers could do it.

By sunrise we all had had breakfast and had a sack of flour, some bacon, and coffee that we had got at the ranch. Just as we were ready to start I called all to attention and suggested we elect Townsend captain of the company, which was agreeable to all. Then we were off, sixteen of us, having picked up four men beside Townsend in the Agua Fria settlement.

What provisions and some cooking tools that we had were packed on the old government mule.

We traveled pretty fast after we got strung out on the trail of the stock until about noon, when we stopped to water and rest our horses. Tom Roddick had been in town drinking pretty hard for several days and was very anxious to have a drink of whiskey, thinking perhaps some of the men had a bottle in their saddle bags. We all had saddle bags on our saddles those days. Tom called to Townsend and said, "Captain, if I can't get a drink I'll die sure."

Townsend replied: "Oh! Not so bad as that, Tom."

Says Tom: "I bet you $200 I'll die in fifteen minutes if I don't get a drink."

He lived, although he didn't get his drink.

The first night we camped on a side hill where there was good grass, and the next morning we were moving by daybreak, and about sunrise we ran into

We traveled pretty fast. OUTING MAGAZINE, DECEMBER 1886.

a soldier camp where they were just eating their breakfast. The soldiers had started from Camp Verde and had a Mexican for guide who had been a prisoner with the Apaches for a number of years,[6] and he knew about where to cross the mountains to strike the trail that he knew the Indians would have to take the stock over. So when he struck the trail they made camp, where we came upon them. There were twenty-eight enlisted men, a doctor, and a young lieutenant named Morton in charge.[7] The lieutenant was fresh from West Point, and as we rode along, Townsend being in the lead, the lieutenant asked one of our party who our leader was, and was told that Mr. Townsend, that man in the lead, was our captain. The lieutenant called to Townsend and walked out a little way toward him, as Townsend pulled his horse out a little to one side and stopped. He said, "Mr. Townsend, my name is Morton, and I suppose we are all out on the same business and I would like to accompany you."

"All right," said Townsend, "come ahead," and he rode on.

We had a bad, slow trail all forenoon, climbing over a rough country, and for long stretches the mescal was so thick that two horses could not pass on the trail. The mescal leaves are as sharp as needles and as hard as steel. It would ruin a horse if he happened to run against one.

The soldiers soon came stringing along and overtook us about the time that we got to the top of what was known as Ox Yoke Mountain.[8] There we found several ox yokes that had been run off in other raids by the Indians. The Mexican guide told us that it was twelve miles down the mountainside to the Verde River from that point.

Here the Mexican guide said that the Indians were liable to fire the brush ahead of us, so we rushed our horses down the steep, brushy trail as fast as we could; but we had not gone more than two or three miles before we saw the smoke rising down the canyon below us. The trail led down the north side of a ridge which was cut with steep gulches, and as it was on the north side and the mountain was very steep, the brush and grass did not burn very readily. Still, nearly all of the soldiers were cut off by the fire and had to leave the trail and make their way around as best they could, everybody for himself.

We reached the Verde River about 2:00 P.M., horses and men all pretty tired and hungry but all safe and sound. We crossed the river at the mouth of the east fork and camped to let our horses rest and graze while we got something to eat ourselves. Here we scoured the country thoroughly to be sure that the Indians had not divided their party, but satisfied ourselves that the whole lot of them had gone the one trail up the east fork. About 4:00 P.M. we started again on the trail, which led up the river for several miles, then turned up the face of a great table mountain which was one mass of lava boulders, and the trail was so steep that most of the men had to dismount.[9] Townsend had told me about this place, having learned of it through some soldiers who had been there and had to turn back as the Indians had rolled boulders down from the top until the whole face of the mountain seemed to be flying rocks of all sizes. The mountain is several miles long, and from the top down for many hundred feet it is a perpendicular bluff, then slopes to the river below. The trail ran along under this bluff, and the Indians could stop an army from passing along that trail, if they were to throw over even small-sized boulders.

Several parties before us had gone as far as the foot of this mesa, where the trail started up, and then had given up the job and turned back. When we got to this point we all bunched up and some of the men started up the trail. Townsend let them go a little while and then called them back; told one of the soldiers to fire a shot to recall them that were out of hearing of his voice. When the men were all turned back we strung out single file, which was the way we traveled all the time, and before sundown were back at the place we had left several hours before.

Townsend said to the lieutenant, "Have some of your men fire a shot or two at a mark."

Townsend wanted the shots fired but did not want the citizens to waste their ammunition. He thought it did not make so much difference whether the soldiers had ammunition or not. When we overtook the soldiers that morning Townsend was mad, for up to that time the citizens and soldiers when they hunted Indians together never could get along agreeably. The officers had always wanted to boss the job and made a failure of it every time. So far, Lieutenant Morton had not made any suggestions at all but had just come along, which was agreeable to Townsend and all the rest of us.

We built up big campfires, fired a few shots, put out a strong guard, and made down our beds, which among the citizens consisted of saddle blankets and saddle for pillow. We knew the Indians were watching our every move from the high rough points which surrounded us on all sides. We got our supper and still kept the fires burning bright, and all lay down to rest, if not to sleep.

The guard was changed every two hours, and at 2:00 A.M. the fires were all out, and as noiselessly as possible we mounted and retraced our steps to the foot of the big mountain, which we reached just as the light began to show in the east. Noiselessly we began to climb up the face of that mountain, and by the time it was light enough to see to shoot we were all over the worst of it; but we had now several miles to travel along the face of the mountain, directly under that great bluff, which seemed to hang over in places.

It was very slow traveling until we got past this big black mesa, then we had rolling hills to cross, with occasionally a pretty rough canyon. About 2:00 P.M. the Mexican guide, who was ahead, threw up a hand, and we all were on the alert. There had just gone over a ridge about a mile ahead of us an Indian on a horse. We were then in sight of quite a large piece of comparatively level land and could see cottonwood trees in the bottom along the east fork, which at this place proved to be dry. Townsend and I jumped off our horses to tighten the cinch on our saddles, which let several of those that were in line behind us go by, and they were going as fast as they could. Among the others that passed was the lieutenant.

When we had traveled about a quarter of a mile, Townsend ahead of me saw an Indian track in the dry dirt which bore off the main trail to the right, and we followed it as fast as our horses and eyes would allow, and of course all who were behind us followed us. Across the flat that we had seen from a distance we all went as fast as our horses could carry us, and on the opposite side of the river we ran into an Indian camp pretty well hidden in the brush. The Indians had most of them gotten out of their camp and were making for the hills through the thick brush, but we were shooting every one we could see that was near enough to make it worthwhile trying our guns on.

As we were crossing the dry riverbed I noticed one Indian running apparently behind a hill, and I started for the top of the hill as fast as I could, and just as I reached the top I caught sight of a big fellow running down a gulch. I dropped him, and as he fell I saw another in a bunch of oak brush about seventy-five yards away. I shot him, and he fell in the brush. Among the soldiers was a Corporal Flynn who had done duty for a long time between Camp Verde and Prescott as mail carrier, and Flynn saw the last Indian that I had shot when he fell, Flynn having followed me up the hill. Flynn said, "You hit, but I think you only wounded him."

So I told Flynn if he would ride up on a little point of a hill that overlooked the place where the Indian fell so that he could see if he ran out and at the same time cover my horse, which I left where we stood, that I would go into the brush and see what I had done to the red. Flynn stationed himself where he could see all around, but could see nothing of the Indian; so I advanced cautiously into the brush and in a few minutes heard shots off to my right. I looked and there were seven or eight soldiers about 200 yards away, and then I heard a bullet strike a rock close to me. Flynn began to yell like a crazy man and said: "What in hell are you damned boys doing? Trying to kill a white man?"

The soldiers had seen my black hat moving in the bushes, mistook me for an Indian, and had all taken a shot without dismounting. I found the Indian, who had crawled into the thick brush, but he was a good Indian.

We had spent so much time looking for the good Indian that there was no use in doing anything but to go and find the balance of the people. We returned to the Indian camp and were the last to get there.

Morton, the trailer, some citizens, and a few soldiers had struck a big trail while running on the main trail that we had been following. This trail crossed the main trail at right angles and led up a small ravine to another Indian camp, but much smaller than the one that we had struck. The lieutenant had no rifle but killed a big buck Apache with his forty-five—about the first one that was killed. Altogether we had killed thirty-five Indians that we knew were dead.[10] We plundered the camp and about 5:00 P.M. took the trail and followed it until dark.

After we had eaten something and were sitting around camp, Townsend asked the trailer what was the meaning of "Wapop" in the Apache language. He said it meant, "Oh, Father!" Then Townsend told of shooting a young Indian about eighteen or twenty years old and breaking his leg. The fellow grabbed hold of a bush and pulled himself up, stood on one foot, and slapped his breast and cried out, "Wapop! Wapop!" two or three times before he got the second shot. This was probably a white man who had been with the Indians so long that he had forgotten his mother tongue, as all who saw the body said it was much whiter than any Indian.

The next morning we took the trail as soon as we could see distinctly, not wishing to miss any sidings, as we were on the rolling country which we knew was the divide between the East Verde and some other streams, and we were expecting the Indians to break up into small parties, as was their custom when followed and pressed by the whites. It was very lucky the Indian the men saw on horseback the day before did not see us, or the alarm would have been spread and we should only have got thirty-five.

⊱——⊰✦⊱——⊰

We traveled on a trot or lope for several hours the morning of the fourth day out, through cedar and juniper timber, over mesa and rolling hills along the foot of the mountain.[11] About 10:00 A.M. the leaders came right into a big rancheria in a big canyon, the banks of which were so high and so near perpendicular that there was no way of getting down into the canyon [except] by single file down a narrow trail. The Indians were getting away. I took in the situation at a glance and saw several Indians skulking into a gulch that ran into the main gulch near their camp. I forced my horse to jump down about ten feet, where he landed on loose, sloping dirt, and made across the big gulch (which was about one hundred yards wide) up onto the mesa on the opposite side, and made a dash to try to head off the Indians that I had noticed going up the mouth of the small side gulch. The mountain to the west of them was so steep and bare of brush that they dared not try to climb it, and I managed to get ahead of them and shot two. One raised up in a sitting position, and I was about to give him another shot when "Hold on, boys!" came from the corporal. He had been right at my heels, the same as the day before. "Hold on, boys! Don't waste your ammunition. I'll finish him with a rock!"

I had seen an Indian down in the gulch when I jumped off to shoot the first one, and I tried to watch the banks to prevent him from escaping; I had never taken my eyes off the place where I saw him long enough for him to climb the steep bank, and the mountain was too bare for him to try that side. Several of the men had followed up the gulch on foot from the Indian camp at the mouth, and I had asked them to look carefully, which they thought they did, but none found him. Still I would not give it up and remained in my position. Finally a young fellow named John Bullard came in sight from among the juniper trees and stopped right above where I had lost sight of the Indian. I hailed him and told him what I had seen, and for him to get into the gulch and hunt carefully while I watched where I stood.

With as little as delay as possible he climbed down, and pretty soon a big boulder hid him from me; then a gun went off, and Bullard's head came up from behind the boulder. Then down it went again out of my sight. Then up came the head again, and Bullard climbed upon the boulder and, holding up his right hand (from which a part of the forefinger had been shot off with the guard of his pistol a couple of years before by Indians who waylaid him while he was on his way from Townsend's ranch to the Bowers's ranch on the Agua Fria), he hallood to me, "I have got even with that finger. I'm very much obliged to you, Charlie."

On all the trip Bullard had not got an Indian until this one.

I went back now to the place where the Indians were camped, and the men had already plundered the camp looking for valuables, and among other things they had bound a buckskin sack with a lot of indigo balls in it, and that reminded me of what my wife had sent me to Prescott for. I poured about a pound of them into my saddle holsters to take home with me. The men had captured several guns, a few buckskins, etc., but nothing of much value.

In the scrap at the Indian camp Townsend had a very narrow escape from an Indian bullet. He was walking through some brush and was within a few feet of a wounded Indian who was lying behind a boulder so that Townsend could not see him, with his rifle cocked and sighted; and if Townsend had taken one step more he would have been within range, but Providence was with him. Jeff Davis caught sight of the Indian, called out to Townsend and stopped him, and in the same breath finished the Indian.

We got a lot of roasted mescal and some horse meat at this camp and took up the trail again, which led to the southeast from this point through low hills and long mesas.

We had traveled some three or four hours and were following a long, low grassy ridge which was skirted on the south and west by a big wide canyon which seemed to run far back into the mountain. The trail ran along the top of the ridge, which in some places was quite narrow as it wound around the head of some short gulch that ran off toward the big valley below to the east.[12] There was quite a little rise in this ridge just before it pitched off into the large gulch to the west of us, and as the Mexican trailer rode nearly to the top of the ridge he threw up his hand and stopped and turned his horse partly around. He had seen what he supposed was two Indians, mounted on horses, going ahead of us on the same trail about 600 yards in advance. Townsend slipped and peeked over the ridge, watched a few moments, then turned and came back and started down a very steep gulch which we could see led down to the big wash. If we could get down it with our horses we should not be in sight of the Indians until we were close to them.

Townsend had brought the gun that came so near killing him and had several buckskins lying across his saddle, upon which rested the two guns. As he passed me he started down the gulch, dropped the Indian's gun, then dumped the buckskins, and was cleared for action. I had no plunder to dispose of except the indigo, and I could not part with that, for my wife had sent me after it. This was a rough gulch, but our horses were sure-footed, and we landed on the level ground, side by side. Here the ground was soft, sandy land, and we turned our horses loose and gave them the spur.

The Indians were going very slowly and appeared to be asleep, for we were in plain sight of them for as much as 300 yards. They were following the main trail and were crossing a grassy flat with bunches of oak brush here and there scattered. We ran our horses at full speed to within forty yards of them and both jumped off at the same time and fired. Both of us shot the same Indian as he was nearest to us, and we could see that he had a long rifle lying across the horse in front of him. We had both noticed before we jumped off that there were two on one horse, and at the crack of my gun the nearest Indian pitched head-foremost off the horse, and with him went the gun and a big quarter of horse meat that he had balanced across the horse's withers.

The other two Indians jumped off the horse they were riding and began firing at me, as I was in the open ground and Townsend was behind a small bunch of brush, and the Indians had the horse between them and Townsend. They fired three or four shots at me, one with a Henry rifle and the other with a six-shooter. I was jumping side-wise and trying to reload my rifle when Townsend sent a shot and broke the right arm of the Indian who had the rifle. Then they both started to run, keeping as much as possible the brush between them and us. They had run only a few steps when they ran together, and the one with the six-shooter got the Henry rifle and gave the pistol to the one with the broken arm. All of this time I was trying to get a shot, but there was too much brush, and they were taking advantage of it.

Then we both made a dash for our horses. Townsend's horse had stood still where he left him, but mine had moved off a little way, and I suppose he did the wise thing, for if he had stood right beside me as the other horse did he might have been shot or killed. When I ran toward the horse he became frightened and would not let me catch him. When I realized that I could not catch him readily, I started running after the Indians. Townsend had started along the side of a low hill, trying to get a shot and at the same time trying to head them off to give me a chance. The Indians kept in the wash, which headed about one-quarter of a mile from where we shot the first one. Along the wash on each side was a growth of oak brush which prevented Townsend from getting a shot. Townsend was on the left of the Indians, which made it necessary for him to turn in his saddle in order to use his gun. He said if he had been on the other side he could have had plenty of shots at them.

At the head of the gulch there was a low divide, and there the Indians separated. One ran down a gulch, and the other through some brush and was out of sight, but Townsend kept in sight of the one with the rifle and followed him for something like a mile before he got a good show to shoot. Then he hit him in the back of the head and killed him instantly. When Townsend rode up to where the Indian lay he took hold of his ankle to pull him down out of some brush, and the grain of his hide slipped like he had been scalded. When I came up to Townsend he was examining the Henry rifle, and he asked me if I had seen the wounded Indian, which of course I had not. He called my attention to the way the hide had slipped on the dead Indian's leg, and while we were commenting on it the balance of our party began to show up on the hills about a mile back on our trail. We got up in sight, and they were all soon with us.

We desired to go back to the big wash that we had crossed in overtaking the Indians to camp, as it was then about sundown and we knew there was water and feed there. On our way back I was riding next to Townsend, the other men having caught my horse and brought him along. I said, "Townsend, why didn't you shoot when you jumped off your horse?"

His reply was "Why didn't you shoot?"

I said, "I killed that big Indian all right," and we both claimed to have shot the Indian. So when we got back to where he lay, we examined the body and found the small Henry-rifle hole, and the bullet must have passed through his heart, while my big Sharp's bullet had passed through right between his shoulders. We had both fired at the same time, and we both thought the other had not shot at all.

Townsend said to me, "How many have you killed?"

I said, "Two yesterday and two this morning."

"Well," he replied, "you count this one. That shot would have killed a big bunch if they had been in line."

"How many have you got?" I asked.

"Eight" was the answer, "and one gone with his right arm shot all to pieces. We will track him up in the morning, and that will be nine for me!"

The gun that had caused us to both shoot at the same Indian proved to be the herder's gun that was killed when the herd was taken. The horse that he rode belonged to the Bowers's ranch, and the other horse belonged to the late Robert Postal. It was quite a noted race horse.

The whole command had sat and watched Townsend and me until the first shots, then came on as fast as possible.

One of the soldiers had noticed a road leading up the mountainside across the valley some eight or ten miles away, recognized it as a road that he had traveled several years before, and said that it led from Old Camp Reno on Tonto Creek to Green Valley. That was the first we had an idea where we were.

From what I can learn from people who have lived in that country the creek that we were camped on is now known as Wild Rye.[13]

The next morning we were out as soon as we could see and tried to locate the wounded Indian. We found his track where he had crawled through the brush and skulked along for nearly half a mile, then in some way he had built a signal fire, and other Indians had come to him during the night and taken him away. So Townsend only counted eight for the trip.

After satisfying ourselves that there was no show to find the wounded Indian, we took the trail, and about 10:00 A.M. struck Tonto Creek and the old wagon road before mentioned. The Indian trail led down the creek to a point below a small canyon that the road was built around. There the Indians had left the road and taken to the hills again, going east. Here we halted for the first time to consult. As our horses were in very bad shape (several being entirely or partially barefooted) and our grub was all gone, that is, the citizens' grub, we concluded that it would be folly to go further on the trail, and we also realized that the Indians were thoroughly aroused, as we had been seeing smoke by day and fires by night on the mountains for the past twenty-four hours.

Some of the party were in favor of going back and trying to get home via Camp Verde. It was also suggested by some that we might as well take our back trail. That suggestion made some merriment among the wise ones, and Townsend spoke up and said 500 men could not get back by the way which we came without losing half of them. Townsend hunted up the soldier who had recognized the wagon road the day before and learned what he could about the country and the road. The soldier had been over the road but once, but he thought we were not more than ten miles from Old Camp Reno, and from there there had been wagons over the Reno Mountains to McDowell. We concluded to go to McDowell, and as we began to mount our horses, Townsend remarked, "We will have to be on our guard from now on or somebody may get hurt."

That was the most talk he had made on the trip at any one time, and the lieutenant had not said that much so as to be heard by the citizen part of the crowd, and we all began to think he was all right. Even Jeff Davis had quit calling him "Corporal" when he had occasion to address him and called him, "Mr. Morton."

We were halted on a mesa of a considerable extent while we were consulting about the road to take. We were among prehistoric ruins of some kind, and they covered many acres of ground.

We had a good road until we reached the old abandoned post.[14] A few miles above the post we passed what had been a garden, irrigated with water taken out of Tonto Creek. This was done by soldiers while the post was occupied, we afterwards learned.

We reached the old ruined post about noon, having traveled some twenty or twenty-five miles that morning, and had spent a considerable time hunting for the Indian with the broken arm. That Indian building the fire with one hand was a puzzle to us. He must have had matches.

As we found a fine large stream or spring near the old camp, we concluded to camp there that night to rest our horses. Several of the citizens had walked all morning to favor their horses. My own horse was very lame, and the first thing that I did after reaching the camp was to hunt up the old blacksmith shop, and I found plenty of old shoes that were good enough to keep a horse's foot off the ground. I also picked up quite a lot of nails, most of which had been bent, but I got enough to put a shoe onto my horse and a lot to spare for the others.

While several other men and I were hunting for the nails, we were startled by seeing some of the fellows in camp run to their horses, while others were running to camp from where they had been picking blackberries, of which there was quite a patch at this place—the first that I had ever seen on the Pacific Coast growing wild. The excitement was caused by a big cloud of dust about two miles up the McDowell road, just at the mouth of a canyon that the road passes through before it reaches the open mesa country. Our first impression was that it was Indians coming with a band of stolen stock, as we could see nothing but dust and a glimpse of something moving. Only a few of us had our horses when we heard a bugle call, and the soldiers said it was a command to charge, and I guess it was, for here they came just tearing up the earth until they were within about 400 yards. Then they subsided and walked their horses into camp, and none of them a bit hurt. It turned out to be a company of cavalry sent out from McDowell to kill Indians, and as our soldiers were all mounted on white horses they were mistaken for a band of sheep, and the officer in command had the horn blown, I suppose to scare them away so that they would not eat him.

The officer stopped and talked awhile with our men and made a strong talk with some of the boys, trying to induce them to join him and go after the ones we had lost.

⊷⊷ ▨✦▨ ⊷⊷

He went so far as to offer to dismount some of his men and send them back to McDowell and mount the citizens on the fresh horses. There were men in our party that would have liked to accept the offer, had it not been for the bugle. The name of this officer I do not recall, but the guide was Hi Jolly, one of the men imported to the United States with the camels that were brought to Texas in the early fifties.[15]

When the McDowell officer struck the trail of the Indians where we had left it he took the back track—the trail that we had followed to Tonto Creek, instead of following the Indians. He was afterwards court-martialed for that. Hi Jolly made the complaint, I believe, which brought him before the court martial. Hi Jolly was a good and careful guide and scout and died a few years since at Quartzsite, Yuma County. In June 1909 Sharlot M. Hall hunted up his grave and marked it with a granite slab.

Our party slept at the old post that night, and we could see signal fires in every direction on the mountains. The next day we started to make McDowell. Townsend spoke to the lieutenant, whom we had all learned to like by this time, and told him to have his men keep close up and not get scattered, as there were liable to be Indians trying to cut off any who might lag behind. It was a long, rough ride over the Reno mountain, and we were all tired after the excitement of the chase, and our horses were badly fagged and sore-footed. We scattered out on both sides of the road, and after we came in sight of McDowell (which we could see ten or twelve miles away), I was riding on the upper side of the road, and Townsend was below the road. I noticed him working his way up toward me, and when he got alongside, he said to me: "Suppose they don't give us rations when we get down there," nodding at the post, "What shall we do?"

I replied, "I don't know."

Says he, in an undertone, "We will take the post," and turned back to go back to his place in the line of march.

As he started off I said: "All right, Townsend."

I will say here that we had been living off the soldiers' rations after the third day out and had eaten everything they had the day before except some mescal that we had found in the Indian camps.

We did not have to take the post, however, as the commanding officer did everything he could for our comfort, gave us good quarters for ourselves and horses and an order for anything that was in the commissary. I believe his name was Major Dudley.[16] We rested at McDowell two days, then started for Prescott, via Black Canyon and Townsend's ranch, where Townsend found his family all safe and well. This woman had been staying at the ranch alone with her small children and no neighbors for several miles. The ranch was more than forty miles from Prescott and right in the heart of the Indian country, but she had dogs and guns. The lady raised a large family and is living somewhere in this country now.

The Indians killed Townsend sometime after; shot him at long range but did not dare to go near him to get his horse. The faithful animal stayed with him several days, then went home. They found the body by backtracking the horse. Townsend had seen signs of a large party of Indians in the country and, having no neighbors to go with him, he went after them single-handed, as he had done many times before. In all he killed thirty-five Apaches in the five years that he had lived on the Agua Fria River.[17]

Our party broke up next day at the Bowers's ranch, having been gone eleven days and recovered all but fourteen head of the horses and mules stolen. The soldiers went to Camp Verde, and those of the citizens that did not belong in the Agua Fria Valley returned to Prescott, where we found the citizens organizing a search party to go out and find and bury us. As they did not know that we had joined issues with the soldiers, they concluded that the Indians had got us into some tight place like the Black Mesa on the East Fork of the Verde and killed us all.

I got to Prescott about 10:00 A.M.[18] and was preparing to start that day and drive through to Skull Valley, where I had left my wife and baby nearly two weeks before, to be gone only two nights, but my friends got around me and persuaded me to stay until next day, as they were preparing an entertainment for me and the balance of the party. That was a day and night of great rejoicing in Prescott, it being the first time that the Indians had been followed, overtaken, and severely punished by either citizens or soldiers for their crimes. It was really the beginning of a long-fought battle in which the Indians got the worst of it every time. While we were at McDowell, we occupied the quarters of a company of cavalry that had gone to meet General Crook, who had just come to the country and was on a tour of inspection of its geography, which he accomplished by going to every military post before he started his campaign, which ended so successfully.

When I had put my team back in Brook and Lind's stable, I walked down across the plaza and someone introduced me to a Mr. John Dunn from Virginia City, Nevada. We talked a few minutes, and he asked me to come into the store a minute (we were standing in front of Levy Bashford's store).

Dunn said: "Mr. Bashford, give me that gun if you please." And Bashford went and brought out a new Winchester rifle—one of the latest models. Mr. Dunn passed the gun to me and said: "See if that is any good. If it is, keep it."

I certainly kept it, until it was burned with my house and all its contents in Salt River Valley.

That act of Dunn must have suggested something, for the citizens of Prescott presented John Townsend with a gun just like it, with appropriately engraved plates on the stock,[19] and also presented Lieutenant Morton with a pair of gold-mounted forty-five pistols, properly engraved. I will say that the older officers at Verde had sent Morton out as a lark, not expecting him to accomplish anything, and were having a lot of fun about it at first; but when he was gone longer than he was rationed for they began to get uneasy about "the boy," as they called him when he first left them. When he returned it was a different name he bore.

That night's entertainment consisted, first, of a wine supper, the table being the full length of a new store that Bashford was building. In the middle of the table was a row of wine baskets, set end-to-end the whole length of the table. This wine was Hammond port, a wine-growing town on Keuka Lake, New York. The first course served was wine, and then Judge Howard made a little speech and winked both eyes. Then we had a course of wine, then a short speech from R. C. McCormick, and another course of wine. We had short speeches and wine until most of the party went wine-ding home. The old Prescott pioneers did do things right when they started.

The next morning, having my load all ready the night before, I started with William H. Smith and Charles Boyce for Skull Valley. Arriving at the Bowers's station, where there were several military officers sitting on the porch, I drove up alongside, and as my wife and Mrs. Bowers came down the steps I handed my wife the holsters that I had put the indigo balls in at the second fight and said to her: "Here is the indigo, wife, and I had a hell of a time to get it!"

The next day I got home to Peeples Valley, having been gone nineteen days when it was my intention on leaving home to be away only five days. There I found John Burger suffering badly from some wounds he had received at the hands of the Apaches on April 1 of that year, when his companion, H. Wycoff, was killed while he and Burger were on their way from Peeples Valley to Wickenburg. Burger had three balls in his right side and was shot through the left thigh, which wound crippled him for life. The wounds were all nearly healed when I left him, and he was getting around a little on crutches. When I returned, the wounds in his side were badly inflamed and were full of proud flesh. One rib had been shot entirely in two and the ends of the rib were growing together nicely when I left him, but when I got the inflammation down and the proud flesh burned out of the wound, I found that there were little ulcers formed on the ends of the new bone. I cut them off with my pocket knife, and with such attention as I was able to give him Burger was out of bed and quite well in a short time. He was one of the early settlers of Phoenix and was killed accidentally in his own mill on Humburg Creek. His wife still lives in Phoenix. Altogether we killed fifty-six Indians and got all of the stock back but fourteen head, and Mrs. Genung got her indigo.

Incidents of Regular Army Life in Time of Peace

FRANK K. UPHAM[1]

The Overland Monthly 5, 2nd ser. (April 1885): 426–29

Our wedding journey began with a trip across the continent over the Pacific railroad, which was then a new thing.[2] Arriving at San Francisco, I learned to my surprise and disappointment that, instead of the pleasant stations in Oregon or Washington territory that had been anticipated, I was fated to return to Arizona, which I had left the fall before with the belief that my term of service in that territory had been completed. But we made the best of it and sailed on the steamer for San Diego after a short delay. From San Diego we proceeded in an ambulance under the scorching rays of a June sun, crossing the arid desert of the Colorado and winding slowly along the Gila, through the sand and alkali dust, which, combined with the intense heat, was well nigh insupportable. In all, we were six weeks on the road from San Diego to my station in a remote corner of Arizona.

The latter portion of this—after leaving Tucson—was traveled with an escort of twenty mounted men, riding near our wagons and constantly on the lookout for hostile Indians; a regular guard was mounted at night as a necessary precaution against the surprise of our camp by the murderous savages who infested the country bordering upon the San Pedro River and Dragoon Mountains, and of whose bloody work we were daily reminded by the lonely graves at the roadside. These were in most instances marked with a rude cross, probably placed there by the friendly hands of those who had known the victims in life, or possibly by the passing stranger, who knew not how soon he too might be in need of the same office.

This was nearly fifteen years ago; now, when I hear others carelessly mention a trip by rail to the same locality and return as a journey of a few days, or a week at most, a momentary feeling akin to envy or anger comes over me, and it is difficult to realize that it has been possible for even steam and the locomotive to accomplish such results—to have apparently annihilated the absolute waste and desolation through which we passed so wearily.

An end came, however, as it always does, and the journey itself is at this distance recalled with even pleasant recollections of the brighter incidents connected with it; for, thanks to that peculiar characteristic of the human mind which enables us to forget all but the brighter spots, those alone have been mainly remembered. The long looked-for station, which was finally reached, and which for a time ended our ambulance and tent life, was then called a camp, though it has since attained the more dignified title of a fort, having been in the meantime, however, entirely rebuilt after the manner of modern garrisons. But at that time nearly all frontier stations were known as camps, as in fact they should have been, for they were not more than the name implied.

This station[3] consisted of a lot of rough log buildings, which had been constructed by soldier labor, and accordingly in the most primitive manner. They were begun a few months before our arrival—when the post had first been located and established—and were still but partially completed. The whole was arranged in the form of a camp of cavalry and was originally laid out with the same military precision, in strict accordance with the plan found in the army regulations. So many outside structures in the way of stables, quartermaster's corrals, a sutler's store, and so forth, besides numerous Indian rancherias, had, however, been permitted or caused to spring up in the immediate vicinity—all of which were out of uniformity with the original plans—that upon approaching the post by the road from Tucson, as we did, it had more the appearance of a frontier town or mining camp, quietly resting on a ridge or knoll which crossed the narrow valley, than of a military post garrisoned by two troops of cavalry and two companies of infantry belonging to the Regular army of the United States. But notwithstanding the want of that regularity in appearance which one might have expected to meet, it was not destitute of a certain natural attractiveness, or even beauty, owing to its picturesque environment especially.

The journey had been a tiresome one, and for more than 200 miles no sign of human life or habitation had been visible; consequently, the satisfaction with which we reached our destination may be understood. As we entered the post, the line of officers' quarters extended for a quarter of a mile parallel to a canyon one hundred yards to the rear. The walls of this canyon were nearly, if not quite, perpendicular, and through it fifty or sixty yards below ran a beautiful mountain stream, whose source was in the distant snow-capped peaks visible against the horizon to the eastward. The officers' quarters faced those of the soldiers, which consisted of six log cabins to each company, running at right angles to the officers' line, about eighty yards from it; the intervening space formed a parade ground. The view from both front and rear of the post, though attractive, was limited, and consisted principally of the immediate and rather abrupt pine and juniper-covered mountainsides. To the east and west, up and down the valley, it was more extended, though also confined to mountain scenery, but of such a grand description that the eye never tired of resting upon it: made up of ridges, crags, and distant peaks, blending with the sky in wild, fantastic shapes. At sunset the landscape was tinted with gorgeous prismatic effects seldom equaled anywhere.

The quarters of the officers varied but little, if at all, in their appearance, manner of construction, or dimensions. All were equally bad, and such as at the present time even the army on the frontier would object to and consider unfit for habitation. Those that we went into were a sample of the others; a building eighteen by twenty feet, the chinks between the logs daubed with adobe mud, both inside and out; the interior, one room, a rough, unplaned board floor, a large fireplace at one end, the chimney on the outside, at the other a door, the only entrance or exit, with a window on one side of the room consisting of a single sash with six lights of glass, swinging inward on its hinges. No ceiling whatever, but the bare rafters covered with rough boards formed an unshingled roof overhead, which, though affording excellent ventilation, was no protection from the weather, the boards having become so warped and twisted by the sun as to admit of frequent streaks of both sunlight and moonlight, and thus partially compensate for the want of more windows.

In this cabin we were soon domiciled, for it was the work of but a few hours to put down the carpet and arrange the few simple articles of furniture which had been brought with us from San Francisco, or had been manufactured by the post quartermaster; and while the weather continued pleasant, we thought we were very comfortable—as much so as our neighbors at least, which is always a satisfactory feeling. But in September, when the terrible rain and thunderstorms came, it was quite a different matter, and we were obliged to go into camp inside the house. This was done by nailing a piece of canvas to the logs on the side of the room, about ten feet from the floor, and stretching the opposite side over a pole supported by two uprights, by this means improvising a shelter after the fashion of a tent, under which it was possible to keep dry until the storm passed. Such articles as we were unable to move under this shelter were also covered with canvas so far as practicable. Fortunately the rains, though frequent at this season, were of short duration; but they came down in torrents while they lasted. The novelty of the situation was, however, something, and it did not then seem so bad as it does now in recalling it.

In our single apartment we lived, slept, and ate our meals, though the cooking was done in a smaller building of the same character which belonged to this establishment, about twenty feet distant, directly in the rear. The one room of this was alike the kitchen and a general storeroom (the cook slept in a tent). Here the meals were prepared, and they were brought hence by "our man" on a tray, into the "large house," where the board was spread—a cow bell which I had borrowed from the quartermaster's storehouse proving to be a satisfactory substitute for the regular call bell with which we had forgotten to provide ourselves while fitting out before leaving San Francisco.

This set of quarters was upon the extreme left flank of the garrison and consequently somewhat isolated from the others, the first that were approached on entering the post by the road already mentioned, and in the event of an Indian attack, the most exposed.

As will be readily inferred, our daily domestic life was a quiet and simple one. Society at first consisted of the invalid wife of our married officer, who rarely left her room and who had, before our arrival, been without female society for more than a year. She was only waiting to gain strength enough to enable her to reach her home in Philadelphia, whither she started a few weeks later. Besides this lady and her husband, there were a few bachelor officers. We came in contact with no others socially, and during the two years passed at this station my wife had no society of her own sex, with the exception of a short period—about six months—during which time the wives of two other officers were with them, so that we were mainly dependent upon ourselves for society. During the pleasant portions of the year we took occasional trips, sometimes on horseback or in the ambulance but more frequently on foot, among the hills and pine trees, or along the river, occasionally looking in on some of the Indian camps, where we were always welcome and where a white lady was an object of singular curiosity. Points and objects of interest were not wanting in a locality for which nature had done so much, and we were seldom at a loss where to go when my occupations admitted of going at all.

But of all the surrounding country the most attractive stroll was through the narrow canyon in the rear of the post, from the entrance to the end of which was about a mile, and through which an abandoned Indian trail was discovered. This the soldiers had made passable by cutting away a portion of the almost tropical growth of tangled vines and bushes which had accumulated and obstructed the trail and felling trees to serve as bridges on which to cross the little stream. The stream abounded in miniature cascades and was filled with trout. Nearly the entire distance was shut in by steep walls on either side; to many of its depths the sun daily penetrated but an hour or two, and during the hottest of summer days one could always be sure of a cool and shady retreat here.

Until the recesses of this canyon had been thoroughly explored, it had not been deemed prudent to enter it unless armed and prepared for an encounter with the bears which were supposed to frequent, if not inhabit it. This impression originated in the fact that one evening at sunset, shortly after our arrival, a large black bear was seen to emerge from the mouth of the canyon at a point above the post and trot deliberately and directly along, passing the open ground in rear of the officers' kitchens, between them and the edge of the canyon.

It so happened that I was the first to observe his approach and had time enough to enable me to go into my quarters, get a carbine—which was always kept between the mattresses of the bed, loaded and in readiness for immediate use—and wait for the bear, who was to pass within fifty yards of the house. I had never killed a bear but was anxious to do so—perhaps too anxious, or possibly the opportunity was too good. At all events, I placed myself behind the corner of the kitchen and waited until I could almost see his eyes, then fired; but to my surprise and mortification—for I had always considered myself a fair shot with a rifle—he only wiggled his stumpy tail a little and shambled on down the line in his lumbering but singularly rapid gait. By this time others had also comprehended the situation and were lying in wait for him in the same manner, though their opportunities were not quite equal to mine; but although at least forty bullets were sent after him from the cavalry carbines and infantry long toms by both officers and soldiers, Bruin escaped. In doing this he was obliged to run the gauntlet of nearly the entire line until, coming to a point on the edge of the cliff which was a trifle less precipitous than the rest, he descended with the agility of a cat and was up the wall of the opposite side of the canyon as quickly, though the firing continued at long range until he was lost to sight among the junipers. No doubt he carried lead with him, but evidently not enough to make him our "meat," and he possibly laughed in his sleeve, as he trotted away, at the ridiculous marksmanship of the "brutal soldiery." Diligent search through all parts of the canyon after this failed to discover any bear sign, and there ceased to be further apprehension about entering it.

As already intimated, my own spare time was very limited. The duties of post quartermaster and commissary had devolved upon me, and these kept me employed—frequently at a distance from the house—the greater part of all the daytime. In addition to the ordinary and customary details which pertained to these duties, the mustering, counting, and rationing of nearly 1,400 Indians was attended to every fourth day; for, up to that time, no agent had been provided for these Indians, and they were in the hands of the War Department.

My wife was consequently left to herself and thrown upon her own resources much of the time. Books and other literature were not wanting, as an abundant supply of magazines and newspapers reached the post. But one can not read constantly, and among other expedients she began to acquire a knowledge of the Indian, or more especially the Apache, language, and very frequently on pleasant mornings, after domestic affairs had received the necessary attention and the simple housekeeping was arranged for the day, a few of the most intelligent young Indians of both sexes would collect outside the little window of our house, where from inside she would hold protracted interviews with them—communicating at first through the medium of signs, or of a few Spanish words which the Indians had picked up. But presently this intercourse was conducted entirely by means of the Indian tongue, with which she rapidly became conversant, to the manifest surprise and delight of the Indians themselves. In this manner she in a few months acquired a more extensive knowledge of the Apache language than any white person who was connected with the post at that time. She did not meet with the same degree of success, however, in her attempts to teach the young Indians [English]. Though she labored faithfully with several of the most promising, she only got so far with "Phillipi," who was the brightest (and had acquired his Spanish name by a short captivity among the Mexicans when very young), that he was able to print in large ungainly capitals on the slate the words, "My sore face," after which exploit even he, apparently, decided that he had sufficiently penetrated the depths of English literature and ceased to apply himself further. The knowledge thus acquired gave her an established reputation with the various bands on the reservation, where, as with the white people, nothing was lost by being repeated—and Indians are notorious gossips among themselves. The chiefs and head men made regular calls to the house, at proper intervals, and seemed by common consent to concede to her a status which was unusual for a woman, and to which one of their own race could never have hoped to attain. Doubtless, had she been so inclined, she might have exerted a strong influence in their affairs, but she was without ambition in that direction. A more practical result of this knowledge was that we were pretty regularly supplied with game of various kinds at a low price—fine wild turkeys, when in season, weighing from twelve to fifteen pounds, for ten pounds of flour; the latter purchased from the post commissary at three cents per pound.

This was, however, only practicable during the summer months. The winter was lonesome and dreary, though fortunately of short duration and not severe. Mail facilities were uncertain and irregular, and frequently during the winter there was no mail for three or four weeks at a time. Once we were five weeks without a mail, though one finally made its appearance quite unexpectedly by way of New Mexico, on top of a load of freight; after this we considered ourselves greatly favored by a weekly mail from Santa Fe, letters from friends in the East reaching us in ten or twelve days. Not long after this the routine of our daily life was changed: a little stranger was within our gates, and we were now three.[4] Our boy was perhaps the first white child born in what has since become a populous section.

In referring to these reservation Indians, I have omitted to explain that they were composed of numerous small tribes, or bands, all of them Apache however and more or less related by blood to each other, as well as to the hostiles in other portions of the territory. In fact, these Indians themselves had once been the enemies of the whites but had been peaceful and had planted corn for many years. The white people in the distant settlements still regarded them with jealousy and believed, or at least asserted, that they maintained regular communication with the hostiles and gave them material aid as well as information, besides permitting their young men to join in their raids upon the settlers or emigrants. But of this we were unable to find evidence, though every measure was taken to that end. At all events, our instructions from the department commander were to watch, feed, and regularly muster and count them at intervals of four days, which duty was conscientiously performed and duly certified to by official witnesses.

At the same time portions of our command were frequently engaged in scouting against the hostiles to the south and west, though mostly in the Tonto Basin, then a region almost entirely unknown to others than the troops but now a rich cattle country. During these periods the post would sometimes be left with a force not to exceed forty men, in the very heart of Indian country, where, in the event of a disaffection, the little garrison could have been massacred without the possibility of assistance, or even communication with the outside world.

And there was at times cause for apprehension on this account, for the Indians did not all like the whites, were quick to observe our weaknesses, and undoubtedly realized the situation and consequent temptation as fully and completely as we did ourselves.

The separate bands had feuds among themselves, probably of long existence if not hereditary, as most Indians seem to have, and these not infrequently resulted in bloodshed. This could not have been controlled had it been attempted, especially as their killing was usually done at night; but it became a source of considerable anxiety, for it was hard to tell where trouble of this character might end if once thoroughly started, and owing to the presence of my family, I experienced a feeling of insecurity greater than I cared to communicate to my wife. One morning in particular six dead Indians, including a small chief known as "The Beggar," were found less than a mile from our quarters as a result of one of their collisions, which had taken place during the night. The dismal moaning of the squaws resounded through the hills for days and nights afterwards.

Most of this trouble followed their drunken orgies, on which occasions their slumbering animosities would be aroused to a pitch of wild fury which seemed to know no bounds. They had a habit of distilling from the corn—which was either raised by themselves or issued to them by the government as a part of the food ration—a villainous compound which they called "tiswin," and although it apparently took a large quantity and a long time to make one of them satisfactorily drunk from its effects, it took still longer to become sober. Deliberate preparations were made for these debauches by the stealthy accumulation of corn in some secluded nook, perhaps a week being required to get the thing in full blast. For indications of this, they were carefully observed, and when the locality was determined, if it was near the post—as it usually was—a detachment, or even in some cases one of the troops of cavalry, was promptly dispatched under charge of a commissioned officer, with instructions to destroy the tiswin. It was not without apprehension and some precaution that the officer upon whom this duty devolved would enter a rancheria in which might be found usually from one to two hundred half-drunken Indians, all of whom were possessed of arms, and to upset the vessels of the vile stuff which they prized so highly. On such occasions the soldiers would remain mounted and be placed in such a manner as to surround and cover the main body of the Indians, with carbine loaded and at a "ready," while the officer himself dismounted and, with a small number of men under his charge, also dismounted, would proceed to spill the troublesome liquor with an assumption of coolness and deliberation which he by no means felt, amidst the black and threatening frowns of the Apaches. This unpleasant duty was shared by me in turn with the other lieutenants and was the cause of anxiety on the part of my wife; but she never complained, though the experience was entirely new to her.

During the second year the Indians became more and more troublesome and harder to control, owing to the cause already indicated and also to others;

so much so that it became advisable to exclude them from the limits of the post by the necessary guard, and my wife accordingly saw but little of them, only those visiting our house who had a special permit for that purpose, and this confined to a few of the more important personages.

One afternoon an unusual commotion was suddenly observed among some of them who had collected at a point near the Tucson road to the eastward of the post, and before it was realized, or any steps could possibly have been taken by the guard to prevent it, a number of Indians fled rapidly in the direction of the post, closely pursued by others in a state of partial drunkenness, hallooing and shooting with guns and bows and arrows, as they closely followed behind.

As I have said, our house was the first and most exposed in this direction, and here the fugitives immediately came, taking refuge in the rear of the house and immediately about it, and behind the chimney which ran up on the outside; either hoping to obtain protection, or for the purpose of making a stand, as they were also armed. But this failed to stop the fire of the attacking party, though their advance was checked. The situation in the inside of the house was critical and alarming; as usual at that time of the day, I was absent. My wife and child were alone, and she fully understood the situation. The man who should have been in the kitchen—he was there but a few minutes previously— or somewhere within call, was nowhere to be seen, and had undoubtedly run away ingloriously or hidden when he saw the Indians coming, though he had served during the whole War of the Rebellion as an enlisted man and was at one time a sergeant.

Immediate action was necessary, for the danger from a chance bullet coming through the chinks in the logs was considerable and not to be despised; besides which, the possibility of the Indians crowding their way inside the house, when they found she was alone, was not pleasant to contemplate. She did not long remain undecided, however, but took a small riding whip which hung against the wall, went at once outside the house, and drove them away by a lively application of the little whip to their bare feet and ankles. Several of these intruders were young Indians with whom she had a personal acquaintance; but they all immediately sneaked off with a sickly smile and would no doubt have greatly preferred to face the fire of the other party to being subjected to the mortification and disgrace of being thus dealt with by a woman. The whole incident occurred in a very short time, and by the time the guard reached the ground, the cause of the alarm was over and the Indians gone. I only learned of its occurrence several hours later, at dinnertime.

Soon after this I started with my family for their home in the Eastern states and reached Santa Fe after another ambulance trip of 300 miles. From this point I saw them again safely on the way to the nearest railroad point, still 250 miles distant, but under the friendly charge of an officer who was fortunately traveling in the same direction. It was months after that they joined me again, but under more favorable and civilized surroundings, at a pleasant station in the Department of the Columbia. It was well that I had taken this course, for but a day or two after again arriving at my station, a courier came in great haste bearing dispatches, which had been telegraphed as far as Santa Fe, from the division commander at San Francisco, ordering the cavalry to march immediately for the Modoc country, and we bade adieu to Arizona.

An Evening with the Apaches

[WILLIAM D. FULLER][1]

Army and Navy Journal 9, no. 25 (January 27, 1872)

To the Editor of the Army and Navy Journal.

SIR: An invitation to a "baile," or dance, had been extended to the officers of the post by Miguel, a chief among the White Mountain Indians, better known as the Coyotero Apaches.[2] It was accepted, and as it promised to be a fashionable assembly, an intimation was given that Miguel might expect his guests about 10:00 P.M. Just after tattoo, the sound of Indian drums and singing indicated that the dance was in progress, and we started for the rancheria.

Miguel's camp was along the side of a ravine, which afforded a grassy bottom of a few hundred yards in length and half as many wide. In this bottom and scattered around the hillside were eighteen or twenty campfires. Each fire had its group of Apaches of both sexes and every age. The fires, though small, burnt brightly, and with their faint moonlight brought distinctly in view the different figures. Not to overestimate their numbers, there must have been at least two hundred of the Apaches lounging about the fires or stretched out for sleep. A few were squatting around an old camp kettle, as if engaged in cooking. To the inquiry what was in the kettle, the cook, who was as naked as when he was born, excepting his breech-clout, answered politely, "bock-e-shee (beef) nada, caballo mucho," at the same time drawing his hand across his throat and pointing to where some dead horses had been hauled from the post.

The dance had not commenced, but large quantities of wood, piled near the fires, were ready to be lighted. Our party had scarcely paid their respects to Miguel when he gave a few brief orders. His instructions were reiterated by some of the others in the Apache tongue amid a succession of hideous yells. One peculiarity of their language is that in calling to each other the end of a sentence is emphasized by raising the voice and lengthening the last syllable into a perfect howl. A novice to Apache manners would suppose them to be in a state of great excitement, when they are only calling each other at very moderate distances. In a little more time, new fires were lighted that displayed finely the bare limbs and sparkling eyes of the Indians. A ring was formed with a fire in the center. It was intimated that the principal dancers were engaged in getting up their costumes, and meantime the Apache women would be happy to dance with the visitors.

Apache etiquette provides two partners for each gentleman. The two ladies, facing their partner, take him by each hand, and all three move a few steps forward and back at a kind of slow trot, marking time to the music and chorus. At intervals, all face about, but do not vary the figure in other respects. For music, there was the monotonous beating of two drums made of rawhide stretched over a jar or kettle. The drumstick was a small piece of sapling, bent into a loop at one end. All this was accompanied by a chorus of a dozen or more singers, who kept up a kind of guttural chant. The time was not fast but quickened towards the end of a dance. The dancing was excellent to warm the feet, and in the sharp air of a November evening, not an unpleasant exercise.

While we had been dancing, the ring of Apaches had increased its numbers, until over two hundred swarthy Indian bucks and squaws were squatting around the fire. Suddenly they set up a howl of applause, the ring opened to the right and left, and the performers of the evening appeared.

The three principal ones were Apache bucks, all dressed nearly alike. All wore moccasins, breechclouts, and a tanned buckskin from the waist to below the hips. Masks, with an immense headdress of horns, feathers, and wood concealed their features. The rest of their bodies were naked, except wreaths of evergreen about the waist and shoulders.[3]

Approaching to within a few rods, they commenced a series of leaps and dances outside the ring. Each one held a wooden sword in each hand, and after a few appearances and withdrawals, they finally entered the ring.[4] Finely formed and the perfection of muscular development, these dancers brought nearly every muscle into action. After half an hour or so of dancing they withdrew, and the music ceased. In a short time they again reappeared, capering about outside the circle and entering it from an opposite direction. An Apache brought a good-looking boy inside the ring, leaving him standing there with his arms folded. The masked dancers would rush by and feign to cut him with their swords, stabbing at him as they passed.

Occasionally, one of the performers would execute a "pas de seul" not discreditable to any ballet troupe. After witnessing these dances for an hour or so, as the night air grew chilly and the performances promised no new feature, our party slipped off for camp; but not until daybreak did the monotonous sound of their music cease, and the tireless Apaches break up their dancing.

Cavalry Life in Arizona

[GUY V. HENRY][1]

Army and Navy Journal 8, no. 43 (June 10, 1871)

CAMP McDOWELL, A.T.

To the Editor of the Army and Navy Journal, May 7, 1871

SIR: Wishing to beguile a few moments, it seemed not to be amiss to give some account of this post, its garrison, their march hither, and Arizona generally. Troop D, Third Cavalry, left Camp Halleck, Nevada, February 21, 1871, and by cars proceeded from Halleck station to San Francisco. The usual commotion and routine of travel was observed till, arriving at Truckee, on the Sierra Nevada, we were switched off at 4:00 A.M. in three feet of snow to await a freight train. Here the men had a chance to prepare coffee, and, continuing our journey, we passed through immense fields of snow and long lines of snow sheds till, arriving at the summit, we detached our locomotive and went for miles on a downgrade regulated by the brakes. The scenery all along the line was fine, but we missed the train we had left, for among the passengers was a theatrical troupe who at the stations afforded us amusement by their dancing, relieving the monotony of the trip.

Leaving the snow-covered Sierra [Nevada] in the morning, where everything was cold, bleak, and dreary, we reached Sacramento in the evening, to find spring in her beautiful garb, forming a pleasant contrast. At Sacramento we remained some hours and had a chance to see the town. It is not unlike others, the only difference being in the number of barrooms and elegance of appointments. 7:00 A.M. the following morning found us at the wharf in San Francisco Bay, with a tug prepared to take us to Angel Island, our destination till we moved for San Diego, California. Our stay here was pleasant, the air delightful, and a fine view of the Golden Gate, Bay City, Goat Island, a former engineer depot, and the artillery posts of Presidio, Black Rock, and Alcatraz, awakening sweet memories of the past, revived still more by a call from Alcatraz of its war-worn and well-known commandant and lady, and some of his subalterns; one of whom, a distinguished graduate of the artillery school, was also accompanied by his wife, he having committed the sin of matrimony since graduating.

A visit to the city revealed nothing of importance. You would meet a Californian who, pointing at a building, would say, "You can't beat that in New York." Their pride, however misplaced, is very commendable. March 1 found us on board the *Orizaba,* and after the usual, routine seasickness, we arrived at San Diego, California, a pleasantly located town, very healthy, a great resort for invalids, fine hotel, and destined, by means of the new railroad and Pacific steamers stopping there, to be an important point. Now you behold cavalry in all its glory, "on the hoof," about to crush sand for 450 miles across a most uninteresting and monotonous country, covered with that beautiful plant the sagebrush, varied once in a while by a cactus. Sad to think of this fate for the gay and dashing trooper and demoralizing; but you are soldiers, and if your Uncle Sam has so little regard for your esprit de corps, Congress so economical as not (after your achievements during the rebellion and hardships required of you in this country) to appropriate the necessary money, then shame on them! We will do our duty at any rate, so at it we go, and by the usual marches we reach Fort Yuma on the Colorado River, supposed to be the hottest place in the country, where (as we are told at least a thousand times along the road), when a man dies and goes below, he sends back for his blankets. We visited some of these graves, but as far as they are concerned they are intact.

Arizona City, just opposite, is quite a town, balls and shootings being the order of the day. Liquor is an unknown article. The quartermaster's depot, which reflects great credit on its builder and on its present incumbent for the excellent order it is in, is on this side. We enjoyed the genial hospitalities of its host. The quarters at Yuma are well prepared for heat, being surrounded by green blinds and having bathing conveniences, water being pumped by an engine into the buildings. May we never be in a worse place.

From Yuma we struck out, still on the hoof, for Camp McDowell, and having the same varied, beautiful scenery, crossing a couple of deserts, in fact all desert, missing the terrible sandstorms west of the Colorado. We in due course of time reached here, and if we do as well on horseback as on the hoof, the Apaches are a foregone conclusion. Here we received our horses, a very fine lot, and relieved Colonel Sanford of the First Cavalry, who has distinguished himself in this country by Indian fighting; he and his troop having their services kindly recognized by Uncle Sam, being allowed as they are to hoof it to San Diego, en route to Benicia, California.

The post is delightfully situated on the Rio Verde, upon a plain, the sun having a fine chance to dry the soil of its frequent rains, and the mountains keeping from us any rough winds. The thermometer never goes above 116 degrees in the shade. The quarters are of mud, and very good green shades of brush add to their comfort. Everything is clean; the kitchen, messing, and table furniture, silver-plated ware, and white tablecloths cannot be excelled. Our stables are as good and as well kept as any in the country; every horse is named with the first letter D, the same as the troop. Each man has his saddle rack and a place for everything, and everything in its place. Owing to so much duty, being the only troop here, we have had but little chance to drill, but every morning at stable call we put blankets on our horses and jump two ditches and a bar, the effect being to give us the best possible seat. A garden is at our disposal, from which we have had spinach and expect soon to have beets, lettuce, cabbage, potatoes, peas, tomatoes, and melons.

We expect in a few days a troop of cavalry, to be followed soon by another, and a company of infantry. Then for a splendid scout, for as it is now, the Indians have their own way; we see their fires at night, find in the morning their tracks through camp, and the garrison had its monotony relieved a few days before our arrival by having at night a volley fired into camp. On guard at night one is not apt to go to sleep when posted. The garrison now consists of Colonel N. A. M. Dudley, Third Cavalry; Second Lieutenant Shelton, First Cavalry,[2] post quartermaster and acting commissary of subsistence; Acting Assistant Surgeon Semig, post surgeon;[3] Captain Guy V. Henry, commanding Troop D, First Cavalry; First Lieutenant W. H. Andrews, absent on detached service; second lieutenant, vacant. Altogether, we prefer to serve in Arizona and reap the many advantages the country and climate offer and do not complain at our lot.

As to Arizona generally, it is a country abounding with beautiful streams, handsome forests, plenty of fine grazing (not costing the government a cent for feeding its animals), cool climate, fine agricultural land, if you could only get the water; splendid mineral resources, if they could only be discovered.

Owing to the unselfish devotion of the inhabitants to the government, the small cost of keeping the troops here, corresponding savings to the national treasury, and great advantages to the country, we sincerely hope that Uncle Sam may continue to make Arizona one of his most important military departments.

———————

Army and Navy Journal 8, no. 48 (July 15, 1871)

To the Editor of the Army and Navy Journal
CAMP McDOWELL, A.T., June 18, 1871

SIR: Since writing you last many changes have taken place here. First, the death of Cushing of the Third Cavalry. He had a reputation for gallantry and perseverance equaled only by that of his brother in the navy, of torpedo fame. We hear also with regret the death of Lieutenants Asbury and Morrison of the First Artillery. The former was known to us as a most excellent officer. General Stoneman has been relieved, and a lieutenant colonel assigned to command a colonel and a lieutenant colonel who rank him. How the matter is arranged we don't know. Brevet rank we thought abolished, but it seems to be again revived.

General Stoneman had an elephant to handle, and he did it well. General Crook has the same, and it remains to be seen how it will turn out. He has a good reputation; but will the government aid him as he needs, or will the Quaker policy still continue to rule, and he go under like his predecessors?

The cavalry picket. OUTING MAGAZINE, DECEMBER 1886.

To show how matters are managed at Verde. In three companies—about 240 men—there are, we believe, about forty horses here. One troop, some eighty strong, have about twenty-five serviceable horses. And so it goes. Economy rules, and the result in the end is double the expense. Wagons falling to pieces; no citizens allowed to be hired; mules unshod, and troop blacksmiths often taken from their work to attend to post matters.

Since my last, Troop M, Third Cavalry, Captain Mills,[4] has arrived from Whipple, the detachment of Troop D having returned from escort duty with the paymaster. We have fortunately had our men together and been able to have drills. Drilling in some regiments of cavalry, we understand, is considered highly improper. On scouts you don't drill, therefore it is unnecessary. On the same principle you might as well give your men a general furlough, to be called together only for a fight, as discipline is not necessary. To have your troop drilled and disciplined (when you can afford on a scout to relax) is a source of laughter. It is told that an officer arriving at this post (then garrisoned by the First Cavalry under Colonel Sanford, well known in this territory and elsewhere as a soldier and gentleman), and being told that they had mounted guard-mounting, shouted with laughter as [at] a good joke and a thing he had never seen or heard of. Such, of course with exceptions, is the feeling.

Fortunately we have been able to disabuse our men of these ideas (some of whom in three years had never drilled, for reasons they say they don't know), and not a trooper but is proud that he is able to manage his horse with his legs properly; knows the difference between a turn and wheel; can jump his ditch and bar; can go through his saber exercise mounted; cut heads on posts, and to the right and left on the ground; take his ring at tierce point; can "disperse as forager" or deploy as "skirmisher"; can load and fire his pistol or carbine accurately mounted; can move from the ranks when told (and not, as I have seen, require a whole troop to back [up] to get one trooper out); can right and left pass and half from a gallop using his legs; is instructed by non-commissioned, who are taught by officers, the anatomy of a horse and treatment of simple diseases. Don't tell me that such a trooper or troopers are valueless, have lost by their drill, and that when told on scout to "Go for them, boys," the redskin is any more certain of getting clear from their clutches than if undrilled. Give me the drilled soldier.

An Arizona citizen, quite celebrated for his Indian-fighting qualities, having just returned from a scout in which he himself had killed fifteen Indians,[5] remarked on seeing Troop D drill that those men could jump a rancheria; that he had seen soldiers so poorly or not at all instructed in riding as, owing to not being able to jump or sit their horses, to fall off; or, failing to have confidence in themselves, did not succeed as they would have done under other training. Some may say that they can't get their men together. Drill six of them; they go off; they don't forget what they are taught; others come who can go through the same drill; and, finally, you get the whole troop drilled. Let us work together and raise the standard—if necessary, have a cavalry school, each regiment being represented, and the tour of detail being for one year. *Essayons!*[6]

We were quite surprised a few days since and agreeably so, as strangers are a novelty, by the appearance at our post of Lieutenant Morton of ours, his troop (A), and twenty citizens. They had returned from the warpath, jumped two rancherias, and killed fifty-six Indians.[7] After resting a few days they returned to Verde and Prescott. Troop M was out seven days, but the Indians, like deer, had taken fright from Lieutenant Morton and made it impossible to catch them. The country they traveled over was very rough. They burnt a rancheria. In the midst of this rough, barren country they struck Greenback Valley,[8] a most beautiful spot; grass for miles; forests of pine trees; and a roaring mountain stream. Remains of old towns and traces of fortifications they saw.

The great question is: What wonderful and powerful people occupied this country? What became of them? Everything shows they must have been numerous, as remains of towns, broken pottery, and *acequias* of enormous capacity for irrigation are to be found. Was the Apache their formidable foe? If so, pleasant for us to contemplate. Say what you choose about Arizona, it has its attractions. Gold there is in abundance; Indians bring in specimens, but so far no white has been able to intrude. Well, I must wind my letter up. We are preparing for an Indian campaign under General Crook. Of us you will hear more anon. How are you off for heat? One hundred ten degrees in the shade here, average 102 degrees; winds cool perhaps when they start, but when touching you, you feel as if you were located over one of the flues of the old boy's dominion. It is, however, what you might call a healthy heat.

Army and Navy Journal 8, no. 50 (July 29, 1871)

To the Editor of the Army and Navy Journal
CAMP ON SANTA CRUZ RIVER, NEAR TUCSON, A.T., July 2, 1871

SIR: I wrote you last from Camp McDowell. As I then predicted, orders were received for Troop D, Third Cavalry, Captain Guy V. Henry, to make ready to join General Crook at Tucson, to participate in his campaign against the noble Apaches. After a few days of delay shoeing horses, fitting extra shoes, getting pack trains, mules, and apparatus in order, we bade farewell to McDowell on May 26. The usual marches were the order of the day and night, as most were done then on account of the heat, arriving here July 1. At Saca-tone we enjoyed the hospitality of Captain Grossman, U.S. Army, Indian agent for the Pima Indians. He has shown a great interest in his work and seems to have won their confidence; speaks the Pima and Spanish languages and has a book forming a very complete dictionary of the language of the Pima Indians. He has a history of this country gained by conversations with the Indians, and parts I heard read were really entertaining; and I trust the *Journal* may be the means of disseminating this interesting article through the army, if not elsewhere.

The Gila River is quite thickly settled. Below Sacatone are the Casas Grandes, ruins of immense buildings three stories high, adding to the mysteri-ous history of this country and its former people. At French John's[9] we saw a lad, only fifteen years old, who had been arrested (and was then on his way to Tucson for imprisonment) for murder, having with a shotgun sent a human being unsummoned before his maker. What a frightful responsibility! They say people don't care out here. I watched him carefully, and although he had only one eye I saw enough to thank God that I was not in his shoes.

A place well worth visiting is the mission of San Xavier del Bac, nine miles from here. It was built by the Jesuits in 1668 and is a splendid monu-ment of civilization. And to be in Arizona! The architecture is Saracenic; the front is richly ornamented with fanciful decorations in masonry. A lofty bell tower rises at each corner, one of which is capped by a dome; the other still remains in an unfinished condition. Over the main chapel, in the rear, is also a large dome, and the walls are surrounded by massive cornices and ornaments appropriately designed. The material is brick, made on the spot. The entire edi-fice is perfect in the harmony of its proportions. In every point of view the eye is satisfied. The Papago Indians are the converts, and the priests, some of whose robes are gorgeously adorned with gold, hold the services. The singing is by the Papago Indian women and is said to be very sweet and harmonious. The church of San Xavier del Bac, with its elaborate facade, its domes and spires, would today be an ornmaent to New York.

Tucson is a regular Mexican town—plenty of greasers, dogs, barrooms.

We had a most terrific and continued clap of thunder last night. It woke us all up, and our captain had time to say, "Stand by your horses!" They came near stampeding as it was. As to heat, it runs up here to 120 degrees in the shade and averages from 107 degrees up. We are now waiting for other companies to arrive before advancing. We may start in a week with four and afterwards with three more companies. General Crook means business and knows his business. He has brought from Oregon his favorite scout and his packer, the two essentials to a successful scout.

You will hear more of us as we progress. We go to the mountains, perhaps the White, and having cool breezes, plenty of game when we can shoot, and the finest trout to be caught, we can, by the presence of a photograph, old letter, or treasured geranium, be forced to imagine we are on the Atlantic coast, surrounded by the fair creatures of our choice. I am writing lying down on my blanket and wish you good luck in making this out; am afraid it will be something like hunting Apaches, but when once found, what a reward awaits you!

Army and Navy Journal 9, no. 5 (September 16, 1871)

To the Editor of the Army and Navy Journal
CAMP APACHE, A.T., August 15, 1871

SIR: When I wrote to you last we were just leaving Camp Bowie. The command as then organized was as following: Major General Crook, commanding; Lieutenant Ross, acting quartermaster and acting commissary of subsistence;[10] Acting Assistant Surgeon Mullin; Troop D, Third Cavalry, Captain Guy V. Henry; Troop H, Third Cavalry, Captain Frank Stanwood[11] and Lieutenant Robinson;[12] Troop B, Captain Meinhold;[13] Troop F, Captain Alexander Moore and Lieutenant Bourke; Troop L, Captain Brent;[14] the packers, mules, etc.; and last but not least, the scouts and guides, Mexicans and Indians. We left Bowie July 14 and arrived here August 12, 1871. Taking the trail running north, we struck out for Mount Graham and by night marches over a dangerous country; by edges of canyons, one false step sending you to the bottom, getting your head knocked by limbs of trees; passing Mounts Trumbull, Arinipa, and White mountains, crossing the Gila, Prieto, and White Rivers, we without casualties (excepting a wounded Mexican) arrived here.

As to the Indians, the Indian Bureau had taken the families of Cochise to their reservation in New Mexico, and of course he was unencumbered and could do as he chose, making it impossible for us to catch him. This is a favorite trick of this Indian ring, and the sooner it is stopped the better. However, we have other things on our hands for the present. All friendly Indians who come in will be organized into bodies of troops and rendered of service to the government.

The country we have passed through is the finest I have seen. The valleys are covered with majestic oak or pine, fine grazing, clear streams filled with fish, and deer and turkey on the plain and creeks. No one can form any idea of Arizona from traveling along the roads on the plains. There dust, stagnant

Gone lame on the march. OUTING MAGAZINE, MARCH 1887.

water, mesquite bush, and hot air; here green grass, running streams, fine forests, and cool bracing air—a perfect paradise compared to the plains.

Captain Henry's troop chased some Indians and took two prisoners; Captain Stanwood's captured some burros; Captain Moore's came near capturing Cochise.[15] Wait till cool weather, when the Indians get together; then we will have a chance, which now, owing to the scattered condition of the Indians, we cannot have.

Two troops of our command have been sent back to their posts to get their horses, which have just come out. General Crook is temporarily engaged in his thorough reorganization, which will show in the future. Our command will be found somewhere in the Tonto Pinal, Sierra Ancha country, or thereabouts, for any inquiring friends. You will hear of us as we progress in our humanitarian work.

We subjoin the following order:

HEADQUARTERS DEPARTMENT OF ARIZONA
IN THE FIELD, CAMP APACHE, AUGUST 14, 1871

Troops D, Captain Henry; F, Captain Moore; H, Captain Stanwood, Third Cavalry, Captain Guy V. Henry, Third Cavalry, in command, will constitute an expedition for the purpose of operating against hostile Indians in this department. This expedition will operate independent of any post, but its commanding officer is authorized to call on any post commander for what supplies or aid the expedition may require. Captain Henry will report to the undersigned for detailed instructions.

Signed,
GEORGE CROOK,
Lieutenant Colonel Twenty-third Infantry,
Brevet Major General, U.S. Army, Commanding Department.

Army and Navy Journal, October 22, 1871

Our correspondent in Arizona writes us as follows in reference to General Crook's campaign:

My last letter was from McDowell.[16] Arriving there, unofficial word was received from General Crook that the peace commissioners had come out and that the war was virtually stopped. Even if the commisioners had only certain fields of operation, the Indians, if pursued, would of course run on and off these reservations as they saw fit, rendering perfectly useless any work of the troops. Troop F, Third Cavalry, Captain Alexander Moore, was sent to Tucson. Troop H, Third Cavalry, Captain Frank Stanwood and Lieutenant Robinson, acting quartermaster, was ordered to Camp Grant; and Troop D, Third Cavalry, Captain Guy V. Henry and Lieutenant W. H. Andrews, was to return to Camp Apache in order to escort to their homes (and at the same time to prevent them from killing any Indians, giving the peace commissioners cause of complaint) the Apache Indians of the tribes of Miguel, Chiquito Capitan, and Pedro, who had served as our allies. These men had done good service and, had our war continued, would have practically illustrated the wisdom of General Crook in arming them the first time the experiment was tried. The usual marches across the country, climbing one mountain to see another higher one beyond—defining cavalry in Arizona to be a corps in which you walk, have the privilege of helping your horse, he in turn carrying your saddle—was our fate till arriving at Canyon Creek.

At this point we were met by a deputation who informed us that the peace commissioners were at Apache[17] and that the Indians were there in numbers, and in their opinion had gone in for fear of our Indian soldiers and the effect upon others, the chiefs fearing that some of their Indians might turn against them, thus proving that General Crook was doing and had done a great deal toward peace, and a permanent one.

The tribes of our Indian friends were all nearly starved, quite a number sick with fever, and fourteen dead. They were indeed in a pitiable condition, and if missionaries wish a place for doing good, they have an abundant field for operations in Arizona, and the sooner they come, the better.

Excuse us, but at this moment we heard our first sergeant say to the cook, "Are your beans boiled soft?" His answer was, "No, sir. If they don't rattle, the boys swear they don't get any."

I suppose a missionary here would not get enough credit, so they do not come. A great responsibility rests upon the American nation for the abject, pitiable condition in which the Indian is allowed to remain.

We will now present two pictures to view, and let the American people judge upon which they prefer the curtain to drop. A picture is a bad simile for me, as I can neither paint nor draw. A theatrical grouping would be equally bad, for we don't have any theaters in Arizona. My first picture represents General Crook as ordered to the department as its commanding officer—a man of character, a soldier (and necessarily a Christian and a gentleman) selected for solving the Indian problem, not by killing all, as people imagine, but, as in Oregon, punishing the bad, causing the rest to be put on reserves and taught the advantages of civilization, in farming, raising stock, etc. At a great expense he organizes pack trains, buys horses for his troops (said troops being composed of the old Third Horse or Mounted Rifles, than whom no finer or gallant regiment ever was organized, and a part of the First Horse, of fine name and reputation, their number indicating their condition), sends word for good Indians to come in, organizes them as scouts, travels over the country to learn all about it for his winter campaign, and when he has all ready to bring about a permanent peace, lo! the curtain drops, and the American nation views Picture Number Two.

An entirely civil scene, the details being as follows: In the foreground is Mr. Vincent Colyer, a gentleman and Christian, and one in whose views every army officer will coincide (that is, do all you can first to civilize the Indians; that failing, kill the bad ones). In the background are his assistants, who we do not pretend to say in this case, but in the generality of cases, far from aid their chiefs. Indians are called in, provided with blankets, shirts, and food. Cost of blanket as charged to the government, $10; cost of quality actually delivered to Indian, about $3—probably a condemned one at that. Shirt as charged to Uncle Sam $2, cost actually, $0.25. The difference in the above amounts I don't say is appropriated to themselves, or if it is, becomes a conscience fund and, therefore, is all right.

After a few weeks the commissioners leave—of course they would not live in Arizona—the Indians become hostile, and the curtain falls on Picture Number Two, and again at great expense is the curtain of Number One raised. How long, ye great American nation, will you [be] beguiled and cheated out of your money? As long as you are Americans, I suppose; at any rate in Arizona, till the curtain of Picture Number One is allowed to remain up one year at least. Look out and decide for yourselves, but don't blame the army.

We will get to Apache tomorrow, and rest a few days and return to our post. If we find any news at Apache, will add a line; if not, when our curtain rises, will let you know what General Crook with the old Third Horse is doing on the stage. Since arriving at Camp Apache, have found Mr. Colyer here. The Indians who ran off the government herd and killed the herder were in and had been treated with greater consideration than those who had been our constant friends. Comment is unnecessary.

An Apache Raid, and a Long Distance Ride

AZOR H. NICKERSON[1]

Harper's Weekly 41, no. 2116 (July 10, 1897): 693–94

In the days of their hostility the Apache Indians were the most expert thieves in the world, and in waylaying a miner, ranchman, or traveler they had few equals and no superiors. They could hide on ground where a partridge would not dare to remain for fear of being discovered. In stalking their quarry, whether it was man or beast, they would glide along undiscovered where a snake could not crawl without being detected. If the animals captured were living, and they wished to so retain them, it was a rare thing for them ever to be caught and their plunder taken from them.

They could get speed out of animals that were apparently about to breathe their last; and instances are quite common where soldiers have abandoned horses as unable to go a step further, and the Apaches have taken the same horses, immediately mounted, and ridden them fifty more miles without any appreciable rest. In fact, they not infrequently made the animal carry a double load, two of the wretches riding, whipping, spurring, and kicking the poor beast at the same time.

One day in the month of May 1872,[2] the ladies and children at Fort Whipple, near Prescott, Arizona, held a picnic at what was known as the sawmill reservation, in the woods back of the post, and probably three or four miles away. Late in the afternoon several of the officers on duty at department headquarters, including myself, rode out to the picnic grove and took tea with the picnickers in the beautiful shade which the ladies had selected as their reception ground. It was nearly sunset when we started back on our return. The women and children came in the ambulances and spring wagons by the regular road in use in going to and from the mill, while we, who had come on horseback, returned by a shorter path or trail. This trail came down the mountain and entered the post by way of a narrow canyon, which in the rainy season contained a small creek but at other times was simply the dry, sandy bed of the stream.

As we were slowly riding down this canyon I saw in the soft sand in front of me a sight that ordinarily would have attracted no attention whatever, but which at that time gave me a thrill of horror. It was only a single footprint, a freshly made moccasin track, but it meant a great deal. As far as known, there were no Indians nearer than the Tonto Apaches, a wily, vicious band that infested the rough mountainous region about a hundred miles southeast from Prescott. General Crook, with the bulk of the troops in the department, was operating far south of this, and the presence of the Indian, undoubtedly a Tonto Apache, indicated the proximity of others, and meant trouble in the immediate vicinity. My first thought, of course, was about the women and children of the picnic party; when, therefore, soon after our arrival at the garrison, and before we could start out to meet them, they came safely in, I was greatly relieved and was congratulating myself on the possibility that nothing serious had occurred when a messenger came dashing up to the post with the exciting intelligence that the Apaches had killed the herder and gotten away with Mr. Stevens's sheep herd. The Stevens ranch was not much more than a mile away from the fort, which was also department headquarters. The herd which the Indians had captured was probably the largest and most valuable sheep herd then in the territory, and its capture as bold and impudent a raid as ever occurred in that locality.

At the post there were at this time only the fragments of two small companies, one of infantry and the other of cavalry, and the men were principally the ailing and the extra-duty soldiers usually employed in the care of the garrison, the abler portion of each company being with General Crook in the field.

As the general had left me in charge of the conduct of affairs in that vicinity, I instructed the commanding officer at the barracks to get together every man he could, and taking them, with a few department clerks whom I armed, and a noted half-breed guide that we had brought from the northern country when we came to the department,[3] I was soon on my way to the scene of the murder and capture.

On reaching the ranch we rode immediately to the spot where the herder's body, riddled with arrows and horribly mutilated, was found. A careful examination showed that the Indians had dodged him for several hours before their opportunity came. Evidently he had set his rifle down and commenced eating his midday meal when they surprised and killed him, using only arrows, which of course made no noise, and so attracted no attention from those stationed at the barracks. It was not until evening, when the man failed to come in, that the alarm had been given and search instituted.

It is only those who have witnessed it that can appreciate to its fullest extent the stampede that an incident of this character created in Arizona at this time. An Apache raid was enough to appall the stoutest heart, accompanied as it always was with sickening scenes of the most savage cruelty.

Having determined the hour of the day when the capture had taken place, we next proceeded to find the trail and direction taken by the marauders. The herd being so large, this would at first seem to be an easy matter; but as it was very dark, it was some time before we found the real direction in which they had gone. They had plunged directly back into the exceedingly rough and rugged mountains lying back of the post, and this accounted for the straggling moccasin track discovered in the canyon so near the station. The Indian who made it had evidently been sent to watch and report when the alarm reached the garrison.

They had taken the herd back in the mountains for two reasons: first, they would be hidden from the sight of any chance passers, and then, if we were to attempt to follow them in the night, we would find it extremely difficult, if not impossible. Immediately upon entering this rough region difficulties accumulated so rapidly that McIntosh, the half-breed guide, was in favor of waiting until daylight before we pursued them further. To this I would not assent. They had already at least six or eight hours start, and if we waited till morning they would have nearly twelve hours more. I had heard such fabulous accounts of the speed with which these Indians had been able to drive even flocks of sheep[4] that I felt certain if they were to have that much more start they would get away entirely. I decided, therefore, to continue following them; even if we were only to make a furlong an hour, we would at least be that much farther on our way when morning came.

It was a moonless night, and when the herd descended into one of those awful gorges that abounded in that locality and which seemed to shut out even the starlight, it was almost impossible to find where the trail left it. One could barely grope his own way, without attempting to find where anyone else had gone. The little tufts of wool which the thorny shrubs had occasionally pulled out of the fleeces proved to be our greatest help in these difficult places. Then, too, a young bugler of the cavalry company developed a great facility in finding the missing trail. McIntosh was an old experienced trailer and one whom General Crook considered to be the most expert he had ever seen, but on this occasion the boy musician excelled him. I venture to say that more than fifty times during the long and tedious night, when we felt that we must give up the pursuit, did we hear his boyish, cheery voice, calling, "Here it goes!" and again we would follow on, till some other obstacle once more brought us to a peremptory stand.

Towards morning we began to find great numbers of lambs strung along the trail with their throats cut. This we correctly interpreted to mean that the trail was approaching the traveled roads, or the vicinity of ranches, and that the Indians had killed the lambs to avoid attracting attention by their piteous bleating.

As the result of this persistent, determined, and ceaseless pursuit, at daybreak the next morning we were still on the trail, where it emerged from the mountains and fully thirty miles from the place where the outrage had been committed. With daylight and the open country, following the broad trail was an easy matter; but the problem now was to follow it as rapidly as possible and yet have enough reserve strength when we overhauled the savages to be able to punish them. I was fearfully anxious, and as the day wore away and it appeared by the signs along the trail that they were still well in the lead, I began to be afraid that night would overtake us before we should overtake them. If this were to happen, I felt confident that by the next morning, at the farthest, they would get across the Verde River, be in the rough region known as the Tonto Basin country, where they would likely break up into small parties and make further pursuit useless. In that event the ranchman, poor Mr. Stevens, would be poor indeed. The loss of that herd, valued at more than $20,000, would certainly ruin him. I well knew that in our front were the savings of his lifetime.

This thought haunted me, and the more I thought of it, the more frequently did I touch with my spurs the sides of my grand old horse "Ben," a splendid animal that had carried me over many hundreds of miles of Arizona desert and which was to carry me over as many leagues more under equally trying circumstances.

About 4:00 P.M. the trail led us down into a little valley that turned abruptly into a canyon, quite wide but very irregular and rough. A number of little pools of water at the entrance were still roiled, showing that they had been disturbed but a few minutes before, and I knew that we were drawing very close to our enemy.

I called the officers of the two companies, Major Boyle and Captain Wesendorff,[5] and told them that, while the nature of the ground would prevent any very strict observance of tactics or command, yet it would be best, as far as possible, for each officer to lead his own men. I should try to be at the head of the clerks and detached men from department headquarters, they and all to follow when I started, which I should do immediately [after] we overtook the savages.

In a few minutes more we were upon them, the poor sheep greeting our appearance with a piteous outburst of bleating, like the applause given on the appearance of the leading artist in an opera. This was really our signal to charge, no other being given or required. It was a fearfully rough place, obstructed by huge boulders, gnarled old trees, and logs. A carpet-knight cavalryman would have considered it the last place into which a mounted squadron should be precipitated, but these hardy frontier soldiers plunged into it as recklessly as if it had been the smoothest esplanade in the world.

Every man was soon virtually his own commander, and between the clattering over the rocks, the clash of the accoutrements, the mingling of the sheep, the Indians, the troops, [and] the shouting and firing, the canyon soon became a pandemonium and echoed to sounds never heard there before, and quite unlike any others likely to be ever heard there again.

One voice in this confusing medley could be heard above all other sounds. I had been told that the saying "he swore like a trooper" was supposed to express the very acme of profanity, but I never until that day fully realized the truth of the aphorism. The first sergeant of the cavalry troop was an Irishman named Barrett. In his demeanor he had always appeared to be one of the most

Every man was his own commander. HARPER'S WEEKLY, JANUARY 14, 1899.

unobtrusive, mild-spoken men in the world. The instant the command had started to charge, however, this silent, inoffensive-looking man underwent a complete change. Spurring his horse to the front like a madman, with each shot from his revolver and every jump of his horse he fairly shrieked every epithet and oath that was ever coined or thought of. The sulphurous stream that poured from the lips of this grim old soldier never ceased until the last Indian had disappeared. I have always fancied that those wild Apaches, who, like all other Indians, seem to learn profanity before they learn any other part of the language, must have thought that he was some incarnate fiend that had seen service as a member of the destroying angel's bodyguard. Most of the Indians slunk away in their usually deft manner, but a few remained long enough to pay the death penalty for their rashness. On my part, I can thankfully say that I was well satisfied to recover the herd so nearly intact—the only losses being the few that the marauders had killed and eaten and the lambs that they had destroyed in the mountains.

Men and animals were so exhausted that we camped very near the place where we had overtaken the rascals, and as soon as we had posted our guards and had our coffee, we each, men and beast alike, selected a soft spot on the bosom of our common mother—Earth; and as we, the pursuers, had had the harder task, I am sure that no crowned head resting on downy pillows could have slept more soundly than did we after our long and perilous ride.

The ranchman was almost beside himself with joy the following day, when I met him and informed him that, with the exceptions above noted, we had recovered his whole herd. Had I permitted him, he would have given me a most substantial reward; and when I refused absolutely, telling him we had simply done our duty, he replied: "Ah, yes, captain; but suppose you had followed the advice of that old and experienced guide and waited till the next day before you pursued the Indians—that would have been doing your duty too, would it not? And yet, had you done so, everybody now knows that today I should be a pauper!"

General Howard's Mission

[GEORGE CROOK][1]

Army and Navy Journal 9, no. 37, April 27, 1872

General Howard's Mission—A correspondent who has had fifteen years' experience among the Indians thinks that "Indian nature interposes an insuperable barrier to the Quaker policy which has led to this mission."

The corn-planting tribes are naturally pacific and under fair treatment entirely tractable. Having already adopted the groundwork of civilization— agriculture, they are the more ready to accept its further adjuncts. Stock-raising Indians are more nomadic and consequently less docile—those whose possessions consist chiefly of horses being especially almost constantly at war, either with the whites or with other tribes.

Between tribes of this class, again, there are distinctions based upon tribal characteristics. The Sioux, for instance, bears among his brethren of the Plains an unenviable reputation for treachery; his tribal name is a vituperative sobriquet signifying "cut throat," conferred upon him by his more honorable neighbors, the Cheyennes. Whenever he finds that he can murder and rob and ravish under peril of no heavier penalty than a moral lecture from friend Broadbrim[2] and a fresh supply of conciliatory presents from his Great Father, all attempts to make a quiet and orderly citizen of him will be futile. He will need correction prompt, frequent, and severe, and then his inherent viciousness, the result of centuries of habit and education, will not be eradicated in many generations, probably not until after the last Sioux has sung his war song and joined his fathers in the happy grounds.

The Apache is as much worse than the Sioux as the hyena is worse than the tiger. Bloodthirsty, cruel, cowardly, treacherous, implacable, incapable of gratitude or any other generous emotion, he has all the ferocity of the most savage wild beast, intensified by the worst human passions and rendered more formidable by human cunning. The outrages perpetrated by Apaches upon the bodies of their living and dead victims would be utterly incredible if they were not strictly authenticated. Their insensibility to kindness, and their total lack of gratitude is only paralleled among the meaner brutes. They have constantly rejected all overtures of peace. They have more than decimated and altogether impoverished the civilized population of Arizona and southern New Mexico. They have requited generosity with the foulest treachery and hospitality with assassination. Driven at length by fear to seek a refuge upon a military reservation, they came with false professions of submission, and while being fed, clothed, and lodged by the agents of the government, issued stealthily forth to murder and prey upon defenseless settlers and sought again when pursued the military protection; finally, when their treachery was discovered, throwing off the mask and boldly taking the warpath, inaugurating a new campaign with fresh atrocities, the merest outlines of which have reached us by telegraph.

General Crook, an experienced Indian tamer, has command in Arizona, and he was preparing an energetic campaign against the savage butchers when the execution of his plan was interrupted by the Quaker policy. General Howard, who is not only a good soldier but an excellent man and philanthropist, is sent on a special mission to induce them to make peace, and meanwhile, General Crook is ordered to stay the chastening rod.

General Howard has arrived on the borders of Arizona and has arranged for an interview with chiefs of pacific tribes. On the day following the announcement of these facts by the telegraph another dispatch informs us of the consequences of General Crook's forced inaction. The Apaches are raiding the settlers in all directions and have captured, near Camp Bowie, a large freight train (consisting probably of from fifteen to twenty wagons) belonging to Messrs. Tull and Ochoa, merchants of Tucson, and murdered the special attendants—number not stated.

This is but a prelude to a long list of robberies and murders by these relentless savages. If under the circumstances it is possible for General Howard to make peace with the Apaches, it seems to us very impolitic to do so until they have been properly punished. Proposals made to them for peace at such a time would be regarded by them as evidence of the pusillanimity of the whites, and the presents usual on occasions of treaty as extorted by fear of their prowess. They cannot and will not understand the spirit that prompts our government to seek their good, and it is useless, nay, fatal, to the white settlers to persist in negotiating with them now. They must be reduced to submission, made to feel that our government is powerful and determined to protect its citizens before peace can be made with them on a secure basis. A terrible mistake appears to have already been made; let it not be followed by equally murderous errors!

General Howard's Treaties

[OLIVER O. HOWARD,[1] ET AL.]

Old and New 6 (November 1872): 620–27

There is no subject, perhaps, which arrests the attention of the general reader in America with so little hold as the condition of the Western Indians, or the relations of our people with them. One account of a murder committed by an Indian, no matter what the scene or what the provocation, is set down as giving the direct contradiction to all that has been said of treaties of peace, or of the good intent of any of the Indian tribes, no matter how distant their homes.

The rumors last spring of wars and massacres in Arizona determined General Grant to send General Howard, in whose sense and humanity he had the same confidence which the country has, to see the condition of affairs for himelf; to bring the different tribes to peace with each other if possible; and, if possible, to establish things on a better footing for the future. General Howard's entire success in this mission is one of the noblest triumphs of his life. At a great council held at Camp Grant, on the very scene of one of these terrible massacres, he brought together the heads of tribes who had never known each other but as enemies. They were in [the] presence of whites, some of whom, as we suspect, had no faith in Indian good faith and no hope in this council. But after a fair talk all round, General Howard brought these chiefs to agree to perpetual peace with each other and with the whites. He has brought several representative men from these warring bands and from their neighbors to visit the president at Washington.

"And did he not have to go right back again," asks an incredulous reader, "because there was fighting again?"

He had to go back to New Mexico, which is a wholly different country, to settle a wholly different affair.[2] As in the Arizona case, every conceivable lie has been circulated by telegraph about his failures; but his own reports will show whether he has failed or not. Meanwhile, we have obtained from Washington copies of the original reports of the caucus-councils he held in Arizona. Once more begging the reader this side of the Mississippi to understand that Arizona is not New Mexico, we will attempt to give him some account of these interesting and important occasions.

The earliest in time of which we need speak is an informal conference with Santo, an Apache chief[3] whom we shall meet again at the Camp Grant council. In a meeting with Santo on April 24, General Howard put to him a crucial question.

General Howard—Do you think it is right to steal horses?

Santo—It is right when there are no friends anywhere. It seems as if there was a difference. God puts us here, and we have no clothes and but little food; but you come here with plenty of clothes and food and good things.

General Howard—When I was a boy, I worked the ground to get a living and worked hard, and so do most all the whites. What they have, they have worked hard to get, and anybody that will work can have good things.

Santo—You are a man that can read and write. You know how to make and do things. You know all about the world. You can make this house; you can do many things. We can't tell you all at once. There are many things we want you to know. You must stay long enough to learn about us. Now, there are the Papagos; we have been trying to make a peace with them. I don't talk about this because I have no way [*sic*] to go. I can travel up the hills, or I can cross rivers.

General Howard—If your children would come into school, they would know as much as I. The old men could not learn much, but the children can.

Santo—Our Great Father has put us here, and why should we not be glad to have every good thing he has to give us?

General Howard—That is right—a good answer. One thing more. We all have one good, Great Father who made us all.

Santo—I know very well this is so. We have one father and mother, but somehow we are not brothers.

General Howard—But I mean the Great Father, God.

Santo—Yes.

General Howard—This is God's book (Bible). It says, "Love one another."

Santo—That is what we want. We want to do right. We are talking now where God Almighty hears us. We thank you.

General Howard—Good men love; bad men hate. Do you know what a thought is?

Santo—It is what I see in the heart, and sometimes I do not see it right.

General Howard—God is like a thought. He loves everybody.

Santo—It must be he likes the Mexicans and Americans better than he does us. He has given them all good things and has not given us anything.

General Howard—He has sent me and your agent and other people to help you.

Hos-Yea (Chief)—You must know from all the books that the Apaches are an old race; they have lived a long time. But you never saw in your books, nor heard anybody say, that the Apaches had good things. They have always been poor.

General Howard—These hills that you run over are full of gold and silver right under your feet. If you dig it out, you can buy all these good things. You can plant these fields and get corn, barley, beans, melons, and pumpkins.

Hos-Yea—That is very nice—to plant wheat and corn; and, if we had been planting long ago, we should have had something now.

General Howard—Would you like to plant now, this year?

Hos-Yea—We could plant, but it is getting late now.

General Howard—It is not too late to plant corn and get a good crop this year. If I and my children were poor and hungry, and Santo had food, would he bring it to me? Would he come to Washington and bring it to me?

Santo—If I knew you the same as I know Hutton[4] and Concepcion[5] and knew that you were suffering, I would take you some mescal or mesquite, if I had any way to get to you. I have been all my life struggling—a wrestling man. Sometimes I have planted. Most of the time I have been on the mountains.

General Howard—If Santo should meet me alone in the mountains, would he not kill me and take what I have away from me?

Santo—If we should see you crossing these mountains, I should follow you and see if you were on good business, and, if not should take you. What about the Americans: Are they all one race? All the same?

General Howard—No.

Santo—Well, we are just the same; we are not all alike. We can't tell what somebody else will do. In times past we were bad when they treated us bad; now you have promised us many good things, and we are getting them pretty well. We know that we are living better than we did in the mountains.

General Howard—Some Americans think that this world, all the land, was made for all God's children; not for one man, or any tribe of men, but for all alike.

Santo—Undoubtedly there must be many other people that we have never heard of, and it must be that the good Father has sent you. The world is getting smoother; the arroyos and canyons are smoothing down, and the thorns are getting pulled up.

On May 11 a formal council was held with some of the chiefs of the Pima and Maricopa Indians, who, as it must be remembered, are people of agricultural habit. They have a real grievance, and one difficult to adjust. Their fields depend entirely on irrigation by the Gila River, and in old times, its waters seldom failed them. But now that settlers have come in upon them on the same river, tapping its waters for their own irrigation, the poor Pimas and Maricopas lose their water and their crops. Antonio Azul, their head chief, stated this admirably well; he and twelve other chiefs cordially promised to go and look at some lands on the Indian reservation to which General Howard hoped to remove them.

Next in order of time came the great council at Camp Grant, to which we have alluded. It was very largely attended, all the white officials being present, with a number of citizens of Tucson, including both Mexicans and Americans. The Mexicans brought with them six captive Apache children, four girls and two boys, who had been taken at what is known as the Camp Grant massacre, April 30, 1871; the Indians, a delegation of Papago Indians, including four chiefs; and forty-two Pimas, including thirteen chiefs; while one thousand Apaches were present in person. This council proved to be a real peace jubilee, though the performers had but little music in them, and the conductor was a simple, brave gentleman, whom the world knows better as a soldier than a peacemaker.

General Howard opened the council with prayer and a short address. After a little exchange of courtesies, Santo, the oldest Apache captain, of whom we have already spoken, said, "I am here with my brothers and sisters in conformity with the order of the great captain (General Howard)."

Taking a stone and putting it down before General Howard:

I don't know how to read and write. That stone is my paper. I want to make a peace that will last as long as that stone. I have the paper and pen of my father, and I want peace as long as you want peace. God put this thought into my head—to make a peace as lasting as a rock. Maybe God gave you everything and put it into our heads to steal from you. Perhaps God made the Indians do as they have done. But it is all past. We won't do so any more. That is the reason why we have put the stone there. As long as the stone lasts, we won't steal any more.

Our friends have come, the Papagos and the Pimas, the Americans and the Mexicans, and they will surely talk to us.

Before the peace, the Papagos and Pimas stole from us, and we stole from them; now we will do so no more. We hunt rabbits, ground squirrels, and deer, as the Papagos do; both have bows and arrows, equally armed. Perhaps we can hunt together without fear now that the Great Father has made peace.

Each of the head chiefs agreed in turn to the peace. The speech of Eskiminzin, head chief of the Apaches, besides being manly and generous, is a model of fine, concise English, when translated.

I am very glad all the captains and these people have come. Just as long as that stone remains, the peace shall be kept, and they shall hear in the city of Washington. General Howard keeps his watch, by which he guides his actions, and the hands tell him what time it is. The sun is Eskiminzin's watch, and while the peace lasts, the hands of Eskiminzin's watch shall never go backward; they shall always be the same.

In the first place, there were two nations. Two of them had possession of two small hills. They had firearms. The Papagos and Apaches were one and had arrows; were originally friends. Then they were hostile; now the time has come when they shall be friends. Formerly they had to betake themselves to the rocks and mountains for fear; now they have made peace; they can come out into the plains and sit down in the shade without fear.

In former years, before the Americans had possession of the country, the Mexicans made a few campaigns against us. Then we had no roads and grounds in the open valleys; now we are thankful to General Howard that we can again take our roads, and we are thankful that being at peace with all made it possible to do so. Formerly the Mexicans and Papagos made campaigns against us, and we made campaigns against the Mexicans and Papagos. Now we have placed that stone there; as long as it lasts, there shall no more campaigns be made on my part. I have placed that stone there in the presence of you, General Howard, and in the presence of all the chiefs and all these people, as a symbol that a new world is to open to all of us. The other day, when you (General Howard) asked if I wanted to see all these people, you made a promise that you would bring them, and you have kept your promise.

To this Antonio, chief of the Pimas, replied,

I believe what Eskiminzin says—that we were once the same people; that we had differences; that we are now friends. We understand and obey the laws of our country, the president, and generals; if you will make peace and keep it, it won't be long before you will understand how to do the same. Tell Eskiminzin I am glad to have made peace with him. Tell him, as the captain of his people, to tell them to obey the orders that General Howard may give them. That is the best instruction he can give his people.

The report goes on to say that,

Antonio then arose and crossed over to Eskiminzin, who rose to meet him. They shake hands and then embrace each other. Then follow the chiefs of the Pimas in like manner, shaking hands and embracing Eskiminzin, together with the chiefs of Apaches; the other Indians, and all the people, clapping their hands and displaying other signs of great pleasure. Not a few shed tears.

"Now," said General Howard, "who will speak for the Papagos?
Francisco, a Papago chief, answered,

I have nothing to say. I have listened to all that has been said and am satisfied. That stone has been placed there as a sign of peace, and

I want to see it verified. If you Apaches will comply with your promises, I will never tread your soil again with evil intentions. If I have done so in the past, it was because I was provoked by your robbing. I obey the orders of my superiors; if you will do the same and comply with your promises, we will dig a hole in the ground and bury everything—all our past differences—in it, and be as if no difference had occurred between us. I have now said all I have to say. We are friends. If you want to come to Tucson, do so; you can traffic with us and visit us without fear.

General Howard's speech at the end of the second day's proceedings, giving his decision in regard to some captive children taken from the Apaches and retained by the Mexicans, deserves to be given in full.
He said,

I have now listened patiently and am prepared to make my decision; but I wish to say first that I think that Mr. McCaffrey, the district attorney, must have misunderstood me. Certainly I *meant* to say that I believed an arrangement could easily be made with the Indians, so that the good people who had the orphans might take them back to Tucson.[6] Yesterday evening, in conversation with Mr. McCaffrey, I said that the faith of the government had been pledged by Mr. Colyer and myself that the children should be returned. I also read to the citizens the proceedings of a former interview with these Apaches, in which I distinctly made the promise to do all in my power to return them. Near the close of yesterday's proceedings, I substantially decided that the children should go back to their people; of course, being willing that any arrangement might be made with the Apaches, through their chiefs, for the retention by the Mexicans of those who were really orphans. I reiterate the same, in accordance with the pledge of a great government.

When I said to the district attorney that Mr. Colyer had made this promise, he replied that when an agent exceeded his instructions by a promise, that promise was not binding, also intimating that I had exceeded mine. I now answer that Mr. Colyer's promise in this thing was confirmed by the secretary of the interior and the president. Again I am fully empowered and make the same promise. Please bear me witness that I have behaved kindly toward the citizens ever since I have been in the territory; almost without exception, you have treated me with kindness in return. You have given me your hospitality and expressed yourselves frankly and pleasantly even when we differed in opinion. But you must not think me so blind as not to know that there are some bad men who have been endeavoring to head me off in this effort for peace—to destroy our mutual confidence. For example, one said, in the circle behind me, when invited to retire, "No, I'm going to see this thing through; I'm going to watch this ring." An effort was made to show that Eskiminzin was not empowered to talk—not a true man; did not mean peace; that much that was said was misinterpreted to me.

Now, let us not allow a few, a very few, bad men to defeat this peace and open up all your roads and farms and people to raids, to murder, and to bloodshed.

Turning to Eskiminzin,

I know that some of you do not believe in this man. Many of you have not the confidence in him that I have. You say you have been in the territory longer than I have and know the Indian better than I can. This is true, but I give you my opinion for what it is worth. I do repose confidence in him. He has kept his word with me and, by universal testimony, with the officers at the post.

Taking Eskiminzin by the hand and standing,

I say to you that I put my life against his life. I am willing to go through any of your canyons with him and such guides as he may select—through any part of this territory. He has promised peace. He has promised to help look up the murderers and thieves, and I believe he will do it. Should he prove utterly false and deceptive, let me know it, and I am at your service.

An appeal having been taken from my decision by a United States officer, District Attorney McCaffrey, I cheerfully entertain this appeal and refer the matter, as is absolutely necessary, to our common superior, the president of the United States.

I therefore now decide that the children shall be placed in the hands of the Indian agent at this post, Camp Grant, and kept by him; he to provide a Christian woman to take care of and teach them at the agency building—this building to be fitted up comfortably for them; that their friends and relatives shall be allowed to visit them freely, both Mexican and Apaches; in short, everything to be done for their proper support and comfort until the pleasure of the president shall be made known concerning them.

The first day of this important council was nearly all occupied with the speeches of the different chiefs, of Governor Safford, and General Crook, who promised peace on the part of the Americans, and of Jesus Maria Elias, who spoke in behalf of the Mexicans. The second day General Howard spent in listening to various opinions expressed as to the disposal of the captive Indian children and in giving his decision. On the third day appeared a delegation of the Santo Apaches with several of their chiefs. A consultation was held by General Howard with them in which they expressed a desire for peace and promised to meet General Howard in eight days with their head chief and a larger number of Indians.

On May 30 General Howard, with Major Dallas, acting Indian agent, met several other captains of Apache Indians, 1,200 of whose followers were encamped in the immediate vicinity. After the captains had been seated according to rank and the rest of the Indians gathered in a circle around them, General Howard opened the council with prayer. He then called upon the different chiefs to say anything they had to say, and some of them responded— Miguel Pedro and an old man named Es-calt-se-tas being the chief speakers. There is something pathetic in the simple character both of their requests and of their grievances: the most ambitious request is for a cow and a bull; the most annoying grievance, that they wanted the rations which they were receiving from the military post to be served out at an earlier hour in the morning.

After this exchange of views, Santo addressed all the Indians and bade them all listen to what the general said. General Howard took a stone in his hand and said, "I want you all to be at peace as long as that stone lasts. I have heard that you have had some trouble among yourselves; I want you now to live in peace as long as this stone lasts."

Here he called upon all of them to stand up and shake hands, which they did, embracing each other also. General Howard asked if they were all friends, and they said "Yes" with earnestness. Old Es-calt-se-tas exclaimed, "You are my father and mother; I wish I could live forever!"

At the close of this council General Howard resumed its proceedings in this speech,

The captains of all your people have again made peace with each other and with me. The Americans never have anything given them to eat; they have to work, plant, raise stock. The German people do the same. The Papagos and Pimas, and a great many Indians north, do the same. If you will all keep the peace you have made today, you will go forward and do better. But you must not sit down and eat your rations and do nothing else. You must plant corn and other things; raise cattle, sheep, and goats; then it will not be long before you will be dressed as well as I am. When I was a little boy, I had to work, raise corn, potatoes, wheat, hay, pumpkins, and melons. I sold them and got money, and went to school and learned to read and write so that I could go anywhere and get my living. If your children can do the same, they can do as I have done. But you must work and learn, learn and work. Do you not want your children to learn? The government is willing to help you, but you must help yourselves. We will help you until you are started, then you must help yourselves. I want you to remember what I have said, for I am your friend. Now, all of you who wish peace, let them clap their hands.

To this invitation the council responded most heartily, all clapping their hands with great enthusiasm.[7]

Something about Cochise

A. P. K. SAFFORD[1]

Tucson *Arizona Citizen*, December 7, 1872

TUCSON, November 30, 1872

Having recently visited Cochise,[2] the Apache war chief, who has for the past twelve years been the leader of the most desperate and destructive band of Apaches in Arizona, and who during that time has seldom been seen except as he sprang from an ambush, who has been reported to be here, there, and everywhere at the same time, and whose deeds of blood have drenched the soil of Arizona, New Mexico, Sonora, and Chihuahua, and whose very name caused a thrill of horror, I have thought it might be of some interest to those who have noted or observed these horrid scenes to be informed of what I saw and heard.

In order to properly understand the true condition of Cochise and his band, I will say that he is the chief of a band of Apaches who in olden times inhabited the country from the Gila on the north to some distance into Sonora on the south, and from the San Pedro on the west to the Mimbres in New Mexico on the east. They have, as far back as the memory of man here runs, been at war with the people of Mexico, and their living has been principally obtained by robbery. When Arizona was first possessed by the United States, for reasons best known to himself, Cochise sought and evidently desired peace with our people and government, and this relation existed until 1860. During that time, however, he constantly raided upon the neighboring states in Mexico and brought back herds of horses and cattle. Occasionally stock was taken in Arizona by his Indians at points distant from his country, but it is understood that when complaints were made in such cases, he made an effort to restore the property.

During the year 1860, a boy was made captive while herding stock in Sonora, and some believed that Cochise had taken him, hence Lieutenant Bascom with a company of soldiers marched to Apache Pass, near his headquarters, and camped at the Overland Mail station.[3] The lieutenant told the station keepers that he was on his way to New Mexico and that he desired to see Cochise and induced them to go and invite him in. When asked by Cochise what was wanted of him, he was informed that he desired to extend the hospitalities of his tent, as he was on his way out of the country. Cochise, with four of his friends and relatives, came in, and when seated in Bascom's tent, it was suddenly surrounded by soldiers. He desired to know the cause and was informed that he and his friends were prisoners and would be kept as such until the boy believed to be with his band was given up. Cochise protested against such treachery and declared that he could not give him up as he knew nothing of him. Watching his opportunity, he drew his knife and cut a hole through the tent and escaped. He immediately called his warriors together and came in force near the station and desired to have a talk. One of the station keepers went to him to hear what he had to say, but as soon as he had reached Cochise's lines, he was seized and made a prisoner. A day or two was spent afterwards in endeavors to effect an exchange of prisoners, Cochise offering to give up his prisoner if the lieutenant would release his (Cochise's) friends. The lieutenant declined to exchange only man for man unless Cochise would surrender the boy, but Cochise steadily alleged that he knew nothing of him.[4]

Finally he came for a last talk, loading his station-keeper prisoner, with a rope around his neck tied to the horn of his saddle. He again offered to surrender him if his four friends were set free. The station keeper begged to have the exchange made, as his life would be forfeited if it was not done, but the lieutenant again refused, and so Cochise turned his horse and dashed away, dragging the poor man at full speed by the neck. The lieutenant then hung the four prisoners, and Cochise took to the road.[5]

The people, not being apprised that hostilities had broken out, fell easy victims, and the horrible murders and tortures that followed for the next few days are sickening to relate, and from that time to the first of last September, scarcely a week passed without the commission of bloody deeds by his band. His attacks were made from ambush and invariably successful. Sometimes he appeared to be supported by a large force and again had but few followers. He was often reported to be at different points at the same time, frequently reported dead, and generally believed to be crippled for life. His force was often reported to have dwindled to mere nothing, while he would, when occasion required, make a stand with a force sufficient to successfully resist all attempts to take him. No matter what impressions were entertained regarding him and his force, one thing was certain, that he had for twelve years successfully resisted all the power of the friendly tribes and what the governments of the United States and Mexico did bring to bear against him, and also that since the first of last April, he had been as successful in taking life and property as at any other period since he commenced hostilities. Having been in the midst of his field of bloody work for nearly four years, and having at times endeavored to find him after the commission of his dire crimes, but generally being compelled to travel in such condition that he was the last man I desired to meet, it will not be a subject of wonder that I had a curiosity to meet him, and see who and what he is. Accordingly, I communicated my desire to the agent,

Cochise's stronghold. NELSON A. MILES. *PERSONAL RECOLLECTIONS AND OBSERVATIONS.*

Captain Thomas J. Jeffords,[6] and was informed by him that he would be happy to accompany me to his camp.

I left Tucson in company with Doctor R. A. Wilbur, agent of the Papagos, on [November 23, 1872] for Sulphur Springs, where I was to meet Captain Jeffords; but upon arrival I found the captain had gone to another part of the reservation to supply a band of Apaches who had recently come in and asked for peace, and I was there delayed one day for his return. He told me he had been absent from the camp of Cochise two days longer than he agreed, and as he had usually been very prompt in all his agreements, he supposed Cochise would think the delay very singular.

Cochise is camped about twenty miles from Sulphur Springs in the Dragoon Mountains, and to this point we directed our movement. When a short time on the way, we saw a large dust rising in the distance and soon discovered horsemen coming rapidly. It was apparent that they were Indians, and Captain Jeffords remarked that they were Cochise's, and as they approached with spears glistening, in full war paint, on foaming steeds, he said, "I wonder what is the matter. They look excited. I fear something has happened." But on they came at full speed, to and around us. Then the leader of the band dismounted and, throwing his long, bony arms around Captain Jeffords, embraced him with the apparent fondness a mother would her child. His example was followed by each one of the party. Captain Jeffords then called us and said, "This is the old man." I asked what old man, and he replied, "Cochise." When informed who I was Cochise cordially greeted me, and we all sat down in a circle to have a talk. He then told Captain Jeffords that his absence beyond his agreement had given him much concern; that he had fear the wild Indians he was bringing on the reservation had killed him; that he had started with his warriors to learn his fate, and if they had done him violence, he intended to kill every one as a penalty.

I now examined his personal appearance, and as so many conflicting stories have been told of him, I will describe him as he appeared to me. His height is about six feet; shoulders slightly rounded by age; features quite regular; head large and well-proportioned; countenance rather sad; hair long and black, with some gray ones intermixed; face smooth, the beard having been pulled out with pincers as is the custom of the Indians. He wore a shirt, with pieces of cotton cloth about his loins and head, and moccasins covered his feet, which constituted his costume. He is thought to be about sixty years of age.

I spread some provisions, which I had with me, before them. All ate with a relish except Cochise. He did not taste my food but remarked that I need not think strange of it because he was afflicted with a pain in his stomach, and nearly everything he ate gave him pain. He then asked if I desired to go to his camp, and upon my affirmative reply, he said that some of his men had drank too much "tizwin" the night before, and he feared if I went that night, I would go away and give a bad impression of what I saw, and hence he preferred I should camp nearby and defer my visit till the next day. I told him if I went to his camp and partook of his hospitality, I did not think it would be proper to afterwards report any irregularities I might observe. Without saying anything further, we started, and upon arriving at the water about one mile from his camp I stopped. He inquired if I had any more food with me. I said no. He then said I had better move on to his camp and eat with him.

I found him camped among the rocks at the foot of the mountains—a place evidently selected with care to prevent surprise, and from which, with five minutes' notice, he could move his band beyond the successful pursuit of cavalry. His lodge consisted of a few sticks set up in a circle and skins placed around the base to break off the wind. Here he has about four hundred Indians of all ages. He has three wives. The last, or youngest, lives with him in his lodge and makes his clothes and does his cooking. Each of the others has a separate lodge and their respective children live with them. Upon our arrival Cochise directed his wife to prepare supper, and we were soon informed that it was ready. It consisted of thin baked cakes, boiled beef, coffee, and sugar. We were not troubled with dishes except tin cups for coffee. A long march and keen appetite made the food very palatable, and certainly our host had no cause to complain that we failed to do it ample justice.

Captain Jeffords told me I need not give myself any concern about articles I had with me as nothing would be stolen. All were curious to see and handle everything I had, and to their credit, I must say I did not lose a pin's worth.

In the morning breakfast was prepared the same as supper, with the addition of cakes made of mescal and covered with flour made of mesquite beans. It was sweet and nutritious, and would pass for a delicacy anywhere. After breakfast, a cloth was spread upon the ground and the head men were gathered around in a circle. Cochise then said he would like to have a talk.

He said he was glad to see me, and the fact that I had come among them unprotected was an evidence that I had confidence in his professions of peace.

He then said that prior to the ill treatment he received from Lieutenant Bascom, he had been a good friend of the Americans, and that since that time he believed he had been their worst enemy; that the time was within his memory when the plains were covered with herds and the mountains were filled with Apaches, but now the herds are all gone and the number of the Apaches greatly reduced; that when he opened hostilities against the Americans, he and his tribe had made a promise to fight until the last one was exterminated to hold the country, but now he was determined to live at peace with everyone on this side of the Mexican line. I told him that the conduct of Lieutenant Bascom was disliked by our people, and if he had not gone to war, Bascom would have been punished and many lives would have been saved. He said he was now satisfied that it was wrong to go to war on that account, and that both sides were blamable and had suffered for it. I told him that the president was anxious that our people and the Apaches should live in peace together and had told me so more than three years ago. He replied that he was satisfied that the president is a good man and loved all his children, that General Howard had told him of the president, and that he liked General Howard because he had the heart to come and see him; but for a long time previous the only friends he had were the rocks, that behind them he had concealed himself, and that they had often protected him from death by warding off the bullets of his enemies.

After talking with him for nearly half a day, I told him I must go. He said there had one thing occurred since he made peace that he did not like, and he wanted to be frank and tell me of it. He then asked if I knew what had become of a certain captive Mexican boy that belonged to him. (In explanation, I will here say that but a few days previous a Mexican boy about sixteen years of age, who had been a captive with Cochise for ten years, escaped and fled to a settlement on the San Pedro, and the people sent him to me for protection, and the day before I started on this visit, I turned him over to an uncle who recognized him.) I told Cochise that the boy had been given to his uncle and gone back to his old home. He said he captured the boy over the line many years ago; that he saved his life; had raised him to an age that he was now of some service; that he had escaped to San Pedro, and the people there had secreted him, and he did not think it was a friendly act on their part; that if I or Captain Jeffords had asked him to give him up, he would have done so; nor did he care much about his value, but as a matter of principle, he thought the people of San Pedro should pay him for the boy and desired to know if I could compel them to do so.

I told him that by the laws of our country the boy was entitled to his freedom, that neither the president nor anyone was allowed by our laws to hold slaves, and if he knew of any Indian that was then held by our people against his will, I would see that he was set free. He replied that he knew that if the boy were an American, he had no right to hold him; but he had captured him in another country from another people, and he thought that the Mexicans only had a right to interfere. I told him that we had a treaty by which we had agreed

Apache signal fire. CENTURY MAGAZINE, MARCH 1891.

to interfere and then inquired of him if he knew we had a war sometime ago among ourselves and why we fought with each other? He said he knew of the war but did not know the cause. I then explained to him that part of our people owned slaves and a part did not; that upon this question they became angry with each other and many men were killed; that those opposed to holding had conquered; that afterwards laws were made prohibiting anyone from holding as slave a Negro, Indian, Mexican, or anyone else. He said he supposed it was all right, and he would say no more about it.

I am informed by Captain Jeffords that when those who yield allegiance to Cochise are all gathered together, they will number from fifteen hundred to two thousand of all ages. In the terms of peace recently made, they have been permitted to retain their property and arms. Those I saw are well mounted and generally have improved breech-loading guns. They are under no control except such voluntary obedience as they choose to give to the agent, and he informs me that so far all have complied with every request; but they distinctly declared at the outset that they would not place themselves within the power of the military authorities. Their fighting condition is undoubtedly better now than at any period since they commenced the war. Probably they number less, but they have been inured to such constant hardship that they are capable of any degree of endurance. With improved arms and their knowledge of their use of them, my judgment is that they are more formidable than ever before.

That he could resist such superior forces as were brought against him for so long a time and protect his women and children is truly wonderful, and shows conclusively that he is a superior man. It is true their superior knowledge of the country has been of great advantage, and by smoke they have a system of telegraphing by which they were able to communicate with their people over the vast scope of country. If necessary, they could subsist on the natural products of the country.

One question is often asked. Will Cochise remain at peace? My impression is that he is now in good earnest and that he desires peace, but he and his followers are wild men, and with the best of efforts on our part some real or imaginary cause may at any moment set them again on the warpath. That a permanent peace may be secured should be and is the wish of every friend of humanity. If he should remain at peace, then, with the energetic war policy General Crook is now dealing out to hostile ones, our Apache troubles will soon be ended; for this band has been the cover for Indians from the Grant, White Mountain, and other reservations to go on raids and return again when their nefarious work was done.

To me, the most singular circumstances about these Indians are the confidence they have in Captain Jeffords and the influence he has over them; and learning that he is respected as an honorable man by all who know him, and that for the past three years he held interviews with Cochise and was the only white man who for twelve years had been in his camp and returned alive, it may be in place to recite the facts connected with their acquaintance and subsequent friendship. He is thirty-six years of age; tall and well-proportioned; was born in the state of New York; came to Denver, Colorado, in 1857 and practiced law for a short time; has since spent much of his time in the mountains prospecting for gold and silver; has been among nearly all the Indian tribes of North America; has made their habits and peculiarities his study, and is by nature well-qualified to deal with them. Several years ago he was superintendent of the Overland Mail Company, and during a short period of time that he was in charge, Cochise and his band killed twenty-one of his employees. He finally went to prospecting again and made up his mind that if the government could not subdue so bad an enemy, he would try and make him his friend, and by the help of other Indians, he visited Cochise in his own camp. This act inspired Cochise with a profound respect for his courage and sincerity. Through Captain Jeffords, Cochise was brought to Canada Alamosa Reservation in 1870, and by him General Howard was led to his camp. General Howard appointed him special Indian agent, and I do not believe any other man living could now manage them, wild as they are, and I have strong hopes, if the government will continue him in charge, that peace may be maintained.

In this connection I desire to say that one of the most fatal mistakes, in my judgment, made by the government in dealing with the Indians is the selection of agents because they belong to any particular religious denomination. No doubt the purpose of the choice is good, but practically it proves not good. To govern and manage wild Indians successfully requires peculiar qualifications. An agent should not only be honest, truthful, and just to both Indians and citizens, but he should also be patient, cool, and possessed of plenty of nerve. Nothing so soon destroys the confidence of Indians as to know their agent fears them; besides it requires years of acquaintance and experience to understand the Indian character. Without this knowledge in advance, few agents attain it in time to be successful. Nowhere can such efficient agents be found as in the country where the Indians live. The fact that General Howard has already selected two in this country to fill the most difficult places among the Apaches is evidence that he is of the same opinion.

The Military and Cochise

FREDERICK G. HUGHES[1]

Tucson *Arizona Star*, January 27 and 31, 1886

General Howard made his treaty with Cochise on October 13, 1872. I arrived at the agency on November 2. In the meantime T. J. Jeffords had been left alone in charge of the Indians after General Howard's departure. The agency was established at Sulphur Springs in a little ten-by-twelve house belonging to Nick Rogers.[2] This was, at that time, the only house upon the reservation (outside of the buildings at Fort Bowie in Apache Pass about thirty miles distant). The reservation was about seventy miles square and included the whole of the Chiricahua and Dragoon ranges of mountains.

I found the Indians upon my arrival still very timid, for it must be remembered these Indians had been constantly on the warpath for fourteen years when they made peace with General Howard. Some of the young warriors had been born and raised during the time the tribe had been at war with all mankind, and quite a number of them had no remembrance of when their tribe had been at peace. A few days after my arrival, Cochise made his first visit to the agency.

To show how suspicious the old fellow still was, he came accompanied by about fifty warriors. They made their camp about half a mile from the agency but within sight; they then commenced sauntering up to the agency building in squads of twos and threes until some fifteen or twenty had reached there, then seeing everything was all right they took Jeffords down to where Cochise was, and he brought him up. This was the first time I met Cochise; that is, in a peaceful manner or to speak to him. I had met him several times while he was on the warpath, when compliments were exchanged with powder and lead. Upon this occasion he came up to me, took me by the hand with both of his, told me he had heard of me before, and that from this day on he was going to be my friend. He kept his word till the day of his death.

Early in the month of December the Janero Apaches, a tribe that lived in the vicinity of the town of Janos,[3] in the Mexican state of Chihuahua, having been notified by Cochise that he had made peace and that they must cease depredating upon the Americans, sent in word they wished to make peace also and fixed a day to have Agent Jeffords meet them in the Pinery Canyon. We both went there on the day set and found about two hundred Indians encamped. They, however, when we met them pretended they had not decided whether they wanted to make peace or not. It was hard to tell what they wanted, and I do not believe they knew themselves, but I have always believed they wanted to be mean and were afraid of Cochise. We were delayed two or three days dilly-dallying with these Indians before they came to terms, which, however, they finally did, the terms being the same as those of Cochise.

This tribe was under the command of a chief named Natiza, and they were in reality Indians belonging to the government of Mexico, as I have said before their homes having been in the Mexican state of Chihuahua. Although these Indians had been at war with both our own and the Mexican government, they had been at peace with the town of Janos, with which place they did their trading, and there is no doubt but what the people of that town sold them arms and ammunition with which to prey upon their own people.

The Indians Juh, Nolgee, and Geronimo, who have since become so notorious, all belonged to this tribe. Geronimo was not thought much of by the Indians then and I cannot believe he has any following among the hostiles now. I always looked upon him as one of the most worthless and cowardly fiends upon the reservation; on two different occasions I saw squaws thrash him soundly. While such Indians as Nahilzay, Cochise's old war captain; Naiche, Cochise's son and a perfect type of his father; Chihuahua, and half a dozen others capable of commanding are with these hostiles, as I have said before, I cannot believe Geronimo has any following. I am inclined to the belief that the military have created Geronimo's chieftainship and kept him as much before the public.

After Cochise's treaty all the Apache tribes in Arizona were at peace, and it was considered safe for a person to travel anywhere he saw fit north of the Mexican line, but wails were continually coming up from our Mexican neighbors that raiding and murdering was being carried out in their country to as great if not greater extent than before the Apaches had made peace. Of course this raiding was being done from our reservations and, as the Chiricahua reservation was established upon the Mexican line, we had to shoulder the brunt, but in reality this raiding was being done from all the reservations. In fact the Indians said they had not and would not make peace with the people of Sonora and Chihuahua. The Indians would come from the Hot Springs and San Carlos reservations to ours, it being directly in their route, and from there they would go on into Sonora or Chihuahua.

About this time it was pretended the agents upon the other reservations were mustering their Indians at a daily roll call. This I afterwards learned was not a fact; and even if it had been the agents must certainly have found many of their Indians turn up missing, for although some of the Indians who came from the other reservations to ours had passes, many had not. (And I want to say right here for Agent Jeffords that at all times he absolutely refused to give a pass to any Indian to go beyond the limits of his reservation, so that if they went beyond the limits thereof, it was at their own peril.)

In February 1873 General Crook, with the intention of trying to stop this raiding, mustered all the troops he could spare in the territory at Camp Grant, in the immediate vicinity of the Chiricahua reservation, and we were given to understand he was coming there to muster our Indians at a daily roll call. Jeffords and I talked this matter over with the Indians, and it became evident to us any such action would drive them on the warpath again. Very likely that is what Crook wished to do for, as I have stated before, he had all his troops in the immediate vicinity ready to cope with them at a moment's notice. I am afraid, though, if he had been allowed to carry out his intentions, the Indians would have flown across the Mexican line, and we would have a continuation of the war which had been going on for the thirteen or fourteen years previous.

Major Brown, then commanding officer at Fort Grant, accompanied by lieutenants Bourke, Ross, and Rockwell, and a company of cavalry, made a visit to our agency, had a talk with our Indians, and returned to Camp Grant.[4] They, I afterwards learned, were well satisfied with the state of affairs at the agency, and after their return to Grant, the troops that had been recently brought there were sent back to their posts. Whether it was on the recommendations of these officers, or by orders from Washington, I never learned.

When peace was made with the Chiricahuas their agency, as I have stated before, was established at Nick Rogers's ranch at Sulphur Springs. This at the time was only intended to be its temporary location, and in the summer of 1873 it was removed to the San Simon Cienaga. The latter place, however, proving to be very sickly, in December of the same year it was again removed to the Pinery Canyon in the Chiricahua Mountains.

While the agency was located on the San Simon, several of the Indians died from malarial fevers, and there is no doubt but that it was while we were camped at that place Cochise contracted the disease which finally carried the old chief to his happy hunting ground.[5]

He died in the month of June following in the locality known as Cochise's Stronghold in the Dragoon Mountains. I do not believe he was off the reservation from the time he made peace till he died.

Cochise was a remarkable Indian, and there is no doubt he would have made his mark among men had his lot been cast in some more fortunate sphere of life. In conversation he was very pleasant, and to his family and those immediately around him he was more affectionate than the average white man; he showed nothing of the brutish nature generally attributed to him. It was astonishing also to see what power he had over this brutal tribe, for while they idolized and almost worshipped him no man was ever held in greater fear, his glance being enough to squelch the most obstreperous Chiricahua of the tribe. Many a one have I seen slink off like a whipped cur from one of his looks without his having uttered a single word; he appeared to be looked upon by them with some superstitious awe, and I have often thought superstition had a great deal to do with the power he had over them.

I remember once while he was ailing, a few months I believe before his death, the Indians had built a campfire in front of the agency building and Cochise was sitting near it. In going to and fro one day about the agency I happened to pass between Cochise and the fire. I noticed the old fellow mutter a few words but paid no attention to it, but shortly some Indians informed me my passing between Cochise and the fire was regarded as a bad omen and asked that I would return and pass back again in an opposite direction. I did as they requested, and as I did so the old fellow smiled, but it did not save his life. Upon another occasion the Indians had got it into their heads that Cochise was bewitched, and that an old crippled Indian belonging to the Hot Spring Indians then on a visit to the agency had bewitched him. They believed they would have to catch the Indian and burn him before Cochise could get well. The poor devil had hid in the mountains for several days but they finally caught him. However, by an extraordinary amount of talk and persuasion by Agent Jeffords and others, they were induced to let him go.

I shall never forget the lamenting over Cochise's death. Quite a large number of Indians were camped near the agency, mostly women and children, and they had evidently gathered there to await the news of their chief's death. When it came, the howl that went up from these people was fearful to listen to. They were scattered around in the nooks and ravines in parties, and as the howling from one rancheria would lag, it would be renewed with vigor in another. This was kept up through the night and until daylight the next morning. Everything then became quiet and throughout the next day almost the stillness of death reigned.

After Cochise's death there was some little contention for the chieftainship between Cochise's eldest son named Taza and the medicine man of the tribe named Eskinya.[6] The latter was one of the worst and most restless Indians of the tribe, while Taza had just been importuned by his father while dying to forever remain at peace with the Americans and he was inclined to respect his father's wish. Taza was selected as their chief, but the friends of Eskinya were ever afterwards dissatisfied.

I remained at the Chiricahua agency till November 1874, when, feeling that I would like to try some other occupation than that of civilizing Apaches, I quit and removed to the Santa Rita and went to mining.

It was while living at the latter place, in the month of April 1876, I heard of the first outbreak of the Chiricahuas, their killing of Nick Rogers and Spence, and the murder of the ranchers upon the upper San Pedro.[7] A few days after this affair, a messenger came to me from Governor Safford asking me to come to Tucson if possible, that he wanted to see me particularly about some Indian business.

Divining it was on business concerning the recent outbreak, I made all haste and met Governor Safford in Tucson the next evening. Sanford informed me that Agent Clum[8] of the San Carlos had received orders from Washington to remove the Chiricahua Apaches to his reservation, but that as the Chiricahuas had then taken to the warpath it was a difficult matter and he did not care to undertake it. But after a short conversation with the governor, in which I informed him I believed the matter could be accomplished, he stated Agent Clem would undertake to remove them in case I would agree to assist him. I immediately assented, and just at that moment Clum came in and matters were settled. It was arranged that I should start out to the Chiricahuas the next day, meet the Indians and inform them of the intentions, and Clum was to follow on the next day to Apache Pass.

I started out the next day as per agreement. I first met the two boys of Cochise, informed them of the intentions of the government and advised them to go peaceably. They said they were sorry, that they and their band had not been engaged in the recent outbreak, that the killing had been done by a band under the leadership of Eskinya. They would also consent to be removed to the San Carlos but wanted me to try and get them a place above the reservation near Pueblo Viejo so they could live apart from the other Indians. I promised to do all I could for them to that end. I next met the then notorious Eskinya. He acknowledged the killing of Rogers and Spence was done by himself and his brother, Pionsenay. He stated Rogers had abused them and they were intoxicated when they killed them. He also stated they would not go to the San Carlos, but if left at the Chiricahuas they would keep the peace.

Agent Clum not having come to the pass I determined to return to Tucson and see what could be done for Cochise's boys in the way of getting them a place near Pueblo Viejo. On my return to Tucson I found Clum still there. He informed me the best that could be done would be to place them at old Camp Goodwin, the nearest point on the reservation to the location they asked for. The next day I started back again for the Chiricahuas. In the meantime General Kautz[9] had been dispatching all the troops he could spare to different points around the reservation, and was on the road from Prescott to take command of them in person.

I had just arrived back at Apache Pass when a courier came in from the Cochise boys to Agent Jeffords, stating they were then fighting with Eskinya's band, who were trying to force them to go with them on the warpath, and they wanted him to have some troops sent down to help them. Major McClellan,[10] who was then commanding officer at Apache Pass, at once ordered Lieutenant Henely[11] and thirty men to the scene. Agent Jeffords and I both accompanied them. We left Apache Pass after dark so as not to be seen by any Indians that may have been on the watch and reached the boys' camp, which was twelve or fourteen miles distant, before midnight.

We learned from the boys that they had killed Eskinya, and they knew Pionsenay was shot, though there had also been some four or five others killed on each side, but they remained masters of the situation. They also stated then and there they were ready to go anywhere I wanted to take them.

As soon as daylight came they took us and showed us the killed of the day previous, and upon our return to camp the party of Eskinya hove in sight, evidently to continue their fight. A volley was fired at them by the troops and Indians, but no one was hurt and they did not return it. They afterwards made signs they wanted to come in, which accordingly they were allowed to do.

After talking awhile they pretended they were willing to go to the San Carlos, but I was suspicious of them. Juh, Nolgee, and Geronimo were all with Eskinya's band. This was Sunday morning; the next day, Monday, was the day set to have the Indians meet Agent Clum and General Kautz and staff in Apache Pass. The Cochise boys agreed to be there at 9:00 A.M., but the other party of Juh and Nolgee stated they did not want to come in with the boys, but would come in at 4:00 P.M. They both came in according to their promises, the former informed the council they were ready to go to San Carlos, but when Juh, Nolgee, and Geronimo came in they wanted a pass for twenty days, as they pretended, to give them time to go and gather up their families.

It was evident to me at once that all they wanted this pass for was to give them a chance to get out of the country, for at this time the reservation was pretty well surrounded by troops. Clum asked me what I thought about giving them the pass and I told him what I thought, and he refused them. They then asked for a ten-day pass, which was refused; finally getting down to four days, Agent Clum granted the pass. This was for their purpose as good as if he had given it to them for twenty days.

I was so satisfied these Indians intended to leave, I went direct to General Kautz and informed him of what I thought. I also informed him of the trail I was satisfied the Indians would take. He informed me he would send Captain Ogilby,[12] who was also then camped at the San Simon Cenaga, up the valley to the trail.

But in military affairs there is always too much red tape to permit of prompt action, and when Captain Ogilby got there he found nothing but their tracks.

When Juh's and Nolgee's party left, they left Pionsenay wounded in their abandoned camp. The latter sent in to Agent Jeffords and asked to be brought in to Apache Pass and cared for, and Agent Clum sent out some of his Apache scouts and they brought him in.

Pionsenay was shot through the right breast and appeared as though he would die, but within a week thereof he escaped from the sheriff and his deputy while they were en route to Tucson with him, and within a month thereof he together with the bands of Juh and Nolgee were spreading death and desolation along the Sonora valley.

Nothing further worthy of note transpired during the removal of the Indians; they went very peaceably and gave no further trouble on the trip.

Crook's Tonto Basin Campaign and After, 1872–78

Crook's Campaign in '72

JOHN G. BOURKE[1]

Chicago Inter Ocean, July 5, 1883[2]

Captain John G. Bourke, of General Crook's staff, in an interview at the Palmer House yesterday with a reporter for the *Inter Ocean*, relative to General Crook and his campaign ten years ago against the Apaches, said:

General Crook in 1871 went to Arizona. At that time he was only lieutenant colonel of the 23rd Infantry, and his assignment to the Military Department of Arizona excited considerable comment among people that did not know him. The Apaches for years had been committing depredations. The settlers were afraid to appear in the highways during the daytime, and they had to do even their work at night. The farmers had carbines, rifles, and pistols, strapped to the handles of their plows when engaged in the fields. An idea of the condition of the country may be gained when it is known that besides robberies by the Apaches over four hundred citizens were murdered in the most atrocious manner in a very short time. President Grant determined to put an end to this state of affairs and to ignore Crook's want of the highest epaulets.

There was then a considerable element in the East very anxious to make an effort to Christianize the Indians. These people did not know General Crook, and they believed the story circulated about him that he would wage a war of extermination against the Apaches. They persuaded the president to restrain General Crook's operations until they had made one more effort with the Apaches to induce them to make peace. The mission of these people to the Apaches after about a year's trial was unsuccessful.

It was then that the president gave orders to General Crook to go ahead and subjugate the Apaches. The movement against the Apaches was commenced in September 1872, and it was brought to a close in May of the following year. The result of that campaign was that six thousand of the Apaches surrendered unconditionally and were placed on the reservation assigned them. At the close of hostilities the chief of the Apaches, Cha-lipun,[3] or Buckskin-colored Hat, said to General Crook at Camp Verde:

"We surrender to you simply because you have too many copper cartridges for us. We have been fighting the whites and Mexicans for I don't know how many years. My father fought them, my grandfather fought them, and my people have met and often defeated them. We never were afraid of them, but you have directed some of our forces against us; you have divided our tribe into two, and when we go out to hunt or for booty we don't know when we return but that our villages will be destroyed and our bucks, women, and children taken away. We have been attacked every day for months and harrassed by your soldiers. So I want to make peace, and I will do whatever you tell me to do."

General Crook told the chief that peace alone would not do; that the Apaches must not only make peace but must become like the white men; in other words, they must go to work. There was some fine arable land near Camp Verde, and General Crook made those Indians prepare it for planting crops. They had no agricultural implements, of course, but with the sharpened ends of burnt sticks and with old hatchets and spades they performed considerable work. It is safe to say that no worse Indians than the Apaches had ever been subjugated, and it is also fair to say that no more orderly body can be found than they are today. There is nothing to hinder the Chiricahuas from becoming just as well behaved if the influence of those who thrive on Indian wars received no consideration. The Apaches planted fifty acres of land and made an irrigating ditch five miles long to bring the water to their fields. They laid out their villages in rectangular streets, which were cleanly swept each morning.

But unfortunately they then began to practice the worst crime of all—they went in for making money. They commenced to deliver wood, hay, etc., to the quartermaster's department at a price not quite one-half that demanded by the contractors. But the contractors, who did not, as one might think, go to Arizona for the benefit of their health, when they could not compete with the industrious Indians had them sent on the San Carlos reservation, and by so doing practically nullified the peace which General Crook had made with them. The Indian is like a white man in many respects, and particularly in this, that if the government does not allow him to enjoy the fruits of his labor, he will cease to labor. The Indian may not know the value of money as well as the white man, but he knows it is money all the same and that he has earned it by his labor. Therefore he has no love for the man or government that deprives him of his earnings.

It is General Crook's personal influence that keeps Arizona as it is today. He knows every one of the Indians by name and he is held in high regard by them. They come to him as they would to a friend and adviser and tell him their stories, which seem to us trifling and absurd. They don't recognize any distinction in shoulder straps or stars. They confide in General Crook because they know him. Should an officer with a dozen or more stars go there, they would treat him the same as any other stranger. The influence of General

Crook with the Indians being of a personal character it will wane unless he is sustained. His success with the Apaches ten years ago would indicate the wisest course now to be taken with this band of Indians.

He would place them on the San Carlos reservation, where all the other Indians would be so many spies upon their every movement. He will have to guard this seventy-five or one hundred male Indians two thousand scouts, all of their own nation, speaking their own language and understanding their artifices in war, and in addition he will have five thousand men, women, and children who will do policemen's duty in watching them, as they are anxious for peace. He succeeded ten years ago in keeping the best of order and discipline among six thousand Apaches, when he had only a small force of soldiers and scouts whom he had employed in the work of their subjugation. At the present time this force would be augmented, he indicated, by the Apaches who would be watching those men. As one of General Crook's Apache scouts said: "It would be better for us to have the Chiracahuas on the reservation here, where we could watch them than to send them back to the Sierra Madre where they would be watching us."

General Crook has been on the frontier continuously for thirty-two years except during the Civil War. He has, therefore, in that time acquired much valuable experience as to entitle him to consideration. The Sioux in the northwest corner of Nebraska are deeply attached to him. So also are all the other tribes. We discovered that the captured Indians had been plundering from the Mexicans. We found that they had a lot of money. Among other things we found on them was a full set of tools for repairing sewing machines. Those who were robbed of their money may find some consolation in the probability that at least one good sewing-machine agent was dispatched to Heaven.

Early Days in Arizona with the Fifth U.S. Cavalry

ANONYMOUS[1]

Winners of the West 1, no. 11 (November 1924): 3

During the years 1872–73 General George Crook, commander of the Department of Arizona, organized a special campaign against the bands of hostile Apaches[2] who were certainly raiding the little settlements scattered at wide intervals in a few of the watered valleys of Arizona. The force consisted of several detachments, each generally consisting of two troops of cavalry, with some friendly Indian scouts. Each detachment had its own field of operations, and I will merely give an account of one engagement with the hostiles, by one detachment, of which my troop formed a part. It was commanded by Brevet Major Brown[3] of the Fifth U.S. Cavalry, his force consisting of troops L and M of the Fifth Cavalry, and a number of Pima scouts under Lieutenant E. D. Thomas,[4] Fifth Cavalry.

The objective of Major Brown was an Apache stronghold known to be somewhere in the frowning canyons of Salt River. A friendly Apache scout who had once lived there agreed to act as guide, provided that the march was made at night, for in daylight he said the command would surely be seen, ambushed, and wiped out. He further stated that the Apaches could in that part of the country easily defend themselves against any available force if forewarned. It must be remembered that in those days the entire army of the United States numbered about twenty-three thousand and was expected to control all the Indians from the Mexican line to the British line, besides garrisoning ocean forts.

The horses, together with the pack train, were left under guard. Each man had a blanket roll, and in it plenty of cartridges to supplement those in his thimble belt. Also a very little food and, of course, a canteen of water. It was bitterly cold, and all night we marched in Indian file along the narrow rocky trail. Shortly before daybreak,[5] a light was seen in front and two scouts were sent forward. They soon returned with the information that the light was made by a party of Apaches returning to their stronghold from a raid on the Pima Indians and the few white families living in the Gila Valley, and that they had left a number of weary mules and horses, stolen from thence, in a little canyon

Lieutenant Ross's attack. CENTURY MAGAZINE, MARCH 1891.

and gone on. Major Brown ordered Captain Burns with his troop to stay where the stolen horses were, so that if any more Apaches came up he could hold them and prevent the command being caught between two fires.

The main body was halted and Lieutenant Ross,[6] with the Indian guide and fifteen men, followed the trail of the returning Apaches toward the stronghold, and in less than one half a mile the guide signaled halt and whispered "Apache." Then he, together with Lieutenant Ross and two scouts, crept along to a turn in the trail, and looking around saw the Apache stronghold about thirty-five yards in front.

It was a long, wide open cave, and a few yards in front of it was a rampart of huge blocks of stone—a natural fortification, but probably added to by the Apaches. Just at the outside of the cavern a fire was burning, and a band of Indians were dancing and singing around it, evidently celebrating their bloody raid through the Gila settlements. A few of the women were cooking a meal, and a number of Indians could be seen sitting in the cave and watching the dance. The men were whispered forward by Lieutenant Ross and sent a volley into the dancers, several falling dead.

The others at once rushed to the cave or manned the rampart, and in less than three minutes opened fire upon the soldiers, whom they could just get a glimpse of in the early dawn. At this moment Lieutenant Bourke, with between forty or fifty men, came at the double down the rocky trail, just in time to save Ross and his handful of men from a counterattack, Major Brown having rushed them forward the moment the first volley was fired. Lieutenants Bourke and Ross hastily posted their men so as to cut off retreat of the Apaches by either flank, and when Major Brown came up with the rest of the men, they surrounded the Indians, the cave being under an unclimbable cliff. For about two hours an interminable fight was maintained, until broad daylight showed that the roof of the cave was all rock and would deflect bullets over the cave.

The men therefore fired volley after volley at the roof, and the effects were soon seen. A number of Indians then made a determined charge, one party at the front, the other at the right flank, while still another party mounted the rampart and fired rapidly, evidently trying to help out the charges, which, however, were repulsed with much loss to the Indians, and several of those on the rampart were also killed.

The troops then commenced firing volleys into the cave, and at this time Captain Burns with his troop came up on the cliff above the cave. It was impossible to get down to attack the Apaches below, so they started rolling rocks down upon them. The Indians, however, still continued defiant, singing and yelling.

After some little time, it was plainly seen that the end was near. The death song had died away, and Major Brown, after assigning Captain Burns to hold up rolling rocks, ordered a charge, and after it was over not a warrior was left alive, except some mortally wounded. In this charge, however, one Apache did get away. He must have thrown himself flat upon the ground in the midst of the charge and wormed his way through, but when he considered himself safe he could not resist leaping upon a high rock and giving a yell of defiance, which brought a shot from Blacksmith Cahill of the pack train which killed the Indian, an eight-hundred-yard shot.[7]

Between eighty and ninety Indians were killed in this fight.[8] The boots of most of the men were well ventilated by this night march over the trail of sharp rocks; many had bleeding feet, and some could not wear their boots but rode barefooted for several days. This is a fair sample of the work done by this Fifth Cavalry during their three and one-half years in Arizona in the early seventies. I may add that our Pima allies all quit temporarily and departed to fast and mourn for their comrades killed in this fight.

The Salt River Cave Fight

JOHN G. BOURKE

John G. Bourke Diary 1: 68–92, United States Military Academy Library

Thursday, December 26, 1872. Awaited in camp the arrival of messengers from Eskiminzin, who sent three men in to Major Brown about 9:00 A.M. A fresh trail has been struck, leading in the direction of Delshay's stronghold. Our command is to go today to the Rio Salado[1] and camp in a canyon. Tomorrow we are to follow down the river and make a camp at a point secluded from observation and from thence we are to go on foot to surprise the rancheria.

11:45 midday. Broke camp, going back on our trail northwest for about three hundred yards—then west to the camp of Captain Burns—about half a mile from our camp—then west a little south over hills for a total distance of two or two and a half miles, halting on a hill about due west from the high mountain we descended yesterday. Hills are now covered with saguaros. We then proceeded down a steep, but not bad grade to the Rio Salado, which we reached at 1:05 P.M.—four miles. Rio Salado here flowing about west and south but only for a short distance, its course being extremely sinuous. Crossed river, passed down its right bank about three-quarters of a mile and camped. Camp is hidden from observation of Apaches,[2] except from west. Weather extremely mild. Distance today about four and a half miles. We have all told 220 fighting men.

Friday, December 27. Remained in camp expecting return of Eskiminzin. All are confident of finding Delshay in his stronghold and, if so, we will make the biggest killing of the campaign. It is rather disappointing to know that our efforts have not been as successful as those of Randall[3] and the others farther north, but we hope to meet with such good fortune during the present week as shall be a fitting recompense for all our past troubles and exertions.

12:40 P.M. Left camp, going back on our trail (north) for about three hundred yards—then due west (nearly) going up very steep and strong grade and through pass on mountain range that lay to west of camp of [December] 26. Halted at top of pass to let pack close up—two miles. We are now south of west about five degrees from High Mountain, [which] we descended on Christmas. Country in this vicinity very badly broken—on left-hand side of this pass mountains are topped by a precipitous ledge of rocks, hundreds of feet high. Upon the highest peak a solitary mescal stalk keeps watch like a sentinel upon the valleys and canyons below. Passed down the mountain on other side, going southwest—trail very bad with loose rocks—went about one mile and half—turned to west—canyon going southwest went over a hill about three hundred yards and then turned northwest, climbed up to top of very high mountain—one mile—Rio Salado to south flowing west southwest through an extraordinarily deep canyon. Mountain we are now on is very narrow—passed down other side, went about half mile. Halted (going southwest). Trail today very bad in every sense of the word. We have not only had to climb steep mountains but had an unusual amount of climbing to do and the trails being filled with loose sharp stones, our animals with difficulty picked their way. A mule died this morning from the effects of eating the insect called "Compra mucho" and "Mayo."[4] Weather fine. The peak we called "Weaver's Needle" is on the south bank of the Rio Salado (apparently).

Went down through canyon to west, about three-fourths mile. Left-hand side a precipice—with an isolated peak jutting out at western extremity. Getting anxious about Eskiminzin, who has now been absent three days. Marched southwest and west, about one mile or perhaps a little more—grade very steep—canyon precipitous on left-hand side—descended into a canyon, with water running south into Rio Salado. Just before reaching camp saw footprints of a squaw who had been watching us descend the mountain and had just run down the canyon. Saw also a fresh pony track.

We are now in sight of the high mesa mountain on the summit of which Delshay has his stronghold, so we are compelled to exercise great caution in our movements. No fires are allowed, the horses and mules are strictly guarded in order that they may not climb up on any of hills commanded by Delshay's mountains. All singing, etc., is strictly forbidden and indeed no precaution is omitted tending to secure the secrecy of our movements. Every preparation is being made for a night march on foot. Each man looks to his weapons, sees that his cartridge belt is full—inspects his clothing—rejecting all that is not absolutely essential to protect him from the cold—provides himself with rations to do for a day or two, and a few matches which are of importance at every moment. Many of us have had our Apache allies make moccasins, which are just the thing in which to climb mountains without giving warning to our foes.

The sky has become overspread with clouds—Major Brown has accordingly allowed the Indians to stew the mule which died today, and whose remains the noble red man brought along. We are to start when a certain star, known to the Indian, rises to its position in our meridian.

8:00 P.M. Our Indians moved out in front, then Burns's company, then Almy, Taylor, and finally the Pimas, under their old chief Antonio; after marching nearly due west about three miles, passing two prominent sandstone buttes of considerable altitude on our right, our trail wound to the left and our general direction became south—after about one and one-half miles' march we came to a steep mountain up the side of which we toiled, using great care to make no noise which might alarm the enemy.

About 12:15 A.M. we were at the summit—a distance as near as I could estimate of about five or six miles from camp. We now rested for nearly an hour, every man closing up to his proper position in the ranks and then lying prone to the ground. Apache scouts were soon sent ahead, who soon returned with the information of fires being discovered in the canyon below. We now advanced one man at a time until we reached the edge of a gloomy abyss; how high and deep it was I could not then discover, and upon this edge we waited in the cold, piercing night air without blankets or overcoats until the morning rays beamed upon the surrounding hills.

We had then an opportunity to examine the locality, so much dreaded by the Pimas, used as one of the strongholds of the Apache-Mojaves and Tontos. Situated upon the crest of a very elevated range, it was difficult of access to large parties from all sides except that upon which we had come and even here the character of the soil was such that a footstep, unless made in the most cautious manner, would be heard for miles.

Granting that an attack could be made, the Apaches could escape unharmed under cover of immense boulders. Looking down into this place, no evidences of recent occupancy could be detected, a disappointment all the more bitter from its contrast to our recent enthusiastic hopes for success.

Most of the command being fatigued sat down to rest, but Joe Felmer[5] and a few others started down the trail towards the Rio Salado, not with any expectation of finding hostile Indians but rather from a disposition to examine into the nature of the country. About three hundred yards from where they left us, in a secluded spot, was found a recently abandoned rancheria of three or four huts. Passing on rapidly, upon descending the mountain somewhat farther, a drove of fifteen horses and mules was encountered and almost immediately a rancheria was seen in an almost impregnable position, which I shall in a few moments proceed to describe.

This handful of our comrades, with a gallantry that cannot be too highly extolled, at once charged the Indians, killing six and driving the remainder into the cave at whose entrance the rancheria was situated. Word having meantime reached Major Brown, the main body was pushed forward as fast as our tired legs would permit, the enthusiasm of the men rising again at the prospect of a fight. To avoid verbose details, let me say the rancheria was situated in a small, elliptical nook. Upon the crest of the bluffs which here enclose the Rio Salado was a small cave or depression in the rocks which overhung this nook by at least five hundred feet, the bluffs first mentioned being one thousand or twelve hundred feet above the Rio Salado. In front of the cave, a natural rampart of sandstone ten feet high afforded ample protection to the Indians, although the great number of boulders scattered in every direction screened our men in turn from the fire of the besieged.

Our policy was obvious—the incorrigible Apaches, at least a portion of them, were now entrapped beyond possibility of escape, and in justice to our men, whose lives should not be rashly imperiled, orders were given to make no charge upon the works, to pick off every Indian showing his head, to spare every woman and child, but to kill every man. Twice the besieged were asked to surrender their families, promises being given that no harm should befall them but, confident in their ability to repel us, their only answers were yells of defiance. These shouts of scorn were soon changed into groans of despair as our shots began to fall with deadly accuracy about them, reckless attempts at escape being made but in each case resulting in the death of those who tried to run our gauntlet of fire. One splendid-looking Indian over six feet, most beautifully proportioned but with a very savage countenance, did indeed succeed in breaking through our front line and making his way down the arroyo full of large rocks, upon one of which he sprang with a yell of defiance, bravado, or joy, I cannot say which. Twelve of us, concealed at this point, leveled our rifles and fired. Every shot must have hit him as he fell dead, riddled from head to foot. This particular instance is mentioned to show the deadly nature of the fire we opened upon them, both as to accuracy and quantity.

A volley was now directed upon the mouth of the cave, and for three minutes every man in the command opened and closed the breechblock of his carbine as rapidly as his hands could move. Never have I seen such a hellish spot as was the narrow little space in which the hostile Indians were now crowded. To borrow the expression employed by a brother officer, the bullets striking against the mouth of the cave seemed like drops of rain pattering upon the surface of a lake.

I must not omit to state that Captain Burns's Company G, Fifth Cavalry had succeeded in gaining a position upon the crest of the overhanging bluffs, whence they discharged deadly volleys upon the wretches fighting below. Not content with the deadly efficacy of bullets, they resorted to projecting large masses of rock which thundered down the precipice, mangling and destroying whatsoever they encountered.

A charge was now ordered and the men rushed forward; upon entering the enclosure a horrible spectacle was disclosed to view—in one corner eleven dead bodies were huddled, in another four, and in different crevices they were piled to the extent of the little cave and to the total number of fifty-seven (seventy-six altogether were killed in this fight) and twenty women and children were taken prisoners. The spoils, very considerable in quantity, were destroyed. We found mescal, baskets, seeds, hides, skins, and the material usually composing the outfit of these savage nomads. Our captives were nearly all wounded, more or less severely, but by good fortune we succeeded in bringing them off in safety. One of our Pima allies was killed, but with this exception, no losses occurred.

Thus ended the most signal blow ever received by the Apaches in Arizona. Not alone did we destroy an entire band, but a band actively engaged in depredating upon the Gila settlements, one that spurned every offer of the government to make peace. Nanni-Chaddi, the chief, had been in to McDowell last year talking with that spawn of hell, Vincent Colyer, from whom he received presents of blankets and other necessaries, promising to return to comply with the demand of the lawful government and obey its orders. He also visited Grant, where in conversation with Colonel Royall, he boasted that no troops ever had found his retreat and none ever would.

A Conference with Cochise[1]

JOHN G. BOURKE

John G. Bourke Diary 1: 125–27, 177–83,
United States Military Academy Library

Wednesday, January 29, 1873. Marched on road to middle crossing of Rio San Pedro and thence to Sulphur Springs. Received dispatches from General Crook. Day very cold. High wind. Sky clear. Night bitterly cold.

Thursday, January 30. Remained at Sulphur Springs. Yesterday a note was sent to Agent Jeffords, requesting an interview with Cochise, and today quite a large band of squaws and children have come over to our camp, but Cochise was not with them. Mr. Jeffords shortly after appeared and had a conversation with Major Brown,[2] with whom he made arrangements for a meeting with Cochise. Express sent to General Crook.

Monday, February 3. Marched southwest across Sulphur Springs, ten or twelve miles to the second canyon in Dragoon Mountains, where we found Cochise and his family with a few young warriors.

Cochise is a fine-looking Indian of about fifty winters, straight as a rush— six feet in stature, deep-chested, Roman-nosed, black eyes, firm mouth, a kindly and even somewhat melancholy expression tempering the determined look of his countenance. He seemed much more neat than the other wild Indians I have seen and his manners were very gentle. There was neither in speech or action any of the bluster characteristic of his race. His reception of us was courteous, although he said but little in the way of compliment. He expressed his own earnest desire for peace—said that in the treaty made with Howard it was understood that soldiers could pass over the roads of his reservation but could not live upon it, nor were citizens to settle there. In reference to the Mexicans, he said he considered them as being on one side in this matter, while the Americans were on another. The former had not asked him for peace as the latter had done. He did not deny that his boys were in the habit of raiding on Mexico, but this he could not prevent as it was no more than was done from all the reservations.

Our interview was quite brief and at its conclusion we returned to our camp at Sulphur Springs. I was very much astonished by the great number of children in the Indian camp.

⇥⇤

Account of the Interview between Major W. H. Brown,
5th Cavalry, and the Indian Chief Cochise, or Cheis,
February 3, 1873

Major Brown: I have come from General Crook to this part of the country to see Cochise. The general hears that Cochise is at peace and he knows by (Cochise's) actions that he has kept it. The general is anxious also to keep this peace in all its integrity, according to the terms of the treaty; but, in order to be able to do this, he wants to know what the terms of the treaty are. He has never been furnished with a copy of the treaty, and although he will receive a copy in time, yet it is a long way to Washington, and as the easiest way to get these terms he has sent me to Cochise to find out what he understands these terms to be, and especially with reference to the movements of troops within the reservation of Cochise—and particularly whether troops are to be permitted to come upon the reservation or not—and also, what has been the understanding about Mexico, whether the peace applies to the people of that country or not.

Cochise: The troops were to pass and repass by the roads on the reservation, the same as ever, according as the emergencies of the service might require, but none were to come upon the reservation to live, nor were citizens to do so.

Major Brown: What stipulations, if any, were made in the treaty with regard to the people of Mexico?

Cochise: (Endeavoring to evade the question) now said that, permission had been given them by General Howard to go to Mount Graham in seed time to gather acorns, mesquite beans, but they were not to live at Mount Graham.

Major Brown: Tell them that is all right; they can go to Mount Graham and get seeds and such things as they may want, so long as they live upon the reservation—but, they must always tell the agent so the troops may expect their coming. Say also if they want to come and see where the new post is going to be placed, some of them can accompany me on my way back. (Major Brown repeated the question about Mexico.)

Cochise: The Mexicans are on one side in this matter and the Americans on another. There are many young people here whose parents and relatives have been killed by the Mexicans, and now these young people are liable to go down, from time to time, and do a little damage to the Mexicans. I don't want to lie about this thing; they go, but I don't send them.

I made peace with the Americans, but the Mexicans did not come to ask peace from me as the Americans have done. I don't myself want to go down to Mexico and will not go, but my boys may go there. I consider that I myself am at peace with Mexico, but my young men, like those at all the other reservations, are liable to occasionally make raids. I don't want to lie about this; I can't prevent it. There are bad people everywhere. A great many of us were one time at peace at Fronteras and some of the Mexicans used to tell us to come up here and steal American horses, which are big and worth a great deal of money in Mexico. But when our people came back there with them, they killed them and took the horses and cattle away. Why don't the Americans tell us to go down there and steal from the Mexicans?

Major Brown: Tell them we are now at peace with Mexico and cannot do them any harm. When we make friends with a man we never do anything behind his back to hurt him. If ever we go to war with Mexico, we shall send word to the Mexicans and tell them we are coming. If we whip them, we shall whip them fairly, but not by doing something behind their backs. I have said all I have to say and when I go back I shall tell the general all about Cochise so that he will know all about him the same as if he had come here himself.

Cochise: It is all right. When this ground was given me it was that we might roam over it as we pleased. I don't intend to let my young men do any wrong on this ground. I like the way in which you talk. (The remainder of this sentence, not being understood by me as Major Brown appeared to understand it, has been omitted.) I am glad of the peace and my people rejoice at it.

The meeting closed as it had begun, with a general hand-shaking.

Incidents of Indian Campaigning in Arizona

WESLEY MERRITT[1]

Harper's New Monthly Magazine 80, no. 459 (April 1890): 725–31

The following events connected with the subjugation of the Apaches, given substantially in the words of an accomplished officer who took part for several years in the Indian wars in Arizona,[2] afford an illustration of another phase of the occupation of the army on the frontier in so-called times of peace.

A parallelogram formed by a line from Camp Verde eastward to the White Mountains, south to the San Carlos, continued westward to Camp McDowell, and thence north to the point first named, would contain fifteen thousand square miles of rocky mountain peaks, deep canyons, heavily wooded mountain streams, and dark pine forests. Here and there beautiful little valleys or parks are found, each an isolated oasis, and it is in this isolation and the intervening barriers that the peculiar difficulties of the region for campaigning purposes are discovered.

After incredible upward toil along the zigzag trail, the scouting party reaches the sharp, rocky ridge, whence the almost precipitous descent begins to the pleasant camp ground far below, and it is plainly seen from the commanding height that the beautiful grassy plain is of very limited extent and shut in on all sides by almost impenetrable mountains. Thus are the anticipations of rest and refreshment sometimes dashed by the prospect of the interminable, heart-breaking, rock-climbing struggle to begin again at daybreak. In most wild mountain regions the narrow berm on the edge of streams, or the bed of the stream itself, is the only passable route, but here the mountain torrents that pour out in every direction from the great ranges pass for the most part through dark, precipitous box canyons, which cut off communication between the parks, strung together like beads by the pure, clear, deep streams, and all who would penetrate the mountain ranges must do so by painfully climbing their rugged sides.

In this Apache paradise many varieties of climate are found. From the cool shade of the pine forests of the Black Mesa to the burning, sandy wastes that form the valleys of the Salt and Gila rivers, one passes from one extreme to the other but would prefer rather to remain in the worst than encounter the torture of a journey over the miles on miles of confused and jumbled masses of rocky mountain peaks to reach the better.

The theater of operations thus fairly outlined, as well as adjacent portions of the immense territory of Arizona, has been for many years the scene of innumerable conflicts between the troops and the many Apache tribes. A record carefully compiled by the historian of one of the cavalry regiments which took its share of the sufferings and hardships of the mountain scouting between the years 1871–75 shows that in that period the regiment had ninety-seven combats with the marauding savages.[3]

Early in the year 1872 it became evident that a portion of the Arivaipa Apaches were using Camp Grant as a base of supplies and pushing their marauding parties out in every direction into the settled parts of the territory. The dread entertained by the settlers for these marauders is best appreciated when the character and mode of warfare of the mountain tribes are understood. As an old wagon master remarked to a cavalry officer: "We have a horror of them that you feel for a ghost. We never see them, but when on the road are always looking over our shoulders in anticipation. When they strike, all we see is the flash of the rifle resting with secure aim over a pile of stones," behind which, like a snake, the red murderer lies at full length.

All the Apaches are footmen, mountain climbers. They will steal horses and use them, but when driven into the mountains the horses become a part of their rations. Graceful, well-formed, with legs of steel wire, light and active as a cat, the Apache on the rocky hillside is unapproachable, and to fight him with any chances of success, he has to be attacked with skill and great caution at gray dawn in his bivouac far up among the rocks. Many a surprise has been effected by night marches against natural fortresses absolutely unassailable in the daytime by any number of men, and where, if the Indians had discovered the ascending columns, even in the night, they could have repulsed them with great slaughter.

As a first step in the campaign, the commanding general[4] directed that all warriors receiving rations should be counted every day, at a place to be selected, within five miles of the post. In order that the officer detailed for this delicate and dangerous duty might be able to identify and keep a record of the young men, a metal tag stamped with a number was issued to each Indian of fighting age.[5] Many of the Indians received the order with sullen dissatisfaction because, if carried out, it checkmated their roving. Seated on their heels in increasing concentric circles in front of the general, the crouching attitude and the steady glare of their brilliant, bead-like eyes made them resemble snakes coiled ready to strike, and it was plain that when the opportunity offered they would resist by the most deadly means this effort to scotch them.

The next day the cavalry officer detailed rode out four miles from the post, accompanied by one orderly, to meet the young savages and make the first count.[6]

The officer selected was one who had seen considerable service and fighting, but he subsequently confessed that he would have been glad to exchange the duty assigned him for a detail to lead a forlorn hope over a breastwork.

However, he had been told by the general that it was undesirable to send a force on the duty, as some of the warriors might become alarmed and in their ignorance make trouble, and that the object was to give the Indians a fair chance. So out he rode, with his heart in his throat, feeling pretty confident that unless he kept his head some young "buck" would stab him in the back and, thus distinguishing himself, take his departure for the warpath. The place selected was at the foot of a hill on which was situated the largest Indian village of the reservation. Arriving at the point, the officer was met by the whole band rushing down the hillside with yells and shouts, and as they approached nearer he had the horror of perceiving that they were nearly all drunk. They had been celebrating the disagreeable order of the day before by a "tiswin" spree.

The lieutenant received the charge by dismounting and standing, with a nonchalance which was far from natural, at the foot of a large cottonwood tree, the orderly, mounted, holding the horses a few yards in rear. It was soon apparent that several of the chiefs had remained sober and were doing their utmost to prevent trouble, and by their exertions the rabble was halted about twenty yards from the tree and seated with some attempt at the usual half-circle formation. The counting officer then approached, with book and pencil in hand, and though appreciating the danger of assassination, he resolutely passed along the front of each circle and checked off the numbers on the tags.

Many of the rascals, with impudent drunken jeers, shook the tags in his face, and one fellow refused to show his. Passing the mutineer for the time being, the lieutenant concluded the checking process. He was now confronted by a formidable problem: either he must capture the drunken young savage or submit to the indignity of seeing the orders entrusted to him for execution treated with contempt, of which the Indians were sure to take advantage, taking it for a confession of weakness.

In this perplexity he called up the orderly with the horses and then turned to one of the most reliable of the chiefs[7] standing near and made signs to him to bring up the young man and force him to show his tag. The young fellow lounged up when bidden by the chief but stood immovable, staring at the representative of the government with drunken insolence. Giving the orderly, who was still mounted, a few words of direction, the lieutenant mounted his own horse as if to ride off, and at a signal the orderly, a fine old soldier, suddenly drew his revolver and covered the young savage, at the same time making an imperious sign for him to jump up behind the officer.

The old chief took in the situation instantly and, seizing the fellow under the arms, almost threw him up on the croup of the horse behind the lieutenant, and so, covered by the steady pistol of the orderly, they rode off. The Indians were quick to appreciate the defeat of the braggart, and the little procession of prisoner and captors was followed by yells, screams, and jeering laughter. The prisoner was safely landed in the post guardhouse, a substantial witness of the nerve and courage of a resolute officer over the savage fury of the Apache.

Such captures were not always made so successfully. A few months later two soldiers approached to arrest a young fellow who was seated on the ground, wrapped in a blanket. Quick as thought the Indian threw off the blanket and, by a right and left stroke with a knife, killed one soldier and severely wounded the other.

No further trouble occurred at the daily verification of the Indians. The young men who preferred war to steady rations slipped away and were seen no more, and a correct estimate of the number of the hostiles was the result of the counting process. There was one exception to the quiet manner of departure. Two desperadoes, Chunz and Cochinay by name, aspiring to be war chiefs, committed a cold-blooded murder within the limits of the military post and then fled to the mountains, followed by their immediate relatives.[8] This party was pursued immediately by an officer and ten cavalrymen summoned from the drill ground.[9]

The soldiers, reinforced by three Apache scouts from the band of Cazador (who had always remained friendly), took up the trail from the scene of the murder, where lay the body of an inoffensive young Mexican, brained from behind by the cowardly assassins. Following the trail, the scouting party soon found a place where a mark drawn in the dust across the path and a red flag stuck up on a stick plainly indicated war.

The trail then led over a country the roughest imaginable. Down deep into the bowels of the earth it seemed to go before the stream at the bottom of the first box canyon was reached and then up, along the slanting slippery path worn in the face of the opposite rocks. Forward all day on foot, leading their stumbling horses over the broken rocks, the little party pushed on, halting only after dark, when the trail could not be followed, to spend the chilly winter night on the bare rocks without food and with their saddle blankets alone for cover. For days the party kept up this pursuit but, unfortunately, without success. This, however, was a prelude to a tragedy in which Chunz and Cochinay, who were natural leaders and desperadoes, were principal characters.

A little later on, the agency having been moved to the San Carlos,[10] these desperadoes, taking advantage of a stormy night and a sudden rise in the Gila River, which separated the camp of the cavalry from the Indians, boldly entered the Apache village.[11]

It so happened that many of the young men that night, feeling secure from the interference of the soldiers on account of the swollen stream between them, were drinking tiswin and fast ripening into a fit mood for any mischief. This habit of the Apaches of intoxicating themselves deliberately by using a liquor made by the squaws from fermented corn was a very difficult thing to deal with. Parties of soldiers under determined young officers were frequently sent into their camp to break up the drunken sprees—a most dangerous duty, always successful for the time, but with all care it was impossible to prevent them from stealing or buying corn and again making tiswin.

In the wake of the destroyer. HARPER'S NEW MONTHLY MAGAZINE, APRIL 1890.

Just what happened in the Indian camp after Chunz and Cochinay with their followers arrived it is difficult to say. Cazador subsequently reported that they harangued the bands and said that all young men not cowards would follow their lead. Taunts, reproaches, and appeals at such a time produced an explosion. A rush was made for a wagon train loaded with supplies for the troops, which was camped on the Indian side of the river directly opposite the cavalry camp. The teamsters were instantly killed and the wagons plundered, and then with wild yells the whole tribe started for the mountains.

Here was work indeed. Hurrying from Fort Apache, the nearest post, two cavalry troops made the seventy miles in one march, bringing with them a company of the gallant and faithful White Mountain Apaches, enlisted as scouts.[12]

Taking up the trail, these troops followed the wake of the devastating Apaches. Straight for the settlements of the San Pedro River it led and was found returning up the valley of that stream and making for the mountains north of the Gila.

No need to follow the trail to the ruined homes of the white settlers down the San Pedro. At the point where it was encountered returning from the raid, torn dresses, children's clothing, and broken household utensils scattered along the path showed that the red devils had swept through the peaceful colony, leaving nothing but the wreck behind.[13] And so it proved, as those who later visited the scene reported. Dead mothers, appealing to the sky with staring eyes, the lifeless bodies of helpless little children, and last the scalped and mangled forms of the natural protectors of the frontier home, composed the too familiar picture presented of the visit of an Indian war party.

The advance troops, after much suffering in the mountains and three days of absolute fasting, finally reported that they had located the whole band of Indians on the top of the Pinal Mountains, in a position unassailable by direct attack. The commanding officer of the San Carlos, a man of nerve and one familiar with the "ins and outs" of Apache character,[14] had by this time secured the services of a renegade from the hostiles, who promised to lead the troops into the natural fortress under cover of the darkness.

The expedition started at once. It included the soldiers from Fort Apache and the cavalry troops summoned from the nearest posts. Marching only at night and halting during the hours of daylight for concealment, it reached at dawn on the third morning[15] a point fifteen miles in an air line from the Pinal Mountains.

As the sun rose the outlines of the Indian stronghold became plainly visible. Towering up against the sky, it looked formidable indeed, and a disheartening evidence of the difficulties of approach was afforded by the very unusual sight of the smoke of campfires which the hostiles made no attempt to conceal.

The extent of their impregnable position along the rocky ridge was plainly indicated by the curling pillars of smoke, and it was apparent that the Apaches felt defiant and secure.

Although only fifteen miles in an air line, the renegade insisted that it would be necessary to make a detour to the north in order to avoid the fearful chasms that intervened, and twenty-five miles of the roughest country in Arizona must be crossed to reach the crest of the mountain.

Early in the afternoon the storming party set out. Only the very best of the men were taken. All marched on foot. The sick and exhausted were left in charge of the horses and pack mules, with orders to keep everything well concealed from any outlying scouts of the enemy.

Single file, in one long column, the troops for the advance pushed out, led by their White Mountain allies. Stripped to their breechcloths, lithe, graceful fellows, the Indian scouts, like a pack of greyhounds, surrounded and guarded the sullen renegade guide. Officers and men alike carried their two days' rations on their backs but had divested themselves of all superfluous weight, and saving their breath by silence, they strove manfully to keep up with their fleet-footed guides.

A terrible task was before them. The country was one mass of broken rocks, and canyons with almost precipitous sides crossed the trail at frequent intervals. All night long they stumbled, struggled, and scrambled forward. How they succeeded in crossing the gloomy, pitch-black canyons no one in the party could ever tell. Keeping within touch of each other and guided by faith, they groped their way to the bottoms of the dark chasms and in the same order toiled, panting for breath, up the opposite sides. Treachery on the part of the Apache scouts would have turned any one of the dark holes into a slaughter pit.

The briefest halts for rest were made, for should daylight come before the crest was reached, discovery, repulse, and death to many must follow. Before the glimmer of the dawn appeared it was apparent that they were climbing up the side of the last and highest ascent, and with increased caution the men pulled themselves upward from rock to rock. From the almost precipitous face of the ridge sharp, rocky spurs ran out at intervals in the direction from which the troops advanced.

The attack was made in three parties, each ascending by one of the natural scaling ladders. So well timed was the operation that when, just at the first streak of dawn, the White Mountain scouts on the right opened fire and with shouts charged the startled hostiles, the troops had gained the top of their rocky spurs, and the fortified camp which, warned of the attack, could have repulsed a brigade, was carried in three places. The capture of this natural fortress, which Chunz and Cochinay, the war chiefs, had labored to prove to the bands was impregnable, broke up the unity of the tribe, shook confidence in their leaders, and increased their fear of the troops. The Indians not killed or captured dispersed in small parties into the surrounding mountains.[16] The expeditionary force in like manner separated, and in small squads scouted the mountains in every direction, giving the hostiles no chance to attack the settlements.

Before long, runners came in to the San Carlos from the scattered tribe, asking for peace and permission to return. The commanding general met every such messenger with the information that any band might come in which would surrender one or all of the four outlaws named. These were Chunz, Cochinay, Pedro, one of the most active leaders in the murders on the river of that name, and Chan-deisi, the tool of Chunz in the killing, a short time before, of a cavalry officer at the agency. They were also notified that if they could not surrender the outlaws named alive, they themselves should mete out the punishment of death, and that upon proof that a just fate had overtaken the desperate criminals, any and all of the other Indians could come in and live at peace.[17]

So it finally turned out: the Indians themselves punished the outlaws, furnishing satisfactory proof that justice had been done, and before summer the Arivaipa tribe was re-established at the San Carlos agency.

On Campaign in Arizona

CHARLES KING[1]

Milwakuee *Sentinel*, March 28, 1880

Just now, while the Cheyenne and Sioux are deriving the benefits of their (very) recent repentance and reformation, and along the Northern Plains and Rockies the frontiersman and the soldier are waiting expectant of the something Indian that is sure to turn up, we read daily accounts of the activity and skill of a chieftain—Victorio by name, victorious by nature—and while we too are waiting Micawber-like for that upheaval among our old acquaintances on the northern frontier, it might interest the readers of the Sunday *Sentinel* to hear a little about the manners and customs of these very fellows whom Victorio is now leading.

In 1874 they were well known to me—perhaps not the very same men—but they were Apaches, all of them, and more intractable rascals than those same Apaches it would be hard to find even in New Mexico and Arizona. Then such a country as they have to fight over when they feel like fighting, or to run away and hide in when that course suggests itself as advisable! The world has nothing like northeastern Arizona. From northwest to southeast run great parallel ranges of sterile mountains, like waves of the stormiest sea—only that the farther you get into the northeastern and northern sections of the territory the more abrupt, jagged, and precipitous they become; the more tumultous is the upheaval, and from broad valleys lying deep and sheltered between, you come upon narrow, tortuous canyons, so deep, so narrow, that while it seems possible to hurl your hat across the widest of the lot, you look down into depths unfathomable, and by winding "goat trails" and hours of dizzy climbing and sliding, sometimes on all fours, you manage to cross.

Cavalry in those regions were as useless as gunboats. We were quartered all over the territory down in some of those deep valleys, one or two companies at each post, and when sent out scouting after the fierce footmen of these strange mountains we in the Fifty Cavalry took our cue from General Crook—rode our horses as far as trails would take them, then, hiding them in some sheltered valley or streambed, kicking off our troop boots and pulling on Indian moccasins, leaving a guard at the bivouac, the rest of us with our Indian

An Apache defiance. HARPER'S NEW MONTHLY MAGAZINE, APRIL 1890.

guides would launch out and go footing it through the crags and canyons until we trailed our foe to his lair and fought it out, every man for himself. It was a wild, vigorous experience—less like soldiering than any service I ever encountered—but it was the only way in the world to whip those Apaches, and it had to be done.

All through those mountains our foe would scatter—some in bands of sixty or eighty, others fewer in number, each with its own chief. When I got to Arizona in the spring of '74 to take a hand in the campaign, I found General Crook at his headquarters at Prescott, had a good talk and some valuable information from his thoroughly experienced aide-de-camp, Lieutenant Bourke, and then went out to the post of Company K, down in the Verde valley,[2] with the intimation that in a week or so I would take the warpath and try my luck after Apaches.

Just then there were two or three powerful bands roaming around in the Sierra Ancha and the Mazatzal range. The chiefs who led them were known as Delshay, Eskeltelsee, and Eskiminzin (Skinn' Jim, the soldiers called him). Far to the south, Captain Hamilton of the Fifth Cavalry,[3] with one command, and Lieutenant Schuyler, with another, were searching through those rocky fastnesses and gradually driving the renegades northward, and now the time was ripe for an expedition from Camp Verde to go down and meet them somewhere in the wilds of the Tonto Basin. One under Lieutenant Heyl[4] was order-ed to skirt the great Mazatzal range, and the other was placed in my com-mand—with best wishes for success on this, my first scout against the savages, and with orders to work well over to the southeast along the base of the Black Mesa and hunt down to the Sierra Ancha.

Now I might have hunted, and my troopers too, for months and never have found a hostile Indian. But the beauty of General Crook's system was that as fast as he whipped one tribe of those Arizona Indians he utilized them as scouts and allies against the others.

All he demanded of the Apache was that he should abandon his forays on the settlements and into Mexico, come in to the reservations, and be fed and cared for. But through his interpreters he gave them distinctly to understand that if they did not come in and accept his terms he would hunt them to the verge of extermination.

It took some time to thrash the Hualapais—a magnificent lot of mountain hunters—but once subdued they became our most valuable scouts and helped to dispose of the Apache-Mohaves and Apache-Yumas, so that when I got into the field the only powerful Indians left in arms against us in northeastern Ari-zona were the Tontos, and they were incorrigible.

My little command marched from Camp Verde on May 21, and, thanks to the admirable noncommissioned officers I had in Sergeants Stauffer and Winser[5] and to the wonderful skill in "trailing" displayed by the allies who were assigned to us for duty, we had a scout that was most successful in its results—two rattling little fights, in one of which we totally surprised the Ton-tos and punished them severely,[6] and then had the satisfaction of seeing Eskel-telsee and over fifty of his warriors surrendered on our return. Four parties in the field at one time was too much for him.

But it is of these Indian allies of ours and their peculiarities that in this article I propose to tell, for I spent many an hour watching them. They were of two tribes—Apache-Mohave and Apache-Yuma,[7] fourteen in all—wiry, sin-ewy, lean-looking fellows, with keen black eyes and coarse matted hair that hung thickly over the shoulders and was banged in front just in line with their eyes. Some of them had portions of our blue uniform and infantry shoes for their equipment, but the majority wore the Apache moccasin, a model of inge-nuity—made to cover not only the foot but the leg well up to the thigh and fit it like theatrical tights, the leg covering habitually falling in folds about the ankle except in snowy weather; the sole of hide with the hair still on (when new) and turned up in a thick wad at the great toe to prevent stubbing that sensitive member on the rocky trails over which they are so constantly roaming. There is nothing ornamental about the Apache moccasin, and the gaudy beadwork so dear to the heart of the Sioux and Arapaho is seldom seen among them. The "buck," as the male is always called, will wear a shirt and these moccasins, and a strip of (originally) white cotton as a compromise for a breechclout, and it is a sight never to be forgotten to see the naked vagabond springing up a mountainside, rifle or bow in hand, agile as a chamois, light and graceful as the four-legged buck, but with this abomination of a cotton streamer trailing after him like the tail of a kite.

We read everywhere of the stoicism and gravity of the Indian, but my Apaches were merry as darkies, laughing, singing (but such singing) for hours at a time. The soldiers delighted in them—gave them tobacco and extra sugar and coffee, made pets of them, as it were, and had nearly all of them rechristened.

The laughter and fun that echoed through the pine-fringed banks of the canyon one bright June evening as I gathered them round me to take down all their names in my notebook was something simply infectious. We were on our way home then and out of all danger of surprise and attack, but of course our pickets were posted and every man's weapon close at hand. The soldiers in their rough dress and bearded faces formed an amused framework to our fire-light council.

The merriest young rattlepate of all was our interperter Arahawa, or Washington Charlie, who had learned his limited English in a trip to San Francisco and who spoke it with so strong a "pidgin" flavor as to suggest that he had acquired it in the Chinese quarters.

"Here, Charlie. Tell them I want to put every scout's name in my book— see? so that I can remember them." And Charlie, with much gesticulation and sputter, makes the wishes of the "Gran Capitan" known. Your readers will understand that in such Apache, the "grande" refers not to stature but to relative rank in the crowd; the littlest man just here happened to be tallest in commission.

Then they all came crowding round to see what their names would look like, inquisitive as squaws and quite full of chatter. One suggested something to Charlie which provoked universal applause, and which he explained as follows:

"Kwonahilka, he say, mebbe so you catchem all some smoke, mebbe so you can get em all some names." So I produced tobacco, and they rolled their cigarettes and we went at it, my efforts to pronounce the gutturals after them provoking shouts of delighted laughter. "Kwonegietha, Wauwamecha, Cholaca, Toyah, Kithaymi, Tomawarecha, Ulnyakoshorah (that was a heathen name), Huskarahma," and so on. Long before, the soldiers had given them such easily spoken and familiar titles as "Jacko," "Popcorn," "Whiskey," and the like, but they had never seen their names in the original Apache until that evening.

When mustered into service they were furnished with a brass tag like a baggage check, with a tribal number (one for Yuma, two for Mohave) and a personal number for themselves. These they were charged never to part with, and many were the devices to which they resorted in securing them about their persons. Then we had a song, and of all the weird, guttural incantations I ever listened to, this was the worst. Squatting about the ground and playing some game with a greasy pack, they set up a shrill doggerel—one taking the leading parts and giving time and tone, the others coming in with no better accompaniment than a positive grunt. When singing rapidly and in "two-four" time, I could not make out the words, but after a while Jacko treated us to something different, a solo of which every numbered line was a chorus of grunts—impossible to accurately translate.

As near as I can copy it without the air it ran like this:

Teyama, teyama
(succession of grunts)
Seyanna, seyanna
Apache Mohave, grunt, Seyanna Gee.

Milwaukee *Sentinel*, April 4, 1880

A recent meeting with an old comrade of the Fifth Wisconsin, later a member of the 12th Infantry, fresh from Arizona, called to mind an incident connected with the first scout I ever made against hostile Indians. It was with the same command and the same Apache allies of whom I told you last Sunday. We had struck Eskeltelsee's band of hostile Tontos on the night of May 25, [1874,] and by dint of shrewd management and total surprise had given them a trashing they never forgot, as fourteen of their dead were left in our hands. Then they seemed to scatter in every direction through the mountains, and we had, after five days hunting, concluded that the Tonto Basin contained not another hostile and determined to try the lairs among the precipices and dark gorges of the Black Mesa.

"Mebbe so try-um Mogy' one[8] tomorrow, mebbe so catchem plenty Tonto," was the way Washington Charlie put it to the commanding officer on the evening of May 30, 1874, and after a guttural consultation with Kwonahilka, the Apache Mohave captain, he added: "Tonto sabby click-click (horse) no make-um climb Mogy' one. Plenty safe."

Charlie is [a] polyglot and prides himself on his fluency. It was a mystery to me when we first started out but is becoming intelligible, not to say interesting.

Sergeant Stauffer, with his bronzed face and great, soft brown eyes, is standing in mute patience awaiting the orders for the morrow. He knows ten times as much about Indian fighting in his little finger as I do in all my educated composition, but unless definitely and distinctly asked for his opinion on each occasion nothing could drag it from him. We are in bivouac after a long day's march and are lighting our cautious fires in a little grove just at the edge of a broad valley that runs with the sun, east and west. The sun has long disappeared behind the great upheaval of the Mazatzal, twenty miles to the west; but, glancing eastward, while all is gloom at the base of that wondrous wall, a like distance to the east, its grand facade is roseate, glowing in the rays of the luminary lost to our view. It looks auspicious and tempting now, if it never did before. "We move at daybreak, Sergeant, and we'll try the mesa." And so, just as the sun comes round again and gilds the peaks of the Mazatzal, we shiveringly mount, for the night has been sharply cold, and with our tireless Apaches bounding along on foot, ahead and on either flank, our pack mules jogging contentedly after Pompe and the bell, we lead off down the misty valley and in a few moments are winding along a mountain trail in single file. The order of march is primitive, a game of follow your leader. We keep old Kwonahilka and six or seven likely scouts well out to the front with Sergeant Winser; then comes the lieutenant commanding on his nag "Bronco"; then the first sergeant and the main body all in a string, as it were; then the pack mules and their guard and attendants. Whenever we reach a steep place, either up or down hill, the rider dismounts and takes the reins behind him, his horse then follows in his footsteps, each man in succession executing the same maneuvers as he reaches the spot where the chief dismounted. The trail leads among rocks, ravines, and canyons—never wide enough for two.

The sun comes out bright and warm overhead; the day grows summerlike; nearer and nearer we draw to the frowning barrier in our front; at last, at 1:00 P.M., right at the foot of the lofty wall, we find a lovely green valley, through which is tumbling a stream cold as ice, clear as crystal, and here we halt for dinner for all hands. Then comes a foot scout, and we spend hours clambering about among the rocks hunting for traces—signs of our savage foe. Late in the afternoon we come upon an abandoned stronghold. Their huts and many of their implements are still here, but the "rancheria," as it is termed in Arizona, is abandoned. By sunset we are back, tired and hungry, at camp, many of our horses welcoming the master with a whinny of recognition and an equine demand for sugar or salt.

Bivouac life has a nameless charm at such a time and in such a climate. With abundant water, grass, wood, game, and fish, and scenery unparalleled in wild beauty, I know nothing like it. Men, horses, and all seem bouyant with life and health, and as we smoke the pipe of peace after abundant supper, in all but our precaution we forget our deadly mission. Jotting down the events of the day in my scouting notebook I turn to a home tie, a pocket diary, a little volume combined with other and holier writ too often neglected amid such scenes, and, looking at the date, I read May 31, 1874. Trinity Sunday. The men are singing some rollicking soldier song in the gathering twilight, swarthy faces of our Indian allies lighting up in the fire gleam and grinning appreciation of the pale faces' fun. Is it homesickness? I wonder, but I drop my pipe and steal away with that little diary still open at its page and wander down the brook, till, out of sight, out of hearing of the camp, I fancy I can hear the far off chime of solemn evening bells and the swelling triumph of the glorious Trinity hymn—it is three years since I heard it last.

Monday, June 1, breaks like a glad carol. Feathered songsters whose notes are new to me are trilling in the branches as we ride away. Two days more we search among these intricate fastnesses, and on Wednesday, just at noon, we are watering our horses in another just such icy stream as that along which we spent our Sabbath evening, when there is a commotion among our Apaches.

Tonto warrior. OUTING MAGAZINE, JANUARY 1887.

Kwonahilka, Toyah, and Charlie are jabbering excitedly up the brookside and pointing to some objects just at the water's brink. Others, bending almost to earth, are jumping up and down along the banks. Sergeant Winser walks quickly up with his quiet salute and says, "Tonto sign, Sir," and with Sergeant Stauffer we join the scouts. At a point where there is a breadth of twenty feet of brawling water between the banks, several boulders lie like stepping stones athwart the stream. The shores are rocky or pebbly, but a little sifted sand, still damp from higher water, is lodged among the crevices, and in one or two places the sand bears the faint impress of the pointed great toe of the Tonto moccasin. I never would have noticed it in the world; an Indian would never have missed it.

"How old, Charlie?" "Mebbe so two day—mebbe so yes'day. Wait. Bimeby catchem some more."

The search is going on. The Indians are creeping almost on all fours through the brushwood and timber now. Presently there is a low call from further upstream. We make our way through the bushes and find Jacko at the edge of a shelving, sandy shore, his eyes aglow, his face eager with suppressed excitement. He says not a word but points to the mud at his feet. There are the tracks of three pair of moccasins, well-defined, and water still standing in those nearest the edge. They are not three hours old. Charlie and his brothers are quick in their conclusions. Somewhere up among the crags and cliffs in the face of the mesa there is what they call "Patchie house."

"Tonto come here for water. Look see," says Charlie, pointing to certain damp splashes where water had evidently been spilled as the carriers clambered up the bank.

Evidently, then, they are either beyond the sources of this stream, which comes tumbling from a black gorge to the east, or so far aloft toward the crest that we must climb skyward to get at them. Gorge and mountainside are densely wooded, and we can see but a few hundred yards in any direction. Only we know that we are at the very base of the cliff and that we can climb at an angle of forty-five degrees for a thousand yards before we reach the vertical.

Somewhere up there they have got their nest, and our orders are to hunt them to their holes and fight it out, hand-to-hand. How long the hunt may last we cannot tell, so we decide on setting forth at once. First we lead our horses farther in among the rocks and trees and secure both them and the pack mules. A strong guard and the three packers remain in charge. Then each man kicks off his cavalry boots and spurs and pulls on the Indian moccasin; the strong sole of thick hide is ample protection to the foot, and in ten minutes my little command is stripped for their work.

What a travesty in "the pomp and circumstance of glorious war" is here. Old slouch hats of white felt, flannel shirts of grey or dingy blue, and hunting breeches of no better color than dirt. Officer and private alike; there is not a vestige of ornament in the army. Each man grasps his carbine and girds himself with his belt of ammunition. One man, ordered to keep well in rear, brings a canteen of water and a little package of bandages and surgical supplies that may be needed.

"All ready, men?" and off we go. No order, no ranks, but in perfect silence. The soldiers come eagerly after me, while Charlie with his Apache brethren spring noiselessly to the front and scatter upward along the rocky ascent. Then follows the prettiest piece of trailing I have ever witnessed.

Close to the stream the bushes and stunted oaks are thick. Once away from it and on the rise the underbrush disappears, and we spread out right and left over the slope. Here, while the trees are numerous, their branches are high above our heads, the trunks straight and bare for twenty feet from the ground. The ground itself is everywhere covered with fragments of rock and slate, the detritus of every storm or avalanche that has occurred since creation. Tiny blades of grass peep up here and there, but we are creeping upwards over a soil on which the human foot leaves no impression. How then can those stealthy rascals in front so unhesitatingly beckon us on? For two hundred yards they cover our front, moving noiselessly from point to point, crouching like panthers on the trail of the deer. Occasionally one of them will call me by a gesture and, proud of the admiration of "Gran Capitan," will point to where a twig is bent and its back faintly abraded, or where a little fragment of rock or slate, crunched from its place by laboring foot, has turned and now lies with a damp face upward. An hour in the sun will bleach it [as] white and dry as its neighbor. On we clamber, steadily, silently, sometimes crossing a mountain ravine, sometimes over rocky ledge, but all the time unerringly our swarthy, half-naked scouts guide us forward. Once in a while we would fain pause for breath. An hour of such climbing is trying to the lungs. But at last Sergeant Stauffer, who is close by my side, holds out a warning hand and points to the right. Two of the scouts are kneeling behind a little rocky barrier and peering over, motioning, "Keep back!" The men, who are spread out unconsciously in skirmish line, halt in their tracks. Presently I reach the ledge and, obeying the signal of their gleaming eyes, peer eagerly over. Five hundred yards away is another and higher rocky point. Above it, boldly outlined against the blue of heaven, towers the great cliff—the western terminus of the mesa.[9] Thick growth of oak and sturdy pine, barren masses of rock and boulder, dark depths of a ravine plunging into the very bowels of the mountain around and beyond that point. A likely place for an eagle's nest perhaps, but not another living thing do I think of or see as a possible inhabitant.

"What is it?" I whisper to Cholaca and Kithaymi, the two Apaches by my side. They point excitedly at the promontory ahead, and still I see nothing. Then Popcorn joins in and whispers "Patchie house" and, waving his hand in small spirals from the ground upwards, indicates "smoke."

Sure enough—my glasses detect what was beyond my eyes—not one, but several shimmering, colorless columns of heat and vapor rising just over the rocks to our front. It is the rancheria beyond doubt. Now for the attack. Sergeant Winser, with Charlie and half the scouts, and Corporal Garner,[10] with ten of the men, are ordered to make their way through rock and tree over to the right so as to attack from the south and, if possible, get around the Indian stronghold to the east. We give them ten minutes to creep into their position, then Sergeant Stauffer and I, with the rest of the men and Indian scouts, spreading well out right and left, creeping from tree to tree, move across the swale to our front and commence the ascent of the western face of the promontory itself. I motion to the men to hold their breath and take it easy, but it is no use. Every blessed one of them wants to be first on top, and so, not to be behind my men, I perforce have to plunge ahead, panting like a broken, winded horse. We are almost on top when from the right comes a double bang, bang, a yell and a cheer, then a scattering volley, and with eager haste we tear up the rocks and find ourselves square in the midst of the rancheria. What followed no man probably could give an exact account of. A few seconds of hot, blasting, exciting work, rapid shots and shouts, a rush of terrified squaws, a whiz of two or three wildly aimed arrows, a dash through the huts, and a firing chase into the ravine beyond in which we were soon left hopelessly behind, shots of pursuers and pursued gradually dying away, and one by one we returned to the rancheria, blown but victorious.

Of the fight itself, lasting only a minute, I have but one vivid recollection—as we sprang in over the rocks, and our leader, some yards in advance, was making for a group of Indians scurrying for their arms, he stopped one brief second at sight of a Tonto form that rose suddenly in his path. The uplifted hands and imploring gaze, the uncovered breast, showed her to be a squaw, and, lowering his carbine, he ran on. Another second and he felt a sharp scratch under his left arm, and a vengeful arrow had pierced his hunting shirt between his arm and side. She had aimed to take the life that would have spared hers.

We burned the huts with all their store of provisions, carried away what we could of their supply of skins and furs, and, leaving to them the duty of burying the dead they had left behind, rejoined that night our guard and horses in the canyon below.

Apache fighting has little or nothing to recommend it.

———

Milwaukee *Sentinel,* March 17, 1880

General Crook was completing in 1874 the task of subjugating a hitherto intractable tribe, and no man ever commanded in Arizona who better knew the Apaches, treated them better when they would behave, or thrashed them better when they wouldn't. All his predecessors had found their methods too slow for so nimble an enemy. Precipitous mountains, jagged and impassable canyons, and scorching deserts all aided the Indians and hampered the troops. Finally the government selected Crook, despite the fact that he was then only a lieutenant colonel, and gave him command of that dismal department on his brevet rank of general, sent him a regiment of cavalry to replace one that had some years of unlucky experience in the territory, and the general himself took the field and practically taught the new troopers how to tackle mountain Indians. He had learned the trick years before the War of the Rebellion. Tribe after tribe and band after band did he whip into submission; finally, in 1874, they were nearly all gathered into great reservations and there remained out in the mountains of northeastern Arizona only a few scattered parties, prominent among them being the adherents of two bull-headed chiefs known as Eskiminzin and Eskeltelsee. These hostiles were nearly all of the Tonto and Sierra Blanca tribes.

All the spring and summer of 1874 the general had scouting parties of cavalry, each with its complement of Indian allies for trailers and its little train of pack mules, hunting through the mountains for these recalcitrants, and the orders were, when we found them, to fight it out then and there. The two northeasternmost stations of the troops were at that time Camp Verde, some fifty miles, by road, east of Prescott, and Camp Apache, down among the foothills of the Mogollon range of mountains, and it was from these points that the detachments sallied forth on their raids. They also served as guards for the great Verde and San Carlos reservations where thousands of the once fierce and untamable Apaches were now living in apparent peace and contentment. The older officers remained in garrison with the infantry and the youngsters were kept at the tireless work.

I was then first lieutenant of K Troop of the 5th Cavalry and stationed at Verde. We had had some lively fights with the Apaches along the Black Mesa and down in the Tonto Basin in May and June, and then came a summer's rest during which we hardly had a scout. Early in the autumn, however, it was demonstrated that the renegades, reinforced by some others, were again showing in the mountains to the southeast of us, and once more the cavalry were called on to find and fight them.

I had been making a survey of the military reservation of Camp Verde and was busy with my maps one warm October afternoon, when some herders came riding into the post and reported to the commanding officer that a war party of Apaches had swooped down from the Red Rock country northeast of us two days before and had run off with a lot of their cattle. They had trailed them, supposing at first the cattle had merely stampeded and strayed; but Tonto moccasin prints soon told the story, and they came back to give the alarm and beg that their beef might be recaptured. The marauders had a big start, of course, but could not go very fast. They had taken a course indicating that they were making for the neighborhood of Snow Lake, over toward the Colorado Chiquito, and in half an hour I was in the saddle and galloping up the Verde valley to the Indian reservation twenty miles away. My orders were to find my comrade, Lieutenant Schuyler, who was there in command, get fifteen or twenty Indian scouts, and return to the post as soon as possible. Meanwhile, Colonel Mason[11] and Lieutenant Eaton[12] would organize a party to be ready to start at daybreak on the morrow.

Unluckily, the scouts I wanted were gone—and instead of the Apache-Mohaves, who had been my trailers earlier in the season, and good ones, too—Schuyler had nothing to offer but some Apache-Yumas whom I did not know and whom he could not especially recommend. Even they were out hunting somewhere, but he could have them sent for, armed and equipped, and hurried down to the garrison that evening. We turned about, therefore, my horse and I, and trotted back to the post, arriving there soon after sunset with appetites for supper, you may be sure, after our forty-mile jaunt.

Meantime twenty men from A and K troops had been selected, and with Lieutenant Eaton for second in command, old Harry Hawes for pack master, and the Apache-Yumas for scouts and trailers, I was ordered to start at dawn and recapture the cattle and "larrup" the cattle thieves. Late that night, while Eaton and I were writing our home letters (sometimes our officers and men never wrote again after these affairs), we heard a clatter of hoofs coming up the hill behind our adobe quarters, and the Apache-Yumas arrived. They were given something to eat and a place to camp for the night, and then we too turned in for a snooze.

At 3:30 A.M. we were up again, dressed in our rough and serviceable mountain rig, and at 5:00 A.M.—just as the trumpets were sounding first call for reveille—we filed out from the corrals, fording the Verde River, and rode swiftly away northeastward. My purpose was to go on as far as Arnold's ranch, bivouac there until dusk, then begin the ascent of the mountains, when the sharpest-eyed lookouts of the Indians could not see us. Of course all the reservations knew by this time that a party was going out, and before nightfall Eaton and I were convinced that our scouts were most reluctant to go with us.

Winding up the valley of Beaver Creek in the early morning, we had reached the ranch at 8:00 A.M. and unsaddled in the grove at the edge of the stream. Here we hid all day long while Eaton and I had a talk with Wales Arnold, the owner, about the trail over the mountains. There was a fair road but a very roundabout one, leaving the valley some miles to the north and making a wide circuit, sweeping around east of us to Stoneman's Lake[13] some forty miles away. It was my plan to make night marches and take the shortcut over the range, feeling confident that we would strike the trail of the captured cattle before we reached the lake, and that once across the range we could soon overtake them. Couriers from Fort Wingate had occasionally taken this shortcut, said Mr. Arnold, and though our Apache-Yumas shook their heads and declared they never heard of it, we had with us a trooper who had ridden across within the last three months and who thought he could follow it by night as well as by day.

Just at dusk we saddled, mounted and, with a "good luck to you" from Arnold and his ranch people, away we went. There was no moon and, though a crisp, starlit night, it was very dark when we began our climb up the rocky sides of the first canyon and the ascent of the range. Riding in Arizona, for mountain-scouting purposes, differed from any riding I had ever done before or have done since, in that it was mostly walking.

The mountains are so precipitous that one has to dismount and lead or follow his horse. The whole command moves in single file with the Apache scouts generally in front, then the commanding officers, then the troopers, and finally the pack train. This march of ours, the night of October 28, was no exception to the rule. Hour after hour we slipped, slid, tugged, and climbed over loose, flinty rocks and jagged stones, up, up, up, twisting, turning, panting, and towing our unlucky steeds by the bridle rein and at last, about 10:00 P.M., found ourselves on the crest of the westernmost spur of the range, and one after another of the men silently clambered to the point; the pack mules followed the tinkling bell of their lead horse, and finally the whole command was grouped along the little mesa under the cloudless and starry heavens—all but the scouts. Long before, they had begun to murmur and protest. "Soldiers go too fast"—a preposterous statement, as we could hardly make two miles an hour. One after another they had slipped back to the rear of the column and when, presently, they came wearily dragging up the cliff and silently grouped themselves at the brink, it was noticed that their "sergeant" was not there to answer questions. He had "gone home," one of them explained. Two others were "heap sick" and could go no farther. More than ever it was evident that for some reason they were mortally afraid to go with this detachment. Never before had I encountered any shirks or cowards among our scouts when we knew the hostile Apaches were all around us. What then could account for the utter weakening of these fellows?

An hour later a partial reason was manifest. Turning a high, rocky spur we came upon a point from which we could see the skyline to the northern horizon; and there, perhaps twenty miles away at the eastern edge of the Indian reservation, glowed against a rocky wall that hid it from all eyes in the valley, a huge signal fire throwing its glare far across the Red Rock country and the pine-covered crests of the Black Mesa[14] beyond.

Later still that night, slipping and sliding down the jagged sides of a dark canyon, Indians again hopelessly behind, we reached a sheltered spot where there was water and grass for our stock, and here we rolled ourselves in our blankets and slept till dawn, and then had a good look about us. Nine of our "scouts" had managed to crawl in, the rest are gone.

Here we breakfasted, inspected our horses' feet, and found that, although every horse and mule had been carefully attended to by the blacksmiths and farriers before we started, four had cast shoes in the scramble up and down the rocks and twenty or more had loosened theirs.

The next night, crossing in its course three deep and rock-ribbed canyons, we struggled along. Three times the Indians were ordered up to the front, but each time they managed to slip back in the darkness. "Tonto" signs had been discovered soon before sunset. Fresh signal fires blazed against the northern sky, and these poor devils were evidently convinced that we were tramping straight into the jaws of destruction. I say "tramping" advisedly, because not until late at night did we mount at all. It was all climb or scramble, but about 10:00 P.M. Sergeant Taylor and Trooper Frank Biffar,[15] who were foremost "feeling the way," halted, and when I joined them, pointed to what appeared to be a broad, dark patch against the low eastern sky, and said: "There are the woods, sir, we must be nearing the road." At midnight we found the trail of the cattle; had looked upon the stardecked surface of Stoneman's Lake; had lost our scouts entirely and half the shoes in the command.

When we left Verde our comrades were wearing light summer clothing all day long and no fires were [permitted] except for cooking purposes. Here we had climbed so high that the water froze solid in our canteens. At 8:30 A.M. seven of our hapless scouts came limping into the bivouac. All heap sick, yet able to eat like hounds. We pointed out the cattle tracks, told them they could rest and sleep until 4:00 P.M., then we would push ahead through the woods until we reached their eastern verge and wait until dark before riding out across the open mesa. If they could keep us, well and good, if they couldn't, they might go to the devil. They were only in the way anyhow.

Through a thick and beautiful growth of pine and cedar we tipped briskly along late that afternoon, noting silently the occasional hoofprints and cattle signs, reached a high transverse ridge at sunset, waited awhile for our valuable allies and, finding that one of them had really cut his foot on a piece of flint, yielded to his importunities and tumbled him up on a spare mule. He thought he was going back home but found to his disgust that he had to come along, and late that night, as we were getting down towards Snow Lake, he fell into a doze, his mule started at something by the trail side and tumbled him off on his head, cutting a big gash and otherwise delaying proceedings half an hour or so while Eaton patched him up. The next day, October 31, we were close at the heels of our quarry and still keeping under cover. We wanted not only to get the cattle, but to include the Apaches.

Late that afternoon, just as the sun began to throw long shadows across the hollows in the mesa, we peered over the crest of a low range, and there, two miles in front and just entering a defile known as Jarvis's Pass,[16] we caught sight of our missing steers. Two or three men and the Indian scouts were left with Harry Hawes to look after the pack train; the rest of us reset our saddles, took an extra loop on the cinches, looked to the breech blocks of our carbines and the chambers of the revolvers. (Officers and men went armed, dressed, and equipped alike in Arizona. We had no more use for swords than we had for shoulder knobs.) Then "mount" was the word and, moving slowly and cautiously at first, we rode to the crest, formed line, and then—there was no help for it since the country was an open undulating surface destitute of shelter for over two miles—struck into a rapid trot; next, as we reached the level below, without a word of command, bugle call, or any of the stirring accompaniments of other warfare, the riders simply conforming to the gait of their leader, away we went at the gallop. Ours were the short, coupled-stock California horses, not very fast but very useful for mountain climbing; it seemed to me an unconscionable time before we were half across the plain, and then the men began to open out a little so as to surround the cattle as we neared them and at the same time be less bunched, in case the Apaches were lurking in ambuscade in the rocks beyond. Eagerly as I looked, not a hostile Indian could I see, nor, indeed, did I expect to see until we hustled them out of their holes. Alarmed by the thunder of advancing hoofs and the irrepressible cheering of some of the men, the cattle were beginning to trot wildly about with tails and heads alike in air, but all sight of their captors was denied us. As we rode around the herd, some north, some south of, and some, in their eager-ness, through them, we closed in a trifle, confidently expecting to be greeted by shots from the rocky entrance to the pass. Even at the gallop quick eyes could detect the print of Tonto moccasins in the soft earth of the roadway, but not a shot nor a sound was there. Warned by the signal fires, they had kept sharp lookout to the crest, and so soon as our coming was detected, they had scattered for the nearest height, shrewdly arguing that so long as we had got the cattle we could afford to let the captors go.

But that wasn't General Crook's idea of dealing with these renegades. As soon as it was dusk, leaving four men and the used-up Indian to drive the herd back by slow and easy stages to the valley, we pushed ahead that night through Jarvis's Pass, forcing our few Apache-Yumas to keep alongside, and at 1:00 A.M. we found ourselves in the heart of the "Sunset Pass" only eighteen miles from the Colorado Chiquito. Here in the wild haunts of the mountains was the likeliest place for the renegades to rest, believing themselves safe from further pursuit, and here we hid in a deep canyon until dawn; and here again our scouts protested, "No Tonto! No Tonto! No Injun," until we showed them the prints of the moccasins under their very noses—and here, on Sunday the first of November, climbing the high mountain to the south, we caught the scamps and carried out the orders. One squad of allies turned tail and ran at the very first fire, and, sure enough, their views were justified; the hostiles were many, and the fight was lively for a while. I wrote no letters for many a week thereafter, nor fired another shot from the right shoulder from that day to this, but there was no more cattle thieving in the upper Verde.[17]

A String for the Bow

GEORGE O. EATON (EDITED BY DON RUSSELL)

Winners of the West 15, no. 8 (September 1938): 1, 3

Editor's [Russell's] Note:

The following manuscript was written by George Oscar Eaton some months before his death September 12, 1930, at Fort Myers, Florida, at the age of eighty-two. Eaton served in the Fifteenth Maine Infantry in the closing year of the Civil War, was appointed to West Point by James G. Blaine, and was graduated in the class of 1873. He was assigned to the Fifth Cavalry, and shortly after his arrival in Arizona, took part in an engagement at Sunset Pass (November 1, 1874), wherein his able handling of a detachment, and the heroic conduct of a sergeant, resulted in the rescue of the seriously wounded commander of the expedition, Lieutenant Charles King, later a widely known novelist. An expedition in the same region November 17 to December 5, led by the young officer, is known as Eaton's scout. It was shortly after this that the incident described in the manuscript took place.

In March 1875 Eaton was given the difficult assignment of moving the Mojaves, Yumas, and Tontos from Camp Verde to the San Carlos reservation—with a fight between the tribes as a complication on the way. At the beginning of the 1876 campaign Eaton was accidently shot during a stampede of the regiment's herds and shortly afterward retired from the army, achieving considerable note as a civil engineer. He was the original of "Jack Truscott" in *The Colonel's Daughter* and other stories by General Charles King.

In the first paragraph "you" refers to General King, to whom the original manuscript was addressed.

Not very long after you left Camp Verde to take your Indian-bullet broken arm to northern climes, I sought recreation by a few days' trip to department headquarters at Fort Whipple, Arizona, three miles from Prescott.

Attended by my orderly and mounted on a good horse, I speedily passed over the forty miles. It being late in the afternoon upon my reaching there, I

177

decided not to dismount until I had formally reported my presence to General Crook. As I rode across the parade ground I noticed that everything was very quiet and the only soldier to be seen was a sentry on a distant post. I dismounted and knocked at the general's door.

"I am indeed glad to see you," he said, grasping my hand, "for I am greatly in need of getting a message through to the commanding officer at Camp Beale Springs. A bad Indian outbreak between here and the San Francisco Mountains has called out all the infantry and cavalry from this post, and with the Hualapais at Camp Beale Springs reported restless, it is vital that I get orders to the commanding officer there."

He said he disliked to order me to go as "it would be impossible to get enough men together to furnish me with even a halfway decent escort."

I said, "I'll go, and perhaps I will not need any escort."

He said, "Do you mean to chance it all alone? There is much chance for Indians to pick up a single man."

I said, "Yes, true, but a single man not traveling over usual trails and quietly going through a more or less wooded country might slip through without encountering any Indians."

"Just what have you in mind?" he asked.

I explained, "The locations of the traveled trail between Camp Beale Springs and this point, over which the paymaster comes with heavy escort of soldiers, has long been a source of unspoken query to me. I have been over it and also stood at both ends and gazed across and wondered."

"As you know, General, the trip from here to Camp Beale Springs is a long, wearisome journey of a full day over a comparatively level country. But the trail followed as a whole is in the shape of a gigantic oxbow, with the two ends represented by Camp Beale Springs and Whipple Barracks. From your front window we can look across the open end of the oxbow and see the general location of Camp Beale Springs, and it is surely not more than one-third of the distance across to it than it is around the traveled trail. Now there likely is a reason why the long-distance trail was first used, but I have often wondered if the fates would not permit me the opportunity of attempting to get straight across from one point of the oxbow to the other—and it seems this is my opportunity, with your permission."

"I am of course glad to give it," he said, "and all good luck go with you. As to the country you will pass over, I have no idea, but if it is a rough and almost impassable country, you are not likely to encounter Indians there. I am glad indeed that you do not propose to go the regular trail, because Indians surely would be lying in wait to pick up any unfortunate settlers who unsuspectingly came along."

At daylight next morning, before any movement in camp, I started with Winchester rifle and a belt full of cartridges, a canteen of water, and a far from fresh horse to brave the uncertainties.

To aid me in pursuing a straight line was the landmark of Cross Mountain, far away to the north, so named because of snow lying in deep ravines on its side taking the form of a cross of white against a dark background.

In ten minutes' time I was traversing a wild but level open glade with scattered trees and no underbrush to impede the horse's fast walk.

Things were going well for perhaps a half hour when in front of and to right angles of my course appeared a very black streak of ground seemingly hardly three or a few more inches high. That I knew by Arizona experience was the very top line of a dreaded box canyon. This section of Arizona is covered by a sheet of lava perhaps three hundred feet deep. In the ages that have passed since this lava cooled, earthquakes had split this sheet like glass from top to bottom here and there (mostly here), leaving the vertically torn apart sides fifty to one hundred feet across at the top. These cracks might extend for miles. Strange to say, these box canyons, as they were called, were mostly parallel with each other, so that if one was laboriously crossed, a few yards' further progress might bring the traveler to a place where he could gaze at the distant bottom of a duplicate to that just painfully negotiated.

There was no way to get across the first box canyon I met save to lead my horse either up or down the ridge in search of some place, perhaps a mile or so out of my way, where the side wall had for some reason partly broken down, at least sufficiently so to enable me to lead my horse down to the bottom without damage to him or myself. Once in the bottom, I must follow along in similar fashion to find a place where I could scramble out.

This I did and only lost about two miles, but I had hardly resumed my general direction when I met another box canyon. This part of my journey is covered by saying I had to cross a regular series of such canyons, all of which used up hours of time and lots of physical and mental energy. But after a while I felt I was safely through that formation, and I tried to think that with distant Cross Mountain still showing white in the midday sun, that while I had surely found the answer to my problem of why the trail went around instead of across the oxbow, yet at least I had not been molested in my investigation.

But just then a serious discovery was made. The forenoon's hot sun poured down through the scattered trees upon us, and there was not a breath of air stirring. My horse and then myself were a reek of perspiration, and we both suffered for lack of water. My canteen had become very hot but the water was wet—while it lasted. From time to time I took a small mouthful from the canteen, moistened the inside of my mouth, and then spirited it directly into the nostrils of my horse. He shied from it at first, but soon got so he did not flinch in the least, and it kept the dust out of his nostrils, which had begun to dry when perspiration ceased.

We were in a bad way from thirst but had reached a more level country, although the trees were very few now, and here and there small, isolated, and ragged buttes stuck up. There would be several of these buttes in sight at one time, perhaps a quarter mile or more away in front of me. Of course it was a part of my business to scan them very closely to see if any Indians might be lurking about them.

All at once I saw, or thought I saw, one of these sizable buttes distant a half mile or more actually move toward me. I said to myself, "You are a sane man, and you know perfectly well that it is your thirst that plays this illusion upon you, and if you will summon all your will power and command that butte to be fixed in the ground where it belongs, it will obey you."

Thus my intelligence spoke, but when I summoned all my resolution and commanded that butte to "stand still," I did not have the luck that Joshua had with the sun, for the butte continued to come on, although fortunately it never reached me. All the buttes in sight by this time were moving toward me in like manner. I did not yield my mind to the illusion for a moment and believe that the buttes did move, but I could not make my vision see them otherwise than as moving.

By this time I was leading my horse, but I did not stop and continued to keep Cross Mountain in view, determined to keep on as long as could be. And so, without hardly knowing it, we passed out of the region of those buttes and into an area where the trees grew more thickly. Then, right on the edge of the new ground, we found water!

A little spring welled up, and a small rivulet led its water away, and around it were plenty of signs that animals of many sorts resorted here for water. It was difficult to control either my horse or myself, but I did have resolution enough to take the water very slowly and if possible get perspiration started over our bodies before becoming gluttons. I did not like to take chances, but I did loosen the saddle girth, which several times I had tightened, to give the horse the best breathing possible, for it was necessary after a moderate rest and safely filling up with water. But it was astonishing to see how the water rejuvenated us. We actually moved away in midafternoon with some evidence of strength and spirit.

I estimated that, if we could go in a straight line from this point to our destination, I would not have more than twelve or eighteen miles to go, and I hoped to get over that distance without trouble, although I was now nearing the old reservation of the Hualapais, and almost anything might happen, for even General Crook did not know anything, save that they had become restless because of other sub-tribes of Apaches being off their reservations.

There could be no secrecy about my movements. It was a clear case of assuming that the Indians hunting trouble just were not there. And if they were off the reservation, obviously they were not on it, and there was little prospect of accomplishing killing or torture in its vicinity to tempt them to linger about. The only thing I had to fear was a chance encounter with a straying band of independent Indians, and that is just what I did run into.

I was pushing along at quite a fast walk, mounted this time, when, as I was passing through a bit of low ground with a rising slope on my right, suddenly there appeared on its crest and leisurely coming toward me five Indians. Seeing me clearly was a great surprise to them. They had no squaws with them, which looked bad for me, as it might be a war party. They also had lots of paint on, but they seemed uncertain and somehow gave the idea they were footsore. They were about three hundred yards away when I first saw them, and I motioned them with my hand to stop, and they did for the moment, but I did not stop and kept quietly urging my horse along to try to get beyond the point where they would cut me off if they continued in their present direction. I would have been glad to get away without any closer knowledge of them, and if they really were footsore I felt that my horse could outrun them into Camp Beale Springs.

But suddenly, as I was quietly moving my horse along and thinking over these things, one of the Indians, without any previous indication, stepped out from his companions and took a quick shot at me, the bullet striking the ground near my horse. I already had my Winchester lying in the hollow of my left arm, and almost as quick as he fired, I pumped two shots, not at any single Indian but at the group of them as they stood in consultation, and they being on my right, I had to twist in my saddle to get in the shots I did.

Evidently one of my shots at least struck something, for instantly they were dragging one at least apart, and in a moment each Indian was covered by a tree. It was a most remarkable thing why they did not, like any other Indians I ever saw, at once seek cover and begin shooting at me. My horse was perfectly gun shy and stood like a rock while I fired my two shots, but immediately after firing I was not interested in anything more there, and before the Indians could think or do very much shooting or anything else, I had started up my good horse for a race from there to Camp Beale Springs if they wanted it.

But I never saw any of them again, and just about sundown I rode into Camp Beale Springs, inquired for the commanding officer, saluted, and said I had a packet that was directed to him, for which at his leisure I would be glad to get his receipt. His response was, "Where on earth did you come from; how did you get through, and where is your escort?"

Report on [the] Coyotero Apaches

L. Y. LORING[1]

Hubert H. Bancroft Collection, Bancroft Library
University of California, Berkeley

The Indians who are now encamped in the immediate vicinity of this post, being settled around it within hearing distance, are what are called the Coyotero Apaches, or more commonly the White Mountain Apaches.[2] They are each divided into about fifteen sub-tribes, or bands, each numbering on an average 110; the tribe, numbering in the aggregate, according to the official count, which takes place every month, 1,650 souls. These sub-bands are variously named. Each of these bands has a chief who occupies his position by reason of hereditary right or election on account of intelligence, decision of character, bravery, or other characteristic.

The hereditary grand chief, Esh-kel-dah-silah,[3] has retired, and Palone,[4] the present head chief, has been appointed by General Crook, and the appointment recognized and confirmed by all the Indians. Palone's character will be discussed further on.

The physique of these Indians to a casual observer does not appear at all to be a striking or unusual one, either as regards size or development; but on a close inspection it will be seen that they are compactly built and are generally well muscled and sinewy. The average height of the men, afforded by about twenty measurements taken at random, is five feet eight inches. The chest measurement of the same men averages in expiration about thirty-four and one-half inches, and in inspiration thirty-six and four-fifths inches; the greatest measurement being that of a man five feet eleven inches in height, whose measurement in expiration forty-four inches, the least being a man of five feet two inches, who measured in expiration thirty-two and in inspiration thirty-three and one-half inches. The lung power was observed to be great, the expansion above indicated not being a good test, as it was difficult to make them comprehend what was required. Their chests are generally deep and square, the sternum and clavicle standing forward prominently and well up, indicating great chest capacity.

The hands and feet of both men and women are remarkably small and delicately formed; the ankles and wrists particularly so. Limbs generally straight and slender rather than bulky; joints small and compact, the apophyses of long bones small and not prominent. Muscles not bulky nor prominent, but hard and firm and well developed, particularly in lower extremities. The women are more heavy muscled than the men, owing to the constant drudgery which they undergo in carrying wood, water, and burdens of all sort. They carry readily two and three hundred pounds upon their backs. The men are generally thin and spare, while the women tend to corpulency, which effect is heightened by a much shorter stature. Their eyes are nearly always black or brown, but few of them being of any other color; they are generally large and bright, are set wide apart, and so situated that a straight, horizontal line would serve for the axis of both balls; they are mild in repose, but during excitement become sparkling and animated.

Eyelashes and eyebrows are generally of delicate growth. Their hair is without exception black and generally coarse and straight and of very heavy growth. Men and women generally wear their hair reaching to [their] shoulders and parted in the middle. A widow wears it banged; a very young woman on the death of her husband cuts her hair short all around. Maidens wear it done up in a knot at the back of the head, ornamented with a piece of flannel or buckskin of an hourglass shape, on which are fastened many glittering brass buttons. The hair of children and old women is generally unkempt and matted and in most cases is the habitat of vermin.

Baldness is never seen among them. Even old men and women whose hair is white are supplied with a thick, heavy growth. Men are usually beardless; any hairs making their appearance on the face are plucked out. To destroy vermin and to render their hair glossy and smooth they sometimes plaster their scalps with a peculiar bluish mud, letting it remain for many days. After washing this off the hair presents a brilliant, glossy black color. They also wash the hair with a solution of the root of a species of plant commonly called soapweed. This makes a fine lather and has peculiar cleansing qualities.

Foreheads are broad at base but become peaked at tops; they are generally low and frequently retreating.

The nose is straight and inclined to be flat. Some cases of Roman noses are observed among the men. Cartileges of ala and septum are thick; nostrils wide and dilated, and but rarely visible. The floor of the nasal cavity dips like that of the Negro and is not on a level with that of the anterior margin like that of the white man. It is said that the first thing that is done after the birth of the child is for the mother to punch up its nose, while at the same time the thumb is pressed upwards against the hard palate to make the vomer and septum project. It may be well to remark here that in their waking or sleeping hours, during active exercise or while at rest, they breathe altogether through their nostrils, thus protecting their teeth from extremes of heat and cold and also from the action of gases generated in the stomach, and guarding the lungs against sudden drafts of cold air, which in too many instances act in an injurious manner upon those who breathe through the mouth. The nose, being the

natural respiratory apparatus, is admirably adapted for its purpose, being provided with small hairs to prevent the ingress of foreign matter and containing
a tortuous canal with projecting bones which afford an immense heating surface for the air of respiration.

The mouth is large and wide, with thick, heavy, projecting, expressionless
lips. It is straight from side to side. Many of them have mouths very similar to
Negroes.

The chin is small, oftentimes peaked and receding.

The ears [are] small and set close to the head. The cheek bones are similar to those of other Indians, being high and prominent, which in connection
with the peaked forehead and chin gives the face an oval shape from above
downwards. The facial angle is smaller than that of the white man.

The skull in the occipital region is flattened and prolonged upwards, making the vertex very prominent and conical. This condition is caused by fasten-
ing the child on its back. As the cranial bones are at this time pliable from
incomplete ossification, the constant pressure from before backwards causes
this elongation. This peculiarity is so marked in some cases as to be almost a
deformity.

The teeth generally are well preserved, which is partly owing, it is
believed, as before remarked, to the fact that respiration does not take place
through the mouth; it may also be attributed to the simple nature of their food
and consequent few disorders from indigestion. Very old men may be seen
with their teeth worn to the gums but yet not carious. Children get their decid-
uous and permanent teeth in about the same time and order as those of the
white race.

Tattooing is not resorted to by them. They paint the face in various colors,
vermilion or some shade of red being the favorite color. They also use bilum-
bago, which gives a metallic black color. White is made from gypsum, yellow
ocher and indigo. As they obtain their paint now from the white man for the
most part, they generally present a variegated appearance when painted, it
being almost impossible to designate the prevailing styles.

A common style is a red background with a horizontal stripe of another
color. Across the nose, cheeks, or forehead sometimes spots or round patches
take the place of the stripes. Sometimes the stripes are perpendicular or diago-
nal. A marriageable widow will have a series of horizontal rows of scroll work
of one color and a background of another color. A man wooing her will color
himself in the same manner, thus making public his intentions. It is entirely
optional with a maiden in regard to her style of painting, but it is generally
understood that she must not paint like a widow. It is observed that the prettier a
maiden is, the more elaborate will she be painted, well knowing that her beauty
will justify the unusual amount of attention and admiration thus attracted to her.

The passion for painting is almost universal among them, developing at a
very early age in both sexes. Mothers paint their infants; children with their
first dawning intelligence daub their faces with any coloring matter that they

can find. Their bodies are never painted. Dark paint is used for mourning and by warriors going on the warpath. The paint is generally moistened with water or saliva and applied with the fingers. The women usually carry small round mirrors, like the cheap shaving glasses sold in the shops, suspended by a necklace, for the purpose of applying the paint properly.

The physiognomy of these people in repose is very mild and as pleasant as their coarse features will admit of; but during excitement it lights up, and every feature, particularly the eyes, betoken deviltry and bloodthirstiness. This ferocity of countenance has been observed by the writer even during the excitement attendant on witnessing a dance by a masked figure.

These Indians at present, with few exceptions, seem to be docile, but it is not known how long they will remain so. It is the prevalent opinion here that it is only the awe inspired by the presence of a large military force which causes them to be tractable, and that were the military removed, they would immediately resume their well-known hostility to the whites. It is only about two years ago since they were compelled to come upon the reservation and remain peaceable.

Their morality as regards truth and honesty is found to be high. A liar is condemned and tabooed among them. Debts are scrupulously paid, both among themselves and when dealing with the whites. Still, it must be said that many of them will steal when opportunity offers, and numerous instances are known of thefts perpetrated by them at this post.

It is thought that their intelligence is above the average Indians, especially so where their advantages are taken into consideration. This is to a certain extent shown by their language, which is carried on almost entirely by articulate words, signs seldom or rarely used.

They are, like most uncivilized people, cunning to a great degree, and examples might be quoted to illustrate. Some of them understand Spanish; there are but few of them who understand much English, and that to a very limited extent.

They have always been a warlike people, having the Navajos, Sonorans, and others as their natural hereditary enemies. The booty obtained in making raids upon their enemies constitutes their main subsistence. Until very recently they have, with few exceptions, been hostile to the government.

Their ability to endure the vicissitudes of heat and cold is wonderful: they have been known to march on foot all day, bareheaded in a scorching sun, without food or water, as far as forty or sixty miles. They have also been known to travel on foot the distance between this place and the Zuni villages in two days, the distance of 120 miles. The writer has seen them during the present winter exposed to a temperature below the freezing point, having on nothing but a breechclout and thin covering of calico. Children especially have been seen stark naked in a temperature below freezing point. Young boys up to the age of fifteen are rarely seen, even during the winter, with any other clothing than a breechclout.

Their sight is keen and remarkable, which may be accounted for by a constant usage to an outdoor atmosphere and the dark color of the iris, which prevents dazzling by excluding a too fine entrance of the sunrays to the retina.

These people are nomadic insofar as their chosen limit of country will permit. They move their "rancherias," or villages, from time to time for various reasons, such as the accumulation of filth or vermin, or from the occurrence of some epidemic disease. They always move on the day succeeding the death of any of their number and burn their deserted residences, this being an invariable practice. They rarely stay in one place more than a few months at a time, and they always select high and dry ground to live upon. It must also be far removed from water of any kind, as they believe that the vapor that arises from the water is unhealthful. They oftentimes live as far as two or three miles from water, the women having to carry all the water that is used that distance.

Their houses, or "wickiups," are built in clusters, without regard to order or rank, those of each sub-band forming a cluster, without which are seen still smaller clusters, which are those of families or near relations. These houses are built entirely by the women and are constructed as follows: a series of poles or sticks are stuck in the ground and arched over, cone shaped, so as to enclose a round space about eight feet in diameter at base and about five feet high; this framework is now covered with bark of cedar, leaves, grass, and sometimes with rawhides. They are not even thatched, but these various articles are thrown up loosely on the framework; a small opening or door is made on the leeward side just sufficiently large to crawl in and out. The opening is not closed, but is provided with one or two wings made of brush and rubbish to protect them from the wind. Within this dwelling, at [the] rear portion, the earth is scooped away something like a buffalo wallow, only on a smaller scale, but sufficiently large to accommodate two persons lying side by side. This scooped out nest, built with straw, leaves, or rawhide, constitutes the bed or sleeping place. The fire is built in the middle of the house, and the smoke escapes by penetrating through the interstices in the roof and wall, giving it the appearance at a distance of a manure pile on fire, or a charcoal kiln in operation.

The atmosphere of these houses, when warmed by a good fire and filled by a good-sized family, has a peculiar, indescribable odor. It is astonishing what a short space of time is required to move out and destroy one village and become established in another. The villages have never heretofore been drained or policed but were deserted from time to time as they became foul, as before stated. At the present time, however, as they are in the immediate vicinity of the post, they are required to be kept clean and are frequently inspected by the commanding officer of Camp Apache. It is ludicrous to see the women run out and begin to sweep and police around their houses in the most assiduous manner at the approach of an inspecting party, ceasing immediately to do so when the party has passed and laughing and joking at the ruse they adopted.

Personal cleanliness, to judge by their appearance, is a lost art among them, although it is observed that they do wash themselves in the stream and sometimes clean their hair when they become overrun with vermin. Yet the generally tangled condition of their hair, especially among women and children, the collection of filth on their faces, hands, and bodies, and the soiled condition of their apparel gives to them a most repulsive appearance. The women have been frequently observed on count days, when sitting down in a row, policing each other's and their children's heads and, what is almost inconceivable, eating the vermin as they found them. Destroying vermin on each other's persons seems to be a friendly courtesy among them and oftentimes a pastime.

Hostile movements are generally conducted on foot, the marching being done in daytime, as they fear to travel at night, having superstitions about the appearance of witches or spirits of the dead in the dark.

Some of the chiefs have horses, but these, as a general thing, are so weak and puny from bad treatment and overriding that they cannot be relied upon. They fight in an ambuscade and under cover generally, but it is said that when contending with the Navajos or Mexicans, they meet them in open fight, as they do not fear them. When they have been successful in capturing much stock or booty, they are then fearless and march day or night. Ordinarily, in moving about at nightfall they carry torches made of cedar bark tied together with strings. In fighting an open battle they charge with their lances, yelling as they run. After the first charge they secret themselves and fight. They are said to be very brave by officers who have commanded them in making war upon renegades and roving bands. Horses captured by them are generally eaten.

Their war weapons are bows and arrows and long lances tipped with metal; the arrows are tipped with metal or flint. The handle or shank of the lance is made of the inner, woody part of the cactus. Another weapon used in domestic fights is made by enclosing a stone about three inches in diameter in the hide of a bull's tail, and then inserting a strong stick for a handle.

The treatment of prisoners is an exception to the general rule among Indians; in this respect they are not only humane but heroic in their conduct. Instead of a cruel death or torture, the captive is adopted and treated in all respects as a relation of the captor. This fact is verified by the number of captives, both Indian and Mexican, that are now among them. Much of the data of this report were given me by such a captive. This man's name is Miguel. He is a Mexican and was captured by these Indians when about ten years of age. With the exception of a few years when he was employed by the government as interpreter, he has always lived among them and is now chief of one of the sub-tribes. He is at present employed as interpreter at this post. He renders the Apache language in Spanish, which is in turn rendered into English by another interpreter. From the spirited manner and striking gestures which he uses when haranguing the Indians in their native tongue, and from the attention which is paid him, it is surmised that he is quite an eloquent orator. Besides Miguel there are other Mexican captives, including some women, who live permanently among them. Sometimes prisoners are killed in the fights which ensue between the captors in regard to the proprietorship of them. At other times it is necessary for the older and more sensible men to secret captives during the time when a general spree or drunk is indulged in, for in those times the captives would in all probability be sacrificed to the vengeance of somebody who had lost relations in the fight in which he had been taken. They do not scalp but are said to mutilate their victims.

The government of these people is effected by their adherence to the time-honored habits and customs handed down to them by tradition. Measures of public safety, such as declaring or prosecuting a war, providing for the tribe in time of famine [or] drought, conduct and means to be observed in an epidemic disease, punishment of infractions of their customs and of offenders, such as thieves or murderers, are discussed and decided upon by a council of the chiefs and other influential or old men who have friends to sustain them. Sometimes in a threatened war some chief noted for his bravery and prowess is selected as a war leader for the time being and is obeyed and respected by everybody accordingly.

It is not an uncommon thing for offenses of every description, even those of murder, to be condoned or pardoned upon the offender paying the sufferers by the offense, or the relations of the deceased man, a certain number of cattle, horses, or other property, the amount and kind to be settled by the council. After this the offender is admitted to all of his rights, social and otherwise. This principle is carried out also in the case of accidents resulting in the loss of life. Here the party the cause of the accident is expected to make good to the survivors of the deceased his loss. Witness the following striking example which recently occurred at this post:

An officer of the army, while out on a hunting expedition in the vicinity of the post, accidentally shot and killed an Indian with whom he was in friendly converse at the time of the accident. Fortunately there were other Indians present who comprehended the accident and witnessed the conduct of the officer in trying to save the man's life and also in getting the man's body into the post in order to deliver it to the family for burial. It was afterwards decided in a powwow between the chiefs and the post commander that the officer should furnish blankets for the purpose of shrouding the body and should also give a horse to the surviving widow. Notwithstanding the tragic nature of the affair, there were many ludicrous incidents connected with it.

The marriage relations and customs which obtain among these people are those of polygamy; each man has from two to eight wives and in some instances ten. Notwithstanding this, many are content with only one. The plurality of wives in this instance, as in all others, has its twin accompaniment—degradation of the women. The women may literally be said to be the "hewers of wood and drawers of water." This is a life of toil and drudgery, and woe to the woman who refuses to perform her appointed task. The writer has frequently seen a woman with an immense load of wood on her back and perhaps her infant on top of this, trudging alongside of a horse, on which was seated her husband. Again, he has seen a woman chopping down a tree, which apparently required all her strength, while her lord lay quietly by, smoking his cigarette and looking on. At certain times of the day a continuous file of them may be observed going from their village to the brook, carrying on their backs huge water bottles filled with water, while at the same time may be seen the men playing at their games of chance and idling their time.

Marriages are effected by purchase. A man takes a fancy to a young woman and, without consulting her, he makes overtures to the chief of the band, the father, and other relations. The price, which ranges from seven or eight head of cattle or horses, is agreed upon and paid, and the bride is carried off. There is no marriage ceremony performed. The finest animal obtained by the purchase is selected from the number and killed to serve as a feast to the bride's relations; the remainder are divided between the chief and her parents. Should the man treat his wife well, he has the privilege of purchasing her sisters, should she have any.

If a woman is guilty of conjugal infidelity her nose is cut off by her husband, but she is not put aside unless her husband chooses to do so. In fact, it seems to carry no other disgrace, for she generally maintains her position. There are a number of women among these Indians who have suffered this mutilation; it imparts to them a hideous and repulsive appearance which must be seen to be appreciated. This custom has been put a stop to by the military authorities, and an Indian is now in the guardhouse charged with this offense.

If a man on returning home from an absence suspects his wife of having been unfaithful, he may tie her up by the hands, keeping her there until she confesses her guilt and the name of her paramour. The husband avenges himself upon the man and may retain his wife or put her aside, as he chooses. If a man violates his brother's wife, he is killed by hanging, and the offspring, if there be such, is choked or hung. Marriage among blood relations is never practiced. Women, almost without exception, marry at some time or other, a spinster among them being a rare bird. Men also, as a rule, marry, there being but two old bachelors known on the reservation. The small amount of worldly goods required to keep house and the scant amount of food and clothing necessary to support a family may be attributed as the cause of these facts.

A most remarkable custom observed among them is the relation between a man and his mother-in-law. He is never to be looked at or addressed by her; their paths lie entirely apart, and should she see him approaching her by accident, she covers her eyes with a blanket or her hands. Should the wife die, the mother-in-law still keeps up the avoidance of her son-in-law, unless perchance he should marry a woman of a family other than her own. This custom, if common report be true, might be an acceptable one among the whites. A man's father-in-law also avoids him as much as possible and never accepts anything from his hands, but the nonintercourse is not as rigid as in the case of the mother-in-law.

A description of the wearing apparel of these people is an undertaking which it is difficult to do justice to, and it is approached with some hesitation on the part of the writer. Their native costume is so blended with that of the various people with whom they have come in contact that it is of the most nondescript character, rendering it difficult to tell where the one ends and the other begins. The following list embraces many of the articles of dress worn by the men. The covering for the head is sometimes a common hat of straw or felt, or a sombrero; sometimes a band of colored cloth tied across the forehead, leaving the top of the head bare. For the protection of the upper part of the person a blanket is generally worn in the wintertime. Occasionally they wear shirts and even waistcoats and coats. Sometimes pants are worn; at others, cotton or cotton-flannel drawers. There is one article which they cling to with a tenacity worthy a better cause, and that is the breechclout. No matter in how modern and civilized a manner they may otherwise dress, the loose ends of this garment, if so it might be designated, will be found hanging over the waistband of their pants in front and rear. This time-honored article is as religiously clung to as the queue is by the Chinaman. Sometimes, instead of wearing their pants in the orthodox style, they are worn folded together and wound around the waist. At other times they, as well as coats, will be wrongside outwards. A man has been seen with the pants simply buttoned around the waist without having drawn them on, the legs of the pants being allowed to dangle behind. Moccasins made of buckskin having long legs and rawhide soles are worn by men, women, and children. To prevent spoiling these are removed in warm weather and carried on the arms. Many of the men, especially those in the service as soldiers, wear many articles of soldiers' clothing, it seeming to be the height of their ambition to be dressed and to appear like soldiers. As, however, their clothing, like any other property they may possess, is freely sacrificed in their passion for gambling, it is not unusual to see a man one day in full uniform and on the following day bereft of everything excepting the most indispensable articles.

The women wear a short tunic with short or long sleeves and made like an ordinary chemise; the skirts of this may or may not be confined at the waist by the band of a skirt which reaches just below the knees. The blanket is also worn by them in the wintertime. The married women in summertime wear nothing but the skirt from waist to knees; even in wintertime they may be seen with only a piece of unbleached cotton, not more than a yard square, thrown over one shoulder and fastened beneath the arm of the opposite side, leaving the shoulder and that side of the chest bare.

These garments of the women are made of unbleached cotton, cheap prints, or buckskin, all of which they buy from post traders. Occasionally a handsome maiden may be seen with a dress such as worn by white women; it may even have a pannier, flowers, or other fashionable additions.

The unclean, soiled condition of the women's clothing gives to them a repulsive, uncouth appearance. They may be truly said to belong to that large family called the "Great Unwashed."

The men wear but few ornaments, these consisting of necklaces of beads, leather bracelets ornamented with percussion gun caps, parti-colored ribbons on their hats or heads, and possibly a string of beads in ears. Occasionally a man who affects foppishness will wear an immense head covering ornamented with turkey feathers, ribbons, etc. His face will be painted in the highest style of art; he will have, instead of a blanket, a cotton sheet with a bright bandanna handkerchief sewed on the middle of it and be otherwise gaudily attired. This character, like his prototype in a civilized community, is regarded in accordance with his deserts.

The ornaments of women consist of innumerable necklaces of parti-colored beads. It is estimated that the beads which one woman will sometimes have on will weigh one or two pounds. They also wear brass rings and bead ornaments in their ears and leather and bead bracelets; the round shaving mirror fastened to the necklace is almost invariably worn. Old men and women wear no ornaments; children imitate their elders and are seen variously decorated.

The various articles of clothing worn by both men and women are for the most part cut and made by the men. There is truly an inverted order of things, the men sewing and making the clothing, and the women performing all of the out-of-doors work.

Families vary in size, depending upon the number of wives. There is generally an average of two or four children for each wife. Children are rarely born deformed or afflicted, either physically or mentally. In a thirty years' life among them, the interpreter Miguel knows of but two cases of idiocy. Congenital malformations, such as clubfoot, strabismus, harelip, cleft palate, hunchback, or curvature of the spine, are scarcely ever seen. Twins are rare. Children are invariably nourished by their mothers, this being continued in many instances until the child is three or four years old. Children are generally kept tied in the cradles until they are two years of age. They are not allowed to walk before the age of fourteen or sixteen months, as it is deemed injurious.

Their cradles are a flat wooden framework about three feet long and one foot wide, so constructed as to form a handle at either end. At the upper or wider end of this framework is fastened a kind of thatched basket, inverted so as to enclose and protect the child's head. A piece of buckskin is now fastened to the flat surface, intended for the child and padded with straw. The buckskin is so shaped as to have two lateral flaps, which when the child is in position are brought forward and laced in the manner of a shoe across its body as high as the neck, the hands and arms also being enclosed in it. Cedar bark is used to absorb the discharges. The child secured in this way is laid on the ground, stood up against a tree or other object, carried on the mother's back, or hung on the pommel of a saddle.

Infanticide and abortion are common among these people. A mother will kill her infant if she has reason to be jealous of her husband. Illegitimate children are deserted or destroyed by their mothers.

Boys and girls are treated alike in all respects until about the age of ten years, when the boy takes the supremacy. He hunts or plays games, and the girl begins the drudgery.

The food used by these people is both animals and vegetable. The animal food is principally beef, venison, wild turkey, and the flesh of the horse, goat, mule, and jackass; the young of the latter is esteemed as a delicacy. The flesh of many smaller animals is also used, such as the various small birds, the rabbit, rat, squirrel, etc. Fish is never eaten, as it is considered unclean. A reverence which is felt for dogs prevents their flesh from being a staple. Vegetable food consists of the various articles of corn, wheat, seeds of many grasses and flowers, acrons, piñon nuts, fruits of many species of cactus, pumpkins, melons, greens of various kinds, mushrooms, etc. Animal food is generally prepared for eating either by boiling or roasting; the latter process is generally accomplished by placing the meal in the fire or holding it over the fire fastened to a stick. Animal food such as beef and venison is preserved by cutting it in strips and exposing it to the atmosphere for the purpose of drying and curing. The various cereals and seeds are usually prepared by roasting and then grinding with a matate, which is a stone hollowed out, into which the grain is poured and then ground with another rounded stone on the principle of the mortar and pestle. These articles, when reduced to a powder, are made into cakes and baked; the seeds of the sunflower prepared in this way constitute a staple article of food. Corn is seldom used for food at present, but is preserved for the purpose of making the national drink, "tiswin." Its place of food is supplied by the flour which is issued by the government. The fruits of the various cacti are eaten when fresh or cut into slices, dried, and stored away. Pumpkins or other vegetables are boiled or roasted.

The cooking, as observed above, is of the most primitive kind, consisting principally of boiling and roasting. The vessels used are simple earthenware pots of their own manufacture and shaped like the Mexican olla. But little fire is used. The cooking is accomplished generally "en famille," the process being watched with eager interest by the several members. Condiments, except a small quantity of salt, are not used. Pepper, vinegar, and mustard are abhorred by them. All the work incident to the preparation of food is done by the women, the men only hunting and obtaining the game.

The soil is cultivated to a slight extent, and their method of cultivation is of the simplest description. Planting is accomplished by making small holes in the ground with a sharp stick; the seed is deposited in these and covered up. Irrigation is understood and practiced by them. As they keep no record of time, their season of planting is governed by the growth of certain weeds or wild plants; for instance, corn is planted, irrespective of weather, when a certain wild plant has attained the height of about three inches. It is observed that they now cultivate more land than formerly, when they were not under government subjection.

Notwithstanding their nomadic, purposeless mode of existence, it is observed that they are provident to a remarkable degree. Their various articles of food intended for winter supply are packed in wickerwork crates or vessels lined with gypsum to protect from animals and cached or hidden in the crevices of rocks or canyons. They have been known to cache a two-year supply of grain. These stores are removed only in small quantities, as required for use. Corn is stored away in large quantities, subject to the demand for alcoholic stimulant, a demand caused by the universal craving on the part of mankind.

The stimulant tiswin, as it is called by these people, is made as follows: a quantity of selected and well-cured corn is placed in a hole in the ground lined with straw. The corn, having been covered with another layer of straw, is now kept wet with warm water for several days until sprouting has taken place; this requires about four days in summer and six in winter. After the process of sprouting has commenced, it is removed from the hole and spread out on the ground to dry. When perfectly dry it is ground up with the matate, and the resulting powder mixed with water to the thickness of gruel. This is now taken and boiled over a slow fire, constantly replacing the evaporated water by a fresh supply, for twelve hours. It is then strained into ollas and allowed to stand until fermentation takes place, which requires about ten hours. The tiswin thus prepared resembles in color and consistency baker's yeast. It contains about one percent of alcohol, will appear rather weak for intoxicating purposes, and so is found to be in practice. The party preparing it sends out two days in advance of the entertainment and invites his friends; this timely notice is the signal to begin to fast, in order to place the system in a condition susceptible to the influence of alcohol. The party having assembled, the drinking begins. There are four or five large vessels containing the fluid, and the company sit about in groups. There are but few women present, as they are generally excluded from these entertainments. One of the party takes a cup and, going around, drinks off a cupful taken from each of the vessels in quick succession. Drinking in this manner nearly a quart at once, he is succeeded by another, and so on. This is continued until the party becomes drunk. The amount usually required to cause intoxication is about six quarts.

To indulge in a tiswin drunk an Indian will part with everything he may possess. An intoxicating drink is sometimes prepared by fermenting the mescal plant.

These drunken bouts seldom last more than a day, as the tiswin is soon exhausted. While drunk they are communicative and quarrelsome; striking themselves on the breast, they boast in their "big Injun me" style of the number of men they have killed. Fights and oftentimes murder are the results. To avoid these the manufacture of tiswin is forbidden by military authority; but in spite of this it is necessary to keep strict watch to prevent its illicit manufacture.

The domestic implements and utensils made and used by these people are few in number and of the simplest construction. The following constitute the principal ones: the water jug or olla is made of wickerwork, and the interstices filled with resin to make them watertight. They vary in size from the capacity of a quart to that of ten or twenty gallons. The ollas are shaped like the old-fashioned water bottles and are constantly used by the women for carrying water; they are provided with two handles, to which is attached a wide strap of leather or rawhide. The vessel is placed on the small of the back and is supported and held in an upright position by the strap, which passes upwards and across the forehead, the woman's body inclining forward so as to make an angle of about forty-five degrees with a horizontal. The mouth of the vessel, which is large, is stopped with straw. Burdened in this way she travels in a sort of dog trot for long distances. There is also an earthenware vessel of nearly the same shape, but generally smaller, used for cooking purposes. A large, conical-shaped basket, the opening of which is at its base, is used for carrying wood, hay, provisions, etc. They are large and generally have a capacity of three or four bushels. These are carried in the same manner as the water bottle.

When not supplied with matches, fire is readily obtained by rapidly twirling between the hands a small stick or reed, so that a rounded, blunt end which is provided may rapidly revolve in a cup-shaped cavity made in another piece of wood to receive it. This cup-shaped cavity has a small groove extending to the end of the stick and contains a few grains of sand to increase the friction. The triturated particles of wood are ignited in the space of a few seconds and run out of the small gutter or groove.

The process of tanning hides, as understood by them, is a very simple and incomplete one. The implements and articles used for the purpose are of the most simple and rudimentary description. It is performed by the women.

As before remarked, the men are inveterate gamblers. The games most indulged for gratifying this propensity being "con-quin," a game of cards somewhat like the game of casino, and also a game called by them "nazus," which is played with a small wooden hoop and two long poles. There are two competitors in this game, each of them having a smooth, delicately tapering pole about ten feet in length. The ground on which they play is covered with a layer of straw, which allows the poles to slide freely. One of the players rolls the small hoop, which is about nine inches in diameter, along the ground, and each player dexterously slides his pole in the same direction with the hoop, so as to cause the hoop to fall across the large end or handle of the poles. The hoop and poles are notched, and the game is scored according to the position [in] which the hoop falls across the poles. This game may be witnessed in every village; it is played almost universally by them at all times.

The children have various playthings, the boys having bows and arrows, whips, etc. Their principal amusement seems to consist in throwing a lasso; this they do very dexterously. The little girls have miniature cradles and dolls made of wood and dressed in Indian costume. Infants are provided with various little articles, such as beads, bear claws, and the beaks of birds hanging on a string from the upper part of their cradles.

The chastity observed among these people, when their low grade of civilization is considered, must be pronounced as comparable with that of many races of a higher order. The sanguinary punishment for violation of its laws, as already mentioned, would seem to make it compulsory, even if it were not a voluntary virtue among them.

Hatred and revenge are marked characteristics of these, as of many other Indians. In regard to their hospitality and gratitude, the writer cannot speak from his own knowledge, but is informed that these qualities exist among them to a marked degree. That they possess the quality of friendship he has demonstrated by experience, having, it is thought, made a few friends among them. Whether such friendships would remain unbroken should they become hostile is not known.

Courage they possess to a remarkable degree, but it is the courage of ignorance and an animal nature. There are many instances of personal, bloodthirsty courage which could be quoted. There are several articles of clothing, handed down for many generations, which they believe to possess the powers of rendering the wearer invulnerable; the chiefs when clothed with these are much more reckless than at other times.

The diseases prevalent amongst them are principally rheumatism, diarrhea, dysentery, catarrh, ophthalmia, malarial fever, etc. But few cases of consumption or allied diseases, such as hydrocephalis, hip-joint disease, etc. have been observed by the writer. Venereal diseases only to a limited extent are known to exist. A most prevalent disease, and one which causes much discomfort and bad results, is ophthalmia, existing in its most simple as well as its most violent form. These cases occur mostly in children and result from the irritation caused by smoke, uncleanliness, and exposure to cold. The disease is caused in many cases by the paint used on the face getting into the eyes. Opacity and destruction of the cornea, with consequent loss of vision, are the results in many neglected cases.

The treatment of diseases is confided to what are called "de-jin," or medicine men. These are generally old men who claim this honor by reason of their experience, age, knowledge, or vaunted supernatural gifts. They use various decoctions and infusions of roots, herbs, etc., and also steam baths, but rely principally on supernatural agencies, which consist in various chants, incantations, dances, and other juggleries. They generally adopt the healing art as a profession by reason of dreams which they claim to have had in which this knowledge was imparted to them. They are divided into various classes, some relying upon the use of herbs and other material remedies, some upon incantations, others upon the laying on of hands.

The steam bath is used as a remedy for disease, as a process for cleansing the person, and by warriors about to go on the warpath. A hut similar to a wickiup, only on a smaller scale, is constructed and completely covered in. The patient is placed within this and subjected to a process of steaming. The steam is generated in immense volumes by pouring water on large heated stones placed in the middle of the hut. This steaming is continued until it can be no longer endured. Immediately on the completion of the steam bath the person plunges into cold water and then dries himself. Many of these huts may be seen on the bank of the creek which runs in the vicinity of the post. The warriors who have undergone this course say they feel much lighter and stronger and better prepared to undertake a long journey.

Sometimes the de-jin places himself at the door of his patient's house and chants a monotonous song, which may be said to resemble the noise made by a person in the distance counting aloud, accompanying himself on a drum. He will keep this up for twenty-four hours, or possibly as long as he has strength to do so. This process of disenchanting a sick man of evil spirits has been heard by the writer; as the performance has occurred within hearing distance of his own house, he is able to speak from an actual knowledge. Sometimes the chant is continued in such a manner that the de-jin is responded [to] by the family of the invalid.

A remedy which is said to seldom fail in its results may be thus described: the patient, in company with a young maiden, is put into a wickiup in which all openings are closed, excepting a small round one at the top. A vessel of water in which floats a miniature boat containing a certain medicine is so placed in this house that the sun's rays must at some time during the day pass through the opening at the top and fall on the water, the duty of the maiden being to watch for this to take place and to tell whether the boat moves or not when the sun's rays fall on it. Should it move, she cries out, and immediately a volley of shots is fired by a party of the male relatives standing outside, waiting for the signal. The patient is now supposed to recover. But should the boat not move, all hope is despaired of, and it only remains for the "doctor" to complete his work. Their therapeutics can at best be regarded as empirical. The doctrine of "similia similibus curantur" has not yet been accepted by them. With this exception, all schools of medicine seem to be in vogue among them.

There are many instances of longevity among them in spite of the fact of their precarious mode of existence and the many violent deaths that occur. It is thought that many interesting data and facts bearing on pathology and thera- peutics might be obtained from a practice of medicine among them. The writer, from his limited experience in this respect (having been stationed here but two months), forbears to enter on the subject.

Death is regarded with awe among them. Mention of the dead is very rare, and if it does occur, the dead person is never designated by name, but as "he that is gone." When a person dies the body is visited by friends and relations, each of whom donates some small personal article to accompany him on his journey. The body is then wrapped up in a blanket and carried by the female relations of the deceased and placed in a rocky canyon or arroyo and covered up with large stones to protect it from wild animals. It was the writer's fortune to witness one of these performances. The corpse was carried by four women, each of whom held one corner of a blanket. They, followed by many other women, uttered the most heartrending cries and lamentations as they carried it to the last resting place. The men never touch the corpse but stand looking on, or remain away.

Should the deceased possess a horse he is killed so as to accompany his master. Should the widow be destitute the horse is not killed, but its mane and tail are cut off. The writer learns that the practice of killing the horse was discontinued by order of General Crook. It could not be regarded as other than sinful and extravagant.

On the day following the death the village has been deserted and burned, the inhabitants having flitted like Arabs to another place. The widow, now having cut her hair, now begins her mourning. She sits in a disconsolate manner and utters a high staccato sort of wail with a falsetto termination. This is kept up day and night with a persistency that is astonishing. She continues to mourn for six months or a year. During this time she does not wash her face or comb her hair. When her period of mourning has expired she beings to paint and show that she wishes to get married. The brothers or immediate male relatives have the preference in taking her as a wife, and should she not be taken by one of them she must obtain their consent to marry out of the family. An infraction of this rule subjects her to the possible loss of her nose.

The mourning on the part of a husband for his deceased wife is much milder. Generally, only a few months elapse when he is painting his face in imitation of some marriageable female to signify his intention of replacing his loss. Sometimes, however, the grief of a husband is intense. He will strip himself of all his apparel and rush about in a frenzied way for days with disheveled hair and bloodshot eyes. Even suicide has been committed by them when in this condition.

The religion of these Indians is similar to the well-known religion of most Indians. It is believed that there are two trails after death, one for the good and virtuous to the happy hunting ground, the other for the wicked leading to a pit of boiling water, into which the traveler steps unconsciously, when all is oblivion thereafter.

Their superstitions are many and of the most absurd nature. A few are herewith given. Lightning is never spoken of among them. Bears are held in great dread and are not even mentioned, though a bear hunt may be in prospect among them. Snakes are considered sacred and are never killed. A medicine man will sometimes capture a rattlesnake and bring it into a village. The bystanders look at it and say "good, good" and allow it to crawl away unmolested.

Dogs are held in great esteem, and it is owing to this fact that there are such wolfish, repulsive looking curs found in every village. They never use abuse either towards or about a jackass or mule; with a horse [it] is different, as nothing can surpass the brutality with which they treat this poor animal.

The superstitions in regard to water, fish, and evil spirits at night have already been mentioned. Sometimes during an epidemic a person, generally a woman, will be suspected and arrested as the cause of it. She will be charged with having taken some of the viscera of a dead relation and, after burning them, of having scattered the ashes about and thus propagated the disease. She is generally sacrificed to the popular fury, as were witches accused of witchcraft in earlier days in New England. Many other instances of their superstition might be cited, but the above, it is hoped, will convey an idea of their nature.

Their traditions, as far as the writer can ascertain, are mostly visionary and incomplete. As they have no record of time it is almost impossible to obtain a clue to their origin or of the land from which they came, or a knowledge of the length of time they have lived in this vicinity. The past is to them but a dim vista, in which the events occurring seem as distorted dreams. Not one of them can tell his age. Parents do not know their children's ages.

They say they came here many years since from towards New Mexico; that they themselves were going further than this, but a coyote told them they must not go beyond the River Prieto, a small river to the south of this. The coyote may have been the name of their chief at that time. Other traditions are given but are of such an obscure, ridiculous nature that they do not merit repetition.

There being no religious customs or forms among these people, there are consequently no feasts or festivals. They have social gatherings which take place at night in the open air and at which their national dances are indulged in. These open-air balls have been witnessed on several occasions by the writer. The scenes presented at them are weird and unique in the extreme. A huge fire is built of pine logs, and around this the men form a large circle, some sitting, some standing. An opening is left for ingress and egress. The women and children are grouped in families around smaller fires which are built on the outskirts of the ball ground.

The music is composed of eight or ten male voices, uniting in a solemn, monotonous chant, with a dull drum accompaniment. The musical strains are short, and each emphasized by a single stroke on the drum, which serves also to keep time.

The music having begun, the females, for the most part maidens, make up pairs among themselves, and one of each pair runs up and touches the man with whom they wish to dance; he, on being touched, follows her, and she conducts him to where her partner stands. The three now arrange themselves by joining hands, the man in the center looking in one direction, and the two females, one on either side, looking in an opposite direction from him. In this way they move backwards and forwards for a distance of fifteen to twenty feet, keeping time by a series of mincing steps to the music.

At a flourish of the drum the music ceases, and the act is concluded, the females running in an unceremonious manner back to their fires. This may take place within the circle or outside of it. The writer speaks from actual experience when he pronounces this style of dancing dull and tiresome in the extreme.

After a while the music changes in character by becoming more animated and emphatic. The family dancing now ceases, and two or three men, dressed in costume to represent evil spirits, make their appearance. They are greeted with loud cries and yells, their faces concealed with masks, their heads ornamented with immense wooden horns. Their almost naked bodies decked with cedar, and holding wooden daggers in their hands, they circle one after the other around the fire, keeping step to the music and contorting their bodies and throwing about their arms. They are cheered by the audience, and this stimulates them to renewed exertions, which in turn excites the audience. It is now that the scene become interesting. The wild and furious movement of the dancers, the excited countenances of the spectators, made hideous [by the] bright paint and lurid reflection of the fire, and their fantastic costumes, the solemn chanting of the singers, and the unearthly yells which go up from every side, furnish a spectacle which is not soon forgotten.

At one of these dances recently at which the writer was present a poor boy, suffering from hip-joint disease, was brought into the circle and placed on a blanket. The maskers, after making a series of circles around the boy, each went up and laid his sword across the affected limb in order to drive out the evil spirit which was supposed to possess it.

During the Christmas holidays past the officers of this post gave a ball of this kind for the amusement of the Indians. The Indian style of arrangement was followed in all respects, excepting that it was on a grander scale. The central fire was very large, and this was surrounded by a line of colored lanterns marking the circle of men, and another circle outside of this marking the family circle. Nearly every Indian on the reservation was present. Several boxes of hard bread, a quantity of fresh beef, and a quantity of smoking tobacco was distributed among them as presents. Fireworks were also provided for entertainment. As they were the first ever witnessed, great consternation was caused among them, but this soon yielded to delight and astonishment. It was the belief of everyone that the affair was the source of much enjoyment for the Indians.

War dances are similar to the above, excepting that the maskers are replaced by warriors who, armed with their weapons, go through various movements, imitating their manner of fighting and making a charge. A war dance was performed the night of the officers' ball.

The characteristics of a few of the prominent men may not be uninteresting and are herewith given in an imperfect and desultory manner.

Es-ka-dah-silah, the hereditary chief, now retired, is old and decrepit. He was once a brave and fine-looking Indian. He accompanied General Howard to Washington some years ago. He now takes great pride in showing a Bible, an autograph[ed] letter, and a photograph which the general gave him. He was hostile at one time but now appears satisfied with the relationship between the Indians and government.

Palone, the present head chief, was appointed by General Crook some years ago. So far he has, by his fidelity and intelligence, given entire satisfaction and demonstrated the wisdom of the general's choice. He is about twenty years of age and is small and delicately formed, and effeminate looking. Although young, he has shown many fine traits and much decision of character. He has been noted for his bravery and coolness in danger from boyhood. He and his father, who was a chief of a sub-tribe, have always been friendly toward the whites. He has never been known to kill a white man. He is now well disposed and demonstrates his loyalty by the assistance which he renders in managing his people in constancy with the wishes of the government.

Pedro, a brother of Palone, is about twenty years older and is a chief of a sub-tribe. He is one of the most intelligent Indians on the reservation; he is thoroughly reliable and trustworthy. He is industrious and is regarded as the richest man among them. He cultivates a large piece of land, having in the year just passed sold seven hundred dollars worth of corn which he raised. He has about thirty-five head of cattle and some mules and horses. He is desirous of having his children educated; [he] wants his favorite boy, who is a bright, handsome lad, to be the first of the tribe and to write a letter to the president. Pedro can boast of being able to sign his own name. He has always been friendly to [the] white man.

Es-ki-in-la, who has the sobriquet of "Diablo," on account of his daredevil character, is about thirty-five years of age. He is noted for his desperate encounters, having been wounded both in battle and in tiswin drunks. He is a large, powerful man with a sinister expression which is often relieved by a smile. He has shown the writer many of his scars. He has within the last two months avenged the death of a brother by killing his murderer, an Indian, in the immediate vicinity of this post and has also assisted in killing an Indian who resisted him when arrested by him for making tiswin. He is a chief of a sub-band, succeeding his father. To give a clue to his character the following incident, which recently occurred, is narrated. He was requested to send a certain woman to ascertain in regard to the illicit manufacture of tiswin by certain parties. He did not send the woman and gave as a reason that he liked the woman, and he feared that she might refuse to go, in which case he would be obliged to kill her. [He] has always been friendly towards the whites and gives promise by his behavior to remain so.

Noch-ay-del-klinne,[5] about fifty years of age, is an honest, sober man. He is chief of the largest sub-tribe, which may be accounted for by his generosity and mildness. He controls his people with a steady hand and is impartial in his dealings with both white man and Indians. At one time he was hostile, but is now well affected toward the government.

These Indians have now a reservation of about eight thousand square miles, situated in the southeastern part of Arizona territory. It embraces most of the land which has always been occupied by them. This tract contains a large part of the White Mountains, which renders it extremely rugged and picturesque. These Indians, from their long residence here, have all the instincts and habits of a mountainous people. They, in connection with the Tonto Apaches and [Cibicue], are the hereditary enemies of the Indians to east and north of this, chief among which are the Navajos, Moquis, and Pueblos. The valley of the Little Colorado, which is a boundary between their respective lands, is considered neutral ground. Here, should parties of these hostile tribes meet, no fight ensues.

The natural intelligence of these people, it is thought, is such as to warrant earnest measures for their civilization. Their docility and willingness to do what is right, as evinced during the past two years, has been remarkable. Practical artisans and mechanics should be sent among them to teach them to house, clothe, and make themselves comfortable, and practical farmers to teach them to cultivate their land to the best advantage and to raise stock. Their children should be taught the English language, as this would bring the rising generation into close relationship with the whites and establish a sympathy which would be more powerful than that arising from any other cause. There will always be more or less estrangement between races speaking different languages.

When they are housed and have beds to sleep in in place of groveling in the earth like dumb brutes, when they have been taught to wear clothes and to keep themselves clean, when they have acquired industrious habits and the rudiments of civilized life, then will they be in a better condition to comprehend and accept the mysteries of the Christian religion. Until such time as this change has taken place, the efforts for their conversion to Christianity will be in vain.

They are now under strict military supervision and do not seem at all restive; many of them are regularly enlisted for short periods as soldiers, and only these are allowed firearms. For any of them to leave the immediate vicinity of this post they must apply for a pass from the commanding officer. The Indian noncommissioned officers are prompt to report or punish derelictions of duty on the part of any of their numbers. They aspire to act and live like the white, and they should be furnished every facility.

At the present time there is a scout absent from this post composed of white and Indian soldiers for the purpose of punishing and driving on their reservations roving and renegade bands of other tribes.

This satisfactory state of affairs is due entirely to the wise and judicious management of the department commander, General Crook. He has made them but few promises, and these he has always fulfilled strictly. He is regarded by them with fear and respect. His humane and firm treatment, if always carried out, would result in them becoming civilized and self-sustaining and eventually a worthy and respectable people. It should be mentioned that to Major George H. Randall, Twenty-third U.S. Infantry, much credit is due for the prompt and decisive manner in which he executed, while in command of this post, the policy of the department commander, and also that praise should be awarded to Major F. D. Ogilby, Eighth U.S. Infantry, the present post commander, whose whole energy and attention are devoted to the improvement and amelioration of the condition of these people.

The writer has, in conclusion, to return thanks for the kind assistance rendered him by the reliable and well-known guide and interpreter, Mr. C. E. Cooley, who is at present in government employ at this post.

To Mr. Cooley's long experience and thorough knowledge of these Indians, as well as to his abilities as an interpreter, he is indebted for most of the foregoing data.

This report is respectfully submitted with the hope that it may serve as a contribution to our knowledge of these Indians.

	(Signed)	L. Y. Loring
Camp Apache, A.T.		Assistant Surgeon,
January 11, 1875		U.S. Army Post Surgeon

Victorio and His Young Men

E. C. KEMBLE[1]

New York Times, November 28, 1880

In the fall of 1875 the Apache chief Victorio,[2] who has been leading our troops such a fruitless chase through New Mexico and Arizona, and whose death was recently reported from Mexico, had a following of less than one hundred of his own band. His reservation was at the Hot Springs (Ojo Caliente), about two hundred fifty miles southwest from Santa Fe. He had been removed thither from Tularosa a year or two before, this being the third removal which had been forced upon him within ten years.[3] In the spring of 1877 these Indians were again marched off to a new "home," strongly against their will, but as a measure of necessity, and placed under the charge of the agent at San Carlos, in Arizona. Victorio and his band straggled back to their old haunts in the neighborhood of Ojo Caliente and Canada Alamosa, from which placed he started off on his last warpath.

While Victorio was on the Ojo Caliente reservation, in the spring of 1876, a discovery was made in the Indian Office at Washington which caused an inspector to leave there in a hurry for the agency, to examine into the method in which its accounts were kept.[4] It was found by the returns sent to Washington that the Indians at the Ojo Caliente had increased in an astonishing manner since the fall before, and that this numerical growth was still going on. From 450 the number had swollen during the winter and spring to 1,200 and 1,300, as shown by the ration returns. Here was a clear case of fraud on the part of somebody, and the inspector, on arriving at Santa Fe, commenced his investigations, in the midst of which a dispatch came up from southern New Mexico announcing that the Apaches had risen and the agent at Ojo Caliente was in danger of being taken off without government interference.[5] General Hatch, commanding the district, was in Santa Fe, and on receiving the message at once ordered out troops from the posts nearest the agency and started the next morning, accompanied by the inspector, for the Ojo Caliente.

The conveyance in which they set out was a small covered mud-wagon, familiar to unhappy travelers in those parts as a "jerky," so named perhaps from its tendency to jerk a passenger out from under his hat and pitch him bareheaded into the bosom of his opposite partner whenever it rocked on its short, stiff leather swings. It started from Santa Fe at the barbarous hour of 3:00 A.M. Riding on the outside with the driver in the cold, bleak morning, he pointed out to me at daybreak where a cloudburst, or waterspout, a few months before had washed away part of the road, carrying with it the up-country stage and drowning the driver and one of his horses.

My companion narrated this incident in an undertone and fell into a serious and meditative mood when he had finished. Rousing himself at length, he added: "Well, Jim said a thing that night that no man ought to say." He then went on to relate how upon leaving the station which we were approaching one of the stablemen called Jim's attention to a black cloud that was forming in the west and told him he was going to get a wet hide before he got into town, and how he said, with a horrible oath, that he expected it and cursed God in language the most depraved I had ever heard, for having "always something agin him." It was a form of blasphemy that made even a stage driver shudder. Jim's body was found half a mile down the ravine on the day following the disaster.

We rode all day and the succeeding night, reaching Albuquerque the next morning at daybreak. We stopped for supper at a low, mud-walled station, where they set before us a dish of stewed pork rinds, the only fare which the dirty cabin afforded. The driver did not sit down with us here, as was the custom all through the country, but "sparred his hash," as he afterward told us, outside, and was indignant when we mentioned the pork rinds. "Did they play that onto you?" said he. "Why didn't you kick the table over! That's the way we settled the business the last time they stuck us with their pigskins!"

Arriving at Fort Craig, General Hatch and the inspector left the stage road and started in an ambulance for Fort McRae, thirty-five miles distant. The road, for a part of the way, lies across the famous Jornada de Muerte, or Journey of Death, so called from the numbers that have perished in the long drives over its parched and arid wastes, where the water stations are thirty and fifty miles apart. Just as the sun was setting we entered upon a still gloomier passage called the Ravine of the Spring of Death, full of bloody memories as an Apache ambuscade. Its cool waters have lured many famishing travelers to a more frightful doom, and the gory legends that are told of Indian surprises and massacres invest each jutting rock in the fading light with an anxious and dismal interest.

From Fort McRae, where we passed the night, it is still eighteen miles to the Hot Springs, or Ojo Caliente Agency. Taking a guide and an escort of six men, General Hatch and his companion started on the afternoon of April 21, hoping to reach their destination by dark.[6] We passed through the cutthroat town of Cañada Alamosa, inhabited by the lowest of Mexican thieves and desperadoes, who derive their living from selling liquor and trinkets to the Indians in exchange for the government goods issued to the latter. On every side one could see government property in the shape of camp kettles, axes, tinware, and clothing. "Greasers" sauntered lazily about in blankets on which the brand U.S.I.D. appeared in letters nearly half a foot long. This town was the favorite resort of Victorio and his swaggering crew when they left the reservation for a little *paseur* down the valley.

The scenery becomes imposing as one approaches the agency. But we were destined to pass another night on the road. Our guide took a wrong trail, and before we could recover the ground lost, darkness had overtaken our little party. Shut in by towering masses of rock, without water or a single ration of food, we prepared to make, in the language of the country, a "dry camp," and after hobbling our animals and putting a man on guard, we spread our blankets on the sand.

Our dry camp was not to be a dull one. We had hardly composed ourselves to sleep when we heard, through the thick pine timber in the direction of the agency, the beating of an Indian drum, and not long after the yells of Indians chanting in unison. They were having an excited dance, and for an hour or more we lay and listened to the increasing tumult. Not long after midnight we were awakened by the sound of a horse's feet coming down the main road. The guard went out to reconnoiter and soon came back with Tom Riley, the agent for the beef contractor of the reservation. As soon as he recognized General Hatch he said there was a mighty bad state of things at Ojo Caliente—the Indians getting drunk and killing one another. The sounds we had heard in the early part of the evening came from a "tiswin dance," and two or three Indians had been shot during the dance. "Tiswin" is the fermented corn drink of the Apaches, brewed by them and, as they use it, one of the most maddening liquors ever distilled. The corn is sprouted, then put in to soak and exposed several days to the sun. Its taste is harmless enough and not unlike lemonade. To get drunk on it the Indians totally abstain from food for two or three days and then drink inordinate quantities. Their tiswin orgies, during which they rehearse with song and dance their warlike deeds, are often the occasion for settling their private grudges, and as an Indian, when he quarrels, usually quarrels to kill, their tiswin dance is not uncommonly a death dance.

"They went into it red hot and greasy-naked," said Riley, describing the scene he had just witnessed, "nothing on but a belt of cartridges, and every mother's son of them with his rifle at the drop. Old Victorio was there, and Loco and Nana, and all the whooping crew." He related how they "picked their steps" hopping from side to side "like as though they were on a hot griddle," and all the time watching one another, looking for a chance to shoot or dodge. "I just said to myself," continued Riley, "that if I got well out of that place they might hold their tiswin fandango by themselves for all me."

All was quiet in the direction of the agency the next morning, and we resumed our journey, reaching there just before noon. The home of Victorio, his favorite refuge, and the reservation from which he was last driven, is a valley surrounded by high hills, approached from the side nearest civilization through a narrow pass, in which a hundred resolute men could keep an army at bay. It had its sawmill, trader's store, school, and agency buildings there, but the school was looked upon by Victorio and his warriors as a snare in which to take away the freedom of his people. So it was patronized almost exclusively by the children of the agency employees. The chief points of attraction to the Indians were the government warehouses and corral, whence the rations were issued, and the trader's store.

The presence in their midst of "El Capitan Grande," as General Hatch was styled by them, and a stranger from Washington, produced intense excitement among Victorio's followers, and, as is usual in an Apache camp when visitors drop suddenly in, the women and children were hurried out of sight. When we drove up to the agency, the *placita* before the trader's store was filled with Apache squaws and their young, and the plain dotted with ponies. Ten minutes later there was neither pony, squaw, nor papoose to be seen in any direction. We ascertained from the agent that the Indians nominally under his control were greatly disturbed by the frequent visits of outlaws from the bands at other agencies, and that they were now feeding and sheltering some Chiricahua refugees who had been concerned in a recent outbreak and murder in Arizona.[7] These visits kept them in a constant state of irritation and turbulence, and rendered them very unmanageable.

While we were talking the agent looked out of the window and suddenly exclaimed, "Here comes Victorio now," and the since famous chief, with his fellow warriors Loco, Nana, Rafael, Vicentio, and half a dozen others, captains of bands, with about thirty headmen and soldiers at their heels, rode up to the gate, dismounted, the chiefs without ceremony walking gravely in. The others remained at the entrance.

Victorio walked boldly up and shook hands with the white men present, his companions following suit. Then they disposed their dirty bodies about on the beds and campstools and sat regarding us in silence for some minutes. Victorio, as he then appeared, was short and stout, with a heavy, firm-set lower jaw, and an eye not unlike the famous optic of a facile Massachusetts politician. He was dressed in a grimy calico shirt and coarse trousers and was without paint, feathers, or ornaments of any kind. Each man of the party was armed and held his rifle across his knee. Victorio was the first to speak, and he bluntly asked General Hatch for what purpose he had come. The general parried the question good humoredly, and the agent set before the company a tin pan containing tobacco and some common straw paper for cigarettes, which is the universal New Mexican smoke. While his fellows were rolling their cigarettes Victorio resumed the conversation, interrogating us in Spanish:

Victorio—I asked my friends why they had come into my country.

General Hatch—I understand you are hiding and feeding some bad Indians here.

Victorio—That was true yesterday, but it is not true today.

General Hatch—How is that?

Victorio—Those bad Indians are all dead.

General Hatch (aside)—Umph! They have learned down here, too, how to convert bad Indians into good ones.

Victorio went on to say that at the dance that morning the three refugees from Chiricahua had been shot. He was very anxious to know if the soldiers were coming into the valley. It was with much difficulty that General Hatch managed to evade the question.

"The great father wants you to be one of his captains," said the inspector. "If you will give him some of your young men he will make soldiers (police) of them to keep the peace on the reservation, and there will then be no need of his white soldiers coming here at all."

Victorio—I am getting too old. If I should mount one of your big American horses he might run away with me, and my young men would laugh at me. Is my father, the agent, going to give us any beef today? When my friends come to see me we should have a feast.

Then an old chief rose up and said: "I am an old man. A good many years ago, before my hair was gray, and when the Americans first began to come into this country, we were sitting in a room like this eating your bread and drinking coffee. We had had some trouble with your people, but we thought it was all ended when they asked us to come to a feast. We left our guns and bows and were ready to smoke with your people. In a moment, and while we were eating, the house was surrounded with soldiers, who put their guns through the windows and shot down all but five of our party. I was one who escaped. I don't know how I got out of that corral. I lost myself when the shooting began, and when I found myself again I was up in the mountains holding tightly in one hand the tin cup out of which I had been drinking coffee. Before that I would have drunk water out of your hand. Since then I cannot lie down beside the road and not be afraid."[8]

Was it for this, I asked myself, that these men sitting now in council with us each held his gun across his knee? And what would be the effect upon this council if one of the companies ordered here by General Hatch should suddenly appear before the windows? The conference adjourned without reaching any satisfactory result. The agent announced that he had given orders to have the cattle herd driven up and that beef would be issued the next day.

The inspector had already begun his investigation into the subject of the muster rolls and the number of Indian families registered, finding, as he expected, that only 450 or 500 Indians were entitled to draw rations at this agency. And yet there was a weekly issue of beef, according to all testimony taken, for thrice that number. How was it to be explained?

Night came on, and, after supper had been finished, we prepared to retire. The herd had been gathered into the corral, and the Indian guards set. I remember that amid all the uncertainties of the situation it was not deemed essential to our safety to lock the doors of our sleeping room, a precaution which I had not neglected at any place where I had passed the night between Washington and the Rio Grande.

In the small hours of the morning we were awakened by the report of a gun fired in the direction of the corral. Another and another shot followed, and

Is it a raiding party? OUTING MAGAZINE, MARCH 1887.

then we heard the shouting of Indians and the bellowing and scampering of cattle, and it was plain that the beef herd was being stampeded. The agent came into the room and without any excitement informed us that the herd was frequently run off in this way by Victorio's young men and that he was power-less to prevent it. "And do you recover any of the cattle stolen?" was asked. "Sometimes, and sometimes not." "And how do you account to the department for the cattle not brought back." "Put them down as issued to the Indians," promptly replied the agent. A light began to break on the mystery of the rapid increase in the Indian population.

In the morning there was not an Apache to be seen about the agency. About the first thing we saw was a group of white employees in front of the trader's store, attentively watching the hills on the north side of the reserva-tion. They said, as we joined them, that they had seen "smokes," meaning Apache smoke signals on one of the peaks. "There it is again!" exclaimed one of the men, and as he spoke a dark column arose straight into the still air, then wafted away, and was quickly followed by two or three lesser puffs. "They are signaling Loco's camp that soldiers are coming," said the trader, who was wise in Apache smokecraft.

The time for action had come. After a short consultation the agent was directed to send a message to Victorio's camp, giving him notice that the cat-tle taken away last night must be brought back before the sun stood above the hills. A half-breed Mexican mounted a fleet little bronco and set out "on the jump" for the camp, distant four or five miles. He had been gone about twenty minutes when, in another direction, we saw a cloud of dust and presently a rapidly moving body of men and animals emerging from behind the low hills to the south, apparently heading toward the agency.

Who are they? Is it a raiding party? Are they on a tiswin drunk? We could see them ride to and fro, passing and repassing each other in a wild, erratic fashion. There were some moments of anxious suspense as we stood silently watching these maneuvers. Then the trader spoke again: "It is a band of Indians driving cattle!" And so it proved, for in a short time we could hear their "hooplas" and distinguish the long horns of the plunging herd as they came on with tails erect. When half a mile distant, some twenty or thirty of the Indians rode swiftly ahead and bore down straight toward the trader's store. As they drew nearer we could see the short, burly form of Victorio, who, with a red handkerchief bound around his moppy head and wearing a coarse, dirty shirt, open at the neck, and not another stitch of clothing on him, cut a rather disreputable figure as a head chief. Crouched upon his fierce little pony, as though he were strapped there, he rode straightly and fearlessly up to where we were standing.

"Buenos dias, caballeros!" he commenced. "I hope you passed a good night." Some of his young men (he went on to say) were a little playful last night and had run off the agency cattle. As soon as he heard of it he called them together and compelled them to go to the ravine where they had concealed the herd and drive them back, and he, with some of his soldiers, had come with them to see that the cattle were all delivered to the agency. And now they are over there waiting to be issued whenever the agent is ready!

Victorio was fully armed, as were his followers, and he and they rode their fleetest ponies. When he had finished his short speech he wheeled abruptly and with his companions galloped over to join the party who were guarding the panting herd near the corral. The agent crossed over also, and some of his employees began to unfasten the gates. We saw the agent exchange a few words with Victorio as we turned to walk back to our quarters, and we were giving vent to our excited feelings and wishing the means were at hand with which to curb this insolent Apache, when two shots were fired, the balls whizzing over our heads. In a moment Victorio's "young men" were shooting right and left among the herd. We saw the agency men at the corral scatter and run, and the cattle dash wildly in all directions. The air seemed full of quavering yells and screeches and humming of rifle balls. The prairie beyond the corral was alive with frantic, bellowing steers and careering ponies, whose swarthy riders, with long locks streaming behind them, seemed to belch flame and smoke.

In the midst of the fierce scene, and while we were rapidly asking ourselves what they would do next, the notes of a bugle fell on our ears. We listened—there could be no mistake about it—the rocky pass environing the road by which we had come to the agency clearly echoed the notes of a bugle; all eyes were turned to the woods in that direction. And now a strange color mingled with the dark green of the pines, as though the blue horizon far over and beyond had broken through them. The pale hues seemed endowed with wonderful animation and advanced in undulating folds; now we traced in them living objects as they stretched out in long line and emerged into clearer space and sunlight, and now our eyes were dazzled with the flash of steel, and we raised a lusty cheer as a column of the boys, in blue overcoats, with Captain Hagen at their head, galloped out and, with the steadiness of veterans, deployed before the agency. We turned to look for the cattle killers and became conscious that their yells had ceased for some minutes, and, though the plain was strewn with slaughtered beeves, Victorio and his band were nowhere to be seen. The friendly mountains had again swallowed them.

Soon after the arrival of the troops I walked into the agency office. The agent and some of his employees were there, and a clerk was taking down in a notebook some memoranda that interested me.

"How many cattle were turned over by Riley?" asked the agent.

"Forty-two," replied the chief herder.

"And how many were brought back by the Indians?"

"Thirty-six."

"And only seven left alive," continued the agent. "Thirty-six times 750 (the average net weight per head) divided by fourteen (the number of pounds constituting the weekly ration to each Indian, great and small) gives 1,875 Indians!"

"Pounds," suggested the inspector in a confused way.

"Indians," repeated the agent. "Total number of Indians represented in this issue!"

The mystery of the astonishing increase of Apache mouths at the Ojo Caliente was out. There was also an agent out in about the time it takes to get a hot order from the Indian Office over the wires. It was ascertained that he had allowed Victorio to issue the rations to his own band in this way more than once, and that Victorio had demanded the privilege that morning when he rode back to the corral.[9]

The next spring Senor Victorio, with Loco, Nana, and the rest, were ordered out of the Ojo Caliente and moved over the San Carlos Mountains. And here began the active troubles with this irrepressible Apache at Ojo Caliente, which made those springs subsequently such exceedingly hot water for that Indian as well as the government and its generals, and, indeed, all of southern New Mexico. The outbreak has at last been quenched in the blood of Victorio and his braves.

PART THREE

Uprisings and Unrest, 1878–83

Campaigning against Victorio in 1879

CHARLES B. GATEWOOD[1]

The Great Divide 11 (April 1894): 102–4

There have been many Apache chiefs whose names have been a terror to the people of Arizona, New Mexico, and the states of Sonora and Chihuahua in Mexico. Among the most prominent were Cochise and Geronimo of the Chiricahua Apaches, and Mangas Coloradas and Victorio of the Warm Spring Apaches. These two tribes have caused more trouble in the last thirty years than all other Apaches combined. While the other tribes fought among themselves, these two, under Cochise and Mangas Coloradas, combined and fought not only the other kindred tribes, but everybody else. While the two chiefs were such in fact as well as in name, Victorio and Geronimo were such only in name. Their reputations were greater among the settlers than among their own people. From 1879 to 1881, New Mexico, northern Mexico, and a part of Arizona were literally terrorized by Apaches whose chief was supposed to be Victorio. The real plotters of this mischief were Nana,[2] Tomacito, and Turrivio. Victorio was a palsied, aged, and decrepit chief, who was barely able to accompany the squaws and children in their forays and who was finally surprised and killed by the Mexicans in 1881,[3] along with many of the women and children of his tribe. Tomacito and Turrivio were killed in 1879, leaving Nana as the only surviving leader of ability among the Warm Springs.

Commanding a company of Indian scouts and on duty connected with the management of the Apaches, the writer took part in all the campaigns against them from 1879 to 1886.

In April 1879, the Warm Springs, nominally under Victorio, left their reservation for reasons which they considered sufficient, chief among them which may be mentioned restlessness, caused by robbery and mismanagement by their agents (the same old story the West over) and innate desire to slay, pillage, steal, and create havoc generally, summed up in the word "revenge." Their trail into Arizona, back through New Mexico into old Mexico, was marked by burned ranches, forest fires, dead cattle and sheep, and the bodies of murdered human beings. Mounted on fresh horses taken from ranches on their way and traveling at a rapid gait, day and night, sometimes for thirty-six hours without stopping to sleep, it is scarcely surprising that they could not be overtaken by troops that had to use the same stock week after week and could seldom follow the trail at night. It is to the credit of the United States army that a body of men in the Southwest, so few in number and belonging to races not trained to endure such hardships, furnished so much protection to settlers scattered over so vast a region, Many a life and ranch, and even hamlet, were saved by the timely appearance of a detachment of Uncle Sam's rough riders.

The Indians soon returned from the fastnesses of the Sierra Madre range in Mexico,[4] and with recruits from renegade Comanches, Navajos, and Mescaleros, resumed their depredations on a larger scale. Encouraged by their fight in September with Captain Beyer, late of the army, they grew bolder.[5] This was the fight, by the way, in which Lieutenant, now Captain, M. W. Day, Ninth Cavalry, declined to retreat and leave his wounded behind, but carried a disabled soldier away under a heavy fire, for which offense the commanding officer, Beyer, wanted to have him tried by court-martial, and for which the Congress of the United States gave him a gold medal.

The few scouts and trailers in the service in New Mexico were enlisted from the Navajos and, compared to the Apache scouts of Arizona, belonged rather to the coffee-cooling class and, with several exceptions, made serious objections to following a trail that was getting warm. So two companies of Arizona scouts, Lt. A. P. Blocksom's[6] and mine, were ordered to report to Colonel A. P. Morrow, then major, Ninth Cavalry and commanding Fort Bayard.[7] We arrived at the post just as the news of Beyer's fight reached the commander. Beyer had withdrawn from the scene of his fight, forty miles distant, and was on his way back to Bayard. There were several troops of cavalry in garrison already, which, with the two companies of scouts, made quite a respectable command with which to take the field.[8] Colonel Morrow issued his orders, and it took but a short time to shoe the horses and mules, draw rations and ammunition, and be on the way to take up the trail where Beyer left it. The scouts, with detachments of cavalry, Lieutenant Blocksom in command, proceeded straight across the Mimbres Mountains to the scene of the fight, while the cavalry took the wagon road around by old Fort Cummings. This was necessary as the latter had wagon transportation, while the former had pack mules.

It took us several days to toil across the Mimbres because most of the way we had no trail and the mountain was rough and precipitous. But the third or fourth day the trail of the hostiles was struck some miles northwest of Animas Canyon, where Beyer's fight occurred. Then, cutting loose from our pack trains, leaving behind all animals, in fact, with the scouts and a dismounted detachment of cavalry, we followed the trail for three nights in succession, each man carrying his rations and equipment.

We laid over in the daytime, concealing ourselves in the narrow gorges and canyons. It rained every minute of the time, and as we dared to build only very small fires to do our cooking by, there was no chance to dry our clothing and the few blankets in the party. The only part of the little we had to eat not

A halt to tighten the packs. CENTURY MAGAZINE, APRIL 1889.

spoiled by the rain was the bacon. Bread and tobacco fell into a pulpy mixture that could neither be eaten nor smoked. Shortage of rations was made up somewhat the second day with some jerked horse meat we found in a deserted camp, and the third day an old abandoned government mule filled the long-felt want. The soldiers some time before had "packed" him till he could go no further and was left to die. Then the hostiles used him till he was not quite dead and left him to live if he could. It was not difficult to see every bone in his body, and his back was a mass of—what you might expect to see on a mule so much abused. From the time his throat was cut by a scout till a stew of bacon and mule was simmering on the little fire in a frying pan picked up on the trail, a very few minutes elapsed. The meat was too tough for mastication and had to be swallowed whole, and, as the mule lay with his back towards the fire, the sight of him was not appetizing. However, it was better than nothing.

We knew from the character of the trail and the signs along it that we were gradually approaching the hostiles and without their knowledge of our approach. On the fourth day we were joined by the cavalry and their wagon train, and by our pack mules—a most welcome reunion. We were then far into the Black Range, northeast of the Mimbres, both being in fact one continuous extent of broken country. It had ceased raining, and the sun was doing his best to dry up the country, in which he succeeded so well that within a few days we had to hunt water. Soaking wet one day and suffering from thirst the next.

From this camp we marched in the daytime, and just before sundown our scouts in advance located Mr. Victorio and his outfit encamped in a deep canyon.[9] They saw each other about the same time, and the fun began. The firing, of course, brought up those in rear "double quick." From the small number of scouts first seen, the hostiles thought themselves already the victors and became quite saucy and facetious, daring them to come closer and even inviting them to supper. My first sergeant Dick answered, "We are coming," and when old Vic's braves saw forty-odd scouts and as many soldiers, white and colored, coming tumbling down the side of the canyon into their camp, they stayed not on the order of their going out of it. Darkness coming on aided them in their flight. Result: two bucks and a squaw on their side; on our side, nothing. They managed to drive their stock away with them, and as they carry very little plunder while on the warpath, their camp was not worth much after we got it.

That night the scouts bivouacked about a mile from the main command in a canyon near the scene of the disturbance of the evening before, being thus separated on account of the limited supply of water. The canyon was perhaps eight hundred feet deep, with steep and rocky sides covered with pine, oak, and heavy underbrush. The other camp was in a sharp bend of the canyon lower down.

Early the next morning, as we had just finished breakfast, a single shot rang out down the canyon, then a volley, suddenly increasing into more shots and more volleys, with shouts of command, all doubled and trebled in reverberation up the valley until it was one roar of pandemonium that was enough to set a nervous man wild, if he had to stay in our camp and listen to it.

Having gotten our men under arms, Blocksom sent me with twenty men on foot to report to Colonel Morrow as soon as possible, and away we went. More noise and more excitement, until I didn't believe there was a sane man in the country except the corporal, who coolly informed me after a while that I was sitting on the wrong side of a rock to be safe from a cross fire. Up to that time, it seemed to me we would all be killed, for every man had lost his head and was yelling with all his might and shooting in the air. But once anchored on the right side of the rock, I was astonished to see how cool they were and how steady was their aim, some even laughing and joking. I afterwards remembered the pleasant smile on the corporal's face as he pointed out to me the folly of protecting a rock. I didn't have to see through the rock either to be aware of the fact that we were above Morrow's camp on the inner side of the bend of the canyon, while the enemy held the outer side, and at lucid intervals nothing but puffs of smoke could be seen over there, at least by me. The scouts had followed the scattering tracks of the hostiles early that morning and were four or five miles away when they heard the firing. The country between us and them was exceedingly rough, and yet within an hour they turned up on the right and rear of our assailants, when, by a further advance of Colonel Morrow's line up the side of the canyon opposite us and a rapid flank movement to the hostiles' left by our party which Blocksom, in the meantime, joined and took command of, our entertainers sought the seclusion of a higher and rockier rendezvous and more inaccessible, so to speak, about a mile further on. When the scouts began to appear, it was impossible for us to tell whether they were hostiles or not from the glimpses we caught of them through the brush and trees. Their firing didn't seem to add much to the uproar, but when we heard above it all the foghorn voice of Sergeant Jack Long bellowing forth,

"Mucho bueno! God damn, come on!" we knew them for scouts and hastened to make our flanking movement. It is very encouraging to see your enemy trying to break the sprinting record, racing with your bullets.

It was useless to try to follow the impertinent rascals into the high and rocky fastness that seemed to swallow them, though occasionally a few would appear on peaks and precipices, shake breechclouts at us, and otherwise dare us over into their backyard. So we returned to our camp and over another breakfast discussed the adventures of the morning.

It seemed that while breakfast was being served to the men, the hostiles sneaked up close to the picket above Morrow's camp (this they could easily do on account of the thick underbrush, rocks, and timber), surprised it, killing one man and getting possession of the heights—well, you can see for yourself how it would be, their position being on the outside of the bend in the canyon. It took some time for Colonel Morrow and his line to climb up the steep side of this deep crack in the ground, and it is just as well that they were not physically able to do so, for a man with the wind knocked out of him can't very well "wrastle" with one who is sitting there waiting for him.

Time was thus afforded for the scouts to return and take them in flank and rear, and altogether to make a pretty little scrimmage, in which everybody got under fire. From pools of blood and bloody rags and sheepskin saddle blankets about the hostiles' position and along their trails it was evident that a number of them had been struck, how many we never knew, for they carried their injured with them. Two colored soldiers of the Ninth Cavalry were killed, shot through the head, and an assistant surgeon stampeded so that he resigned his commission and afterwards went into practice in civil life.

Apache Indians seldom make an attack on troops so bold and daring as this one. They never tried it on that column again.

Water was scarce, and as we couldn't get to our tormentors, there was nothing to do but withdraw and seek an entrance to their stronghold from some other side. Getting the animals out of this canyon was no easy matter. The trail we came in on was too steep to ascend, and a new one had to be broken. Blocksom of the Sixth Cavalry, with a dismounted detachment, took the advance. The writer had the pleasure of being in a safe place in the middle of the column, in charge of the led horses and pack trains. Wright of the Ninth Cavalry, with a dismounted detachment, was rear guard, and the scouts were flankers. The rest of the command was held in readiness to go wherever needed. The doctor concluded that it was safest to accompany the advance, as it was the furthest from the enemy, but some of the impudent devils got around in front of Blocksom and gave him a salute, just for fun apparently, that sent the medical man along the column, down the side of the canyon at a breakneck pace to Wright. Then he came flying back for a like reason and concluded to journey with the mules. Pretty soon the scouts were withdrawn from the flank towards the enemy, and while the doctor and myself were sitting in a safe place watching the mules go by, those infernal heathens came to the opposite bluffs and caused us considerable uneasiness until we could get under cover. After the scouts had run them away again, we came out from behind our pine trees and overtook our riding mules at the top of the ridge. Late that afternoon we made our camp only a few miles from the hostiles.

II

It was after a month of weary marching that we were able to overtake them again. From the stronghold in the Black Range they scattered in small bands over the greater part of southern New Mexico, pillaging isolated and unprotected ranches and now and then committing depredations near the towns.

Rumors of their bloody work came from all directions. All the murders that occurred were attributed to the Apaches. A man could wear moccasins, kill his neighbor, and succeed in laying the blame on the dreaded Apaches.

On one occasion my scouts found the bodies of two white men only a few miles from San Jose, on the Rio Grande. We followed the tracks of two Mexicans into the town, but nobody would believe that moccasin tracks were made by Mexicans or whites; but these they were, all the same; any sane man could recognize the difference between an Indian's footprints and those of a Mexican or a white man when pointed out to him. The size, the shape, the way the foot is planted on the ground and raised, infallibly indicate the race to which the men belonged. Ranchers would tell us that this man and that actually sold arms and ammunition to the hostiles, and they had proof of it.

"All right, give us the proof and we will arrest them and bring them before the proper civil authorities." No, they were afraid of being murdered if they testified, but the military ought to take such men out and shoot them, and so on. The people and the newspapers abused the military in every way imaginable. General Hatch, commanding the District of New Mexico, was called all sorts of names because he would not station cavalry at the ranch of every man who applied for them that he might sell forage at an exorbitant price. Infantry bought no supplies. Every officer was a coward and every enlisted man a hoodlum and a thief.

There were many ranchers who realized the difficulties to be overcome by the troops, appreciated their efforts, and took no pleasure in deliberately starting false rumors of depredations and then make fun of them for believing their lies. But these were exceptions.

III

Across the mountains and deserts of New Mexico, up and down and across the valley of the Rio Grande, we followed Victorio for nearly a month, marching every day and often at night, on foot and horseback. The wary old fox (we gave him the credit, though he didn't deserve it) redoubled his watchfulness, particularly at night. Several times we almost had him, but he was too smart for us. They overcame their superstitious fear of darkness and kept sentinels and scouting parties out all night, thus rendering surprise exceedingly difficult.

Finally, the latter part of October, our fights having occurred on the twenty-sixth and twenty-seventh of September, they concentrated their parties, killed Bill Jones and his posse of fourteen men who came out from Mesilla to settle the war, and headed for Mexico.[10] We were several days behind them. In the meantime the term of service of Blocksom's scouts had expired and they had returned to Arizona. With two troops of the Ninth Cavalry, Captains Purington[11] and Dawson;[12] one of the Sixth Cavalry, Captain Campbell,[13] since resigned; and seventeen Indian scouts, less than one hundred men all told, Colonel Morrow took up the trail again near the boundary line between the two countries, below Lake Palomas, Mexico.

As we were going into an unknown region, where water was said to be scarce and the little to be found strongly alkaline and therefore not fit to drink, everybody filled their canteen at Palomas Lake before we left there. We marched in the broiling heat all that day in a southwesterly direction and about dark found a small tank of water in the rocks near the foot of the Goodsight Mountains, which furnished perhaps half a pint to each man and animal. There we camped for the night. Early in the next morning, as soon as the trail could be seen, we were on our way. All day long again the command plodded along through the sand and heat, across the desert north of the Guzman Mountains. The trail wound around in every direction among the sand hills and lava beds, tending generally southward. Horses and mules began to grow leg weary and suffer from thirst and the heat, and for every horse that was shot by the rear guard a soldier was placed on foot. Thus man and beast trudged along, frequent halts being made to allow a little rest for the weary. About 9:00 P.M. we found a pool of mud in an alkali flat and camped there for the night. It had been a pool of impure water, but the hostiles that day had driven their horses through it and it had so thoroughly stirred it up that it was about the consistency of thin mortar. Men and animals tried to drink it but not with much success. In the two days' march fully seventy miles had been covered, and not a drop of water in the whole command.

An unknown country, still ahead of us, and the outlook was not encouraging, but the hope of finally overtaking the enemy and giving him a well-deserved punishment spurred the men to extra efforts. Besides, it was more than probable that by proceeding on our way water would be reached sooner than by retracing our steps, or by making a day's march to the west into the Hatchet Mountains, where it was known water could be had. So, bright and early the next morning the march was resumed. The number of animals killed by the rear guard increased, the sun seemed to beat down hotter and hotter as the march continued. Men began to offer a month's pay, or all they had, for just one swallow of water. There was no singing, no joking, no conversation, no smoking in the column, and the banjo of a colored soldier that used to enliven the men on the march and around the campfires at night was silent.

The Indian scouts, who always marched on foot, were more used to hardships and could stand it better than the others, but even they began to show the effects of marching under such conditions. Several times we passed places where the wily savages had laid in ambush for us but had abandoned them evidently on account of the extreme caution with which such places were approached. In the afternoon we found a tank of clear and cool water, but a coyote had been killed and disemboweled in it, and it had been otherwise disgustingly poisoned. It was difficult to keep many of the men from drinking it. Several had been made very sick by swallowing it. Some of the dismounted men were in serious condition and had to be packed along on the best of the remaining horses and mules.

Thus the command dragged its weary length along, until after dark[14] we had entered the projecting ridges of the Guzman Mountains, twenty miles perhaps from the towns of Janos, Chihuahua, Mexico. Here the very plain trail ran between two parallel ridges, covered with bushes and rocks, and a line of warriors on each ridge, hidden in the bushes and behind the rocks, waited for us to march along in the open, within easy range. But our scouts were not to be deceived by the evidences on the trail that the enemy had passed through hurriedly and was trying to get away. The full moon had just risen, and in that clear atmosphere one could see a man at considerable distance. How they must have chuckled to themselves as they watched us coming and gloated over the victory so easily to be obtained! But they didn't chuckle long. Some of our scouts had succeeded in getting to the rear of one of the lines without attracting attention, and a volley from them, followed by the advance of a line of dismounted soldiers, caused a precipitate evacuation of their strong position. They rallied, however, on a higher ridge a few hundred yards further on, which they held until the flashes from the two opposing lines almost overlapped. But Apaches can't stand close quarters; they broke and ran, as they will always do. Our men steadily advanced, though it was evident by this time that the enemy outnumbered us considerably and we were following into a rougher and more broken mountain region, with which, of course, they were perfectly familiar, and of which we were totally ignorant. Water was probably there if it could be found. Again they took up a position still higher, and again the men responded to the "Forward, march," of the commander and splendidly climbed the mountainside. The Indians seemed to have plenty of ammunition, which they rapidly expended in improved Winchester rifles, for when our line arrived within point-blank range, the whole top of the mountain was a fringe of fire flashes.

Stationed with a few men on a peak to the left and rear of our skirmishers, I had a good chance to witness this part of the fight. Nearer and nearer to the top of the ridge approached the flashes from the Springfield carbines, and the reports from the Winchesters above were so frequent as to be almost a continuous roar. It seemed to me that fully half the men must be disabled, yet their return fire was brisk enough as they slowly advanced. Suddenly the firing ceased; the rumbling and crashing of large stones down the side of the mountain could be distinctly heard; the line had run up against a palisade of solid rock, twenty feet high or more, which they could not climb and which had not been noticed because the moon was rising behind the enemy's position and the palisade was hid in shadow. From this place the hostiles were rolling heavy stones down among our men, but luckily none were hurt, though several had been killed and several more wounded during the heaviest fusillade.

Unable to reach the enemy and have it out hand to hand with him, if he would only stand, Morrow withdrew behind a small ridge at the foot of the inaccessible one. My detachment was recalled, and Captain Campbell, with his troops of the Sixth Cavalry, which had not yet been seriously engaged, occupied a position to our right and rear that protected our horses and pack mules. He was ordered to advance with his troop (about thirty men), to march around our right flank, and as the ridge occupied by the enemy seemed to slope more gently in that direction, to proceed far enough to allow the main line to swing in on his left by a right-flank movement and thus assail the hostile position on the left flank with a good chance of carrying it.

As Emmet, Day, Finley, and Schaeffer, lieutenants of the Ninth Cavalry,[15] had been with the advance in the hard work already done, I was sent with six men to reconnoiter in the direction Campbell was ordered to take and in advance of him. The reconnaissance was made and the lay of the ground found to be about as it appeared. In spite of the precautions taken to proceed under cover of the growth of stunted bushes, the hostiles discovered us and evidently took in the situation and paid us marked attention. There was no substantial shelter, but by hugging the ground pretty close we escaped the damage intended. Pretty soon the tramping of men hurrying towards us, firing as they came, could be plainly heard, and heads bobbing up among the bushes not a hundred yards in front could be seen. It was hoped that, by shifting positions and firing rapidly, they might be held in check till Campbell's arrival, by causing them to believe our numbers greater than they were. This worked all right for a while, but Campbell didn't come, and the Indians were getting uncomfortably near a line between the small detachment and the main body.

I don't know how long we waited for reinforcement, but it seemed an age. At last Colonel Morrow ordered us to run for the home base, as it were, and the three or four hundred yards were covered in a remarkably short time, at least by me, for having to report to the colonel, I was the first to get there. Instead of doing as intended by Morrow, Campbell, by a circuitous route, turned up on the left of the line, some distance from where he was wanted, according, as he claimed, to the orders he actually received. However this may be, the chance to rout them was lost, and for two reasons. The enemy had taken up and well fortified a strong position over there, as was afterwards found out; and the men were too exhausted from thirst, fatigue, and want of sleep to do any more climbing. When they halted, after withdrawing from the bluffs, every man lay down, and most of them went to sleep. In fact, many of them fell down and slept every time they halted during the hotter part of the fight and had to be wakened by the officers and made to resume firing. The only noise to be heard about this time was the "tumtum" beaten by Victorio himself all during the fight, accompanied by his high-keyed, quavering voice in a song of "good medicine." He was at this junction holding forth to our scouts, trying to persuade them to desert and join his men, and together they would kill the last white and black soldier present. He didn't succeed.

After discussing the situation with his officers, the colonel concluded that the best thing he could do was to take his command to water. Our guide, for we had one, knew nothing of the surrounding country but said that there was an old ranch at the foot of a peak about eighteen miles to the west which we could see from the plain we had crossed the day before.

It was now about 2:00 A.M. and very cold, being October 28. Officers were then ordered quietly to wake up their men and conduct them to the rear, where the animals had been left. This was not an easy matter. Many of the men showed symptoms of that wild insanity produced by great thirst and had to be handled with tact. Two months' pay and as much as one hundred dollars were offered for just one swallow of water, but there was none. Considering what they had gone through, however, they were remarkably tractable and amenable to discipline. Some of them had to be watched to keep them from straying off in search of water. With the weakest on horses and mules and the strongest afoot, they struggled along the eighteen miles to the deserted ranch. The moon had gone down, so that it was dark before they reached the place. Some of the scouts had gone on in advance and had built large fires along the little stream that ran from the spring, to light the water. Then occurred a scene not often witnessed in a lifetime. White, colored, and red men, horses and mules, all rushed pell-mell for the water. They drank of it, they rolled in it, they got out of it, and returned to it. They wept and cheered and danced in it, and the mud they made seemed to make no difference in drinking.

It would have been impossible to regulate the amount taken by any individual. Nobody tried to do so, or even thought of it. Every man and beast was busy drinking it in by the quart, mud and all. As their stomachs became literally full, they crawled out on dry land and threw themselves on the ground, apparently dead. A few of the strongest were able to ease the horses and mules out of their saddles and packs and turn them loose with the bell horses. There was no danger of their straying away; the grass was good nearby and there was the water. They had suffered along with their masters, poor beasts, as swollen tongues hanging out of their mouths amply bore witness. There were a few men yet strong enough to keep guard over the exhausted and prevent surprise by the Indians. These duties were performed cheerfully.

About 10:00 A.M., a dash of cold water in my face aroused me. Those who were able to do so were passing around among the sleepers, pouring water over them to protect them from the heat of the sun. What a sight! Men lying in all attitudes under the scorching sun, for there was no shelter, none had been sought.

Fully half of them were carried to the stream and plunged into the cool water to revive them. None of them were injured by drinking to excess, nor were any of the animals. Rations were running short, and after a rest of a day or two, the command slowly made its way back to its base of supplies, Fort Bayard.

In seventy-six hours, from Palomas to the ranch, it had marched 115 miles on the small allowance of water indicated, besides making the fight at night in the Guzman Mountains.

In forty-nine days, from Fort Bayard and return, it marched 975 miles, and the Indian allies, including side scouts, on foot covered 1,125 miles in the same time. That command marched further, suffered more hardships, and fought oftener with the Apaches (there were several fights not alluded to in this article for want of space) than any other one command before or since, and, so far as I know, this is the first time its work has been alluded to in a public manner.

In the course of time the Mexican government complained of Morrow's entrance into their territory, whereby he came near getting into serious trouble. But as he had fought those who were enemies to both republics, he was forgiven. Nana told me some years afterwards that they lost several killed and had quite a number wounded in the Guzman fight. Our loss was several soldiers killed and six or seven wounded, if I remember right, and one scout killed and one wounded, the redoubtable Sergeant Jack Long. He killed two Chiricahuas afterwards to make up for it. From what Nana said, there were fully one hundred fifty bucks against us, being recruited from renegade Navajos, Mescaleros, Comanches, and Lipans.

The Campaign of 1880 against Victorio

JOHN CONLINE[1]

The Palestine Bulletin (Lodge No. 357, Detroit), November 15, 1903: 80–81

On April 4, 1880, the Second Battalion of New Mexico troops, composed of companies A, D, F, and G, Ninth U.S. Cavalry, comprising seven officers and 148 enlisted men commanded by Captain Henry Carroll, Ninth U.S. Cavalry, moved from Tularosa, New Mexico, to Malpais Springs, New Mexico, a distance of twenty-eight miles, to take the field against Victorio's band of hostile Indians, then supposed to be located in the San Andreas Mountains, a range running parallel to and about twenty-five miles east of the Rio Grande in southern New Mexico and only a few miles westward from Malpais Springs.

Arriving at the springs two hours before dark, we went into camp for the night. The next morning, April 5, my Troop A, Ninth Cavalry, was ordered in advance to ascertain the location of Victorio's band in the San Andreas range and communicate with and assist Major McClellan's command,[2] a part of the force operating against Victorio from the west.

I made a rapid march of about thirty-seven miles nearly due south to Hembrillo Canyon, San Andreas Mountains, and at 4:20 P.M., I struck a fresh trail of about fifty horses and ten or more head of cattle, leading up the canyon a short distance from its mouth. I followed the trail about one and a half miles, to a point where the canyon became much narrower, or boxed up. Here the troop was halted and dismounted; and, owing to the strong impression gained that the Indians were not far away, a small guard was placed over the horses in rear and the company on foot was immediately formed in a concave line of battle, in open order, with right and left flanks resting against the steep sides of the canyon and facing toward the head. I posted a vidette about four hundred yards in front of the line up the canyon and another on the left rear. The vidette in front and the men in line were posted behind rocks and small boulders. I also sent two citizen guides and four soldiers up the canyon to examine and report, and upon their return no Indians were reported in sight.

I felt morally certain, however, that Indians were in the neighborhood. After all preparations had been made for an attack and to prevent a surprise by the Indians, in accordance with my usual habit I made a careful examination of the canyon in every direction through a pair of field glasses, and a little before 5:00 P.M., I saw up the canyon first two Indians, and upon turning the glasses to the right, I discovered about thirty-five to fifty more Indians coming down the hillside into the canyon on the run. I informed the men in line of their approach, and at 5:30 P.M. the first shot was fired from our line. When the Indians advanced to within about two hundred fifty yards, a heavy fire was opened which caused them to halt and seek cover. The Indians fired rapidly in the beginning, and afterward kept up a desultory fire until 7:30 P.M., when the engagement closed and the Indians fell back.

The Indians made several attempts to turn my flank, but their efforts in this direction were repelled.

When the Indians were about three hundred fifty yards in front of us, Victorio was heard giving orders to Chavanan, one of his sub-chiefs, then opposite our right, to turn our right flank.

Victorio's Indians—having been defeated in their attempt to take us by surprise, rush our camp, [and] stampede and capture our horses—retired up the canyon and built a large fire about five hundred yards in front, near the dry riverbed, at 7:30 P.M., and another fire on top of a hill about two and a half miles farther up the canyon.

The action or fight lasted two hours and ended at 7:30 P.M., sometime after dark. There was no water where the engagement took place, and as I did not know of any except on the trail on which I came, I decided to rejoin the main body of the command, which was met on the road at 11:00 P.M., on the way to join me.

The casualties were Corporal Hawkins and Mr. Enbank, citizen, slightly wounded; one public and one private horse killed, and one public horse wounded.

On the morning of April 6 the reunited battalion marched westward to the mouth of San Jose Canyon, where the command was divided into two columns, F and D troops under Captain Carroll, and A and G, under Lieutenant Cusak. A and G troops of cavalry attempted to ascend a very steep mountainside and, finding it impracticable to do so, turned to the left and went over the foothills southward until opposite the mouth of Hembrillo Canyon.

Here a courier overtook us with orders to take Captain Carroll's trail and rejoin him, which we at once proceeded to do, marching until 10:00 P.M., when the trail was lost in the darkness and we were obliged to go into camp at midnight.

In the morning at daylight, on the seventh, having found the lost trail, we moved forward and joined Captain Carroll's command near the head of Hembrillo Canyon at 8:30 A.M. While marching up the hillside to the position occupied by Captain Carroll, the Indians opened fire upon us from the opposite hills but did no damage in Troop A. While the officers were consulting as to the best course to drive the Indians from positions covering the water, their deliberations were interrupted by two or three volleys fired into the group of officers by the Indian scouts of Major McClellan's command, who mistook us for Victorio's band. These volleys were fired from the crest of a high hill in rear of and commanding our position; and although about one hundred fifty or two hundred shots were fired at four hundred yards' range into the four troops of the Second Battalion, including horses, no damage was done except the wounding of one mule in the knee, showing very poor shooting on the part of the friendly Indians.

Soon after 9:00 A.M. companies A and G, Ninth Cavalry, Lieutenant Cusack commanding, with part of the Indian scouts, deployed as skirmishers covering a front of about seven hundred yards, advanced and drove the Indians from the hill nearly east of the water and from which they opened fire on us in the morning. The Indians retreated in a southeasterly direction up the side of a high mountain. After remaining some time on the skirmish line, Lieutenant Cusack left me in command and went back to confer with Captain Carroll.

At 3:30 P.M. I moved to attack the Indians posted on the hill south of us and commanding the water. While moving in this direction, Lieutenant Cusack about 4:00 P.M. sent word to have the whole command marched by the right flank to the water, which had been taken by the Indian scouts, covered by the fire of the Second Battalion. The first water was taken at 11:00 A.M. and the second and principal water was taken not later than 4:00 P.M. The positions occupied by Victorio's band were naturally very strong and covered a front of about two and a half miles.

Victorio, having been driven from all the hills covering the water, retreated rapidly over the hills to the southeast into the great plains of San Augustine, in the direction of Whitewater, the southern point of the White Sands. Captain Carroll was severely wounded twice. No one was killed on our side, although a considerable number were wounded and some dangerously.[3] In this campaign our battalion marched 1,031 miles.

A Scout among the Havasupai and Hualapais Indians

WILLIAM R. PRICE[1]

WHIPPLE BARRACKS, PRESCOTT, A.T.
JULY 1, 1881

To the Assistant Adjutant General,
    Department of Arizona,

SIR:

In compliance with Paragraph 5, Special Orders No. 60, dated May 30, 1881, and letter of instructions from Headquarters, Department of Arizona, with letters from War and Interior departments, I left Fort Verde, A.T., with Lieutenant H. P. Kingsbury, twenty-five men of Company K, Sixth Cavalry, Assistant Surgeon Elliott Coues,[2] U.S. Army, and pack train of thirty-five animals, and proceeded to Spaulding's Ranch, twenty-six miles; June 2, to American Ranch, twenty-one miles; June 3, to Williamson's Valley, thirteen miles. I was here joined by Lieutenant Carl F. Palfrey, Corps of Engineers, one man of Company B, Twelfth Infantry, and three wagons.

June 4—Went to Roger's ranch, Chino Valley, eighteen miles.

June 5—With cavalry and pack train took Indian trail, bearing a little west of north and moving along the base and west of the Picacho Mountains;[3] arrived at Kerlin's Tanks[4] (improperly called on several maps "Cullins Wells") after an almost direct march of thirty-two miles. This tank is in the head of a ravine and lies due south of the highest peak of Mount Floyd, five miles from the base of that mountain. There is another prominent landmark in the shape of a round butte, or small mountain, five miles south of it. This water is on the old Beal road and was named for one of the members of that expedition,[5] the name being deeply engraved on the rocks in letters three inches in length. I took great pains to determine whether there was living water here. I ascertained beyond a doubt that there was no seepage or renewal of supply at this season of the year and that a command of seventy animals would consume the entire amount in three days. We could not have remained there another day.

Marching in the desert. CENTURY MAGAZINE, APRIL 1889.

My three wagons were obliged to make a detour, and by making a dry camp, reached Kerlin's the next day at 5:00 P.M., having traveled over fifty miles.

June 6—Made a reconnaissance to find Kisaha Water, an Indian tank northwest of Mount Floyd, but the trails had been obliterated, and the guide was with the wagons, and I returned to Kerlin's Tanks, having marched twenty miles. We afterwards learned from Indians that the tank was nearly dry, and we could not have watered there.

June 7—Moved eastward on the Beale road for several miles, leaving Mount Floyd on our left, then turned northward and, after a march of nineteen miles, reached Black Tanks, which is fifty-five miles south of the Havasupai villages.

From this point I sent two noncommissioned officers, a Hualapai Indian, and a packer familiar with Indians as interpreter to give warning to the Indians that I was coming and requesting their main chief, Najavo, to meet me "in three sleeps" at a point six miles to the right of our trail after it entered Cataract Canyon,[6] he holding the two soldiers as hostages for his safe return should he so desire.

In the afternoon of June 9, after watering the animals, moved with cavalry and pack train, traveling in a northerly direction far into the night; made a dry camp after a march of eighteen miles. June 10, a twelve-mile march brought us to the edge of Cataract Canyon, twenty-five hundred feet below us; a very steep, zigzag, rocky, hazardous trail over a mile long which consumed an hour in descending brought us to the bed of the canyon, and we were soon joined by

Navajo and several of his people; the packer was with him; the two soldiers had remained in the villages. The water, of poor quality, which was in two springs, was not sufficient to supply more than half my command, the animals crowding around the springs all night to catch the few drops that seeped from the earth.

Navajo, the Supai captain, was at first nervous, excited, and very suspicious—fearful that an effort would be made to remove them to some other reservation. They subsequently regained confidence and said that all they wanted was to be allowed to retain the little land they cultivated; that they were self-sustaining, and that they would cause no expense or trouble to the government. I assured them that our intention was to locate and set aside for them all the arable land they had ever cultivated and to secure for them all the water they had ever used for irrigation from any encroachment of the whites.

June 11—Moved to the head of the water in the vicinity of the Indian villages, thirty miles. Later in the afternoon Navajo brought to our camp all his people, over two hundred in number, to whom he wished me to explain our mission. He brought with him apricots, dried peaches, and jerked venison, which he presented as a friendly offering. I gave him some flour and tobacco in return, which he distributed among the Indians. There was some hesitation among them in accepting anything, they being very suspicious that it might be the opening wedge toward their removal from their country. They had evidently been misinformed (probably by the Hualapais) that the discovery of mines in their country would necessitate the abandonment of their lands, as the whites would take them for their own use.

The explanation of my orders and intentions was accepted by them in good faith, and they subsequently seemed to understand the matter perfectly and expressed themselves as glad that we had come to settle their troubles and their minds. I had several talks with them during the next succeeding days.

For numerous reasons, viz.: that the Indians might feel more assured of our intentions; as the grazing and water was bad, and some of the animals might stray upon and destroy their crops; as the heat was intense and gnats and mosquitoes very annoying to men and animals, I directed Lieutenant Kingsbury to return with the cavalry to Black Tank the next day, I remaining with interpreter Charles Spencer and such men as Lieutenant Palfrey required to perfect his survey of their land and reservation.

On the twelfth the command moved to the top of the canyon, twenty-four miles. On the thirteenth, to Black Tank, thirty miles.

THE HAVASUPAI INDIANS

This curious and quaint, self-sustaining community, cut off from the entire outer world in an almost inaccessible canyon three thousand feet below the surrounding mesa land, consists of 60 men, 53 women, 101 children—total 214. They are polygamous, as are most Indians, but only ten or twelve have a plurality of wives. They have so constantly intermarried that they are all rela-

In the Havasupai country. NELSON A. MILES. *PERSONAL RECOLLECTIONS AND OBSERVATIONS.*

tives of more or less close consanguinity. The result of this inbreeding is man-
ifestly observable.

They are evidently a branch of the Hualapai tribe, as their language and
affiliations are with that people, the former being almost identical, whereas
they say they cannot understand the Moquis, their nearest neighbors on the
east, with whom they do much trading. Their traditions are that they occupied
the country eighty to one hundred years ago, when it was abandoned by the
Moquis; by this they evidently mean the prehistoric race who inhabited all
arable portions of Arizona, as is known by their pottery, artificial tanks, crum-
bled villages, and acequias, and of whom the Moquis are at present the nearest
living representatives. Remnants of cliff dwellings and pottery are observed
fifteen or twenty miles above the villages, which would indicate that at some
previous date the water had come to the surface much higher up the canyon
and that much more land was susceptible of cultivation.

The water bursts out from under the red and sandstone formation and
almost at once obtains its full volume, which I should consider is equal to
about five thousand miner's inches, or a creek eight feet wide and over four
feet deep. The water is thoroughly saturated with lime, forming stalactites
wherever the spray touches twig or shrub. Many beautiful and fantastic petri-
factions were obtained by us, noticeably the maidenhair fern, but they were so
frail that it was impossible to keep them in any state of preservation on pack
animals. The water is of deep blue color, and from this they very possibly
derive their name—they speak of themselves as the Avasuz, a very slight devi-
ation from the *agua azul* (blue water) of the Spanish.

Just below their cultivated land the water falls away in three beautiful cataracts, varying in height from fifty to two hundred feet; below these cataracts the water drops off probably in successive waterfalls for fifteen hundred to two thousand feet, where it enters the canyon at a point presumed to be eight miles below.

The trails around and about these cataracts are considered very dangerous, even by these remarkably surefooted Indians, as several of their number have fallen off the cliffs, to be dashed to pieces on the rocks below. The last victim was an Irishman, who last year, against the appeal and protestation of one or two mining friends who were with him, insisted that he would go to the Colorado River; they refused to witness what they considered his self-destruction. He had three hundred feet of three-eighths-inch rope which he knotted some distance down, fastened to a root, and let himself over the abyss. He probably reached halfway down, when he let go and was dashed to pieces on the rocks below; his body was not recovered for many months afterwards.

The land is cultivated entirely by irrigation. I should estimate the acreage at not exceeding three hundred acres and that there were not over four hundred susceptible of irrigation. They raise eight articles—corn, beans, watermelons, musk melons, peaches, apricots, squash, and sunflower seed. The men do most of the outdoor work, planting and irrigating, the latter being done in the primitive way, in small squares, as the Mexicans, Moquis, and Navajos cultivate.

THE MINES

We found two miners in the canyon who represent Jones, Beckman, et al. They showed us a faint streak in dolomite formation which they said laid horizontal for a distance of sixty feet, the vein showing two to six inches. They showed us some small samples of ore which they said would assay forty dollars per ton.

I cannot conceive of any capital going in there to work, unless they find very large deposits of very rich ore. There is almost every possible obstacle to successful mining: the enormous expense that it would require to get any kind of a road into the canyon; the great distance between water, a fifty-mile march being required in any direction; scarcity of wood, grass, etc.; and the thorough inaccessibility of the place would tend to keep out capital until the many other promising prospects of Arizona have been developed. I believe these men will prospect for a few months and then abandon the place.

Navajo and all the Supais seemed much gratified when the monuments were erected, at points they themselves indicated, covering all their arable land and all the water they required, and that they would be maintained in their right to possess it against all intruders. For the small party of eight or ten miners who were there, they thought that if they would take ordinary care of their horses, the fences now around their crops would answer; but if the mines proved valuable and more men and more horses came in, they would require a better fence. There would be no trouble concerning the right of way, if a substantial fence of two miles was built by the government.

In the fall of the year these Indians go up on the eastern side of their canyon and hunt. They kill many deer and make fine buckskins. They are good traders and merchants; in fact, they trade extensively their mescal and buckskins with the Moqui Indians for Navajo, Moqui, and Zuni blankets. These they again trade with the Hualapais for horses and buckskins.

Lieutenant Palfrey, U.S. Engineers, will, I presume, furnish his report, of whom it is required. He was ordered to accompany me—I have no knowledge of his instructions. He informed me that the monuments erected in the presence of the Indians were within the line of the reservation, as would appear when accurately surveyed.

Left the canyon on the fourteenth and reached Black Tank on fifteenth. The four days in the canyon, although interesting in so many ways, were attended with great discomfort on account of the intense heat and prevalence of gnats and mosquitoes; the two days' march back was accompanied by considerable suffering on account of water. A courier was sent to Black Tank to have men with canteens meet us on the trail. The water in the Black Tank was almost exhausted, and we learned from the Indians that Kerlin's Tank was dry. It was necessary to send the wagon with grain via Young's to Peach Springs, making one dry camp and reaching Peach Springs the third day.[7]

It would have been impossible to have retraced the route over which we came without great suffering. Peach Springs, the nearest water, was forty-five to fifty miles to the westward.

On the afternoon of the sixteenth, Black Tank had become almost exhausted; I had caused the depth of water to be marked after each watering of the stock and demonstrated that it was simply a tank and received no fresh or living supply of water. It furnished water for my command (71 animals, 39 men) for six days, which at 10 gallons per head for the stock would be 4,260 gallons; I presume the tank contained nearly five thousand gallons of water when I first arrived there June 7. The kegs and water barrels were filled, and the wagon with grain moved out, to make two dry camps and, passing through Young's, to meet us at Peach Springs on the third day.

June 17 at 3:00 P.M.—After watering the animals there was left a small mud hole which contained probably as much animal and vegetable matter as water—we had fished from the tank a number of water dogs (the Spanish *Axolotl*),[8] a disgusting looking, low order of animal about nine inches long with four legs, tail, gills, and head not unlike a dog's. Taking our water kegs, which had been filled the previous night, we moved westwardly over an unbroken trail for eighteen miles and made a dry camp at 9:00 P.M.

June 18—Continued in the same direction for twenty-eight miles, reaching Peach Springs about 3:00 P.M. Here was the first pure, living water we had drank since we left Roger's ranch on June 5. Remained at Peach Springs June 19. A portion of the command went down Peach Springs Canyon to the Grand Canyon of the Colorado at the mouth of Diamond River. I started the pack train for Barley, which was to meet us the following night at Milkweed Spring. June 20 we moved to Milkweed Spring, eighteen miles. The wagon, which had been loaded with the baggage of the whole command, was obliged to make a large detour over an unbroken road; did not reach us until late in the night. The Hualapai Indians had kept themselves advised of all our movements, and Scherum and his brother[9] met us several miles this side of the water. A large number of these Indians had gathered at this place for a council, to many of whom I was personally known, and to all of whom I was known by tradition. Remained at Milkweed until the twenty-fifth in council with Hualapais. A portion of the command went to the [Grand] Canyon of the Colorado.

THE HUALAPAI INDIANS

In 1867 this band of Indians consisted of over fifteen hundred people, between four hundred and five hundred fighting men. They were a wild, capable, implacable foe. They had scarcely any wants, except the powder, caps, and lead necessary to contend against the white. They went summer and winter almost entirely naked and lived on rats, lizards, and rabbits. They were relentlessly pursued by me for over two years and in 1869 surrendered and asked for peace; several of their prominent men were sent to San Francisco in irons and remained for months as prisoners on Alcatraz and Angel Islands. It was ascertained that 175 of their people, mostly warriors, had been killed.

They were thoroughly subdued and have never since caused any serious trouble to the government. They furnished fifty guides and scouts for the subjection of the Apaches-Mohaves, or Yavapais, while I was in the territory, and General Crook made his first organization of one hundred of them for the subjugation of the Tontos and the southern bands of Apaches. They were at one time sent to the Colorado River reservation; being mountain Indians they died there very rapidly. They sent word to General Crook that they did not want to fight, but that they could not live there and that they would rather die fighting on their native mountains than sicken and die as they were doing on the river bottom. General Crook made many appeals for them, and the present department commander, General Willcox, has done the same, but as they have committed but slight depredations and caused no serious trouble, there has been but very little done for them. Sherum, Soquonya, Soskuorema, Cowarrow, and a majority of the tribe, in council assembled, wished me to aid them and represent to the proper authorities the following:

They say that in the country over which they used to roam so free the white men have appropriated all the water; that large numbers of cattle have been introduced and have rapidly increased during the past year or two; that in many places the water is fenced in and locked up, and they are driven from all waters. They say that the railroad is now coming, which will require more water and will bring more men, who will take up the small springs remaining. They urge that the following reservation be set aside for them while there is still time; that the land can never be of any great use to the whites; that there are no mineral deposits on it, as it has been thoroughly prospected; that there is little or no arable land; that the water is in such small quantities, and the country is so rocky and void of grass, that it would not be available for stock raising. I am credibly informed, and from my observations believe the above facts to be true. I therefore earnestly recommend that the hereinafter reservation be, at as early a date as practicable, set aside for them.

RESERVATION

Beginning at a point on the Colorado River five miles eastward of Tinnahah Spring; thence south twenty miles to crest of high mesa; thence south forty degrees, east twenty-five miles to a point of Music Mountains; thence east fifteen miles; thence north fifty degrees, east thirty-five miles; thence north thirty miles to the Colorado River; thence along said river to the place of beginning; the southern boundary being at least two miles south of Peach Springs, and the eastern boundary at least two miles east of Pine Springs.[10]

All bearing and distances being approximate.

There is, I believe, but one legitimate claimant on the above described land—that is Charles Spencer, who has lived with these Indians several years; he, I believe, claims Milkweed Spring and another location far down in the canyon north of that spring. Peach Springs has at once time been claimed, but I understand no one has been living there for more than a year.

These Indians seem very destitute, and it is miraculous how they are enabled to secure an existence in this barren waste of a country. They say they live on grass seeds and mescal; we did not see even a rabbit in several hundred miles of the country they occupied.[11] It will be necessary to issue them beef about every third or fourth day. Peach Springs would be the proper place at which to feed them.[12]

LITTLE CAPTAIN

They complained that Little Captain had been lying and causing much trouble since his return from confinement at Fort Yuma; that he claimed to have a paper direct from Washington; that he owed no allegiance to the tribe; that he had caused my command to move through the country; that I was going to arrest four of Soquonya's people; that he had terrorized the Indians by firing at some women and old men; that he had gained a good deal of influence, had drawn a good many of the young men about him and had taken them to the Juniper Range, beyond the limits of any country they had ever inhabited. They feared he would get them all in trouble.

I sent for him to meet me at Oaks and Willows.[13] He was very insolent and defiant, confirmed and repeated all the lies the Indians had reported and gave evidence that he was gathering around him a very strong following and that he was liable to draw to him a sufficient number to divide the tribe, as the hunting was quite good in the section he had selected. He recognized no authority in the department and would have soon caused serious trouble. I decided to arrest him and bring him to this post and would recommend that he be placed in irons and obliged to work with the other prisoners until he gives sufficient evidence that he will go back and conduct himself properly.

We left Milkweed on June 25 and reached Hackberry, distant about eighteen miles. We then followed the main road to Prescott the next day and had no incident except the arrest of Little Captain at Oaks and Willows. Reached Prescott on June 30; distance from Hackberry to Prescott, 111 miles. Total distance marched 433 miles, portions of the command marching 70 miles farther.

Lieutenant Kingsbury and the men of Company K, Sixth Cavalry were at all times most efficient and cheerful during the scout, and credit is due them for its success. Assistant Surgeon Coues, U.S. Army, and Lieutenant Palfrey, Corps of Engineers, who accompanied me were cheerful and uncomplaining under much suffering from want of water and hard riding.

I have endeavored to comply with all instructions received.

I have the honor to be,

Very respectfully,

Your obedient servant,

WM. REDWOOD PRICE,

Liuetenant Colonel, Sixth Çavalry.

On Campaign after Cibicue Creek

JOHN F. FINERTY[1]

Chicago *Times*, September 18 to October 21, 1881[2]

FORT THOMAS, Arizona, September 13—I have been so busy in moving from place to place and in sending telegrams, and in waiting until answers were received thereto, since I received orders to come into this God-forsaken region and write up the Apache "war," that I have been quite unable to do anything except send what news I could by telegraph for several days. My rush from San Francisco to Tucson was too rapid to permit me to see much of the intervening country. What I did see in California was, for the most part, a wheat-producing region, and millions of sacks of grain were piled on the platforms of the stations we ran by. The long drought had parched the landscape to a disfiguring extent, and the atmosphere was so smoky and murky that I could see but little of the general features of the southwestern portion of the Golden State.

A large freight train ran off the track about one hundred thirty miles from Los Angeles, and we were detained in a desert ravine for over eight hours. I never saw such another smash up. The cars were chiefly freighted with groceries and liquors, the latter ranging from whiskey to champagne. About one hundred Chinamen were employed to clear the wreck, and they managed to get away with enough of the loose wine to become very imposingly drunk. Doubtless this circumstance was accountable for our long detention. The Southern Pacific Railroad has been quite unfortunate during the last few months and will have to pay out large sums for damages. The track, owing to the great cloudbursts in Arizona, is in miserable condition and will continue so for some time.

There were very few passengers on our train because people are afraid of unreasonable detention and also because of a very lively Indian scare. I was struck by the admirable consistency of the railroad authorities, who, having asked for arms from the government for the use of their employees, allowed their baggage men to take away such weapons as the passengers had with them. This seems to be an order on nearly all Pacific Coast railroads and appears very absurd on the face of it.

The baggage man charged for carrying the guns in his car, and, as the money goes into his own pocket, no Irish or Russian constable was ever sharper in spying out a firearm. As they are under orders to disarm passengers, nothing is left for the latter but submission. But is not the custom an infringement on the right of American citizens to have and to hold arms? Who gave the railroad people authority to override the constitution? Perhaps the railroad "kings"—merry monarchs they are—feel themselves mightier than the constitution. If so, let us brag no more about "the best and freest government under the sun."

We ran off the track near Tucson, which delayed us three hours. General Willcox and Acting Governor Jasper were on the train, which made a narrow escape from being a total wreck.

Tucson is so nearly like an old Mexican town—which in fact it is—that I need hardly pause to describe it, even if I had the time. The houses are chiefly built of the repulsive-looking adobe, one story high in most cases and with no pretensions to elaborate architecture. I met some very unpleasant people there. It seems as if their whole business was to tax travelers heavily and give as little as possible in return. There are many honorable exceptions to this rule, I suppose, but I failed to discover more than three or four during my stay.

From Tucson I proceeded to Willcox, eighty-five miles further east, and found great difficulty in sending through my dispatches because of the official diarrhea which seemed to have seized upon department headquarters. This has continued ever since and, not satisfied with taking the lion's share at Willcox from the Western Union Company, the superintendent of the military line, acting under orders I suppose, has instructed military telegraph operators not to send any dispatches over their wires from newspaper correspondents unless approved by the nearest commanding officer. This Russian rule, which can be found in Section 41, series of 1880, of the signal service instructions, ought to be wiped out. It is a disgrace to the American government. I have no time to comment at great length, as I leave here for Fort Apache within a few minutes and have been delayed and distracted, as have been the military, by the number of contradictory telegraphic orders emanating from department headquarters. Fort Apache is about ninety miles by the Indian trail from this place, which is over seventy miles from Willcox and is reached by stage.

It is singular, looking at the campaign from a business standpoint, that Carr was not heavily reinforced to start with and a vigorous scout made after the revolted Apaches. But, then, there are things in the philosophy of military genius that civilians cannot possibly undertake to understand.

I will write at greater length when I reach Fort Apache.[3]

ASH CREEK, Arizona Territory, September 15—Major Tupper's command, to which I had attached myself for the purpose of joining General Carr, left the weedy and alkaline banks of the Gila River in front of Camp Thomas at daylight this morning. It consists of thirty-six noncommissioned officers and privates of the Sixth Cavalry and of fifty Yuma and Mojave Indian scouts recently enlisted, and three or four packers, mostly Mexicans, thoroughly versed in the ways of that noble and intellectual animal, the mule. The caval-cade was glad to get away from the military telegraph office, because it thereby escaped the ever thickening orders and counter-orders from General Willcox's headquarters in the field—on the railroad. Once out upon the Indian trail, which shortens the dilapidated wagon road by many miles, it was impos-sible for the A.A.I.G. and A.A.A.G. to reach the commanding officer unless by courier. What everybody most dreaded was an order to garrison the banks of the abominable Gila for several days, by which time half the command would have been laid up in the hospital because of the unheroic and unromantic effect of the worst running water in the world on the bowels of the country's defend-ers. It should always be a consolation to a soldier who is dying of intestinal laxity to remember that such heroes as Edward the Black Prince and Henry V of England perished of that unsavory complaint.

The weather was balmy and breezy when, at the first rays of the sun, the Indians, under a typical young Virginian, Lieutenant Gatewood, all armed with the latest improved army musket and all wearing a red band resembling an ori-ental turban around their long black hair, set out on foot to scour the canyon in the line of our advance, which was directly northward from Fort Thomas. These aborigines are not horsemen by nature, like the red men of the plains, but they prefer to ride any kind of animal, if they can get him, to going on foot. They are more efficient as scouts acting as infantry than otherwise, because they can more easily hunt up the lurking places of the hostiles, who generally wait in ambush behind rocks and trees awaiting a favorable chance to "jump" the unwary. The scouts preceded the soldiers about one hour, and Major Tup-per, wishing to see how they would work, left Lieutenant Cheever in charge of the company and pack train and, accompanied by a couple of couriers and myself, set forward to overtake them. So rapidly did they cover the ground, which is very broken and rugged, that we did not catch up with the natives, although we trotted most of the way, until we had cleared the first canyon and halted beneath the shade of some large trees that grew upon the summit of the defile. I have seen so much mountain country of late that very little impression is conveyed to my mind by ordinary highlands. Nevertheless, as we waited there for the rest of the command to come up, I could not refrain from admiring the boldness of the view—Saddle Rock Mountain, above the Gila, in the near distance; savage rocks all around us; enough timber to relieve the landscape from monotony; and weather such as Italy in its most favored season could hardly have excelled.

In front of us the walls of the canyon spread out and diminished, revealing an extensive prairie, with pine bluffs, evidently well timbered, in the back-ground. The plain looked emerald in verdure, and it was so, because this year the rainfall has been unparalleled and grass has grown upon the mesas with a luxuriance unknown in the previous history of Arizona. It took the company and train more than an hour to come up to where we rested—the Indians having meanwhile gone ahead at what might be called a sling trot, their muskets glittering in the sun, and their red turbans reminding me of descriptions of the Sepoys on the march that I had read of somewhere. Beside these picturesque savages the soldiers looked commonplace enough, because in the field the United States army dresses nearly "at will" and there is no attempt whatever at producing a theatrical effect. So long as a soldier keeps his arms clean, he may dress about as he has a mind to.

"You will find it a long, weary march over that prairie to Ash Creek," said Lieutenant Gatewood to Major Tupper as he rode off at the head of the scouts.

"It doesn't look over ten miles," said the major.

"I'll bet it's fifteen," said Lieutenant Cheever when he came up.

Distances, as everybody should know, are very deceptive in mountain regions, and this we found out, to add to numerous experiences of the same kind, before we reached Ash Creek. Our horses stretched out bravely, but the distance did not seem to diminish. The ground, where it was not rocky, was sodden from the great cloudbursts that had recently occurred and made rapid traveling difficult, not to say dangerous. In one place, by the banks of a rain-produced stream, the major's horse went down almost to his belly, and mine, which was following and bearing a greater weight, sank still lower. I had to get out of that saddle with celerity and then had quite a job in extricating my animal, which was so frightened that he would have run away, had the ground been harder. The major sent the troops by a better path, and all got across in safety.

It was quite late when we reached Ash Creek, having traveled at least thirty-five miles, and there found our Indians in camp. They had killed an immense deer, on which all hands feasted that night. How pleasant it would be if the denizens of the great cities could produce, to do justice to their viands, the appetite born of a thirty-five-mile march and the air of the highlands.

⊷⊷ ≣✦≣ ⊶⊷

CREEK BEYOND BLACK RIVER, Arizona, September 16—We slept last night, as usual, under the dew and were on the march at 6:00 A.M. We had to pass first through a pass known as Rocky Canyon,[4] where the Indian runners said the hostiles had threatened to fight Major Tupper's command. The major paid no attention to the threat but took the usual precautions against surprise, as every good soldier does in passing through a dangerous defile. The Indians were in front and on the flanks, and then came the soldiers, the packs well up with the column and everything neatly in hand in case Mr. Sanchez[5] and his cutthroats should be willing to try his hand upon us. We were more than an hour defiling through the canyon, but we saw no hostiles and no sign of any—at least none that were very recent. After clearing the pass we entered a charmingly wooded country which presented the appearance of a gigantic orchard because of the peculiar shape of the handsome scrub oak trees which are found in such abundance in this territory. There was plenty of rainwater lodged among occasional rocky courses, so that neither man nor beast suffered from thirst. It was past noon when we reached the wild, weird, but beautiful canyon of the Black River, on the west bank of which Major Biddle, who was there with a weak command soon after the outbreak, had erected very creditable fortifications, the only drawback being that he was too high above the river to obtain water, without which a long defense would be impossible.

We descended the rugged and difficult path—the wagon road has been completely swept away by the floods—to the crossings, and there, to our surprise, found the rope ferryboat, which the hostiles, no doubt appreciating to use in their own behalf, had left intact. Our Indians crowded at the landing, not caring to wet their precious hides in the deep and rapid river. The boat was moored at the other side, so Major Tupper ordered a very handsome young Yuma chief to swim across to it on horseback. The native complied at once, and then we found that it was not necessary to swim at all, as there was a narrow ford, a few yards on either side of which the water was of great depth. All of the soldiers, led by the major and the other officers, then crossed the river by fording, although the water reached above the saddle bars. My California horse, used to the business, did about as well as the rest, and we were subsequently fortunate enough to cross the whole outfit without accident. We ferried the foot Indians over and also transported the mule packs, as the stream was too savage to allow of the poor beasts crossing loaded down. The braying of the mules on the other bank, when they had crossed this Rubicon, was amazing. They evidently had a thankful appreciation of the perils they had escaped.

It would never have done to go into camp on the river bottom, as we would have been murderously commanded from the cliffs on every side. Major Tupper, who is an officer of great experience and tried courage, marched the command about four miles further north, across the mesa, and went into camp at the place from which I write. It is a very pretty camp—the only drawback being damp ground and a fair average of active mosquitoes. The country has not varied in appearance to any noticeable degree since we left the Gila. We must have marched twenty-five miles today.

———— ≡♦≡ ————

CAMP APACHE, Arizona, September 17—Last night at about 11:00 P.M. our Indians reported prowlers around the camp.

They discovered them by the moonlight, but, finding they were observed, the intruders, whoever they might be, took to their heels. Preparations were made to give them a warm reception if they, or their fellows, should again reappear, but they did not. Leaving watchfulness to the pickets, the rest of the outfit fell asleep and did not awake to the troubles of frontier life until the gruff voices of the sergeants announced that the marching hour was at hand.

We had all plain sailing through the orchard-like country until we approached Seven-Mile Hill, beyond Turkey Creek, down from which slopes the canyon that leads to Fort Apache. Just as we approached the plateau we observed two oblong heaps of stones on our right hand and one upon our left. "They are graves," said the major. "No doubt there are buried the two soldiers who were employed at the ferry and the man who went to warn them." This subsequently proved to be the fact.

A hundred yards further on we came upon another grave on the right-hand side of the road. A red pocket handkerchief, held by a stone, waved from its summit and produced a ghastly effect. Another grave appeared on the other side of the road, and, almost abreast of it, a box of empty cartridge shells. These latter had been discharged by that heroic Mormon, Henderson, before he fell a victim to the ambushed savages. There were nearly two hundred cartridge shells. In the trees, fifty yards off, we saw the debris of his wagon, in which the Apaches burned the poor fellow to death while helpless from his wounds. He had some kerosene oil on his vehicle, and with this the bloody wretches consummated their infernal work. A few charred bones, no fragment being over an inch square, are all that remain of gallant Henderson.

Both the soldier and citizen victims traveled carelessly enough by daylight and ran into the Indians where they least expected. They are supposed to have been murdered the second day after the attack on General Carr—that is, September 1.[6] Their graves will long be a terrible reminder to travelers along that lonely road. General Crook's chief aide, Lieutenant John G. Bourke, accompanied by Mr. Moran,[7] the artist, passed right over that ground the day before the massacre. Lieutenant Bourke had a narrow escape and will now, no doubt, live to complete his scholarly book on the Indians of Arizona and other parts of America.

The murdered people were buried by a party of the Sixth Cavalry under Lieutenant Overton. The mail carrier was killed down in the canyon near the post, while a man named Cullen was shot at Phipps' ranch, a mile or so from where the soldiers and Mormon perished.[8] Phipps himself escaped by hiding in the underbrush until night. He had heard the shots that killed his hired man and guessed they were fired by Indians. It was a lucky guess for him. Poor Cullen was at dinner when the dastards shot him through the head.

The scouts proceeded cautiously down Seven-Mile Canyon, led by Gatewood. Major Tupper with all his force followed closely behind. The road was a very bad one. Twenty brave men could almost arrest the progress of an army there, but we met with no interruption. When within a mile of Fort Apache the column halted, and the major rode ahead to report to General Carr. We were not long in getting in, and as the post appeared in sight an orderly rode forward and designated to Lieutenant Cheever the place of our encampment behind the corral. We had hardly unsaddled when Major Tupper came up and said: "We march with General Carr to the Cibicue in the morning. Let everything be ready."

I walked up to the officers' rendezvous and there found General Carr, whom I had last seen on Whitewood Creek, near the Black Hills, in September, five years ago. He had not changed much in appearance, and no shadow of the Cibicue seemed to be upon him. He recognized me at the first glance and treated me with the hospitality which friends and foes alike accord to the officers of the American army as a body, both in the field and out of it. You may very occasionally meet a snob, a peacock, or a damn fool on general principles among them, but the great majority are as pleasant companions, as obliging, as good-humored, at least to strangers, as I want to meet with. If they sometimes have disagreements among themselves, that is none of my business, and, indeed, the inertia and ennui of a military post on the frontier, in peace times especially, would try the temper of the angel Gabriel himself.

The general was impatient to be in the field, although I thought I could gather from his manner that he had little hope of catching any large body of the hostiles just then. He knows the Apaches too well to suppose they will hold together until an overwhelming mass of troops is brought against them.

It would seem, as I learned from General Carr, that the late revolt had its origin in wild superstition. A talented medicine man with an unconquerable name impressed the White Mountain Apaches with a belief that he could raise some of their favorite chiefs, killed in old battles, from the dead within a certain time. "I'll do it when the corn is ripe," said he. The corn ripened, and his promise was not fulfilled. He feared violence and told his credulous hearers that he had been in conference with the spirits of the departed and that their bodies would not arise from the dead until the whites had left or were driven from the country. This was a direct inducement to revolt, and no doubt the movement would have been widespread and, for a time at least, successful, had not the cunning medicine man been killed on Cibicue Creek when Captain Hentig and some of the soldiers were murdered.

All Indians are brutes, more or less. They cannot help being treacherous, because men can hardly recreate themselves. People who hate each other cannot be rationally expected to love white men, who are aliens and conquerors to their estimation. If Indians remain attached to white interests at all, it is from fear or self-interest, but never from love.

In its dealings with the Indian question, the Interior Department seems to be a dead failure. In that regard the whole government is weak, and our Indian policy is too disgraceful to be mentioned in the same breath with decent statesmanship of any kind. I personally doubt exceedingly whether the government is really in earnest about putting an end to Indian misconduct. White men are generally hanged or imprisoned for committing murder. With Indians the case is different. The killing of white men by them seems to be regarded as a piece of harmless frolic, and though households are bereaved, though widows weep and orphans wail, no justice seems to overtake the copper-colored butchers who are responsible for all this misery. The American government, in my humble opinion as an observer of Indian matters, is prodigiously afflicted with a chronic case of misdirected benevolence, which, although wondrously merciful to the savage, is outrageously cruel to the white population of the territories.

I could easily see from the surroundings of Fort Apache that it is an assailable position, commanded by eminences from nearly every side. Still, I have no faith that Indians can ever bring themselves to capture a post if defended with resolution, even though the defensive force be inadequate. To use the favorite frontier phrase, they haven't got the requisite amount of "sand" for such an operation as that. They came near enough to burn some outbuildings in the garden, a quarter of a mile perhaps from the parade ground. Their attack would have been far more serious had not General Carr returned from the Cibicue in the nick of time.

CEDAR CREEK, Arizona, September 18—This camping place is fifteen miles north by west of Fort Apache, from which General Carr marched out at noon today with 11 officers, 185 enlisted men (cavalry), 50 Indian scouts, and 20 packers. As I have already given the organization and the names of officers by telegraph, I'll refrain from repeating here.

We struck a trail, about four days old, this afternoon, leading toward the San Carlos crossing of the Black River. This indicates a stampede of the hostiles—perhaps frightened by the unexpected death of the magical medicine man—toward the agency, where they are now most likely being fed and strengthened, after the venerable fashion in such cases, to do some more throat slitting at their leisure.

Beyond an unusually pretty landscape of great extent, I have seen absolutely nothing in this day's march to write about. I don't believe there are any hostile Indians hereabout. General Carr is obeying orders from the railroad and is, therefore, not left free to follow the bent of his own judgment. In any case, I hardly think the red rascals want to do much fighting if they can avoid it. They made a bad miscue to start with, and it has taken the heart out of a big majority of them. All, I firmly believe, would gladly surrender now if they thought they would escape being hanged. And yet they have cheek enough to enable them to believe anything of white forbearance.[9]

GENERAL CARR'S CAMP ON CEDAR CREEK, Arizona, September 18, via FORT APACHE, Arizona, September 19—The command under General Carr, which left Fort Apache at noon today,[10] arrived at this point, about halfway to the Cibicue, without finding any hostile Indians or any very recent signs of their presence. There are, as usual, many rumors concerning them, but none can be called authentic. The fine growth of grass due to the unprecedented rainfall in this region is of great benefit to the cavalry. The animals cannot suffer while nature has so well provided for them. No part of Arizona is so fine as the country which the White Mountain Apaches have forfeited by their murderous folly. The *Times* correspondent has not seen, in all the territories, any finer grazing tract than that which extends from Fort Thomas to this point.

Water is, however, rather scarce, except in the rainy season like the present. If we are going to have an Indian war it will be developed within the fifteen days during which this scout is to last.

The most cheeky thing in connection with the whole outbreak is the sending of their women and children by the hostiles to the agency. They cannot certainly help themselves if white people neither have common sense nor natural resentment. The newly made graves of the victims of their treacherous cruelty, three soldiers and three citizens, killed about the same time that General Carr was attacked on the Cibicue, at the head of Seven-Mile Canyon,[11] remind every traveler on the road from Thomas to Apache of the devilish nature of the rebellious savages. The *Times* correspondent saw the heaps of cartridge shells lying in the roadway near some rocks which Henderson emptied at the enemy before he died. His covered wagon and burned bones are also there. The scene of death is as lovely a landscape as can be imagined, and no one in looking at it could associate the place with the infernal horrors enacted there some two weeks ago. There are still, no doubt, small skulking parties hanging around to cut off couriers or people traveling in small parties.

The latest phase of Indian insanity is a belief that their medicine man can raise the dead. The *Times* correspondent asked General Carr whether the idea was borrowed from the Christians, and he said he did not think so. He believed the superstition, which it amounts to in the Indian race, has existed for centuries among the tribes of the Pacific Coast.[12] The slain medicine man incited the White Mountain scouts to mutiny by impressing upon them that the dead could not be resurrected until the whites had left the country. His prompt taking off has no doubt cured him of that belief. The scouts about two miles from this place came on a trail of about forty, a week old, going southeast toward the San Carlos crossing of the Black River.

The personnel of General Carr's command is as follows: commander of column, Eugene A. Carr, colonel of the Sixth Cavalry; adjutant, First Lieutenant William Carter; Surgeon G. W. McCreery, Company B, Sixth Cavalry; Second Lieutenant Blake, Company C, Sixth U.S. Cavalry;[13] Second Lieutenant Thomas Cruse, Company D; First Lieutenant William Stanton, Company E; First Lieutenant Overton, Company F; Major T. C. Tupper; and Lieutenant B. H. Cheever.[14] The Indian scouts are commanded by Second Lieutenant C. B. Gatewood, with the cavalry. The whole force numbers about two hundred fifty effective men, including the Indian scouts. We march on Cibicue Creek in the morning.[15]

CHIEF SANCHEZ'S CORN TRACT, Carrizo River, Arizona, September 19—We reached here, after a pretty rough twenty-mile march, early this afternoon. It is a fine valley, planted to a great extent with Indian corn. Sanchez, who owns most of it, was the ruffian chief who numbered Carr's forces on the Cibicue, after shaking hands, and then joined in the treacherous attack upon him. Gatewood's scouts found some mules and a donkey, which they seized as contraband of war. Most of the corn crop was destroyed and a good deal carried away for horse feed. The valley is deep and somewhat narrow, the bluffs well wooded, and the water heavily alkaline. We had to lead our horses a good deal of the way while crossing from Cedar Creek. No fresh trails were discovered. The sun was fiercely hot, and our horses seemed to feel the effect more than ourselves. I am tired and will close at this point.

━━ ☰♦☰ ━━

GENERAL CARR'S CAMP, Cibicue Creek, Arizona (Scene of Indian Attack), September 20—We made another twenty-mile march or more, from Sanchez's farm to this place today. The trail was pretty bad all through until we cleared the ravines and came out on this fine valley, which witnessed a few weeks ago one of the most exciting episodes of Indian history. As we passed the defile we came upon a dead government mule with the aparejos still on. This animal had been shot in the fight and, of course, stunk infamously.

We noticed the Indian scouts in a group down by the river bank, where the plain was broadest, and rode in that direction. As we approached, the air was filled with a horrible odor, which we had no trouble in distinguishing as the dreadful smell that exhales from decomposed humanity. We were not long in discovering the cause. The Indians, after General Carr retired, had desecrated the graves of the slain, and there on the polluted ground were extended in mutilated, unrecognizable hideousness the bodies of the once stalwart and handsome Captain Hentig, of the Sixth Cavalry, and four soldiers. An attempt had been made to cut them into pieces. One of the captain's feet had been carried off, and the leg bones lay bare in the sickening sunlight. A hand had also been carried away, and he was otherwise cruelly dismembered. His face had been smashed in with a rock. His blue shirt still clung to his frame, which lay partially face downward, and his pantaloons, with the stripe of his rank on, were cast beside the repulsive remains. Maggots wiggled around his head and neck, and it was utterly impossible to identify in that terrible wreck the finest man physically, and the most popular officer personally, of the Sixth Cavalry. What poor, miserable worms we are anyhow! I pity the vain creature who is proud of a physique that a few days of sun and wind can destroy almost as utterly as if it had never existed.

The four soldiers equaled, if they did not excel, the unfortunate captain in horribleness. All were more or less cut up, and the air for hundreds of yards all around stunk so desperately that some of the recruits vomited.

Down in the brush lay another body, that of a soldier named Miller,[16] who had gone down to gather firewood, also badly decomposed, and the head entirely gone.

General Carr detailed Lieutenant Cruse with a party to rebury the remains. This was done effectually, the graves being marked carefully; but the odor still remained, because of the decomposing matter which had drained from the bodies while above the earth.

I have seen so many awful sights that I have grown somewhat case-hardened, but I think the remains of Hentig and his unfortunate companions capped the climb of my [horrible] experiences.

General Carr looked on with the stoicism of an old soldier, but I don't think he could have helped reflecting how near he came to be one of that hideous company on the river bank. The same thought must have stirred in Adjutant Carter and Lieutenant Cruse, who were also of the party jumped by the mutinous scouts and their confederates.

Had the attack been made in the narrow part of the valley, or rather if General Carr had not selected so good a camping ground, few if any who went to arrest the medicine man of the Cibicue would have lived to return to Fort Apache.

Campaigning does not, fortunately, leave much time for gloomy reflection. We were soon in camp, out of range of the charnel smell, and enjoyed our suppers as if we had seen nothing of an unusual nature.

GENERAL CARR'S CAMP, Cibicue Creek, September 21—The Indian scouts found three superannuated old squaws—abandoned by their relatives because they could not walk far—in a corn field today and brought them in. The poor old wretches were badly scared. One looked to be at least a hundred years old. The scouts would not doubt have killed them only for the intervention of the guide, Byrnes,[17] who accompanied them. The general turned them over to the four White Mountain Indians who are supposed to have remained faithful and who accompany him on the expedition. These quieted the fears of the hags, and they ceased to jabber with fright. They belonged to the medicine man's village and say they have seen only one man and one woman since the day after the massacre.

General Carr ordered them to be left at their hut and cautioned the scouts against molesting them under penalty. The savages obeyed with evident bad grace. What better comment can be made on the brutality of the Indian nature?

WARM SPRINGS, Near Black River, Arizona, September 25—General Carr hung around the Cibicue Valley long enough to convince himself that there was nothing there beyond a few old squaws, a lot of miserable huts—something like those used by the Zulus, as represented by the illustrated journals, and enough Indian corn to supply a cavalry command for several weeks at least. Our native allies—no doubt great scoundrels if opportunity offered—would have killed the old women if they had not been prevented by the officers. They found bain for their wounded feelings in the capture of about a dozen jackasses, which they were allowed to retain. They mounted the little animals two at a time and present, with their long guns and peculiar costumes, a most ludicrous appearance. The jackasses get even by braying infernally day and night, creating such echoes among the canyons as no yelling savages could produce.

We had a slight rain on the twenty-first. On the twenty-second, the general, having received news to the effect that Sanchez and other blackguards had surrendered, considered that he had only the mutinous scouts to deal with and resolved to divide the command in pursuit of them. Accordingly he ordered Major Tupper to take companies C and G of the Sixth Cavalry, with Lieutenant Gatewood's Indian scouts, and scout the rough country lying along and between Cibicue and Carrizo creeks, to the line of the Black River. The remainder of the column was moved, with headquarters, toward Fort Apache. I determined to go with Tupper; first, because I wanted to see some new country, and next, because I messed with him and knew that if he could get something to write about out of the Indians he would not shirk the amusement. Besides, I felt confident from previous experience that all was not as smooth as it looked, and that Brevet Major General Willcox and Agent Tiffany would be sure to find something new for the troops before many days. This campaign so far has been, in my opinion, run according to the temperamental fluctuations of the Indian agent at San Carlos. One day he is for peace, it would appear, and the next his voice is all for war. I don't know the circumstances of Mr. Sanchez's arrest. It is good to have him in irons, no doubt, but it would be much better if the troops had been sufficiently strong in the neighborhood of the agency to capture the whole band of miserables and string them up all at once. It was only natural that the other Indians, who at first appeared willing to surrender, should take to their heels the moment their most prominent chief was placed in disgrace. I don't know who gave the order, but whoever did has immeasurably increased the difficulty of bagging the game.[18] But this, I discover, is anticipating my narrative.

Major Tupper moved out of Cibicue bottom on the morning of the twenty-third, accompanied by Lieutenants Craig,[19] Cheever, Gatewood, and Sands, sixty-five soldiers, fifty Indians, six packers, and your correspondent. We saluted the graves of Captain Hentig and his murdered companions as we rode past and held straight down the canyon, past a small Indian village, entirely deserted, until we came to a deep ravine, in which we struck a large Indian trail, apparently ten days old, which led out of the canyon in the direction of Carrizo Creek. The major halted his column and sent the scouts down the Cibicue to find out whether there was an outlet to Black River by that route. They followed it a couple of miles and then found that it was utterly impracticable for animals, forming what is known as a "box canyon"—a ravine with precipitous walls, out of which it would be difficult to extricate even a command on foot.

After ascertaining this much, there remained but the trail to follow. The day was already pretty far advanced. The animals were somewhat jaded, and it was determined to go into camp where we were and make an early march on the morrow. There is not much variety in camp life on a scout. The average feeling is one of disgust. It is different on a march. Then the blood circulates freely; there is a probability of action—it is soldiering in earnest. That is, it is soldiering insofar as the Interior Department and the confusing shower of orders that is pelted on the command from the railroad and the agency will permit it to be.

There is an intense satisfaction in cutting communication with headquarters when that institution is in the neighborhood of a military telegraph wire. The very sight of a red-ink endorsement to a contradictory order is a terror to the average old campaigner. The American army proper is composed of much good material, but it suffers confoundedly by too much "major general by brevet" and also of ingenious gentlemen who attach, by order, a heap of capital letters to their distinguished names.

I remember once upon a time in 1864 that the colonel of a certain volunteer regiment became strict with his men and had occasion to punish one of them severely. The man had influence in a certain New York ward, and a politician came over to Governor's Island to interfere in his behalf. The colonel listened for a time and, at last losing patience, said: "Mr. B——, if you have any business to attend to, oblige me by doing it, for this is war, Mr. B——, this is war."

And so in a certain sense this is "war." It is true that the generals—there are heaps of them—have not, to all appearance, grasped the situation, but I respectfully hope that, under the inscrutable ways of divine providence, the situation may not grasp them. Generals have been grasped by situations before. Braddock was grasped by a situation. St. Clair was grasped by a situation. So was Custer. So would Carr have been, only that he is a practical, fighting general and broke the grasp of the situation as a skillful fisherman has often been compelled to break the grasp of a lobster's claws. These situations are terrible things—especially near a telegraph line.

Talking of Carr, his conduct at Cibicue has won for him the lasting respect of his soldiers. He never took to cover, and when a sergeant called out: "For God's sake, General, get under cover or you'll be killed sure," the gallant old chief replied coolly: "Oh, God damn these whelps, they can't hit me, God damn 'em." And they couldn't.

I asked a soldier who was in the fight how the general happened to escape. "Damned if I know," said he. "The general waltzed around there in the open, and the bullets seemed to shun him. I expected him to fall every moment, but devil a fall did he. He issued his orders just the same as if he was on the parade square, only a damned sight cooler. It was the same in the defense of the post. He ordered all around under fire on horseback. Bullets rained around him. His horse was hit in the hoof, but nothing touched him. Hang me if I can explain it at all. Lieutenant Gordon[20] no sooner showed himself than he was hit in the leg."

One of the ludicruous incidents of the Cibicue affray was the query addressed by Lieutenant Stanton to Lieutenant Carter, in a most matter-of-fact tone of voice, as to whether the latter had an extra pair of clean socks in his saddle bags.

A soldier named Sullivan,[21] who happened to be about the last man mounted, was shot in the breast at the first fire. "The sons of bitches," he exclaimed as he alighted from the saddle. Another bullet took him in the heart, and he fell dead in his tracks.

Poor Captain Hentig only ejaculated "My God!" as he fell, shot through the heart.

Foran, a young Irish recruit,[22] refused to lie down under fire and was shot through the bowels. The brave young Dr. McCreery placed him on a horse and brought him more than halfway in, helping him to mount and dismount, which he did frequently, owing to the intolerable agony of the wound. He had to be tied on his horse finally but broke the rope and hung head downward, writhing in torture. He was straightened in the saddle, but on reaching the top of the great hill he said: "It's no use, Doctor, I'll never live to get to the bottom of this." He begged to be untied, and when his request was granted he suddenly sprang a yard into the air and fell at full length, perfectly dead. General Carr's son showed much coolness and proved himself the worthy offspring of a fearless sire.

All the foregoing are campfire jottings and, although a little old, will serve to illustrate the character of the fight and the retreat. The mule packs were the chiefest means of defense, and the safe retreat was due in a great measure to the well-known dislike of the Apaches, who are very superstitious, to attack at night.

It became very cold—by "it," I of course mean the weather on the night of the twenty-third, and I fairly shivered under my blankets, but the morning of the twenty-fourth dawned cheerily, and our whole outfit was en route, the scouts leading, before the sun had climbed to the top of the environing hills. We followed the Indian trail through a not over-difficult country for some miles. Our scouts reported United States troops in camp some miles from us in the direction of Cibicue. As the major had his orders, he resolved to look for nothing but Indians and held his course. We soon came upon the cross trail made by the other soldiers—since discovered to have been Major McLellan's column—and a few miles beyond it struck an Indian trail that led to the right, in a southwesterly direction, which was the exact course we wished to take. We moved, after climbing one of the most damnable hills, or mountains, that I have ever breasted, over a lovely mesa all studded with beautiful trees, and this lasted for miles. Suddenly the tableland terminated, and Byrnes, the chief white scout of Lieutenant Gatewood's command, said we were coming to the "devil's own country."

This proved to be no exaggeration, for we were very soon in the bowels of a most formidable canyon, down one side of which we slid and stumbled, leading our horses, to an astonishing distance. The sun beat upon us terribly. The chaparral tore our clothes, and the whole proceeding was thoroughly

A pool in the desert. CENTURY MAGAZINE, APRIL 1889.

uncomfortable. The novelty of this kind of thing has worn off for me, and that, perhaps, is the reason why I don't think it's a heap of fun.

After scrambling down the wild mountainside for some time we suddenly came in sight of water, and then we knew we had struck an almost unknown portion of Carrizo Creek Canyon, over which white troops on horseback had never, to all appearance, marched before. There was a pretty well-defined Indian trail, which we knew was the best guide to follow. Climbing up and down mountains is an exercise that soon destroys the morale of horses and mules. Even our Indians showed signs of fatigue. It was a devil of a place in which to encamp, if an enemy should chance to be around, as it was hopelessly and helplessly commanded in every direction. But we had to make camp somewhere, and we made it there, for the troops found the canyon worse lower down. Fortunately there was plenty of good grass and water, and we were also so tired that the rough rest proved grateful. Our indefatigable cook, Foy, was not long in getting up a good soldier dinner, and when the shadows began to lengthen we were as happy as it was possible to be under the circumstances. To be sure, we hankered somewhat after a good cigar and a glass of beer, but such luxuries belong enduringly to those who never quit civilization. Soldiers and correspondents cannot expect to have everything their own way; and if an Indian bullet should make a hole in their stomachs, what the devil do you care, gentlemen, sitting in your neat sanctums, or sipping your pleasant toddies by your own firesides? Yea, verily, unless a battalion is massacred, to make a Chicago or a New York seven days' wonder, or unless a correspondent is scalped, the average American citizen rarely knows or cares what soldier or journalist endures in this kind of a life. And perhaps the average American citizen is right when he says, after hearing of some accident to the historian of a campaign: "What, Smith killed? Served him right. What business had he there? Why didn't he stay in the rear?" My illustrious friend, I have never had before occasion to remark that there is no rear in Indian warfare. It is like a Boston belle without her bustle.

But, then, the percentage of slain war correspondents, it must be admitted, is very small. "Bull Run" Russell still survives, and this knowledge somewhat props up my spinal column.

At this moment a huge campfire is blazing in front of an "A" tent, in which I write. A candle stuck upon a board affords me light, and Major Tupper's undershirt, which he has just succeeded in washing, is drying on a stick by the blazing logs. I feel already the first symptoms of an active population around my person. I shall adopt the English method of dealing with such a difficulty and inflict a famine upon them.

We resumed our march down Carrizo Canyon this morning, through mountain walls of extraordinary ruggedness, where a large and determined band of enemies would have had our small force entirely at their mercy. But what could we do? An order is an order and must be obeyed, and General Carr issued it supposing, because of advice from the telegraph office, that we had only a feeble foe to fear.

Within a few miles of the mouth of Cedar Creek we came upon a great salt spring of singular beauty. The mineral had aggregated there for centuries, until now there is a salt bed of prodigious dimensions, which would be extremely valuable to some company that could work it. The spring itself is about twenty feet square, very deep and of extraordinary clearness. It is one of the most beautiful natural curiosities that my eyes have rested upon. As it has no place on the maps, the command christened it, after the energetic commanding officer, "Tupper Spring." This title I hope it will be allowed to retain, as I am almost certain ours was the first cavalry column that ever came down that valley.

After leaving the spring we had to breast some more steep mountains, and just as we descended to Cedar Creek we saw a group of horses in the valley below. They were saddled, and we had no difficulty in recognizing General Carr and the rest of the command with which we parted company on the morning of the twenty-third. We knew at once that there was something up, and we were correct.

The general, who had moved down by Cedar Creek, was very glad to see us and said that advice received from General Willcox informed him that the hostiles refused to come in, and that Sanchez and other chiefs who had come in were arrested and in irons. The latter piece of information explained the rest. How in the name of common sense could the authorities, whoever they were, expect a suspicious people like the Apaches to remain within their power, while they had a chance to escape, after the arrest of their chiefs?[23] It is General Trevino's blunder with the Mescaleros over again,[24] and if the escaped hostiles do not make the scattered settlers pay for this insane piece of statesmanship in blood, Indian nature must have changed. If all could have been taken and ironed and hanged together the case would be essentially different.[25]

━━━━━✦━━━━━

GENERAL CARR'S COMMAND, San Carlos River, Arizona Territory, October 3—Perhaps no campaign—not even an Indian campaign—has ever been conducted on the peculiar principles that have distinguished the present affair. It may do to regulate the movements of civilized troops by chart and compass, but the same experiment tried against the Apaches has resulted in a military botch, the like of which, up to date, is almost without parallel. General Willcox did perfectly right in getting all available troops into his department. The comparative slowness of their mustering could hardly be avoided because of the want of properly organized transportation—something that should always claim the strict attention of a commanding officer; but having placed the troops in the field finally, the department commander should have allowed the leaders of the different columns to act according to their discretion and not confine them, as in the case of General Carr, strictly to orders. Indians who go upon the warpath rarely confine themselves to old traveled trails. They generally strike out on new paths, and the province of officers commanding in the field should be to follow the new traces until the Indians are hunted down. Under the positive orders issued by General Willcox it became impossible for the chief of this command to follow his own judgment. If he failed to carry out his orders and follow the trails indicated by the department commander, he would have left himself liable to be made a scapegoat of at the end of the campaign in case of failure—something that has often occurred to subordinate commanders before. Therefore, orders were strictly adhered to, and as a result nothing was accomplished beyond the arrest of forty-seven White Mountain Indians, forty of whom surrendered of their own free will, and the rest were brought in by Indian police at the agency without any trouble.

Colonel Tiffany, Indian agent, claims that he could have procured the arrest of all the White Mountain mutineers if there had been less display of force around the San Carlos and Gila River agencies. At the latter place the chief trouble was that there was not sufficient force—only just enough to flush the game, as in the case of the Chiricahua tribe, who to all appearance had no intention of running off before the attempt made to arrest George and Bonito of the White Mountain tribe, concerned, it is popularly believed, in the murders at Seven-Mile Hill, south of Fort Apache.[26]

The threatened chiefs cunningly aroused the fears of the Chiricahuas, who, by the way, had nothing to fear from the crimes of recent date, and the result was that seventy-two of the best fighting Indians in Arizona went upon the warpath. I am forced to believe, however, that they only needed a pretext to resort to the deviltry they practiced so successfully under the notorious Cochise for many years. The strangest part of all is that, while the Chiricahuas are out killing people on the highways, George and Bonito still linger on or around the sub-agency on the Gila River, fifteen miles from here, apparently afraid to come in and equally afraid of going out. The cunning chiefs, who have a band of about fifty well-armed bucks under their command, have scattered their women, children, and property among the "friendly" White Mountains, so that it is next to impossible to jump them effectually. Something in that direction will, I believe, be attempted within a short time. At all events, the Indian problem can not be considered settled in this neighborhood until George and Bonito are captured or destroyed. The great obstacle in the way of this achievement is the strong probability that the other White Mountain Indians, reported to be amicable, might join in with their kindred. This would give them at least three hundred fighting men, quite a formidable force in such a rugged country as this.

Within a few miles the Indians can get into a rugged country, where three times their number of troops could hardly make an impression upon them. Of course there are the Indian scouts; but, since the Cibicue lesson, grave doubts of the fidelity of a majority are entertained by a great many officers. Some of the latter say it would be better to have all the Indians on the warpath than have half of them friendly and the other half hostile. While in this divided state the danger to white settlers and travelers is much increased because it is impossible to tell a hostile from a friendly Indian unless troops accompany the latter. In this way a good many citizens who might otherwise have taken necessary precautions have been slaughtered when they were least expecting an attack.

Nothing prevents, in my opinion, a general outbreak of all these Indians except the bitter hatred that exists between the different tribes, although they are all of the same race. It is possible to bribe any of them to hunt down a brother Indian and bring in his head in a bag for a stated reward, the same as if it was that of a wild beast. With all this hatred of each other, they individually and collectively hate the white man most of all and are on good terms with him simply to procure rations, arms, ammunition, and other luxuries which they can not produce themselves.

When they have laid in a sufficient store of these they are prepared to do any amount of murder and robbery and, having had their fun, are equally prepared to return and "repent," and then enact the same game over again at the first convenient opportunity. No amount of kind treatment will cure the Indian of his desire to murder somebody. The most petted band of Apaches, both by the agency and the military, was the body of scouts that played traitors on General Carr at the outbreak of this infernal business. It is becoming more evident every day that the reservation system is a failure. I cannot suggest a better system, except, perhaps, a declaration of war against all the Indians outside the limits of Indian Territory, with the choice of death or retirement to that section of the country. This wholesale removal of the savages from the settled portions of the states and territories of the Union might prove both expensive and bloody. I have no doubt that it would; but in the end it would be cheaper and every way more efficient than the present tinkering policy. The peace of the country is disturbed year after year by a few recalcitrant savages, commerce is put back, settlers are discouraged, and the loss of life on the side of the whites is so great in proportion that it is hardly wonderful [that] there is a widespread stampede every time one insignificant tribe takes a notion to kick over the traces and bid defiance to the government.

The inherent nature of the Indians is so devilish that fear alone can make any impression on it—fear and superstition. He may have, in a few relations, some kind of a moral nature, but it is so distorted that it may be called, without injustice, an immoral impulse. This may sound paradoxical, but it is illustrated by the reply of an Apache chief to a man who charged him with killing a settler who had been his fast friend for years, and whom the Indian was supposed to have loved as a brother. "A coward," said the Apache, "can kill an enemy— any coward can do that; but it takes a brave man to kill a friend!"

With such notions as that impressed upon his mind, which is not so benighted as it is constitutionally depraved, how can the most hopeful of missionaries ever hope to Christianize these lazy and treacherous vagabonds?

It is a general remark here and elsewhere that the signal service telegraph line is an almost useless institution. The operators are all right enough, when they have a chance, but the wire is down so often that no reliance can be placed upon it. Between Grant and Thomas, the trouble is no doubt partly attributable to the raiding Chiricahuas, but between this place and Thomas the defect is due to the very imperfect manner in which the line is constructed. As a result, all here is in a state of incertitude. Major Biddle has sent a slim telegram, which announces a skirmish with hostiles near Fort Grant, but we have received no particulars.[27] Hostilities were not expected in that direction, so that the report came as a surprise. If the troops have struck the savages at all, I hope they have done so to the purpose. The demolition of the Chiricahuas would have a most salutory effect on the remaining malcontents. I am sorry, if there has been a fight, that it was not my fortune to witness it, as it might have afforded some opportunity for a letter out of the ordinary channel. However, I am consoled by the reflection that I cannot be in two places at one time, and the seat of an Indian war is about as uncertain as the winning card in a game of monte.

If George and Bonito fail to come in, I think General Carr will attempt something against them very soon. He is only restrained from attacking them by a desire to avoid stirring up the other tribes to immediate hostilities, which in the present scattered condition of the troops might prove decidedly embarrassing. The future movements of the chiefs alluded to will doubtless be determined by the fortunes of the Chiricahuas. If the latter have succeeded in escaping severe punishment, the chances of a more formidable outbreak in this region will be vastly increased. Some Chiricahua scouts who have been in the service of the government for some time were paid off yesterday, and it is not improbable that they, or some of them at least, will also take to the road, plundering and murdering. I can see no sense in giving money to members of a hostile tribe to render them more formidable than ever. And yet, to refuse payment would be accepted as a declaration of war. It might be just as well that way now as at any other time.[28]

SAN CARLOS, Arizona, October 4—Telegraphic communication has been reestablished since morning between this point and Willcox. All the events that have occurred since Saturday below the line of Camp Thomas have undoubtedly been reported to the *Times* before. The barest outlines are known, but from all sources of information it is learned that ten citizens, mostly Mexicans, and five soldiers have been killed by the raiding Chiricahuas.[29] All danger of an outbreak has not yet been removed from this locality. The band of Chief George hangs around the sub-agency on the Gila River, fifteen miles from here, and is likely to give trouble. All friendly Indians have been notified to cross to the south side of the river today and to report themselves daily at roll call to Subagent Hoag. An attempt to arrest George and his faction will be made tonight by the forces under General Carr that can be spared from the agency, unless a counterorder should come from General Mackenzie,[30] whose force is reported in sight of Camp Thomas, which he has doubtless reached by this time. The operating force will consist of about seventy cavalry, thirty infantry mounted, and nearly one hundred scouts of the [San] Carlos tribe, dividing in two companies. The chance for a good-sized battle was pretty strong. The *Times* correspondent will accompany the expedition if allowed to go ahead. George's band alone will not be formidable if the other Indians at the sub-agency should not undertake to make common cause with him. In that case Mackenzie's forces are near enough to render any necessary assistance. All will be decided in the way of arrest, or otherwise, before tomorrow noon.[31]

GENERAL CARR'S HEADQUARTERS, SAN CARLOS, Arizona, October 6—Everything has been in extraordinary confusion around this country for sometime. The arrest of the White Mountain Indians at this agency was easily accomplished, but a similar attempt made at the sub-agency on the Gila River with too weak a force has led to the stampede of Indians who might otherwise have remained on the reservation, and the prolongation of a very tiresome and apparently unprofitable war. The Chiricahuas, formerly led by Cochise, who have taken to the warpath are a small but formidable band and will no doubt create a reigning terror in the northern part of the territory before they are again reduced to subjection. The most alarming feature of the situation around here is the refusal of Chief George of the White Mountain tribe and some of his colleagues in the Seven-Mile Hill murders to come in. They are hanging around in this vicinity, and a movement in some force against them within a very short period is contemplated. Should they assume a hostile attitude, the road between this place and Thomas will be rendered very unpleasant to travelers. The telegraph line (military) has been down between Thomas and Grant since Saturday: consequently, no news can be sent through. It has not even yet been repaired. The line was also disabled between here and Camp Thomas during most of the day. A meager dispatch from Major Biddle at Thomas informed General Carr that some skirmishing had occurred between the troops guarding the Indian prisoners from here and the hostiles. There has been no confirmation of the intelligence, but there is apparent confirmation of the statement that six Mexicans and two white men have been murdered by the Chiricahuas between Camps Grant and Thomas at Cedar Springs. Until telegraphic communication is fully restored there will be slow work getting information of importance through.[32]

THOMAS, Arizona, October 9—The White Mountain Indians who have remained on the reservation are excited over a report that Jack, one of their number, first sergeant of Bailey's company of scouts, was murdered by the eight Chiricahuas who deserted from this post the night before last. Jack's hat and turban have been found on the banks of the Gila River, half a mile from here. It is supposed that the Chiricahuas knifed him and allowed his body to go downstream, believing that he would betray them to the military authorities. The White Mountains were about to murder the remnant of the Chiricahuas' camp last night but were prevented by Cook, chief of scouts.[33] They are now dredging the river for the remains of Jack, and if they find the body it will be difficult to prevent a massacre. The killing of the Chiricahuas would in itself be well enough, if the slaughter went no further, but once killing begins it is impossible to say where it would end. General Mackenzie is expected back from San Carlos today. His talk with the Indian chiefs was peremptory. He gave them plainly to understand that he would have no more nonsense from them and said that the guilty alone need fear the presence of the troops. Fresh reports of trails breaking away from the agency have come in, but they are no doubt exaggerated.[34]

WILLCOX, Arizona, October 12—The Apache war has, to all appearances, fizzled out rather ignominiously. The advantage in the way of slaughter, rude as it was, has been with the White Mountain and Chiricahua warriors, especially the latter, who are the murderous chivalry of the widespread Apache family. In returning from Camp Thomas to Camp Grant with the detachment of Lieutenants Blake and Willcox, I had an opportunity of seeing, near Cedar Springs, the riddled wagons of Samaniego's[35] ill-fated train. The Indian fire directed against the half dozen brave and unfortunate Mexicans, headed by the

The brave and unfortunate Mexicans. OUTING MAGAZINE, FEBRUARY 1887.

teamster's young brother, must have been simply infernal. The number of bullet holes in the vehicles is enormous. It is wonderful, contemplating this fact, how the doomed half dozen held their own against seventy-five Apaches for upward of two hours. The bodies found beside the wagons were full of lead. These men died hard, and the rude cross in front of "Shotgun" Smith's ranch that marks the common grave of five of them throws its sacred shadow on the dust of heroes. Dead mules pave the roadway, and the grass, trampled all around for miles along the thoroughfare, indicates the desperate nature of the struggle.

The troops did not come up until all the Mexicans but one, who with splendid presence of mind feigned death, were dead for some time. The Indians had had leisure to plunder the wagons to a considerable extent before the soldiers made their first appearance. This the Mexican teamster observed as he lay, partially on his face, in the grass. An Indian came up and pounded him with the butt of his gun between the shoulder blades to ascertain if any life was left in him. The Mexican took the pounding and saved his scalp. Had Lieutenant Overton's cavalry come upon the Apaches while they were in the open around the wagons, many of the savages must have been killed or captured. But the Chiricahuas were aware that they were followed and did not tarry too long. They retired east by south to the foothills of the Graham Mountains, along Norton and Stewart's new stage road, between the railroad and the Gila River. It was here, in a small ravine that crosses the road, that they killed the two telegraph repairers and three soldiers.

The bodies were still warm when the companies of the Sixth Cavalry under Lieutenants Overton and Glass[36] came suddenly upon them. Overton ordered the bodies to be examined, and while so engaged the Indians, from ambush, opened upon him. He deployed the soldiers, and the skirmish began. Colonel Sanford's two companies of the First Cavalry, escorting the White Mountain prisoners, heard the firing and hastened up. General Willcox directed Captain Bernard's company and a portion of Captain Carr's to support Overton and Glass. With the remainder of the escort, he took the road to Eureka Springs and had the prisoners conveyed to Camp Grant. Afterward they were taken to the railroad and shipped to Fort Lowell. General Willcox, to do him justice, appears to have done all he could to punish the Indians in the fight, but fate was against him. The soldiers struck the savages at a point where they were at an immense disadvantage. The women, children, and ponies had had several hours' start and were already far up to the Graham Mountains, the warriors fighting the soldiers simply to gain time. This they accomplished effectually. They took post in a spur of woods running down from the mountains to the foothills—a natural fortification, as it is filled with rocks, and the Apaches have no superiors in the art of taking cover.

Their fire, although heavy, was nearly as ineffective as that of the cavalry, which is wonderful, seeing that the latter were compelled, as the attacking party, to expose themselves much more than is usual with their adversaries. Quite a number of cavalry horses were killed, but only one sergeant was shot dead and four soldiers wounded in the affair. This skirmish continued until night, and the cavalry fired off over four thousand rounds of ammunition, as I am informed, without any discernible effect. I make no comments, because I wasn't there, and I have no right to criticize an engagement of which I was not an eyewitness. I have no doubt that Bernard, Overton, Glass, and their companies did all that lay in their power, but they were out of luck. The Chiricahuas, in this rear guard fight, had decidedly the best of it. This, I think, everyone will concede. It is only fair to add that the Indians, as marksmen, have little to brag about in this instance.

When night closed the soldiers found themselves nearly out of ammunition and entirely out of rations. Many were dismounted, and all were despirited at the bad success of the day. I state this merely as a matter of information. It is hardly news at this hour of the day. But people will ask: "Why did not the soldiers keep after them?" This is a very natural question. But the answer comes in the fact that Bernard's men were entirely unprepared for a long chase and had no idea that any Indians were near them until they heard the firing. Overton and Glass had already made a long march and used up their rations. As I have said, most of the ammunition was exhausted. This caused the cavalry to halt at Camp Grant until morning.

Meanwhile the Indians, with the admirable genius for irregular warfare that their greatest haters, among whom I number myself, must concede to them, came down from the Graham Mountains, struck right across the plain to the southwest, and went into camp on a stream that runs down from a near "point of mountains,"[37] and composed themselves for a further retreat by early dawn. Some citizens made a futile attempt to dislodge them, but they were not more successful than the soldiers. For soldier or citizen the noble savage is an exceedingly hard nut to crack. The valorous gentlemen of the east, who are forever annihilating them on paper, ought to come out to Arizona and try their hands at the game. I don't wonder that so many excellent military reputations have been wrecked upon those Indian breakers. Napoleon Bonaparte himself would be as an infant among these damnable mountains, pitted against Apache generals who know the exact value of a rock, large or small, as a breastwork. "Fire and fall back" is the Indian motto. It works first rate, but most frequently it is the white man who does the most artistic falling back. No wonder that generals who made a reputation in civilized warfare dread the ridicule inevitably attached to failure in such a "campaign" as the present. These Indians run like quicksilver and fight like brigands. (If they were better shots, the vacancies in the army list would be amazingly increased.)

You know the result of Bernard's pursuit of the hostiles into Dragoon Mountains. It was the old, old story, and no carping critic can doubt Bernard's bravery and ability. If any man is fitted to cope with the Apache he is, but what can be done in mountain fastnesses with this wily, irritating, and all but intangible enemy? Will some military genius or some editorial prodigy solve this problem? If so, he can become governor of Arizona. I don't want the position.

As a result of this outbreak the army is terribly out of humor, and no wonder. General Willcox is mad over it. General Carr is displeased with it. Colonel Bernard swears over it. The staff quarrel about it. The line officers curse their luck, and the soldiers sulk, feeling more or less humiliated.

I desire to say a word about the Regular army of the United States. I have a right to, as I have been with it on several campaigns. It has fine material, both in officers and men, but it is, let me humbly suggest, badly managed. The companies are allowed to become depleted by expiration of term of service or by desertion, and when an emergency arises, they are partially filled up by recruits, who are usually next to worthless on a first campaign. The trained soldiers of this army are, in point of intelligence, obedience to orders, and a high order of courage, equal to any body of troops of their number in the world. The overwhelming majority of the field and line officers are attached to the profession of arms and are fully competent to lead their men anywhere. There is a certain proportion in field and line that might be honorably retired as a benefit to the service and to themselves. They have outgrown their usefulness and belong to another age. We want young, fresh blood in this army, more than dignity allied to servility, and we want to spare that young blood to a sentiment of martial glory by abolishing in service regiments—by which I mean all the cavalry and most of the infantry—the moth-eaten, musty, demoralizing system of promotion by seniority. This, of course, all the old fellows waiting for dead men's shoes will howl against. Let them howl. So much the better. If Congress will recognize Indian campaigning as legitimate warfare—it is infinitely more dangerous than civilized warfare—and promote an efficient young lieutenant who accomplishes a brilliant exploit over the head of some slow old captain, major, or colonel who fails to accomplish anything, they will put into our army an esprit such as that which led the ragged Frenchmen, under republican generals, to drive the Austrian sharpshooters from the Alpine passes and achieve the conquest of Italy. Men are mortal, and to win victories their ambition must be aroused. There is a vast difference between a lieutenant simply doing his duty in a cold, unimpassioned manner and the same individual pushing against an enemy, savage or civilized, with the hope of rapid promotion gleaming resplendent before his eyes. And this hope of promotion should extend all the way down from the general to the private soldier. Under the present slow-coach system our best Indian fighters remain lieutenants or captains. Very few have risen higher in rank, and these only by virtue of seniority. If a fighting officer receives any reward at all he is taken from the field and made a paymaster, a quartermaster, or something of that kind, destroying his most important usefulness as a soldier in active service. This I regard as the crowning idiocy of the American service. I could give many instances in point, but it is needless. The army knows all this better than I can tell it.

"Promotion for merit will bring the army into politics," is the chief valid objection raised against this proposition. I have no doubt there would be some lobbying, as there is in the matter of staff appointments, but when it is distinctly stated that meritorious promotion in the field and line must be for deeds accomplished in actual warfare and recognized by the army actively engaged in the operations, I don't see how any officer who has performed no brilliant exploit can possibly have the face to lobby for rapid promotion. I admit that the reform will involve many complications and that the conservative element of the army—by which I mean gentlemen who are rapidly approaching "the shelf" in the matter of health and age—will vigorously oppose it, but the hale and young element will, on the other hand, be as strongly in its favor. Under the present dullard system, a line officer who may display the genius of a brilliant warrior has to wait for promotion until some person above him retires, resigns, or dies. What system can be meaner than this? It places the army officer in the position of a man waiting to be shaved in a barber shop on Sunday morning, when numbers are issued, and the tonsorial artist shouts, "Next." I admit there is something to be said on the side of seniority, but in my opinion the arguments against the system immensely outweigh those in favor of it.

One other point, and I drop this subject. I don't believe a brevet gained in the Civil War should entitle an officer who has no knowledge of Indian affairs and who has never distinguished himself as an Indian campaigner to override, or command, in the field an officer who knows Indian habits and who has proved his ability to deal with the savages in their peculiar mode of warfare. They is too much humbug about alleged "rank" and too little common sense in our army. Rank, like tactics, is excellent for dress parade but not worth a continental, with the usual reservations, where real work is to be performed. I don't know anything more demoralizing to soldiers and more paralyzing to military movements in the wilderness than a general officer experienced only in grand warfare, with a top-heavy and ambitious staff. The greatest curse that can befall any officer of rank is to be completely in the hands of his staff. He might just as well, for all useful purposes, be in the hands of the enemy. The general should always run the staff, and not the staff the general.

This reminds me that General Mackenzie, as commander of the forces in the field, is in his proper sphere, but it would be much better if the government would form the territories of Arizona and New Mexico into one department and place them under his command.

From Hembrillo Canyon to Chevelon's Fork

THOMAS CRUSE[1]

Charles P. Gatewood Collection, Arizona Historical Society, Tucson

Fort Lowell, A.T.,
May 25, 1883

My Dear Abbot,

Your request for a letter was received, and as I saw the history of the Class of '77 and thought the letters a very interesting part of it, I take pleasure in complying.

After leaving the Point, Shunk[2] and myself took a trip to Boston. I had received my assignment to the Sixth Cavalry and to Fort Apache, Arizona. The latter name was found on the maps, but they utterly failed to reveal any such name as Fort Apache, and I never did find out its location until my arrival in Arizona.

I left home for my post September 10 so as to have time to get there. Once started, the question of "land-grant roads" gave me some anxiety, but I discovered that I had to pay my way through. I traveled on until I found out where Fort Apache was and also that it was quite a problem to get there, even after its location was known. I finally arrived at Camp Thomas, which was as far as I could go by stage or buckboard.

The post commander[3] was very glad to see me, and soon after my arrival rushed over to the telegraph office and sent off a message. When I spoke to him the next day about going on to Apache, he informed me that I was to remain at Thomas for temporary duty and added that the paymaster had just been there. The latter sentence conveyed no particular idea to my unsophisticated mind at the time, but an order detailing me as recorder of a garrison court-martial, and thirteen payday drunks for trial, soon enlightened me on the subject.

The post commander and "Ives" didn't agree, and the result was that I wrote nearly all the proceedings nearly two or more times before they satisfied him. I ultimately reached my post in November and was immediately sent on detached service to take some Indians to San Carlos. Killed my first deer in December.

January 1, 1880, I was made quartermaster of a company of Indian scouts, and on the third of that month left the post with Gatewood, Class of '77, in search of blood and glory, which were to be obtained by the total annihilation of Victorio. Traveled around in New Mexico and Arizona and finally wound up at the end of March on the Rio Grande under command of General Hatch. During this time we had frozen in the mountains and roasted on the plains, and I had seen some of the terrible effects of Indian warfare, having buried a party which had been massacred by Victorio's band.

About April 2, the scouts located the hostiles in the San Andreas Mountains, and we started after them in three columns. One arrived at the rendezvous a day too soon, and the Indians attacked and surrounded it.[4] When we arrived there at 6:00 A.M., April 6, the hostiles were making things extremely lively for Captain Carroll and his command, who had been two days without water. I didn't feel afraid when I first went in, but when several bullets had come uncomfortably close to me, I came to the conclusion that they were <u>actually</u> trying to shoot <u>me</u>, and that put a different light on the matter, and I didn't feel half so comfortable or confident. I am sure that I did not kill any Indians, because I did not see a single thing to shoot at; in fact, I saw nothing except a long ridge from which came white smoke and bullets.

After it was all over I met Taylor of our class,[5] and he told me how the Indians had put it to them. If he wishes, he can no doubt write more eloquently than I can about the fight. I saw my first dead Indian after the affair.

The Mescalero Indians had given aid and encouragement to the hostiles, so General Hatch moved there to interview them. They would not interview, so on the night of April 16 we received orders to go out and kill any Indians found three miles from the agency. About daylight we jumped a camp and killed six or eight, and the remainder ran in to the agency fast enough.[6] Met Grierson[7] and Finley[8] at the agency. We then went after Victorio and traveled on his trail until May 10, when the Indian company was ordered home to Arizona, where we arrived about May 22. I was then put in command of the Indian company, much to my disgust. All the remainder of the summer and fall it was scout and travel, and travel and scout, the only variation being a trip into Old Mexico after Victorio. But we did not get him, and I returned to Apache November 17. I was very nicely mentioned in the reports of the fights and felt very proud about it, because there had existed a good deal of doubt in my mind as to whether I would get wild and run or not.

Matters went on nicely at Apache, garrison duties being varied with an occasional scout, until the latter part of June 1881. At that time the Indians around the post began to show some signs of discontent, on account of the doings of a medicine man who said that he could bring back the spirits of their forefathers if the whites would only get out of the country. In August he became more decided and said that the whites must go when the corn ripened. I noticed discontent and murmuring among my Indian scouts, and when the commanding officer, General Carr, asked me for my opinion, I told him that, if I had my say, I would discharge every one of them and employ a company of

Yumas, as the present company belonged to the tribe that was most discontented and were unreliable. The commanding officer telegraphed for permission to act on my suggestion and also requested that two more companies of cavalry be sent up there, as matters were critical.

Just about this time a request and an order came, the first from the Indian agent, the latter from the department commander, but both with the same meaning, to arrest or kill the medicine man; and then the line went down, and we had no more news for some time. General Carr had a meeting of the officers and resolved to carry out the order and also to take my scouts along, as it was even more dangerous to leave them behind than to take them.

So on August 29 we left Apache with seventy-two white soldiers and twenty-two Indian scouts. On arriving at Cibecue Creek, much to my surprise, I found the medicine man at home. General Carr then came up and told him that he must go back to the post with us. He attempted to delay until the next day, but his request was refused. A sergeant and ten men were detailed to guard him, with instructions to shoot him if he attempted to escape or his friends attempted to rescue him.

The command then went down the creek for about two miles to go into camp. On the way down the Indians kept coming out from the adjacent bluffs and ravines, and when we reached the camping place there were about two hundred armed Indians around us, and I felt as if I was standing on a can of dynamite with a quick fuse attached. Some of the Indians came into camp, and General Carr ordered the company commanders to put them out. I had dismounted and reported for duty as officer of the day and was turning to see about securing the medicine man when suddenly there came a war whoop; a cry, "Look out, they are going to shoot," and then it seemed as if lightning had struck. How did I feel? I was stunned for a moment, for I saw that our scouts had fired on us, then I didn't know whether I was shot or not, because they were not twenty feet from me. Then I saw it was live or die right there, and as another volley came, I dropped to the ground and then got up and got my gun and went in for shooting—shooting at something.

The Indians fell back [at] the first volley from us, and then General Carr made his dispositions for defense. When we counted noses, one officer and six men were killed, another mortally wounded, and another slightly so. The Indians had run off a portion of our herd. They fired at us from the bluffs until dark and then left.

At the first volley, the sergeant[9] stepped up to the medicine man and shot him; his son attempted to run in with a pony and was killed; and his squaw grabbed a revolver and attempted to shoot a soldier and was killed by another one. After dark we buried our dead, and if I live to be as old as Methuselah I shall never forget how taps sounded over the grave, because it was an extremely doubtful matter if we could manage to keep from being killed ourselves the next day.

At 11:00 P.M. we pulled out for the post, and after severe marching reached it the next day about 2:00 P.M., distance forty-five miles. The Indians followed us closely, and the next day jumped the post, but we were all tired and angry and just wanted them to come on. They saw that they had stirred up a hornet's nest and soon gave up the job.

During the fall and winter we had the pleasure of reading our own obituary and scouting after the Indians.

In January 1882 I went to my home in Owensboro, Kentucky, and on February 14 married Miss Beatrice Cottrell.

Returned to Apache in March, and in April the Chiricahua Indians broke out, and we made some of the vilest marches on the trail that I have ever experienced and then didn't get in for the fight.

But in July my renegade scouts and some other of the Cibecue Indians made a dash into the agency, killed some of the police, and started off. The whole [Fort] Apache command was ordered out, and Converse[10] and myself were among the officers, the Third Cavalry having in meantime taken station in Arizona.

We took the trail and finally caught up with them at Chevelon's Fork, or Big Dry Wash, strongly entrenched and with a deep, precipitous canyon between us and them, and they had laid their plans for fighting one company.

About 3:30 P.M. the fight began, and it was hot, I tell you. Converse was the first fellow hit, but we all thought at the time that he wasn't much hurt. One company was left on the edge of the canyon to amuse the Indians, while two companies were sent out on either flank to cross the canyon and surround them. This was done about 5:00 P.M., and then things became decidedly lively, because the Indians were not more than one hundred yards from us, and I saw something to shoot at and have a chance of hitting for the first time in all the fracases that I had seen.

After about thirty minutes fighting there was a lull on my flank, and as there were four or five dead Indians in sight I thought the camp was deserted, so I called four men to me and we dashed across the ravine and got into the camp, but the Indians were not all dead by a good deal, and the first thing I knew I was within fifteen feet (actual measurement the next day) of the muzzle of a gun, with the livest kind of an Indian holding the trigger. Bang! it went, and I thought I was a goner, but one of my men about two feet to my left toppled over. I dropped also, and my captain said that he thought I was a dead man too. Then the firing was deafening, and in the while it lasted, Morgan,[11] Class of '80, killed an Indian, and about the next moment an Indian plugged him. We also had four other men wounded. We dragged my man back and asked him where he was hurt, and he said that his arm was broken, and I was actually envious of him, because I had an idea that it would be one of the nicest things in the world to have a nice wound and take Mrs. Cruse home and be a hero. But as is often the case I envied the wrong man, because that fellow had something more than a broken arm and died that night.

I went over the ground the next day and saw eleven dead Indians and was

Wounded soldiers on an escort wagon. CENTURY MAGAZINE, MARCH 1891.

told that there were three more.[12] The next morning the festive ranger was on hand bright and early—not to fight, thank you—but to claim all the captured horses and ponies.[13] We returned home, and I was much complimented in the report for my "gallant charge" into the camp, but to tell the truth, I didn't know the danger at the time or I might not have gone.

The department commander concluded that we needed a change of climate, so in November 1882 we were ordered to take station here and most gladly complied, as it is a nice post and near a town of some six thousand inhabitants, the only objection being that the thermometer has a queer way of running up to 115 and 120 degrees in the shade during summer.

Present station—Fort Lowell, A.T.

Yours sincerely,

Thomas Cruse,

Second Lieutenant, Sixth Cavalry

The Apaches' Last Stand in Arizona: The Battle of Big Dry Wash

WILL C. BARNES[1]

Arizona Historical Review 3, no. 4 (January 1931): 36–59

On July 6, 1882, about sixty White Mountain Apaches swept down onto the San Carlos Agency, captured and took with them half a dozen squaws, rode up the San Carlos River, and a few miles from the agency waylaid and killed chief of scouts J. L. Colvig ("Cibicue Charlie") and five or six of his Indian police.[2] Colvig succeeded chief of scouts Sterling,[3] who had likewise been killed in an encounter with recalcitrant Apaches only four months before.

The band then rode to the north, passing to the east of Globe, then westward through the Wheatfields region above Globe, across Pleasant Valley and up by Payson and the East Verde, leaving behind a sickening trail of burned ranches and murdered settlers.

Following the news of the outbreak and Colvig's death, five separate bodies of U.S. troops were in the field after the raiders.

Troop D, Sixth Cavalry, Captain A. R. Chaffee and First Lieutenant Frank E. West, were first in the field from Camp McDowell on the west side of the basin, under orders to move to Wild Rye Creek and await developments. Chaffee had with him Al Sieber and eight Tonto Indian scouts.

Troop D, Third Cavalry, Captain Albert D. King and Second Lieutenant Franklin D. Johnson; Troop E, Third Cavalry, Lieutenant George L. Converse commanding; Troop I, Third Cavalry, Lieutenant Francis Hardie commanding; Troop K, Third Cavalry, Captain George A. Dodd commanding; Troop E, Sixth Cavalry, Captain Adam Kramer and Second Lieutenant Thomas Cruse commanding; Troop K, Sixth Cavalry, Captain Lemuel A. Abbott and Second Lieutenant Frederick G. Hodgson commanding, all under command of Major A. W. Evans, Third Cavalry, left Fort Apache on the east side of the basin, under orders to scout the country and follow the hostiles' trail vigorously.

Company E, twenty-six enlisted Indian scouts, Second Lieutenant George H. Morgan, Third Cavalry commanding, also followed Chaffee's troop from McDowell with orders to scout the region and keep Chaffee advised of the hostiles' movements as far as possible.

Two troops of the Third Cavalry, Captains Gerald Russell and Henry Wessells commanding, hurried from Whipple Barracks near Prescott.

From Fort Verde, Troop K, Sixth Cavalry, First Lieutenant Henry Kingsbury commanding and Troop A of the Third Cavalry, Lieutenant George F. Chase commanding, were rushed out of that post eastward on the old Verde or Crook Road, which followed closely the rim of the Tonto Basin, to scout for signs and intercept the hostiles if they should attempt to climb up the bold escarpment known as the rim of the basin, swing around to the east and thus back into the Apache Indian reservation and safety.

From Fort Thomas on the Gila above San Carlos went four troops of the Third Cavalry with Captains George A. Drew, Peter D. Vroom, and Emmet Crawford, and Lieutenants Charles Morton, John M. Porter, and Britton Davis.

Thus we have a record of no less than fifteen troops of cavalry, probably three hundred fifty men in all, one company of Indian scouts, and fully one hundred fifty pack mules with many civilian packers, all searching the country for the hostiles and converging on them from every side.

Those who today ride over this country on well-built auto roads; who drive easily from Phoenix to Payson, under the rim, in six hours, can have little real appreciation of the difficult task these army men faced in 1882. There is no rougher, more broken terrain in the United States. The granitic formation is peculiarly hard on horses' hoofs, and a lost shoe on a cavalry horse or pack mule means a lame animal, if not shod at once.

Writes Lieutenant Britton Davis in his very interesting book *The Truth about Geronimo*:

A pack train of thirty packs accompanied the command from Fort Thomas. The mules were in poor condition, and the packers were having trouble keeping them up with the command. I was detailed to see that they did keep up. That night Drew decided on a night march. The trail led through a creek bottom with reeds and underbrush higher than a mule's head. The bell had been taken off the bell mare for fear of alarming the hostiles. Fifteen minutes after we got into the creek bottom you could not have heard the bells of St. Paul's Cathedral. It seemed to me there were mules scattered all over central Arizona. They were all lost—wanted to get back to the bell mare and determined that I should know it if their voices held out.

That night I completed my education in pack-train profanity. What those packers said in English, Spanish, Indian, Irish, and German left nothing more to be desired. We overtook the command about 10:00 A.M. the next morning but left two packers still hunting for lost mules.

Captain Chaffee was the first to cut the hostiles' trail above Payson on the East Verde. He knew the command from Fort Apache under Major Evans

On the march—the advance guard. CENTURY MAGAZINE, JULY 1891.

("Beans" Evans the men called him) was some miles distant and sent word by courier that he could use another troop of cavalry.

Troop I, Third Cavalry, under Lieutenant Converse made an all-night ride and reached Chaffee at daylight of July 17, 1882, the day of the fight. Morgan and his company of Indian scouts had previously overtaken and joined Chaffee's command and went with I Troop.

The Indians had evidently planned to climb out of the basin and slip along the Crook Trail on the rim and reach the sheltering depths of their reservation, a comparatively few miles to the east. They chose a most rugged and hazardous section of the two-thousand-foot cliff which forms the rim at the head of the East Verde. The place is known today as Tunnel Hill, due to the fact that in 1885 a company from Globe established a camp here and began to dig a tunnel, which they claimed was to be a part of a railroad from Globe to Flagstaff. It may be seen today, a bore in solid rock, 16 feet square at the entrance and about 112 feet long. It is very close to Zane Grey's cabin.

Up this tremendous cliff those hostiles forced their barefooted ponies. Halfway up they could view the whole country as from an airplane. They realized, of course, troops must be after them.

Chaffee's troopers of the Sixth rode white and gray horses. So did the troopers of Converse's command of the Third. These white horses showed among the green pines below like a long line of geese.

The hostiles did not count them. They felt themselves able to whip one troop of cavalry. It never occurred to them that in the U.S. Army there might be more than one white-horse troop.

Moreover, so secure did they feel that they failed to look farther back on their trail, hence they did not see several more cavalry troops riding blacks and bays; nor Lieutenant Morgan's company of Indian scouts, with Al Sieber at their head, slipping along under the pines—hungry wolves, eager for a feast or a fight.

On top of the hill the Indians rode boldly to the north. A few miles from Generals Springs, not far from the present Forest Service's Pinchot Ranger Station, the trail plunged abruptly into one of the numerous canyons that form the head waters of East Clear Creek. It was a veritable maze of deep, precipitous canyons surrounded by a heavy pine forest, but fairly level and free of underbrush at that time. Here the wily Apaches thought to give Chaffee and his troopers the surprise of their lives.

They built rock and log breastworks at the head of the canyon down which the trail led, assuming that the soldiers would ride blindly into the trap and, scattered in single file down the rough trail, fall easy victims to the Apache rifle fire.

Unfortunately for their plans, they quite overlooked the presence with the soldiers of Al Sieber and the thirty-two or more Tonto scouts. Chaffee pushed them ahead of his command to uncover just such a trap. This they soon did, and then the tables were turned.

The following account of the fight is taken from Britton Davis' recent book *The Truth about Geronimo* by permission of the Yale University Press, and also with General Cruse's consent:

For the following description of the fight, the most successful our troops ever had with the Apaches after they had obtained modern arms, I am indebted to General, then Lieutenant, Thomas Cruse, U.S. Army retired, whose gallantry in the action won him the Congressional Medal of Honor.[4]

The hostiles had seen Chaffee's troop, which was mounted on white horses, and had kept it under observation from about 3:00 P.M. until dark. They counted his men and concluded to ambush him the next day under circumstances favorable to themselves. But they had not seen the Fort Apache column at all, and their watchers reported the next morning that Chaffee's troop was still alone.

Colonel Evans told Chaffee to keep ahead the next morning as if he were acting alone, and he would follow at daybreak. Troop I, Converse, Third Cavalry, also on white horses, would be in the lead at the head of our column, so that if the Indians did stop to fight Chaffee he would have two troops on white horses to engage them at once, and the other troops could be placed to the best advantage as they came up.

At daylight on July 17 we moved out cautiously and saw Chaffee climb the rim of the basin unopposed; then we followed, reached Generals Springs, and saw signs of the hostile camp of the night before; then went on, cursing our luck over the prospect of a tedious campaign in the rough, waterless Navajo country. About a mile farther a mounted courier from Chaffee dashed up. Converse with his white-horse troop rushed forward at a gallop, and word was passed along that the Indians were camped on the far side of a deep crack in the earth, a branch of Canyon Diablo (Big Dry Wash), with all arrangements to give Chaffee the fight of his life.

The location was about three miles from where we were, and as we rapidly approached we could hear casual shots and an occasional volley crash. Sieber and the scouts located the hostiles on the far side of the chasm. Chaffee then dismounted his troop and sent a few men forward to the brink. When these were seen the hostiles opened fire; then Converse galloped up, dismounted almost in plain view of the hostiles, sent his horses to the rear, and advanced in line of skirmishers along the edge of the canyon as if intending to go down the trail. Both troops and hostiles then opened up a heavy fire across the canyon. The scene of action was in a heavy forest, thickly set with large pine trees (parklike, with no underbrush or shrubbery whatever) on a high mesa at the summit of the Mogollon range. Across this mesa from east to west ran a gigantic gash in the face of the earth, a volcanic crack, some seven hundred yards across and about one thousand feet deep, with almost perpendicular walls for miles on either side of the very steep trail which led to the Navajo country. This crossing point was held by the hostiles, and their fire covered every foot of the trail, descending and ascending.

Colonel[5] Evans and his troops rode up and quickly dismounted about three hundred yards from the brink of the canyon. Chaffee reported to him, outlined the situation, and started to suggest some dispositions of the troops. Evans stopped him, told him to dispose of the troops as he saw best, and gave him full control, saying that he, Chaffee, had located the Indians and it was his fight.

This was one of the most unselfish actions of relinquishing command that ever came to my notice during a long career in the army because, mind you, Chaffee was not only Evans' junior (a captain) but also belonged to another cavalry regiment, the Sixth, while Colonel Evans belonged to the Third, and there is always rivalry for honors between regiments so thrown together.

Chaffee got busy at once; ordered Kramer and Cruse with Troop E, Sixth Cavalry, his (Chaffee's) own troop, Sixth Cavalry, commanded by Lieutenant Frank West, and part of the Indian scouts under Sieber to go cautiously to the right of the trail and cross where possible about a mile to the east. When the far side of the canyon had been gained they were to form for attack and close in on the main trail. Converse and his troops were told to keep up a heavy fire across the chasm. Troop K, Sixth Cavalry, Captain L. A. Abbott and Lieutenant F. G. Hodgson; Troop E, Third Cavalry, Lieutenant F. H. Hardie and F. C. (Friday) Johnson; and the remainder of the Indian scouts under Lieutenant George H. Morgan, Third Cavalry, were sent across the canyon to the west and then to move east.

A small group from each troop was left with the pack trains and led horses to protect them from surprise should any of the hostile succeed in gaining our side of the canyon unperceived.

These movements began about 3:00 P.M. and the sun was shining brightly. As we moved out, we heard that Converse had been shot in the head and was being brought in. I saw him as we passed and rushed up for a second and spoke to him. He said something was the matter with his eye but thought it would soon pass.

Poor fellow, it has never passed. A .44 caliber bullet had struck a piece of lava rock, split it in two, and one-half had penetrated the eye, wedging firmly in the eye socket where, in spite of the ministrations of the noted surgeons of the world, it has remained ever since. He is still living, a colonel on the retired list, after a most useful life to the government, punctuated at periods by almost unbearable pain from that wound.

Our column finally found a place where we could climb down the precipitous side of the chasm, and had gained the beautiful stream that flowed at the bottom, when someone exclaimed and pointed up. Every star was plainly visible in the sky at 3:30 P.M.

By dint of strenuous climbing we finally reached the crest on the other side, formed a skirmish line, I Troop on the right with Sieber and his scouts, and moved rapidly forward. Just as we started we heard the crash of several volleys and knew that the other encircling column was in action. Sieber and his Indians with I Troop ran into the Indian herd just then, and as the hostile herd guard's attention had been attracted by the firing in the other direction, our people soon placed them hors de combat. The scouts rounded up the ponies, placed them behind our column with a guard, left them there, and moved on.

The other column, Abbott's, finally negotiated the descent into the canyon and started up the other side. When almost at the top it ran into a party of Indians coming down a little side ravine with the evident intention of getting to the rear of what they supposed was Chaffee's white-horse troop still keeping up a fire from the edge of the canyon on the other side. As they thought there could be no opposition on their side they were proceeding rapidly and without the usual precautions when Abbott opened fire on them. Several were killed and wounded, and all were thoroughly stampeded.

The fugitives, rushing back for their main camp and the pony herd, were joined by those of the camp who had been firing across the canyon. They were sure there was something wrong but could not tell what. As this main body of the hostiles came sweeping through the woods, we saw them and at first imagined they were trying to rush us and recapture the pony herd, but as a matter of fact they were totally unaware of our being there until we fired directly into them, causing further casualties, which drove them back.

West had swept the right of his line across the Navajo trail by this time, so that line of retreat was cut off. We then swung our line in a semicircle toward the Indians' camp, driving the hostiles in front of us and penning them against the edge of the canyon.

By this time, 5:00 P.M., and the shadows heavy in the dense forest, I found myself in command of the left flank of Troop E, next to the brink of the canyon and probably two hundred yards in front of what had been the main camp of the hostiles, indicted only by some scattered blankets, cooking utensils, etc. Sieber was by my side.

As our line closed in there was a furious burst of fire from the hostiles, causing several casualties among the troops, among others, Lieutenant Morgan, Third Cavalry, who had joined West after his Indian scouts had been left behind the line, and Sergeant Conn,[6] Troop E, Sixth. As the line advanced from tree to tree, Morgan had chances to fire at hostiles several times and finally dropped one. Elated over his success, he called out, "I got him." In doing this he exposed his position to another Indian in the same nest who thereupon fired and got Morgan through the arm, into the side, and apparently through both lungs. The soldiers got the Indian.

We thought sure that Morgan would die that night, but he is still living and in good health, a colonel on the retired list. The surgeon found that when the bullet broke the arm bone its force was so lessened that it did not break the rib, as from the hole made we supposed it had, but slid around it under the skin and lodged in the muscles of the back, where it was finally dug out and presented to Morgan.

Sergeant Conn was a character in the Sixth Cavalry and had been with the regiment for about twenty years. The bullet hit him full in the throat, made a ghastly hole, pushed aside the jugular vein (so the surgeon claimed), grazed the vertebra, and passed out, leaving a hole as big as a silver dollar; all this in a neck that wore a number thirteen collar.

In the meantime I had pushed forward with Sieber, whom I saw kill three hostiles as they were creeping to the edge of the canyon to drop over. He would say, "There he goes," then bang would go his rifle. The Indian that I had never seen, strain my eyes as I might, would, when hit, throw up his arms as if trying to seize some support, then, under the impetus of his rush, plunge forward on his head and roll over several times. One shot near the brink plunged clear over and, it seemed to me, kept falling for ten minutes.

It was now about 5:30 P.M. and getting dusk; only about seventy-five yards and a little ravine some seven feet deep separated me and my men from the Indians in the camp. I knew that unless the camp was taken pretty quick the Indians would escape under cover of darkness, so I resolved to cross the ravine and take it. I told Sieber that I was going to do it, and much to my surprise he hastily remonstrated.

"Don't you do it, Lieutenant; don't you do it; there are lots of Indians over there, and they will get you sure."

"Why Al, you have killed every one of them," I replied and instructed my men what to do. They were to rush forward to the ravine, halt under cover, then, when ordered, were to advance at a run into the camp with some cartridges in hand, guns loaded. We did just that and had no casualties, due, I think, to the fact that Captain Kramer's men and Sieber smothered the hostiles with their fire.

As we rushed forward on the other side of the ravine I soon discovered that, as Sieber had said, there were lots of Indians there, and we had business on our hands. But I had with me Sergeant Horan,[7] Sergeant Martin, and six or eight other old-timers whom such things did not disconcert in the least. Things were going slap-bang when suddenly, not over six feet away, was an Indian with his gun leveled directly at me. It seemed he could not miss, so, raising my gun, I stood awaiting the shock of the bullet. He was nervous and jerked the trigger sufficiently to barely miss me and hit a young Scotchman, McLernon,[8] just to my left and probably a foot in the rear. McLernon fell. I fired and threw myself to the ground.

Sieber, Captain Kramer, and several others saw me go down and thought for sure I had been hit. I found I was not but saw McLernon lying almost beside me and asked if he was hit; he replied, "Yes, sir, through the arm; I think it is broken."

I told him to lie quietly and we would get back to the ravine. In a lull, I rose up and found he was unconscious; dragged him back about twenty feet where the slope protected us; rested a little, then back a little farther. Finally Sergeant Horan and myself got him to the bottom of the ravine.

In going back with McLernon, Abbott's men saw several hostiles rise up to fire whom they had not seen before. Every man in the line turned loose on them, not knowing that I was in their direct line of fire at two hundred yards' distance, and the way the air was filled with bullets showed that they were coming close inside their target. Several pieces of gravel and small fragments of rock or lead struck me in the face, making it bleed. I was sure that I was hit and would soon collapse. Kramer's men swarmed into the hostiles, but darkness soon came on, and the fight was over.

I grabbed some blankets from the Indian camp and made a nice bed for McLernon, but the bullet had smashed his rib and gone through both lungs. He passed away quietly about an hour later.

＋＊　Ⅲ＊Ⅲ　＊＋

This concludes General Cruse's statement. From notes the writer [Barnes], then military telegraph operator at Fort Apache, made at Fort Apache in discussing the fight with officers and men of the command, army records at Washington, and also, in later years, General Cruse and Colonel Morgan, the following particulars of the fight are given:

About dark the day of the fight a terrible thunderstorm such as are common in the mountains of northern Arizona swept across the country. The rain turned to hail, which covered the ground four or five inches deep. When they found poor Conn he was half buried in hail. Under these difficult conditions the Indians slipped away during the night, nearly all afoot. It was not more

than twenty miles to the Apache reservation line, where they were secure from
further attack or punishment.

A night guard or patrol under the command of Lieutenant Hodgson, Sixth
Cavalry, was left on the battlefield while the rest of the command moved back
and made camp on an open flat a short distance from the canyon.

Early next morning, July 18, Hodgson's men heard groans as from a
wounded man. A wounded Apache at bay is a dangerous person. The men cautiously investigated the vicinity from which the groans seemed to come. While
they were doing this a shot came from a sort of breastwork of rocks on the
edge of the canyon. They hunted cover and, locating the point by the rising
powder smoke (there was no smokeless powder then), they fired at the rocks.
Two or three more shots came from the nest, then ceased.

The troopers blazed away at it for some minutes, then charged. Curled up
behind it they found a young Apache squaw—the hostiles had but five or six
women with them—with a young baby by her side, together with a very old
woman who seemingly had taken no part in the firing.

The girl pulled a knife from her belt and attacked the soldiers fiercely.
When she was overpowered and disarmed she had a rifle. The three shots she
fired were her last cartridges. She proved to have a bullet through her leg
above the knee which had broken and shattered the bone.

The men rigged up a rough litter of pine saplings, and with a soldier carrying the baby, got the poor thing down the rough trail to the bottom and up
and out the other side to the camp. It must have been a terrible ordeal, but she
stood it without a groan.

The following day, September 19, the army surgeons amputated her leg
close to the thigh, doing it without anesthetics or stimulants of any kind. The
soldiers who helped in the operation said they never saw such fortitude and
apparent indifference to pain as that young Apache squaw displayed.

On September 20, 1882, the troops, having made their wounded as comfortable as possible, buried the dead, shot a lot of the horses and pack mules
that had lost shoes, and started for their separate posts.

The column from Fort Apache took a gentle saddle mule, covered the
army saddle with many folds of blanket, making a sort of broad seat, on which
they placed the wounded woman. With a soldier to lead the mule, her baby at
her breast, she rode for seven long, hot days across those rough mountains to
Fort Apache.

The writer saw her not so long afterward hobbling around the post with a
crutch. Eventually they fitted her up with a peg leg, with which she got about
very nicely.

The casualties to the troops were First Sergeant Taylor, D Troop, Third
Cavalry, wounded in the arm; Sergeant Daniel Conn, E Troop, Sixth Cavalry,
shot through the neck. I saw him a few years since, hale and hearty, at the soldiers' home near Washington, D.C. Private Joseph McLernon, of the same

troop, died on the field from a shot through the lungs. Privates Timothy Foley, James Muleca, and John Witt, of K Troop, Sixth Cavalry, all were badly wounded, but they recovered.

Private Pete of the Indian scouts was instantly killed by a bullet through the head very early in the battle.

Second Lieutenant George H. Morgan, Third Cavalry, and Second Lieutenant George L. Converse, Jr., Third Cavalry, were both severely wounded, as told by General Cruse. The two officers were sent from the battle to the nearest military post, Fort Verde, where everything possible was done for them. Later Converse was sent east for further treatment.

As I recall it, there was no surgeon with the command until two, hurriedly summoned by Chaffee, reached the battle ground from Fort Verde the day after the fight.

Within a week after troops had returned to Fort Apache, scouts reported the presence in nearby White Mountain Indian camps of a number of Indians badly wounded in the fight. The commanding officer, being a wise soldier and well acquainted with the habits and peculiarities of the Indian service,[9] instead of sending a troop of cavalry after them, first wired the department commander, General Crook, at Prescott, for orders. Crook sent the wire to the division commander at San Francisco; he, in turn, asked army headquarters at Washington for orders, which, in its turn, took it up with the officials of the Indian service.

In the course of time came a brief dispatch from Washington to the effect that no Indians who were living on the reservations peacefully were to be interfered with, regardless of their past history. The Indian Right Association was in the saddle, as usual, and nothing was done to the renegade Indians.

Within six months we were discussing the fight with Indians living around Fort Apache who took part in the fight. They told us many of the details.

It was from some of them that we understood how they were misled as to the size of Chaffee's command. They declared they saw only the white-horse troopers and believed no other soldiers were near.

Lieutenant Cruse told me he was directed by Chaffee the next morning after the battle, July 18, to make as close a count of the dead on the battleground as he could. He found and marked twenty-two dead bodies but believed a number of others were in inaccessible places among the rocks, where his men were unable to locate them.

As a matter of fact, civilians who came on the field after the troops left claimed to have found several that Cruse had missed.

According to War Department records, only five troops of Cavalry—D and I troops of the Third; D, E, and I troops of the Sixth, and Morgan's Indian scouts, E Company—were engaged in the fight. The others arrived on the field the morning of the eighteenth, after the battle was over.[10]

Major Evans in his official report called it the "Battle of the Big Dry

Wash." It was said to be a branch of the Canyon Diablo. This was because it was so designated on the only map available then. On Sitgreaves' map of 1851, and on Smith military map of 1879, it is called Big Dry Fork. On both it seems to flow into the Canyon Diablo. It is now known to be an eastern tributary of East Clear Creek, which in turn empties into the Little Colorado River about three miles east of Winslow, on the Santa Fe. The battleground is on the extreme eastern end of the Coconino National Forest in Coconino County.

On present-day forest maps the battleground covered the northern end of what is shown as Battleground Ridge. This ridge ends at the point where the canyon heads, in which the fighting occurred. Battleground Ridge is about three and one-half miles northeast of Generals Springs, near the rim, and some eight or ten miles southeast of the U.S. ranger station in Long Valley.

The troops from Fort Apache returned there on the afternoon of July 27, 1882. I stood in the doorway of the old log telegraph office as they marched in review past the commanding officer standing on the walk in front of it. The wounded squaw was with the pack train, rather excited and pleased at the attention she attracted. Every one guyed most unmercifully the soldier trooper who, astride of his horse, carried the baby, done up in a willow papoose basket one of the Indian scouts had made for it.

The Sixth cavalrymen rode western horses of California stock—small, active, surefooted animals, with good hard hoofs and used to rustling their food at night hobbled out on the range. I think every Sixth cavalryman came back to Apache on the same mount he left with.

On the other, the Third Cavalry, which had but recently come to Arizona from Fort Hayes, Kansas, were mounted on big, fine-boned Kentucky-bred animals. They had huge and very brittle hoofs; let one of them lose a shoe, and unless reshod at once, they went dead lame and had to be left behind. Also, they knew absolutely nothing about "hobbles" and rustling for their forage on the range at night after a hard day's march.

In the command that passed us a number of the men and at least one officer of the Third regiment were riding Indian ponies captured from the hostiles. Their mounts had played out. Also, a large number of those handsome cavalry horses from old Kentucky were limping along, just about able to make the post and no more. Practically every troop of the Third lost horses on the trip from various causes. I have before me a copy of the muster roll for July 1882 of D Troop of the Third. It states that Captain King on arrival at Fort Apache called for a board of survey "to relieve him from responsibility for seven troop-horses lost during the campaign." All the other troops of this regiment had about the same luck with their mounts.

A day or two after the outbreak of 1882 a small party of citizens around Globe organized what was called the "Globe Rangers." Amid much local enthusiasm and with much criticism of the military authorities for their failure to protect the settlers, they started after the hostiles. The second or third night out they camped at a cattle ranch on Salt River, put some of their horses in the corral near the cabin, and hobbled the others out to graze on the nearby range.

About daylight the next morning the Indians raided the place, fired a few shots into the cabin to wake the sleeping warriors and let them know they were around, then skipped out with all the horses in the corral and every animal they could find on the outside range. Two or three of the men, mounted on what animals they could pick up, followed the Indians, arriving at the battleground after all was over.

Of these Lieutenant Davis writes:

The morning after the fight two of these men appeared in our camp looking for their horse stock. They began claiming every good horse in the herd that our troops had captured from the Indians.

I was standing beside Chaffee, who with his hands in his pockets was letting them go as far as they would but getting madder and madder every minute. Finally one of them claimed Chaffee's own saddle mare and his companion backed him up in the claim.

Then the air around us took on a blue tinge. The two sneaked out under Chaffee's barrage. They got no horses. A few hours later the rightful owner of the horses they had been claiming, the wounded Sigsbee brother (Lieutenant Davis erroneously calls him Bixby— W. C. B.) came into camp and recovered his stock.

As a matter of fact, several officers present at the fight told me that a number of citizens who had heard of the battle put in an appearance a day or two later and proceeded to loot the dead Indians' corpses and their camp, including taking off their scalps. Major Chaffee, however, promptly suppressed this, but they hung around until the troopers left and then scalped and robbed the dead bodies to their hearts' content.

A number of these so-called rangers followed the command over to Fort Apache, and a few days afterwards I myself saw half dozen freshly taken Indian scalps in the hands of soldiers around the post. They had purchased them from these civilian warriors.

It should always be remembered that the Apaches do not, nor never did, scalp their dead enemies. Many of the Sixth cavalrymen had served on the plains where the Indians did scalp their fallen foes. From them they had learned how to preserve scalps according to Indian practice. A small wooden hoop about six inches in diameter, such as ladies use for making fancy work upon, was first made. Inside this hoop the fresh scalp was stretched by sewing it along the edges and over the hoop with heavy thread or twine, just as small hides are stretched for tanning purposes. Several well-cured Apache scalps fixed up in this original form, with the original owner's long black hair attached, were peddled around the post and offered at ten dollars each.

There has been considerable criticism of the military forces for not burying the dead hostiles after the battle. This was practically impossible. The country there was very rocky, they had no suitable tools for the purpose, and the bodies were widely scattered over the terrain, amid the rocks and deep fissures of the rough canyons where the fight took place. They buried their own dead, which was about as far as they could under such conditions.

(Letters from civilians who saw the battlefield soon after it was over.)

C. P. Wingfield of Humboldt writes:

In regard to the battle between U.S. troops and Apache Indians. It was fought on the point between Generals Springs Canyon and Miller Canyon and in some small canyons on the east bank of East Clear Creek. I think you have the date right, July 17, 1882. The battle started at 11:00 A.M. and lasted two or three hours. It was a pretty hot fight for one or two hours, then the Indians began to scatter and shoot wild. They reported about forty Indians killed, and about that many got away through side canyons. I mean warriors—they had quite a number of children and squaws with them. They all managed to make their escape in some way. Some were picked up by U.S. troops about thirty-five miles north of there. All had guns and tried to put up a fight. (This is an error on Mr. Wingfield's part, or at least the officers made no report of such an incident—W. C. B.)

This fight took place about Rock Crossing or near there and about ten miles from the rim of the Tonto Basin—not on Canyon Diablo. Battleground Ridge is the place. I was with the pack train and about half a mile back of the firing line. I have been in Clear Creek Canyon at all times of the day but never remember seeing stars in the daytime.

The Indians came up out of Tonto Basin where the tunnel road comes up to Generals Springs; went out west on the big flat ridge and pitched camp; rolled some big oak logs together and built a big fire, then killed two mules and a horse and had a big barbecue.

The fire was still burning when we came up that night. Al Sieber sent out two Indian scouts to spy on the Indians and report their movements. They came into camp sometime before daylight the day of the fight and reported they—the Indians—had made camp and were fortifying and preparing to fight. The packers were given orders to get the pack mules as soon as it was light enough to see and proceed to pack up the camp outfit and follow after the troops with all haste, which we did.

If you have been on the rim of Tonto Basin at Generals Springs, you know you can see pretty well down into the basin.

Well, those Indians could look off down there and see what we called the "White-Horse Troop" mounted on grey horses. They supposed that was all that was after them, so they thought they would fortify and the soldiers would ride right into their nest and they—the Indians—would massacre the whole troop. So an Indian said that got back to the reservation. They did not know there were two companies of cavalry and one company of Indian scouts after them.

The Indians said all they could see from the top of the hill were the white horses.

Casualties on the troops' side, one private killed and Lieutenant Morgan shot through the lungs below the heart. We packed him up to the Fort Apache and Camp Verde Road and from there hauled them all to Verde in a government ambulance. Next day the lieutenant was taken to Fort Whipple. He was killed in the Philippines afterwards. (Colonel Morgan please take notice—W. C. B.) The troops rode to the top of the mountain and dismounted. Every fourth man held horses. Then they charged down the hill as fast as they could—Indian scouts and troops, Lieutenant Morgan in the lead. The Indians got excited and were shooting high. The bullets were cutting the tops off the pine trees up where we were with the pack train.

Right in the thickest part of the fight one of Al Sieber's scouts saw two of his brothers and his father with the Indians. He threw his gun down and started to run to his folks. Sieber told him to halt. He did not heed him. Sieber raised his rifle and fired, shooting him in the back of the head. The trooper that was killed on the battlefield was buried there and the grave marked with stones.

I was there in the summer of 1886, four years afterward, and saw the grave, also found the skeleton of an Indian in a cave about half a mile up the canyon from the battleground.

Humboldt, Arizona,
August 18, 1929.

(Considering Mr. Wingfield writes wholly from memory, this account fits very nicely into the official and other accounts written at the time, besides giving several additional incidents not elsewhere recorded—W. C. B.)

Fred W. Croxen, at that time forest ranger stationed at Payson, Arizona, in the Tonto Basin, has written the following account of the incidents concerning this battle. It is published by his permission.

The last real Indian raid in Arizona occurred in the summer of 1882. This was started by a band of renegade Indians concerned with the fight at Cibicue where Captain Hentig and several soldiers were killed. This occurred on Cibicue Creek on the Apache Indian reservation on August 30, 1881, and such an occurrence could only be followed by further trouble.

Eighty-six Indians ran away from the reservation and went in a westerly direction through Pleasant Valley, where they killed several horses and stole others belonging to the Tewksbury family and Al Rose. After leaving Pleasant Valley the Indians went in a northwesterly direction, next attempting to raid the Bar X Ranch, which is about nine miles from Pleasant Valley. This ranch was occupied by Bob and Will Sigsbee at that time. There was a man with them, a Swiss by the name of Louie Houdon, who had discovered a rich mineral deposit at Spring Creek Canyon, directly under Diamond Butte.

Houdon had come up to the ranch to get the Sigsbees to help him do some work on his claim. Early that morning, Bob Sigsbee and Houdon were up on the ridge east of the house wrangling their saddle and pack horses when they were attacked by Indians, both being killed.

Will Sigsbee, hearing the shots and suspecting what they meant, grabbed a water bucket, ran to the spring, filled it, and ran back to the house, which was an adobe with thick walls. This house, by the way, is still in use as the head-quarters' ranch house. As Will ran to the door, an Indian shot at him. He slipped, and the Indian no doubt thought he was hit. This made the Indian rather careless, and Sigsbee was fortunate enough to kill one in a very short time as he raised his head up through the forks of a walnut tree a short distance from the house. Sigsbee was besieged for three days, during which time he killed an Indian who tried to cut the saddle from a dead mule in front of the house—killed by the Indians—and got another Indian hiding behind a stump on an elevation several yards east of the house. I am told the Indians found the troops after them and left, which was a great relief to poor Sigsbee in the house, for it broke the siege. When the troops came they buried the two white men on the ridge where they fell. Their bodies still rest in those hastily made graves.

After leaving the Sigsbee ranch the Indians continued in the same direction, next coming to the Isadore Christopher place. Christopher was a French-man; had settled the place and swore he would stay there and make a stake or lose his life in the attempt. He did stay in spite of the many hardships and made himself wealthy. At this place the Indians burned two log houses, all he had built at the time. Fortunately, Christopher was away at the time and no doubt escaped death at the Indians' hands in that way.

The soldiers were on their trail so close that they came to the still smol-dering ruins of the cabins. Christopher had killed a bear, and the carcass was hanging in one of the cabins. The soldiers saw this body in the fire and were sure Christopher had been killed and burned. After leaving the Christopher place the Indians went in a westerly direction, passing north of the Diamond Rim over the old Indian trail, past what was then known as the Jim Roberts place—now owned by Zane Grey, the writer. They went on west, passing near the present E. F. Pyle ranch and camped on the East Verde, on what is now the old Belluzzi ranch.

From here a part of them went down the East Verde nearly five miles and attacked the Meadows family at what is now known as the Hendershot place.

Jim Burchett and John Kerr had already ridden out from Globe and warned the settlers at Marysville, Payson, and surrounding country. The peo-ple had been fortunate up at Payson. Tiring of this inaction, old man Meadows determined to return to their place on the East Verde, saying he didn't believe there was an Indian outbreak, and if there was, the bullet had not yet been cast that could kill him. So the family returned home.

Henry, one of the Meadows boys, was at the army post of Camp Verde and returned home to warn his people of the Indian outbreak. He arrived there about 11:00 P.M., and as all were in bed and asleep, he did not waken them, thinking the Indians were far away from there.

As day was breaking the father heard the dogs barking on the north side of the house. He thought it was a bear after their stock, some of which had been left in the corral. Taking his Long Tom caliber-fifty rifle, he went out to learn the trouble. As he walked round the top of a pine tree that had fallen there he was shot by two Indians, a ball piercing each breast and coming out at the back. The boys heard the shots, grabbed rifles and cartridge belts, and ran outside. Henry was shot between the bones of his forearm, and another bullet hit the cartridge belt in his hand, exploding three cartridges and driving one, brass end foremost, into his groin.

Doc Massey and John Grey, who first settled the Cold Spring ranch, were notified by messenger from Payson that the Indians were on the warpath. They rode to the Meadows ranch, and Mrs. Meadows told them her husband had been killed and the two boys wounded. They rode to Payson and notified the men, who went to their relief. They buried the father and hauled the rest of the family to the Siddle place, farther down the East Verde. The old man they buried under the floor of the cabin so the Indians would not find and mutilate the body, should they return. His body was removed a few years later to the Payson public cemetery, where it still lies in the Meadows plot.

Major A. R. Chaffee, at Camp McDowell, near the mouth of the Verde River, who was in command of Troop I, the White-Horse Troop of the Sixth United States Cavalry, had received notice from San Carlos that the Indians were out. He left for Pleasant Valley, arriving behind the Indians, and learned of their depredations near that place.

It is not known whether he brought his Indian scouts from McDowell or not. (He did—W. C. B.) Old-timers, however, say he brought forty soldiers and forty Indian scouts with him, together with his pack train. Al Sieber, Pat Kehoe, and Mickey Free, all noted scouts of the time, were also with the troops, having come from San Carlos and caught up with them, according to Tom Horn, who claims to have been chief of scouts at the time. (He was not chief of scouts, however—W. C. B.)

Chaffee took their trail, and when they found they had climbed the Tonto rim at the head of the East Verde over what is now known as the Old Tunnel road, he allowed his men only time to eat and feed their horses. They took the trail up over the rim and jumped the Indians at Generals Springs, where the battle opened and was fought down what is now known as Battleground Ridge.

The Indians were putting on a big feed and jerking meat when the soldiers jumped their camp. The had also stolen a little fat mare belonging to the Tewksbury family. Before fleeing from the soldiers the Indians stabbed this mare to death with their knives for no other apparent reason than to show their cruel and savage nature. Chaffee had been on so many Indian campaigns in Arizona that he gave the order to shoot to kill. Eighty out of the eighty-six Indians were accounted for, and only six captured, some of them badly shot up. (This is an error according to Lieutenant Cruse's statement—W. C. B.)

One soldier was killed near the close of the battle at what is known as Rock Crossing, on East Clear Creek. His body was buried in a lonely grave on the rim of the canyon, unmarked and forgotten, but that of a soldier nevertheless.

There is a story current in this country now that a squaw was wounded in this battle, having one leg shattered. She was captured after a day or two at what is known as Hunter Spring on Blue Ridge, about two miles northwest of Rock Crossing, and when captured she asked the soldiers to cut the other leg off so she could walk again. The leg wasn't cut off. Tom Horn mentions a squaw in his book which is probably the same squaw but does not tell about her asking to have both legs cut off, although he says the surgeons amputated one leg when they brought her back to camp. This squaw, according to Horn, had a papoose concealed in the rocks and brush and made a big fuss until the soldiers looked and found it, bringing it along with them.

It is said by reliable parties that for several years after this battle skeletons of Indians, wounded and later dying, could be seen in the shallow caves along East Clear Creek from the Rock Crossing up to what is now known as Jones' Crossing.

As previously stated, when the people of Payson and vicinity heard of the Indian outbreak they "forted up" at the Siddle place, an adobe house on land now owned by August Pieper. The married men and families held the fort while the single men did scout duty.

Some of the single men caught up with the troops and were in the battle down the Battleground Ridge and Rock Crossing.

The scene of this battle has ever since been known as Battleground Ridge, and the canyon on the west side of this ridge where the pack trains made camp and the troops camped after the fight is now known as Cracker Box Canyon, because of the cracker boxes left there when the camp was broken up after the fight. A part of one of these old boxes was nailed to a tree and the writer saw it, old and weather-worn, thirty-five years after this battle.

One of the Indian scouts who took part in the battle resides now in Payson. He is Henry Irving, but his command of English is so poor that it is impossible to get an account of it from him. He claims to have killed two Indians in the battle.

Most of the above account was given me by William Craig, who still resides in Payson, Arizona, and who helped move the Meadows family after the shooting of their father and sons. Other parts have been gathered from time to time from old residents, from stories told by the older inhabitants to the younger generation, and from Tom Horn's book.[11] Some may be in error; the greater part is just as it happened. However, it is the account of the fight as remembered by the old-timers and recited by them after more than forty-five years have passed away.

Mr. Craig recently told me that shortly after this fight six wild Apache Indians came into San Carlos and gave up. These Indians, four bucks and two squaws, had been in hiding on the head of Deer Creek, on the east side of the Mazatzal Mountains in Tonto Basin. They had never before been to an agency, and no record of them had ever been made. They would not have given up, but they realized after the disastrous fight on Battleground Ridge that their time would come before long and they would probably be captured or killed—the latter in all likelihood. They were the very last wild Indians to give up in the Tonto Basin country.

Payson, Arizona, July 28, 1929

These two personal narratives, written by men who took part in those early Arizona days, are invaluable from the historian's point of view. They offer an entirely different point of view from the official and military reports upon which much of our early Arizona history is based.

If in some particulars they do not fit exactly into the facts as generally accepted, we can be very lenient with them, remembering that these matters happened nearly fifty years ago and that the human memory is very unreliable after a lapse of years. Moreover, most of these old-timers were grown men in 1882, hence must now have many, many years of life behind them.

The story of old man Christopher's bear left hanging in the log cabin is well recalled. One version of it is to the effect that the soldiers really thought it was a human body and so buried the charred remains in a grave near the burned cabin without ever realizing they were performing the last sad rites over the remains of a bear. The civilians of those days were inclined to poke fun at the army people.

Tom Horn was not chief of scouts at the time. He was a packer in one of the pack trains—at San Carlos, if my memory serves me right. Reliable army officers have told me Horn was not in the fight but was with the pack trains back of the lines. The quartermaster records at Washington have been searched for Horn's record as a scout. They show that the one and only time he was employed by the U.S. government as a scout was at Fort Bowie, Arizona, from October 13, 1885, to September 30, 1886. This was during Miles' Geronimo campaign in Mexico. His long yarn in his book telling of his presence at the Battle of Cibicue is an outrageous, barefaced lie from start to finish. I knew every soldier, officer, packer, and scout who took part in that fight. I saw the command leave Fort Apache and met it four or five miles west of the post the afternoon they returned from the unfortunate affair. Tom Horn was not with the command at any time. General Cruse says his yarn about the Cibicue fight was false from beginning to end.

The soldier and Indian scout killed and buried on the Dry Wash battlefield were taken up by the military authorities a few years later and moved to Fort Apache, where they were laid away with a full military funeral in the post cemetery.

I established a cattle camp at the head of West Chevelon Canyon in 1887 a few miles east of the battlefield and rode over to the battlefield several times in the following years. There were then plenty of skeletons, skulls, etc., of both humans and animals scattered around on the ground. Most of them, however, were carried off eventually by visitors to the scene.

The cracker box mentioned was still on the tree, just as told by Mr. Craig. These boxes, by the way, were those in which hardtack for the troops in the field was packed. They used a lot of hardtack in those days.

The muster roll of Company E, Indian Scouts, a copy of which I have before me, shows no Indian named Irving. But there is one named Henry on the list, and it's an easy matter to guess that he was later called Henry Irving. Anyhow, that's a fairly good guess.

The story of the six wild, bronco Apaches that gave themselves up after the battle is an interesting one. I never before heard it. Probably it is based on facts. Stranger things than that happened in those days.

One thing always stands out in my memory of this fight. It is the fact that the company of Indian scouts that took part in it were in large part relatives, friends, and members of the same band of Apaches from which came the renegades—the White Mountain Apaches. That only one deserted to the enemy during the fight is a fine tribute to their loyalty to the government which they were serving as enlisted men.

Rafferty's Trail

WILLIAM A. RAFFERTY[1]

Tucson *Arizona Daily Star*, May 17, 1882

The *Star* prints this morning the subjoined diary of Captain Rafferty, whose successful pursuit of the Indians[2] has won for him the plaudits of the territory. The account briefly recites incidents and is devoid of elaboration. Here it is:

We had a lively old trip of it last time. Leaving Fort Bowie at about 11:00 P.M., April 24, found an immense trail at Galeyville at 5:00 P.M. on the twenty-fifth. We rested a few hours at Cave Creek, eight miles below Galeyville; joining Tupper's command[3] of his own company and Mills'[4] scouts, who did not desire being seen crossing San Simon Valley during daytime. Started again at 6:00 P.M., and at a walk and trot crossed the valley, the trail leading southeast and striking Peloncillo about thirty-five miles south of the railroad crossing. The hostile trail was much broken, the Indians evidently looking for water. So at 2:30 A.M. we lay down in our overcoats and saddle blankets till morning, the pack trains not having arrived.

Next day we had a very hard march over a new pass the trail took,[5] and we next camped a few miles above Cloverdale, on the east side of Peloncillo. Next day, the twenty-seventh, the trail led within two miles of Cloverdale, and about six miles further south they crossed Animas Valley almost due east, then over the very highest peak of Animas range by a trail they used for the first time. This proved a terrible hard pull for the boys. It was about five or six miles south of the pass, near the boundary line and in Mexico. At 6:00 P.M., having got near the eastern end of the pass, we stopped two and a half hours to cook supper, having made about thirty-five miles since 6:00 A.M. At 8:00 P.M., leaving our trains in camp with a guard, we started on, as the trail at this point was very fresh. About 10:00 P.M., Sieber and a few Indians in advance thought the hostiles were in camp a short distance ahead. One or two of the scouts crept on three miles and found it was so. It was then arranged to try and get the scouts placed in the mountains above this evening. Mills and Darr[6] succeeded in this before morning, fairly creeping along the mountains to get their position. Darr took off his shoes so as to make no noise on the rocks. A plain, very level, on the west of the Indian

On the Mexican border. OUTING MAGAZINE, OCTOBER 1886.

camp was to be taken up by the troops. To the right of the rough hill,[7] the Indians were camped. From 12:00 A.M. till 4:30 A.M. we were moving cautiously forward, leading our horses and stopping every ten yards to listen. There was no talking and no smoking. At last we got to the position we were aiming for, about eight hundred or one thousand yards from the camp, just as day was breaking.

The signal for the charge was to be a volley from the scouts as soon as they could see well. About 4:45 A.M. a blaze of fire from the mountains announced the beginning of the fight.[8] At the same instant the cavalry sprang on their horses and with a yell charged into the basin fronting the camp, and within one hundred yards of the rocks lay camped the Indians. They then jumped from their horses and began firing rapidly at the Indians, who were running for the rocks. As soon as they got in the rocks they made it very warm for us, we were so close. We then scooped in the greater part of their herd and returned at a walk to a great distance. Goodrich of my company was killed and Miller badly wounded at this place. We then formed a dismounted skirmish line on the plain and kept up a good fire till 11:30 A.M.

By that time we were satisfied that we could not get the savages out of the rocks and that no good could result from further firing, which would reduce our supply of ammunition, and hence we concluded to withdraw, which was done slowly, one company holding the skirmish line at a time. The Indian scouts first filed out close to the mountains, we trying to keep a heavy fire on the Indians to prevent them from giving their whole attention to the scouts while they were withdrawing. The Indians were mighty glad to suspend operations and did not fire a shot after we began to retire.

The cavalry with a yell charged into the basin. R. F. BERNARD. *ONE HUNDRED THREE FIGHTS AND SCRIMMAGES.*

We returned to our camp of the previous night, or rather the place we had started from at 8:00 P.M. on the previous night, about eight miles from the scene of the fight. We had had nothing to eat for twenty hours. We got our dinner when Colonel Forsyth's command of several companies of cavalry and two or three companies of scouts joined us—and gobbled us.[9] They were a little chagrined to think that they had not had a hand in the fight. We had not the least idea there was another body of troops within seventy-five miles of us. If we had known it we would have held the situation till their arrival, though we would not have waited for them before attacking.

Next day Forsyth took us all with him, though we were almost tired to death and of little account, and we went thirty-five miles into Mexico, going south. The next day, the morning of the thirtieth, about forty miles south of the line, we met Colonel Garcia's regiment of 273 men[10] and found that early on the morning of the twenty-ninth, about six hours after our fight, he saw the dust on an immense plain and knew the hostiles were coming. He "laid for them" along a little creek in the plain, and the grass, etc., concealed his men—all infantry. He killed seventy-eight Indians and lost twenty-three of his men killed and thirty wounded. We all went with him over a part of his battleground. I counted over thirty Indians. He requested General Forsyth to return to the United States, saying all the Indians that escaped were broken up into such small parties that further pursuit was useless. General Forsyth then relieved the Arizona troops, and we set our faces homeward, he going to Separ with the Fourth Cavalry.

We believe we killed at least twelve bucks and five or six squaws. This estimate is carefully made by Sieber, Kehoe, etc., who kept a sharp lookout. We got seventy-five animals, good ones, of their herd, and they left twenty Indian saddles on the field and fifteen dead Indian horses. A good many hostiles must have "hoofed it" over the twenty-five-mile plain to meet their death the next morning.

I lost three horses, among them the one I rode, old Jim. He was wounded, and I had to have him shot. I had ridden him for over seven years. But he could not travel, and to put him out of his misery, I got————to put a carbine ball through his head. Poor fellow, I felt sorry for him. In the fight, M Company had twenty-eight men, Tupper twenty-seven or twenty-eight, and the Indian scouts numbered forty-nine, with Kehoe, Sieber, Mills, Tupper, Toney, Darr, Blake, and myself, beside Drs. Burns and Carroll. I suppose every man fired from fifty to eighty shots; some more. I used about forty cartridges, shooting very deliberately at intervals.

Military and Indians

AL SIEBER[1]

Prescott *Weekly Courier*, May 27, 1882[2]

Considering the shameful manner in which the late fights with the Warm Springs Indians have been represented, I wish to give you a few facts which in no respect shall be anything but the truth. I shall begin with the fight at Stein's Peak and end with Colonel Garcia's in Mexico.

On April 23 Colonel Forsyth, with about six companies of cavalry[3] and twenty-five scouts, attacked the Indians in Doubtful Canyon, near Stein's Peak, and after three and a half hours fighting withdrew his entire command, he says for want of water; and I wish to say right here that there is water in Doubtful Canyon.[4] The Indians then pulled out, crossed the San Simon Valley, and camped about six miles north of Galeyville,[5] in the Chiricahua Mountains. Colonel Forsyth, with his six companies of cavalry, started in pursuit, but took the back trail towards San Carlos and followed it till he met Captain Gordon's[6] Sixth Cavalry about twenty miles from Stein's Peak. He then concluded that the Indians had not gone back to the agency, so he took possession of Captain Gordon and his command and started back to Stein's Peak.

This peak is about seven miles from the railroad. Colonel Forsyth had attacked the band with six companies of the Fourth Cavalry and in a place where he could have held them as long as he might wish. If he could not handle the band to any purpose, why did he not send for more troops, as plenty of them were near and he could have had as many as he wanted inside of twelve hours? If the hostiles had withdrawn, they could have gone nowhere but into a valley, and in that case, what better could he wish? Captain Tupper's Sixth Cavalry, with only thirty-nine soldiers and forty-five scouts for actual fighting, fought the same band in a very strong place, killed, if eye evidence is worth anything, seventeen bucks and seven squaws and captured seventy-four head of their stock. If eighty-four men can do this, why is it that five hundred men can't do anything?

Captains Tupper and Rafferty performed their duty well as United States officers and infinitely better than could have possibly been expected, and at a time when they did not know there were any troops nearer than 125 miles. Colonel Forsyth's own guides say that they saw the dust of Tupper's command at different times for two days and yet failed to overtake it. Be it remembered also that Colonel Forsyth made a dry camp on [April] 26 only five miles in Tupper's rear and on the twenty-seventh left Tupper's trail, went twelve miles to Miners Creek, watered his stock, went back twelve miles, took the trail, and then after following it a short distance went into camp again. On the same day Tupper and Rafferty crossed the Animas Mountains, made a short march at night, and discovered the Indians in camp. Colonel Forsyth, it is said, got lost when he was only five miles in Tupper's rear, at least that is the excuse given. If a man cannot follow a fresh trail, well beaten by a large body of Indians, a command of cavalry, and four pack trains, would it not be better for him to stay at home that someone else might go who could follow a trail and travel as if he wished to catch Indians?

On the night of April 24, Captain Tupper with his command at San Simon station and Captain Rafferty with his command at Fort Bowie were informed that the Indians were near Galeyville, so both commanders started at once and arrived there at 5:00 A.M. next morning. On learning that the Indians had crossed the valley during the same night on their way to the Cloverdale country, Tupper concluded to lay over during the day and hotly pursue them at night. He did not wish the Indians to know that anyone was following them, and the only way to keep this information from them was not to go out into the valley, where they could see him for thirty-five miles. At 5:00 P.M. on the twenty-fifth, he left camp and marched at a trot and a gallop for about thirty-five miles.

At this point the hostiles had scattered, so the trail disappeared. As it was dark he remained here a few hours longer till it became light enough for the scouts to find the trail. They found it very early in the morning, so pursuit was kept up till the following night, when camp was made that the pack trains might catch up and give the men something to eat. Colonel Forsyth made a dry camp five miles in the rear of us the same night. The pack trains came in that evening after traveling forty-six miles; the men got some bacon and bread, a little sleep, and pursuit was resumed early next morning. The Animas Mountains and valley were crossed on that day. Just before entering the valley on the opposite side, the command stopped, got a little to eat, and resumed the march, notwithstanding it had already come thirty-five miles that day.

After marching about seven miles, I told Captain Tupper that I thought the Indians were camped about two or three miles ahead and that if he would halt the command, I would go and investigate. I took three scouts and in half an hour discovered the camp. One of the scouts crawled up to the camp and saw they were making medicine. As soon as I familiarized myself with the location,[7] I went back and reported to Captain Tupper how the camp was situated and what could safely be done if proper care was taken. Lieutenants Mills and Darr took their scouts and crawled into the rocks between the hostiles and the main mountains, the hostiles being at the base of these rocks. I conducted Captains Tupper and Rafferty down the valley and brought them in position nearly opposite the Indian scouts.

It was by this time getting tolerably light, and the scouts were forced to begin battle because Loco's son and two women unknowingly came upon the scouts while in search of some mescal which had been hid in the rocks.[8] The scouts began firing at once and killed Loco's son and the two squaws.

The cavalry began to prepare for business immediately. Lieutenant Touey[9] deployed Captain Tupper's company about a round, rocky hill detached from the main mountains about four hundred yards. Captain Rafferty cried out, "Forward, you men of M Company," and with Captain Tupper and Lieutenant Blake charged for the rocks where the hostiles were.

Every horse seemed to struggle for the lead into the terrible snare into which they were charging. The company was halted about five hundred yards from the Indian camp, owing to the presence of one buck and three squaws who were hearding the stock. Rafferty saw the mistake at once, so he mounted the company and charged till he was about one hundred fifty yards from the hostiles. Captain Tupper started for his own company, but the hostiles afforded him plenty of music about the head as he passed by them. The hostiles received Rafferty's company with heavy and repeated volleys. Being almost surrounded and in close quarters, every man in the company became aware of the few chances of escape left him. In fact, if the hostiles had kept cool, there would have been no chance at all and every man would have been shot down. As it was they fired too high, and the bullets passed over our heads every time.

There was but one thing left for everyone to do, and that was for each man to get out the best way he could. They withdrew slowly and continued firing into the rocks where the Indians were hidden. About one hundred fifty yards to the rear there was a small sink in the ground in which five men and myself concealed ourselves. There was not room for another man, and the rest of the company continued to move back. We soon saw that we could do nothing, so we concluded to get out, and as the safest way, one man would get up and run about twenty or thirty yards and drop on the ground for a few seconds. In about five minutes another man would do the same thing. Bullets hailed about every man, but all got out safe with the exception of Miller, who was wounded, and Goldick[10] killed. Captain Tupper's company and the Indian scouts were firing with all their might to attract the attention of the hostiles, while Captain Rafferty was withdrawing and driving off seventy-four head of the Indians' stock.

Loco tried to get the scouts to turn against us, but they would abuse and curse him and fire into the rocks where he was. As soon as Captain Rafferty got his company out he formed a skirmish line on the right of Tupper and continued firing until 12:00 P.M.

There was no hope of doing anything more, as the hostiles could not be surrounded and kept there because there were only thirty-nine soldiers in all to put on the line. To have moved the men toward the rocks where the Indians were hidden would have been to murder every one of them without the hope of killing an Indian. The command was withdrawn and moved back about ten miles and went into camp. Up to this time not a man in the command had closed his eyes for thirty-six hours, nor had the horses been unsaddled for the same time.

Captain Tupper is highly deserving for the brave manner in which he conducted himself through the fight and the great energy he showed in his endeavor to annihilate the entire hostile band. Lieutenant Touey, entirely unprotected, deployed Tupper's company about the rocky stronghold, and there remained during the entire fight and undoubtedly did good work. Captain Rafferty and Lieutenant Blake were conspicuous objects in the charge and held their places in the front. M Company stood with them and showed no signs of excitement. Lieutenants Miller and Darr pulled off their boots and crawled into the rocks with their scouts during the night and there concealed themselves. This was certainly risky on their part, for if they had been discovered many if not all of them would have been shot down. They certainly executed their parts in a beautiful manner. Pat Keogh and Rower,[11] the guides, urged on their Indians boys and reveled in happiness over the good work they were doing. The whole affair was a success adorned with coolness.

Tupper had been in camp but a short time when Colonel Forsyth with seven companies of cavalry and two companies of Indian scouts came up. On learning of the fight, he told Captain Tupper that he wanted his command to go with him that night after Indians as they were only ten miles away. Tupper told him that he could not go as his command must have sleep and rest, but said that he would overtake him the next day. Being determined to have a large command that the Indians could see for fifty miles, Colonel Forsyth went into camp for the night with his small detachment of four hundred soldiers and fifty scouts. The truth of the matter is that Captain Tupper with thirty-nine soldiers and forty-five scouts for fighting duty had attacked the Indians in one of the strongest places I ever saw (and I have seen a great many), while Colonel Forsyth, then in command of four hundred fifty soldiers and scouts, did not pursue and attack the same Indians because he wished to display a larger command. A long column of troops makes a big show, but they don't catch Indians.

Tupper's fight was on the morning of [April] 28, and on the twenty-ninth the hostiles ran into Colonel Garcia in command of 275 men on the Corralitos River. Here a bloody fight took place, in which, as far as I was able to see, there were eleven bucks and plenty of squaws and children killed, and fourteen squaws and eleven children were captured. The Mexicans had twenty-three killed and about thirty wounded. More bucks may have been killed, but I failed to see them. As soon as Garcia opened fire all of the young bucks belonging to the Warm Springs band put spurs to their horses and made escape. The old bucks stood and fought for their families, and there they died with them. Young bucks look out for themselves; old bucks fight for their families. The band of Warm Springs Indians will be heard of no more since the old bucks and nearly all, if not every one, of the squaws have been killed. The young bucks will unite with Juh and there will be formed one of the strongest bands of Indians that has existed for years in this part of the territory.

The time will come when we will have them to fight again. Many a poor man will fall at their hands before their final destruction. Juh can now muster a force of 150 young bucks, all experienced in the arts of Indian warfare and all brave and daring. No small command of troops will ever be able to do anything with them, and nothing but a small command will ever be able to catch them. By keeping small commands of 150 men, each in supporting distance of each other, when once their trail is found, there is hope of catching and killing the entire band. But unless this is done, there will be no hope of making any progress towards their final destruction.

If Colonel Forsyth had shown the same energy as Captains Tupper and Rafferty, he could have overtaken us before the fight, and the entire band of Warm Springs Indians and about sixty of Juh's band would have been good, in other words dead, Indians, and the territory of Arizona would today be in a fair condition to continue prosperous and happy, peaceful and undisturbed. Major D[avid] Perry, Sixth Cavalry, so distributed his troops in small commands that it was actually impossible for the Indians to escape without striking one of them. His commands were necessarily small because he had but few troops, but by placing them in supporting distance of each other, he saw that he could annihilate the entire band. But Colonel Forsyth's cavalry, on reaching Arizona, took possession of every command, or tried to, that Major Perry had started in pursuit of this band—at least, of all those he was able to reach by courier or otherwise. He thus upset every arrangement that Major Perry had made. He is the sole cause of two commands of the Sixth Cavalry not overtaking us in time for the fight and thus, instead of destroying the whole band, we, with a small command, were only able to cripple them as above mentioned.

If the Indians had been attacked by the Mexicans where Tupper fought them, the Mexicans would have been wiped out before breakfast. If Tupper had not fought them on the twenty-eighth, the Mexicans would never have seen them, as they did not know that any Indians were coming and were simply camped on this river for the night while en route for Janos; that is, if their own statement is worth anything. I have now given a detailed review of the whole affair from first to last, and no one can truthfully deny anything I have said because I have not deviated in the least from actual facts.[12]

The Apache Story of the Cibicue

ALCHISAY, ET AL.

John G. Bourke Diary 60: 21–63,
United States Military Academy Library[1]

Fort Apache, A.T., September 22, 1882
Present: General Crook, Captain Bourke, A.D.C., Assistant Surgeon J. O.
Skinner; C. E. Cooley and Severiano as interpreters; Pedro (a deaf chief, using
an ear trumpet), Cut-mouth Moses, Alchisay, Uclenny, Esketeshelaw, Noqui-
Noquis, Pelti, Notsin, Mosby, Chile, Eskiltie, and some forty others.

General Crook: I want to have all that you say here go down on paper,
because what goes down on paper never lies. A man's memory may fail him,
but what the paper holds will be fresh and true long after we are all dead and
forgotten. This will not bring back the dead, but what is put down on the paper
today may help the living. What I want to get at is all that has happened since
I left here to bring about this trouble, this present condition of affairs. I want
you to tell the truth without fear and to tell it in as few words as possible, so
that everybody can read it without trouble.

Alchisay:[2] When you left here, everything was in good shape; there were
no bad Indians out. We were all content; everything was in peace. The officers
you had here were all taken away and new ones came in—a different kind. The
good ones must all have been taken away, and the bad ones sent in their places.
We couldn't make out what they wanted: one day they seemed to want one
thing; the next day, something else.

Perhaps we were to blame; perhaps they were; but anyhow, we hadn't any
confidence in them.

We were planting our own corn and melons and making our own living.
The agent at San Carlos[3] never gave us any rations, but we didn't mind that, as
we were taking care of ourselves.

One day the agent at San Carlos sent up and said that we must give up our
own country and our corn patches and go down there to live, and he sent
Indian soldiers to seize our women and children and drive us all down to that
hot land.

Pedro:[4] When you (General Crook) were here, we were all content—but
we can't understand why you went away! Why did you leave us? Everything

General Crook and (behind him) Alchisay. JOHN G. BOURKE. *ON THE BORDER WITH CROOK.*

was all right while you were here. There came a commissioned officer—a man with large whiskers all over his face (General Carr).

He sent for me; I was lame and could hardly walk, but I went up to his house from my place over yonder. He said, "I am going out on a campaign." I said, "Why? There are no bad Indians in the country. Why should you want to make a campaign now?"

When he said that he was going on that campaign, I told him that the Indians had permission to plant on the Cibicue, the Carrizo, and over by that hill (pointing), and in other places, and that they were all contented; they all had passes and were planting corn and had cattle in plenty and were very contented. I asked him why he wanted to go out and make a campaign against them. When he made that campaign, all that the Indians had was destroyed, their corn cut down, their cattle driven away.

Severiano:[5] A lot of my own cattle were taken away by soldiers and citizens.

Pedro: When I asked him why he was going on that campaign and told him that when I was in Washington the president had said we were all good Indians and all at peace, he looked at me in a very foolish way and just snickered—but did not reply. The interpreter Charlie (i.e., Charlie Hurrle, known to the Indians by his first name) was there, but I could get no information out of him.[6]

Then I came right back to my home, and I saw the troops starting out through the pass (pointing), and that's all the satisfaction I got.

Then I sent this Indian, Notsin, to overtake General Carr and ask him what he was going for, and General Carr said he was going out to the Cibicue to arrest the Indian who was having all that dancing, Noch-ay-del-klinne—the "doctor."

At this I was not alarmed, because I knew that there was no trouble with the Indians and that they were all good. Then Major Cochran[7] told me that he had received word from the agent at San Carlos that all the Apaches had to go down there and he said: "You (Pedro) had better get back to your own corn-fields over at Forestdale." This was after General Carr and the soldiers had left for the Cibicue.

When Severiano brought us in word of the fight at the Cibicue, everybody was much excited, and I thought best to take all my women and children up to Cooley's[8] house. When Major Cochran told me about the message from the agent at San Carlos, I intended starting for my cornfields, but when I heard of the fight, I thought best to go up to Cooley's.

This thing is all past now, and I have said all that I want to say about it, but I have something else I want to talk about. I don't understand this thing; I am getting to be an old man now. I have always done what was right.

Often when I have wanted a little fun, I have sent word to all the women and children and young men to come up and have a dance; other people have done the same thing. I have never heard that there was any harm in that, but that campaign was made just because the Indians over on the Cibicue were dancing.

Why this change? When you (General Crook) were here, whenever you said a thing, we knew that it was true and we kept it in our mind. When Colo-nel Green was here, our women and children were happy and our young peo-ple grew up contented. And I remember Brown, Randall, and the other officers who treated us kindly and were our friends.

But why should the other who came after them be so different? I used to be happy; now, I am all the time thinking and crying, and I say, where is old Colonel John Green and Randall and those other good officers, and what has become of them? Where have they gone? Why don't they come back? And the young men all say the same thing.

Alchisay. When you (General Crook) came here, you made me a soldier in Major Randall's company; I went on your first campaign. I have always been a friend of the soldiers—and now, in this Cibicue affair, I have suffered without cause, and I am sorry to say that I have been in the guardhouse for five or six months, and all because I tried to be a friend to the whites and to benefit them. Cooley went with me when I went to General Carr and offered him my services. General Carr told me to go back to Cooley's house and try to find out all I could about the Apaches who were out; I did so.

After all that, he sent out in the night and had me arrested, and I was in the guardhouse for six months at the San Carlos and at Camp Thomas.

Uclenny and I were doing all we could to help the whites, but we were both taken off by General Carr and put in the guardhouse.

All that I have ever done has been honest; I have always been true and obeyed orders. I made campaigns against Apache-Yumas, Apache-Tontos, Pinaleños, and all kinds of people, and even went against my own people.

When the Indians broke out at the San Carlos when Major Randall was here, I helped him to go fight them; I have been in all the campaigns. When Major Randall was here, we were all happy; when he promised a thing, he did it; when he said a word, he meant it, but all that he did was for our own good, and we believed in him and we think of him yet.

Where has he gone? Why doesn't he come back? Others have come to us since he left, but they talk to us in one way and act in another, and we can't believe what they say. They say: "That man is bad and that man is bad." I think that the trouble is they themselves are bad. Oh! Where is my friend Randall, the captain with the big mustache, which he always pulled. Why doesn't he come back? He was my brother, and I think of him all the time.

Cut-mouth Moses (first sergeant of the company of Indian scouts concerned in the Cibicue fight). General Carr sent for me and told me that he wanted me to go to the Cibicue and tell the Indian doctor that he, General Carr, wanted to see him. The doctor wasn't at home, but another Indian told me that the doctor wasn't at home, but would come in to see General Carr in six days. When I told this to General Carr about three days afterwards, he, General Carr, went to the Cibicue with the soldiers. When we got to the crossing of the Carrizo Creek, General Carr gave the Indian scouts twenty rounds of ammunition apiece.

When we got over to the Cibicue, General Carr sent me with another Indian over to where the doctor had some corn planted; the troops got there almost as soon as I did, just as I had begun talking with the doctor. When I told the doctor that General Carr had sent me after him, he made no reply, but sat with his head hanging down. When I took the doctor down to General Carr's camp, I sat down and he sat down alongside of me. A soldier came up and began punching the Indian soldiers and telling them to "ugashe" (go away).

Then General Carr's cook began firing at the Indian soldiers. We had hardly reached camp when this happened. I was up on a bank with the doctor, General Carr and Captain Hentig were down in a little ravine close to me, but I couldn't see them. The next thing after the shot was fired, the Indian and white soldiers began firing at each other; the other Indian soldiers ran into the brush, but I stayed where I was. I was sitting alongside of the doctor. The first shot fired at the doctor didn't hit him; the second shot wounded him, and then I laid down behind a pile of aparejos.

The doctor was hit in the head and fell without a word; I got behind the aparejo. That's all I saw. I could hear the doctor breathing.

I came back here with the troops. General Carr came to me and said three times, "Good! Good! Good! You are going back with us to Camp Apache!"

When they gave the Indian soldiers cartridges at the Carrizo, an officer asked me, "Whose friends are you; are you for us or are you going to help the Indians at the Cibicue?" There was nothing said by the Indians. I didn't hear them say a word about fighting the troops.

After the doctor was killed, the troops left there and marched all night to get back here. I couldn't tell how many Indians were in the fight; I was with the soldiers. There were four or five chiefs there, but I don't know how many men they had.

When I arrested the doctor, he was alone; all the white soldiers from the post were out there. I heard the Indians say that General Carr took the troops from here to make war on them, but that they (the Indians) didn't want war. If they wished, they could have killed all the soldiers in that rough country.

I was one of the first soldiers enlisted and have been a soldier ever since. I saved my money and put it into stock and had a good deal of property; it looks to me as if General Carr went out there just to destroy everything. The Indians and whites both stole all I had; now I haven't got anything.

Camp on Rio Prieto, A.T.
September 23, 1882

Present: General Crook, Captain John G. Bourke, Assistant Surgeon John O. Skinner; Mr. C. E. Cooley and Severiano as interpreters; Alchisay, Cut-mouth Moses, Chili, Kulo, Notsin, Nagataba, Yank, Comanche, Charlie, Naudina, Louni, Nita, Tzi-di-ku, Cliche.

General Crook. I want you to tell the truth: I know a great deal of what has transpired, and if I find that you don't tell the truth in what I know, it will shake my confidence in all that you tell that I don't already know. No harm shall come to any of you here for speaking the truth; so you must tell the truth, all the truth, and nothing but the truth; so, speak without fear.

Kulo (one of the ex-scouts) said here that he would speak first.

General Crook. I want you to speak about what you know of what happened at the Cibicue.

Kulo. I started away from Camp Apache with the soldiers and when we got over the crossing of the Carrizo, ammunition was given to us. Then an officer asked us, "Are you going to be for or against us?" At the time the question was asked us, we had confidence in the officer in charge of us; the captain with the long beard—General Carr. We answered that we had confidence in him and would be for him. After that, Moses here (i.e., Cut-mouth Moses, then first sergeant of the scouts) detailed myself and Charlie here (pointing to one of the ex-scouts), to go over and notify the doctor that the soldiers had come to arrest him.

When we got over to where the doctor was, the soldiers came right behind us. When the troops came down to where the Indian doctor was, Moses and the Indian soldiers took the doctor and went with the troops down to where they were to make camp.

While they were unloading the mules, General Carr's cook had a fire built. The cook fired a shot at us, and we all started to run away from him and ran to the pack train and aparejos, which were in the willows near the stream. As we ran there, the white soldiers opened fire upon us. After the firing on both sides had lasted a little while, we scattered and went off in parties of one, two, three, and four. After we scattered, I saw no more of that body of soldiers. We were all much frightened and worried because those officers had treated us so badly.

We have been out ever since and have not shown ourselves to any officers because we have been afraid after the treatment received then. Alchisay came and told us that you (General Crook) were here, and we have come in, trotting all the way.

I don't know of an Indian being killed, except the doctor, but I have heard that there were several Indians wounded. I don't know how many white soldiers were killed.

The white soldiers got back to Camp Apache before I did, and I then learned from Indians living near there that some of them had been killed. I didn't go to Apache myself; I went up to the headwaters of the Carrizo, near where Severiano had his cattle, but I learned from Indians living near the post what I now tell you. We didn't want a fight with the soldiers. The fight was unexpected by us as, up to that time, the soldiers had been our good friends. When the firing began, we ran away to hide and get out of range.

I am glad that you (General Crook) have come in; I have confidence in you and want to tell you all I know and would have followed you down to the San Carlos sooner than not see you.

Charlie. What kind of a man was that officer (General Carr)? What could he have been thinking of? What had he put in his head that he should act that way? Everything seemed to be going on all right and much to his satisfaction. Here we were, his soldiers—I have been a soldier since I was a boy, and he said he was content with us. He never said a word against us, either to us or to the interpreter, and yet he suddenly turned and treated us in that way. What kind of a man must he be?

We had many other commanding officers before he came; they were all good men and treated us well. And so did this man too until this time. What was the matter with him? He never gave us a reason; he never said a word to us. We used to be his soldiers, and if he wasn't satisfied with us, he used to punish us; he used to put us in the guardhouse for not finding water on the trail—that was all right, we expected that, but we can't understand why he should treat us as he did at Cibicue.

I was with the party under Moses that arrested the doctor and brought him down to the soldiers' camp. There was a big crowd of white and Indian soldiers and women and children, all close together. I went to the cornfield, got some green corn, and was making bread out of it when the firing commenced. I don't know who commenced the firing. I ran off with the other Indian scouts when they scattered. I started down Cibicue Creek; when I got away, below, an Indian came to me with a woman and said there had been fighting, the doctor had been killed, and some white soldiers—how many, he did not know. I only know of the doctor being killed on the Indian side.

We didn't want to fight the soldiers because they were our friends; we were all of that opinion.

I wasn't in that party, but one of the chiefs of the Cibicue, when all were running away, found a mule loaded with ammunition.

We have been waiting for someone to come here in whom we could have confidence. Many of our people blame the soldiers. I am glad to see you. I have told you the truth.

Louni (an ex-scout, son of One-Eyed Miguel). I have just the same thing to say that the others have said, and I have the same opinion of that officer at the Cibicue. I think that there was something wrong with his head. I know that his cook fired the first shot, and then the soldiers opened fire on us and we ran in every direction.

Nita (an ex-scout). We were out on herd, herding government mules, with Comanche over there, and when we got back in the evening and unsaddled, I went into the room where a white sergeant—Burns—was; there was a box of cartridges. I looked through a broken window and saw the box of twenty cartridges. I reached for them. The sergeant arrested me, put me in the guardhouse, put chains on me, cut all my hair off (a degradation in the eyes of the Indians equal to what the lopping off of the queue of a Chinaman would be in the view of his countrymen), said that I would have to stay in the guardhouse thirty days and pay fifteen dollars.

When Alchisay was sent down to the guardhouse at San Carlos, I was sent with him; I was in the guardhouse four months. I don't know anything about the Cibicue.

Ziddi-ku (ex-scout). I saw the cook. I was standing close to the woodpile where he was, near the aparejo. I saw the cook fire the first shot with his pistol, and almost as quick as anything the white soldiers grabbed their guns and began shooting at the Cibicue Indians who were near the doctor, and then the fighting commenced.[9] I saw but one Indian shot; the Indian who killed Captain Hentig. I was right close to Captain Hentig when he was shot; the Indian who shot him was Haw-she.

⦁—⧓⧗—⦁

At this point, General Crook asked for the names of those who had been in the affair at the Cibicue; they answered that all now present had been there with the exception of Alchisay, Chili, and Notsin. Cut-mouth Moses had remained with the soldiers; the rest had escaped to the mountains. Nagataba, Yank, Comanche, Nita, and Tzi-di-ku had also been in the fight on the summit of the Black Mesa, July 17, 1882.[10]

The strange aversion of the Apaches to giving their own names was here manifested in a ludicrous way. Not a single Indian evinced the slightest desire to shirk any responsibility, but not one would give his own name, and when asked for it would always refer to either his right-hand or his left-hand neighbor, who would furnish it; but when his turn came would refer back to the first one. The moon was so bright and our heaped-up fire sent such a stream of crackling sparks skywards that we had light enough without needing lanterns or candles.

The five Indians who had participated in the fight on the Black Mesa said that Na-ti-o-tish came and told them that the Indians of his band had taken their families away from San Carlos, and he wanted them to go with him. The Indian—Na-ti-o-tish—had charge of all the Indians of the Carrizo bands on the San Carlos. The trouble began between Sanchez and Na-ti-o-tish. Na-ti-o-tish told these five Indians that the whites were going to kill all the Apaches and that the soldiers would fire on them just as they did on the Cibicue, and so he persuaded us to go with him. "We were in that fight on the Black Mesa. We lost fifteen or sixteen killed and eleven wounded. We left him after the fight and don't know whether any of the wounded died or not. Down in Tonto Basin, there were two Indians killed and two wounded, one of whom died afterwards."[11]

◆━ ▆◆▅ ━◆

General Crook. It's getting late; we'll have another talk in the morning.

Alchisay. I want to say a few words. I am very well satisfied with everything that has been said and done here this evening. These Indians are not to blame. There has been so much said and done that they hardly know what to do, but there are bad Indians of the Cibicue band at the San Carlos Agency.

I am glad of this talk. I have understood all that you (General Crook) have said to me.

These Indians are not to blame. They have been forced into this thing by the way in which they have been treated. I have given you my hand, and you have given me yours. If you knew everything as well as the Indians do, I don't think you would blame them. When you are in command, all the Indians feel that they can go to sleep without fear. You talk straight, and I think that I do also. When you give your hand, you mean it, and when I do, I mean it. You have given us pleasure by telling us that we shall not be harmed.

General Crook. I have heard all that you have said and think I understand you. It is believed by the white people that these Indian soldiers turned against the white soldiers at the Cibicue. When white soldiers do such a thing as that, we always kill them. The whole matter seems to be wrapped up in a good deal of mystery and confusion—each side has a different story.

The promptness with which you have come in here makes me think you are telling the truth as you know it. I don't do things halfway; I either do one thing or the other.

I want all those who have government guns to turn them in and return them. When they do that, we'll wipe out the past and commence on a scrubbed floor, on a new basis. In a short time, I'll send an officer up to Fort Apache to enlist soldiers, as we did when Major Randall was here, and I'll expect these soldiers to control all the Indians, just the same as they used to do. They must report everything that is going on, so that the guilty may be punished and the innocent may not suffer with them. That officer will report directly to me. Of course, if he doesn't suit, I'll send another, and keep on doing it until I get one who will suit. You will know when that officer arrives, and you can turn your guns in to him.

Alchisay. We have not had a good interpreter for a long time. When Stanley was with us, Severiano was our interpreter, and we had no trouble in understanding what was required of us. There are many Indians who speak badly of me, but you and I have talked together; you understand me, and I understand you.

(Conference broke up at about 10:30 P.M.)

————————

Camp on San Carlos River, A.T.
Four miles north of San Carlos Agency
September 26, 1882, 12:00 P.M.

Present: General George Crook, Captain John G. Bourke, A.D.C., Assistant Surgeon J. O. Skinner; Mr. C. E. Cooley and Severiano as interpreters for the Apaches, and Dick, an Indian of the Apache-Yumas, for his people and the Apache-Mojaves.

Present: Navatane, Nodikun, Santos, [Sanchez], Jun, Podilkun, Bonilke, Chunatil, Capitan Chiquito, Gudi Guya (Sierra Blanca Apaches); Eskinospos, [San Carlos Apache]; Chalipun, Apache Tonto; Chunahuevi-Gal, Apache-Yuma.

General Crook. I want to hear what has transpired since I was last here and what the trouble has all been about, and to have it in as few words as possible.

Capitan Chiquito.[12] When I first came in to make peace at Camp Apache, Colonel Green was in command; he was kind to us, and we were contented and remained so until we were moved down here; since then we have not been contented. When I first met Colonel Green, he told us that we should remain satisfied in our homes; after that talk, I went back to my home in the Cibicue—I was contented there and remained there; the land was good, and the water good, and I was satisfied. Then, I would come into Camp Apche and find brothers and friends, and there were letters written about us to Washington, and we had friends and were satisfied.

Whether I received a written paper or not, an officer's word was good to me; all he said was good; all the roads were safe. We were always satisfied so long as we remained in our own country on the Carrizo.

When you, General Crook, were here some years ago I was very contented, and since you've been away I've often thought of you and of my old land, and I wish to God I was back there again. In this country (San Carlos) the water is bad; everybody is sick. The ground is bad, the climate is too, and we wish we were back in our own country again. When we were first brought down here, we were treated kindly. We are not contented here. When I was in my own home, I knew where the reservation lines were, and if I went outside the soldiers would bring me back, and I was contented to remain within the boundaries.

I ask of you the favor to use your influence to get me and my people back to my own country, where the soil is good and the water plenty, and where, by working with my hands, I can get enough to eat.

One reason why I want to go back is I don't get enough to eat here; the food given me to last for seven days doesn't last for three. The treatment here is not good, nothing is good.

Sanchez.[13] A great while ago, I was not a captain, I was a soldier, but now I am a chief, and I want everybody to hear what I have to say. Since I've been here, I've never been contented; I couldn't sleep well and didn't feel at home, but now I am glad that you (General Crook) have come and hope that you'll let me go back to my own country. I am not satisfied here and ask as a favor that I be allowed to go back to my own country. Things are sent here for us which we never get; they are kept from us. The agent here is not kind to us, nor are any of his people. Pants and shirts are sent here for us but are not given to us. These I have on, I got from somebody else; the agent didn't give me any. (Sanchez was wearing a cast-off suit of officer's clothing.) I am not content here; none of the agents have ever been good to us. I would sooner be in my own country without rations than live here, even if the agent were to give me rations and all that was promised to me.

I know that stuff is sent here for us from Washington, but I don't know what becomes of it; it never gets to the Indians. Therefore, as I have said, I would sooner be back in my own country without rations than remain here with them. You know very well that lots of stuff is sent us here in wagons; what becomes of it? It is very sickly here; my people have been very sickly all the time. The agent doesn't give us enough. We get three yards of manta (calico) for a family of six, and one blanket for each family. For twenty persons for seven days' rations, we get the shoulder of a beef.

There was an agent came here some time since with a big belly (Tiffany). I don't know what he was sent here for; he was the worst we ever had. None of his papers were good; none of his passes, none of his orders were good, and nothing he said was good. He said on paper that he was feeding a good many Indians. This was a lie, as there were many Indians who never got any rations. I give you my hand and ask the favor of being allowed to go back to my own country. Nothing suits me here, but there I was always contented, so I ask the favor of being sent back.

Juan Cliche. I have talked with General Crook before and haven't forgotten what he told me. I am glad to be able to talk with him once more, and I want him to listen to what I have to say.

The reason I went in to Camp Apache was because while I was fighting the whites, you (General Crook) killed all my relatives and many of my people; so, I was obliged to submit and go in to Camp Apache, where I was kindly treated.

After my talk with you, I became satisfied. I have not forgotten it. I was contented until I was brought down here with my people; since then I have been unhappy. Everything is blamed on the Indians, but it is the agents who are to blame for the treatment they give us. They steal from us and we don't get what we are entitled to. The agent tells me that when he gives me a cupful of flour. (A squaw cried out, "It's not a cupful, it's only a spoonful." Laughter among the Indians.) When the agent gives me that much and tells me that it is the ration for seven days for each person, you know he lies. I know better than that; he is stealing our rations.

We eat all the meat from the hoofs to the horns and the insides too. When we want a piece of rawhide to make soles for our moccasins, we have to buy it from the agent. He trades in everything. He trades in the hides. Every twenty persons get for seven days only one shoulder of beef; that isn't enough. Wagonloads of blankets, shoes, and boots come here, but we never get any. All we get is that kind of a shirt and pants (pointing to an Indian near). Great piles of blankets come to the agency; we never get any. What becomes of them? Do they fly away? He wouldn't give us any pass to hunt, not even in these little mountains close by; we didn't get enough to eat, so we had to ask a pass for hunting. Neither me nor my family get enough to eat; our bellies are always empty and we ask of you, General Crook, the favor of being sent back to our homes, where we can get enough to eat.

When I want anything and ask the interpreter about it, he always says, "How much will you pay me for it?" Everything here is to be bought. Where I used to live, I had white people on both sides of me and I never had any trouble, but here I am not contented and would like to get back.

I got permission to go out and cultivate my land. I planted lots of corn and everything. When the corn was knee-high, the agent changed his mind and brought me back, and I was never allowed to go after it, so it rotted in the ground. I could go there easily in one day from here. When I would go to the interpreter to ask him to speak to the agent on this subject, the interpreter would say, "How much will you pay me?" I became discouraged and stopped asking. I want you to do me a favor in Washington. With my own hands I can make my own living in my own country.

I have understood thoroughly all you have said in former days and I want you to believe what I tell you now; it is all true.

Chalipun. When I first met you (General Crook), a long time ago, you gave me your hand and said, "Remember what I tell you, I am your friend." I have not forgotten those words. I have given you my hand again and am your friend and will tell you the truth. I have never forgotten what you told me. You told me to sit down and behave myself, and I have always done so. We have been waiting for you a long while. You told me you'd always be my friend, so I've been waiting for you to come back for a long while and thinking about you every day. Now that you have come, I haven't many people; they are nearly all dead.

Once you were here, and then you went away and were gone for a long while. Now that you are here I want to tell you that we are living in a fire; we are not contented, we are unhappy. I have no family now. My mother, wife, and children—nearly all are dead. I ask the favor of living again in my own country, where I can be happy again. Here is a paper you gave me years ago. I want you to look at it to see if I have taken good care of it or not (handing a commission as chief, dated August 1874).

Now I want you to do the best you can to get us out of this country; we shall soon be dead if you do not soon get us back to our own land. When I made peace with you at Camp Verde, you put me under an officer of the army. We always got our full rations—meat, flour, coffee, sugar—everything; we never were hungry, our bellies were always full. Since we have come here, we often have to go without food; we don't get our rations. We can't raise anything here. I have tried to do so every year until this year, but I failed to raise anything, so this year I wouldn't try anymore.

I have stood this as long as I can. I have held my people together, but I don't know what will happen to them if the same kind of people have charge of us much longer. We have failed in everything, and my people won't stay here much longer. That is all.

(As all the other chiefs expressed themselves as of one opinion, no other testimony was asked from the Apaches.)

Chunahuevi-Gal (head chief of the Apache-Yuma). I have heard what the other chiefs have said; they have said the same as I think of this business. I want to talk with you, because I have known you for many years as our good friend. A long time ago you talked to me and told me to behave myself and settle down to live like a white man. I remember all you told me, and I've been trying to do as you told me. These other chiefs have told you everything that has happened and of the bad way in which the agents have been treating us. I have had some of my people serving as scouts; four of them were killed in the last campaign. We have always helped the whites. I have planted a great deal of corn, pumpkins, watermelons, etc., but it is hard to raise anything, as water is scarce and the sun dries everything up.

The agent has always treated me kindly. The first agent that was here gave me three blankets for my family of five; the next agent gave me two, but I have tried hard to raise crops and gain my own living.

Gudi Guya (a Sierra Blanca Apache). I am glad that you, General Crook, have come. When you were here before you were our good friend and all our people were contented.

I want to return to my own land. I like it better than this. Our own land is cool, and when we were there, we were all contented and happy; in this country, everybody is sick. It is very hot and water is bad. When I was in Camp Apache I got all my rations—beef, sugar, coffee—everything—and was happy; here, I don't get one half enough. With my own work, I was supporting my people in my own land without rations; all that grows here, grows just as well there. I ask the favor to be allowed to go back to my own country.

Eskinospos (San Carlos Apache chief). This has been my country. I have nothing to say against it. I was born and raised here. These other Indians are from the cool mountains and they don't like it. I get enough to eat.

(Conference ended at 3:15 P.M.)

Camp at San Carlos, A.T.
Four miles north of San Carlos Agency
September 27, 1882, 3:00 P.M.

Present: General Crook, Captain John G. Bourke, A.D.C., Assistant Surgeon J. O. Skinner, Mr. C. E. Cooley and Severiano as interpreters.

General Crook. I want to know why you went out on the warpath.

Manuel. I can't think of all that has taken place since you, General Crook, were last here. I have been a soldier for a long time; I was one of the first soldiers Major Randall had; everything at that time was all right. But now everything is like a dream and I can't account for how it all happened.

The agent gave us permission to plant on the Cibicue and gave us hoes and spades to work with. Our crops were fine. I don't know why the soldiers were sent up there unless our fine crops made the agent mad. All Mexicans and Americans raise corn—take pleasure in raising it.

After he found out that we were raising corn, why did that fat agent send out soldiers after us? What had we done? We had an abundance of everything planted—corn, watermelons, musk melons, beans—everything. We couldn't understand why the agent should always be sending men up to see what we were doing; their horses always trampled down our fields of corn. Up where we planted was an open road. No stolen horses ever found their way in there; we never did anything wrong; then why did the agent send soldiers in there?

If the commanding officer of Camp Apache—General Carr—wanted to arrest the doctor, why didn't he send out and do it? He could have done it without any trouble. But he brought out soldiers with him to make a campaign, and they began firing on us. Of course, some of our people fired back; but who wouldn't? We couldn't understand why the soldiers should treat us in that way; we had always been their good friends.

After that fight, we came down here to the agent, who was our captain. But he was very unkind to us and we were afraid that he would fire upon us also. The agent said, "Go away." I said, "I want to remain here where I belong.

Why did you tell that officer at Camp Apache to make war upon us? We are your people; you are our commanding officer. We want to stay here." But he said, "Go away, go off to the mountains." I told the agent I hadn't done anything wrong; I hadn't gone on the warpath, I hadn't stolen anything, I wanted to stay here, where I belonged. But he took me, tied me all up, tied my hair, put irons on my feet and hands, and put me in the calaboose. I hadn't done anything wrong, at least I don't think I have.

When I heard tell that you, General Crook, were coming, I said, "Would to God he would come soon! Would to God he would come tonight! Would to God he would come today!" And when at last I heard that you had come I got on my horse and here I am!

I have trotted all the way from the Carrizo. When we were living up above here on this river—when I was let out of the guardhouse, everybody told me that I was going to have everything taken away from me, that I was going to be put in irons and sent to Tucson, and when at last the Apache-Yuma scouts came out to our camp and fired two shots at us, all of us thought that, instead of staying here to be killed, we had better run off to the mountains and hide.

When the officers at Apache were here in your time—Major Randall and Major Ogilby—everything went along nicely. They were very kind to us. But after you went away, another set came in that somehow didn't seem to care anything for us; they never had any patience with us and everything seemed to go wrong. But now you are back, we think that you'll straighten everything again, just as it used to be. I want you to understand that I have told the truth and have not told a lie.

Camp on San Carlos River, Arizona
(As above) September 29, 1882
5:45 A.M.

Present: General George Crook and Captain John G. Bourke, A.D.C.; Mr. C. E. Cooley and Severiano as interpreters.

General Crook. I want to find out exactly why you went out.

Nodeski.[14] When I was in Camp Apache in early days I liked it very well. I can remember four commanding officers who were kind to me. When Major Randall was in command at Apache, all the Indians, young and old, got everything they were promised and were content. After we were brought down here from Apache, we were also kindly treated for a while by the white-faced agent (Clum); but soon everything changed, everything became poor. We were treated badly and didn't get enough to eat. While Merejildo was interpreter everything went on all right; we could understand everything. After he went away, we couldn't understand anybody. They gave one blanket to every ten persons—the rest went to the mining towns around here. So it was with the shawls and everything else.

I don't know what kind of a man that fat agent was. (In speaking of Agent Tiffany, the Indians always used an expression which Severiano rendered into Spanish as "Hijo de puta panzon"—it will not bear translation.)[15] While he was here, everything was wrong, everybody around him was wrong. While that fat agent was here, we had a great deal of corn planted out in the western part of the reservation, near Globe. One day he sent for us. He had two sacks of Mexican dollars—the kind that is worth at the store six bits each. He said: "You mustn't go back there, you must give up that country. You must take this money." I said, "Why? I don't want that money, I want my own land. It is mine." Then he said, "If you don't take that money, I'll have you all killed."

The land here is good enough, but when we plant corn, it comes up nicely and then it dies. So it is with the agents: they commence nicely, but they soon quit their pleasant ways and we suffer. The agent counted everything for rations: even our dogs were counted as having rations given them. I ask a favor. We are not treated right here. We have to pay for everything. Even the interpreters rob us. If we ask an interpreter to go with us to talk to the agent, he always says, "How much will you pay me?" Everybody is unkind to us. The agent is sent out here to be kind, but he is unkind. He steals from us and we all know it.

Pedro's band is living up at Forestdale, making its own living; his people don't have to beg from the agent for everything they want. When there were soldiers here, we didn't have any trouble; we got along with them very well. We were good friends; they were very kind to us. But when the soldiers went away, everything changed. The agents' men were very unkind; they were always threatening us. They would threaten us with the guardhouse for nothing at all. They said that they were going to take our arms away. They were always knocking and pulling us around.

When one Indian did wrong, they never made any effort to get him, but punished the whole band. They would fire into a band for nothing at all; that's how they killed that squaw, she wasn't doing anything at all. They were going to arrest another Indian, but that's the way they did [it]. When Major Randall was in charge of us up at Camp Apache, if an Indian did wrong, he would send to arrest him and would say to the band he belonged to that he didn't want to hurt the innocent, but the guilty had to be given up. That was the right way. The bad Indian we always gave up, and he would be put in the guardhouse. But I think that this fat agent, Tiffany, wants to drive us out on the warpath— and we all thought that he wanted to kill us anyhow, and we might as well go off to the mountains at once. I want to ask a favor; let me go back to my own land. With my own hands I can make my living and shall not want rations.

<u>Tubucasinda</u>. The first time I ever saw you, General Crook, I saw Major Randall, and all the time that you were here it seemed as if Randall had his arms around us all. We were happy and contented until you both went away; since then, we have been miserable. Lately, every day, every night since the Cibicue, we have been told all sorts of things; we were to be put in the guard-

house, have our arms taken from us, and be sent away from this country. A man would be suddenly put in the guardhouse without any cause and then let out again without any explanation; we couldn't make out what was meant by such treatment.

We had permission to go over to the Carrizo to plant. We had a splendid field of corn. We had over one hundred cows. Over on the next creek, Cibicue, we had over two hundred cows and a good many mares and young colts and another fine field of corn. We were getting to be very rich. When the captain came out with the soldiers from Fort Apache (General Carr), he let his soldiers turn their horses in upon our corn—it was all destroyed. Our cows were killed or stolen, and the same with our mares. It looked to me as if the Americans didn't want us to work and didn't like the idea of having us make our own living; wanted to destroy all we had and drive us out on the warpath.

After the trouble on the Cibicue we never had any peace. First, one man comes and tells us that we were going to be put in the guardhouse; then another would say that we were going to be arrested, disarmed, and taken far away to another country; and, in this way, we were very much excited and didn't get any rest. Some thought it better to go on the warpath at once and have the business ended. We thought it would be better to die fighting in the mountains than die in this place.

After the Cibicue trouble, after General Carr left, we blamed all our new troubles upon the big fat agent, Tiffany. He was always sending up and having us brought down and was wronging us in every way he could.

(Conference dissolved at 6:50 A.M.)

The Apache Troubles

GEORGE CROOK

Army and Navy Register, October 21, 1882

General Crook has written the following letter, giving the result of his investigations and his opinions and views upon the vexed Apache question:

HEADQUARTERS, DEPT. ARIZONA, IN THE FIELD
CAMP NEAR SAN CARLOS AGENCY, A.T., September 29, 1882

Adjutant General Military Division of the Pacific, San Francisco, Ca.—
Sir: I have the honor to report that, since leaving my headquarters at Prescott on the eleventh instant, I have had several conferences with Indians of the Apache tribe—renegades and others—of which I send you herewith a record as made at the time. This record imperfectly outlines the sentiments of the Indians as I learned them from private conversations and in my own way, but it will serve to give an idea of the condition of affairs viewed from their standpoint. It should be remembered that in the council, when statements are put upon paper, Indians are much more guarded, timid, and distrustful than when talking privately.

I learned to my own satisfaction that the Indians are so firmly of the belief that the affair of the Cibicue last year was an attack premeditated by the white soldiers that I am convinced any attempt to punish one of the Indian soldiers for participation in it would bring on a war. Without wishing to express an opinion on that affair, I have no doubt, from what I know of the Indians and the country in question, that if these Indians had been in earnest, not one of our soldiers could have gotten away from there alive. Of course, afterward, it was perfectly natural for the Indians who had lost friends and relations to commit the depredations which they did in the vicinity of Fort Apache.

When I first visited the Indians I found them sullen and distrustful, and it was only with much difficulty that I could get them to talk with me. After breaking down their suspicions by railing at them and shaming them for not trusting me, who had always been straightforward with them, they finally came around and talked freely with me.

They all agreed that affairs could not well be worse; that one officer of the government would tell them one thing and another something else, until finally they lost confidence in everybody and, not knowing whom or what to believe, lent a credulous ear to every story which Mexicans or other irresponsible parties throughout the country concocted.

They were constantly told that they were to be disarmed and then were to be attacked, as at Cibicue; the interpreters were incompetent and some of them prejudiced; and probably as a consequence of this incompetence and prejudice, innocent Indians had been ironed and put in the guardhouse. No one knew when his turn would come, and they were fast arriving at the conclusion that they were all to be killed anyhow and that they might as well die fighting as in any other way.

I have but very little doubt that in a short time there would have been a general outbreak, and when we consider the hundreds of exposed ranchmen and prospectors through the country in which they would depredate, the deplorable consequence of such a contingency may readily be imagined. Furthermore, I became satisfied from the explanations the Indians made that all the troubles of the past season, terminating in the engagement on the summit of the Black Mesa in July last, were but an outgrowth or a culmination of the ill feeling engendered at the Cibicue.

Over nine years ago I put the White Mountain Apaches on their reservation; at the same time, these Indians were put on their present ground. The White Mountain band soon became self-sustaining and, up to the time of the unfortunate trouble at the Cibicue, had raised considerable property in the way of livestock, of which the campaign since waged has almost entirely deprived them.

When I reached here, those living on the Gila and San Carlos flocked to see me, bringing doleful tales of the unhealthiness of the climate and the difficulty experienced in getting a sufficiency of goods; their former agent had not made adequate provision for them; they had not been allowed to hunt; and it had been impossible, on account of the character of the soil, the burning sun, and meager water supply, to raise crops of any consequence. All begged to be allowed to go back to their old homes, promising that they would work for their own living and ask nothing from the government.

The taking of these Indians down to their present location has been of very much the same pattern as it would be to transfer the inhabitants of the cool mountains of Vermont or Nebraska to the fever-ridden swamps of Florida. This reservation, as at present constituted, is abundantly large enough for all the Indians belonging to it and contains every variety of soil and climate suited to their different requirements. Under this feature of the case, as there has been no necessity for concentrating all the bands at one point, I see no reason why those belonging to the mountains should have been deprived of the privilege of living in places more agreeable to them, and I earnestly recommend that they be allowed to return to their former homes. In my judgment they can never be self-sustaining here, and as they can be better controlled with full stomachs, I am anxious to have them located in places congenial to their dispositions and more healthful for them. If sickness be kept from them, and they be encouraged to farm, they will not long need rations and will soon acquire property, with which acquisition contentment and peaceful thoughts will arise.

There are now no hostile Indians out excepting the Chiricahuas who have taken refuge in Mexico. The Mexicans do not seem to be making much headway against this particular band, which is likely at any moment to return across the border. Pursuit by our troops will be almost certain to result fruitlessly, as under the terms of the recent convention with Mexico, if my interpretation be correct, we can only follow Indians on hot trails; whereas, to ensure success, campaign against them must be incessant. From their present position they can depredate at will on either side of the line, and it will be utterly impossible for us to prevent them. Very respectfully,

> Your obedient servant,
> GEORGE CROOK,
> Brigadier General,
> Commanding Department Arizona

General Crook's Return

MURAT MASTERSON[1]

Prescott *Arizona Democrat*, November 25, 1882

Learning of General Crook's return last night from his two months' trip to the Southern portion of the territory among the Indians, and knowing that any information in regard to the Indian question would not only be read with interest by readers of the *Democrat*, but by citizens of the entire territory as well, the editor of this paper this morning went out to headquarters and had a very pleasant and sociable interview with him which we present to our readers. We were introduced to the general by Captain C. P. Eagen, who, by the way, is very well and favorably known to the citizens of Prescott, and whom we found to be a very courteous and affable gentleman and an exceedingly interesting and entertaining conversationalist.[2]

The general received us very courteously and, on stating our mission, very kindly consented to answer any questions which we might ask him, when we at once applied our A number-one, double-acting, automatic interviewing apparatus by propounding to him the following questions:

General, in what condition of mind did you find the Indians in regard to their relations with the white people?

Answer—Very uneasy and unsettled.

Question—Is it true, General, that they confessed to you that they contemplated a general uprising.

Answer—It is. They said that everybody seemed against them and that they could trust no one as their friend. One officer would tell them one thing one day, and the next they would be told something different by someone else. Someone would place them in the guardhouse without their knowing the cause of it, and probably the next day they would be released, only to be put in by someone else, so that they did not know what was expected of them, or what they should do, and that the least idle rumor would stir them up and arouse their hostile nature. They frankly acknowledged that they had at last come to the conclusion that they had to die and that they might as well die with guns in their hands and on the warpath as any other way.

Question—How many Indians did you find on the reservation?

314

An Apache rancheria. JOHN G. BOURKE. *ON THE BORDER WITH CROOK.*

Answer—About thirteen hundred bucks in the different bands—there being some fifteen or twenty bands belonging to the reservation. They were very much scattered, only a small proportion being in the vicinity of the agency, and some being entirely off the reservation. Those who were inclined to go on the warpath were away from the agency, scattered through the mountains.

Question—How did you induce them to come in to the agency?

Answer—Well, from my former dealings with them, they reposed a great deal of confidence in me, and I sent out to them to come in and have a talk with me and sent word to them that even if my decision would be against them that they should not be harmed in any way by coming in and having a talk. At first they were very reluctant and hesitated considerably. One fellow whom I knew very well when I was here before, hesitating about it, I asked: "Why, do you not know me?" He replied, "Well, really, I am not sure about it; you look like the same man, but I cannot tell now who is my friend and who is not." Finally, when a few of them came in, the rest came all right.

Question—How were they pleased with the arrangements you had made with them?

Answer—They seemed perfectly satisfied and unless some causes should arise over which we have no control to arouse them to hostility, there is no danger in the least now of an Indian outbreak as far as those on this side of the Mexican boundary are concerned.

Question—Well, General, having seen some statements in the newspapers in regard to the regulations you made for their government, would you kindly give me the details of it?

Answer—The Indians in each band were all numbered and each given a brass tag or check, the different bands having different-shaped tags, so that the tag shows not only the band its owner belongs to but his number in the band. A record of these together with a full and complete description of the owner of it is kept in a book. They were then instructed that anyone found outside the reservation or without his tag would be considered as hostile and treated accordingly. The reservation is also being resurveyed, and they will be provided with seed in the spring and allowed the privileges of selecting any location they may choose within the reservation to plant them. Heretofore they were only allowed the privilege of cultivating around the agency, and San Carlos Agency is located in the most barren and uninviting portion of the territory, which is saying a good deal. The Indians have also been suffering greatly with malarial fevers and have died off in great number around the agency, which naturally discourages them. Now, as they can make their own selections of location, they are better satisfied.

Question—In what condition did you find them, as to any progress in civilization, as compared with their condition when you were here before?

Answer—Worse off, a great deal worse off, as far as taking care of themselves is concerned. Before I left here, many of them had accumulated quite a little property and had made a fair start. I enlisted a number of them, and with the pay they received I encouraged them in buying stock—horses and cattle—which they did, and were doing fairly well. Now, with the exception of a very few bands, they have absolutely nothing. Everything has gone, though they are tolerably well and comfortably provided for the winter, except in some cases a little short of clothing.

Question—I believe you discharged most of the old scouts who had been enlisted among them?

Answer—Yes, as fast as the time was up for which they were enlisted, they were discharged, as they were mostly boys and young bucks without standing or influence among their own people. A few, however, were reenlisted, and others will be enlisted under an entirely different system. We shall hereafter enlist only those who have character and standing among their bands and who will have influence with them, to keep them under control. To send strangers in among the citizens to govern them would arouse their jealousy about the same as to import Europeans to govern and run our affairs. We have two officers stationed at San Carlos, and there are two civilians, who are called chief of scouts, to look after them, and two interpreters.

Question—How are they pleased with the change of agents?

Answer—Very well. Agent Wilcox gives them all that they are entitled to, and no one appreciates that more than an Indian does.

Question—Did they complain any of the former agent, Tiffany?

Answer—Yes, they were loud in their denunciation of him, saying that he sold their supplies, what they knew belonged to them, right before their eyes.

That he did not give them enough to eat, and that he showed favoritism, allowing some to do as they pleased and being very severe and stringent with others.

The general was then shown an item clipped from the Tombstone *Republican*, in which it was stated that it has at last been definitely decided to establish the headquarters of the Military Department of Arizona at Fort Huachuca, and asked what he knew of it.

"The fact is simply this," he replied, "The headquarters were established here by order of the secretary of war and they can only be changed by his order, and of course I have heard nothing of it, nor do I think that he will be likely to go the expense necessary for the transfer. So far as I know the officers are very well satisfied with the present location."

In speaking of the government of the Indians, he remarked that the great secret of success in that direction was to deal justly with them. They knew pretty well what they ought to have and expected it.

Agent Tiffany Torn to Tatters

JAMES H. TOOLE

Tucson *Arizona Star*, October 24, 1882

To the Hon. Wilson W. Hoover, district judge:

The United States Grand Jury for the present term of the United States District Court for the First Judicial District has concluded its labors and begs to submit the following report.

Thirty indictments have been found and a thorough investigation has been instituted regarding all matters coming within its jurisdiction. The greatest interest was felt in the examination into the cases of the eleven Indian prisoners brought here for trial from San Carlos. The United States district attorney has spent much time in preparing this investigation and had entered into an extensive correspondence throughout the territory in order to secure all the testimony possible which might throw any light on this matter. The Department of Justice had peremptorily ordered that these cases should be disposed of at this term of court. Indian agent Wilcox[1] had notified the district attorney that he should release these Indians by October 1 if they were not brought away for trial. The official correspondence from the various departments with the district attorney, which was presented to the grand jury, included a letter from Agent Tiffany to the Interior Department, asking that these Indians be at once tried, and yet Agent Tiffany released all the guilty Indians without punishment, or any report or request for their punishment, and held in confinement these eleven men for fourteen months without ever presenting a charge against them, giving them insufficient food and clothing, and permitting those whose guilt was admitted by themselves and susceptible to overwhelming proof to stalk about unblushingly and in defiance of law. This, too, under the very shadow of his authority and in laughing mockery of every principle of common decency, he says nothing of justice. How any official possessing the slightest manhood could keep eleven men in confinement for fourteen months without charges or any attempt to accuse them, knowing them to be innocent, is a mystery which can only be solved by an Indian agent of the Tiffany stamp. The whole proceeding is a burning shame.

The investigation of the grand jury has brought to light a course of procedure at the San Carlos reservation, under the government of Agent Tiffany, which is a disgrace to the civilization of the age and a foul blot upon the national escutcheon. While many of the details connected with these matters are outside of our jurisdiction, we nevertheless feel it our duty as honest American citizens to express our utter abhorrence of the conduct of Agent Tiffany and that class of reverend peculators who have cursed Arizona as Indian officials and who have caused more misery and loss of life than all other causes combined. We feel assured, however, that under the judicious and just management of General Crook, these evils will be abated, and we sincerely trust that he may be permitted to render the official existence of such men as Agent Tiffany, in the future, unnecessary. The investigations of the grand jury also establish the fact that General Crook has the unbounded confidence of all the Indians. The Indian prisoners acknowledged this before the grand jury, and they expressed themselves as perfectly satisfied that he would deal justly with them all. After an exhaustive analysis of a large amount of testimony and a critical examination of the prisoners themselves, no evidence could be found to implicate them in any crime; but the grand jury, by their careful research, have discovered the real perpetrators of the offenses under investigation but do not deem it advisable at this time to disclose their action in the premises. We have made diligent inquiry into the various charges presented in regard to Indian goods and the traffic at San Carlos and elsewhere and have acquired a vast amount of information which we think will be of great benefit.

For several years the people of this territory have been gradually arriving at the conclusion that the management of the Indian reservations in Arizona was a fraud upon the government; that the constantly recurring outbreaks of the Indians and their consequent devastations were due to the criminal neglect or apathy of the Indian agent at San Carlos, but never until the present investigations of the grand jury have laid bare the infamy of Agent Tiffany could a proper idea be formed of the fraud and villainy which have been constantly practiced in open violation of law and in defiance of public justice.

Fraud, peculation, conspiracy, larceny, plots, and counterplots seem to be the rule of action on this reservation. The grand jury little thought when they began this investigation that they were about to open a Pandora's box of iniquities seldom surpassed in the annals of crime.

With the immense power wielded by the Indian agent almost any crime is possible. There seems to be no check upon his conduct. In collusion with the storekeeper and chief clerk, rations can be issued *ad libitum* for which the government must pay, while the proceeds pass into the capacious pocket of the agent. Indians are sent to work on the coal fields, superintended by white men; all the workmen and superintendents are fed and frequently paid from the agency stores, and no return of the same is made.

Government tools and wagons are used in transporting goods and working the coal mines, in the interest of this close corporation, and with the same result. All surplus supplies are used in the interest of the agent and no return made thereof.

Government contractors, in collusion with Agent Tiffany, get receipts for large amounts of supplies never furnished, and the profit is divided mutually and a general spoliation of the United States Treasury is thus effected. While six hundred Indians are off on passes, their rations are counted and turned in to the mutual aid association consisting of Tiffany and his *confreres*.

Every Indian child born receives rations from the moment of its advent into this vale of tears and thus adds its mite to the Tiffany pile. In the meantime, the Indians are neglected, half fed, discontented, and turbulent, until at last, with the vigilant eye peculiar to the savage, the Indians observe the manner in which the government, through its agent, complies with its sacred obligations.

This was the united testimony of the grand jury, corroborated by white witnesses, and to these and kindred causes may be attributed the desolation and bloodshed which have dotted our plains with the graves of murdered victims.

In conclusion, we desire to express to the court our gratification at the prompt and thorough manner in which the business of this term has been dispatched. We desire also to return thanks to District Attorney Zabriskie for the able and vigorous assistance which he has rendered to the grand jury, always prompt and efficient. To Marshall Tidball and his deputies for their activity and zeal in the discharge of the responsible duties which have devolved upon them at this time, and to all the Federal officers generally, for their courteous and kind attention, all of which is respectfully submitted.

FOREMAN OF THE GRAND JURY.

The grand jury has given the Indians rather a lively deal, and Parson Tiffany has been exceptionally distinguished by its attentions.

The grand jury pays a high compliment to General Crook and trusts that his administration will undo the evil that Tiffany has done.

Motto for the grand jury: Let no Indian agent escape.

———

Tucson *Arizona Star*, October 25, 1882

In the publication of the grand jury report in Tuesday's issue of the *Star*, the name of James H. Toole, the foreman, was unintentionally omitted. The circumstance is to be regretted, inasmuch as the admirable document and the splendid work it foreshadowed does Major Toole an honor which the entire community is ready to endorse. His ability, fairness, and energy in all matters subjected to the investigation of the jury has been conspicuously worthy of mention and praise.[2]

An End to Indian Outbreaks

PHILIP P. WILCOX

Denver *Tribune*, November 2, 1882

Mr. P. P. Wilcox, agent of the San Carlos Agency, returned to Denver yesterday, going to the St. James, where he was kept busily engaged for some hours, shaking hands and explaining that he yet possessed a whole scalp; that he did not come up to escape the dreadful savages, but simply to claim this city as a place of residence and to cast a vote on election day. He is greatly pleased with his new charges and says that he has no fears for his own personal safety while on the reservation, or no fears of an outbreak. "Why," he said to a *Tribune* reporter last evening, "the days for general outbreaks are over; there will be no more of them; the last wrinkle has been taken out of their war blankets, and they are as gentle and docile as lambs."

"But do you not expect trouble from the fact that you have so many factions and tribes in your care?" asked the reporter.

"Oh, of course there may be some domestic trouble and internal dissension among them, but they will never amount to a great deal. We have the means of quelling any disturbances that may occur."

"How many tribes are there in your care?"

"There are six different tribes now under my care—nearly all branches of the great Apache nation. They are the San Carlos Apaches, the White Mountain Apaches, the Chiricahuas, the Yumas, the Mojaves, and Tontos."

"Do they all live together?"

"Oh, no. They live separately and speak three different languages. They have but little intercourse with each other, and visits are rarely interchanged. However, no hostility exists between them. The Yuma, Mojaves, and Tontos are the most closely allied, as they intermarry and speak the same language."

"To what do you ascribe the peacefulness of the Indians?"

"Well, first of all the rigid discipline enforced by General Crook, who, with some of his men, is now on the reservation. He has inaugurated a system of watchfulness by which we are able to tell if one Indian leaves the reservation. It has a wholesome effect and keeps the savages within bounds."

"What is this system?"

"It is one of counting the Indians every day. The different camps are visited daily and the inhabitants are drawn up in line and counted. If one is missing the chief is held responsible, and he must send out for the absentee. This has the effect of keeping all renegades within the reservations, and whenever any of them are heard of on the outside they are sent for and brought in. Once inside the line they do not get out again, for we issue no passes. You can see that this has a good effect, as it impresses them with the fact that we are in power and intend to remain so."

"But do not the Indians object to this daily count?"

"They did object strongly when this policy was first commenced some three weeks ago, but they are becoming accustomed to it. Besides that, they do not care to make any vigorous protests, for they are now being treated better than ever before. They are well fed, and all they do is to hunt and lay about their tents and sun themselves and gamble for tobacco and blankets."

"By the way, Mr. Wilcox, in case of an outbreak, how many bucks could the Indians muster?"

"About twelve hundred; all told, there are over five thousand Indians on the reservation."

"How does it occur that there is no clash between you, of the Indian Department, and General Crook, of the War Department?"

"Well, it is strange; and do you know that it is the first time in the history of Indian affairs that such a thing has occurred? Such a thing has never before been heard of. General Crook has been fair and wise in all his propositions, and I heartily concur with him in his policy. He is doing splendid work, and I will aid him all I can. We do not disagree on any subject. When one makes a suggestion, the other acquiesces in it and acts upon it. It is encouraging to work in this way, and the result has been that many a roving band of Apaches has been broken up."

"How is the general regarded among the Apaches?"

"With a feeling of awe and respect. He has explained to them that they could prosper and increase by confining themselves to peaceful pursuits, and he has made a lasting impression upon the majority of them. They will heed his words in the future."

"By peaceful pursuits does he mean the old agricultural theory and the policy of self-sustenance?"

"In a measure, yes. The agency is situated on the banks of the Gila—a most barren and unproductive spot, and the general and myself understand perfectly that the soil there cannot be cultivated. Next spring, however, about two thousand of the Indians will be removed to the northern boundary of the reservation, which is thoroughly watered by the numerous Apache streams, making the soil very fertile and easily treated. Timber and grass also abound in profusion, and there they will be allowed to hunt and fish and farm to their hearts' content. This prospect greatly pleases the savages, and they are anxiously looking for the time to arrive."

"What protection have you in case of trouble?"

"Oh, we are amply protected. Thirty-five miles from my headquarters, just outside the reservation, is Fort Thomas, with five companies of infantry, and seventy miles away in another direction is Fort Grant, with an equal number of men. But we do not rely upon them for aid. There are in the reservation, besides my force of scouts, thirty-nine in number, two companies of Indian soldiers, and they are all we require."

"But can you count upon these Indians?"

"They have before been tried and not found wanting. These companies and the corps of scouts are composed entirely of Mojaves and Yumas. They have always been loyal and have never failed to come to our assistance when desired. General Crook has a scheme on hand by which the Indian soldiery will be increased. He will form several additional companies, and by so doing will gain their good will toward the government. The extra pay they will receive will bring that about."

"What kind of soldiers do they make?"

"I speak truthfully when I say they make the best soldiers I ever saw. I went to the agency with a natural hatred toward all Indians and an especially great prejudice against their soldiers. But I soon saw that I was mistaken as to the latter. They know nothing but discipline and do whatever they are ordered to do. They have but one end in view, and that is to please their captain, and they generally succeed in so doing. They want a white man to lead in everything, and what they learn from him they learn well. Charles Wilcox of Denver is my chief of scouts, you know, and he is giving great satisfaction. He has his men well trained, and they will follow him anywhere. He is a great favorite among them. The appointment of Charlie was a good one. I am surrounding myself entirely with Colorado men, and I find the plan a good one. They are reliable, and I know what to expect of them. I cleaned out the old outfit when I took charge, as I want men whom I can trust."

"How are the coal mines on the agency?"

"Oh, they are all there," said Mr. Wilcox, "but you can reply upon it that they are not being worked for the benefit of the agent, either."

At that moment a fresh delegation of friends of Mr. Wilcox appeared, and the reporter bid him goodnight.

A Profile of the San Carlos Agency

FREDERICK LLOYD

SAN CARLOS AGENCY, ARIZONA,
February 10, 1883.

Medical Director,
    Department of Arizona,
        Whipple Barracks, Prescott, A.T.

Sir:

In compliance with your direction of the fifth ultimo to furnish such general statistics as I may be able to obtain, with information as to the number, character, arms, diet, clothing, habitations, occupations, etc., of the Indians residing at the San Carlos Agency; also the relative proportion of males, females, and children; the diseases observed among them, and their remedial measures, and all other information that may prove useful in studying the habits and peculiarities of the Indian portion of the population, I have the honor to submit the following:

My service here covers a period of only three months, and my previous opportunities for observing Indian character and customs have been but slight and casual.[1]

The Indians at present residing at this agency are one tribe of the Yuma and another of the Mohave nations, and the San Carlos, Coyotero, Tonto, and White Mountain tribes of the Apaches.

The Yumas and Mohaves are bands detached from their tribes or nations, whose homes are respectively in the valleys of the Colorado and the Verde. It is common for these Indians to be spoken of as Yuma-Apaches and Mohave-Apache, but this simply signifies that they are associated with the Apaches at this agency.

The philologist encounters difficulty in distinguishing names originating with the Indians themselves from those bestowed by Europeans. In translating Indian names into English, the Indian pronunciation seems to have been better preserved than when changed into the languages of Spain or France. There is nothing in the vocalization of the tribal title of the Iowas or the Musquakas to arouse suspicion of their being of derivation foreign to the Indian, while the Assiniboin and Ouisconsin betray the French origin, and the Mexican-Spanish derivation is not disguised in such names as those the tribes I am considering. Coyotero evidently coming from the Mexican word coyote, the jackal, and Tonto being Spanish for foolish, this latter term having been applied to the tribe now bearing it, it is said, by visitors who found them talking two languages, the Yuma and Apache, probably a corruption of both. However this may have been, there is no doubt that the Tontos speak both the Apache and Yuma dialects.

The Yumas and Mohaves here are but small fragments of those tribes of the same names who still dwell, the one on the banks of the Colorado, and the other in the Verde valley, and for purposes of description may be classed together as they speak the same tongue, intermarry constantly, and differ little in customs and manners. The Yumas here number: adult males, 131; adult females, 99; male children, 49; female children, 34; total, 313. Of Mohaves there are: adult males, 209; adult females, 171; male children, 108; female children, 95; total, 583. These two bands are regarded as reliably peaceful toward the whites. They are more reserved, dignified, and industrious than the Apaches and in the primitive arts, such as making pottery and weaving baskets, are a short step in advance of their neighbors, and exhibit skill and taste in their work. Their customs permit plural marriages, but comparatively few of their men have more than one wife, and none more than two. They cremate their dead, whereas the Apaches bury theirs under the rocks in the mountains, heaping brush above to mark the spot.[2] Like the Apaches, upon a decease of a person they destroy, by burning, all effects pertaining to the dead—[wickiup,] clothes, and cooking utensils. Some of these people present a Jewish cast of countenance, not displeasing in the men and lending beauty to the women, a fact which may tend to confirm the belief of those who think the Indians a portion of the lost tribes of Israel. The men are more considerate in the treatment of their squaws than the Apaches, bearing some of the burdens of the day. On the contrary, in the morals of the women, the Apaches are superior.

The Apaches are more athletic, daring, and restless than their associates, and their countenances and physiques are more typical of the American aborigines. Their heads are round, their faces broad, and their cheekbones high, and in these characteristics the White Mountain Indians are the most pronounced.

The four bands of Apaches here number conjointly: adult males, 1,090; adult females, 1,247; male children, 673; female children, 668; total, 3,678.

It will be seen from the figures given that the total Indian population here is 4,574, of which number 1,430 are men, 1,517 women, 830 boys, and 797 girls, the children being of all ages, from infancy to adolescence, and that the males in all classes are in excess of the females, except in that of adult Apaches, in which the women have a majority of 157; also that the proportion of children to adults is not as great as might be expected. This shortage of children does not support the theory of the fruitfulness of polygamous marriages, as the Apaches are a polygamous people, some of the bucks having as many as six squaws, while few of them, in the married state, restrict themselves to one.[3] Notwithstanding the excess in the number of women at present among the Apaches and the liberal customs which obtain on the subject of marriage, rape is an offense quite commonly complained of. The Apache, in accordance with the general Indian custom, buys his wife from the father or people, giving generally one or more ponies, and she is thereafter his chattel property. If there are other younger sisters in the family, he often buys one or all of them also, even though no more than five or six years old, and takes them to his camp to participate in aforesaid cohabitation before the approach of pubescence. In these matrimonial bargains, even when the bride has reached years of discretion, her wishes are not consulted. However repugnant to her inclinations, if the cupidity of her family is satisfied, she must submit with the best grace she can.

Of the four bands of Apaches here, the White Mountain Indians are the most warlike, and their women the most virtuous. Their physical proportions seem greater on an average than the others. They may generally be distinguished by the breadth and prominence of the cheekbones. The symmetrically arched mouths and regular teeth often lend a rude beauty to the females of this savage people. The Apaches are a gay and lighthearted set, full of laughter and hilarity; they exhibit warm affection for comrades and relations, couples of the same sex being often seen walking about with their arms entwined about each other. They are courageous and patient. Although most of their time is spent in idleness, this seems to be more from want of employment than from natural sloth. They seem to be destitute of any feeling of gratitude. They do not appear to be conscious of inferiority, but stand unabashed in the presence of the greatest. Against all the good traits that can be accorded them, they must be accounted as adept in treachery and cruelty, delighting in torture and blood. When prompted by a morbid desire for the display of prowess, no bounds of consanguinity are strong enough to stay their murderous hands. Brothers and sisters, vainly crying for mercy, go down before the rifle and the club, and children's brains are dashed out against the trees or stones.

The Indians at this agency are said to be well supplied with good arms and plenty of ammunition. If so, they make no display of them, only carrying them when hunting. The bow and arrow seem little to be depended on by them for defense or aggression and have become the playthings of the boys, who amuse themselves lying in ambush, waiting the approach of the meadowlark, whose body generally receives the steel-pointed arrow. The long lance, once a formidable weapon with them, has fallen into disuse and is only occasionally to be seen now.

These Indians generally evince a willingness to engage in husbandry, and at this writing a considerable breadth of barley has already been planted by them. Their clean and prepared fields, enclosed with improvised fences of brush and saplings, line the bottoms of the Gila and San Carlos Rivers for a number of miles east and west of the agency, and many of them are tilling the soil at great distances from San Carlos.

The industrious perseverance with which they engaged in cutting, collecting, and transporting hay for the uses of the military at the agency is a contradiction of the charge that all Indians are inherently lazy. Within a period of six weeks these people supplied two hundred tons of hay. To appreciate this statement, it must be remembered that every blade of this hay was cut with knives, that most of it was carried on the backs of men, women, and children an average distance of four miles, and only an inconsiderable portion on the backs of "burros" (donkeys) and ponies. When the haying season was at its height, the scene around the agency was animated in the extreme. From dawn to sunset the panorama presented was a plain of moving hay. Bucks and squaws, boys and girls, burros and ponies were the motive forces, but they, for the most part, were invisible, being covered and concealed by bundles of hay tightly bound with thongs made from the leaves of the "soap-weed," a species of the "Spanish Bayonet," and all converging toward a central place, where it was stacked.

The chief amusement of the Indians, participated in by both sexes, is dancing. The war dance admits only warriors with arms. The corn dance is a sort of festival. The squaw dance, in which the women join, is purely social. A game similar to that known to American youth as "shinny" is played by the men, and a game called in Yuma tuderbe, played by rolling a hoop, on the top of which the two competitors engaged throw a pole which knocks down the hoop, is a masculine game very popular. Footracing is another pastime much enjoyed by them. Several footraces have lately been run, graduated prizes ranging from five to two dollars having been awarded by some of the spectators to the best three runners. The Indian has little conception of musical harmony. He often warbles, but his vocal efforts are the merest singsong. I have never heard a squaw hush her papoose to sleep with a song. Both sexes take the supremest pleasure in gambling. The favorite game is "monte," played with Mexican cards. The stakes are generally money, but in its absence, cartridges, blankets, ration tickets, or the clothes from their backs are risked to indulge this universal passion. This view often occasions much suffering to women and children, who are often in this way deprived of their rations.

The Apache is a free dispenser of hospitality. The nature of his dwelling, with doors always open, probably tends to foster this trait. It is not common to find an Indian's meal shared in only by his own family. The wife, though esteemed only in the light of property, maintains her place at the repast, generally replenishing it as it progresses with fresh supplies, which she supervises the cooking of while she herself partakes.

Their diet at present consists chiefly of the ration issued by the Indian agent. This consists, for each week, for each man, woman, or child of whatever age, of five and one-half pounds of flour, ten and one-half pounds of fresh beef (sometimes reduced to six pounds), with four pounds of coffee, seven of sugar, two of salt, two of soap, and half a pound of tobacco to each hundred rations. In addition to the above, they have the surrounding mountains and valleys, rich in game, from which to draw. Fish is not eaten by them. Venison is their favorite wild meat. The turkey is not absolutely rejected as an article of diet, but his flesh is not a favorite. The feathers of this bird, however, next to those of the hawk, are valued for their uses in the decoration of the war bonnet. In the line of vegetables, they have the wild potato, indigenous to Arizona (and thought by some to be the progenitor of the Irish potato), which the children dig and gather early in the spring when no larger than peas. Its size at maturity is nearly as great as that of the cultivated Irish potato and seems to be as rich in starch. Mescal is a favorite luxury. It is derived from the pitch of a plant growing like a cabbage. The heart, with the outer leaves stripped off, is baked in the earth and afterwards beaten into shreds with stones and put away in masses for use. When used it is dipped in water to moisten it. It has a sweet taste and evidently contains sugar. This is a species of the same plant from which the Mexicans distill the mescal liquor. Another delicacy is the preserved fruit of the saguaro, a species of giant cactus. It ripens in the latter part of June, when the Indians go in flocks into the mountains to gather it. Much of it is converted immediately into wine and drunk on the spot to intoxication, but large quantities are dried and kept in irregularly shaped cakes. It has a deliciously sweet taste. The wild fruits and berries that abound in this semitropical country form a considerable portion of the diet of the Indians in summer and autumn. The acorn of the stunted white oak, one of the commonest bushes (for it does not attain the stature of a tree) that adorns the sides of the Arizona mountains furnishes a nut used as an edible addition to soups. It is also eaten roasted or raw. They reject as food the direct product of the hog, though in the form of bacon, as issued by the army commissary, it is partaken of with relish.

The Indian, like the people of all races, seems to have inherent appetite for alcohol. The alcoholic product of Indian corn, subjected to rude processes of fermentation, which is termed tiswin, is their almost only source of this supply. It is a comparatively weak beverage, and to experience its full effect, those intending to partake of it generally precede the indulgence of it by a long fast, experience having taught them that it will more readily affect them through an empty stomach. The manufacture of tiswin is strictly forbidden by the government authorities, and a violation of this inhibition subjects the detected offender to a long imprisonment. Nevertheless, the inclination for this use is so strong that the rule is frequently broken. In a word, the manufacture and use of tiswin among the Indians, like the overindulgence in alcoholic beverages by the whites, are the most frequent sources of an Indian's troubles at this agency.

The use of tobacco is a universal habit with the male Indian from the age of ten years and upwards. Smoking is the favorite manner with them of enjoying it, though it is often chewed as well. I have not noticed that the women generally acquire the habit of using tobacco.

There is considerable variety in dress presented by the Indians at this agency. Since the reception of their annuities the latter part of December, their appearance in this respect has improved. It is very common to see both men and women dressed entirely in the apparel of the whites, and it is rare to meet an adult wearing nothing but blanket and breechclout. Children, however, are constantly to be seen in the camps entirely nude, playing in a winter atmosphere, apparently comfortably unconscious of their immersion in a freezing air. If clothing could be issued to them at shorter intervals, or if they had better facilities in the way of permanent abodes for preserving what they get, these people would soon discard the Indian and adopt the white man's dress. It would perhaps take longer to induce them to leave off painting their faces, as they seem to attach prophylactic virtues to this custom. Red seems to be their favorite color in dress. Red blankets and red calico are flaunted on all sides. As a single grain in the weight of testimony that a taste for colors, like other mental or physical peculiarities may be inherited, I may state that "Mickey Free," of Irish-Mexican parentage but captured by the Apaches when a child and to all intents and purposes one of them ever since, selects a green blanket.

The habitations of these Indians are not superior to those of the lowest savages. They consist almost universally of [wickiups], made of boughs and saplings stuck in the ground so as to inclose a circular space about eight feet in diameter which has first been excavated to the depth of about a foot. The ends of the boughs are bent together at the top, so as to form a dome. The top and sides are covered with canvas or thatched with brush or hay to shed the rain, and the loose earth thrown up in excavating the floor is thrown around the base to make the foundation firm and protect the inmates from the wind. A single opening, from one to three feet wide, permits entrance and exit. The height in the inside is sufficient to admit of a man standing upright. The floor is covered with leaves or hay, on which blankets are spread, which serve for beds at night and a lounging place in the daytime. In cold weather a small fire near the door warms the interior. The top and sides of the wickiup afford supports on which are hung meat and other supplies and spare clothes. No attempt is made to imitate the whites in supplying the comforts of furniture. The ground forms at once bedstead, table, and chairs.

Engaged as they already are in an attempt at agriculture, which they seem generally desirous of adopting as a means of livelihood, if an attachment could be generated in them for a certain limited locality, where their buildings, fences, and implements would remain undisturbed till recurring seasons should recall them into requisitions, and such other accumulations as they might require would be preserved, a great step in their permanent improvement would be reached. It seems to me it would be a forward movement toward civilizing these people, and even an economical one, to supply them with small but substantial dwellings whenever they declared a willingness to occupy as a permanent abode a definite parcel of ground. I am aware that some prejudices and superstitions on the part of the Indians would have to be overcome to make such a plan feasible, but I believe them to be not insurmountable.

In this locality the Indians are subject to malarial fevers, dysentery, and diarrhea. Syphilis is said to be common among the Yumas and Mohaves. Consumption is almost unknown among them and when occurring can be traced to a syphilitic origin. Their exemption from constitutional pulmonary disease is probably due to climatic influences. It seems probable that Arizona, when the superb winter climate of its valley becomes extensively known, will become a popular winter resort for persons threatened with, or suffering from, pulmonary complaints, especially consumption. At present the territory is generally decried as a summer furnace, and the story of the dead soldier at Yuma and his blanket is rife everywhere, while the truth probably is that, except in a few very low localities, the heat in Arizona in summer is no greater than on corresponding parallels in other sections of the country. [Be] this as it may, it is certain that, with a winter climate more equable in the valleys and as warm as that of Florida, an atmosphere so dry that no dew is precipitated, and rain infrequent except in the hottest months, leaving out of account the cheerful influences of constant sunshine and the exhilarating effects of a pure mountain air, Arizona must soon become the favorite winter home of those laboring under chest complaints. Pneumonia, pleurisy, and rheumatism are not common; diseases of the digestive tube, due to irregularities in diet, gorging, and badly cooked food, in addition to those of malarial origin, are the complaints which affect the Indians here.

The office of the "medicine man" has not yet come to an end. He seems to be given the first chance generally at the en-dee, or patient, and if he does not afford speedy relief is discarded in favor of the white za-hon-ton, or doctor. In ministering to the sick, the medicine man sits in the wickiup near the patient and chants in a loud, monotonous tone, seemingly repeating the same words over for hours night and day. The Indians attribute their sickness to the power of witches, and women are killed, probably much oftener than is known, as such events are concealed from the whites if possible, on the supposition that they are witches. An instance of this kind has happened here within a few weeks. An Indian who had lost several children through sickness, impressed with the belief that their deaths were caused through the witchcraft of a certain squaw, shot her and attempted to escape, the fact becoming known to the authorities. The woman is recovering and the man is in prison. The medicine man therefore encourages the patient and his friends with such cheering intelligence as that kan, the good spirit, will drive away ilkas, the witch, sent by Chetin, the devil, to disturb his comfort and repose. From time to time he rests his voice, while he applies, if the disease is local, some mysterious medicament, generally in the form of a powder.

Although not embraced in the order calling for this report, a subject presenting so many phases may perhaps be allowed in suggestion as supplement. Every political economist has a plan for the amelioration of the condition of the Indians and the prevention of Indian outbreaks. The allotment of parcels of culturable land to Indians in severalty has been authorized and practiced, I believe, whenever the Indians are willing to sever their tribal relations. However, so far as my limited opportunities have enable me to observe, this plan seems to work well only when the Indians are under the direct supervision of white superintendents. If every Indian novice in agriculture could be surrounded by white farmers, he would soon become a proficient, progressive, and permanent tiller of the soil, but clustered with others no better enlightened than himself, he has no one to copy from superior to himself.

A system that would surround every Indian with industrious whites engaged in every calling of civilized life would soon transform him from a savage to a citizen and forever end Indian outbreaks, with all their horrible concomitants. I would distribute the Indians among the several states according to population, exempting the late slave-holding states, already burdened with a Negro population. Each state would then divide its quota of Indians among its several counties according to their population, and the counties in their turn would subdivide their spaces among the townships, and these latter would distribute them among families, if necessary. No separation of nations, tribes, bands, or families would be required. One or more nations might go to a state, one or more tribes to a county, one or more bands to a township, and families, unbroken, or individuals would become allied by neighborhood to, or incorporated with, white ones. The government, at probably no greater expense than it now incurs on their account, could make generous provision for their removal and temporary maintenance, and the proceeds of the sales of the lands now occupied by them might be devoted to the accumulation of a fund for their benefit, certain disconnected sections or portions of sections being held for the occupation of such as desired to return to their homes and own lands in severalty.

To such a scheme there may be constitutional objections which would make it impracticable, but if not, some such system, in a single generation, would convert the Indians from murderous savages to thrifty citizens, and in a few more generations the most of them would be consolidated by intermarriage with the bulk of the white population probably without detriment, but with improvement to the latter.

I am, very respectfully,
Your obedient servant,
[Signed]   FREDERICK LLOYD,
A.A. Surgeon, U.S.A.

Life in Arizona Army Posts during the 1880s

ANTON MAZZANOVICH[1]

Arizona Daily Star, Fiftieth Anniversary Edition, 1927

I landed at Camp Lowell from San Francisco, California, in the early spring of 1881, having enlisted in the Sixth U.S. Cavalry to serve five years. Got a good idea of Arizona after the train left Yuma. One vast desert—mountains, cactus, and sand for miles. On reaching Camp Lowell, seven miles from Tucson, I reported to the adjutant's office. Camp Lowell was regimental headquarters of the Sixth U.S. Cavalry, Colonel Carr commanding; Lieutenant J. B. Kerr was adjutant of the regiment.

I was detailed for duty with the regimental band. Found army life at the post rather dull. The officers stationed at the post gave a ball now and then, and the Who's Who of Tucson were invited to attend. But with the rank and file it was sure a dull life between pay days. After pay day some of us would get a twenty-four-hour pass, go to Tucson, and squander our two months' pay over the Congress Hall, Palace Hotel, or Fashion Bar. And many would buck the tiger, or Mexican monte game. Some of them would put too much Cowboy's Delight under their belt and get tanked up and overstay their passes. In such cases, as soon as they got to camp they were put in the guardhouse.

The daily routine at the post was as follows: Sunrise, reveille. The morning gun. Troop would fall in in answer to their names. Raising the stars and stripes. The officer of the day would stand on the parade ground and receive the report from the first sergeant of each troop. Everyone present and accounted for. After payday some of the troopers would take French leave. And the sergeant would report, "Private So-and-So, absent without leave." Anyone who got a mounted pass and skipped by the light of an Arizona moon was severely dealt with if caught, court-martialed, and sentenced to serve in the military prison at Alcatraz Island from four to five years, also got a dishonorable discharge from the army. The same applied to men who made a getaway on foot. But they would only draw a sentence of two or three years.

After reveille, stable call was sounded. The troops were marched to the corral to groom their mounts. At 9:00 A.M. all troopers detailed to mount guard would fall in in front of their quarters. The band played the march, and the

Pay day. OUTING MAGAZINE, JANUARY 1887.

men would assemble in the center of the parade ground. Then the adjutant would inspect arms and equipment. The band marched in review. Then the new guard would proceed to the guardhouse and relieve the old guard.

After guard mount came sick call. After sick call two or three men from each troop, including the band, were detailed to take the horses out on herd. Between 10:00 A.M. and 12:00 P.M. the band would practice for the evening concert, which was held at the bandstand in front of the commanding officer's quarters.

We did not have a sutler store at Camp Lowell, consequently the soldiers would pass the time playing cards and reading or writing letters to folks back home.

At 4:00 P.M. the cavalry horses came in from herd. Then the bugler would sound stable call. The men would fall in and march to the corral and attend to the horses. At sundown came the evening gun, and a file of the guard would lower the stars and stripes.

At 9:00 P.M. the bugle sounded taps, and all lights in the soldiers' barracks went out. At Camp Lowell we had a baseball team. On several occasions we played the Tucson team at Levins Park, which was located at the end of Congress Street.

Many times soldiers were arrested for being drunk or trying to stage a real wild and woolly stunt and put in jail. The next morning they were taken before the justice of the peace on Meyer Street. No matter, guilty or not, the judge would sentence the prisoner to pay a fine of fifteen dollars or fifteen days in the lockup. Nine times out of ten the victim said: "I have no money." The judge would ask him if he had any friends in town who would lend him the amount. If he did, he was allowed to go out and raise the cash. A constable went with him.

The writer was pulled in one night for riding into Congress Hall, going to the bar, and ordering a drink. Pronto, horse and rider were placed under arrest. I was ordered at the point of a .44 frontier Colt to dismount. Needless to say, I obeyed mighty quick and was dragged to the lockup. Next morning at my trial I pled not guilty. Then the constable went out and brought in more witnesses. Again I pled not guilty, but the judge said fifteen dollars or fifteen days. I told the court that he could make it a million, as I did not have any money, and furthermore, I had no friends from whom I could borrow. This answer was a bombshell. After whispering to the officer who arrested me, the judge said, "Discharged." When I arrived at the post, I was put in the guardhouse for overstaying my pass and kept there for ten days.

The tenth day after guard mount I was sent out under guard to scoop up water from a small ditch that went around the parade ground and wet down the camino in front of the officers' quarters. It was sure hot! I'll bet a Mexican jumping bean against a horn[ed] toad it was 110 in the shade. Now and then I would lean against a cottonwood tree to rest up some. After doing the sprinkling act for an hour or so, the orderly passed by and gave me a letter from my brother in New York City. I opened it and backed up against a tree to read it. Shortly after, my attention was attracted by a tap on my shoulder. I turned around and found myself face to face with Captain Chaffee, the officer of the day. He asked me a number of questions, also inquiring why I was in the guardhouse. I answered all the questions. When finished, he turned to the guard and ordered him to take me back to the guardhouse, with an order to the sergeant of the guard not to send me out again for the day. He said it was too hot for me to act as a sprinkling wagon. After taps that evening the orderly came to the guardhouse with an order to the sergeant of the guard, which read: "Release Private Anton Mazzanovich from the guardhouse."

The troopers were always mighty glad when boots and saddles was sounded. That meant hit the trail after the Apaches.

On many visits to Tucson I formed the acquaintance of a fine young man who was connected with the Palace Hotel. He was always mighty good to the boys from the camp. No trouble at all for some of us to get an eye opener when our coppers were hot and dry. His name was Knox Corbett. The first time I met him after many years was at the annual ball given by the Arizona Society of Southern California at Los Angeles.

In May the White Mountain Apaches were creating trouble. Colonel Carr was ordered to proceed to Camp Apache. At the time, I had a scrap with a couple of German horn blowers in our band. And before anyone could stop me I floored them both for the count. Next morning after guard mount, the orderly came with an order for me to report to the adjutant. When I got to the office I received an order to get ready and proceed to Fort Grant and report to Lieutenant Overton for duty with Troop F, Sixth U.S. Cavalry. It sure was welcome news. I boarded the Southern Pacific the next day [and] arrived at Willcox in the evening, where an ambulance was waiting. In less than three hours I was at my new station.

Fort Grant was situated at the base of the Graham mountain range twenty-seven miles from Willcox. An ideal location; one could see for miles. Looking east and north you got a fine view of Sulphur Springs Valley. And to the west as far as the border line to Old Mexico lay the alkali plain between the Dragoon and Dos Cabezas mountains. The famous Cochise Stronghold is in the Dragoon range.

After sunrise the alkali plain looked like an island lake, and one could see wonderful mirages. Three miles from Fort Grant was a settlement called Bonita, consisting of several saloons, a store or two, and a dance hall. Miles M. Wood lived there with his family. Everyone in the valley knew Judge Wood. Judge Wood is now living in Los Angeles.

When the settlement was first started, a plot of ground was set aside for a graveyard. The natives built a fence around it. But the place was so healthful that no one ever hit the long, dim trail. And after waiting two years for someone to kick in, someone killed a Mexican so as to give the graveyard a start. In that plot of ground lies the first man killed by Billy the Kid.[2]

Fort Grant was not much of an improvement on Camp Lowell. The troopers' barracks in both Lowell and Grant were built of adobe. The firm of Norton and Stewart from Willcox ran the sutler store at Grant.

Several days after I joined my troop, boots and saddles rang out, and everyone in the troop let out a mighty shout, tickled pink because they knew that the call of boots and saddles meant to hit the trail. The orderly came from the adjutant's office with instructions that we were to start and make a forced ride to Camp Thomas. Everyone made a rush for the corral to saddle up. At the quartermaster corral the pack-train crew were busy loading up our supplies. In less than an hour everything was in shape to hit the camino. The two troops, A and F, were assembled on the parade ground ready for the order: Prepare to mount. Major Gordon,[3] First Lieutenant Eugene Overton, and John Glass dash up. We hear the first sergeant of each troop shout attention; right dress; front; count fours. They right, about face, and salute the officers. At last the command rings out: Prepare to mount, mount, twos left into line, march. Soon after, the bugle sounds double-quick time, and we settle down to a brisk trot.

Early in the evening we reach Cedar Springs,[4] where we stop to feed our mounts and get supper. That over, again we are on the move. The cause of our hurried departure from Fort Grant was brought from Camp Apache by courier, who volunteered to cut through the hostile Indian lines. The White Mountain Apaches, after the Cibicue fight, had surrounded the post and cut the government telegraph lines. Two men volunteered. One started over Seven-Mile Hill; the other took the airline trail and succeeded in getting through. He managed to reach Camp Thomas, ninety miles away. His name was Will C. Barnes. He is now assistant forester with headquarters in Washington, D.C. Two weeks after, the other, who answered to the name of Owens, was found dead almost in sight of the post. He stumbled into a party of Indians and had been shot from his horse.

Early in the morning finds our small command at Camp Thomas, where we went into camp. Our mounts are made secure to the picket line. Guard mounted. And the tired troopers turn in, or rather turn out, as we did not have any shelter tents. We were not disturbed until 9:00 A.M. After breakfast we learned that the commanding officer at Fort Grant received orders from headquarters of the Department of Arizona to head Troops A and F for Camp Apache to reinforce the garrison, as well as one troop from Camp Thomas.

General Willcox was in command of the department, stationed at Camp Whipple. The Gila River was in flood, so that we could not cross. We were to wait until the swollen stream got low enough to get across. The quartermaster issued us shelter tents, which protected us from the rain. At the end of two weeks the water got higher, and we were ordered back to our home post.

Two weeks after, orders came from headquarters to get under way for Camp Apache at all hazards. Believe me, everyone was mighty glad to get away, and all eager for excitement and adventure, as a trooper's life at the post between paydays was certainly a lonesome job.

We arrived at Camp Thomas and directly pitched in to provide some way to cross our supplies and mounts across the raging Gila River, We got over, and for the remarkable campaign which followed against the White Mountain Apaches and Geronimo's band, read my story, *Trailing Geronimo*.[5]

At last we made Camp Apache, a fine post. The men were able to pass dull hours away in hunting and trout fishing, as the surrounding mountains and streams were well stocked with game and trout. Before the campaign ended I was ordered from the trail to report at Fort Grant for medical treatment. My eyes were in a bad way, caused by alkali dust and exposure.

Doctor J. B. Girard[6] did all he could for me. After several months I was transferred to Camp Thomas for treatment. Camp Thomas was situated several miles from the Gila River. A little frontier town close by, called Moxey, was a hangout for the troopers, as there was a dance hall, several saloons, and gambling joints.

Doctor Shouey did not succeed in effecting a cure, so I was ordered back to my home post, Camp Grant. Several months afterward I was discharged from the army for disability.[7]

Norton and Stewart hired me to work for them at the sutler store. A young man by the name of H. A. Morgan was the chief clerk. Mr. Morgan is now in the government land office at Phoenix, Arizona. Horace Hambler and Barney Norton served drinks to the thirsty troopers over the bar. My duty was as counter jumper and to relieve the bartenders when feed time came, sort out the mail, and look after the officers' club.

While at the store I became personally acquainted with the following named officers: Colonel Shafter, Major Biddle, Captain Gordon, Captain Faulk, Captain Rafferty, Captain Chaffee, Lieutenants M. P. Maus, Slocum, Blocksom, John Glass, Blake Overton, Willcox, Kingsbury, J. B. Kerr, and others whose names have slipped my memory; also, contract doctors Marshall M. Wood, Skiner, and Carroll.

Among the troops I discovered some talent and conceived the idea of organizing a minstrel troop. I asked Colonel Shafter if he would allow me to use the post chapel to present my show, a request he gladly granted. I informed him that I would give two performances a week—one for troopers, and the other for the officers and civilians. Colonel Shafter gave me permission to use members of the First Infantry band for my orchestra.

Everybody at the camp eagerly waited for my opening show. With the help of several troopers, we built a stage, and one of the boys, who was a sign painter, did his bit as the scenic artist. After several weeks of rehearsing I opened my all-star minstrel show. The first performance was for the troopers, and it sure was a grand success.

The boss of the pack train, Mickey O'Hara, asked me one day if I would like to accept a job as cook in the pack train. Believe me, he did not have to ask it a second time. I grabbed the job pronto. A few days later I quit Norton and Stewart, moved down to the quartermaster corral, and got busy on my new job.

The boys who worked as packers were a fine, honest-to-goodness bunch. I recall the following names: Mickey O'Hara, Al Glendenning, Peterson, James Sheridan, George Dunn, Ed Johnson, Give-a-Damn Smith, and Joe Perry. I continued presenting my all-star minstrel show, which was much appreciated by everyone at the fort, as well as everyone within reach in Sulphur Springs Valley.

At the corral something was doing all the time; gambling was the rule. Between paydays the boys sometimes rode down to Bonita, where one could liquor up or take a whirl with the senoritas at McCrintick's Dance Hall. The above also applies to the soldiers at the post. I got acquainted with M. L. Wood and family, also the Vangosick family. M. L. Wood contracted with the quartermaster to cut hay for the post and was known for years in Sulphur Springs Valley as Judge Woods. He is now living in Los Angeles. In those days I used to visit them often and spent many happy hours with them. One of Vangosick's daughters is now living at Safford and is married to Mr. Basco, and they have grown-up girls.

The sutler store at Fort Grant was sure a great institution, and on paydays the troopers lined the bar three deep, liquoring up. Hambler and Barney Norton had them trained not to call for any fancy or mixed drinks, consequently everyone had to drink their favorite brand straight. It did not require much time for the troopers to squander the two months' pay, which was at the rate of thirteen dollars per month.

The bar had to close when taps sounded, 9:00 P.M., and after that some of the troopers would get by guards number Two and Three and go down to

Bonita and continue the celebration. However, the next day many of them found their way to the guardhouse, which gave them a chance to sober up.

Gambling at the barracks after pay day was in full swing, and what money the sutler bar did not get would go against the banking games which were conducted by noncommissioned officers of each troop, so that in the long run all the money the soldiers got would find its way over to Norton and Stewart's bar, or in the pockets of the men who dealt the games of chance in the troop quarters. Government packers and teamsters were paid by check. Their pay was seventy-five dollars per month. We conducted a gambling casino of our own at the corral while I was cooking for the packers. Mickey O'Hara, the chief of the pack train, gave me lessons every day how to handle the diamond hitch and the art of packing. I was an apt scholar and soon acquired all the points of this branch of the government service.

The pack train is the life of our government troops when out on the scout. In less than two months I became as good at the game as any hombre in the outfit. Shortly after, one of the packers was transferred to the wagon train, and O'Hara advanced me to his place.

It was now within one week of Christmas, and preparations were under way by the officers for a grand celebration on Christmas Day 1882, in this out-of-the-way army post: running and jumping, a heel-and-toe match, three times around the parade ground, boxing—in fact, everything that goes in field sports. I entered the heel-and-toe race, as I considered myself quite an expert in that line, because several years back I had participated in two six-day, go-as-you-please races at Portland, Oregon, and San Francisco, California. I won the first heel-and-toe race by fifteen yards.

It was a perfect day, and all had a good time. The sutler store did a good business serving tarantula juice over the bar, as many people throughout the valley managed to attend. I gave my all-star show to standing room only in the evening. On that day I received the first telegram I ever got in my young life. It was sent by my brother and his wife. "A Merry Christmas and a Happy New Year, Jack and Jesse." I still have it in my possession.

After Christmas, O'Hara was ordered to proceed to the Mexican border with supplies for General Crook, who at the time was doing in Sonora his best to round up the Apaches. Only one-half of our outfit was used. Lieutenant Barry,[8] the post quartermaster, informed me that Colonel Shafter had appointed me to assume charge of the twenty-eight mules left over, so that in four months I advanced from cook to chief of pack train and scout. And while acting in that capacity I hit the trail three times: twice under Colonel Shafter and once under Lieutenant Willcox. In the meantime General Crook succeeded in inducing the Indians to come back on the reservation. We met the command at the borderline with the pack train loaded with supplies.

In due time we reached the San Carlos reservation. From there I was ordered back to Fort Grant and placed in charge of the wagon train. The commander of the Department of Arizona had a standing offer of a fifty-dollar reward for the arrest of army deserters; consequently, very few men managed to get by, and those that did escape arrest got hard-boiled and desperate and cast their lot by joining cattle rustlers' gangs, which operated in the Southwest in the eighties. As boss of the wagon train, I had to learn how to drive six or twelve-mule teams by the jerk-line route. It did not take me long to learn. The boss of the wagon train had to drive the government ambulance to Willcox and get the post mail every Sunday. Willcox at that time was indeed a lively frontier berg. All freighting for Globe, the Indian reservations, and army posts to the east started from Willcox, as well as points west of the Southern Pacific Railroad. One could buck the tiger or Mexican monte and play stud or draw poker. I used to hit the whole bunch. Sometimes I would make a killing and more often go flat busted. But getting down to bedrock, those good old frontier days meant nothing in my young life. I was a happy-go-lucky soldier of fortune. And believe me, many good pals of mine were in the same boat. Many of us underwent danger and hardships, and those who remained at their jobs doing their best to make Arizona a fit place to live in should indeed be proud that they have accomplished their task. For surely the great state of Arizona today is one garden spot on earth. It is true that it has much desert land left, but what her pioneers started to do will be accomplished by their sons and daughters.

PART FOUR

The Sierra Madre
Campaign and After,
1883–85

Mexico: Reciprocal Right to Pursue Savage Indians across The Boundary Line

FREDERICK T. FRELINGHUYSEN

Agreement
Between
the United States and Mexico

Signed and exchanged, July 29, 1882

Memorandum of an agreement entered into in behalf of their respective governments by Frederick T. Frelinghuysen, secretary of state of the United States of America, and Matias Romero, envoy extraordinary and minister plenipotentiary of the Republic of Mexico, providing for the reciprocal crossing of the international boundary line by the troops of the respective governments in pursuit of savage Indians, under the conditions hereinafter stated.

ARTICLE I.
It is agreed that the regular federal troops of the two republics may reciprocally cross the boundary line of the two countries when they are in close pursuit of a band of savage Indians, upon the conditions stated in the following articles:

ARTICLE II.
The reciprocal crossing agreed upon in Article I shall only occur in the unpopulated or desert parts of said boundary line. For the purposes of this agreement the unpopulated or desert parts are defined to be all those points which are at least two leagues distant from any encampment or town of either country.

ARTICLE III.

No crossing of troops of either country shall take place from Capitan Leal, a town on the Mexican side of the Rio Bravo, twenty Mexican leagues (fifty-two English miles) above Piedras Negras, to the mouth of the Rio Grande.

ARTICLE IV.

The commander of the troops which cross the frontier in pursuit of Indians shall, at the time of crossing or before if possible, give notice of his march to the nearest military commander or civil authority of the country whose territory he enters.

ARTICLE V.

The pursuing force shall retire to its own territory as soon as it shall have fought the band of which it is in pursuit or have lost its trail. In no case shall the forces of the two countries, respectively, establish themselves or remain in the foreign territory for any time longer than is necessary to make the pursuit of the band whose trail they follow.

ARTICLE VI.

The abuses which may be committed by the forces which cross into the territory of the other nation shall be punished by the government to which the forces belong, according to the gravity of the offense and in conformity to its laws, as if the abuses had been committed in its own territory, the said government being further under obligation to withdraw the guilty parties from the frontier.

ARTICLE VII.

In the case of offenses which may be committed by the inhabitants of the one country against the foreign forces which may be within its limits, the government of said country shall only be responsible to the government of the other for denial of justice in the punishment of the guilty.

ARTICLE VIII.

This agreement shall remain in force for two years and may be terminated by either government upon four months' notice to the other, to that effect.

ARTICLE IX.

As the Senate of the United States of Mexico has authorized the president of that republic in accordance with Paragraph III, Letter B, Section III of Article Seventy-second of its constitution, as modified on the sixth of November 1874, to allow the passing of Mexican troops into the United States and of United States troops into Mexico, and the constitution of the United States empowers the president of the United States to allow the passage without the consent of the Senate, this agreement does not require the sanction of the senate of either country and will begin to take effect twenty days after this date.

In testimony of which we have interchangeably signed this memorandum the twenty-ninth day of July, 1882.

[Seal] FREDK. T. FRELINGHUYSEN
[Seal] M. ROMERO

With Crook in the Sierra Madre

JOHN G. BOURKE

John G. Bourke Diary 66–68, United States Military Academy Library[1]

<u>May 1, 1883, Tuesday</u>. General Crook gave orders to Colonel Biddle[2] to move his companies back to better ground, two to take station at Mud Tanks (our bivouac of the twenty-fifth ultimo) and two at Silver Creek, where we had remained the night of the twenty-sixth.

The general himself, with Captain Bourke, Third Cavalry, A.A.A.G, Lieutenant Fieberger, aide-de-camp; Chaffee's company of the Sixth Cavalry (Captain Chaffee, Lieutenants West and Forsythe, and 42 enlisted men); 193 Apache scouts under Captain Crawford, Third, Lieutenant Gatewood, Sixth, and Lieutenant Mackay, Third Cavalry; chief of scouts Al Sieber and Archie McIntosh; interpreters Mickey Free, Severiano, and Sam Bowman; and a train of 266 pack mules, tended by 76 packers—also Private A. F. Harmer of the General Service[3]—broke camp at 5:30 A.M., moving south down the San Bernardino River, passing the mouth of the Guadalupe, almost dry, and making a slight detour to the east, striking Elias Creek, a good-sized stream of pellucid water, flowing rapidly over bottom of sand and gravel. Width, twenty feet; depth, ten inches. Banks lined with cottonwood, ash, and walnut. At end of eighteen or twenty miles went into camp in a bend, heavily matted with sacaton.[4]

Here our Apaches killed several deer and captured a couple of wild turkeys. Formation, in early part of day, broken lava; in latter part, alluvium. At this camp, wood, water and grass plenty. (Goody-Ganya and three other Indians left back, sick.) A rattlesnake of good size and the thickness of my wrist, crawling across our blankets while Fieberger[5] and I were dozing thereon, furnished a source of pleasurable excitement in chasing and killing it, and a theme of animated conversation afterwards.

One of the turkeys captured alive by our Apaches and tied to a walnut sapling in some manner got loose and started full jump across lots, our savage scouts after it, yelling and howling; it was run down and, to avoid any possibility of its getting away again, had its neck wrung. After lunch, the Indians scattered up and down the valley for miles, the slump! slump! of their rifles telling that they had run in upon deer or other game; as they shoot always with

General Crook on the trail. CENTURY MAGAZINE, MARCH 1891.

a couple of crossed sticks for rests, they are successful hunters; the limbs of the walnut and ash trees in whose grateful shadows our blankets are spread are already laden with fore and hindquarters and viscera of mule deer and with wild turkeys, plucked and unplucked.

Fresh moccasin tracks have been seen this A.M., but whether of Mexican smugglers or Apache Indians is not yet definitely known.

Made a visit to the rude shelters of boughs erected along bank of stream by our Apache contingent. They were playing monte, cooking, and eating. They pointed to different articles of food, of which I learned the names as well as those of the utensils.

Mickey Free showed me a medicine bag fastened with brass-headed tacks. Inside this were some twigs and other matter deposited by the medicine man from whom obtained. This bag, Mickey says, is only to be opened in great exigencies, when the stick is withdrawn and set upright in the ground. The owner dances around it and sings and never fails to receive a prompt and favorable response to his supplication. It is impossible for a bullet to hurt a man provided with one of these talismans.

With our expedition is a medicine man—a mere boy in years but looked up to by his fellows as a phenomenon. The night before last, he communed with the spirits and announced that we shall catch the Chiricahuas and whip them on this trip. He backs up his prediction with a bet of forty-five dollars.

May 2, 1883, Wednesday. Breakfast at 4:00 A.M. General Crook and aides are taking their meals with Frank Monach's train. This is composed of equal divisions of Americans and Mexicans; so, when the cook spreads his canvas on the ground, one hears such expressions as "tantito azucarito quiero," "sirve pasar el jarabe," "pase rebanada de pan," and "otra gotito mas de cafe," quite frequently alongside of their English equivalents—"I'd like a little more sugar," "please pass the syrup," "pass over a slice of bread," "another drop of coffee," etc.

The shady foliage along the creek banks has been alive from the earliest tinge of dawn with the chatter of melodious birds—a most agreeable contrast to the aridity and tomb-like silence of Arizona, where songbirds are so rare.

Broke camp at 5:00 A.M. Moved south down the San Bernardino River but could not follow its valley on account of the jungle of sacaton, cane, willow, and ash blocking up the course. Took to the hills and had a rough time climbing up and down a constant succession of low but steep bluffs of metamorphic rock, chiefly of fragmentary and half-disintegrated porphyry and basalt.

These hills were masses of small, water-worn stones, with a vegetation composed of equal parts of mesquite, ironwood, greasewood, mescal, and nopal. The ironwood flaunted its plumage of crimson flowers much like the fuchsia but growing in clusters; the greasewood, ordinarily as homely, half redeemed its reputation by putting on a garniture of cream blossoms, almost rivaling the gaudy, lotuslike cups upon the nopal and putting to shame the modest, caterpillar-looking tendrils pendent from the tips of the branches of the mesquite.

The country today has been very severe upon our mules, which have not been able to go more than eighteen or twenty miles. Fieberger and I got lost in a dense canebrake and, after fighting our way through that, ran into a forest of mesquite and were badly scratched by the thorns. Thinking to come upon a better trail back to the command, we crossed the river and I was nearly drowned in a quicksand.

Camp this afternoon has been lively. The warm and genial sun has wooed all to the water, the whites stripping and plunging at once into the cool current, the Apaches preferring to first enter a sweat lodge and sing and cook for a while before following their example. It is a fact worthy of comment that an Apache will never expose his person; he may be so poor that he does not own a shirt, but at all times he wears a loin-covering, of which he doesn't divest himself even while bathing.

One might readily fancy himself in Acadia, there are so many flutes sounding in the wickiups. The Apaches have been making them all afternoon from the cane growing in such plenty. They call these four-holed flutes "tzyl." The head medicine man has been busy singing and crying over a youngster who sprained his ankle badly by slipping down a rocky hill soon after leaving camp; he has certainly put him to sleep, but I wish I could get a bottleful of arnica or liniment to supplement his incantations.

The game of monte is kept up with fidelity, and the fumes of meat baking in the ashes attest that the Apache hunters are not to live by bread alone.

Sergeant Nott, a Tonto Apache of the Saguaro (Juniper) or Yakuyikaydn clan, comes to see me each evening. He is unusually intelligent and is advancing rapidly in the knowledge of English and is keen to learn all possible about us and our modes of life.

Saw a number of old ruins today; merely the traces of walls—square—of lava boulders—not well defined. Metales of lava of large size; also mortars. Have seen fresh moccasin tracks all day. Our Apache scouts indulged in a "medicine song" lasting until long after midnight. With this I am almost convinced that the sweat baths of this afternoon and yesterday had some connection.

May 3, 1883, Thursday. Left last night's bivouac at 5:30 A.M., crossed the San Bernardino River (gravel bottom), marched nearly due southeast, leaving the stream, which made an abrupt turn to the west.

Our advance took us out over a rugged mountainous country—a series of steep hills running in every direction and composed of a nondescript accumulation of lava, basalt, sand and limestone, porphyry, etc., half rounded by the action of wind and water and so loosely held together as to slip apart and roll away the instant the feet of horses or mules touched it.

The vegetation was an unpleasantly thick growth of mesquite, Spanish bayonet (which at some points actually made chevaux-de-frise for hundreds of yards), soapweed (of which the Apaches cut bunches to clean their hair tonight), cactus growing ten and twelve feet high and terminating in gaudy flowers of yellow, some mescal of large size—a new cactus springing out from the ground, the branches being eighteen inches long and tipped with a beautiful white flower of the size and shape of the camellia and almost as delicately perfumed as the magnolia—and acres of ironwood, every branch bearing its cluster of crimson buds.

There was some grass of excellent quality. The country apparently abounds in game, and two or three different bands of white-tailed deer were sighted quite close to the road. Signs of hostile Apaches increased in number and freshness. A party of them must have passed over this road not long since, mounted on ponies; our scouts pointed out where they had slept under the bushes and brought out a headband made of yucca fiber, still green and pliable, and a string for carrying meat, also of fresh yucca.

Ten miles out, in a deep ravine, was a spring where Mexican soldiers had bivouacked a month or so ago; within sight of this we came upon a sudden bend of a broad, fine-looking stream, an affluent from the southeast of the San Bernardino; upon this tributary, a few miles further on, we camped for the night in a recess in the hills; wood plenty, grass good—water from the stream fifty feet wide, four to eight inches deep—rocky bed, current three miles, flowing generally through a steep canyon but having easy approaches at this point. Distance today (bad country) twenty miles.

Our Chiricahua captive[6] pointed out this afternoon the range of mountains in which is the Apache stronghold; this did not seem to be more than forty miles south of us, although it may be fifty or sixty. He also indicated the rough sierra, almost upon the boundary, in which the Chiricahuas hid for five months; this is seamed with deep, ugly canyons which contain plenty of good water and are full of mescal, which the Chiricahuas cut and roasted in quantity. In such a position they enjoyed absolute immunity from punishment. They might raid upon Mexicans and, retreating to this inaccessible mountain, convince the plundered ranchero that they had gone to the San Carlos Agency, or kill and destroy within the territory of the United States and, scattering as they approached the boundary, obliterate tracks by which they could be pursued. If American officers learned through spies of their position, the convention between the two governments was not elastic enough in its provisions to permit them to cross this imaginary line dividing the desert of southern Arizona from an uninhabited portion of Sonora; they could only send notification to the Mexican officers. Without telegraphic communications, with irregular mails and a difference in language, it needs no argument to show how and why the hostile Indians have thus far been enabled to defy two nations and elude two armies.

Immediately below our camp, the river (it is the Bavispe) runs over rapids and collects in opaque, glassy pools of unknown depth, said by the enlisted men to be at least thirty feet. In one of the minor bathtubs, as we call them, white soldiers, packers, and Apache scouts splashed in the cool and limpid current. Upon the banks were two or three sweat houses, each filled with patrons.

These lodges are hemispherical in form, four feet high and about five feet across on the bottom. They are made in a moment by planting ten or twelve willow twigs in the ground and uniting them at the upper extremities. Blankets, boughs, and pieces of shelter tents are laid on to exclude air and retain heat. A fire is kindled, in which are heated a number of siliceous boulders; calcareous rocks are not used because the Apaches know that when heated they would fly asunder. To take these heated rocks to the sweat lodge, the Apaches make use of willow switches bent into a loop, enclosing the stone. Half a dozen of these heated boulders are placed inside the sweat lodge, and with them a tin cup or other vessel of cold water.

The Indians pack themselves together like sardines; the one who acts as leader spills a few drops of water upon the hot stones; all of his comrades join him in a weird refrain, which they keep up with energy and unison until the perspiration pours from them in streams, when they walk into the river and splash about for a moment or two and then dress and return home.

When I applied for admission the lodge was so full that I couldn't see how a leg or an arm, much less a body, could find a place, but the master of ceremonies encouraged me with a smile, and as my experience with New York omnibuses has been considerable, I determined to push in as far as I could. First, a leg, and then an arm; finally my whole body. Thump! sounds the damp blanket as it fell against the framework and shut out all light and air.

The conductor of affairs inside threw a handful of water upon the hot rocks, and steam in the instant filled every crevice of the den. The heat was that of a bake oven. I couldn't breathe. "Sing," said in English the Apache boy "Keet," whose legs and arms were sinuously intertwined with mine; "sing heap; sleep mucho tonight; chiningoinyu—heap" (meaning "sing all you can—it will make you sleep well tonight and enjoy a good dinner"). I sang; that is, I joined in the chorus and wasn't put out, as a more critical or less kind-hearted audience would have insisted upon doing; I was allowed to remain and howl with the rest. Something ran down my back. I started; it might, for all I knew, be a centipede, but before I could explain to any satisfaction, it was followed by another and another, and I rubbed my hands over my legs and body to find them beaded with perspiration.

The flap was lifted; we all rushed out and dipped in the grateful coolness of the Bavispe. It seemed like a couple of hours, but it was only about two minutes that I had been occupied in a most refreshing ablution.

Doctor Andrews[7] caught a fine string of blue catfish at sundown.

One of our mules was shot by order of Major Chaffee[8] this morning; it had snagged itself last night upon a mesquite bush, which had pierced the lungs, and the poor brute's body was badly swollen with air, which had entered the wound.

I find that our scouts camp as much as possible by clans; thus, the Apache-Mojaves keep together, as might be expected, and also all those of the Chatchin, Destchin, etc.

Before going to bed, I went over to the bivouac of the scouts, about thirty yards from our fire and was told by those with whom I sat down that they represented in that circle the Destchin (four), Satchin (two), Klokaydekaydn, Kyakanni (three), Tzibinaztije, and Ustedinnaye clans, or twelve men in all. While chatting, they were roasting white-tailed venison on spits made of ramrods. They told me I ought to be a Kyakanni or a Destchin; I replied that I was a member and a brother of each clan—a rejoinder which tickled them greatly.

May 4, 1883, Friday. Broke camp at 5:30 A.M. Moved southeast up the Bavispe, crossing the stream four times, passing through several fine groves of cottonwoods, and then leaving the river on our right (west) and taking to the mountains.

The country was broken up beyond conception; all kinds of formations cut in upon one another; basalt, traephyte, lime, huge cliffs of sandstone battered and gashed into ravines without number, feldspar and granite crags cutting skyward in needlelike pinnacles or rent asunder into passageways just wide enough for our single file of animals.

The vegetation did not differ from that noted yesterday. There was a painful abundance of Spanish bayonet and much mesquite, in the shade of whose foliage grew in luxuriance the mesquite grass eagerly plucked by our animals. The trail was well defined and followed the best lines of travel; we marched rapidly along it, despite the loose stones which so annoyed our horses.

Campfires in two places witnessed the presence of civilized man at some date not far gone, while on a smooth rock in a narrow gorge through which passed the trail were dozens of Indian hieroglyphics, the most common and most striking of which I copied. Many of these were with difficulty decipherable. Two hundred or three hundred yards from this point struck the Bavispe once more near the trace of stone habitations, no doubt prehistoric, but of small extent. Here were a few cattle running loose in a dense grove of mesquite, whose gnarled branches almost shut out the light of the sun. Our scouts, seeing that camp was at hand, began to run at full speed, uphill and down, jumping from rock to rock in their eager haste to see which should first reach the water. In this camp, wood, water, and grass—all plenty and good. Distance today (bad country), sixteen miles.

I had unsaddled my horse and turned him out to graze, when Nott came up to say that there was a snake in the tree above where he was going to make his wickiup. I seized a carbine, took careful aim, and sent two bullets through its body, much to the delight of the Apaches; "But why didn't you shoot him yourself?" I inquired. Nott explained that, although the Apaches looked upon snakes as "tonjinda" and would kill them if they met them on the trail, they never would harm them when they came around the Apache wickiups. That would be a bad thing to do; yet they had no hesitancy in asking me to do it. I tried to learn what their opinion was of these reptiles but effected nothing beyond starting a Babel-like jabber among themselves. The snake, measuring something over six feet, was thrown on top of a bush close to my blankets, a proceeding which apparently displeased a fraction of the Apaches.

General Crook killed a queenly little hummingbird of peacock blue; Mr. Randall[9] secured the nest, no larger than a thimble.

Two of our packers had a fight; one had his "snoot busted"—served him right. Mr. Randall and I took another bath in a "ta-a-chi," or sweat house. For a song, I gave "Our Captain's Name was Murphy" with thrilling effect. The Indians assured me I was a good Apache and repeated what they had said yesterday, that I would sleep well tonight.

One of my comrades, when we got in the river together, looked around to see if anyone was within earshot and then told me in a low tone that he was Destchin. Bought a reed pipe, one of the few specimens I have seen in use among the Apaches. Eskay-ti-al-ti, a fine young boy (Destchin), sold it to me.

May 4, 1883, Friday (continued). Two of our Mexican packers, natives of Bavispe, left our camp and went to that town to see their relatives. One of the inhabitants came out to see us and remained all night. He reported that eight or ten days ago the national guard from Bavispe and Bacerac had had a fight with the Chiricahua, having three of their men killed and two wounded. They reported having killed twelve of the enemy—doubtful story.

May 5, 1883, Saturday. Bright, lovely morning. Marched upstream nine miles to the old town of Bavispe, said to be about two hundred years old. On the trail met the alcalde, coming to see General Crook. As one of our Mexican packers, Jose, was with him, I did not turn back to interpret and remained only long enough to take a drink of mescal from one of the two bottles in the alcalde's possession. There were some bands of Mexican cattle, but no signs of human occupancy until we got to the town itself, every one of whose population—men, women, and children, four or five hundred in the aggregate—had gathered in the corners of the streets and on the roofs of the houses to feast their eyes upon the strange procession. We were spoken to kindly by everyone on the way, and many bright eyes looked gently as we removed our hats in salutation.

One of the older men politely urged me to dismount and try a drop of mescal, which, pure and unadulterated from the still, is not bad liquor but rather too fiery for general acceptance. We bought a couple of dozen fresh eggs, the only thing in the way of food worth purchasing; talked with a number of the people; entered the old church, San Miguel, of poorly burnt brick— old-fashioned, good example of the groined arch. On coming out, I addressed a few words to a small boy, asking him in Spanish to hold my horse; one of the bystanders remarked, "Surely that man can't be an Americano; he must be a Cristiano; he goes to church and he talks the Castilian perfectly."

All the people of northern Sonora are armed to resist the Apaches; they work in their fields with arms in their hands and have organized into patrols, which in bands of twenty-five or thirty each day explore the country, looking for trails or other signs of the hostiles. Twenty-five of these men came back to town as we were leaving.

Last week a "conducta" of mules bearing tobacco, panocha, mescal, and oranges left here for Janos, Chihuahua, seventy-five miles off, escorted by the infantry detachment on duty in Bavispe.

Nine miles farther up the river is Bacerac, a town of 876 souls; if possible, more dilapidated and down at the heel than was Bavispe. Here also the whole population turned out to get a look at the strangers; curiosity alone was to be gratified, not idleness; for the latter, no excuse was even offered, it being the normal state of their existence.

Both these towns and the "haciendas" between were environed by large belts of fertile land, under irrigation and bearing crops of wheat not yet ripe; but notwithstanding the groundwork of prosperity, or at least of comfort, the mass of the people are living in a condition of squalor and poverty beyond description.

In former days there was [a] better state of affairs, and some broken-down evidences of respectability are to be encountered, made more conspicuous by the surrounding degradation. Superstition, illiteracy, and bad government have done their worst and left the people in a worse position than that now occupied by the Chiricahua Apaches who formerly lived peacefully here at Bacerac, as well as at Bavispe and at Janos, Chihuahua.

There are two stores—miserable affairs—in Bacerac: the main article of traffic is mescal—excellently made—but the worst thing in the world for a man to put inside his mouth. No matter how dangerous the road may be, mescal always finds its way, and every pack train encountered today has had from one to three packages in kegs or bottles.

The inhabitants invited us into their homes, where I must say that the women were much superior in breeding and good looks to their husbands and brothers. Mescal was offered as refreshment; there seemed to be no lack of this fiery beverage. There were no chairs or tables, no looking glasses—nothing but the bare walls and bare earth, with two or three strips of matting; mescal, however, was always to be had.

Fieberger and myself met the families of Davila and Montoya—the ladies pretty and of good disposition, but hopelessly ignorant, lazy, and disposed to be fat and dirty.

Passing through town, we descended the bend of the river; here a limestone formation, corrugated by the action of floods; noticed a square vat, filled with limewater used in tanning leather. After a march of twenty miles went into camp on the left bank of the river in a mesquite thicket, wood and water abundant, but grass poor and scanty.

Hardly had we unsaddled and unpacked when camp was filled with a delegation of men and boys from town, among them three of the "Guardia Nacional," who had been sent out by the "presidente" of Bavispe to show General Crook where they had had their fight with the hostile Apaches two weeks since. They gave the same account of the fight as we had received in the morning but added that they had found two rancherias, one burned and the other burning, and much meat of domestic cattle, slaughtered by the Apaches, who had driven them off from the country below. The fifty men of the Guardia Nacional had started to climb the face of a steep ridge and were allowed to approach within twenty feet of parapets of stone, concealed under a matting of grass, when up jumped the Apaches from their ambush and fired into the advance from three sides, killing four and wounding two very badly. Colonel Aguerre, with the regular troops, hurried up the hillsides, but the Apaches escaped.

The presidente of Bavispe sent a message to General Crook by Mr. Monteverde; he had ordered three of the national guard to go with General Crook and show him the place where the Apaches had last been fought. He had also intended sending Lazaro Colosio, the best guide in the country, but could not do so as Colosio was sick abed. Should General Crook need assistance, he wanted him to send back a dispatch, and he (the presidente) would come up with all the national guard. He would do all he could to help General Crook in his work, such being his orders.

This afternoon, General Crook bought four beeves at twenty dollars each and had them killed for the command; the meat was stringy and tough. Fieberger and I crossed the river at a ford where it was very narrow (thirty feet) but deep, flowing swiftly over a solid rock bottom.

Two Mexicans with a horse lent us the animal to cross upon, Fieberger throwing the rope back to the other side of the stream. One of these gentlemen took us to see the church. A much homelier structure than that in Bavispe, it is partly of brick, partly of adobe, and at one angle has a low, square belfry of the first material. The roof of the church is flat and rests upon beams, painted and rudely carved and set very close together. There were a dozen statues—

wretched monstrosities, all of them, and wall paintings to match; this miserable apology for a church bore the elaborate title of the Temple of the Holy Sepulchre and of Our Lady of the Trance. Adjoining were the ruins of a convent, long since abandoned.

The misery of the inhabitants was extreme. In one of the houses I saw a whole family seated at a supper of "atole" alone (thin flour paste, much like the paste used by paper hangers).

The bells of the church were ringing a mad peal, announcing that tomorrow would be Sunday, when a prolonged thumping upon a drum gave the signal that a "baile" was about to commence. Winding our way to the corner from which the noise proceeded, we found that Sieber, Frank Monach, Hopkins,[10] and several others had bought out the whole stock of a "tienda," which seemed to deal only in mescal. Everybody passing along the street was collared and run in and made to take a drink. An orchestra was recruited of a bass drum, a snare drum, and two squeaky fiddles to play for the drinks. None of them knew a note of music, and whenever any special piece was called for, it was first necessary to whistle the air, which the players readily caught and rendered with enthusiasm, emphasized by the two drums. This orchestra was augmented after a while by the addition of a man with a sax-horn. He couldn't play, and the horn had lost several keys, but he added to the noise and was welcome with screams of applause. It was essentially a stag party, but a funny one. The new player was doing some good work with his horn, when a couple of dancers whirled into him, knocking him clean off his pins and astraddle of the bass drum and drummer. Confusion reigned, but only for a moment, and good humor was restored by the liberal administration of mescal.

It was about 11:00 P.M. when Fieberger and I started to make our way back to camp. When we had reached the riverbank and taken off shoes and stockings, Fieberger advanced to the edge and called out, "Come along, it's only ankle-deep!" The words had only left his mouth when his feet slipped from under him, and with a dull, sickening thud, he went squash! into the water, waist-deep.

We made our way to bed in a silence that was painful.

May 6, 1883, Sunday. There were many swelled heads among our packers this morning, but we moved out at an early hour, going nearly due south in the morning and more to southwest towards evening. The country was rough and hilly, but the trail, although stony, was first-rate.

Outside of Bacerac was a fine ranch of green wheat, with pomegranates, peaches, quinces, and grapes. Cattle and horses looking well.

Six miles out was the hacienda of Estanco, where fifty men, women, and children lazily gazed at us from the fences. Ten miles out, the town of Huachinera, population three hundred, a squalid hole, with a squalid church—that of San Ignacio de Loyola, originally dedicated to San Juan but, burning down, had its patron changed to Saint Ignatius, who, my informant thought, would take better care of it than Saint John had done. On the walls hung five or six well-executed paintings in oil brought from Spain and still valuable, although badly marred by dust, smoke, candle drippings, and bird manure.

Eggs and children are plenty in this town. The "kids" are often handsome, a peculiarity disappearing as they approach maturity. I bought a dozen eggs from an old lady who produced them from an earthenware receptacle reserved by ourselves for baser uses.

Made a march of from eighteen to twenty miles to the ranch of Tesorababi, abandoned on account of Indian depredations. This is not far from a fine oak grove. Camp made in a fine mesquite grove with plenty of wood, water, and grass; the water, from springs, cool and sweet (sycamore trees). The days on this whole trip, thus far, have been quite hot; the nights, extremely cool.

Our Chiricahua prisoner says that the Chiricahuas came through this place when they started on their raid in March, and he asserts unqualifiedly that sixteen of them entered the plaza of Huachinera in broad daylight and purchased tobacco. All our scouts manifest an open contempt for the Mexicans.

This camp, the finest on this scout, has not so much running water as some of the others; General Crook remedied this by having the springs dug out and walled up with rocks. The scouts made sweat houses and bathed or played monte all day; at least twenty of them found diversion in stoning a squirrel running among the branches of the sycamores shading the springs and pools of water.

May 7, 1883, Monday. Remained in camp all day at the springs of Tesorababi. An ideal morning; a sky of sapphire, a genial, invigorating, but not too fervid sun, and a refreshing zephyr, just strong enough to sway the tender branchlets of the mesquite. The four men of the national guard left at 2:00 A.M. last night with dispatches from the president of Bavispe to General Garcia,[11] informing him that we were on a scout in the country, and two at sunrise today, going back to Bavispe. Four Mexicans riding mules and donkeys came into camp about breakfast. They were coming up from a place called Bacadehuachi to Bacerac. From them I learned that Colonel Aguerre was going today or tomorrow with four hundred regular troops for a scout in the Sierra Madre and that he would be assisted by all the available force of the national guard of the District of Moctezuma, which, it was expected, would be about three thousand strong.

Mexicans in squads of two and three having been coming and going all morning. Mr. Randall has gathered a nosegay of flowers of varied and attractive hues. Overlooking this camp is a bluff, seventy-five to one hundred feet high, upon whose summit is a dense copse of mesquite. Fieberger, Randall, Harmer, and myself scaled the rocky walls and saw, under the thick growth of timber and grass, the foundations of an Indian pueblo, not easy to trace but built of boulders from the arroyos surrounding the bluff. Mr. Randall was the fortunate finder of a very small, round mortar of black lava. The rest of us gathered flakes of obsidian and shards of pottery, painted and decorated almost exactly like those found in the valley of the Verde, and others marked with

Mexicans in squads of two and three. OUTING MAGAZINE, MARCH 1887.

incised lines with punctured, circular spaces. Harmer made colorful drawings of them. Five parrots flew over camp early in the afternoon. At 3:45 P.M. took the trail, going southwest, approaching timbered foothills of Sierra Madre country. Rough hills, liberally covered with oak and cut up by a thousand steep ravines. Grazing of the best quality.

While we were halted on top of a high ridge, Mr. Randall displayed on the pommel of his saddle a young owl, still in the down. The Apaches declined to come near, saying that the "bu" (owl) was a "chi'ii dn" (bad spirit).[12]

The oak gave way to scrub cedar in great quantities; the hills and ridges became steeper, and we soon struck the trail, followed by the Chiricahuas when driving off and horses and cattle from Sahuaripa and Oposura. We were fairly in the Sierra Madres and began descending a canyon with steep sides, along which grew pine and cedar, with some oak.

The darkness was so great and the trail so rocky and dusty that we were glad to come to the little box canyon in which the Chiricahua prisoner said we were to remain until the break of day (twelve miles). Altitude of this camp, 4,600 feet. Wood, of course, was in plenty, and the pasturage good, but water for the animals was not accessible and for the men was obtained only by climbing down over steep rocks to tanks in the bottom of the canyon.

The pack train had much trouble in getting into position, no fires being allowed. All night long they ran round our bed, to the great annoyance of Fieberger and myself.

May 8, 1883, Tuesday. Made fire for coffee in the early mists of morning; saddled and took the trail at 6:30 A.M. One of our packers—Vaca—picked up a large pattern of cotton cloth, dropped by the Chiricahuas. Moved in an easterly direction up the canyon, extremely rocky, with water in pools sufficient to slake the thirst of all our animals. Trail well beaten out by passage of stolen cattle; fresh cow manure frequently seen, also the carcasses of five horses killed only a short time since. The path next wound up the side of the canyon and was so precipitous that if a horse slipped his footing, he would roll hundreds of feet to the bottom. At one of the abrupt turns, we saw below the bones of a steer which had fallen from the trail and been dashed to pieces against the rocks. On top of ridge, another dead beef. Climb! Climb! Climb! Up the summit of one crest, only to learn that above it towered another, the country fearfully corrugated into a perplexing alternation of ridges and chasms, pine in small amounts and a great deal of oak marking the surface. Trail remained plain, several articles of Apache wearing apparel lying alongside it.

Climbing up and down this rugged pathway, we marched through the site of a camp of Mexican soldiers, ashes still bright and the signs showing that a large detachment had been there not many days previous.

Ten miles from camp of last night, descended into a deep, narrow gorge with running water; here also were fresh ashes of Mexican campfires. Less than half a league beyond this, on the other side of a low, grassy hill, had been the bivouac of a band of Chiricahua raiders returning with booty from the low country. There were the ashes of twelve fires and the burnt and unburnt remains of two beeves and two horses. Here we went into camp—under the shelter of a clump of pines; good grass and water in abundance, the last from a running brook. In this place once lived some people—Mexican or Indian—very likely the latter—who built houses of stone and dammed up the narrow gorges of the mountains. Distance today, eleven or twelve miles. Altitude of this camp, 4,600 feet. Pack train did not get to camp until from two to six hours after the column; many of the mules, wanting water, had gone back all the way to the bivouac at Tesorababi, to which ranch they were followed and caught.

The camp of this evening was especially charming in every aspect. The reports from our pack train were that they found the trail of today so bad that half a dozen of the animals tumbled off and rolled over and over until they landed on their backs at the foot of the precipitous slope; none of them were badly hurt.

At 8:00 P.M. the scouts, under the leadership of four medicine men, set to work to sing and "see" the Chiricahuas. I seated myself quietly alongside of Jim, who spoke some little English and who with good nature gave me a translation of all that was said. The chorus, in which nearly all the Indians joined, was the same as that of the dance before leaving Willcox and much like the refrains chanted in the sweat boxes.

The principal medicine man thumped himself violently in the breast, pointed to the east and north, and soon had worked himself into a hysterical condition. Jim said that he told the Apaches, "I can't see the Chiricahuas; bimeby, me see him, me catch him, me kill him, me no catch him, me no kill him. Mebbe so six days me catch him, mebbe so two days. Tomollow, me send twenty-five men hunt him thail; mebbe so tomollow catch him squaw. Chiricahua see me, me no get him; no see me, me catch him. Me see him little bit now, mebbe so me see him more tomollow. Me catch him, me kill him; me catch him hoss, me catch him mule, me catch him cow. Me catch Chilicahua pooty soon, bimeby. Me kill him heap, catch him squaw." These vaticinations bore a strong family semblance to the predictions of American clairvoyants, but they were listened to with rapt attention and reverence by the circle of Apache scouts.

Our Apaches, in looking around this evening, discovered two live heifers hamstrung by the Chiricahuas and left behind. Found also a bloody rag, the bandages of some wounded Mexican.

May 9, 1883, Wednesday. Last night was extremely sharp, and Fieberger and I shivered under our blankets until the call for breakfast. The trail continued unusually rough; as fast as one knife edge was surmounted, another yawning chasm had to be descended. We wound around the noses of promontories with vertical faces of rock; the least misstep would have sent our animals rattling to the bottom. We led our horses and mules up and down, up and down, the animals sweating, and we bathed in perspiration. In two places, saw dams for reservoirs and filled up with sand and having trees growing upon them. The Chiricahuas had killed five beeves and one pony close to our line of travel, and our scouts picked up five ponies, two of which were, however, too stiff to travel.

In every ravine, gorge, and canyon was water. Either in tanks or running brooks of good volume, but in either case of good quality. The timber encountered was pine, oak, and cedar, the oak in greater frequency than the other two. After slipping and climbing as best we could for four hours through this terrible series of precipices and abysses and seeing two other slaughtered carcasses of beeves, we halted on the crest of an elevated peak to allow the pack train to close up. In our front, the mountains were full of smoke. The Chiricahua captive pointed out a rocky gorge immediately below this ridge where he wanted the camp to be made; the point indicated was attained after about an hour's hard work, or after a total of five and one-quarter hours on the trail. We had come about nine miles, and knowing that the pack trains would experience still greater difficulty, General Crook wisely took no risk in attempting a long journey, but bivouacked in this gorge and awaited the descent of the mules, which was not effected for four hours longer, or a total of nine and one-quarter hours for a distance of as many miles. The gorge widened into a small ampitheater, very rocky, very steep, thickly mantled with a growth of small pine and some oak, while down the middle trickled a brooklet, whose water collected in large tanks in the rocks. The accommodations for men and animals were very slender, and grass was not any too plenty, although wood and water were at hand in abundance.

In this secluded and thoroughly protected nook the Chiricahuas had established two of their "rancherias," whose remains our scouts examined with care. I went over one of the seven jacales, or houses, of branch and brush. There wasn't much to be seen. The food of the Chiricahuas had beyond a doubt been mainly the flesh of beeves and ponies. There were three heads of cows inside the village and two a short distance off, up on the trail. There was a very slight amount of mescal and some onions, which the Apache boy with me said must have been captured from Mexicans. A squaw's dress—old and ragged—and a fragment of Mexican blanket constituted all the clothing left behind.

From the appearance of the grass all over the amphitheater, there must have been a large herd of horses and beef cattle grazing here until a few days ago. Mickey Free picked up what he said was part of the equipment of a young Apache going on the warpath for the first time. It consisted of a small reed pipe (one and a half inches long), through which the young warrior had to suck water, as it is not considered the proper thing, so Mickey says, for him to put his lips to a spring or brook. Neither can he touch his head with his hands, but he has to provide himself with a fragment of sharp, hard wood for doing the necessary scratching.

All around us are walls of rock taken from the ravine—generally not over six inches cube—but occasionally large enough to tax the energy of two or three strong men. What these walls are for, no one is able to tell; they run across the narrow clefts in the amphitheater, but they can hardly have been intended to collect water, which flows in such plenty a dozen rods below them.

General Crook is of the opinion that they were retaining walls for terraces, upon which the primitive inhabitants erected their stone dwellings. The more I look at them, the more do I incline to this view. They occur in two different places, one across a petty ravine and the other in a smooth part of the amphitheater, and number altogether about twenty. Their height is from twelve inches to three feet.

Five of our pack mules, in advancing along the trail this morning, fell over the precipice and killed themselves, three breaking their necks and two having to be shot. One of them was laden with Mr. Randall's photographic apparatus, which was crushed to smithereens.

The Indian scouts and the packers have gathered together from the Chiricahua rancheria a hairbrush of grass and a boy's bow and have discovered where the squaws had been cutting the children's hair, as well as where the children had been sliding down smooth rock.

With Fieberger, made my ablutions in a deep stone tank of cold, pellucid water, a bathing place worthy of Diana. Altitude, 5,500 feet.

May 10, 1883, Thursday. Passed another very cold night, but with little discomfort, having placed our bundle of bedding in a hollow between two big rocks.

Moved (at 5:40 A.M.) back half a mile to the top of nearest ridge; this was covered with small pines; here had been a rancheria of over forty houses, all standing. Apaches had killed many horses and beeves for food. One or two hundred yards farther on were the ruins of a couple of old buildings; foundations forty feet by fifty feet for each. Within ten feet of one of the foundations was a well-cut "metate"[13] with grinder of lava twenty inches by twelve inches, deeply hollowed, of the pottery common to Arizona.

The trail from this on was, if anything, more dreadful than it had been yesterday, but the line of travel of the hostile Apaches was very plain, having been made only a few days ago during wet weather. After two miles more of fatiguing work, climbing up and down, we slid down the almost perpendicular face of a high bluff of clay and shale and, rounding a corner of rock, entered another deserted rancheria with jacales so scattered about amid the oaks and cedar that it was impossible to discern them all at once, although I counted thirty. In this rancheria, the Chiricahua young men and boys had been playing their favorite and tribal game of "cool," or "Apache billiards." Two white-tailed deer ran straight into our long file of scouts, streaming downhill; a shower of rocks and stones greeted them, and there was a great deal of suppressed merriment, but not the least bit of noisy laughter. A fearful chute led down into the gloomy chasm, along which trickled the headwaters of the Bavispe, gathering in basins and pools, clear as mirrors of crystal. A tiny cascade babbled over a ledge of limestone and filled at the bottom a reservoir of much capacity. In this gorge the ashes of Indian fires and the straw of Indian beds at every shaded and sheltered corner.

Up! Up! Up! Perspiration running from every brow, the trail zigzagging up the vertical, or almost vertical, slope of a ridge, very nearly a thousand feet above the water. "Look out!" comes the warning cry from those in the lead, and then those in the rear dodge nervously from the trajectory of some piece of rock which, dislodged by the feet of horses or men, has shot downward, gathering momentum each second, as if shot from a catapult. To look at this country is grand; to travel in it is Hell.

And yet, up and down these ridges our Apache scouts, when the idea seized them, ran like deer. In every conceivable place of secrecy and security the remains of the rancherias of the Chiricahuas presented themselves; the captive said that the Chiricahuas never made fires by night but waited until 9:00 or 10:00 A.M., when they cooked the meat needed for the day. He pointed out the grove of pines where they had all met to have a big dance before breaking up into small bands and starting out on their last raid. A flat stone, covered with the flour of acorns, showed where and how the squaws made bread.

Far up on the flank of the mountains, almost at the very crest, were to be discerned the rock walls built by the people once occupying this region. While we were on this last hill our Apache scouts came running in much excited, saying that they had discovered two Chiricahuas coming through a gloomy ravine a short distance away. Before I had finished making this note they had skinned off their trappings and darted like wolves along the ridge, intending to capture the two pilgrims, if possible. In less than an hour they returned and reported that the two supposed Chiricahuas were a couple of our own packers, who had made a detour in the hills looking for strayed mules. Away off down in the depths of the gorges could be dimly made out our pack trains, the mules no bigger than jack rabbits, struggling and panting up the long, steep, tortuous grade.

A thousand yards beyond this cliff, and at a distance of not much more than six miles from last night's bivouac, we halted in a narrow canyon with broken sides, having plenty of timber, most of it pine, and some good grass. The Chiricahuas had lived all around here scattered in bands of two and three families, making surprise of the whole band an impossibility, but close enough to each other to be of mutual assistance in any exigency. Here they had been roasting mescal; here were the bones, horns, and paunches of cattle and ponies. In this nook, some warrior had been twisting for himself a rawhide rope; on this smooth sward, in a circle of graceful pines, numbers had been dancing and playing the game of cool. Mickey Free brought in a nice-looking black pony left behind by the enemy.

We may now say confidently that the Mexicans lied when they told of having killed eleven of the Chiricahuas. We have followed this trail, have seen no graves, no dead bodies, no exploded shells, no marks of struggle, and no fortifications. We are reluctantly compelled to accept the theory advanced by Mickey Free that the "Mexicans heap lie—mentiras muchas"—and that the Chiricahuas simply jumped them, killed and wounded a few, and drove the rest pell-mell out from the mountains.

We are taking the greatest precautions not to be seen and not to be surprised; detachments of scouts cover the country like swarms of locusts, going to the advance and to both flanks and taking in with the keen, painstaking glance of the hawk the slightest detail transpiring near them. Others remain with the pack trains, the company of cavalry remaining with them.

The packers are having a grievously hard time. Today they have been from eight to ten hours in moving over a distance of six miles. In front of each train marches a man with an axe to chop down young saplings or remove, as far as may be, particularly bad obstructions.

Since our departure from Willcox (April 20) the sun has shone brightly by day and the stars by night; this afternoon a change is to be noted; the sky is overcast, and a rainstorm is impending.

General Crook found a "fire stick," the presence of which would seem to indicate that the hostile Apaches are short of matches; let us hope that they are short of ammunition too.

Five mules roled off the trail today, but were all rescued without much injury.

General Crook held a conference with the Apache scouts this afternoon; they told him that they hoped to find the Chiricahuas and surround them; that if they had a fight and the Chiricahuas refused to submit, they would kill the last one, and if they did submit, they thought that some of the bad ones, like Juh[14] and Geronimo,[15] ought to be put to death anyhow, as they would be all the time raising trouble. General Crook replied that if the Chiricahuas thought proper to fight, they should have all the fighting they wanted, and the scouts couldn't kill enough to suit him, but he wanted them to save the women and children and grant mercy to all who asked for it. We should take prisoners back to San Carlos and there teach them how to behave themselves.

Mickey Free discovered a Winchester sixteen-shooting rifle in this camp, perfect in all save one screw at the breech block. The scouts then organized a scout of 150 men—under Crawford,[16] Gatewood, and Mackay; with them Sieber, McIntosh, Mickey Free, Severiano, and Bowman—to examine the country carefully for signs of the hostiles; the pack animals, with the cavalry command, packers, and rest of the Apache scouts remaining in this bivouac, which is easily defensible, has plenty of wood and grass, and a sufficiency of water.

Fires are burning hotly, and upon the bright embers the Apache scouts are baking bread in quantities to be carried with them. Mills are grinding coffee, or where the Indian is not the possessor of a mill, the fragrant berry is mashed between rocks. Careful attention is bestowed upon their moccasins, and full repairs are made. One man is sewing upon a new shirt, some are playing monte, and a few of the more cleanly are patronizing the sweat bath. A reservoir of water has been found in the rocks almost in the center of camp. A dead pony lies in the canyon one hundred yards or so from our position. Twenty-five or thirty of our Mexican packers, guided by half a dozen Indians, climbed over the ridges for two or three miles in a southeasterly direction until they came to the scene of the fight recently had between the Mexicans and the Apaches. Their stories varied greatly, no two agreeing, but that the Chiricahuas had given the Mexicans a good drubbing was evident. They found three Mexicans buried under piles of rocks, and down in the canyon alongside the battlefield, they claimed to have seen the grave of a dead Chiricahua. There were two parapets of stone and numbers of exploded copper cartridges, caliber fifty (used by the Mexicans) and Winchester (the weapon of the Chiricahuas). The scout brought back four ponies.[17]

The care taken by the Apaches in making down their couches at night may explain in part their ability to sustain the fatigue of travel in such rugged mountains. Unlike white soldiers, who flop down in the nearest level space, the Apache picks his ground, clears it of the smallest pebbles, spreads upon it a bed of grass, willow boughs, sagebrush, cedar or pine branches, as the case may be, surrounds himself with a windbreak of rock or brush, "spoons" in with five or six of his comrades, and snoozes comfortably until midnight, after which someone of the party is constantly on the alert.

There was another medicine song after dark, precisely like the one described a few pages back. The medicine man said that in two days the scouts would find the enemy and in three would kill a heap.

May 11, 1883, Friday. One hundred and fifty Apache scouts under Crawford, Gatewood, and Mackay, having with them Al Sieber, Archie McIntosh, Mickey Free, Severiano, and Sam Bowman, left our camp at daybreak with rations for four days. Five Chiricahua ponies came in with our herds and were promptly gobbled up by our scouts, who have altogether picked up sixteen at present writing. In this camp have remained all the pack trains, guarded by seventy-six packers, Chaffee's company of cavalry, and forty-eight Apache scouts; these last have busied themselves in erecting fortifications of stone and brush, commanding all approaches.

The Chiricahuas don't seem to have brought many cows into this rugged retreat. Their meat has been that of ponies only, unless they jerked some of the beef killed in their camps farther back.

General Crook established picket stations on three high hills overlooking camp; five men in each picket—Apaches by day, American soldiers by night. The afternoon was occupied by almost all not on guard or other duty in bathing or in washing clothes. Speaking for myself, I can truthfully say that the clouds of dust through which we had marched had made me blacker than a Negro. General Crook went bird shooting; he has secured three unusually small and beautiful specimens of the hummingbird. Yesterday morning, five of our white soldiers and two of our packers became separated from the command, the packers while following a trail, and the soldiers while in pursuit of horses which had stampeded. The packers rejoined early this morning, and one of the soldiers, Harmer, General Service, General Crook's orderly, at sundown. He reported that the horses had gone back to Huachinera and that the men following them had come upon a mule with a load of bacon and yeast powder.

Two Chiricahua babies were picked up on the ground in camp this evening; one was given to me, one to Fieberger.

While we were eating supper three Indians came back from Captain Crawford with a message in writing to the effect that he had found a good camping place for us about twelve miles from present position and that the trail was good and the march could be effected in one day.

May 12, 1883, Saturday. Morning warm and cloudy. Our pickets, upon being drawn in, reported that upon the top of one of the hills occupied by them had been another rancheria, well defended by parapets of stone. Started at 5:30 A.M., following Crawford's trail southeast up the ravine holding the water flowing past camp. Passed a dead pony one mile out. The trail, in the element of roughness, bore a striking resemblance to those toiled over since our first entry into the Sierra Madre (May 8). Having attained the crest of this ridge and awaited the coming of the pack trains, we continued our progress, still about southeast, going over a comparatively level mesa, well grassed and heavily timbered with pine and some oak. Saw four dead ponies, also great amounts of rawhide dropped by the Chiricahuas, and several caches of old clothes, a saddle, and stirrup. Again going down the flank of the ridge, entering a heavy growth of oak. Trail well defined and strewn with plunder dropped by Chiricahuas. One of our Apache scouts showed me a cloth toilet case, marked in red with letters S. C. Z.

In a little depression the Chiricahuas had made a mescal pit but had hurried off before burning any of the plant. Three ponies had been killed, and our

Indians gathered up three mules. Our progress became much more rapid with the improvement in the trail, and the pack mules kept close at the heels of the Apache scouts. There was water in every deep ravine. Close to our left was a ridge with bright green sycamores and cottonwoods fringing a spring. Wherever water was to be expected, we saw the peculiar walls of masonry which Fieberger thinks were put in position to retain earth in terraces for gardens; this theory derives strength from the total absence of soil in the valleys, as the streams flow over beds of boulders and gravel.

Our course led us down into the canyon of a beautiful brook, flowing to the south to add its waters to those of the Bavispe, coming in from [the] southeast at a bend one thousand yards distant. This creek was from thirty to fifty feet wide, six to eight feet deep, hollowing out in its path dark and deep pools, overshadowed by the walls of the canyon and flowing with the velocity of four or five miles an hour over a bed of gravel and rock. The Bavispe was of same character, only of greater dimensions: in width from twenty to thirty-five yards, depth from twelve inches to three feet.

Pushed east-southeast up the Bavispe for several miles, going through a burnt oak grove. Met Lieutenant Gatewood and Apache scouts coming back from Crawford's advance; they had gathered together seven of the mules and ponies. Gatewood reported that along the whole trail could be observed castaway plunder, abandoned ponies, and other signs of a hasty retreat on the part of the Chiricahuas. We went into camp at this spot in an amphitheater formed by high hills. Pine grove, with some oak. Water from river in abundance and of best quality; grass good and in some quantity. Distance today, twelve miles.

Rained a little and blew with violence this afternoon, the sky massing over in inky clouds. The Bavispe and the creeks flowing into it are much resorted to by ducks; whippoorwills can also be heard sounding their calls towards evening.

General Crook suggested an examination of the ruins at the lower (south) end of camp. They were so concealed by an overgrowth of sacaton that we could only make out that the total length was about one hundred twenty feet, breadth half as much, rooms twenty and thirty by ten feet, walls two and three feet thick of heavy blocks of water-worn lava, eight-inch cube, from the stream bed, fifty feet below. No pottery found and no traces of "acequias,"[18] although it is more than likely that the inhabitants were an agricultural people, tilling this rich flat of forty or fifty acres. Last of his race, abandoned by his former masters, the Chiricahuas, a little black burro wandered disconsolately in these ruins, nibbling at the sprigs of grass, until one of our Apache allies relieved him of his sense of loneliness and provided him with a new owner. The Chiricahuas dropped on the ground near here a very good Mexican "petate," or mat. Rations for five days sent back on the trail to the four men of Chaffee's troop who have been absent in pursuit of stampeded horses and mules.

May 13, 1883, Sunday. The brief rain of yesterday, to dignify it by such a title, had the effect of making the air delightfully cool and invigorating without being at all cold. Apprehending a storm, we had improvised all manner of shelter out of canvas, branches of trees, etc., but the night wore on without trouble, and our eyes opened upon a morning perfect in serenity and temperature.

Eight mules, loaded with rations, under care of four packers and guarded by twelve Indians, were sent forward on the trail to overtake Crawford's command. Fieberger made the ascent to one of our picket posts, on a peak twelve hundred feet above camp, and found the ruins of a pueblo of good area; some pot shards, incised and painted, two metates, and an unusually well-cut mortar.

The packers and soldier sent out with rations on the back trail rejoined at dusk, reporting having left the rations on the trail but, seeing nothing of the soldiers, concluded to return.

May 14, 1883, Monday. No message came back from Crawford yesterday, so we did not move from our camp. This day also we'll remain as we are. A more charming spot it would be hard to discover; our animals are enjoying their rest and filling up with nutritious grass; officers and men are bathing in the shoulder-deep pools of icy cold water, with bottoms of rocks and clean pebbles, in the grateful shadows of graceful pines. Others are stretched lazily upon the ground, reading, writing, or chatting, or languidly listening to the twittering larks in the branches. The more active have gone fishing, the stream being well filled with "blue cat." Upon each of the high peaks overlooking camp, vigilant pickets scan the horizon in each quarter, on the lookout for adventurous assailants. The sky is immaculate, the sun shines with brightness but without fervor, and the gentlest of zephyrs toys with the delicate foliage of the pines.

Last night was very cold and frosty, compelling Fieberger and myself to hug close for warmth, in spite of our four blankets of cover. Breakfast was not announced until 6:00 A.M., an agreeable change from the scheduled time of 4:00 A.M. of marching days.

Crawford dispatched four Indian runners, who entered camp as the sun was passing the zenith; from one of them I gathered that our advance had followed the advance of the Chiricahuas to a sheltered ravine, where they had indulged in a grand dance, killing and eating many ponies and then scattering into three or four bands. But let Crawford speak for himself; here is his letter.

Camp on Bavispe, May 14, 1883

Dear Gen'l

We ran on the Indians' deserted camp yesterday morning on the top of the divide. They had camped there for several days; from there, their trails ran in several directions. Peaches and the Blind Sergeant say they are going to a mountain across a big valley, about three days' march from here.

My plan now is to move out in the morning and keep one day in advance of you. I will leave here in the morning, so you can easily move here tomorrow night; it is only about thirteen or fourteen miles. The scouts I sent with this will bring you to the place. The pack mules you sent with rations, I will take with me so you can follow right on. When we reach the open country Peaches speaks about, I will wait for you and have it thoroughly scouted before you get up. Peaches says in the other side of this open country there is a rough mountain, and there is where the Indians have gone.

I counted ninety-eight wickiups in their village on the mountain; several bloody bandages were found. They have a large herd with them and some cattle. They killed quite a number of horses and cattle in their camp and jerked the meat. Some of the trails are about four days old.

Respectfully,
(signed) Crawford

Orders were issued this afternoon to exercise unusual care in extinguishing all fires before leaving camp, this to prevent conflagrations from high winds. A large tract of land has been burned over from the scene of the engagement between the Mexican troops and the Chiricahuas—extending well along the ridge. Special mention is deserved by the peerless bathing places in which yesterday and today so many of us have sought healthful relaxation. Of water, so clear that it has been a pleasure to count every pebble at the bottom, or the graceful fishes stealthily darting within the shadow of moss-grown rocks, and so deep that, sinking slowly with uplifted arms, we have not always been able to touch bottom with our toes; its width has been such that twenty-one good, nervous strokes barely sufficed to speed the swimmer from shore to shore. The transparency of the current has been equaled by its purity and coldness; the water is soft, sweet, and refreshing, and a plunge beneath its surface soothes away the wrinkles of care.

May 15, 1883, Tuesday. Sky overcast. Our course lay southeast or east-southeast up the Bavispe, here cutting its way through deep canyons; forded it three times. On trail, one dead pony and one live one. Upon the first hillock after leaving camp was an old ruin, whose foundation walls were of unusually large rocks from the riverbed, most of them being as much as sixteen and eighteen inches cut. The trail left the river and crossed several ranges of considerable height, upon which grew a thick sprinkling of scrub oak, from fifteen to thirty feet high. The grass had lately been burned from the slopes, and the trail, although not bad, as we had learned to consider such things, was bad enough. Two other dead ponies lay on the flank of the ridge first crossed after our halt, making four in all noticed this morning. There were also several series of the "retaining walls" closest to the very apex.

The rock on the trail this day has been a half-disintegrated, reddish feldspar with thin seams of quartz (crystals), some granite, sandstone, shale, quartzite, and round masses of basalt.

Every hour or less, or upon gaining [the] top of some steep bluff, the command halted in order not to let pack trains get too far behind. The advance guard had all it could do in chopping down trees, rolling boulders out of the way, or in other modes, helping the mules along.

In the bottoms of the ravines were all kinds of "float"—granite, basalt, sandstone, porphyry, schist, limestone, etc.—but no matter what the kind of rock, when struck upon the mountain flanks it was almost invariably split and broken and grievously retarded our advance. Saw on trail two dead ponies. Total today, six. Ten miles of climbing and marching, the last league over an area of burnt country, brought us to the bottom of a narrow gulch with a pretty stream winding northward to the Bavispe.

In this place, General Crook came face-to-face with two packers and nine Apaches sent back by Crawford. They bore this message.

May 15, 1883

Dear General,

Scouts out yesterday report fresh trail of Indians going west, with horses and cattle. You had better camp at place packers designate until you hear from me again. I thought it best not to take mules with me.

Resp't,
(sig.) E. Crawford

P.S. I don't think the Indians know we are in the country.

The packers amplified this report to the extent of saying that the Chiricahuas had had a mescal cutting and dance about four miles beyond this; that Crawford had yesterday moved out fifty scouts, who discovered the reunited trail and had gathered in some twenty or twenty-five ponies, mules, and burros left behind by the Chiricahuas, and a live steer.

In this secluded bivouac there was a sufficiency of running water, pine and oak in the greatest plenty, and much good grass not burned over in the recent fire. The dust from the trail and the soot from the burnt ground have added greatly to the discomfort of the command; faces, feet, and hands pure as snow in last night's bath are this morning foul and black, as if pulled through a chimney. Distance today, ten miles.

While I was bathing in a deep pool a short distance down the gulch an Apache runner arrived with a dispatch from Crawford, which was delivered at 1:05 P.M. By examining dates it will be plain that the runner must have come the intervening distance, six miles over the mountains, in something of a hurry.

12:15 (A.M.?), May 15, 1883

Gen'l:

The scouts ran across the Indians this A.M. in a canyon. Two shots were fired at two bucks and squaws by scouts, which alarmed them, and the whole camp is on the move. We will push after them as rapidly as possible. I think you had better come after us as rapidly as possible. Send whatever men can be spared. The scouts became very much excited. The bearer will bring you after us.

Resp't,

Crawford

At 2:00 P.M. reports of distant musketry shots sounded in our ears. Crawford and his scouts were fighting the Chiricahuas! There could be no mistake; Nott, our Apache friend, came up to call attention to the skirmish.

Sergeant Purcell and detachment of three men, who had been sent back after stampeded horses, reached camp at 3:00 P.M. He reported having followed the two horses, of which he was in pursuit, as far as the village of Huachinera, where all traces were lost, the Mexicans, beyond question, having stolen them. While trying to overtake us, the party caught two stray mules— one, a saddle; the other, a pack—and brought them into camp.

Captain Chaffee and company left to advance to the support of Crawford and the scouts. They took no rations with them. In anticipation of an encounter of some sort with the Chiricahuas, the Apache scouts left with us have lost not a moment in fortifying themselves. They have taken a position in a little wash in the bottom of the gulch, every two or three putting up a wall of rock, so as to be able to shoot upward at any object outlined against the sky.

Desultory firing continued at long intervals during the afternoon, just enough to attract attention and to convince listeners that our Indian scouts were still hanging to the trail of the fleeing hostiles. I could not help indulging the fancy that the Chiricahuas were fighting without energy simply because they had no ammunition to throw away.

Their constant attrition with the Mexican state and federal troops must have worn out their resources to a considerable degree, and my own belief is that they have such an amount of impedimenta in the way of horses, cattle, women, and children, they must fight to save them.

If they pause to resist, their lack of ammunition will put them in a fearful predicament. Taking everything into consideration, I am strongly of the belief that we can end the major part of this business by the first of the coming month. The moon is becoming so large that pursuit can be kept up by night as well as by day. Our camp was picketed with unusual precautions, and the mules and horses left with us herded close.

Crawford returned with the scouts late in the afternoon. They had jumped Bonito's[19] rancheria at 2:00 P.M., killing seven and capturing five—two boys, two little girls, and one young woman, the daughter of Bonito. From the Chiricahuas killed were obtained four first-class, nickel-plated, sixteen-shooting Winchester rifles and one Colt's new-model revolver. They (scouts) destroyed the rancheria, burning up the wickiups (between twenty and thirty) and loading down forty-seven animals—thirty-five mules and twelve ponies—with plunder. This included the traditional riffraff of an Indian village—saddles, bridles, meat, mescal, blankets, and clothing—and an occasional piece of more valuable booty obtained in their countless raids upon Mexicans and Americans.

I saw a fine gold watch—American made, bought in Saint Louis—elegantly but simply cased and having a seal of dark stone cut and set in gold and platinum. The darkness was so far advanced that a more minute description was impracticable, and the same excuse must be offered for not learning more about the silver watch also shown me.

Alchisay's band had a small purse containing a twenty-dollar gold piece; three silver dollars, all of American money; and a fifty-cent Mexican paper note.

The procession coming down the mountains was unique and, at times, laughable. The captured animals were weighted down with all manner of stuff, and the scouts themselves puffed and struggled under burdens, most of which had been carried home for glory only and would be thrown aside upon the first opportunity. The captives appeared to be much frightened but behaved with great self-possession, considering their tender years. Crawford's command consisted of 143 Apache scouts under Lieutenant Mackay, Archie McIntosh, Al Sieber, and Sam Bowman. Mickey Free and Severiano were also present as interpreters.

The impetuosity of the younger scouts precipitated the engagement and impaired its effect; had it been deferred until next morning, the result would, of course, have been more brilliant; but as it turned out, we have no cause to complain.

The fight was made by our Apache scouts alone, no white troops being present; although the result might have been better, yet it might also have been worse. Our scouts were eager to engage; a serious fault, it is true, but a virtue compared with a disinclination to do the same thing. The excellent conduct of the captive Peaches was attested by the unanimous voice of all who took part in the action. Not a casualty happened to a man on our side. This is the first time that the Chiricahuas have suffered so great a loss without inflicting any punishment whatever upon their assailants.

The attack has been made in the innermost recesses of what they have so long regarded as an impregnable stronghold—a fact, of itself, sufficient to disconcert them greatly. One of the young captives turns out to be the child of Naiche and the granddaughter of Cochise. The vicinity of the rancheria was so cut up with arroyos and ravines that the enemy's loss cannot safely be stated: the numbers reported are those actually seen, but there is every reason to believe that at least several others were killed or badly wounded.

Chaffee's company returned at 8:00 P.M.; they reported having seen two very fine American mules near the line of return march. All night long, the mountain—the scene of the action—blazed with fires from the burning rancheria.

May 16, 1883, Wednesday. Heavy rain clouds palled the sky. A sprinkling shower began at 6:30 A.M. but lasted only a few moments. Al Sieber came over to see Fieberger and myself. He said that he had noticed that when fighting, Indians as much as possible go by clans, just as they encamp.

One of the Indians handed me a note, dated Moctezuma, April 19, 1883, addressed to Señorita Doña Regina Maria de Mendez, Bavispe, telling her that he was on his way to Hermosillo, whence he would write again. By Don Ariano, he was sending her a dozen yards of black velvet ribbon, five dollars in money, and eight oranges. The note concluded with expressions of regard for herself and family.

I also examined a photograph album, which there was some reason for believing once belonged to Judge McComas[20] of New Mexico Territory. It was in pocketbook style, with red leather covers much discolored by age and wear, made by Hardin, 630 Chestnut Street, Philadelphia, Penna. There were twelve portraits. Nearly all the faces were decidedly intellectual. Although no portrait of Charlie McComas was contained in it, yet we all thought that it might be one of the old-fashioned pocket albums, with pictures of man and wife and living relatives at time of marriage. The third picture bore a striking resemblance to those of Charlie McComas, which I examined most carefully at Dos Cabezas on the march down.[21]

This morning has been full of very interesting points. General Crook had a talk with the oldest of the Chiricahua captives, who stated that she was the daughter of the chief Bonito, to whom and to Chatto[22] belonged the rancheria destroyed yesterday. It seems that we made pretty good time in getting even with Mr. Chatto for his raid into Arizona in March and April, from which the captive said he had only a short while ago returned. In this very rancheria, she said, was a white boy about eight years old, captured by Chatto on his raid. General Crook conjectured this must be Charlie McComas. He gave the girl provisions to last her back to her people and sent her with the older of the two little boys to open negotiations for the surrender of the young American. The girl asserted that the Chiricahuas were anxious to make peace and had talked of dispatching two messengers to San Carlos to ask for terms. General Crook replied that he would move camp tomorrow to a point on the Bavispe a short distance (four miles) from here and would there await for three days any communication the enemy might wish to make.

Included in the plunder exhibited by our scouts is a leather-backed mirror marked "J. W. Clark, Tombstone, Cochise County, Arizona." A new driver of a sewing machine and some other appurtenances would favor the hope that the Chiricahuas had been the instruments under Divine Providence of making a horny-cheeked sewing machine agent bite the dust; we can do no more than clasp the gratifying illusion to our breasts and trust that time may not dispel it as a delightful dream.

The other three captives are too young to give much information. Everybody is exceptionally kind to them, and no one more so than the Apache scouts, who keep them well provided with roasted mescal from their own village and with bread and meat from our supplies. The eldest, a bright girl of six or seven, is sewing assiduously, but like another Penelope, as fast as her pattern is finished rips it up and begins all over again, apparently afraid that idleness will entail punishment; the other two—brother and sister—a girl of five and a boy of three—sit wrapped in one blanket, the poor little girl gasping and sobbing convulsively, and the boy—a handsome brat—gazing stolidly at the world through eyes as big as oysters and as bright as jet.

There was a chance which I improved of buying two pretty Chiricahua flat blankets. Fieberger has employed most of the morning in repairing his brogans, torn to pieces by the sharp rocks. He merits small praise as a cobbler. Cool showers dampened the ground at noon. We are all hoping that their effect will be to extinguish the fires burning in the mountains.

All around us in this ravine are the curious walls already mentioned so many times and for whose construction no perfectly satisfactory explanation has yet been suggested. Gambling has been carried on with energy by the Apaches; monte the game, and the stakes bills of American money as high as five dollars and of Mexican issue of various denominations, the spoil of the constant warfare carried on by the Chiricahuas upon the hapless people of Sonora and Chihuahua. Rumors of the most contradictory character have been flying around, crediting our Apaches with having fallen upon considerable spoil; one man is said to have taken $140, another $110, both in gold, but I think that these amounts have been exaggerated. All that can be said with certainty is that our savage allies are now flush and are bucking the tiger with the air of Wall Street brokers; several of them are arrayed in Mexican sombreros of the loudest patterns, embroidered in gold and silver and entwined by a silver rattlesnake.

As alluded to already, our little captives are receiving gentle treatment. When the fitful showers of this morning suddenly turned at midday into a chilling, driving, and soaking rain, the little girls and boy were the first to be looked after. A comfortable bed of grass was made for each and blankets spread upon which they might recline when so disposed. The wickiup where they lived was tightened against rain and wind and plenty of coffee, bread, and stewed meat set before them. I should also say that when the two captives set out to go back to their people, they were provided with presents of handkerchiefs and of tobacco by the scouts. Much of these came from their own people, who in turn had levied it as tribute from the Mexicans. This tobacco is conceded by smokers to be of an excellence second only to that of Cuba; there is enough of it in camp now to keep the command fairly well supplied for several days.

After my examination of today, I am more than ever of the belief that the wildest savages are ever solicitous to provide their children with means of diversion and amusement proper for age and sex. The toys supplied are correct imitations of arms or implements to be used in after life; thus, a little girl's hours of play are enlivened by making dresses for minute dolls or in learning the purposes of small baskets, ollas, etc. The pack or saddlebag, carried on horseback, in which squaws place scissors, awl, thread, and domestic nostrums, I saw copied today in a little arrangement which faithfully repeated the contents of the original, even to the herbs and roots enclosed there.

Major Chaffee told me in the afternoon that the Apaches yesterday, after the fight, made five smoke signals from one mountain; there is no mistaking the straight, opaque, inverted cone which rises so rapidly from the ridge nearest the scene of a defeat.

The setting of the sun was the signal for another sharp shower, cold and dispiriting as the others had been; with it came a stiff wind, chilling everyone's blood.

Elevation of this camp, 4,950 feet.

May 17, 1883, Thursday. The severity of the cold this morning was the sole souvenir of yesterday's tempest: water froze in pails and the general keenness of the air was more like that of early fall than of the first days of summer.

The personnel of our pack trains is not up to the usual standard of excellence; there are many good men who work faithfully and with intelligence: indeed, they work more than their share, having to make up for the deficiencies of the bummers alongside them.

Every night our mules have been allowed to stray, thus entailing unnecessary fatigue in catching them and delay in leaving camp. Last night all of Hopkins's train wandered off, the herders no doubt being asleep on post; and so, instead of starting at 5:30 A.M., we were not able to get away from this bivouac until 9:00 A.M.

We had gotten over the first high ridge, traveling not quite so slowly as we expected, when we descried, on the summit of a bald knoll directly in our front, a thin curl of smoke wreathing upward. This was answered by our scouts, who heaped up a quantity of pine cones and dry branches, which, in a second, shot a bold, black, resinous signal above the tops of the tallest trees.

Five miles up and down mountains of small elevation but great asperity ended in a camp at the junction of two canyons, each of which had water. Pine and oak in plenty, and grazing quite good. While horses were unsaddled, the Indian scouts sent a detachment to the apex of a crucial butte overlooking our position and there set up a signal smoke.

The captives have been riding ponies. Numbers of the Apache soldiers have been doing the same thing; animals, both saddle and burden, are numerous. There must be an aggregate of over seventy-five picked up on road or taken in the recent fight.

At noon, answering signals curl upward from the mountains beyond us; at 12:45 P.M., Severiano came up to inform General Crook that two Apache squaws were approaching; in another moment, their movements could be followed down from where our scouts had made the fire—and at exactly 1:00 P.M. they had met General Crook. They were the sisters of To-klan—one of our scouts, himself a Chiricahua—the only one of that band who had not broken out from San Carlos. The squaws said that they had lost heavily in the fight of the day before yesterday, and while they were retreating in a bunch up the canyons, our scouts played sad havoc among them. They admitted that there was in their village a young American boy who, in appearance, corresponds closely to what we have heard of Charlie McComas. This first brief interview ended, General Crook ordered Archie McIntosh to conduct them to one of the pack trains and provide them with food.

The elevation of this camp is 5,050 feet. The country marched over the morning is well watered; two miles back of this camp was a large branch of the Bavispe, and due south, just across the ridge, another one is reported.

A cry sounded from our picket post at 3:00 P.M., and two new squaws— one afoot, the other on a pony and waving a white flag—came slowly down the trail to open negotiations with our commander; four others sat themselves with our pickets on the hilltop and looked down upon the strange scene of animation so far beneath. I went with Mackay to a lovely pool in the rocks one hundred yards from camp and there enjoyed a delicious bath.

Sauntering back, we mingled with a score of Apaches killing a pony for meat. They avoided defilement from blood as much as possible. The most interested spectator was the little Chiricahua boy. The number of prehistoric walls—some almost cyclopean in type—seen on all sides today is worthy of mention. The two squaws, one of whom was a sister to Chihuahua,[23] one of the head men of the Chiricahuas—told General Crook that Chihuahua himself would come in early tomorrow morning with his whole band and surrender. The women did not tarry long with us after the interview.

May 18, 1883, Friday. All traces of Wednesday's storm have disappeared, and a more lovely early summer's morning could not well be imagined.

Four Chiricahua squaws, one buck, and a boy came into camp at 8:30 A.M. Within an hour sixteen men, women, and young children able to walk had descended, including Chihuahua himself—a man upon whose lineaments great decision of character was imprinted. At various times, and in squads of from two to eight, nearly all women and children, Chiricahuas came down to our camp until, at 4:00 P.M., we had an aggregate of forty-five, captured or surrendered.

Chihuahua had a very satisfactory talk with the commanding general, after which he was given permission to go out and hunt up the remnant of his band, promising to have them all back by tomorrow. With him went two men of his people. The women showed the wear and tear of a rugged mountain life and the anxieties and privations of an Ishmaelitish war, but the children were models of grace and beauty, which revealed themselves through rags and dirt. Two young girls, wearing the brass-tacked headdress of the unmarried, were comely and clean, although rather too muscular to be handsome from an American standard. The property in their possession consisted mainly of mescal, ready-roasted. The main stem is a delicious morsel, highly deserving of attention as an addition to the diet of the Southwest. Very many of the Chiricahua women and children are wearing ornaments of fragments of nacreous shells and necklaces of what I am told are pony teeth, bored and polished. Three of the young boys—models of youthful beauty and ease of manners, paid a visit to our mess fire and supped bountifully on bread, sugar, and coffee.

Sergeant Nott and half a dozen Tontos spent the evening with us, explaining the expressions of the Apache language.

May 19, 1883, Saturday. An unusually cold night, succeeded by a bright, sunny morning. We halted at end of this morning's short march in a "cienaga,"[24] furnishing a sufficiency of water and almost concealed in a black forest of tall, slender pines, none over twelve inches and most only six inches in diameter, height from six to eight feet. Our accommodations were ample, and we had no cause to complain of anything except the danger of losing our animals among the trees. We made about two and a half miles an hour, ascending a canyon, narrow, steep and rocky, with pools and springs of water, and a rough but well-beaten trail. There were to be seen walls encountered all through these mountains; in one instance an escarpment eleven or twelve feet high, of a structure almost cyclopean, confronted us. The summit gained, [we] entered the forest; the trees had grown over the foundations of the homes of a people who had left no other trace, not even pottery, behind them. These houses, as nearly as could be determined under the circumstances, were from thirty to forty feet long by twelve to fifteen feet wide.

The camp of today, southeast of that of yesterday, is within easy reach of the scene of the fight with Bonito's and Chatto's rancherias and had been placed in pursuance of directions given by Chihuahua. Elevation, 5,700 feet. Indians have followed our trail and come into camp; with those previously enumerated, we have, at this moment, over seventy, not counting Chihuahua or others absent with him, who would swell the total by five or six. Before noon the number present was an even 100.

After dinner half a dozen especially handsome boys paid a visit to headquarters and were the recipients of bread and sugar. Harmer made a successful sketch in colors of [boy] number one.

The report was brought in by the squaws surrendering today that Loco had gone on to the San Carlos reservation with twenty families, there to deliver himself home.[25]

An unusually good example of the Apache squaw's upper garment was worn by one of the younger girls; it was of buckskin, open at the sides, where a fringe of buckskin strips supplied ornamentation, that around the neck being a triple line of the conical pendants of tin so much admired by them. It reaches no lower than the swell of the back.

The kind treatment accorded the surrendered by our Apache scouts has had a most happy effect; victors and vanquished are eating together. Kettles are steaming with pony ribs and steak, and loaves of very good bread are browning by the ashes. Supper concluded, the scouts called the captives together for a council in which they told them that since they were going to be brothers and sisters, it was not proper that they should keep the Chiricahua ponies and mules.

"You can go tomorrow morning," said the gallant Alchisay, "and lariat all the ponies and mules. Going home to San Carlos, we may have long marches, and the youngsters and babies can't walk. We have told all this to the Nantan-cha,[26] and he says it's all right." A chorus of grateful squaws praised to the echo the generous victors.

The silvery moonlight flooding through the pine branches made camp as bright as day; in wandering from point to point, I was more than ever struck by the care the Apaches exercise in making down their couches. American soldiers, American packers, and American officers sprawled upon the ground wherever blankets happened to fall; on the contrary, the native Indians carefully leveled the ground, removing even the smallest stones and replacing them with a thickness of two or three inches of hay; large rocks and branches of trees made a serviceable windbreak and covering.

Samaniego, a packer belonging to the command, is well acquainted with one of the surrendered squaws, having been brought up with her. Twenty or thirty years ago, when a very little girl, this woman, with a dozen other children, was captured by a Mexican scouting party and taken to Bavispe and there was kept for six years, a servant in the family of Samaniego, to which this packer belongs. The encounter was very cordial. It amused me to listen to this squaw (who spoke Spanish fluently) inquiring after all the Mexicans she knew—Don this and Doña that, much as if they were of her own blood.

A young girl wounded in the left hand recalls the fight of a few days ago, now almost forgotten. Another souvenir of the same episode is a battered tin coffeepot struck by a glancing bullet and knocked from the fire.

<u>May 20, 1883, Sunday</u>. Remained in camp. We were eating breakfast comfortably, when an exclamation from the cook caused all to look up and see a perfect avalanche of squaws and children pouring down upon our supplies. They had been playing the scavenger at all the other trains and were ending with ours. The occasion was a favorable one for making a count; they numbered 121, nearly 60 being squaws.

At 8:45 A.M. great commotion arose in camp. The scouts grasped their guns, took to the trees, and set up a fearful yelling; the captive squaws and children were much more collected but still added a fraction to the turmoil and yelled in response to cries directed at us from a pinnacle one thousand feet high, commanding the camp. It was a band of Chiricahuas, asking to come in but first anxious to learn how far they might commit themselves with safety.

After a brief parley, a couple of squaws ventured within the lines, and then Peaches and a Sierra Blanca Apache went up the mountain to hold a colloquy with the new arrivals.

But it was fully 1:00 P.M. when the first band of bucks—five in all—preceded by a squaw, concluded to trust themselves to the mercy of the troops. Upon seeing the commanding general, they were provided with food. Ten minutes after this first detachment, two other young men followed, each armed with a repeating rifle as their avant couriers had been. From my seat on a burnt and prostrate pine log, aided by the Apache scouts alongside, I made out the descent of each Chiricahua, whether he continued bold enough to keep on inside our lines or faltered and turned back. The scouts are dexterous in the use of the field glass and ask for the loan of one always, when obtainable.

A quarter of an hour elapsed, and then three more men, without arms and preceded by a young squaw, followed in the footsteps of the first two batches. By small driblets they kept coming in through the afternoon. From our Apache scouts I obtained the information that this was a big raiding party which had been raising hell in Chihuahua. These Indians had with them a large head of beef cattle and five Mexican women and one child. Those who didn't dare to come down perched on the battlements of the high, rocky bluff overhanging the camp, where they looked like so many hawks, or vultures perhaps, greedy for blood. They could not comprehend our behavior; they sent word that they wanted to talk with General Crook. His reply was to the effect that if they wished to see him, they could come in without fear of molestation; that he did not intend to hurt them for the present and would refrain from active work for a day or two to allow such as were so inclined a chance to surrender.

Half the camp or more improved the day by going down to the creek and bathing, or washing soiled clothing; the word "soiled" conveys no idea of the amount of dust and grease matted into all our garments and yielding slowly to the effects of soap and a vigorous thumping upon the rocks.

There is one glad heart that greets the Chiricahuas with unfeigned joy: the youngest of the captives, a bright baby boy, has been recovered by his mother, who has been wild to find him. Whenever he cried, and he cried very often, his savage guardians made desperate efforts to soothe him with "baby talk" and gave him chunks of bread or cups full of coffee to occupy his mind and stay his hunger. I predict that the young brat will one day be a distinguished astronomer, from the profound interest he now manifests in the Milky Way.

While we were eating supper, Geronimo was ushered in to have a talk with General Crook. His men entered in the usual Apache style, two by this trail and two by that, the fear of treachery and ambuscade ever present in their minds. Seventeen or eighteen had filed in when I, supposing that all had come, went out to a small spring two hundred yards from camp. This gurgled behind a bold rock, which I turned; to my amazement, I came plump upon half a dozen fierce-looking Chiricahuas, every one with a Winchester rifle. I greeted them pleasantly and was responded to in same tone. "John, you catch him natu (tobacco)?" asked one. "Elle (No). Ihi chikun nuku, natu, tagayn, dungua (I have matches here—tobacco in camp." "Good!" they replied, with words and motions, "when we wash our faces and hands, we will go to camp!" I turned on my heel, saying "yellon (good-bye)," when the one who had addressed me first, and whose ablutions were completed, called out, "Ho! John, me go," and walked up with me to where Geronimo and a score of others were seated on a fallen log.

The aggregate imperceptibly swelled to forty or more—a piratical gang, surely, one that would have made the fortune of any manager who should place them on the stage as the "Pirates of Penzance." There wasn't a weak face in the line; not a soft feature. Each countenance was indicative of boldness, cunning, and cruelty.

General Crook received them coldly. The conference did not last many minutes, and amounted to but little, but was followed by another and longer one as the night advanced.

Among the Chiricahuas who have come in up to the present writing I have observed one feeble-minded young man, one cross-eyed boy, and one stuttering child.

The San Carlos scouts and the Chiricahuas had a grand dance, interspersed with singing of a joyful type, which lasted until daybreak.

May 21, 1883, Monday. Remained in camp. When Fieberger and I sat down to breakfast, we were not alone. Four of the chiefs of the Chiricahuas invited themselves to our festive board: Geronimo, Tchanolpaye, Chatto—the leader of the raid into Arizona—and Naiche, the son of Cochise. They seemed to be in pleasant humor and consumed with relish the bread, beans, and coffee set before them; pork they would not touch, Geronimo saying it was "Tonjinda."

Breakfast over, I should have been at a loss for some new item to be inserted in my journal, had it not been for the kindness of Captain Crawford and Lieutenant Gatewood, who put me on the scent for fresh data of importance.

Gatewood described the ceremony of blessing the war bonnet, in which the treasured headgear was carried about by the medicine man, placed upon the shoulders and heads of the warriors, greeted with yells, and sprinkled with "hoddintin," or sacred meal.

Crawford told me I ought by all means to get a peep at one of the Apache war shirts worn only in time of ritual conflict—that Alchisay had an unusually elegant one. Going to Alchisay, he told me that he had left his at Camp Apache, but his brother Shika-shlani (Big Foot) had brought one with him. Getting Severiano to act as interpreter, I went to Shika-shlani, who at once produced the priceless garment. It was a sleeveless shirt of the finest white buckskin, reaching to the waist, open at the sides, ornamented with eagle feathers and smooth chips of nacreous shells, and decorated both front and rear with figures and symbols in colors. On the breast were the full-length figures of two "santos" (saints)—one with a halo, the other without, each holding crosses in their outstretched hands. The border enclosing the design stood for the mountains of the world. In the upper corners, stars were symbolized, and in the lower left, a circular design, quadrated in diverse colors and motleyed with small round polka dots, was accepted as the representative of a "sierra pintada" (colored mountain). This figure was almost three inches in diameter. The lower right-hand corner was taken up with a pair of crescent moons and a series of small stars. The ornamentation upon the back was somewhat different. Here also were the bordering of semicircles standing for mountains, eagle feathers, and iridescent shells, but the santos were replaced by two wind gods, which, however, counterfeited them almost perfectly. Between these gods was a small eagle. A small, rectangular bluish block near the lower right-hand corner was the emblem of hail. The other decorations were stars, small crescents, larger ditto [crescents], and under the right-hand god, one terminating in two circles like those of the Navajos, Zunis, and Moquis. Porcelain buttons filled the eyes of gods and santos alike, and each had sewn to one of its shoulders a pretty fragment of shining shell.

Shika-shlani said that he was not able to give a complete explanation of all the designs portrayed on the shirt. The winds were powerful gods, and the wearer of the garment enjoyed immunity from danger in a fight with an enemy. For that reason he had brought this one along. If the Chiricahuas assailed the camp by night, their bullets couldn't hurt him if he wore this medicine shirt; they would fly off in the air and hurt no one.

There was an old man in Pedro's camp, back at Camp Apache, who knew everything; he was a great medicine man. He had made this garment and could explain all about it.

Early in the afternoon, a detachment of nine Indians—two men, four women, and three half-grown children—gave themselves up; the men were armed with the Winchester repeater. Immediately behind them [were] two other men—one on a very good pony, both armed.

Five minutes had not elapsed before there wound through the pine timber a curious procession, mostly men, but having also some women and children. They were driving before them fifteen steers and work cattle, and many were riding ponies and burros with Mexican brands. For arms they had the Winchester and the Springfield breechloaders, with revolvers of various patterns and lances, the blades of which were old sabres. The young boys carried revolvers, lances, and bows and arrows. The arrows are made with a hardwood stem in a reed shaft, without barbs, and [have] a crosspiece within two inches of extremity, so that when they shoot birds the dart can be withdrawn without delay. The good condition of cattle and horses made us believe that they must have been grazing in the mountains for some time. Besides the meat on the hoof, there were several loads packed on mules and horses. This band numbered seventy-nine, twenty-three being full-grown bucks.

One of the mules of Hopkins's train was bitten by a rattlesnake day before yesterday; it was promptly bled and ammonia injected, and it is now reported out of danger.

The closing hours of the day were enlivened by the butchery of most of the cattle in the possession of the Chiricahuas. Their intention is to jerk the meat to make it serve as food on their march to the San Carlos. Standing within six feet of a steer, a young buck prodded the doomed animal one lightning thrust immediately behind the left foreshoulder, and with no noise, other than a simple bellow of fear and agony, the beef sank upon its knees. The issue of rations to this swarm of hungry mouths has added new wrinkles to the forehead of Archie McIntosh, who has assumed the functions of commissary, and is causing a perturbation in our calculations as to the time of our absence from the United States. Should nothing occur to delay the surrender of the rest of the tribe (one-half has now been heard from), we ought to get away from here by June 1 at the outside and strike the boundary as soon as the women, children, and tired animals can march there, which will hardly be more than ten or twelve days. The Chiricahuas deny that in their recent fight with the Mexicans they had even one man killed.

Another long talk took place late this evening between General Crook and a party of Chiricahuas—those who came in this afternoon.

May 22, 1883, Tuesday. Camp presents a medley of noises not often found united under a military standard. Horses are neighing, mules braying, and bells jingling as the herds are brought in to be groomed; the ping of axes against the trunks of stand pines and the hum of voices, the squawking of babies, the silvery laughter of children at play, and the occasional music of an Apache flute combine in a pleasant discord which leaves the listener uncertain whether he is in the camp of grim-visaged war or among a band of school-children.

Doctor Andrews was not suffered to wear his soul out in idleness. The moment his breakfast was over, sick Indians surrounded him, petitioning for medicine and service. Two of his patients—both Chiricahuas—are in a bad way. One of them is an old squaw who fell against a rock, breaking her arm at [the] elbow; the other, a half-grown boy, also fell upon a sharp rock, severely injuring his knee.

Alchisay let me have his medicine sash, worn from right shoulder across body to the left hip. He says that it is very old, formerly belonged to his father, and is a sure guarantee against arrows and bullets; in fact, against all dangers.

A wave of excitement rippled through camp. The distribution of the meat slaughtered last evening has given rise to fierce war among the Chiricahua ladies. Two of them rushed for each other like a couple of infuriated Texas steers: hair flew, blood dripped from battered noses, and the two human forms divine were scratched and torn by sharp nails, accustomed to this mode of attack. The old squaws chattered and jabbered; little children screamed and ran; the warriors stood in a ring and, from a respectful distance, gazed stolidly upon the affray. No one thought of interfering; there is no tiger more dangerous than an infuriated squaw—she's a fiend incarnate. The packers and soldiers looked on, discussing the points of the belligerents. "The little one's built like a hired man," remarks one critic. "Ya'as, but the old un's a He, en doan' you forgit it." Two rounds settled the battle in favor of the older contestant, although the younger remained on the ground, her bleeding nostrils snorting defiance, her eyes blazing fire, and her tongue volleying forth Apache imprecations.

In pleasing contrast to this picture of fury was the peaceful attitude of Blinkey, a one-eyed Apache veteran, who watched the fiery embers whereon, brown and savory, steamed and broiled a narrow gut, to the savage the most delicious morsel of the beef. I ate a small portion and confess I was surprised at its richness and delicacy.

Aroused by a cry from our Indian scouts, I ran out of my shelter, where I was dozing at 10:00 A.M., and had pointed out to me by Alchisay a file of five women, slowly and painfully moving up the trail from the bottom of the canyon. "Nakaydi" (Mexicans), said Alchisay; we all ran to where the wretched creatures had halted under a tall pine. They gave names of Rafaela Mendoza, Valentina Marquez, Refugio Hernandez, Maria Jose, and Antonia Hernandez, who bore in her arms an infant, Maria Catarina Hernandez, going on two years old.

They gave a doleful account of their sufferings since their capture fourteen days ago from the village of Alamo, or Carmen, nine leagues from Casas Grandes, Chihuahua. "We have been beaten constantly and maltreated in every way you can think of," said one of the unfortunate women, her eyes filling with tears. "We have had to keep up, whether we were tired or not; an old woman who was captured with us, named Maria Caballero, was threatened with death because she fell a little behind; but Geronimo, the chief, let her go free, and she started back to Chihuahua. We have not had anything but meat on the way; for three days we have not had anything at all from the Indians; all our food has been gathered from one of your old camps, where we picked up some meat and bread thrown away by your people. We first ran in upon one of your deserted camps four days ago." Such was the disconnected tale poured out in a paroxysmal series of ejaculations. "But don't let's have any more talk; come up and have something to eat." "But won't those men beat us?"—pointing to the scouts. "No, I guess not—come along." It brought tears to the eyes of our stoutest soldiers to look upon this line of unfortunates—of the same sex as our mothers, wives, sisters, and daughters. The one who had acted as spokeswoman up to this time continued, "It seems as if Heaven has opened today, when we come here to the camp of friends. It must have been our Blessed Lady, the Most Holy Mary, Virgin of Soledad, who has taken pity on us." "Truly, before you close your eyes tonight, you ought to give thanks to Heaven for this unexpected blessing." What was my astonishment upon making this innocent remark to hear myself called to account by Archie McIntosh, one of General Crook's principal scouts—a very good man in his way but, like Severiano, who stood alongside him, spoiled by too much consideration and attention.

"You'll interfere with General Crook's plans if you talk with those women and give them an idea they are released. He's trying to make a point about that boy." "I want to second all of General Crook's plans," I said, "but God damn any plans which will hinder us from feeding women who have not had anything in their stomachs for three days. I don't want to receive a lecture from you, anyhow, so get out."

The women ate nervously and ravenously but were carefully guarded by Felipe, who remonstrated with them and admonished against want of caution in overloading their enfeebled stomachs. They accepted his advice and partook only sparingly of the food spread before them by Hale.

These were the fragments of our dinner, increased by a can of peaches and one of jam brought out from the secret compartments of the mess kit. The suddenness of the change from degradation and misery to comparative comfort and superlative respectability was too much for the captives, who were almost overcome by the transition.

Besides these six people, the five grown ones being, as they stated when they had recovered from their first fright, wives of Mexican soldiers, this day has not seen any additions of note to our stock of Chiricahua captives. (The little baby became sick.)

As the evening drew nigh, clouds gathered above and around us, rain sprinkled the ground slightly, but there was no storm. Five Apache squaws and two bucks came in with four sorry-looking plugs. The sky became so threatening that a rope was run from tree to tree, ground smoothed off, canvas from the pack train stretched as a tent by Frank Monarch, and blankets made down for a couch for the Mexican captives. So far as our means would allow, they were cared for tenderly. Water was brought in basins, soap and towels given them for their first toilet in a fortnight. They opened themselves up in a very little while and assumed to some extent the appearance of human beings. The scared look had not yet left their eyes, and the spokeswoman begged me not to let them be taken away by the Chiricahuas to be killed. I promised that no harm should befall them and that all of us would protect them. My words were put to the test. An insolent Chiricahua buck swaggered up to the trembling wretches and ordered them to go down to where his people were camped. I stepped forward, bade the women sit just as they were until General Crook returned, and told the red-skinned bastard to mind his own business. He hemmed and hawed, uncertain what to do, and then went off to where McIntosh was reclining under a tree. I saw at a glance that McIntosh had put him up to the whole business; the Indian, however, came back. I told the squaws to remain where they were until they saw the Nantan-cha.

The fall of the sun was the moment chosen by the Sierra Blancas for a grand dance. The drums used are the ordinary iron camp kettles, covered tightly with a piece of manta or bagging, soaked; inside the kettle is left a very little water. The drumstick is of willow sapling, curved into a hoop at one extremity.

My watch recorded the beats at one hundred to the minute; the sound is the dull, solemn thump which scared Cortez and his followers during "La Noche Triste." No Caucasian would refer to it as music; nonetheless, it has a fascination all its own, comparable to the bewildering whir-r-r-r of a snake's rattle. And so the song chanted to the measure of the drumming had about it a savage harmony that held listeners spellbound. When the dance began, a ring was formed of thirty-six Sierra Blanca and Chiricahua Apaches, six being squaws and eight children; two other squaws, gray-headed and bent with age, but warming up under the music until they became as lively as crickets, danced in the center. Around them pranced the two naked boys, not over two years old. The figure was the one, so often described in my journal of past years, of moving in the circle from right to left, the four persons inside the ring keeping up an independent movement.

This turned out to be the overture merely of the main dance, in which, when the moon had sailed over the shades of the forest, fully two hundred Indians of both sexes must have engaged. The dance was for the purpose of stealing cartridges from our scouts; but in this, the Chiricahuas were disappointed.

The Mexican captives were today exercised over the probability of being remanded to the tender mercies of the savages. Washington, the chief, claiming them as his property, made several efforts to frighten them into going to his wickiup, but his efforts were foiled by the vigilance of our packers, who quietly determined to kill the Chiricahua the moment he laid a hand upon one of the women. General Crook, coming back from [a] bird-shooting walk along the camp lines, ordered that the women and child be kept at headquarters. For this misunderstanding none to blame but McIntosh, himself a half-breed, who to ingratiate himself with the Chiricahuas has, by using the commanding general's name, made concessions and promises enough to satisfy them that we are in fear of them. The Tonto Apaches and most of those from the San Carlos have a dignified aversion for the Chiricahuas, and neither make nor receive advances; the Sierra Blanca band is outwardly more friendly.

Before turning in, I went to the shelter arranged for the Mexican women; they had as yet no thought of retiring but, as one said with pious simplicity, were sitting up, talking over their miraculous escape and giving thanks to Almighty God, the Blessed Virgin, all the Saints, and the most Holy Sacrament. Felipe was present, questioning them upon all they had observed during their detention among the Chiricahuas. The replies were straightforward and circumstantial, so far as the observation of the women went. The Apaches had been raiding and killing people in Chihuahua for months without cessation. On the present raid, three hundred head of cattle had been driven away from the Mexicans and hidden in the gorges of the range in which we now are.

The Chiricahuas are almost destitute of ammunition. The women insist that they have not lately killed a man by a bullet; they have laid in wait, alongside the trails, watching through field glasses for all wagons and pack trains, as well as for pedestrians.

When they have made an onslaught, they have rarely failed to capture the panic-stricken men or women. Men they have stripped of clothing and then brutally murdered, slashing them with lances or crushing them to a jelly with heavy rocks and stones, the hapless women in their hands being in each case compelled to witness the massacre. One man was taken, his arms tightly bound behind his back, before Geronimo, who cross-examined the trembling prisoner upon the prospective movements of the Mexican soldiery. Of all these, the poor man protested that he knew nothing; he could say only that fifteen men in one detachment stationed in a small village had left it to rejoin the main body.

Geronimo, irritated at his failure to elicit information, called out to his men, "Kill him!" In the phraseology of the women, they rushed upon him "lo mismo como lobos" (like so many wolves). They dragged him over the ground, beating him, stamping upon him with their feet, mashing him with rocks, and gashing him with knives and lances.

Another man had his privates smashed between two flat rocks, and when he writhed in agony, lances were darted through his body. But why recapitulate? The poor women, with arms bound behind them and all tied together, were the fear-frozen eyewitnesses of this holocaust of Christian blood.

Then Geronimo bade one of the women write a letter to the commanding officer of the Mexican forces and leave it on the trail where it could be found by any party in pursuit. In this he said that he had two hundred warriors and could make bitter war, but was tired and wanted to make peace and remain at peace for a long while. He would keep the women as hostages, to be exchanged for the squaws and children of his tribe captured during the past year. He promised that if no expeditions were sent against him, to go in to Casas Grandes for a talk in fifteen days from date of note. The date fixed, however, was May 23, 1883, so his promise was not observed.

The women say that there are two other captives among the Chiricahuas; one a boy named Nicolas, whose origin I have suspected, and the other a half-witted one of sixteen or eighteen years, who wanders around camp in a dazed, stupid manner. They are too well under the surveillance and power of their tyrants to try to run away. The women knew nothing of Charlie McComas. Speaking of their own treatment, they said that when they slipped and fell down, they had to crawl on all fours, the men thumping them and yelling, "Anda mula!" (Get along, she-mule). Several of their captors spoke Spanish with some degree of fluency.

The dances of the Apaches did not end before three on the morning of [May 23].

May 23, 1883, Wednesday. Sam Bowman has collected a dozen or more shards of pottery, colored and incised, or both, from the ancient ruins of this camp.

Rations have been issued this morning to 199 Indians of both sexes and all ages; the squaws say that yesterday there were 220 in camp.

Two bucks, mounted and armed, rode into camp: one of them, Nana, the chief so often reported killed. In the good old days, the seeing alone of this brute would have been evidence enough to cause him to be thrown to the lions.

The squaws are prattling and laughing over the "stick" game of Tzet-tish, and our scouts are not behind in staking their money upon the result. The women wager all personal decorations, necklaces of beads, and other trinkets, in which one generally notices a strange blending of Indian medicine and the medals of the Catholic Church, the small picture of Mexican saints encased in cheap frames, or the crosses of wood and metal.

Nana had an interview with General Crook. This old chief has a very strong face—one showing he is powerful, for good or evil. He has been reported killed no less than a dozen times in the past three years but seems to be able to get around at a lively gait yet. He is still prominent and influential among the Chiricahuas, although the principal chief seems now to be Looking Glass, a quite youthful man. Looking among the Chiricahuas for wounds, old or recent, to show to what extent our bullets have injured them, I find that the old chief Nana himself is a cripple in one foot; one of the young chiefs has a fresh cicatrix of a dreadful thigh wound at the knee joint; the two patients treated by the doctor (Andrews) for broken arm and bruised knee indubitably fell upon rocks while running from our men in the late skirmish; and so on. The camp is in the enjoyment of the best health, excepting two of the scouts, seriously ill with pneumonia. Fifteen Indians, all told, formed the band of Nana. "Another delightful musical reunion" was given by the Chiricahuas; the last squawk was belched forth at dawn, along with the closing strains of the medicine song intoned by the Tontos on behalf of one of their number sick with pneumonia. With this cacophony, Aurora opened the portals of day.[27]

Where Is Crook?[1]

U.S. GRANT, et al.

El Paso *Times*, May 20, 1883

Your correspondent had an interview at length with General Raguero[2] today. He says that there was no express understanding as to General Crook's crossing the Mexican frontier, but he was simply told that he might follow the Indians over into Sonora so far as interference from the state was concerned. Under the treaty it was not possible to give General Crook permission to make a campaign in Old Mexico. Among the people of Sonora and Chihuahua there was no objection whatever to Crook's coming over, but it was of doubtful legality.

The country into which Crook has attempted to penetrate is virtually inaccessible, and no courier or scout could possibly reach him. No attempt to do so would be safe without an escort of at least one hundred men. This, he thinks, is the real reason of Crook's silence. Crook told him (Raguero) that he would stay out for three months, and this length of time, he thinks, in view of all the circumstances, is not unnecessarily long. He believes that Crook has not sent back couriers owing to the danger anyone away from the main body would run. The general has himself been for two months on a campaign without being able to communicate his whereabouts to anyone. He thinks it was most unwise to have trusted so much to Apache scouts. He (Raguero) would not trust himself with them under any circumstances. Still, as Crook has outside them close on one hundred men, he would not be likely to be taken in except by surprise. The country, unfortunately, affords only too many chances for this, and as a measure of precaution the general ordered a column of 250 men under command of Lieutenant Colonel Emilio Gallardo to advance from Casas Grandes in the Sierra Madre mountains to General Crook's support. This column started on the fourteenth. No one, the general says, except those who have made a campaign in the Sierras can form an idea of the difficulties and danger it presents and of the ease with which the Indians can conceal themselves from the most experienced scouts. He has frequently, on a scout, passed within a few yards of a large Indian camp without being aware of a single Indian being anywhere nearer than fifty to one hundred miles.

The band of Chatto,[3] "Flat Nose," which numbered sixty men, did not enter old Mexico until the ninth, according to latest information at headquarters. The band came into the country through the Sierra de Fierro, or Iron Mountains, situated east of the line of the Mexican Central Railroad. They crossed the railroad line about fifteen miles this side of Ojo Caliente, going in a westerly direction. At Magueys, in the Iron Mountains, they killed a Mexican, and at Ojitos, in the foothills of the Sierra del Nido, some thirty miles northwesterly from Gallegos station, on the Mexican Central Railroad, they killed another. Both of these places are so insignificant as to be unnoticed on even the larger maps. A little south of the San Buenaventura, in the same part of the mountains, two Mexican herders were killed. All the Indians were on foot and seemed to be heading for the very heart of the Sierras. This is the tribe that had Charlie McComas, but the dispatch to the general says that the boy is no longer with them, and it is supposed that he was killed when unable to keep up with the brutal march of the savages. The Indians of Chatto's band sent runners on ahead, who pretended that the Indians following them were friendly, and in this way managed to take in the poor Mexican freighters and herders, who were slain without being able to raise a hand. Troops from the nearest post, numbering 110 rank and file, started at once but were twenty-four hours behind the Indians. This force, with that already in the Sierras under Gallardo, makes 310 Mexican soldiers in active pursuit of the hostiles, who on the opposite slopes of the mountains are faced by General Crook's command. The great difficulty in fighting the Indians, General Raguero says, is that their intimate knowledge of the mountains gives them a vast advantage by enabling them to double on their pursuers. On the plains the troops can keep well up with them, but once they get into the mountains they almost always lose them. General Raguero says the largest number of hostiles in the field does not exceed three hundred. They are composed of Juh's band, Loco's, and Chatto's. Juh's band is the smallest and numbers only thirty men. It belongs to Mexico, and all the rest belong to the United States and have come off reservations. Captured squaws put the number of bucks as low as two hundred, but as there are several small bands roaming through the mountains, three hundred is nearer the truth. So certain is he that this number is not underestimated that he has his columns composed only of two hundred men each. The Mexican troops stationed in Chihuahua and Sonora numbered eight hundred in all, but should any disaster have happened, there are thirteen hundred additional troops ready to move at the shortest notice. The general spoke strongly against the policy of the United States in keeping at the public expense hordes of Indians on reservations situated in the immediate neighborhood of a friendly power, a perpetual danger not only to the frontiersmen of the United States, but peaceable citizens of Sonora and Chihuahua. General Crook had told him of the tag system, and it had rather amused him, as there was not the slightest way of preventing an Indian from leaving or punishing him properly when he came back. The Mexican military authorities and the citizens of Sonora and Chihuahua are bitterly and intensely opposed to the reservation system of the United States, which has barely left a frontier home without a lost one.

Chicago *Times*, May 24, 1883

Major General John M. Schofield, commander of the army of the Division of the Pacific, stopped in the city yesterday on his way to California, going at once to the residence of his father, Reverend Joseph Schofield, at No. 582 West Adams Street. A reporter for the *Times* called upon General Schofield yesterday for information regarding the command of his subordinate, General Crook, and the probable result of the Mexican expedition against the hostile Apaches. The general was found in comfortable pose, enjoying an after-dinner cigar and engaged in a pleasant visit with members of the family and a few friends.

When asked if he thought the expedition across the Mexican border was liable to terminate disastrously for the troops, with a smile of confidence he replied: "I think Crook understood the situation perfectly before he made the venture, and I do not think he would imperil the lives of his men in what promised to be a hopeless undertaking."

"Have you heard from him lately?"

"I have received no communication from him for about one month, but I attach no unpleasant significance to this. You see, he is in a wild, desolate region, and the only means of communication with the outside world is by messengers. He needs every one of his men, and unless absolutely necessary, he would not weaken his force by lessening them for that purpose. When he starts back we will hear from him, but lack of news now is evidence that he is going ahead."

"How many men did he take with him on this expedition?"

"In Regular troops he had Captain Chaffee's company, numbering about fifty men. Besides these, he had about two hundred Indian scouts. He might have taken five times as many soldiers, but he thought that number would be adequate for the purpose, and besides, it would not be easy to carry supplies for a larger army."

"How long do you think it will be before his return?"

"General Crook wrote to me that he expected to be gone about two months, and as one month has already been occupied by the expedition, I confidently expect to hear of his return within four weeks. He knows just what he has to contend against and can probably estimate the numerical strength of his enemy to within ten rifles. I do not think he has gone blindly into the thing and believe he will come out all right."

"What do you think of the prospect of further trouble with the Indians after the Apaches are conquered?"

"There is now no indication of any of the reservation tribes breaking out;

all seem to be well contented and peaceable. The Apaches are really the only race that has never been subdued. The Mexicans recently killed all their women and children,[4] and they are desperate and will fight to the bitter end. If the troops are surprised or entrapped, they can hope for no mercy, but all will be killed. But General Crook's scouts are so familiar with the country that there is hardly a possibility of being taken at a disadvantage."

———————

Tucson *Arizona Citizen*, May 25, 1883

CHICAGO, May 25—In an interview with General Grant the question was asked, "Do you regard Crook's failure to make his whereabouts known as an indication that he is in danger?"

General Grant replied: "No; General Crook is an able officer and Indian fighter. I have every confidence in him; he has not entered into this engagement with the Apaches without considering the obstacles that are sure to spring up before him. His progress must necessarily be slow, and in the mountainous region of Mexico, the Indians, accustomed to the country, may temporarily entrench themselves, but that is to be expected. That Crook will dislodge and capture them there is no reason to doubt."

Question—"You have no idea he has been drawn into a situation where the Apaches could massacre him?"

Answer—"I do not believe he has met any such fate. My knowledge of General Crook's character, his support being with him—he has Indian scouts of great experience and some cavalry at his hand—forbids me entertaining a thought that Crook has met with a defeat. At any rate, it will take official information to convince me he is not gaining advantage of the hostile Apaches and that he will not drive them to the wall."

———————

Omaha *Herald*, May 27, 1883

General O. O. Howard, commandant of the Department of the Platte, accompanied by Lieutenant Guy Howard, his son and aide-de-camp, is at the Merchants', en route to Omaha. The general is on his way home from Fort McKinney, where he has been looking up the condition of affairs in the country tributary to that post. Two companies of the Ninth Infantry have been transferred to Fort Russell, near Cheyenne, to give place to two companies of the Fifth Cavalry, as that arm of the service is more effective at that point than infantry. There are now three companies of cavalry and one of infantry at McKinney. The general expressed himself as pleased with the development of the country where he followed the Nez Perce on that long and wearisome march over rugged mountains, through forbidding canyons, and over trackless plains. The great civilizer has opened up the wild wastes to settlement and cultivation.

"Have you any fears as to General Crook's safety at present?"

"No. I think—as he would think of me if I was in his place and he in mine—that he will act judiciously. I can't tell as to the probabilities of success, as I don't know the number of Indians with whom he will have to contend. I should not suppose they numbered more than a couple of hundred, but as I said, I am without information on that subject. The band is desperate. They have lost all, or nearly all, their women and children, and in my judgment none will ever be taken alive. The Apaches are said to run away when attacked. So they do; it is their method of fighting, but they are the most dangerous antagonists in the world, so far as ambush is concerned. You may ride right through their country and never see head nor hand, so perfectly do they conceal themselves, and you can ride right into an ambush when you least expect. The first indication you are likely to have is the ping of a rifle bullet."

"How about Crook's scouts?"

"The Apache scouts are excellent for a time. So long as you keep them moving, so long as you give them active work, something to interest and excite them, they are excellent. They cannot stand inaction, however, and are very apt to get tired, want to go back and, if permission to do so is refused, to desert and take the back trail."

A Diary of the Sierra Madre Campaign

WILLIAM W. FORSYTH[1]

Tucson *Daily Arizona Star*, June 17, 1883

May 1—The command left San Bernardino ranch. It consisted of General Crook and escort as follows: Captain J. G. Bourke, Lieutenant W. Fieberger, Captain F. Crawford, [Captain] A. R. Chaffee, Lieutenant Frank West, Lieutenant W. Forsythe, Lieutenant C. H. Gatewood, Lieutenant W. O. Mackay, and Surgeon G. E. Andrews. All of the above officers, with the exception of Mackay and Fieberger, the former of the Third Cavalry and the latter being the chief engineer officer of the Department of Arizona, are attached to the Sixth Cavalry, mostly to Troop I. Accompanying them were 193 Indian scouts and about 40 white men employed as packers, etc. The first day the command marched eighteen miles in a southerly direction, camping at night on Elias Creek. Nothing occurred on the march worth special mention. The entire command felt that they were going on a perilous expedition, but they had faith in their commander.

May 2—Broke camp and marched twenty miles, camping on the Bavispe River, about thirty miles east of the town of the same name. The country is beginning to grow rough. Captain Crawford and the scouts are in the lead.

May 3—Marched twenty miles, following the course of the Bavispe River, and again camped near it. No signs of the Indians as yet.

May 4—Made about the same distance and camped at night about five miles from town, on the Bavispe. Still nothing to indicate the presence of the hostiles.

May 5—Marched through the towns of Bavispe and Bacerac, where we were greeted by the inhabitants with every demonstration of welcome. Accomplished about twenty-five miles this day. Here it was determined to change the course, and the following morning the command struck out due east for the heart of the Sierra Madres, where "Peaches" informed Crook that the main body of the hostiles are to be found.

May 7—Camped during the day and made a night ride of ten miles over a very rough trail. The country is getting rougher and apparently more inaccessible as we penetrate the Sierras.

May 8—Continued to march east about fifteen miles over a trail so rough that the entire command, including General Crook, were obliged to dismount and proceed on foot. Camped at night on a plateau on a mountain crest, seven thousand feet above the sea level. The country is grand and gloomy, the whole face of nature being cut by immense gorges and mountains apparently piled one on top of the other.

May 9—Broke camp at 7:00 A.M. and continued to march on a general course east and made camp at night on a small tributary of the Bavispe River. Here it was discovered that the Indians had set fire to the grass, burning it off to such an extent as to leave no feed for the animals, and a forced march of ten miles was necessary before reaching feed and water. Twelve hours were taken up in making this ten miles and causing the loss of five pack animals, which, missing their footing, were hurled down hundreds of feet into the chasms below.

May 10—The country is almost impassable and looks as if the passage of men had been barred by the hand of the Almighty. But nine miles were made during an entire day's march of about ten hours.

May 11—Captain Crawford, Lieutenants Gatewood and Mackay took 150 scouts and provision for a foot scout of three days, Peaches having informed General Crook that the command was nearing the stronghold of the hostiles. Late the same day a scout from Crawford returned with a notice to bring the entire command about fifteen miles further up, where a better camp could be found on a tributary of the Bavispe River.

May 12—Made for the new camp over a rocky and precipitous country.

May 13—Remained in camp to take a needed rest. Crawford, with the tireless scouts, and himself as tireless, is still ahead.

May 14—Received another message from a scout from Crawford to move nearer to his camp with supplies; that he had found fresh Indian signs and would be able to surround the stronghold in about three days. He is satisfied that the hostiles do not know of Crook's presence in the Sierra Madres.

May 15—The command had marched about six miles when again they were stopped by a scouts from Crawford with the following dispatch: "15th— 1:10 P.M.—Indian scouts ran upon one buck and ten squaws and killed them before I intended to attack the camp, but I must now, Crawford." Upon receipt of this news the command pushed rapidly on, not making camp until after nightfall.

May 16—Crawford came into our camp on the evening of this day with five Indian prisoners, twenty-eight ponies, four Winchester rifles, two revolvers, and a quantity of other plunder. He reported a fight with the Indians, resulting in the killing of four bucks and six squaws and the wounding of some others; that he had their stronghold surrounded, and it was only a matter of time when the Indians must surrender.

May 17 to 22—The time was occupied in maneuvering about the stronghold and selecting the best plan of attack, if it became necessary. During this time General Crook sent one of the captured squaws to the stronghold to inform the hostiles that he would give them three days to surrender, and if they did not do it in that time he would kill them all.

May 23—The squaw returned and informed Crook that Loco wanted to talk to him, and the two had an interview. Loco said he wanted to surrender and go back to San Carlos and would do so if "Gray Fox" would promise him that he and his people should not be hurt. Crook told him that he would make no promise; that he must surrender unconditionally, telling him at the same time that he would kill the last one of his tribe if he did not bring them. Loco returned and the same evening came back with Geronimo, Nana, Bonito, Chatto, a chief known as a brother to Navajo Bill, and 204 others, mostly women and children.

May 24—Five Mexican women and ten Mexican children came into camp, nearly starved. They said they had been captured by the Indians about fifteen days previously in Chihuahua and were with them at the time of the first fight; that at that time the Indians whom they were with had decamped, leaving them, and they had subsisted since on garbage picked up about the deserted campfires. While with the Indians they had been subject to all manner of drudgery and abuse; had been beaten and obliged to submit to the hostile lusts of their captors. They were overjoyed at their release from a fate worse than death and invoked all manner of blessings on the heads of their deliverers.

From the twenty-fourth until the twenty-ninth Crook remained in camp to give the other Indians who desired a chance to come in and give themselves up. Quite a number took advantage of it and came into the camp by twos and threes. On the twenty-eighth a grand round up was made and the Indians counted. They numbered 123 bucks and 251 women and children, a grand total of 374.

May 29—The day was entirely devoted to rest and preparations to start on the return trip.

May 30—Broke camp and started for home, arriving at Silver Creek, Colonel Biddle's headquarters, June 10, just forty-one days after leaving there, including a stay of a few days at Elias Creek, where the first camp was made when the command started.

In the Heart of the Sierra Madre

A. FRANKLIN RANDALL

El Paso *Times*, June 20, 1883

May 14 [1883]—After thirteen days' march from the camp at San Bernardino, we strike fresh trails in the outer strongholds of the hostiles; good running water and grass in abundance. We find the old camps of the Chiricahuas; have been eating horses and mules, also burnt mescal; find used-up stock all about the stream; some left to be cached in the mountains.

May 15—Our scouts came in after an attack; Captain Crawford and Lieutenant Mackay in command. Al Sieber, chief of scouts, and Mickey Free, interpreter, went along. Force makes attack on the camps of Bonito and Geronimo and takes twenty-five prisoners. They return at sunset with prisoners and plunder, including horses and mules to the number of one hundred.

May 16—Indian scouts looking over the plunder. An album found, with pictures of the McComas family; gold and silver watches, stuffs, wearing apparel of all kinds, and silver, gold, and greenbacks amounting to two thousand dollars. A squaw prisoner [is] sent out to her people and told to say that if they wanted to surrender they could do so; if not, they would be treated as hostiles and hunted down.

May 17—On leaving camp in the heart of the mountains, we march to the scene of battle. As we ascend a large mountainside a signal fire meets our eyes. By order of General Crook we answer and proceed to camp. Then we signal where the general can be found, and soon we see six squaws running over the mountainside one by one. They talk with General Crook. We lay in camp and see the hungry eat, after months of hardships. The squaws are sent in by Chihuahua, who is the only chief in camp; he wishes to come in tomorrow and is sent a captured horse.

May 18—Chihuahua, chief, comes into camp with a number of bucks and squaws and has a talk with General Crook. The McComas boy is in the mountains and was in camp when it was attacked by our scouts, but he must have gone into the mountains with some of the families in their fright. We make a photograph of the battlefield, surrounded by young bucks and squaws, who gaze with much curiosity. The women report that the Indians were much dismayed to find the country full of Apache scouts from San Carlos. They will drop all resistance.

May 19—We leave camp and march to the main stronghold, a camp agreed upon by Chihuahua, who is hunting up the scattered bands; after being in camp about two hours the families came into camp for our protection and number ninety-eight squaws, bucks, and children.

May 20—Lay at camp at the headwaters of the Bavispe River to give the Indians a chance to come to us. All day long the strangers came in. The raiding Indians appear on the mountainside overlooking the stronghold; are seen by the squaws, who give them the white-flag signal. Geronimo, Naiche, Bonito, Washington are among the band, numbering in all twenty-seven bucks. A squaw come and says the chief wishes someone to come and talk. Peaches and a medicine scout go to meet them. They are urged to go with us or they will be hunted down. They come into camp, talk with General Crook, meet him with hands shaking, are surprised to learn that Tiffany had left San Carlos, and are in favoring of returning.

May 21—Hostiles have a peace dance all night. Geronimo and chiefs go out to get the hostiles together. Five Mexican women and one child stray to the camp. They were left in the mountains by the hostiles after suffering the most brutal torture; had nothing to eat for three days. They are cared for by Captain Bourke, on Crook's staff.

May 22—Hostiles in camp number two hundred fifty, with three hundred cattle taken on their Mexican raid. Loco and Nana come in, surrendered today. Geronimo promises to bring in Charlie McComas; nothing from him as yet, but that they will bring him in. No Mexican troops seen during the campaign. We are to arrive in San Bernardino June 10 and will wait there for all straggling hostile Chiricahuas.

Apache Affairs: An Interview with General Crook[1]

GEORGE CROOK

New York *Herald*, July 9, 1883

G eneral Crook, having completed the business for which he was ordered to Washington, left for Oakland[2] tonight and, after spending a day or two there, will proceed to Omaha, where private business will detain him for a few days. From thence he will go to San Carlos Agency, in his department, to execute the agreement reached this afternoon between the War and Interior departments in regard to the future administration of discipline at that place. General Crook says the agreement is entirely satisfactory to him. It will be, in his opinion, productive of lasting peace and the development of the self-sustaining energy which the Apaches are in a preeminent measure capable of showing. The general thinks that within a very short time every Apache outside the reservation will be glad to join their comrades, and that with a wise administration of affairs at the agency nothing more need to be apprehended from the former pests of civilization in Arizona, New Mexico, and the upper part of old Mexico.

General Crook speaks very well of the ability and fidelity of Agent Wilcox at the San Carlos Agency, and will have in him an efficient promoter of the intention of the government in making this agency an exception to the regulations governing other Indian reservations. Under the agreement men, women, and children will be kept together on some part of the reservation. It will be remembered that Secretary [of the Interior] Teller said he would take the children and put them to school. General Crook says, however meritorious this plan may be in the future, at present it could not be done without arousing all the suspicion which belongs to Indian nature. The Apaches would regard such a separation not only with distrust, but it would awaken the most wicked suspicions in their minds that the government was not dealing fairly with them. Until their confidence in the goodwill of the government toward them is firmly established, it would be idle to talk about removing the children to an educational school or place to learn a trade. The treatment received by the Apaches from the Mexicans has made them more than cautious in their present position, and this, General Crook says, is one of the causes which led to the agreement made today to give him absolute authority at San Carlos, that the Indians may know that their confidence will not be betrayed.

Captain John G. Bourke, who has been on General Crook's staff for some time, will now receive a leave of absence for six months to enable him to recuperate his strength. He left for Philadelphia today.

General Crook, in an interview with your correspondent today, went over the story of the Apache troubles in Arizona and gave his reasons why the captured Chiricahuas should be left to the control of the army until the disposition to go on the warpath is entirely subdued. The general had been in consultation with the secretary of war and secretary of interior as to the manner in which this could be accomplished without involving the friends of the so-called peace policy in a wrangle with the administration.

General Crook said very plainly that he had long since ceased to have any political views in regard to the management of the Indians. His experience had been gained where he took his life in his hands, and if sentiment was to be superior to discipline, of course he did not want to be involved in bad faith with those who had already confided in his promises.

Seated in a cane chair, with the thermometer ninety-six in the shade, and not a breath of air stirring, General Crook divided the time between answering questions, opening telegrams, receiving callers, and scanning a large number of letters which had followed him from his headquarters in Arizona. In his quiet manner he went over the ground recently traversed by his command in search of the Apaches, and in the whole conversation showed little enthusiasm but a wonderful degree of observation and tact in dealing with the greatest of the Indian warriors known to history.

During the interview Colonel G. A. H. Blake, now on the retired list and well known to the army as an Indian fighter, was among the visitors, and he ventured the remark that Indian fighting forty years ago was about as dangerous as it was now. General Crook smiled and asked the colonel what he would have done had his enemy been armed with repeating rifles, and every rifle certain death to a dozen or more soldiers. The venerable colonel began to think Washington was good enough for him, and without disputing the modern view, he turned to social matters of personal interest to them both.

I said to General Crook in a moment of rest between official and unofficial claims upon his time:

Q. It is suggested that you would be a proper person to write a book on Indians and Indian warfare, and thereby not only make a valuable addition to American literature, but also render a great service to the rising generation, whose mind is filled with the wildest ideas of frontier life.

A. I think there is a great field for a work that will give Indian life and customs as they really are. I am satisfied that if this Indian question were put in its true light, it would be entirely different from anything now in print. The eastern and western ideas are too far apart. Take the Fenimore Cooper idea and the western impression—that the only good Indian is a dead Indian—and see how widely they differ. Of course, this extreme view, taken by the people of the West, is not the correct one. However, it has never occurred to me to write this subject up.

Q. Are you of opinion that it is practicable to convert the savage warrior into a peaceful and self-sustaining citizen?

A. Yes, I know it is. The Indian himself knows it is to his interest to leave the warpath and take up the peaceful pursuits of the white man. In nearly every instance, the Indian is forced upon the warpath, and we shall always have trouble with him until the government adopts a settled and fixed policy. Whatever is done toward civilizing the Indian must be done gradually, and it is not reasonable to suppose that he can be converted into a farmer in a few months.

The band of Apaches whom I punished so severely ten years ago are now located on the San Carlos reservation, and they are getting along well. They have put in good crops and will harvest enough this fall to feed themselves through the rest of the year. I told them if they behaved themselves they would not be molested and I should protect them, but if they were bad I should punish them. Indians are like children but differ in this, that they are not so harmless. They must be taught and educated, not forced. Because I have been fighting the Indians, there seems to be an impression among many that they dislike me. There never was a greater mistake made, and I believe if the question of my departure from Arizona was put to a vote, every man, woman, and child would vote against it.

In this connection I will mention that just before we started on this last trip they protested against my going. They feel that they are protected when I am present and do not like me to take any risks, fearing that if anything should happen to me my successor would not look after their welfare as I do. I do not mention this through egotism, but rather as an illustration of the fact that if the Indian is protected in his rights he is appreciative and docile. During the trip into Mexico the Indian scouts protested against my going out of camp and constantly evinced great anxiety lest harm should befall me. In fact, they were not only faithful to myself, but also to the very object of the expedition.

Q. And you had no fears of your Indian scouts turning against you.

A. I never had the slightest doubt as to the faithfulness of those Indians. I knew many of them personally, but that would have made no difference if they were not heart and soul with us in the undertaking. Upon this expedition they left their families back upon the reservations, who became, as it were, hostages for their good conduct; but I have often been out with Indian scouts when I really had no hold upon them except the confidence which they had in me.

Q. But your scouts on this occasion were part of the same band that you were pursuing, where they not?

A. Yes, but they were as anxious to bring in the remainder of their band as we were, because they had to bear the responsibility for what their pillaging brothers did when they were innocent. They knew they could have no peace

Indian scouts on the trail. OUTING MAGAZINE, OCTOBER 1886.

and quiet on the reservation so long as these other Indians were depredating, and they wanted them where they could control them.

After the raiding of last March a company was formed in Tombstone, and it marched to the reservation for the purpose of attacking that portion of the band which was living in peace, holding them responsible for the acts of the others. But those San Carlos Apaches had no more to do with the matter than I had. Now the Indian problem has reached a point where the Indians understand thoroughly the situation. They know that if they go to war with the whites, while they may kill a great many more of us than we will of them, eventually it will result in their being wiped out. They wanted to be located where they will have a future home. Now that is the feeling of all these Indians, and when they go on the warpath they are compelled to, or starve.

Q. Cannot they support themselves on the reservations?

A. No, sir. Now here the Indians claimed all of Arizona, and had all that territory from which to gather their subsistence. Our government says you have too much country, and we will only allow you a certain part of it. Now the country given the Indian may not contain sufficient products to feed him, and if he cannot feed there, he must depredate. In cases like this, where the government does not feed him, the Indian must go on the warpath or starve. This should be corrected, and I will say here that some of the papers speak of my making an individual arrangement, and not a government one, in treating with the Indians. The fact is the Indians do not understand the government. They have a confused idea of what it is, at best. The government sends out an agent to treat with them, and he informs them that he is sent by the government. When the Indians are bad he is afraid of them, and when they are good he steals from them. As I said before, I tell them that I am there to look after them, and when they are good I will protect them. Now what idea do you think they can have of the government? And so it is that an individual confidence is the only means of controlling them.

Q. How many Indians were there on the San Carlos reservation?

A. When I put them there ten years ago they numbered about six thousand, but they are divided up, and there are not quite that many now; they can nearly take care of themselves and if kept up another year will need little or no assistance from the government.

Q. What is the direct cause of your late campaign against the Apaches into Mexico?

A. In the month of March [1883] those Apaches whom we now hold as prisoners made raids through Arizona, killing citizens, depredating, and committing all kinds of outrages to such an extent that the entire country was aroused, and the people [were] so incensed that it was absolutely necessary that something should be done.

After they had spread terror through the country and had moved further south, I had information that they were coming back to renew their raids, and of course there was only one way to stop that, and that was to go down and meet them in their strongholds, because it is impossible to catch a raiding party of Indians while they are on the rampage. I was satisfied they could not be brought into the reservation unless we punished them, and I felt that if we could not locate them from this side, it would be necessary to extend the expedition into Mexico.

When I found they had gone so far into Mexico, I went to Sonora for the purpose of having an understanding with the Mexican authorities, and did it upon my own responsibility. We found the people kindly disposed, and they assured us that they would do everything in their power to assist us.

To supply my expedition I got all the pack mules I could raise in that country—about 350. I obtained two months' rations to guard against any possible contingency, for I did not want to stop at a critical moment for want of food. I knew about what force the hostiles had, and I kept my own force down to the minimum because I did not wish to take along a larger number than I could transport rations for during the time I expected to be out. All our supplies were transported on these pack mules. My force, including fifty packers, whose duty it was to look after the mules, was about three hundred. This force hardly equaled the Apaches, because fifty of my men, the packers, were noncombatants and not available. The hostiles had 120 warriors, and a lot of boys could fight in a tight place.

Q. How was your force divided with respect to Indian scouts and soldiers?

A. I had forty-two soldiers, 193 Indians, and fifty packers, but the latter I do not include in my fighting force.

Q. What is the distance from the border to the rendezvous of the Apaches in the Sierra Madre Mountains?

A. About two hundred miles, and one hundred miles from the railroad to the border.

Q. And it required how much time to march to the place where you discovered the Apaches?

A. We started from the border on May 1 and arrived on the fifteenth of that month.

Q. What method of strategy did you adopt in pursuing the savages?

A. Of course, my plan of fighting Indians is first to locate them. When located we make forced marches and attack them. You cannot surprise them with a large command, particularly in a mountainous region, where they occupy positions overlooking many miles of territory. When we got to within twenty or thirty miles of where they were located, I sent Captain Crawford in advance with the Indian scouts, who carried with them three days' rations and blankets, which were strapped to their backs, in order that they might more readily climb precipices and canyons, the mules and soldiers remaining in the rear. It was a case of playing Indian on Mr. Indian.

Q. By what means did you locate the hostiles?

A. Our Apache scouts told us where they were. Peaches, our leading scout, said they were in there somewhere.

Q. Had the Mexicans rendered you any assistance up to this time?

A. No, we had no assistance from them whatever. Come to think of it, though, the Mexicans sent us two guides several days before we reached the point where we stopped, to show us where the Mexicans had a fight with them eleven days before, but we told them it was no use for them to come, as we were sure we could find the position of the Apaches. The character of the country is fearfully rough and cut up, with canyons and crevices crossing each other at right angles and forming knobs and ridges that are almost impossible for a white man to ascend.

It was upon a series of these peaks, within a circuit of ten miles, that the Apaches were camped. The ascent to some of the knobs was almost perpendicular, but the Apaches are wonderfully active and muscular, and can scale these walls with amazing alacrity. They are great runners and climbers. By sending Captain Crawford ahead with the Apache scouts, we surprised the hostiles, whereas if we had taken along the white command they would have discovered us.

There is a great difference between fighting Indians and fighting white men. The savages always get in a position where they will be shielded and only fight when they want to, and our soldiers are forced to fight whether they want to or not, and these scouts knew better how to surprise them than our soldiers, for they are intelligent warriors and take advantage of every little circumstance.

Every Indian is a general and knows exactly what to do under any circumstances. He knows which is the best position for him and how to take the enemy at a disadvantage. He is always, under all conditions, perfectly self-possessed, and there is an individuality about him at all times. The soldier is mechanical and part of a great machine, and thereby loses his individuality. If there is a weak spot in our line and a lot of Indian boys are in front of us, they will drop on that point and make as much out of it as a Caesar, Napoleon, or Hannibal could do, for they will do exactly right, and that is all the best general in the world could do.

The Apaches are the shrewdest and best fighters in the world. They will strip themselves and ascend a precipice like a cat, and they will do all this after making a day's march. During this expedition they danced through one night, to the discomfort of our soldiers, who were trying to sleep, marched all next day, and climbed places where a coyote would have trouble in getting. I have known them to run suddenly on a quail and kill it with a stone, and run down a wounded antelope. They are just as much smarter than any other Indian as anybody could be. They have wonderfully good eyesight, being able to follow a trail on a starlit night as well as I could in daylight.

Evidences of their prowess are visible all through that country, and they and the Mexicans have been fighting for hundreds of years, and upon every hand are to be seen the remains of Pueblo settlements which have evidently been wiped out by these Indians, and it is a tradition among the people of that section that the Apache is unconquerable. Yet they have wiped out every band of Pueblo Indians, except the Moquis and Zunis, who I am satisfied are the same class of people. I have seen these fellows ambuscade in a place as level as a floor.

There was a wagon train in 1871 going out of Arizona into California, with an escort in advance. The Indians saw them coming and ambuscaded in the road, which was perfectly level, with here and there a clump of grass. The Apaches lay upon their stomachs, threw dust over themselves, and tied grass in their hair, and were passed by the escort unnoticed. After the escort was some distance off the Indians jumped up and captured the wagons in the rear and killed the teamsters. These fellows took all the chances, whereas other Indians seek a place where they will be safe and shoot the enemy.

Peaches, our principal guide, knows that whole country, and we left everything to him. I was not afraid to trust him, and I believe I am the only man who has used these Indians against each other. I do not know how to describe the way it is done, but I have never met a case of treachery. I have taken these same Indians in a battle who were in open arms against me and have had them to turn around immediately against their own people. Peaches came in on that raiding party that killed McComas and his wife and took their little boy a prisoner. Just before the expedition started he was brought to me in irons. I took the irons off and he accompanied us and did the most valuable service, for he was the only man who knew the strongholds of the hostiles, and he led us directly into them. Peaches is a full-blooded Apache and a member of the Chiricahua band. He had two wives among the Chiricahuas. Peaches did not, of course, know the names of the mountains and, like all Indians, has no idea of distance as to miles. He computes distance by the day's travel, and that is very uncertain, so that we could not form any idea of how far down we had to go when he put it upon the basis of number of days' travel it would require to bring us to the objective point, as some days we traveled faster than on other days.

Q. What was the result of the fight, General, in killed on either side?

A. We did not lose a man, neither Indian nor soldier. We found nine dead bodies of the enemy. If they had surprised us instead of our surprising them, we would have had a hard time of it, for they would have penned us up in a country that is rough and inhospitable. The Apaches themselves cannot live on the country and can only get their subsistence by plunder. About all that grows there is a little mescal, and they prepare a very fair food from that. They hid on these peaks until nearly starved and then started forth on their raids. The raid they made in March was divided, one band being sent to Sonora to steal stock and another to Arizona to get ammunition, but they got so little from the people whom they killed that they carried out no more than they brought in. Geronimo led the party though Sonora, and Chatto headed that which went through Arizona.

Another evidence of their success in predatory warfare is the fact that about 120 bucks have paralyzed all business interests for hundreds of miles around their rendezvous and have totally depopulated that country. General Tapete, commanding the Mexican forces, says they have gone after the Apaches with civilized troops and found that it was no use, for they may just as well have hunted coyotes. He said that we had one advantage over the Mexicans in that we could use the Apaches against each other.

Q. You seem to be certain, General, that the little son of Judge McComas will be found and brought in. Is there any particular reason for your confidence?

A. The little fellow is six years old, and my reason for feeling confident of his return is this—there are two Indians, Chatto and Naiche, who lost members of their respective families when the Mexicans induced them last summer to come in and make peace; after they came in, however, the Mexicans got them drunk, killed some of them, and held others as prisoners, including these members of their families. They are very anxious to recover their families and asked me to do what I could for them. I told them I would do the best I could, but that I feared the Mexicans were so bitter against them on account of their repeated outrages that my efforts would not be successful. They asked me to do my best, and I promised them I would. I told them that the recovery of this boy would aid me more in accomplishing the recovery of their families than anything else. Chatto, whose eyes filled with tears, said solemnly that if that boy was above ground he should be brought in with the squaws who are now out.

Q. What route did you follow into the heart of the Sierra Madre?

A. We started from the San Bernardino ranch on the border and marched down the river of that name to a point near its mouth, then crossed the country until we reached the Bavispe River, which we followed until we came to the rough country. Then we worked through the mountains until we got into the country where the Indians were.

Q. What is your policy upon this Indian question?

A. I never disarm Indians under the present circumstances, because it has been my experience that in order to govern the Indians you must not allow them to think you are afraid of them. To take their guns from them while the whites about them are allowed to carry guns would have the effect to impress the Indian at once that you were afraid of him.

Another thing is that when these Indians surrendered, they only brought in lances, or indifferent arms, expecting to give them up. Where the Indians contemplate surrender they always take the precaution to hide their good weapons. Now if I had demanded these arms they brought with them they would have credited me with fear, while I would get only those weapons which they did not attach much value to. This is always the case where the attempt is made to disarm them.

Since the introduction of the breech-loading gun, the Indian problem has undergone a change. A breechloader in the hands of an Indian makes him a very formidable enemy, for every rock affords a fortification for him, and he can keep us at bay while he deals death and destruction to the pursuing party without the latter gaining anything in return. They handle the breechloader with remarkable quickness and are good marksmen.

Q. What is your impression of the Sierra Madres as compared with Colorado scenery?

A. It is extremely rough, but not as sublime as the Yellowstone country. There is no game to speak of, although there is grass, an abundance of woodland, and plenty of good water. We had to rely solely upon the supplies we carried with us. Our cook had been graduated as a teamster, and his bill of fare was very limited as to variety and extremely unpalatable with respect to manipulation. Some of our soldiers were wont to criticize him on one occasion, but he put a summary stop to all dissatisfaction by stating that if any man grumbled at his cooking he would kick a lung out of him. Our rations consisted of fat pork, beans, bread, and coffee. The scouts were supplied with rations and did their own cooking, while the officers and men messed with the packers, the ration averaging about three pounds a day to each man.

Q. Are there any hostile Apaches now at large, or have you brought them all in?

A. We have about cleaned them up, except Juh, his brother, and their immediate families, who were run out. When they find that all the others have surrendered they will come in, so that the Apache raids have been brought to an end.

An Indian Reservation under General George Crook

CHARLES P. ELLIOTT[1]

Military Affairs (Summer 1948): 91–102[2]

For the first time since the occupation of Arizona by Americans, the spring of 1884 came and passed into summer in peace. The rains fell, were soaked up by the dry soil; grass sprang up and matured; and the Apache Indians, the Yumas, Mojaves, Tontos, San Carlos, White Mountains, and most astonishing of all, the Chiricahuas remained on the San Carlos Indian reservation, contented and hard at work, taking out irrigation ditches where necessary and raising good crops of small grain. The reason for the contentment was not hard to find. General George Crook was in command of the Department of Arizona, and Captain Emmet Crawford of the Third U.S. Cavalry was in immediate command of the White Mountain reservation, with his headquarters at San Carlos, at the junction of the river of that name with the Gila River.

The peaceful condition of Arizona enable the War Department to effect the transfer of the Sixth U.S. Cavalry, which had done long, arduous, and distinguished service under General Carr, its colonel, and other of its officers, among them General Chaffee, who was then captain and whose name whose known and respected as an Indian fighter, but not as now to the world as a soldier well fitted to maintain the dignity of our country in far distant China among most trying surroundings.

The transfer of the two regiments was effected by marching and was but little of a change for either the Sixth from Arizona to New Mexico or the Fourth to take its place. The sun seemed just as hot and the dust as thick and full of alkali on one side of the imaginary boundary line as on the other, and both columns appeared, from a short distance, as moving clouds of dust, with no animate object visible.

I was ordered as second lieutenant of Troop H, Fourth Cavalry, to Fort Lowell, and soon after reaching that post was detached and ordered to report to Captain Emmet Crawford for duty as provost officer on the San Carlos reservation.

I went from Tucson by rail to Willcox, by stage to Fort Grant, where I met Captain Crawford and went with him to San Carlos via Fort Thomas by ambulance, as the government conveyances were called.

The heat and dust on the ride down the Gila can only by appreciated by those who have experienced it in midsummer, and one can fully endorse the wish expressed by an officer leaving the territory that when next he saw it he hoped the whole country would be turned into a duck pond. San Carlos itself is no paradise but requires such a ride to bring out its good points.

From the crest of the hills about opposite the mouth of the San Carlos River, one catches [a] glimpse of the agency buildings. The valley of the Gila widens out slightly, and with the flats at the mouth of the San Carlos, an open space is formed, surrounded on all sides by more or less high and rugged hills and mountains, the two rivers breaking through from the east and north and flowing out together through a mild canyon to the west.

On the left bank of the Gila were numbers of huts or brush "wickiups," the home of several bands of Mojave and Yuma Indians. On the flats between the San Carlos and Gila were the camps of the government pack trains, thoroughly equipped, constantly in use, and always ready to move at a moment's notice to any part of the reservation where trouble might threaten.

Near the pack trains were the corrals for C Troop, Third Cavalry, when at San Carlos. On the bench just above the flats and towards the west stood the school buildings, occupied as store rooms, officers' quarters, and living rooms by the commanding officer and his assistants. Still further to the west down the Gila River on the same bench stood the agency buildings, storehouse, and trader's store. Below the agency building on the flats near the river were the corrals and slaughterhouse for Indian cattle. The buildings were of adobe or sun-dried and mud-colored brick, differing not at all in color from the sun-baked plain on which they stood.

On one of the buildings with walls 18 inches thick I have seen a thermometer register 114 degrees at 2:00 P.M. The only good point that I can recall about San Carlos is its winter climate.

Opposite the agency building across the river were the Indian camps spoken of before and below, on both sides of the Gila, and above, on the San Carlos, numbers of camps were scattered.

Down the Gila and opposite the mouth of the San Pedro (on the right bank) was a considerable band, and on the San Pedro, Eskiminzin, formerly a noted outlaw, had a camp and thriving fields. On the Aravaipa were several small camps, one of them the home of Capitan Chiquito, with his six lusty young wives. And so, over the reservation wherever the ground was favorable, camps were located.

Frequent reports were received from the outlying camps, and visits were made when necessary by the commanding officer or provost officer.

In July 1884 the civilian agent of the Interior Department was still in control of issues to the Indians, and the presence of two influences, civil and military, were bound to lead to friction. The presence of the military was a very unwelcome restraint upon the agents, if, as too often happened, it was considered necessary by them to eke out an insufficient salary by small deals with mining towns outside of the reservation.

The successful handling of 5,500 Indians, the wildest ever known to us in this country, on a reservation ninety by sixty miles, rough beyond telling, with bands scattered all over it, was a task sufficiently difficult with the governing influences in perfect accord. The discord at headquarters multiplied the difficulties, but Captain Crawford had mastered them, and his watch over the agent and his employees was as strict as that over the Indians, and he allowed no interference with the police control of the reservation. He, with his officers, Lieutenant F. O. Johnson, quartermaster, T. B. Dugan, adjutant, both of the Third Cavalry, Doctor Thomas Davis, and Lieutenant Charles P. Elliott, occupied an old adobe building, formerly used by schoolteachers who had vacated at the last outbreak and had never returned.

There were no troops in sight upon my arrival, and there were, in fact, none nearer than Fort Apache, many miles away.[3]

To the north of the school buildings was a cluster of huts, where the Indian scouts with their families lived: two companies, so-called, but there was no effort at that time to make trained soldiers of them.

There was a third company called home guards, whose members were scattered among the various camps of Indians, tributary to San Carlos. These reported to the provost officer direct and were under his orders, acting for Captain Crawford.

There were about ten enlisted men at San Carlos in July 1884, acting as clerks, storekeepers, and hospital attendants. The only military organization having station there was C Troop, Third Cavalry, Captain Crawford's Troop, under Lieutenant Parker West, temporarily absent in the mountains. It was there only because Captain Crawford happened to be and was not utilized in the police control of the Indians, but was subsequently relieved, leaving only a few enlisted men for duty as indicated above.

Captain Crawford had immediate control at San Carlos of all Indians tributary to that place. Lieutenant Britton Davis was in charge of the Chiricahua Apaches near Fort Apache, and Lieutenant C. B. Gatewood, Sixth Cavalry, with Lieutenant Roach,[4] 1st Infantry, controlled the White Mountain Apaches, with headquarters at Fort Apache, all under command of Captain Crawford, who reported direct to General Crook. The latter's interest in and supervision of the reservation was keen and direct, and he knew in person all of the prominent Indians as well as many of the young men and enjoyed the perfect confidence of all, never making a promise he could not fulfill and always keeping one made, whether to help the Indians or to punish them, as the case might be. They may have been more successful Indian fighters than General Crook, but in the management of them on their reservations, he was far ahead of any officer that the army has ever produced. His experience with Indians had been continuous during his service, except during the war of 1861–1865. He had studied their nature and habits; was himself a quiet and retiring man, thoroughly familiar with nature, a great hunter, and perfectly fearless. Those Indians who did not like him respected him and trusted him and in turn gave him the full measure of trust to which their conduct entitled them. During hostilities he utilized friendly Indians against hostile ones, and in their reservations, he made them govern themselves.

On the San Carlos reservation were two distinct tribes of Indians, the Mojaves and Yumas constituting one, and the Apaches, of different appearance and language, the other. The latter was designated according to the locality formerly most frequented by them, as San Carlos, Tonto, White Mountain, and Chiricahua.

The Mojaves and Yumas had blended somewhat with the others, the result being known as Apache-Yuma and Apache-Mojave. These Indians had at different times been gathered in from all over southern Arizona within the borders of the San Carlos reservation.

In 1884 a complete census had been made, the tribes being enumerated under their head chiefs, and each camp of Indians of the same tribe under its head man. Brass tags of different shapes, with one shape for each tribe, had been provided. The band or subdivision of a tribe was designated by a letter of the alphabet, and each member of a band had his number, stamped by the provost officer on the tag of the proper shape and given to each Indian, whose name was recorded in books kept for the purpose. Each man was required to wear his tag at all times and to produce it when called upon by the proper officer. Any failure to comply with these regulations was severely punished, and in a short time the system worked to the perfection I found it on my arrival.

Any American who would attempt to burden himself or his memory with a number of Indian names would soon be hopelessly lost, but tag numbers and the records made it very simple to locate a special individual.

In addition to the home guard of scouts mentioned above, there were a limited number of secret service employees—Indians who rendered very efficient service.

One of the greatest menaces to the peace of the reservation was due to the efforts of white men to sell or trade guns, ammunition, and whiskey to the Indians, as well as to prospectors insisting on crossing the reservation line and looking for minerals on forbidden ground; many of the latter lost their lives probably without anyone being the wiser for it. The duty of arresting such trespassers was a frequent and most unpleasant task, and it was never possible to convict and punish them in the territorial courts, though the sales made by them to the Indians were often directly responsible for outbreaks resulting in the death of innocent and isolated ranchers.

At San Carlos the guardhouse, where all offenders were confined, was under the control of the provost officer with Indian scouts as guards. Offenders could be arrested and imprisoned at all times, at near or distant camps, by member of the home guard or by scouts sent specially for that purpose, but before being confined were, if possible, examined by the provost officer to see that no flagrant injustice was done before a thorough trial could be had. If witnesses were convenient, the commanding officer or provost officer, if present, would hear the case and award the punishment; if not, Friday was recognized as the day for hearing all cases, civil was well as criminal, and then all parties and witnesses, willing and unwilling, gathered before the officer, who faithfully attempted to sift out the facts and administer justice. Two interpreters were necessary to convert from Apache to English. First, Antonio Diaz, a Mexican (captive for years among the Indians), translated from Apache to Spanish, and Jose Maria Montoya from Spanish to English. If the case required a Mojave or Yuma witness, then a third to interpret from Yuma to Apache was necessary. The use as interpreters of young Indians, educated at the Indian schools in the East, proved most unsatisfactory.

There was a zealous effort on the part of all officers to assist the Indians in all possible ways and to aid them in making progress in agricultural pursuits.

The younger officers selected sites and laid out irrigating ditches, showing the best places for fields, superintending the digging of the ditches and regulating the distribution of water. The result of their efforts was most gratifying and was evidenced by the raising of some two million pounds of small grain in one season, a large part of which was bought by the government at good prices. The effort was also to uplift the Indians in their domestic life and to discourage the custom of having more than one wife, six being the greatest number known. A very thrifty old chief, with an eye to cultivating a good farm with labor entirely under his control, took six young wives, all good workers, and the result was so satisfactory that it was impossible to induce him to reduce his family.

The habit of beating their wives was one that gave the officers a great deal of trouble and led up to the following occurrence, which given in detail will exemplify the methods employed.

A secret service report came from an Indian camp just across the river from headquarters that a certain Mojave had given his wife a brutal beating the night before and, fearing arrest, had early in the morning taken to the hills south of the Gila River, carrying his gun. On the receipt of this report two scouts were sent to arrest him, one an old and reliable man, the other a young Mojave. They struck his trail and about noon came within sight of him near a spring. The older scout, who was a friend of the wife beater, went towards him; the younger remained on the ridge about the spring. The hail of scouts was answered in a friendly spirit, and upon the older scout joining the fugitive, both went to the spring and ate a simple lunch together, the scout telling what was wanted and the other consenting to accompany him when they were through eating. In a few moments the scout was told that if he would start the other would follow at once. He had not gone twenty feet when he was shot dead, and another shot directed at the younger Mojave above (it was his baptism of fire) sent him flying to San Carlos with news of the murder.

A party was put on the trail of the murderer, but a lone Indian in those mountains is too much even for Apache scouts, and all trace of him was lost. He held no communication with any of his people for months, and they thought him dead. Several months elapsed, when an Indian runner from the Havasupai reservation went to General Crook at Prescott and sent the description to San Carlos. He was the man wanted for murder, and the chief of scouts, Al Sieber, was sent to Prescott to bring him back to San Carlos. In due time Sieber arrived with his prisoner, who was a splendid specimen of Indian manhood, six feet tall, broad-shouldered, and in perfect physical condition, due to the life he had been leading in the mountains for so many months. There was a little excitement among the family and friends of the murdered scout, but no effort was made to try the prisoner, who was kept working under guard with other prisoners until it was decided whether he should be tried by the civil authorities or by tribal custom.

The civil authorities really had no jurisdiction of this particular case, so the trial was conducted according to the custom of his tribe.

Twelve men of his tribe were selected and under the direction of the provost officer proceeded with his trial, which was open to all.

The testimony of all witnesses was interpreted into English so that intelligent revision of the case could be made.

Deep interest was manifested by all of the Indians, and every effort was made to arrive at the true facts. The evidence was very clear, and the man in his statement gave no excuse for the deed, admitting that the murdered scout was a friend of his, but that having beaten his wife, he knew if he came back to San Carlos he would be punished for it and saw no other way out of his trouble.

The deliberation of his peers did not take long.

They concluded that having killed a good man, his friend, while in discharge of his duty, the murderer should be shot to death himself.

When this decision was imparted to the provost officer, the prisoner was wild with rage and, ironed though he was, with one bound he reached the spokesman of his tribesmen, wound one hand in his long hair, and endeavored to stab him in the throat with a piece of hard wood he had sharpened and concealed on his person. The provost officer jumped on him and pinioned him while Al Sieber caught him by the shackles, tripping him, and in falling, his hold on the other Indian was broken, the provost officer going down in the fall with the prisoner.

The excitement among the Indians was intense and spread to numbers who were at the agency drawing rations. Al Sieber and the provost officer, one on either side, hurried the prisoner to the guardhouse. Before putting him in the cell, Sieber was directed to search, lest the prisoner should have some weapon concealed there with which he could injure his guard. The provost officer stood with his hand on the prisoner's shoulder, and while Sieber was at the far end of the long cell, the Indian wheeled and grasped for the officer's throat; a push on his shoulders was just sufficient to deflect his hands so that they passed under the chin instead of around the neck; then it was a close fight with odds in favor of the Indian, who was desperate and as strong as a bull, nor was there time to talk or ask for help, but Sieber heard the scuffle, ran out, grabbed the Indian by the hair, pulled him away from the officer, swung him off his feet halfway around a circle, and knelt on his head. It was a wonderful exhibition of strength, and one that afforded no more pleasure to witness than any I have seen before or since. The prisoner's head had hardly touched the ground when Sergeant Smily of the guard had the muzzle of his gun at his ear, looked up, and said, "Shoot?" "No, no shoot," was the answer, "give me a piece of rope."

After having been bound for some time, the prisoner asked to see the provost officer, who found him quiet and resigned to his fate. He was released from his bonds, and after several days, the excitement having quieted down, he was started with a firing party toward Fort Thomas, up the river.

The sentence of his tribe was executed upon him, and his life paid for his crime.

The effect on the other Indians was most beneficial, both as regards wife beating and resisting arrest.

The relatives of the murderer made threats to revenge his execution, but no attention was paid to them, and no overt act was committed.

To revert to the brass tags in detecting individuals, I cite the following instance. A complaint came in from the Silver King Mine that Indians had been off the reservation killing deer and that several had visited the store at the mine. The provost officer was ordered to investigate. There was no evidence that the Indians had killed deer, but they had been off the reservation, trading at the store, and one of the clerks, noticing the brass tags on them, had taken, out of curiosity, the letters and numbers on a slip of paper. These were transferred to the officer's notebook. A two days' ride brought the detachment to the camp at the mouth of the San Pedro, where the officer crossed the Gila on his mule, called the band of Indians together and, walking along the line without a word, only looking at their tags, selected the men he wanted to see at San Carlos and rode off. The chief and all the band were astonished but promptly complied, and their culprits were duly punished.

Infinite patience was necessary in listening to the various complaints made by Indians at the weekly sessions. Every trouble, large and small, was gone into most minutely, and every new complainant began his talk by a complete family history, reaching back as far as he could go. It made no difference that ninety-three times out of a hundred the family history had no bearing on the case. As their responsibilities increased, the disputes multiplied, especially as regarded their grain fields, a fruitful source of discord, the differences often very difficult of adjustment, and it was never possible to satisfy both parties. In an attempt to settle a dispute of this kind, Lieutenant Mott[5] of the army, who was on duty at San Carlos after me, was murdered by the party against whom the decision was rendered. Many of the complaints were very childish, but the Indian requires about the same treatment as a child. There was no sickly sentimentality about Captain Crawford's method of handling the Indians. We allowed them to take no liberties with him, expected them to behave and do what they were told, any failure being visited by swift and sure punishment. The guardhouse was kept clean; the prisoners also kept the premises around the headquarters thoroughly in order and were kept at healthy work during the day.

The Indian has a well-developed taste for whiskey or any other strong drink that will intoxicate him. It was difficult for them to obtain whiskey, but the older ones knew how to make an intoxicant called "tiswin." Their tiswin drunks were responsible for many fights amongst themselves, but they were so secretive in making and hiding their liquor that it was only after the resultant fight that the fact of tiswin came to our knowledge. It was never my good fortune to get possession of any of this liquor, but I was told that it was made usually by the very old women from corn and was a sort of "sour mash."

In order to reap the full benefit of a tiswin drunk, the bucks fasted for three days beforehand and then had a royal time, occasionally allowing a woman or two to join in for the pleasure of beating them when they had all reached the proper stage.

The Apache Indian is as perfect a savage as this country has ever produced, and it is impossible to conceive of greater cruelty and less natural affection in any creature that walks on two legs. The fiendish cruelties committed by them when on the warpath give one a creepy feeling while among them, and when a son brings in his father's head on which a reward has been placed, not because he had trouble with him, but because he happened to know where he was in hiding and wanted the reward, it makes one doubt whether they are human.

During my duty at San Carlos, the "Kid" was one of our most trusted scouts. Afterwards he was a terror to Arizona for years.

In the spring of 1885 the Third Cavalry was relieved from duty in Arizona, and Captain Emmet Crawford was relieved from command of the San Carlos reservation and went with his regiment to Texas.

The peace that had prevailed in Arizona for nearly two years soon came to a sudden end, and it was only a few months before Captain Crawford was ordered back, at General Crook's earnest request, to command the battalion of Apache scouts put in the field in pursuit of hostile Chiricahuas. It was my good fortune to be with him for many months during his campaign in Arizona, New and Old Mexico, nor could a young man hope to serve under a better soldier in a better field of instruction. Captain Crawford was killed by Mexicans in Sonora in 1886 just as, after months of arduous service, he was, with the surrender of the Indians in sight, bringing his campaign to a successful close.

General Crook was called by the Apaches "Nan-tan Cle-pa," which has been wrongly interpreted by many as "The Gray Fox." As a matter of fact, it means "Gray Captain," from his general appearance. There was less of the fox in his character than any man I ever met.

Captain Crawford was "Nan-tan En-das-en," "The Tall Captain," and when I arrived, just as tall but much younger, the Indians were puzzled to name me until I was placed in charge of the guardhouse, when I became "Calaboose Nan-tan."

The quartermaster was "Nal-soos Nan-tan," writing, or letter, captain because he give little written slips as receipts for hay and grain. One officer was "Big Foot," another "Long Nose," a third "Billy Goat," from his imperial.

Into their own names it does not do to inquire too closely. One baby was called "White man scratched him on his back," from the marks of an officer's fingernail made on his little brown back. One very young officer was "Nan-tan Bijaji," Baby Captain.

Resolution Adopted at Meeting of Residents of Cochise County, Arizona, Regarding Outbreak of Indians From San Carlos Reservation

G. GORDON ADAM

Thomas McGill & Co., Law Printers, Washington, D.C. [c. 1885]

COCHISE COUNTY, ARIZONA,
TOMBSTONE, June 15, 1885.

At a meeting of the residents of Cochise County, Arizona, held at Tombstone, June 13, 1885, the following resolution was unanimously adopted:

Whereas, The attempt to keep the Apache Indians on the San Carlos reservation in this territory has repeatedly proved disastrous to the lives and property of the residents of this and the adjoining counties situated between that reservation and the strongholds of those Indians which are in that portion of the Sierra Madre range of mountains extending into the Republic of Mexico and has recently resulted, and still results, in the serious sacrifice of the lives of our people, and the military forces of the United States have proved powerless in preventing the outrages committed by them, or in assuring the peaceable prosecution of the industries in which our people are engaged; and

Whereas, We believe that it is the unanimous sentiment of all the residents of this territory and of all nonresidents possessed of property in it, except those who furnish arms, ammunition, and supplies to the Indians, that the Apache Indians should be removed from this territory to some region where it will be impossible for them to continue the outbreaks which result in sacrificing the lives and property of our people, prohibiting all immigration and continuously preventing the growth and prosperity of the territory; and

Whereas, We can look only to the government of the United States, by which the territory was created and is controlled, to protect us from murder and rapine:

Resolved, That we call upon that government to look upon the mutilated bodies and desolate homes of our people and to remove the Apache Indians from this territory.

After several speeches and other proceedings, the meeting referred to a committee, composed of W. H. Stilwell, E. B. Gage, L. W. Blinn, J. V. Vickers, and C. S. Abbott, the selection of some person to present this resolution to the authorities at Washington and to advocate its purpose.

WILLIAM HERRING,[1] Chairman
CHAS. D. REPPY,[2] Secretary

TOMBSTONE, June 15, 1885

G. GORDON ADAM, Esq.

DEAR SIR: At a meeting, held on this day, of the subscribers to the expense of going to Washington and presenting the resolution adopted by the residents of Cochise County at a meeting held on June 13, 1885, to the authorities at Washington, and advocating the purpose of said meeting, you were selected by a unanimous vote of the subscribers.

Yours, respectfully,
W. H. STILWELL,[3] Chairman
J. V. VICKERS,[4] Secretary

WASHINGTON, July 1, 1885

THE PRESIDENT.

SIR: As it was expected by those who adopted the foregoing resolution that it would be presented without delay, I cannot indulge in any extended comments upon the general policy of our government in relation to the Indians, but must be confined to the presentation of facts which bear directly upon the matter presented and suggest that, if they are not stated with sufficient particularity, the reports of Indian agents and other documents on file in the public offices will, it is believed, corroborate all that is stated.

The reservation, called the White Mountain Indian Reservation and generally known as the San Carlos reservation because San Carlos is the place where the agency is situated, has irregular exterior boundaries and covers an area of about six thousand square miles. It is occupied by about five thousand Indians, comprising several tribes called by different names, which are all known by the general name of Apaches.

Those Indians who discontinue their savage life and occupy an Indian reservation and afterwards leave it to indulge in their former savage pursuits are called renegades, and Geronimo, a Chiricahua chief, is the instigator of the outbreak of Indians from the San Carlos reservation which occurred about May 17, 1885, and their leader and chief.

John P. Clum was the first Indian agent at the San Carlos Agency, having in charge about eight hundred Apaches at that agency, and in August 1874 there were about eighteen hundred Apaches at Camp Apache, about one hundred miles north of San Carlos. In 1875, prior to the month of June, about fourteen hundred Mohaves, Tontos, and Yumas (Apaches) were removed from Rio Verde to the San Carlos Agency, and in June 1875 Clum was ordered to, and did, remove the eighteen hundred Apaches at Camp Apache to the San Carlos Agency.

In 1876 Pionsenay, a Chiricahua chief, had instigated an outbreak of the Indians which resulted in the murder, on April 6, 1876, of two men at Sulphur Springs; and in May 1876 Clum was ordered to, and did, remove from Apache Pass to the San Carlos Agency about 350 Chiricahuas, and Geronimo was included in this removal. On June 8, 1876, he also arrested Pionsenay and turned him over to the civil authorities, who failed to keep him under arrest. Geronimo then asked and obtained permission to leave the reservation for the sole purpose of bringing in his women and children; and immediately, at night, accompanied by from 100 to 150 other Indians, left the reservation and went to Sonora in Mexico. This band was followed by three companies of United States troops and one company of Indian scouts, without any result. After June 1876 Geronimo was considered the leader of the renegades who were committing outrages in New Mexico, Arizona, and Sonora.

In March 1877 Lieutenant Henely of Fort Bowie saw Geronimo at Polomas, on the Rio Grande, opposite to the Southern Apache Agency; and this information being communicated by telegraph through the department commander to the secretary of war, the commissioner of Indian affairs ordered Clum to take his Indian police and arrest the renegades at the Southern Apache Agency. To obey this order Clum and his police were obliged to go to Ojo Caliente, a place 150 miles north of Silver City, in New Mexico, and a distance of about 350 miles, the march occupying about three weeks. He had been informed that a military force would join him at Ojo Caliente, but on his arrival at that place he received a dispatch from the commander of that force stating that he could not join Clum in less than three days. Victorio was the chief of the Ojo Caliente Indians, who had been induced to join him and six other Chiricahua renegades, and Clum did not await the arrival of the troops but on April 21, 1877, by strategy, surrounded and captured Geronimo and his band, whom he soon afterwards was ordered to remove to San Carlos. He put Geronimo and the six other Chiricahuas in irons and carried them in wagons to San Carlos, also taking with him about 450 Ojo Caliente Indians, and arriving at that agency on May 17, 1877, he confined the seven prisoners in irons in the guardhouse and offered to turn them over to the civil authorities for trial, but they did not take them. They were kept so confined, guarded by the Indian police, till July 1, 1877, when Clum resigned his office as agent and left the agency. In August 1877 they were released from confinement, but by whose order I am not informed. The order to Clum from Washington was "to hold him [Geronimo] in confinement for murder and robbery." After his release, he remained on the reservation for four or five months, when he left it and again became a renegade for about eighteen months, when he surrendered to Captain Haskell at Camp John A. Rucker as a prisoner of war and was taken to San Carlos, where, after a brief imprisonment, he was again set free and remained on the reservation till 1881, when he again became a renegade, and his trail was followed to the Sonora line. After this, he and his band made the Sierra Madre in Mexico their base of operations and continued their usual killings and depredations to such an extent in Sonora and Arizona that in 1883 General Crook, with about forty-five soldiers and a company of Indian scouts, made a long and arduous march into that portion of those mountains in which was situated the principal stronghold of Geronimo's band, and surrounded and captured a considerable number of old men, squaws, and children, whereby Geronimo and his fighting men, usually called "bucks," were induced to surrender as prisoners of war. I have no knowledge of the exact terms of this surrender, but it will suffice to say that sometime after the date of it, Geronimo and his bucks went with some troops under the command of Lieutenant Davis to the San Carlos reservation, carrying with them some stock which they had stolen on their frequent excursions, and that on June 26, 1884, this stock was sold in pursuance of the following printed notice:

GOVERNMENT SALE OF CATTLE.

HEADQUARTERS DEPARTMENT OF ARIZONA,
OFFICE OF CHIEF COMMISSARY OF SUBSISTENCE,
WHIPPLE BARRACKS, PRESCOTT, A.T.

May 26, 1884.

There will be sold at public auction, to the highest bidder, by the acting commissary of subsistence at San Carlos, Arizona, on Thursday, June 26, 1884, commencing at 12 o'clock M., about ninety head of cattle, consisting of steers, cows, and calves. Terms: Cash. Cattle to be removed from reservation immediately after sale. This lot of cattle was brought in from Mexico by the Chiricahua Indians.

CHAS. P. EAGAN, *Captain and C.S., U.S. Army*

In this connection the following memorandum of a conference between the authorities at Washington and General Crook may be of importance:

MEMORANDUM OF THE RESULT OF A CONFERENCE BETWEEN THE SECRETARY OF THE INTERIOR, THE COMMISSIONER OF INDIAN AFFAIRS, THE SECRETARY OF WAR, AND BRIGADIER GENERAL CROOK, JULY 7, 1883.

In view of the difficulties encountered in making satisfactory disposition of the Apache Indians recently captured by General Crook

under existing methods of administration, it is determined by the secretary of war and the secretary of the interior, after consideration, that
the Apache Indians recently captured by General Crook, and all such
as may be hereafter captured or may surrender themselves to him,
shall be kept under the control of the War Department at such points
on the San Carlos reservation as may be determined by the War
Department (but not at the agency, without the consent of the Indian
agent), to be fed and cared for by the War Department until further
orders. For the greater security of the people of Arizona and to insure
peace, the War Department shall be entrusted with the entire police
control of all the Indians in the San Carlos reservation and charged
with the duty of keeping the peace on the reservation and preventing
the Indians from leaving, except with the consent of General Crook
or the officer who may be authorized to act under him.

The War Department shall protect the Indian agent in the discharge of his duties as agent, which shall include the ordinary duties
of an Indian agent, which shall remain as heretofore, except as to
keeping the peace, administering justice, and punishing refractory
Indians, all of which shall be done by the War Department, as above
stated.

(Signed)   ROBERT T. LINCOLN, *Secretary of War*
H. TELLER, *Secretary of the Interior*

On or about May 17, 1885, Geronimo and other renegades left the San
Carlos reservation and committed the outrages which have not yet ceased.

I feel confident that the above statement of facts will be substantially corroborated by the reports of all the United States officers, civil and military, and
bearing in mind the full meaning of the word renegade, as given above, it may
be condensed as follows:

In May 1876 Geronimo is a renegade under Pionsenay and is captured and
put on the reservation. In April 1877, having become leader of the renegades,
he is again captured and held in confinement for murder and robbery. In 1879
he surrenders to an army officer and is held as a prisoner of war. Thus we see
this Indian four times in the custody of the United States officials and are at a
loss to imagine why he was allowed to escape from custody. How much longer
are the rules which apply to warfare between civilized nations to be applied to
savages who utterly disregard them? The Indian policy, as to Indians like
Geronimo, has been to treat them as prisoners of war, rely on their parole that
they will cease committing murder, and sell the property which they have
obtained by robbery of our citizens as we sold captured Confederate cotton.

Those who have suffered, or are still suffering, by this policy are unable to
understand what delicate sense of honor or charity or forbearance can justify his
being allowed so often to be at large. If so many homes had not been made des-

olate, the narration of these facts might be received with an incredulous smile; but this will vanish when the actual result thus far, and the probable result in the future, of the last outbreak of Geronimo and his followers are shown.

The list of killed which is attached to this paper was, with the exception of the soldiers killed (which will be reported by their commanding officer), and the Mexicans found by soldiers, and those killed in the Black Range, prepared from the statements of those who saw the bodies of the slain or aided in burying them, and the list of wounded from the account of those who knew and saw them. They show twenty-eight residents and three soldiers killed and nine residents wounded. The number of horses and stock stolen or killed is impossible at present to estimate.

In the list of killed, the one described as "Prospector Unknown" may be considered a doubtful addition to the number; and to those not familiar with mining regions it may be well to explain that one whose occupation is to wander over the mountains for the purpose of discovering mineral veins is called a prospector. He generally has no fixed habitation—often his relatives are unknown—he is sometimes called by a nickname—when he leaves one place, it is uncertain at what place he will next appear, and his occupation is known by the small tools he carries. Undoubtedly later on the skeletons of others, picked bare by the coyotes, will be found.

The name "Oucha" in the list also looks doubtful. He was a Mexican herder. Cochise County is settled principally by Americans, and the names of those Mexicans employed as herders are seldom correctly known by their employers.

These renegade savages did not kill or wound, or their squaws mutilate, the bodies of the peaceable people with the purpose of obtaining anything of value to them. They kill purely because they have been reared from childhood to do so.

In considering the probable effects in the future of the last outbreak, it is necessary to understand the topography of the region in which it occurred and what portion of it will be affected by further Indian outrages.

The San Carlos reservation lies about 170 miles north of the Mexican line, and the counties of Graham and Cochise lie south of the reservation, the southern boundary of Cochise County being the northern boundary of Mexico. The renegades under Geronimo are now in the Sierra Madre range of mountains in Mexico, south of Cochise County, and deep snows will cover their principal stronghold in that range in the fall, when they will be obliged to obtain means of subsistence from the nearest settlements. As it is hazardous for them to go far in a northerly direction, the experience of former outbreaks has shown that they will then commit murder and rapine in Sonora and Cochise counties. In this country, therefore, Cochise County will be the principal sufferer from the outrages of this band.

As renegades always attempt to reach the Indian stronghold in Mexico, which is inaccessible to any considerable body of our troops, and Geronimo, knowing that he would be expected to do so, and probably fearing that he might be intercepted by the troops lately stationed in the southern part of Arizona, led his band at first eastward to the Black Range in New Mexico, as is shown by the bodies of those first killed, and before our troops could reach him, divided his force into several small bands, whose numerous trails rendered it almost impossible for our troops to know which way to go to intercept them. These small trails united in a large trail about thirty miles south of the northern line of Mexico, and not a single renegade has been captured or killed by soldiers. When this outbreak commenced, some troops were sent from Camp Huachuca, in Cochise County, to guard the mouth of Guadalupe Canyon, situated near the southeast corner of that county and supposed to be the pass by which the renegades would attempt to reach their stronghold in Mexico; but Geronimo was probably informed of this, as the small trails above described united at a point in Mexico far west of that canyon. By examining these small trails where they united, some estimate could be made of the number of the renegades, and the lowest estimate made by an old and intelligent resident on the spot was that they numbered 300. Moreover, another band, which must have taken some other route, was seen fifteen miles south of Fort Bowie, and seen and counted in Sulphur Springs Valley, in Cochise County, comprising seventy-five Indians. These estimates are given because it has been published that the renegades numbered 125, of which only 50 were bucks, and it is fair to presume that the number of renegade bucks is at least 100.

It having been shown that the residents of Cochise County will undoubtedly suffer, as formerly, from the raids of those renegades, and that our military forces have been, are, and will be unable to protect them, and that the capture of Geronimo and his followers will probably only have the effect of furnishing them with better arms and ammunition and provisions with which to indulge in further outrages and depredations, those whom I represent make their unanimous appeal to the government to adopt some means by which they may be effectually and permanently protected against a recurrence of the outrages which they have been suffering. As to the means to be adopted, I make these suggestions:

When pioneers settle on our frontier in the vicinity of savages, they must expect to incur more risk of losing life and property than in a more civilized region, but Arizona is not a new territory. If a citizen of the territory had committed one of the hundred crimes of which Geronimo has been guilty, he would have been punished for it. A few years ago we were afflicted with bands of train robbers and outlaws, and every one of them has been either killed whilst resisting arrest or tried and punished by due course of law. For some time prior to this last outbreak one could travel, unarmed by day or night, without fear of molestation, through any portion of Cochise County. Geronimo, however, because he is an Indian, seems to possess some potent charm to protect him from punishment. If it is asked why the civil authorities do not arrest and punish him, the first reply is that when he was last on the reservation, he was in the custody of General Crook, who has never turned him over to them. The second reply is that he is now, through no fault of the civil authorities, in Mexico, and they cannot be expected to arrest him when the United States troops cannot do so. And the third reply is that these Indians never fight in the open field, even against half their number, and always kill from behind bushes or rocks; and if Geronimo were arrested and tried, it would be impossible to prove that he fired the fatal shot or was guilty as an accessory, and he could not be indicted for treason, because he is not a citizen.

If the civil authorities can afford no protection, what other means can be adopted? All experience has proved that against Indians like these renegades, whose methods of warfare are different from those of any other Indians, in a region peculiarly adapted by nature to their methods, soldiers like ours, however brave, are of no avail, and that Indian scouts only, who have been reared and can subsist and fight like these Indians, can kill or capture them. But if, as is reported, these scouts are to be organized and used for that purpose, and should succeed in capturing Geronimo, what assurance have we that he will not be again set free and be permitted to instigate another outbreak? If he should be killed and the others captured, there will always be a chief ready to succeed him and follow the same career, if the military policy of treating them as prisoners of war and depending upon their honor and good faith is to be continued. Though many of the Indians upon the reservation are disposed to be peaceable, many of them also yearn for their former mode of life. The latter are of an inflammable character, and one or two Geronimos can at any time apply the torch that sets the flames ablaze.

Those whom I represent, believing that they express the unanimous sentiment of all the residents of our territory, ask that the Indians be removed from the San Carlos reservation, making no suggestion as to those peaceable Indians who are on other reservations; and I offer in support of their application the following considerations:

The San Carlos reservation, in the middle of our territory and peculiarly situated, as above described, is a standing menace to the lives and property of those who have made their homes in those valuable portions of Arizona and New Mexico which are affected by the biennial Indian outbreaks, and also to all nonresidents, warning them not to settle or invest in any industries in such portions. It also retards the growth and prosperity of the whole territory, because nonresidents generally believe that the whole of it is subject to the effects of these outbreaks.

There is abundant precedent for the removal of Indians from regions where their close contact with any civilized population imperiled its growth and prosperity.

This policy was inaugurated by Thomas Jefferson and was continuously enforced till about 1840, and probably later. The Creeks, Cherokees, Chickasaws, Choctaws, Cheyennes, Kiowas, Arapahos, Comanches, Apaches, and other tribes were removed to the Indian Territory, and it is a notable fact that the larger portion of those who were so removed made a much greater advance in leading peaceable and civilized lives than those who remained in the states. The advantage of placing them in that territory is easily seen. The Indian Territory is surrounded by civilized populations; and all immense ranges, deep canyons, and inaccessible strongholds are too remote from it to afford places of refuge for them. In making any outbreak, they must traverse long distance, in regions in which our troops could easily intercept them, and the expense of keeping them peaceable by the military force is much lessened.

The northwestern portion of the Indian Territory, usually called Oklahoma, embraces a larger tract than the San Carlos reservation and contains lands much better fitted for agriculture without irrigation and stock raising than the reservation. Its value for such purposes is shown by the trouble which the government has had in preventing settlers from occupying it. The Indians on the reservation, like all other Indians in their first attempt to lead peaceable lives, are engaged in farming and stock raising. If, when the present year's crops are harvested, those Indians, with their horses and cattle and agricultural implements, were removed to Oklahoma, it will cost the government much less than to sustain the San Carlos reservation and effectually prevent any further attempts by others to settle upon and occupy it, thus relieving the government from all further trouble on that subject.

It may be suggested that such a removal will work hardship to some of the Indians who have acquired homes by their industry and always been peaceable. If there are such Indians, why cannot their dwellings be sold by the government and the proceeds of the sales be turned over to them to build dwellings in a much better locality, where lumber is much cheaper? Would this be treating them worse than the residents were treated when, in 1884, the cattle stolen by Geronimo and other renegades, marked by brands which plainly showed from whom they were stolen, were driven to the reservation and sold at public auction by the United States commissary, and no part of the proceeds of that sale was ever paid to any of the owners? If these peaceable Apaches will, by removal to better homes, suffer present inconvenience, or even some pecuniary loss, is this consideration to have any weight if, by such removal, peaceable residents will no longer be outraged, robbed, and murdered?

How much longer are the rules which apply to warfare between civilized nations to be applied to savages who utterly disregard them? The Indian policy as to Indians like Geronimo has been to treat them as prisoners of war, rely on their parole that they will cease to murder, and sell the property which they have obtained by robbery of our citizens, as we sold captured Confederate cotton.

If it should be deemed impracticable to remove all the Indians from the reservation, surely none of those who have engaged in outbreaks, or will possibly do so, ought to be permitted to remain on or to return to it; and if this is done, the size of this enormous reservation and the expense of keeping troops on it or in its vicinity will be materially reduced.

I trust that I shall not return to those whom I represent without being able to assure them of some definite measures to be adopted for their protection now and in the future.

To avoid prolixity, I have omitted to mention many details which might be of interest in considering this matter and shall be gratified by being afforded the opportunity to communicate orally some minor considerations which might influence the action of the administration on this subject.

Very respectfully,

G. GORDON ADAM

LIST OF KILLED

Robert Benton, ranchman.
Christian Lutter, ranchman.
Frederick Lutter, ranchman.
  Blue Creek, Graham County, Arizona.
James Montgomery, prospector.
Robert Smith, ranchman.
Peter Anderson, ranchman.
Prospector unknown, buried by Captain Smith, 4th Cavalry.
  Little Blue Creek, Grant County, New Mexico.
Nat. Luse, prospector.
Calvin Orwig, rancher.
E. W. Lyons, English capitalist.
  San Francisco River, five miles from Alma, Socorro County,
  New Mexico.
J. J. Baxter.
——— Bunting.
  Mogollon Mountains, near line dividing Socorro and Grant Counties;
  buried by Captain Madden, 4th Cavalry.
Felix Marquez, wood hauler.
Juan[ita] Marquez, wife.
Maria Marquez, child.
Marqueta Lechuga, wood hauler.
Paz Rascom, wood hauler.
  Four miles north of Silver City, Grant County.
James Cummins, prospector.
  Dry Creek, Socorro County.
Edward Ford, ranchman.
John Frachel, ranchman.
  Lower Gila River, about eighteen miles southeast from Carlisle mines,
  Grant County.
Charles Stevenson, ranchman.
Harvey Moreland, ranchman.

Easy prey for Apaches. NELSON A. MILES. *PERSONAL RECOLLECTIONS AND OBSERVATIONS.*

Frank Adams, ranchman.
 Near Grafton, Black Range, Sierra County, New Mexico.
W. A. Daniel, mounted United States customs inspector.
 In Dixie Canyon, Mule Mountains, Cochise County, Arizona,
 near Mexican line.
——— Oucha, Mexican herder.
 Found by soldiers in Sulphur Springs Valley, Cochise County.
Fred. Huntington, miner.
Peter McKurtan, miner.
Peter Palma, miner.
 Twelve miles from Nacosari, Sonora, near Mexican line.
Three soldiers, near Guadalupe Canyon, at southeast corner of
 Cochise County.

LIST OF WOUNDED

Thos. Welch, prospector. On Little Blue Creek, Grant County, New Mexico.
Charles Prather, rancher. On Mogollon Creek, Grant County.
N. C. Stahlworth and wife, ranchers. On Devil's Creek, Socorro County,
 New Mexico.
Mrs. Holloday, wife of rancher. In Devil's Creek Park, Socorro County.
Green Batterton, teamster. At Moulton's mill, on Sapillo Creek,
 Grant County.
Pablo Marquez, wood hauler. Four miles north of Silver City, Grant County.
Navaricio Guerra. Near Chenowitz's store, on Gila River, Grant County.
Names unknown. At Gebhardt George's ranch, three miles from Fort Bayard,
 Grant County, and seen by G. G. Posey, attorney-at-law, of Silver City,
 New Mexico.

PART FIVE

Chasing Geronimo, 1885–86

The Geronimo Campaign of 1885–1886

CHARLES P. ELLIOTT

Journal of the United States Cavalry Association 21, no. 80 (September 1910): 211–36

The Chiricahua Apache Indian tribe is one of the families of Apaches who have but little in common with the other Arizona Apaches and differ even in language. The habitat of the tribe was Arizona and northern Mexico, where they had reservations on both sides of the line. They were for years a scourge to both Americans and Mexicans, and it was not until the close of the campaign against them in 1886 that the troubles with them were terminated. The beginning of that campaign I am about to describe. Since the death of Victorio, the Warm Springs and Chiricahua Indians have combined and blended and are both known as Chiricahuas.

In 1883 General George Crook, with a command of regulars and Indian scouts, entered the Sierra Madre in Mexico, followed the Chiricahuas to their stronghold in the heart of the mountains, and induced the entire tribe to return to the White Mountain Indian Reservation in Arizona, where they were held as prisoners of war under the military command of Captain Emmet Crawford, Third Cavalry, in whom General Crook reposed great trust and confidence.

They were held at the San Carlos Agency for a time, then, at their own request, were allowed to remove to Turkey Creek, ten miles from Fort Apache, and were placed in the immediate charge of Lieutenant Britton Davis, Third Cavalry. A number of bucks and their families started farms on Turkey Creek and White River, worked hard, and were to all appearances perfectly contented.

The first trouble occurred at Turkey Creek in 1884 with one of their war chiefs, Ka-ya-ten-nae. His prompt arrest, trial by Captain Crawford, and sentence to three years' imprisonment at Alcatraz Island, in San Francisco Harbor, put a stop to all further trouble.

The fall and winter of 1884 passed in peace and quiet, as did also the early spring of 1885. In April 1885 the Third Cavalry, Captain Crawford's regiment, was ordered from Arizona to Texas. Captain Crawford applied to be relieved from duty over the Indians in order to go with his regiment. His request was granted in an order paying high tribute to his valuable services. Lieutenant

Davis, Third Cavalry, was retained in charge of the Chiricahua Indians and came to San Carlos in the latter part of April to draw annuities for them. He reported that all were quiet and seemed thoroughly satisfied with their condition. On his return to Fort Apache he was accompanied by Captain Pierce, First Infantry, the new commanding officer of the reservation, and Agent [C. D.] Ford, who represented the Interior Department. On their return to San Carlos they reported the Chiricahuas to be in a thoroughly satisfactory state.

Immediately thereafter a telegram came to Captain Pierce[1] stating that several of the prominent leaders had gotten drunk, camped together, evidently intending to defy authority and avoid punishment, and that an outbreak was feared. In a few moments after the receipt of the message, the telegraph wire to Fort Apache was cut by the Chiricahuas, and of course it did not require an experienced cook to tell that the "fat was in the fire."

An extract from General Crook's report explains the situation very clearly:

> My first information of impending trouble was a telegram received on the afternoon of May 17, 1885, and before a reply could be sent, the wires between Fort Apache and San Carlos were cut. The next afternoon I was informed that Geronimo, Nana, Mangus,[2] Naiche, and Chihuahua, with a considerable party, had left their camp on the preceding evening. Within a few days the exact number of renegades was fixed at thirty-four men, eight well-grown boys, and ninety-two women and children. I learned that on May 15, Lieutenant Britton Davis, Third Cavalry, sent a telegraphic dispatch which I did not see for months afterwards. Had the telegram reached me I feel morally certain that the trouble would have been settled without an outbreak. Troubles of minor importance were constantly occurring on the reservation, which were quieted down by the officers in charge by reporting them to me and receiving my instructions.

TELEGRAM FROM LIEUTENANT DAVIS, MAY 15, 1885

There was an extensive tiswin drunk here last night and this morning; the following chiefs came up and said they with their bands were all concerned in it: Geronimo, Chihuahua, Mangus, Naiche, Fele, and Loco. The whole business is a put-up job to save those who were drunk. In regard to the others I request instructions. The guardhouse here is not large enough to hold them all, and the arrest of so many prominent men will probably cause trouble. Have told the Indians that I would lay the matter before the general, requesting, at the same time, that their captives in Mexico be withheld. I think they are endeavoring to screen Naiche and Chihuahua.

(Sgd.) DAVIS, Lieutenant

The above is the telegram which had caused so much comment. When I reached San Carlos, the commanding officer told me that he had received the telegram, but did not forward it.

Embodied in the reports of General Crook are the interesting reports of Captain Allen Smith, Fourth Cavalry, commanding a squadron sent to pursue the renegades and head them off if possible before they left the reservation, also Lieutenant Davis' report of his pursuit with Indian scouts.

The Indians retreated, however, without loss to themselves, but leaving a trail of blood behind them, until they finally escaped into Old Mexico.

REPORT OF GENERAL CROOK

Within an hour after the renegades left their camp on Turkey Creek, two troops of cavalry (the Fourth) and a party of White Mountain and Chiricahua scouts under Lieutenants Gatewood and Davis left Fort Apache in pursuit, but such was the rapidity of their flight that it was impossible to overtake them. It subsequently appeared that they traveled nearly 120 miles before stopping for rest or food. Captain Smith's report is attached.

As soon as the departure of the Indians was known, troops were immediately put in motion to endeavor to overtake or intercept them. Captain Pierce, with a party of scouts from San Carlos, moved toward Ash Park. The commanding officer of Fort Thomas, without waiting for orders, sent two troops of cavalry towards Clifton. The commanding officer of Fort Grant was ordered to send all his available force of five troops of cavalry towards the Gila, with orders to cut their trail if possible and to pursue vigorously, regardless of departmental or national lines. The commanding officer of Fort Bowie was directed to ambush his cavalry at proper points in the Stein's Peak range, which had been a favorite trail in former years. The commanding officer at Fort Huachuca was instructed to send three troops to Guadalupe Canyon to scout the whole country in that vicinity. Information was sent to the commanding officer, District of New Mexico, of the departure of the Indians and the movement of the troops, and finally, every effort was made to warn citizens at all points within reach of danger.

A few days before the outbreak of the Chiricahuas I was ordered, as provost officer of the reservation, to take two packers and what riding and pack mules were needed, and make an inspection of the Indian camps on the Aravaipa Canyon and San Pedro River. En route to the Aravaipa we stopped to examine a fine spring, reported by the Indians as flowing through a rough, rocky canyon a few miles north of the Aravaipa. I found the spring as reported to be of clear, pure, and cool water, a treasure indeed in Arizona.

Just after leaving camp in the morning for the Aravaipa, my saddle mule was struck by a rattlesnake, and having no remedies, after lacerating the wound, I made one of the packers lead the mule back to the spring and tie her in the mud near it with a weak rope. That the remedy worked was proven by the mule being found, twelve months later, among the Indians on the San Pedro. The delay caused by the accident caused me to meet the mail carrier at the foot of the trail into the Aravaipa, and from him I learned that the Indians had broken out and started southeast from Fort Apache. I concluded that they would endeavor to elude the troops and escape into Old Mexico, in eastern Arizona or western New Mexico, and that my best chance to join an expedition against them was to strike diagonally across through Fort Bowie, Arizona, get the latest intelligence, and continue to the east until one of the pursuing columns was met. At the mouth of the Aravaipa a courier from Lieutenant Walsh[3] at San Carlos overtook me, suggesting that my return to San Carlos was advisable, but as he was junior to me, I could not resist the temptation to continue on my way and follow out my original plan.

Our route took us up the San Pedro, as long as possible on the wagon road, then across country towards Fort Bowie, laying a course as nearly straight as possible in such a rough country, using the stars at night as a guide.

The first news was obtained at Willcox that the Indians were in the mountains near the Gila but trying to work south. At Fort Bowie I secured all the supplies that my mules could carry and started southeast, going by the Double Adobes in Las Animas Mountains, across the line and to the Janos River in Old Mexico. There I found that I was south of the Indians and started north toward Deming, New Mexico.

At the noon camp on the Janos River an incident occurred rather characteristic of the country. We had killed, on an average, more than one rattlesnake a day traveling across the country, but had never encountered one in camp. The cook had just spread our meal on a canvas manta, near a water hole, and we were setting to in good earnest when, with an exclamation in Spanish, the Mexican packer jumped over the improvised table. I looked around and saw, about six inches off, the head of a rattlesnake appear between where he had been and myself; as quick as thought, the American packer, with one stroke of the ax, cut off the snake's head. We had spread our table directly over the hole of a five-foot rattlesnake, but in breaking down the fennels to make a level place had not been able to see it. Sleeping on the same ground was not pleasant, but excessive fatigue is a good sedative.

While we went north from the Janos, the hostiles went south within a short distance; just when or how far apart we passed in the night I am unable to say.

I found that a battalion of the Tenth Cavalry under Major Biddle, which had returned from pursuit of the band gone south, was camped near the Florida Mountains. General Crook had gone to Fort Bayard, New Mexico. I reported to him by telegram and awaited instructions.

Captain Pierce, who had succeeded Captain Crawford in command at San Carlos, was expected in from the east with his Indian scouts, the command to which I belonged, by rail from near the Ojo Caliente. Captain Crawford had been ordered back from Texas to organize and command an expedition composed of Indian (100) scouts and one troop of the Sixth Cavalry, and one pack train, to pursue the Indians into Old Mexico.

REPORT OF GENERAL CROOK

Captain Crawford, Third Cavalry, who had reported to me, was ordered with the battalion of scouts which had been operating in the country about the Warm Springs reservation to Separ by rail, and thence to move with a troop of cavalry to the south end of the Animas Valley, with the hope that the Indians might cross into Mexico through the Guadalupe Mountains. The result proved that the main body of the hostiles crossed the line to the west of the Mule Mountains, though a small party surprised a camp of the Fourth Cavalry in Guadalupe Canyon, guarded by a party of seven enlisted men, killing four of them, and another small party crossed the line near Lake Palomas. Lieutenant Davis, who, with sixty White Mountain and Chiricahua scouts, had been following the trail of the Indians as rapidly as possible, was ordered to report to Captain Crawford, and on June 11 the combined force, consisting of ninety-two scouts and Troop A, Sixth Cavalry, followed the hostiles into the Sierra Madre.

My duty while waiting at Deming was to collect and forward to General Crook all information possible about the movements of the Indians, especially that gathered from the employees of the two railroads running into Deming. The shameless lies told by some of the employees, who would go into the most minute details about seeing a band of Indians breaking camp and moving south, caused me to ride many useless miles in the hot sun and to learn by experience that residence in New Mexico and Arizona, if too prolonged, produces the champion breed of liars.

Lack of veracity on the part of the civilians in reporting movements of Indians was frequently the cause of unnecessary loss of life among themselves, by causing the troops to go on a fruitless search in the wrong direction for Indians raiding and killing elsewhere. In a sparsely settled country with few railroads, few roads, high and very rough mountains, with water long distances apart, information was hard to obtain, and when wrongly given, many weary miles were necessary to discover the error.

The campaign now opened in real earnest; all the troops in both territories were on the move. Our command was loaded on cars and taken to Separ on the Southern Pacific Railroad. From that point the course lay south towards the Animas Valley, the scouts covering the country on both sides for signs of the trail of the hostiles. News reached Captain Crawford that the hostiles were to the west of us and that the troops from Fort Huachuca had left their camp in Guadalupe Canyon in pursuit of them, the Indians working to the south. He took his command over to Skeleton Canyon but, seeing no signs of the hostiles, went to Lang's Ranch, New Mexico, and from there crossed the line and mountains into Old Mexico. The band of hostiles, soon after crossing the Guadalupe Canyon, evidently noticed the white-topped army wagons in the camp at Guadalupe Canyon and, rightly concluding that they belonged to the command that they had just eluded and left behind, doubled back, crawled up on the camp down the backbone of a ridge, terminating in a steep bluff just opposite it, watched the soldiers until the sentinel on duty was called to his dinner and, contrary to specific orders, left his post to get it; then the Indians got within a few feet of the unsuspecting men and opened fire on them. The soldier acting as cook and two others were, I think, killed instantly. The sergeant in charge was shot, but Private Snitzer of C Troop, Fourth Cavalry, took him on his back and climbed with him out of the canyon on the north side. The sergeant was shot a second and third time while on Snitzer's back and killed. The Indians took what they wanted and burned the rest. On the return of the troops, the men that had been killed were buried, their graves remaining as a warning to the soldiers in that camp during the rest of the campaign. Private Snitzer was duly rewarded for his gallant conduct.[4]

The first camp made by Captain Crawford in Old Mexico was at Sierra en Medio (Middle Mountain), the scene of a severe engagement between the Sixth Cavalry and Indian scouts under Major Tucker and the Chiricahuas during a former outbreak. Some of our scouts had then been hostiles and, during the night of our camp on their old battleground, celebrated, by the most fiendish singing, their former successful escape from a rather desperate position. From Sierra en Medio, no signs of hostiles having been seen, the command went northwest towards the mountains south of Guadalupe Canyon. The scouts still failed to develop signs, so we turned south towards the Sierra Madre, camping at Dos Carretas Creek. Captain Crawford's intention now was to get south of the Indians, keep a sharp lookout for sign of them, and if possible, surprise and capture them, as it was nearly impossible to get a fight out of them otherwise.

In pursuance of this design, the command crossed into Sonora, notifying the presidentes of all towns of the outbreak and asking that any movements of the hostiles be communicated to it at once. The country was very thoroughly covered, and it was evident that the hostiles were in the mountains to the north of our position. An incident occurred about this time that resulted in the killing of one of our scouts and the wounding of another by an American living in Mexico. The scouts were, as usual, well ahead of the command and spread out, looking for signs. The American, who had heard of the Indian incursion into Mexico, was driving his cattle to a place of safety, when suddenly he saw coming towards him three Indians. He took up a favorable position, biding his time, killed one, wounded another, and put the third to flight. He did not know that we were near with Indian scouts and thought he had run into the Chiricahuas. The heat at this time was frightful.

The following is Captain Crawford's report:

Camp on Batepito River, Six miles above Oputo, Mexico.
June 25, 1885.

General Crook, Whipple Barracks, A.T.

Camped in Texas Mountains, vicinity of Guasaoas, on the nineteenth instant, and was informed the following day that Indians had been seen near Oputo the night of the nineteenth. Acting on this information, I ascended the river to this point and on the morning of the twenty-second discovered the fresh trail of about eight or ten Indians leading into the Bavispe Mountains northeast of here. That afternoon Chatto left camp with a picked body of scouts to overtake and capture the men whose trail we had seen or, failing in that, to locate the camp and hold the hostiles, if possible, until the rest of the command could overtake them. Some of the scouts returned night before last and the rest yesterday morning with the following report: After leaving camp they marched until about dark, when it began to rain heavily and washed out the trail, when they camped. Starting again the next morning, they entered the range of mountains toward which the trail had been leading and about 9:00 A.M. came in sight of the rancheria. The camp was in such a position that Chatto thought it impracticable to surround it without being seen by the hostiles, in which event the chances of capturing any of them would have been very poor. The best position practicable was obtained, and Chatto then opened the fight. As soon as the firing commenced the hostiles fled and endeavored to escape, with their women and children, through several deep canyons which joined near the camp. The scouts followed as rapidly as the nature of the ground would permit, and for several miles a running fight was kept up, but the canyons were so very rough that the pursuit was slow, and the bucks, eight in number, with four boys and three women, escaped to the mountains. Fifteen women and children were captured, and one of the women was sent by Chatto to see if she could not induce the surrender of the others of the party. This woman has not yet returned. There was also captured all of the property belonging to the party, five horses belonging to the Fourth Cavalry, three saddles, two revolvers, cartridge belts, ammunition, etc., belonging to soldiers killed in Guadalupe Canyon, one white mule, branded "U.S.," and other property of less value. One Indian was killed and several others wounded in the fight.[5] Two of the captives, one a squaw and the other a child, were wounded; one scout, a White Mountain, known as Big Dave, was shot through the elbow, his arm being broken. The camp was that of Chihuahua, whose entire family is among the captives. Naiche is supposed to have left him several days before the fight and is now thought to be with Mangus and Geronimo on the eastern slope of the Sierra Madre. Expect to leave here tomorrow morning, continuing to follow Naiche's trail into the Sierra Madre. Country through which trail has led so far is extremely rough and with scarcely any water, so that time will be necessary to accomplish satisfactory results.

The Mexican citizens and officials of the different towns have shown us every consideration and attention, expressing themselves as more than pleased to have us here protecting them. The Mexican troops are said to be south fighting the Yaquis.

(Signed)
EMMET CRAWFORD, Captain, Third Cavalry, Commanding.

The command had been subject to every possible hardship up to this time, excessive heat, very little water, poor rations, bacon made rancid by unusual heat, and at night were pestered not only by mosquitos, but by ants, large and small, with an occasional centipede. I killed one of the latter at Dos Carretas Creek that measured eight inches. At the camp on the Bavispe River, while waiting for the return of the scouts with their captives, the insects had been particularly annoying. Due to the rain mentioned in Captain Crawford's report, the river had risen a foot or more and then receded. I concluded to spread my rubber poncho on the wet ground near the river, put my head in a pillowcase that I was fortunate enough to have, and try to get a little sleep. The air was rather vibrant with suppressed excitement; the scouts in camp knew the hostiles were not far off and seemed to think they would try to recover their squaws or run off some of our stock. The mule pack train was herded across the river from where I went to sleep. I was awakened out of a sound sleep by loud cries all around me and a great splashing in the river. It flashed across my mind that I was just in the way if the mules stampeded towards camp. Of course the pillowcase stuck, but I could not allow a small thing like that to stop me, and being young and active, I went blindfolded for the high ground. When in a place of safety from the mules, I got the pillowcase off and found Lieutenant Davis, Al Sieber, and all hands armed and ready to receive an enemy. What I had heard coming through the water were our scouts, some of whom had camped across the stream, who had imagined that the Chiricahuas were upon us and had stampeded to our side of the river to join forces. All of the excitement was caused by a lone burro crossing the river just below where we were.

The following morning the captives were brought in. Captain Crawford directed me to go to Oputo to get a guide and some grain, if possible, as he wished me to go by forced marches to Fort Bowie with his report to General Crook. I succeeded in getting a Mexican smuggler for a liberal consideration, who undertook to take me by the shortest possible route. Captain Crawford allowed me my choice of all animals in the command, as he wanted the dispatch to get to Fort Bowie in three days.

With my smuggler guide, one pack mule, loaded with a half sack of corn, a loaf of Dutch-oven bread, a piece of bacon, and a coffeepot, we left camp at 8:00 A.M. on June 25.

The first part of the route was entirely unknown to me; in fact, I had never been into Bowie from that direction, but near the post is a prominent landmark visible for miles down the valley towards Mexico, and I knew if my guide would get me out of the mountains that I could be independent of him. About two hours from camp a deer jumped up in front of me, ran a short distance up a side canyon, and stopped in easy range. I shot it from my mule, cut off a hindquarter, and hung the carcass up on a tree for the pack train that I knew would follow me. Had we not been engrossed with the deer, we would undoubtedly have noticed that the hostile bucks had crossed the canyon just before we got there, and the officer in charge of the train said that finding the signs all mixed up together, he expected at any moment to find our mutilated remains. However, I was spared to make one of the hardest and most trying rides of my life.

By riding sixteen hours a day in two periods of eight hours each, as nearly as possible, stopping to water the mules and make coffee where possible, the ground was covered quite rapidly. Making camp consisted of taking the saddles and blankets, wet with sweat and rain, off the riding mules and the aparejo with its light load from the pack mule. With the ground or a wet blanket to lie on and a saddle to rest your head on, your housekeeping arrangements were soon completed.

I had the satisfaction of delivering my dispatch to General Crook at Fort Bowie at 8:00 A.M. on June 28, on time. I had to finish the last stage on foot, leading my mule, worn out and unable to bear my weight. The Mexican and the pack mule did not turn up until the afternoon. The distance covered was between 190 and 200 miles.

General Crook was glad to learn of the whereabouts of the hostiles and ordered me on the second day to go with a fresh mount and a packer to Lang's Ranch to await the arrival of fresh supplies and a fresh cavalry troop for Captain Crawford, Troop A, Eighth Cavalry having been worn out by the work with the scouts. The ride to Lang's Ranch was made in two days, the distance from 90 to 100 miles.

Within a few days of my arrival at Lang's Ranch, the pack trains with fresh supplies for Captain Crawford's command were ready to start for Mexico with Troop C, Fourth Cavalry, under Lieutenant Guy Huse,[6] Fourth Cavalry, as escort. Nothing of consequence had occurred since the time of my leaving Captain Crawford, near Oputo, and my reporting to him with the new supplies.

Being now thoroughly equipped for further scouting, the search for hostile Indians was resumed with fresh vigor. The heat in the deep, rocky canyons of northern Sonora was something frightful, and water, except on the rivers, was scarce and poor when found.

On August 9, near Nacori, in Sonora, Captain Crawford met Lieutenant Day, Ninth Cavalry, with a detachment of Indian scouts who had just attacked and captured a camp of Chiricahuas, women and children, back in the mountains from where we were. Captain Crawford took up the trail of the bucks of the party, and our pursuit of them across the Sierra Madre is well described in the report of Lieutenant Britton Davis, who led the pursuit:

> The mountains at that point were so abrupt that we experienced great difficulty in crossing them; a detachment of packers and scouts was kept continually ahead of the pack trains for the purpose of making a trail; but even with these precautions the difficulties of proceeding were so great that several mules were killed and injured each day through rolling down the mountains.
>
> After reaching the summit of the Sonora slope of the Sierra Madre, I was detached and sent forward with a party of scouts under Seiber to follow the trail of the hostiles, who were moving east and traveling rapidly. We took with us six days' rations, which, with the aid of horse meat, beef, and game, when obtained, lasted us eleven days. Heavy rains fell almost daily, and at times it was almost impossible to keep the trail. The hostiles, on the contrary, had nothing to carry but themselves and were also driving a number of fresh animals. As soon as their horses would give out, they would kill them and mount the fresh stock they were driving. They lived upon the flesh of the horses they had killed and upon such wild fruit as they could gather along the route. Fearing that we would run upon them at any moment and be discovered before we saw them, it was necessary to keep a few scouts eight or ten miles in advance each day, and our progress was necessarily slow. The country through which we passed was so soft that our mules, with even their light loads, sank to their knees in the mud, and riding at times was out of the question. Had the Indians caught sight of us they would have scattered in every direction, and further pursuit for the time being would have been useless.
>
> After leaving the scene of the fight (with Lieutenant Day), the hostiles moved nearly due east across the Sierra Madre, a distance of nearly 250 miles, reckoned from Nacori on the western slope to Via de Buenaventura on the eastern slope. Arriving in the vicinity of Via, the trail turned towards the southeast, avoiding the larger towns and ranches until the town of Santa Clara was reached, at a point, following the Indian trail, about a hundred miles further to the east.

We must also leave Lieutenant Davis' trail here, however interesting it may be, and return to the main command under Captain Crawford. The difficulties encountered by Lieutenant Davis with his small command of selected mules, not too heavily loaded, were of necessity less than those of the main column. Mules hate mud, and the more that go through it, the worse the mud becomes, and the more they balk at it. For eight days in succession we were wet through all the time, and with no shelter at night, in those high altitudes, the cold went to your very bones.

There was only one compensation, and that was the view we got from the high points on the west of the Sierra Madre. I shall never forget the scene that was unfolded to us one morning that broke clear, after a very severe rainstorm the day and night before. We were then camped on the top of the range with a view limited on both sides only by the length of your vision and the rotundity of the earth. We were above the clouds, which filled all of the valleys with a mass of white, billowy vapor, the rough and forbidding mountains of Sonora falling in tier after tier toward the Pacific Ocean, which we imagined that we could see. Captain Crawford was much impressed with the grandeur of the scene and, as fate would have it, within less than six months, lost his life on one of the cloud-environed mountains at which we were looking.

It soon became evident to him that at the rate we were traveling, it would be impossible to overtake Lieutenant Davis with the whole command within double the time, six days, for which Davis was rationed. The captain therefore detached me, with two good packers, six selected pack mules, and eight Indian scouts, to push forward and overtake Davis before he got out of food, as it was of the utmost importance that some of the command should keep in touch with the hostiles, touch meaning on a hot trail, a hot trail being less than twenty-four hours old.

I started out as directed and had no difficulty in following rapidly the plain trail left by Davis and his mules, except in such places where he had experienced trouble due to the nature of the country. As the trail led east, we were bound to get out of the mountains sooner or later, and at noon of the day on which we finally emerged from the main range and got into the foothills, three of Lieutenant Davis' scouts, coming back on the trail, met me with a request to Captain Crawford to forward supplies to him, Davis, at once. On reaching a cattle range in the foothills I put my small detachment into camp at the same place where Davis had camped with his scouts a few day before. They found the remains of three head of cattle that Lieutenant Davis had killed and butchered for his Indians. Before killing them he had tried in vain to communicate with a Mexican cowboy, whom he saw on the range, but the sight of the Indians with Davis was too much for his nerves, and the valiant greaser vanished. Both Davis and I had orders to kill what cattle were necessary for food and to give receipts, to be taken up by Captain Crawford on his arrival. Whether the receipts were ever taken up is more than I know; but there can be no doubt about my having been, and it is only due to execrable marksmanship on the part of the Mexicans that I am here to tell of it.

The Mexican herder who had seen Lieutenant Davis and his scouts did not stop until he reached San Miguel, many miles from the camping place. There he roused the town and turned out the voluntarios to suppress the invasion of the Tejanos (Texans) and broncos (as they called the wild Indians).

Lieutenant Davis had broken camp very early and had followed directly on the Indian trail across a range of high hills. Neither he nor his scouts, who had come back to guide me by a shortcut through a canyon, and had thus missed the Mexicans on his trail, had the faintest idea that he was being pursued.

On breaking camp at 4:00 A.M. I was guided by one of the Indians through the canyon in question and drove my mules to their utmost capacity. At about 2:00 P.M. the Indian guide could not be found; he and the other two had slipped off to look for game whose sign they had seen. The trail became faint just here, and rather than get off it or overrun it, I determined to take the packs off the mules and give them a rest for an hour or so, knowing that I could make Davis' camp before night with an hour or two of daylight.

While we were pushing down the canyon, the Mexicans had followed the trail over the mountains and were just in advance of us. They had formed an ambush just a few yards ahead of where I stopped and would have murdered us beyond doubt had we not stopped just where we did.

While helping the packers to unload and cover the cargoes from an approaching rainstorm, one of my Indians said in Apache, "Nantan, No-ki-ai," ("Captain, Mexican"), pointing to a mounted man against the skyline. I looked at him, and he was like any other range rider in a similar country riding on high points to look for cattle. I reassured the Indians and went on with my work, arranging the rations under a cottonwood tree, when a volley burst from the crest of the hill where the Mexican had been seen, and the leaves were cut from the tree over my head. I had put my rifle and revolver on my bedroll and started for them, but concluding it must be mistake on the part of the Mexicans, ordered the packers to take cover; the Indians had needed no warning, had gotten in a strong position, and the two tame Chiricahuas who had come back from Davis to me promptly returned the fire. I ordered them to stop firing, but knowing the Mexicans better than I, when they could not shoot, they lit out for Davis as soon as my back was turned.

I ran from under the tree to open ground and toward the hill, calling to the Mexicans that I was a friend and American officer. In a moment the firing ceased, and I went and stood on a small bare mound, waiting for the commander to come down. While I was standing there, alone and unarmed, the fire was by command, for I heard it, concentrated on me. It was a noble specimen of Mexican chivalry, and profanity was the only weapon I had to meet it with. The vigor of my remarks had the desired effect, and the firing ceased. Three men detached themselves from the main body and came towards me. On seeing them start, I called to one of my packers, who spoke Mexican fluently, to come to interpret for me. The Mexicans came up, shook hands most cordially, passed the compliments of the day and season, and just as I was about to warm up into friendship and forgive them for having tried to pot me, with one accord they raised their carbines on us and wanted to know why we had killed those three head of cattle. At once it flashed over me that they had mistook me and my little squad for Davis and his fifty scouts. I told them I had killed only two and that the man they wanted was just over the hill with fifty Indian scouts.

That made them think quick and hurry. They had me where I could do nothing to help myself, and my Indians could do nothing to help me. Finally we were all started, the two packers and I mounted bareback on our mules, the Indians tied together on foot, toward Buenaventura. I declined to go unless they untied the Indians, whom they had forced me to disarm, and they did so.

En route to Via we met Lieutenant Colonel Mesilla of the Eleventh Mexican Cavalry, with cavalry and infantry marching to repel the invasion of Mexico by me and my poor little eight Indians.

My explanations were listened to but evidently doubted. We were marched to Via, where the entire population turned out to see the show, and I was called many vile names, which fortunately I did not understand.

We were turned over to the Mexican Regulars, the officer of the day, a courteous Mexican gentleman, giving us into the charge of the officer of the guard. The Indians were put in the barracks, and the two packers and I were allowed to remain in the room of the officer of the guard. On entering the compound a little Mexican soldier, moved by pity, handed me a very nice-looking ear of corn, roasted to a turn. I accepted with thanks and slipped it into my pocket. It was my only ration from 4:00 A.M. that day until the next morning. The officer of the day kindly gave us a large glass of aguardiente; as I needed my head, I gave my share to the two packers.

The two Indians who went from me to Davis when the firing started confirmed a report made to him by one of his own scouts, who had seen the trouble from a high point, and Davis at once started with his command to my assistance. Before he could reach us, we had been hurried towards Via, no guard even being left over my property. He followed with his scouts just over the crest of the hills, beyond which we were being taken, and halted just outside of town, concealing his command. He had seen the meeting with Colonel Mesilla from a distance. At dark Davis, who spoke Spanish with ease, entered town and placed himself in communication with the presidente. That official refused to act until the return of the military commander. Upon his return, my statements having been proven true by the marks on the property and aparejos, after a consultation between Colonel Mesilla, the presidente, and Davis, I was paroled and ordered to report to headquarters at 9:00 A.M. It was then a great pleasure to hear Colonel Mesilla give the voluntarios "Hail Columbia" for the part they had taken in the affair, made them restore what they had tried to steal, and express his regrets for what had happened and his pleasure at my not having been killed, to all of which I heartily agreed, especially the latter.

My love for Mexico and the Mexicans had not been added to by my experience, and when, after joining us, Captain Crawford told me that he wanted me to take dispatches north to General Crook at Fort Bowie, I was very keen for the start.

I am happy to state that Captain Crawford complimented me very heartily on getting out of the scrape as well as we did, saying that had I allowed my Indians to return the fire and open a fight, Davis would have been drawn into

At dark Davis entered town. OUTING MAGAZINE, MARCH 1887.

it, then Colonel Mesilla would have joined in the battle, and as we were two hundred miles south of the line and with nothing but Indian scouts, Troop C, Fourth Cavalry having been sent north from the west side of the Sierra Madre, we would have been in a desperate state even if victorious, not to mention international complications.

The ride north with dispatches was uneventful, except that we stood, the packer and I, and counted ninety-five antelopes file slowly down to a small stream to drink and did not fire a shot. We were under orders not to shoot on the trail. It was not the first time. Once on the west side, in Sonora, Captain Crawford and I, while riding in the lead, came upon a buck and two does within twenty yards, standing perfectly still and looking at us with wonder in their eyes. They had probably never seen a man or mule before. I begged to be allowed to shoot; fresh meat had long been a stranger to us. He only laughed at me. Finally I dismounted and threw a rock at the buck to ease my feelings. Within a few days we returned over the same trail; the order about shooting had then been revoked, and the packers were busy all day picking up deer left by the Indians on the trail, to be packed into camp.

Once while in the heart of the Sierra Madre, while the shooting embargo was on, I had a most exciting chase on muleback after a flock of young turkeys. They got mixed up and I very nearly caught one. The Apaches are reported to have frequently run them down on foot. That I have never seen, but I have had them bring to me a well-grown fawn that had been run down by them and caught.

After crossing the stream where the antelope went to drink, we knew of no water for many miles to the north of us, none, in fact, short of Media, on the Janos plain. We rode all day, and as the sun was sinking caught sight, over to the left of our course, of the vivid green of the cottonwood. It did not necessarily mean water that we could get at, but we had to camp somewhere. On reaching the spot we found the worst-looking brown mess, wet, and by filling the coffeepot and cooking its contents, we got a half potful of stuff soft enough to flow and the color of black coffee. By making a strong infusion of coffee, we were able to moisten our dry mouths and tongues during the night. The mules had to take theirs straight.

The next morning we started out very early with no hope of water within twenty-five miles. Just before noon my mule, that was in the lead and was beginning to show symptoms of great fatigue, suddenly sniffed the air, pricked up her ears, and took a smart trot. The other mules, the packer, and I knew she smelt water. Within a short distance she came to a beautiful, clear spring of pure water, bubbling up on the open prairie. The mules kneeled and stuck their heads in nearly to the eyes, and we were not slow in assuming a position where gravity assisted the flow of an elastic fluid. Oh, how good it was—the remaining twenty-five miles of the day's march seemed a mere step compared to the same number of miles from the cottonwood mud hole to the spring.

Captain Crawford did not return to the United States but went with his command to the Carretas Ranch, where I joined him later with fresh supplies and with Lieutenant Faison, First Infantry,[7] to replace Davis, who had requested to be relieved, in order to resign and take advantage of a good business offer.

The hostiles had led Davis a dance after he left us at Via de Buenaventura and had finally escaped into New Mexico, where they stirred things up for a while.

Soon after my return to the command at Dos Carretas news came to us that Major Wirt Davis, with his command of soldiers and Indian scouts, had an engagement in Sonora with a band of Chiricahuas and that the hostiles were heading east toward Dos Carretas.[8] I was ordered to get rations for fifty scouts ready at once and scout towards the north for signs. I left camp at 3:00 A.M., and at 4:00 A.M. came within sight of a campfire too large for Indians and found Major Davis with his command just come out of the mountains, having left the trail of the hostiles about four miles to the north of where we were. I at once moved on, and at daylight my scouts picked up the trail. We followed it on the open prairie until noon. I say we, but a large part of the time I saw no sign, but my Indians could run on the trail, it was so plain to them, and led as straight as a crow flies towards the waterhole, which we reached at noon. My mules and men both needed water and rest, having been on the road since 3:00 A.M., so I concluded to take off the packs for an hour or so. At 1:30 P.M. we started to pack up and at 2:00 P.M. took the road. On leaving camp the Indians started out ahead, as usual, and traveled straight across the prairie in our original direction. I will say here that we left the Indian trail about a half mile to the north of the water hole. I took it for granted that the leading Indian had the hostile trail and was following it. After a while I noticed that the Indians in front spread out and hesitated. I at once rode forward to ask what was the matter and found that they had assumed that the hostiles would keep on as they had been traveling but had not really had the signs since we left the water. I told them that when they had found and followed the proper trail we would think about making camp, but not before. I was mortified at my own carelessness and mad at the Indians. We picked up the trail and camped on it when it was too dark to see farther. Major Davis, with his command, and Captain Davis, with his, joined us early the next morning and started as lively a chase across the mountains as had ever been seen in Arizona. The hostiles, when abreast of the water hole where my Indians made their noon camp, had turned at right angles to their original direction and started due north for Arizona. It is safe to say that my Indians covered at least fifty miles during the day's march.

The nature of the pursuit of the Indians from the Janos plain is clearly set forth by the following extracts from the reports of Major Wirt Davis, Fourth Cavalry, and General George Crook:

At 8:00 P.M. September 25 the command camped on the Dos Carretas Creek. Just before daylight on September 26 Lieutenant Elliott, Fourth Cavalry, with fifty Indian scouts, who had just been sent out by Captain Crawford (whose command had been camped on Dos Carretas Creek, four miles above my camp, and who had received my dispatch about 10:00 P.M., September 25), passed my command, going in the direction of Middle Mountain to cut the hostiles' trail. Just as I was leaving on the twenty-sixth Captain Crawford joined me with the balance of his command. After considerable work and much time spent in following the trail of single horses, we struck the main trail in the Raton Mountains, ten miles west of the point where they had scattered. Here I sent a courier to Lang's Ranch with dispatches for General Crook, stating that the hostiles were traveling in a northerly direction towards Guadalupe Canyon. His trail again led out four or five miles in the plain and then returned back in to the Guadalupe Mountains. It is probable that they saw Lieutenant Elliott's scouts, who, coming from the Middle Mountain, joined me on the twenty-seventh. The whole command followed the trail as rapidly as possible. We reached Guadalupe Canyon September 28. The hostiles had crossed the canyon sometime in the morning, about five miles above the cavalry command stationed there. Before daylight on September 29 Captain Martin,[9] Fourth Cavalry, with his troop ("H") and some Indian scouts, started in pursuit. As my scouts had followed the trail rapidly about 270 miles and had torn moccasins as well as torn feet, I sent Captain Crawford and his scouts (who were comparatively fresh, as they had been in camp on Carretas Creek, so Captain Crawford told me, for two or three weeks) on the trail. I sent a courier to General Crook, at Fort Bowie, informing him of my whereabouts and of the situation, and stated that it was believed the hostiles (between twenty and twenty-five) intended going to the reservation to get recruits, or to make a raid on other Indians, Chatto and several of the other Indians concurring in this belief. This party of hostiles (Chihuahuas) killed on the trail between Nacosari Mountain and Guadalupe Canyon, while my command was pursuing them, thirty horses, mules, and burros.

EXTRACT FROM REPORT OF GENERAL GEORGE CROOK

The Indians, having been driven out of Mexico by the scouts, crossed into the United States through Guadalupe Canyon within a few miles of a camp of two troops of cavalry about daylight on the morning of September 28. They were closely followed by both Major Davis and Captain Crawford. It being evident that the hostiles intended to raid the White Mountain reservation or go into the Mogollones or Black Range in New Mexico, dispositions were made to prevent this. Cavalry were directed from different points by converging routes toward the Gila. Troops were established in positions to prevent the Indians crossing the San Simon Valley into Stein's Peak range; others were placed along the railroad, where they would be available for instant transportation by rail to threatened points. The scouts followed the hostiles, and several troops of cavalry were moved to points where it was thought possible they might ambush them. The renegades took the roughest possible trails over the Chiricahuas, twice endeavored to cross the San Simon Valley, but each time were frightened back into the Chiricahuas either by seeing the dust of moving columns or discovering their trails across the valley. They then crossed the Sulphur Spring Valley, by night, into the Dragoons, whither they were followed by Crawford's scouts. Through this range back into the valley, south towards the Mule Mountains, where their trail suddenly turned sharp to the east and went back into the Chiricahuas, Crawford's scouts followed them persistently.

The stock of the hostiles by this time was worn out, and though they had gathered all possible along their route, they were finally absolutely dismounted, and troops were in such a position that it seemed the entire band would be captured or killed. But just at this juncture they succeeded in remounting themselves with the best stock in the country, and finding that it would be impossible to get north of the railroad, they returned to Mexico. Captain Viele,[10] Tenth Cavalry, followed them with two troops as far as Ascension, Chihuahua, from which point, further pursuit being useless, he returned with his jaded command to his camp in Cave Canyon. The remounting of the Indians was, in this instance, particularly exasperating.

The cattlemen of the San Simon had gathered in the White Tall Canyon on the east side of the Chiricahuas for the beginning of their fall roundup.

In spite of the warning they had received the evening before that Indians on foot had been seen in their vicinity, they lariated their cow ponies, the best stock in the country, around a ranch in which they all slept. In the morning all their stock, with the exception of two or three, were gone, and the Indians had secured about thirty of the best horses in Arizona. Several times before and since, parties of Indians have been dismounted by persistent pursuit and escaped in the same way by securing remounts; and this, too, in spite of constant warnings and importunities to ranchmen to secure their stock. The Indians acted as if they could secure stock with perfect impunity. At one time they took a quantity of stock from a corral belonging to the Sulphur Springs Cattle Company under circumstances that made it evident that several men who were in the ranch knew what was going on, and although there were only three Indians in the party, no attempt was made to prevent the stock being taken.

At another time, early in June, a party of Indians, numbering perhaps a dozen men and forty or fifty women and children, drove up and shot down several beeves within a mile of the largest ranch in Arizona in broad daylight. There were twenty cowboys in the ranch at the time and all fully armed, and yet the Indians went into camp and cooked the meat, and some time during the night left; and during all of this time not the slightest attempt was made to interfere with them, or even to give information to troops.

The Indians having returned to Mexico, the troops were sent back to their proper stations. The scouts having been constantly on the march since the beginning of the operations, and the terms of service of many of them having expired, it was thought best to discharge them and enlist others, and while the new commands were being organized, as thoroughly as possible refit and reorganize the pack trains, which by this time were almost worn out.

The chase described in the above extracts was lively in the extreme. On turning north from the water hole in the Janos plain, where my scouts lost the trail, the Indians made for the Raton Mountains, entered them, circled again out into the open plain, reentered them, and took up a position on a point, which they, as usual, fortified with stone breastworks commanding all approaches from the front and with an open line of retreat along the hogback from the point to main range in case of attack. They left this position during the night and started as straight as the country would permit for the Guadalupe Canyon, both commands following in hot pursuit in the early morning. The trail was warm, aye, red hot, the coals still glowing in what fires they had made. Though there were many chances to ambush and kill the leaders of our party had they wished to do so, the Indians made no stand, and the nature of the country was such that it was impossible to take precautions against being ambushed. One or the other of the younger officers was always in the immediate advance with the leading Indian, and at no time did any of our Indians show the least disinclination to drive ahead, and all seemed keen for a fight, which the hostiles seemed as keen to avoid. Luck was against the two troops of my regiment stationed in Guadalupe Canyon, otherwise they would have had a pretty fight with the hostiles and could have probably struck them on open or nearly open ground north of Guadalupe Canyon. Major Davis had sent word to Lang's Ranch how the Indians were heading; this message was transmitted to the commanding officer at Guadalupe Canyon. By one of those circumstances fortuitous for the hostiles, but fatal to the chances of the officer in question, a sleepy head on the shoulders of the officer in charge of the Indian scouts in his camp prevented two scouts being sent out with the couriers scouting for Indian signs between Guadalupe Canyon and Lang's Ranch, as was always done, and the two soldiers rode over the trail and did not notice it.

As soon as I reached Guadalupe Canyon in the lead I saw at once that no troops had taken up the trail, rode forward on it to make sure, and then sent word back to Major Davis to that effect. On his arriving there, where we had been ordered to stop, he sent word to the camp four miles below me on Guadalupe Canyon, and the commanding officer knew for the first time that the Indians had slipped by. Major Davis was rather wroth and made a few caustic remarks, but the Indians were gone. Our trains were somewhat demoralized by the forced marches, and as they did not come in, late at night I returned over the trail to bring them in. They were wrecks when I found them, but a little discipline soon put them in shape and we returned at once to our camp in the canyon. From there, as shown in Major Davis' report, we took up the hostile trail, following it to the south of the Chiricahua Mountains, where the Indians nearly ran over a camp of the Tenth Cavalry, who immediately pursued them hot foot. Nothing yet invented has ever caught a Chiricahua in the mountains, certainly not from the rear, and the hostiles got away. Other troops of cavalry took up the cry, dashed in, were distanced, and the twenty or twenty-five bucks seemed to enjoy the sport. We were constantly on the trail, and as our Indians were good trailers and had not forgotten the lesson when they overran the trail on the Janos plain, there was no similar occurrence, and the hostiles knew we were always after them and would stay. We chased them out of the Chiricahua Mountains over to Cochise's stronghold, from there across Sulphur Springs Valley, within a mile or two of White's Ranch, back into and across the highest part of the Chiricahuas, and out of them near White Tail Canyon, where they got new horses and near where Captain Viele with the troops from Cave Canyon, over whom they had nearly run on their excursion north, took up their trail and ran them back into Mexico.

Having been absent from my regiment and troop since July 1884, and Troop H, Fourth Cavalry, of which I was second lieutenant, being left by the absence of the first lieutenant on recruiting duty, and of the captain on sick leave, without a commissioned officer, I applied, upon the reorganization of the command, to be relieved from duty with the Indian scouts and placed in command of my troop in Guadalupe Canyon. The application was at first refused in the most complimentary way, but upon my making it plain that service in Mexico, where I had suffered such indignity at the hands of the treacherous natives, would not be at all agreeable to me and might tend to spoil my usefulness with scouts in that country, I was allowed to join my troop. Within four months Captain Crawford was attacked in Sonora, Mexico, by Mexicans from Chihuahua, Mexico, and murdered. Though he was the only support of his widowed mother and sister, no reparation was ever obtained from Mexico for the outrage against an American officer acting under orders from his government and under international agreement.

Though General Crook did not write this, the closing paragraph of his report, until he was about to leave Arizona, I will quote it here:

Before closing this report I desire to express my appreciation of the conduct of the officers and men during the many months they have been engaged in the discouraging and well-nigh hopeless task. Where all have done well it seems invidious to mention individuals, but while my thanks are due all, it seems proper to mention the names of Captain Wirt Davis, Fourth Cavalry; the lamented Crawford, who sleeps in a soldier's grave; First Lieutenant M. W. Day, Ninth Cavalry; First Lieutenant M. P. Maus, First Infantry; Lieutenants Britton Davis, Third Cavalry; Charles P. Elliott, R. D. Walsh, and H. C. Benson, Fourth Cavalry; Leighton Finley and W. E. Shipp, Tenth Cavalry; and S. L. Faison, First Infantry, who commanded expeditions or scout companies in Mexico and bore, uncomplainingly, the almost incredible fatigues and privations as well as the dangers incident to their operations.

Assistant Surgeon Henry P. Birmingham, U.S.A., at his own request was sent with the expedition into Mexico under command of Capt. Wirt Davis and earned the thanks of the department commander by his efficient and valuable service.

The Geronimo Campaign

HENRY W. DALY[1]

"The Capture of Geronimo," *Winners of the West* 11, no. 1
(December 1933): 1, 3

In March of 1885 I was ordered from Fort Apache to Whipple Barracks, at Prescott, to take charge of the pack train at the headquarters of the Department of Arizona. I found the mules run down. The clerks at headquarters had been riding them into Prescott to take in the sights of the town. Not that the sights of Prescott were any great shakes in the view of a young fellow looking for a little excitement. There were saloons aplenty and wide-open gambling, but Prescott had the name of a quiet place by the standards of the West of that day and date.

By April the pack train was in condition to take into the field. General George Crook and a small party went to the Grand Cataract, a tributary of the Grand Canyon of the Colorado, to settle a little Indian trouble between the Havasupai and the Moqui tribes. This business was so soon over that the excursion turned into an outing, more than anything else, much appreciated by me after a winter of sleeping under a roof for the first time regularly in a good many years.

In May we were at Whipple, with nothing but garrison duty to pass the time. For nearly eighteen months now, the Apaches, the terrors of the Southwest, had trod the white path; that is, had been at peace. A long and bloody road indeed had been traveled to this end, and it had been my fortune to have traveled most of it in person, serving through the Tonto Basin war of 1872–84, the Mescalero outbreak of '79 and '80, the Warm Springs campaigns against Victorio and Nana in '80, '81, and '82, and the Sierra Madre campaign that wound up with the surrender of Naiche in the fall of '83.

I had perforce acquired some knowledge of the Indians, who were subtle, treacherous, and cruel. They were, in fact, what the uninformed think nearly all Indians have been. There was just about one thing an Apache wouldn't do, and that was shoot a man in the back. I have seen that curious point of honor demonstrated more than once, and one time I myself figured too close for entire comfort in a test of it. Out of the tail of my eye I saw Geronimo, mad and drunk, coming up behind me with a pack of braves armed to the teeth. He just wanted to kill a white man to relieve his feelings. He halted a few paces in my rear and used every artifice by way of grunts and clatters of arms to make

A packer and mules. CENTURY MAGAZINE, APRIL 1889.

me turn my head. Once facing him my life would not have been worth a copper cent, but from my understanding of Apache character I knew that with my back toward him my life was safe. This performance caught the fancy of Geronimo, as he later told me.

My professional acquaintance with Geronimo was made during the Sierra Madre campaign against Naiche, head chief of the Chiricahuas, the most bloodthirsty of the Apache clans. This campaign took part in northern Mexico, where by special arrangement we were permitted to pursue the Chiricahuas. This campaign brought Go-yath-lay, or Geronimo, as he was known to the whites, to the fore as a war leader.

Geronimo was then no longer a young man, being forty, I should say, and about medium tall.[2] His frame was well muscled and, like most of the Apaches, capable of fabulous endurance.

He could march seventy miles during a night, fight all day, and appear no more weary than an ordinary man after an ordinary day's labor. Unbelievable, perhaps, but I have seen him do it.

The countenance of Geronimo was the most arresting I have ever seen on a human being. There was in it a look of unspeakable savagery, or fierceness, and yet the signs of an acute intelligence were also present. Geronimo was of a nervous type, which is, or was, rather rare among Indians. His countenance was mobile, rather than masklike. When he was mad he simply looked like the devil, and an intelligent devil at that. This type of leader was well calculated to advance himself under Naiche, an able Indian but a loafer when he could find a subordinate capable of assuming his responsibilities.

Geronimo. A good likeness, but the tepees in the background are inappropriate. NELSON A. MILES. *PERSONAL RECOLLECTIONS AND OBSERVATIONS.*

"The Geronimo Campaign," *Journal of the United States Cavalry Association* 19, no. 69 (July 1908): 68–103

In giving a narrative of the principal events of this memorable campaign, it may be well to remember that they are given as a dry statement of facts coming under my personal observation as packmaster in charge of the pack trains with Captain Emmet Crawford's command, and later with that of Captain H. W. Lawton (afterwards General Lawton), the operations being under the direction of the department commander, General George Crook, and his successor, General Miles.

Late in May 1885, it was reported at Whipple Barracks, Prescott, Arizona, that Geronimo, with about 150 of his band, had broken out from the Fort Apache reservtion and started for the Sierra Madre in Old Mexico, and that Lieutenant Britton Davis, Third Cavalry, under whose control the Chiricahuas were, was in pursuit with a company of Indian scouts, having with him Chief Chatto as first sergeant of scouts. On May 29 I received orders to pull out for Ash Forks with my pack train and to proceed thence to Deming, New Mexico, by train, and there report my arrival by telegraph to General Crook, then at Fort Bayard. On June 1 I received orders to await the arrival of Captain Crawford and to report to him.

He arrived on the evening of June 6, and I met him at the train. On his invitation, I went with him to the Railway Hotel, where we had a full conference as to the situation. I had known Captain Crawford for years on numerous Indian campaigns; and as he knew that I was personally acquainted with Geronimo and other chiefs of his tribe, many of whom had served as scouts in New Mexico and Arizona, it is but natural that he should have taken me into his confidence.

We discussed the probable duration of the expedition, the personnel of the scouts, the reliability of Chatto, and knowing the extreme caution of these renegades, their natural selection of terrain to avoid surprise, and their mode and rapidity of travel, either on foot or mounted, we also discussed freely a plan for scouting both flanks of the Sierra Mountains and for guarding all waters along the line. Captain Crawford stated that General Crook would have sufficient troops to guard every waterhole on the line, and a small number of scouts with every troop to "sign ride" the country between waters, and that a second line of troops would be stationed along the railroad, as water might be available.

It was thought that this disposition would afford ample protection to the settlers within a radius of one hundred miles from Guadalupe Pass, should hostiles attempt to reenter Arizona or New Mexico, and that the troops, with the aid of the scouts, would give them a warm reception. It was considered that it would be best to exercise the greatest vigilance in the vicinity of Guadalupe Pass, inasmuch as it lay in the direct line of travel from the Sierra Madre to the Apache reservation.

Captain Crawford said that Lieutenant Elliott and Al Seiber, with a company of Indian scouts and pack train, would join him on the next day, and that his movements would depend upon what news they brought of having cut any signs of the hostiles; also that Captain Kendall and Lieutenant Hanna, with a troop of the Sixth Cavalry then at Deming, would form a part of his command.

On the morning of June 8, Lieutenant Elliott and scouts having reported, we proceeded by special train to Separ, a station on the Southern Pacific, due west from Deming. On reaching Separ, Captain Crawford learned of the whereabouts of Lieutenant Britton Davis and his scouts, and we detrained and pulled out for Skeleton Canyon, due south of Separ, where we went into camp to await the arrival of Lieutenant Davis. He arrived the following day with sixty scouts and a pack train.

On the morning of June 11 the command broke camp and traveled in a southeast direction, passing by Black Springs, Fronteras, and the hamlets of Bavispe, Bacerac, Huachinera, and thence in a westerly direction to the Oputo Mountains, and about three miles west of the village of that name, reaching this point on June 21. Here it was learned that the hostiles had rounded up and killed a few beef cattle and headed north for the Sierra Madre. The following morning we moved about two miles east of Oputo and camped near where the hostiles had killed the cattle.

From the reports brought in by the scouts it was learned that the hostiles were in camp in the foothills of the Sierra Madre, not far from our camp. That night Captain Crawford sent Lieutenant Davis, Lieutenant Elliott, Al Sieber, and fifty scouts, with Chief Chatto as first sergeant, to locate their camp, attack them and destroy their camp, and if possible to cause them to surrender. Next day, June 23, a runner came in with the information that one of the hostiles had been killed, one or more wounded, and fifteen captured, without any casualties among our men.[3]

Lieutenant Davis returned that afternoon with his command and brought in the fifteen prisoners, composed of women, boys, and girls of all ages. Old Chief Nana, of the Warm Springs Apaches, was among the number.[4] This old rascal was the war chief of Victorio's band that made life a burden to the people of New Mexico for the three years 1879, 1880, and 1881, and led the troops of the Fourth and Ninth Cavalry in many a long and weary chase. With the exception of himself and twenty-five warriors who were absent on a raid, the remainder of Victorio's band were massacred in the Tres Castillos Mountains, Chihuahua, Mexico, by General Terrazas with two troops of irregulars and some Tarahumari Indian scouts. By the way, it was these same troops that killed Captain Crawford in 1886.

On June 24 Lieutenant Hanna with a part of Troop A was sent to Fort Bowie with the prisoners, and with him was sent a scout named "Dutchy," a most incorrigible and vicious scoundrel who had made the night hideous in camp by his overindulgence in mescal, obtained in the village of Oputo the day before. Dutchy was ordered to be confined in the guardhouse at Fort Bowie on arrival there. That afternoon was spent in rearranging cargoes to be carried by the two pack trains, giving an average of three hundred pounds to the pack mule. On the morning of the twenty-fifth the command moved in a southeasterly direction, and by easy marches, until the hamlet of Nacori was reached, and thence fourteen miles south of that village, where a permanent camp was eastablished on a little tributary of the Haros River, where there was an abundance of wood, water, and succulent grasses for the animals.

Captain Crawford, having realized that it would be utterly impossible to overtake the Indians by following their trail and that it was their policy to encourage pursuit and thereby wear out our stock, determined to remain quiet and to send the pack trains back to Lang's Ranch, New Mexico, for supplies. He directed me to bring back all the supplies and ammunition possible and, if practicable, to get another pack train, and thereby return with about three months' supply for the command.

So far I have not attempted to give a narrative of each day's travel, the terrain and distance traveled, and it is sufficient to note that our scouting was along the southern flank of the Sierra Madre, which were cut up by seemingly impassable ravines and hills covered with pine, fir, oak, mountain mahogany, scrubby cork trees, giant cacti, and of thorny undergrowth. The small tributaries of the Haros River rushed madly down between boulders of immense size, making fording them a perilous undertaking. Game was plentiful, there being an abundance of small white deer, black and brown bear, and wild turkeys, with which the scouts kept our camp supplied.

On the route to Lang's Ranch we passed through the villages of Huachin-era, Bacerac, and Bavispe, thence in a northerly direction across the Bavispe range and the Janos plains toward Loco Pass in the San Louis range. We passed by the Sierra Enmedio, the scene of the Tupper and Rafferty fight of 1881. Three miles north of the pass is Lang's Ranch, where we found Lieu-tenant James S. Pettit, in command of the supply camp, and one troop of the Fourth Cavalry under Captain Budd.[5] Lieutenant Huse, in command of Troop C, Fourth Cavalry, with another pack train, arrived soon after, he (Lieutenant Huse) being under orders to relieve Captain Kendall's troop, which was to take station at Alamo Waco, New Mexico.

The three pack trains were loaded with the necessary supplies, and under command of Lieutenant Huse, the return trip to Crawford's camp was made in ten days. On the following day Lieutenant Davis and myself were ordered to select twenty of the best pack mules from the pack train that had joined us at Lang's Ranch, Carlisle's pack train and two of his packers, and the remainder was ordered back to Fort Bowie. The supplies were divided between the two remaining pack trains, Daly's and Hay's, making a cargo of over three hundred pounds to the pack mule.

On August 2 the command broke camp and traveled in a northeasterly direction, which led us into the steep spurs of the Sierra Madre, which towered above us grand and gloomy, hidden at times by fleecy clouds, truly well chosen as a suitable home for the fleet and vindictive Chiricahua Apaches. After five days of continuous climbing over rugged spurs, a runner came in with the report that five of the hostiles had been killed by the scouts of Lieutenant M. W. Day's company, and that some women and children had been captured. These scouts were a portion of Major Wirt Davis's command that had been operating on the northern flank of the mountains and had crossed the divide and come in touch with our party.

Later in the evening of that day Chief Chatto and Al Sieber returned and reported that the hostiles had been caught by surprise by Lieutenant Day's scouts, and many were forced to jump over a steep bluff in order to escape being captured. Had this happened a day later the scouts of both commands would have caught the hostiles in a trap of their own choosing.

This occurrence scattered the hostiles, a part taking down the divide in a northwesterly direction, and the main party taking across the divide in an east-erly direction.

Crawford decided to follow this latter party; but realizing that the condi-tion of the troop horses was such that they could not stand the rough climbing, he concluded to send them back to the line, and on the next morning Lieu-tenant Huse started back with them for Lang's Ranch, taking ten pack mules and two packers to transport their supplies.

On the afternoon of August 8 we pulled out from camp and picked up the hostile trail. On the third day, on reaching the crest of what we assumed to be the summit of the Sierra Madre, we bivouacked at a camp made by the hostiles two days before. The remains of some slaughtered ponies found here testified that they were not only short of meat, but also that their animals were playing out. From here Crawford sent out an advance scouting party under Lieutenant Britton Davis and Al Sieber with three days' rations in hopes that they might overtake the hostiles.

Toward sundown, heavy clouds, laden with moisture, hung on the summit, and as they sank down the steep sides of the mountain, vivid flashes of lightning shot downward, revealing the cavernous depths along the flanks.

As we were encamped on a hogback, the water flowed down on either side, north and south; on the northern, a precipice of unknown depth would reveal itself as the lightning shot down into space. The frightened animals huddled together as if for protection, and the hair of their tails stood out straight, as if supported. On the southern side, mountains, or what appeared as such when traveling in the lowland, now looked like hillocks in the distance and stretched as far as the eye could reach—a magnificent panorama, never to be forgotten.

On the twelfth the scouts returned and reported the trail of the hostiles as having scattered. Crawford then decided to send a stronger force, with fifteen pack mules and with instructions to hang to the trail at all costs and to force a fight or surrender. They were to keep him informed of conditions, and he would keep as close touch as possible. The hostiles were evidently hard-pressed, as they were dropping their ponies on each day's travel. The trail also showed that there were not more than five or six ponies with the renegades. The scouts reported that they were climbing the steepest portion of the Sierra Madre and that many pack mules would be killed in the climb after them. Crawford asked me what I thought about it, and I replied that I had no fears on that score, knowing that every mule in the train was as sure-footed as a chamois and as careful with the load on its back as a mother with a child in her arms. Every mule was a pet with the packers, and each knew their name when spoken to in a voice of caution or word of encouragement as well as a human being in a similar situation would understand it. I may add the mules evidenced approaching danger quicker than a man would and knew instinctively how to avoid it.

On the afternoon of the thirteenth Lieutenant Davis, Al Sieber, and fifty scouts, with Chief Chatto, started, taking with them fifteen pack mules and three packers.[6] Knowing Sieber to be as true as steel when on a trail of a hostile, I cautioned him as they pulled out: "Don't forget that Chatto is with you, if it comes to a fight, or trying to surprise the hostiles." They left camp in a drizzling rain, and it kept up for the next five days, until every blanket and piece of canvas was water-soaked.

Climb[ed] up one side and down the other of a series of broken ridges that seemed to be without end, and with an occasional bog, waist or belly deep, that tried the mettle of both men and animals. On the eighteenth the sun rose bright and clear, and with it the spirits of everybody.

Captain Crawford expressed uneasiness in not hearing from Lieutenant Davis and decided to send Lieutenant Elliott, with twenty-five scouts, ten pack mules, and three packers,[7] to endeavor to overtake him and be guided by circumstances, but in any event, to send a runner back with the first information obtainable. By noon the following day the heart of the Sierra Madre had been crossed, and the downward trend of the broken ridges was noticeable. On the twenty-first the headwaters of the Casa Grande was reached, and the valley could be seen spreading out in the distance, bright and green. The sight of the green valley, with numerous beef cattle roaming at will, gladdened the hearts of man and beast.

On the twenty-second the valley of the Casa Grande was reached, and the Sierra Madre had been crossed by mounted men and pack animals, a feat considered impossible by the Mexicans on the other side of the divide.[8]

The pack mules appreciated the fact, as they sailed in cropping big juicy mouthfuls of succulent wild timothy and white grama grass. The animals had been subsisting on pine grass for the past fourteen days, and this being utterly devoid of sustenance, they had fallen off in flesh very considerably.

On August 24 we entered the hamlet of Casas Grandes and learned that Lieutenant Elliott, scouts, and packers had been captured and put in prison or guardhouse by the Mexican forces (irregulars), and that Lieutenant Davis and his party had crossed the river about a mile above the town, on the trail of the hostiles, and were in pursuit of them.[9]

As I had to care for the scouts with Crawford, in the absence of both the lieutenants and Al Sieber, the captain, on entering the plaza and before riding up to the commandant's house, instructed me to keep a sharp lookout in case of treachery. As the captain entered the house, every packer had his gun across the saddle in front of him, the mules being rounded up and held there by the scouts, and every street leading into the plaza was watched for any indication of trouble. I dismounted and stood in the doorway.

Possibly this may seem an act of bravado, but I had occasion to remember that Lieutenant McDonald of the Fourth Cavalry and his company of Indian scouts and pack train had been made prisoners in the little hamlet of Ascension in 1881. The "alcalde," or mayor, had received him and party most royally and gave a dance in honor of the occasion of his friendly visit. During the evening, and before the dance opened, a courier was sent posthaste to notify the commanding officer at the town of Janos that one hundred Americans had entered the town armed to the teeth and to make all haste possible in coming to their rescue. The scouts were placed in a corral enclosed by a strong adobe wall, and the lieutenant was given a room in the mayor's house. In the early grey of the morn the corral and packers were surrounded by Mexican cavalry and the lieutenant placed under arrest. The whole party was marched to Janos under guard and kept prisoners for two weeks, and fed on parched corn, until General Mackenzie effected their release. It was well that they turned them loose as they did, as two troops of the Fourth Cavalry were starting out from old Fort Cummings, New Mexico, to open negotations in force.

In the meantime, I noticed the captain rising from his seat, and the mayor all bows and smiles. The lieutenant, in brass buttons on his short coat and down the legs of his trousers, stepped forward and saluted, and the order was given for the release of Lieutenant Elliott and his party. In fifteen minutes up they marched, as sorry-looking an outfit as I ever saw, barring Lieutenant McDonald's, and in a few minutes more the pack mules were led up, about as sorry-looking objects as the men. The firearms of the scouts and packers were restored to them.

Eveything being in readiness, we rode out of town and bivouacked on the Casa Grande, about five miles west of the hamlet.

The following day Captain Crawford struck out in a direct line for the boundary, going into camp three days later close to the scene of the "Garcia" fight, on the western edge of the Janos plain,[10] and sent dispatches to General Crook, then at Fort Bowie, Arizona.

In the first days of September the captain sent Hay's pack train to Fort Bowie to recuperate. This pack train was afterwards divided into sections and apportioned among the troops on the line. About the middle of September Crawford sent me to Fort Bowie for a similar purpose, and on arrival at Bowie I was ordered to the southern flank of the Chiricahua Mountains, about twenty miles east of Bowie, with instructions to turn over ten pack mules and two packers to Captain Carpenter,[11] stationed at Galeyville. His camp was situated in a little park, with an outlet through a box canyon on its northern side, through which could be seen the San Simon flat and the Stein's Peak range in the distance.

On the night of my arrival a courier, Navajo Bill, arrived in camp with dispatches from General Crook to Captain Carpenter, with the information that the hostiles were reported coming down the Stein Peak range, and with orders for him to cut across the valley and endeavor to intercept them. Everything was in readiness by 3:00 A.M., and the two troops pulled out through the box canyon. On the following morning Navajo Bill and I struck out on the back trail for Fort Bowie. On the western edge of the little park it narrowed toward a dry ravine, up which the trail went to the top of the divide. At the mouth of this ravine, a family lived in a frame shack, who at this time were rounding up a bunch of horses on the divide. A short distance from the mouth of the ravine we cut hostile signs, scattered somewhat, the droppings of their ponies still steaming. I remarked to Bill, this is valuable information for General Crook to know as soon as possible, and determined to ascertain for a certainty their probable destination.[12] A little further on we found a burro and its rider shot dead. This man belonged to the shack we had just passed. Further on up the trail we found that the hostiles had captured some ponies from a shack on the crest of the hill about two miles from the first shack.

We followed the trail on up as it ascended towards the divide until we became satisfied that this hostile party would bivouac on the top of the divide for much-needed rest, and also to watch the movements of the troops cutting across the valley.

Not wishing to give them the impression that their location was known, we traveled back on the trail and then pulled over a saddle of the range to the main-traveled road to Fort Bowie. Having traveled about five miles toward Bowie, a bunch of horses were seen on our left coming down the slope at a two-forty gait, a rider in front waving his hat and one behind driving the horses. On they came for dear life, shouting "Indians! Indians!" On coming up they stated that they had been run off the divide by the Apaches, and they thought the family at the ranch had all been murdered. I informed them that they were alive, with the exception of the one man we found dead by his burro. I advised them either to drive their stock to Fort Bowie or down to the railroad station. This latter advice they followed.

Having lost fifteen or twenty minutes, Bill and I hastened on to Fort Bowie. On entering the parade ground we were met by Captain Cyrus S. Roberts, General Crook's adjutant general, and informed him of our discovery of the hostile party. He immediately took us to headquarters, where we gave our information to the general. I stated to the general that it was my impression that the hostile party would bivouac on the divide that night, keeping pickets out watching the flat for any movement of the troops in their direction, and also watching Fort Bowie; that they had undoubtedly seen the dust of Carpenter's troops on crossing the valley.

Soon after, the general left and took the train at Bowie Station for New Mexico, with the evident purpose of making a fresh disposition of the troops in that quarter.

On the afternoon of the following day Captain Roberts informed me that Captain Crawford was on the trail of the hostile party; that they had stolen a number of horses from the ranch and were beating back toward the Chiricahua range again. Also that he was sending out Captain Thompson's troop of the Fourth Cavalry[13] to pick up Crawford's trail and render him any assistance possible.

Knowing Captain Roberts well, I ventured to question the advisability of sending the troops to follow Crawford, as they would be of no practical assistance. I therefore advised that Thompson's troop be sent down the Chiricahua range, as I believed that the hostiles would follow an old wood road that led to the top of the range and thus they would be caught between two fires. However, Captain Roberts was obeying orders, and Thompson started out to follow Crawford. It was found that the hostiles did follow the old wood road over the range and thence into Mexico.

This practically ended the campaign for the summer.

A few days later I met Al Sieber, who gave me an account of their trip after the hostiles since they left us on the summit of the Sierra Madre. He stated that the hostile party kept one day's march ahead of them; that in passing Casas Grandes, Lieutenant Davis left two scouts to inform Captain Crawford that they would follow the hostiles as far as possible, and that they seemed to be heading for New Mexico. They knew of the trouble Lieutenant Elliott got into, but as they felt that Crawford would settle it, they did not think it advisable to lose any time in pursuing the hostiles. He stated that Chatto and some of the scouts had been very ugly on the trip, and that at times their lives were in danger. He also said that he and Lieutenant Davis were then going to headquarters to discuss the cause of the outbreak, which he would tell me later.

I told him not to be too aggressive, or he would be taking his blankets back to San Carlos, and that I would hate to be in Lieutenant Davis's boots, for I knew the "old man" would know the cause of the outbreak.

A few days later Lieutenant Davis told me he had resigned his commission, and Al Sieber "took his blankets" back to San Carlos.[14] I felt sorry for him, as a better scout, one who understood the Indian in all of his numerous phases, I never met. He was utterly fearless but still had sense enough to know when numbers were too many for him. His services to the government ever since the close of the Civil War had been invaluable.

In the early part of November Captain Crawford rode into camp and stated he was starting for Fort Apache to enlist a new company of scouts, the term of enlistment being six months, and that he wished me to have everything in readiness so as to be able to start by the end of the month.

On November 29 we left Fort Bowie. The party consisted of 100 Indian scouts, divided into two companies of fifty each, Lieutenant M. P. Maus in command of the first section, and Lieutenant William Shipp that of the second. Tom Horn was chief of scouts for the first, and William Harrison that for the second company. Dr. Davis was the medical officer, and hospital steward Nemeck, two pack trains, Hay's and Daly's, of fifty pack animals each, and twenty-eight packers, completed the command. Captain Emmet Crawford was in command of the expedition.

The route taken was by the way of the Dragoon Mountains, Tombstone, Fronteras, thence through the Cumpas Valley range of mountains. From this point the route took a northerly course toward Nacori, arriving at the summer camp, fourteen miles east of Nacori, in the latter days of December 1885.

From this camp, as during the summer campaign, scouts were sent out daily to endeavor to cut any sign of hostile trails. Perhaps I ought to state here that during the summer campaign at no time were we on the trail of Geronimo, Naiche, and their band.

In the Chiricahua tribe each chief had his own following, and each was extremely jealous of the other. Chatto operated in New Mexico and joined hands with old Nana of the Warm Springs tribe after Victorio was killed by General Terrazas. In one of Chatto's raids he killed Judge McComas and his wife on their way to Silver City, New Mexico, and captured their little son Charlie.

This led to the campaign of 1883, known as the Sierra Madre campaign, by General Crook in person, with the expectation of rescuing Charlie McComas. Peaches, a White Mountain Apache who led the expedition to the stronghold of the hostiles, stated that a white boy was with the renegades, but he was never found. No doubt he was killed by the squaws.

Chihuahua, another chief, had his following, and with him were some of the brightest of the Chiricahua tribe, such as Josanie and others of that ilk. This chief was first sergeant of a company of Indian scouts in New Mexico under Lieutenant James A. Maney of the Fifteenth Infantry in 1880, and after the outbreak of Geronimo from Fort Apache, or rather their camp on Turkey Creek, in May 1885, Chihuahua and Josanie led our force during the summer campaign. Geronimo during all that time lay hid in his stronghold in the Sierra Madre, and neither he nor any of his following made a raid during the past summer, as far as came to my knowledge. The killing of a few of Lawton's troop, left at Guadalupe Pass by Captain Lawton to guard the camp while he was absent with the main body of the troop, was done by a party of Chihuahua's band. The capture of a band of ponies at White's Ranch, the raid into Fort Apache, or the Apache camp on Turkey Creek, resulting in the killing of twelve of the friendlies and the capture of six women and children in the month of November, were also by Chihuahua's band.

The capture of fifteen women and children of Chihuahua's band on June 23 was effected by Chatto in the mountains north of Oputo, not as a feat of arms to please the white race, but to show the followers of Chihuahua, as well as Josanie, that he was their master.

In the early days of January 1886 I became convinced from certain signs of our scouts that they knew more about the whereabouts of the hostiles than they had reported to Captain Crawford. One night I questioned Corporal Juan, a White Mountain Apache, and accused him of this, and after I had become satisfied of it, I told him to bring Noche to me. They came, and after questioning him, I told them they must go to Crawford in the morning and tell him all they knew. Later, after the scouts and packers had retired for the night, I went to Captain Crawford, who was in bed but still awake, and informed him of my impressions and of the talk that I had with Juan and Noche. The next morning Noche and the medicine man approached Captain Crawford, and the latter commenced a harangue to him and the scouts that had assembled in a half circle about him. After talking for some time, he, the medicine man, produced a small buckskin bag, which he took around to each scout to kiss, and each repeated after him some form of vow or obligation. I then became convinced of their sincerity and that they would find the hostiles.

That day a scouting party was sent out, and on their return they reported that they had located the camp of the hostiles and that they were engaged in sun-drying some meat, evidently beef from some cattle that they had rounded up from a raid on some Mexican hacienda.

The next day Captain Crawford formed a party to go on foot to attack the hostile camp. He left six scouts and the packers, except three, with me to look after the camp and gave me instruction to store the officers' baggage, which was very little, with several hundred deer skins that the scouts had accumulated, at the village of Nacori, where the alcalde had promised to care for them. Three packers with eleven pack mules were selected to accompany the command, to carry the rations and extra ammunition. Orders were given that each man and officer should carry his own blanket, and all surplus impedimenta was cut out. That night, after supper, the officers and packers and a few of the scouts sat around the campfire discussing the proposed scout on foot through the mountains. Some did not think the scheme practicable and so expressed themselves to Captain Crawford. He, however, insisted that if they expected to surprise the hostiles, it would be necessary to take as few animals as possible, and to keep those taken well to the rear, and to travel light. The officers and chiefs of scouts were ordered to provide themselves with moccasins, as their heavy boots would make too much noise. He also ordered that a rope corral should be made around camp each night, outside of which no one would be allowed to pass except under guard. The captain told me he would like to take me with him but that I was needed more with the pack train, as one upon whom he could depend to bring it up when needed.

About sundown on the night of January 3, 1886, they pulled out in single file with Crawford in the lead, followed by the other officers, the scouts and the packers bringing up the rear. The captain called out a cheery "good-bye," as I watched the command from the top of a neighboring hillock, as it started up the slope. As they disappeared from view in the gathering darkness, I turned back with a feeling of depression, a choking sensation that I could not shake off that night.

The following day was spent in preparing dugouts, in which we stored all the supplies and settled down to await news from the command.

On the morning of January 9 Corporal Juan with three scouts came in with a note from Captain Crawford, saying that he was on the trail of the hostiles and directing that I take the pack train loaded with all the supplies, except the deer skins stored at Nacori, and to join him as soon as possible. He said that Juan would show me a shortcut, whereby I could avoid his tortuous and difficult trail and save much distance.

The pack train was immediately gotten ready and sent to Nacori for the supplies there, and then, returning by the way of our camp, we pushed on for the Haros River, where we bivouacked that night, having made about forty-six miles in all.

Our camp that night was on the bank of the river, at the mouth of a small box canyon. On the other side rose a steep, rugged mountain, so high that its top was lost in the clouds, while at its base was a narrow ledge, with scarcely standing room for animals, and between it and our camp the waters rushed down over rocks and boulders, a maddening river that bespoke an ugly crossing in the morning.

At daylight on the morning of the tenth, the crossing was made without accident, and we started up the mountain, the steepest I have ever ascended. We made a dry camp, or rather a wet camp, that night, as there had been a drizzly, misty rain falling all day that made the climbing very laborious for man and beast, and at times dangerous. Sufficient water was caught in canvas for making our coffee, and we laid down to spend a dismal and uncomfortable night.

The following morning, the ill-fated January 11, the sun rose clear and bright. After half an hour's travel, we struck Captain Crawford's trail, and the traveling became much better. About 11:00 A.M. a courier came in with a note from Lieutenant Maus, stating that Captain Crawford had been shot and mortally wounded by Mexican troops, that they were out of rations, and urging me to rush forward the supplies.

I immediately "cached" all impedimenta and started forward to make a forced march to join the command. About three hours later another courier arrived with orders for me to select a camp and the information that they were bringing the captain on a litter. Soon thereafter I could see their party coming slowly down the side of the opposite mountain. I selected a camp at the foot of the mountain, where there was running water, and anxiously awaited their arrival.

About half an hour later they came in, the scouts carrying the litter, and very soon poor Crawford was lying on the ground before me, apparently unconscious.

Having put up the only tent in the command, a common "A" tent, the captain was made as comfortable as possible in it. I spent the night at his side, watching for any sign of returning consciousness, but without avail.

The following day a "travois" was constructed, and I made a "wickiup," or shelter, of withers and canvas for the travois, to protect the captain from the sun and rain. The supplies that I had cached on the mountain the previous day were brought into camp and everything put in readiness for the return trip to Nacori. During the day Dr. Davis had prepared a little nourishment, made from a can of extract of beef, which Captain Crawford swallowed with difficulty and evidence of great pain. Soon after this was given him, I noticed signs of returning consciousness, and taking his hand, I asked if he knew me and if he could understand what I said, to which he replied by a pressure of my hand. I then asked him if, in case of his death, he wished to be buried by the Masonic fraternity, and he again replied by pressing my hand, and also by a grateful look in his eyes.

This was the only occasion in which he showed any signs of being conscious, although I spoke to him several times. I asked him if it was the Mexicans or the scout Dutchy that shot him, but he made no reply.

That night Lieutenant Shipp and I remained with him, he taking the first and I the latter half of the night.

On the afternoon of January 13 Lieutenant Maus decided to return to the line, in the neighborhood of the Cañon de los Embudos, and there await instructions from General Crook, first sending a courier in advance to inform the general of the conference with Geronimo.

An account of this conference and also of the events of Captain Crawford's operations will be related later.

Having made the captain as comfortable as possible in the travois, we pulled out of camp, ascending a steep and ugly mountain, with one packer leading the mule with the travois, and with the other two packers, one at each pole, to ease it over rough places and to bring them into proper line when making abrupt turns in the trail. The scouts were continually on the lookout for as smooth a trail as could be found, so as to make the trip as easy as possible for the poor captain.

On January 17, while on the march, one of the men lifted the canvas that protected Captain Crawford and saw that he was dead. He immediately reported the fact to Lieutenant Maus, who at once selected a suitable camp, and we bivouacked for the night. That evening I improvised a stretcher for carrying the body.

On January 21 we reached Nacori, and there, near the unfenced cemetery of that hamlet, we dug a grave in which we lowered the body to rest, wrapped only in his blanket, but with some slabs about it to protect the body from the earth. There was no funeral oration, no dirge, no taps, but we moistened his grave with our tears and on bended knee repeated the Lord's Prayer and "So mote it be."

I cannot pass, in this poor account of his untimely death, without paying a tribute to this remarkable, manly man, whose character and worth were so well known to me. He was the bravest among the brave; gentlest among the gentle; he forgave and overlooked the faults and frailties of others while being the most chivalrous and gentlemanly officer and man that I have ever known, in or out of the service. His loss to all those who knew him, and particularly to General Crook, was irreparable.

There was but one officer that could have taken his place in that campaign, but unhappily he was at that time not in good standing with General Crook on account of his trouble with the postmaster at Holbrook. I refer to Lieutenant Charles Gatewood of the Sixth Cavalry. Gatewood knew the Indian character thoroughly; they knew and trusted him, and had he been in charge of the Chiricahuas at Fort Apache, as he had been formerly, this outbreak would never have occurred.

Now to return to the events of the expedition of Captain Crawford that ended in his receiving his death wound.

The Indians had left the camp where our scouts had located them before Crawford's command reached there, and their trail led off over the mountains but, as he wrote me in the note brought to me by Juan, towards an unknown objective.

The trail was followed with all possible speed until the night before the hostile camp was attacked, when Captain Crawford formed a corral by stretching ropes around the bivouac and allowed no one to go beyond it.

This was done to prevent, if possible, any chance for the scouts to get out and give a warning to the hostile camp of his approach. This was a factor that always had to be considered, for the Chiricahuas expected or hoped that their friends among the scouts would give them timely warning of approaching danger. This would enable them to pack their camp outfits and saddle up, and also give them time for a parley in case they desired to surrender, or for their families to escape in case they wished to fight. In the former case a squaw was sent into the American camp to pave the way for a talk, they knowing that no harm would befall her.

On January 10 the hostile camp was located, and disposing his scouts to the best advantage, the command was given for the attack. The rush on their camp was so sudden and so unlooked for that the hostiles had only time to grab their rifles and break for the river, scattering in all directions and leaving everything in the hands of the scouts. Their ponies, dried meat, and camp outfits were all abandoned.

Crawford knew full well that it would be folly to attempt to follow their scattered trail and soon gave up the chase and went into camp on the site of their camp. That evening a squaw made her presence known by calling to our scouts and told them she had been sent to have a talk with the captain. When she came in she said that it was Geronimo's camp that they had jumped, and that he (Geronimo) wanted to have a talk with Captain Crawford.

Crawford told her he would talk with him the next morning, and she left camp to deliver the message. The command, being worn out with the tiresome marching and climbing mountain trails, all retired to rest with a sense of security and with the feeling that the campaign was practically ended.

Such, however, was not to be the case, as the light of the coming day brought forth an unforeseen occurrence that changed the whole aspect of affairs, an occurrence that was destined to prolong the campaign for another long nine months, that led to a change of departmental commanders and to international complications.

To understand fully this unfortunate affair, it will be necessary to go back some five or six years or, to be more definite, to the year 1880.

In the state of Chihuahua, Mexico, especially along its southwestern boundary, where the Sierra Madre divide it from the state of Sonora, there were in these mountains numerous strongholds for the Yaqui Indians and their neighbors, the Chiricahuas. The depredations committed by the latter on the little hamlets along its northern flank made life a burden to their citizens. Women and children were captured, and cattle in droves were driven to their strongholds, where they were secure from molestation by Mexican troops.

General Terrazas, brother of the governor of the state of Chihuahua, organized two companies of irregulars, made up from volunteers from the various hamlets of Ascencion, Janos, Casas Grandes, etc. For scouts and trailers, a company of Tarahumari Indians was enlisted. These scouts were as fleet of foot and as bloodthirsty as the Chiricahuas. This organization was known as the S.P., "Seguridad Publica," similar to the state rangers in Texas.

In 1880, at the close of the Victorio campaign (General Buell's), Lieutenant James A. Maney, Fifteenth Infantry, with a company of Indian scouts and a pack train, traveled with his command from the Candalaria Mountains to within a day's march of Tres Castillos, a range of mountains which formed a basin with but one outlet, through a box canyon. Owing to the hostiles having retreated to the interior of the state, it was deemed unnecessary for the American forces to accompany General Terrazas further, and Lieutenant Maney returned, rejoining the expedition at El Paso, Texas. The following day General Terrazas bivouacked in the Tres Castillos, where his pickets soon after signaled approaching dust, which, by the aid of field glasses, was made out to be the Apaches moving rapidly in the direction of their camp. Terrazas deployed his men on either side of the canyon, having put out all signs of his campfires and allowed the hostiles to enter the basin, where he annihilated the band, with the exception of twenty-five women and children, which were taken as captives to Chihuahua to grace a triumphal entry. The war chief Nana was absent with twenty-five warriors making a raid on the little hamlets, or else Victorio's tribe of the War Springs Apaches would have been dstroyed. This established the reputation of this organization as Indian fighters.

In the Geronimo campaign of 1883, Major Wirt Davis, Fourth Cavalry, operated on the northern flank of the Sierra Madre in the state of Chihuahua, having two companies of Indian scouts, about one hundred, with Lieutenant M. W. Day in command of the scouts, and Frank Bennet[15] as chief of scouts. He also had two pack trains of fifty pack animals each, and twenty-eight packers, with packmasters Patrick and Houston in charge of trains, a force similar to Captain Crawford, which was operating on the southern flank of these mountains, in the state of Sonora.

When Captain Crawford crossed the Sierra Madre with two pack trains and entered the little village of Casas Grandes the previous summer, it became known for the first time that the mountains were passable in that section to beasts of burden. The organization referred to, the Seguridad Publica and Tarahumari scouts, got together under the leadership of a captain whose name I find blotted in my diary of those days, and not to be outdone by the Americanos, crossed the Sierra Madre in quest of Geronimo. On coming down the steep sides of the mountains on the Sonora side, they located the smoke of the hostile campfire the same day that Captain Crawford jumped their camp and planned to attack the hostiles the following morning.

In the meantime, Captain Crawford had made his attack, and when the hostiles fled across the Haros River, he occupied their camp. Crawford's command being worn out by continuous day and night marching through thorny undergrowth and laborious climbing up and down the steep sides of mountains, their clothing literally torn to shreds, they laid down for the night for the rest they sorely needed. They knew that now there was no danger of an attack from the hostile camp, and no doubt they had visions of the successful termination of the hard campaign.

In the gray light of the morning of January 11, 1886, the camp was startled by the rapid firing of rifle guns, the balls striking the ground in their midst.
In an instant everybody was out of bed, gun in hand, the scouts shouting,
"Nacoya, Nacoya, Mucho!" (Mexicans, lots of Mexicans.) As the Apaches
hate and despise the Mexicans, the firing soon became general on both sides.

Captain Crawford ordered out Lieutenants Maus and Shipp, with scouts
Horn and Harrison, to cause our scouts to cease firing, and as Lieutenant Maus
and scout Horn spoke Spanish fluently, it was expected they would explain
that they were American troops and not hostile Indians. However, the Mexican
troops paid no heed and kept up their fire.

Captain Crawford took scout Dutchy with him and, handing his gun to
him, climbed on top of a large boulder so that he could be seen distinctly by
the Mexican troops. He was in the uniform of an American officer, although it
was literally torn to shreds and disfigured from all semblance of an uniform.
Taking a handkerchief in each hand, he waved them about his head, shouting,
"No tiro, no tiro, Americanos, Americanos!"

About twenty-five yards distant from him and across a small ravine, a
Mexican, taking a rest against a pine tree, took deliberate aim and shot down
poor Crawford. In falling from the boulder, his right arm was broken and one of
his eyes blackened, and when found a few minutes later he was unconscious.

The scout Dutchy claimed that he killed the Mexican that shot Crawford,
as well as another that was approaching in rear of the one shot. However,
before notifying the officers, Dutchy first took occasion to go through Crawford's pockets and appropriate what money he had on his person.

Scout Horn received a flesh wound in the left arm, and three Apache
scouts were also wounded. On the Mexican side, the captain in command was
killed and seven men wounded.[16]

By this time the firing had ceased, and Dr. Davis and the hospital steward
did all that was possible for Captain Crawford, as well as for the wounded.

In the meantime, Lieutenant Maus had sent Concepcion, a Mexican and
Apache interpreter with our command, to the camp of the Mexicans requesting
information as to why they continued firing on our party after they had learned
that we were Americans. Concepcion did not return and soon called out that he
was a prisoner and that they would not let him return.

Lieutenant Maus then went in person to their camp and was promptly
made a prisoner also.[17] He informed them that he was an officer of the United
States Army and that the scouts were in the employ of our government.

They then used threatening and villainous language towards him, and
finally they said they would only release him when he had furnished a certain
number of ponies for transporting their dead and wounded. Thereupon he called
to Lieutenant Shipp to send the required number of ponies to the Mexican camp.

As the ponies had been captured by the scouts in the attack upon the hostile camp, they refused to give them up and said that they would fight and die
before giving them to the Mexicans. Lieutenant Shipp reported this to Lieu-

tenant Maus and informed him that we could spare eleven pack and three riding mules that could be sent instead of the ponies. These were sent, and Lieutenant Maus and Concepcion were released.

That night,[18] just before midnight, while I was sitting by the side of Captain Crawford, Geronimo, Chihuahua, Josani, and others of the hostiles came into our camp and squatted around the campfire of the scouts. I could see them plainly, but as they chatted in low tones I could not always hear what they said. I knew there was no danger from their being in camp, and I made no report of it until the following morning.

On the following afternoon, while the preparations were being made for the return trip, the officers had a council with Geronimo and his followers, which resulted in an agreement that Geronimo would meet General Crook at the Cañon de los Embudos, near the line, but on the Mexican side and not far from Contrabandista Springs. This he said he would do as soon as he could round up his people, which would take about five or six weeks, and that he would make his approach known by signal smokes.

Lieutenant Maus stated that he did not know what Captain Crawford's instructions were and that it was not within his power to make any promises or agreement with Geronimo as to what would be the result of the conference with General Crook.

Feeling sure that the hostile chiefs would return to our camp again that night, I was anxious to watch their movements and hear what they said, in order that I might judge of their sincerity. When I relieved Lieutenant Shipp about midnight in watching Captain Crawford, we discussed the situation and wondered what would be the outcome of the agreement with Geronimo, as well as what steps would be taken by our government after the news of this sad affair should reach Washington, especially as there was plenty of evidence to establish the fact that the Mexicans had continued firing on our command after they knew that we were United States soldiers and scouts. Lieutenant Shipp was worn out by the marching, the attack, the worry and excitement of the affair with the Mexicans, as well as by his care of Captain Crawford, and was inclined to take a gloomy view of the results of the campaign.

Shortly after he retired, Geronimo and several of his party came in and remained about our campfire for two or more hours, when they left. A little later I heard one of the hostiles calling to Noche that the Mexicans were on the move and coming towards our camp, and for him to tell the "Captain with Glasses" that if they attacked us, Geronimo and his party would help him with every gun they had. This was said partly in Apache and partly in Spanish, and evidently with the intention that I should hear it, as they knew that I was awake and had been listening to them.

Our scouts at once gathered around and asked that more ammunition be issued to them. As I knew that they had plenty of ammunition, I felt that this was a ruse to obtain more for their friends, the hostiles; not to be used against us, however, but on the Mexicans, or anyone else that came in their way.

To resume our narrative, on January 22 we left Nacori for the rendezvous, where the conference between General Crook and Geronimo was to be held, passing through the hamlets of Huachinera, Bacerac, Bavispe, and Fronteras, and thence on to San Bernardino Creek. Here a camp was established, about ten miles southwest of the Cañon de los Embudos on the Mexican side of the line, and there [we] awaited the signal smokes that would indicate the coming of Geronimo.

About the middle of March 1886 smoke signals were seen at several points on the southern flank of the Embudos, and Lieutenant Maus at once proceeded with a party of scouts to the canyon to investigate them. He learned that Geronimo would arrive the next day, and he moved the command to the canyon, where he selected a camp on a low mesa, or terrace, at the base of which a clear stream of water ran through a dense growth of timber. On the western bank a small clearing was made for the kitchen of the pack train, and on the terrace the packers' camp was made in the usual formation.

Immediately back of our camp, a small rise gave a commanding view of the country in the direction of San Bernardino and Contrabandista Springs. Looking up the creek, the valley was bounded by a series of jagged terraces of "mal pais"[19] formation, which at the summit broadened out into a mesa, from which the country in every direction could be viewed. It will be seen that Geronimo had especially selected this place for his talk with the general with a view of guarding against surprises, as he could watch the approach of troops from any direction.

About 10:00 A.M. the following day Geronimo, Naiche, and Chihuahua, with their respective followings, swept around the base of the foothills on the opposite side of the stream like a whirlwind, dashing by as if in review, and rode on by our camp until lost from view in the timber. They crossed the stream about three hundred yards above our camp and made camp on the upper terrace on our side of the creek, having, however, the mal pais formation between their camp and ours. Geronimo could be distinctly heard giving orders to his warriors as he carefully selected the site for their camp.

None of them came near us that day, but on the next day a few of the Chiricahuas came into our camp, guns in hand, and chatted with our packers, many of whom they knew when they had served as scouts at one time or another. A few moments later, as I was standing alone watching these visitors to our (the packers') camp, I heard a rustling in rear of me, and Geronimo appeared, bringing his gun down to the ground with a thud. He evidently expected to startle me and then to laugh at me. I slowly turned around and spoke to him by name, and he, after eyeing me for a moment, came forward and shook hands with me, calling me their Apache name for "mule captain."

We had quite a talk there, he questioning me closely about several things, but particularly as to when General Crook, the "Gray Fox," as they called him, would arrive. Chihuahua also made me a visit, and we chatted of the days in 1880, when he was first sergeant of scouts under Lieutenant Charles W. Taylor, Ninth Cavalry, now lieutenant colonel, Fourth Cavalry, on our trip in the San Andreas Mountains, out from old Fort Cummings.

In the meantime, a beef contractor for the troops along the line named Charles Tribolett had put up a small shanty about three miles from Slaughter's Ranch at San Bernardino, where he kept a supply of mescal, vile whiskey, and tobacco for sale to anyone, white man or Indian, who had the cash. Our scouts patronized him, and we knew that the Chiricahuas would not be slow to do the same. On the night of their arrival pandemonium reigned in their camp as a result of their indulgence in this vile liquor obtained from Tribolett.

This, together with the nonarrival of General Crook, put the hostiles in an ugly mood, and their camp, as well as ours, was in a state of feverish excitment the following day, and many looked for trouble, while many bets were made that the hostiles would not surrender.

On the forenoon of March 25 the scouts reported that General Crook was coming, and soon thereafter he with his party arrived in camp. As was usual with him, he visited the packers' camp almost the first thing, expecting to get a good meal with us. Blair, our cook, was sadly disappointed that a fine wild turkey that he had been saving for the occasion had become spoiled. I told the general that while we were glad to see him, we had hoped he would come sooner, when the hostiles, especially Geronimo, were not in such an ugly mood as a result of their debauch.

After dinner, Ka-ya-ten-nae, a Warm Springs Apache of old Victorio's band who had never been on a reservation since a boy until he surrendered to General Crook in 1883, with Nana came in and shook hands with the general. Soon after, Geronimo and Naiche, with many of the Chiricahuas, gathered around our kitchen fire, and General Crook decided to have the council then and there, and soon our camp was alive with hostiles and scouts, all anxious to hear what Geronimo would have to say. Among them was also the beef contractor Tribolett. Lieutenant Maus, on seeing Tribolett, told him that his presence was not desired. While I had no doubt that this rascal was the cause of the ugly and excited condition of the hostiles, yet I did not think it wise to send him away, and so intimated to Lieutenant Maus, but he scouted the idea and said that the rascal ought to be hung. This man was the undoubted cause of the breaking away of Geronimo from Lieutenant Maus later, after his surrender, and his shack should have been destroyed then, as was done later by Lieutenant J. B. Erwin, Fourth Cavalry.[20]

Captains Bourke and Roberts of General Crook's staff were also present. The former, seeing me sitting aside on the cargo, called to me as he passed and said, "Come down and hear the old man give Geronimo hell." Having known Captain Bourke for many years, I thought this was a good time to warn him, and through him General Crook, that Geronimo, as well as the other chiefs, were in a bad humor and that it would be well to go slow in giving them hell; that had the general come a week before, he could then have talked as he thought best, but that it was too late now if they hoped to have them surrender, as he and his people had been on a continuous drunk ever since they came in.

General Crook selected the ground for the council and seated himself on a little ledge at the base of the knoll. Captain Bourke, with interpreters Montoya, Antonio Besias, and Jose Maria, Lieutenant Maus, and scout Noche were on his right in the order named, while Charles Roberts, a son of Captain Roberts, Lieutenant Faison, and Lieutenant Shipp were on his left. Opposite to the general sat Geronimo, clad in his usual simple costume of the Apaches—shirt, vest, and breechclout, and with a bandanna handkerchief about his head in the Negro-mammy style. On his right sat Naiche, the chief of the Chiricahuas, Geronimo being the second in command, or the war chief, and on his left was old Nana. In his rear stood Josanie and other chiefs, while in rear of the general were many of our packers and Mayor Strauss of Tucson.[21]

All being in readiness, General Crook turned to Captain Bourke and told him to have the interpreters ask Geronimo to speak and to tell him plainly what his reasons were for leaving Camp Apache, and for him to remember that all he said would be taken down in black and white; that he was here at the appointed place to listen to what he had to say. Captain Bourke repeated this in Spanish to Montoya, who in turn repeated it to Jose Maria, who understood the Chiricahua language thoroughly. In rear of old Nana sat Concepcion, another Mexican interpreter, who also understood Chiricahua and who repeated or nodded assent as Jose Maria gave the message to Geronimo.

Geronimo then addressed Naiche, the head chief, and after quite a discussion with him, began his talk, or address, for it was a speech full of fire and eloquence. It will be impossible to give his talk in full, and only a synopsis of the main points of it is noted.

He said that in accordance with the promise made two years before (1883) in the mountains, he had gathered his people and taken them to Camp Apache, where he was glad to be, and to the general as a "father," as he had promised he would be to them; that he gave them the long-nosed captain (Lieutenant Gatewood), who was their friend, to care for them, and that there they were happy; that he then took our friend, the long-nosed captain, away from them and gave another, who created trouble among them in many ways. That this new officer in charge of them gave the people of Chatto's village all they wanted and them what was left; that he decided against us in all games and races and punished our people for slight offenses, while Chatto's people went free under like circumstances.

He said that they had asked to have the long-nosed captain sent back to them; that his people had prayed with their medicine man at night to the moon and the stars, and in the day to the sun and "Good Spirit" to keep the darkness and evil spirits away from them, and to have their friend sent back to them, but he never came; that troubles and quarrels grew among his people like grass after the rain, until they felt that they had been forgotten by their promised father, and that their young men felt that they were becoming old women.

When he closed his long harangue he was covered with perspiration; he brought his legs close under him, straightened his back, and throwing his head forward with a jerk, his whole body quivering with emotion, he fairly hissed, with all the venom of his wild nature, "I want no more of this!"

It was a critical moment, and the excitement was tense among the Chiricahuas, and Naiche, who was watching his people, waved his hand to them to keep quiet.

During all this time the general had kept his eyes fixed on the ground, although Geronimo asked through the interpreters why he did not look at him; why he did not say he was glad to see him; why he did not smile and talk to him as he did formerly.

General Crook, at this time, wore a light brown canvas coat and overalls, a pair of Apache moccasins, and a low, double-crowned cork hat, and on his hands a pair of buckskin guantlets. His long whiskers were braided in two plaits, as he always wore them when in the field.

Turning to Captain Bourke, he told him to ask the following, and as it was being translated, he watched Geronimo closely:

I have heard what you said, and why is it that more than forty men were afraid of two or three; why did you, after leaving the reservation, kill innocent men, women, and children and steal their horses? The white people hold me responsible for all the innocent people that you have killed. You are no child to listen to every foolish story told you by the old women in your camp, and you know better than to believe them. You say that you heard that you were to be arrested at Apache, which was all nonsense, as there were no orders or thought of them. Yet you spread this story among your people to make them disatisfied. You promised me in the Sierra Madre that the peace made then should last forever, but you have lied to me about it. When a man lies to me once, I want something better than his word before I will believe him again. Everything that you did on the reservation is known to me, and it is useless for you to talk nonsense to me. You sent some of your people to Lieutenant Davis's camp and then spread the report among your people that they had been killed by him, and by that means persuaded them to go on to the warpath, sneaking through the country like a pack of coyotes, killing innocent people. You must make up your minds whether you will keep on the warpath or to surrender unconditionally. If you decide to stay out, I will keep after you until the last one of you are killed, if it takes fifty years.

He then told them to think it over during the night and to let him know their decision in the morning.

After the conference General Crook, the officers, scouts, and packers returned to their camps, and the Chiricahuas went up the stream until opposite their camp and then crossed over and to their camp near the summit of the ridge.

Remembering that on the occasion of the former conference with Lieutenant Maus, I had found the guns of Geronimo and his party stacked up against a tree near our camp, with a squaw guarding them, I wished to know if they had done the same thing on this occasion. During the conference I walked back behind them in the edge of the timber near the stream, and there, not fifteen yards away, were their guns, stacked against the trees in a similar manner, ready for any emergency. On the other hand, not one of our party was armed at the conference. I could not help commenting on this incident, which so plainly indicated that Geronimo was as fully entitled to the title "Red Fox" as was General Crook to his Indian name of "Gray Fox."

During the day following the conference our interpreters, Maria, Antonio, Montoya, and Concepcion, together with the friendly Apaches Alchisay, Mike, Noche, and Ka-ya-ten-nae, were busy in the Chiricahua camp endeavoring to bring about an amicable settlement on the question of a surrender. They kept us in the packers' camp posted on the favorable and unfavorable signs and the probable outcome of the final conference. All agreed that there was too much mescal in the hostile camp to bode any good results.

The Chiricahuas were at this time split up into three bands under as many different chiefs and war chiefs. The main band was under Naiche, with Geronimo as war chief; the second was under Chihuahua and Josanie; and the third under Chatto and Martinez. Since the surrender of Chatto in 1883, his band had remained on the reservation, and it was through his efforts principally, when he was first sergeant of scouts under Captain Crawford, that the capture of the fifteen Chiricahuas was made in 1885, as related before. I believe that it is not overstating the facts when I say that ninety-five per cent of the men, women, and children killed during the Geronimo campaign was done by Chihuahua and his about twenty "Cossacks of the Sierra Madre." He slipped through all the snares laid for him by the scouts of Major Wirt Davis's and Captain Crawford's commands. The troops guarding every water hole along the line could offer no resistance to his whirlwind dashes through their lines. He slipped into Fort Apache in November 1885 and killed twelve of the friendlies and carried off six of their women.[22] He stole a bunch of horses out of a corral at White's Ranch when there was a lot of cowboys guarding them who had remarked that they would like to see the color of a redskin that could get away with their horses. His party dashed into the various hamlets across the Mexican line and purchased what supplies of ammunition, mescal, etc., that they wanted and made love to the Mexican women of those villages. When occasion demanded, they could ride one hundred miles in twenty-four hours and could nearly do the same on foot with as much ease.

When on these raids they cached their old men, women, and children in the mountains so as not to be encumbered with any impedimenta. Their commissary was tied on their saddles, or strapped on their backs when on foot, and consisted of dried beef or horse meat. The leaves of the agave (mescal plant) were roasted and furnished a good substitute for bread, meat, and sugar. They carried water in a canteen made from the large intestine of a horse, and which, empty and dry, made no weight to carry.

In their raids they always traveled along the summits of the ranges, the better to observe the movements of pursuing troops, and so that they could rest when necessary without much danger of molestation. Miners and prospectors were their legitimate prey, they believed, and could, by killing them, obtain guns, ammunition, and other supplies, as well as fresh ponies. Yet, while they had many opportunities to shoot soldiers when they were hidden behind rocks or other protection, yet they seldom attacked them except when in self-defense. This, then, was the character of Chihuahua, who now proposed to surrender unconditionally to General Crook.

On March 27, about noon, another conference was held, about fifty yards above the place where the first council took place and in a thick growth of timber. General Crook seated himself at the foot of a large sycamore tree, while Geronimo and the other chiefs squatted about ten paces in front of him.

At this conference Chihuahua took a leading part and, after making a long and eloquent talk, surrendered his band unconditionally. He surpassed Geronimo in his resourcefulness of expressions and flowery similes, and it could be seen readily that he was doing his very best to make a good impression on the general. However, General Crook knew his man perfectly and landed the slippery eel like a diplomat.

While not being able to give all of Chihuahua's long talk, the following is in substance what he said:

The sun is looking down today on us, and the earth is listening to what we say; the one who makes the wind and the rain is now speaking to us, and tells me to speak the truth as he has told you to come here to listen to us. You have never lied to us, and I will not lie to you. I am satisfied with all that you have said to us, and I and my people will surrender to you, and want you to be a father to me and my people and treat us as your children. The rain, the grass, and the wind seem softer when you are with us, and we feel that you must be the one who brings it. I have traveled from mountain to mountain, and from water hole to water hole, and have never felt happy until today, when we know that all this is over and that you are to be our father. We want you to feel good towards us and not listen to what bad men say about us. I now surrender to you and will go with you and will shake your hand.

After the conference was over, and while I was talking with Captain Roberts, I noticed Geronimo watching us closely, as if trying to judge from our expressions what we were saying. I instinctively felt that he had no intention of going back to Fort Bowie; but to make certain as to the result of the conference, I went up the creek and mingled with the Chiricahuas to learn, if possible, their intentions.

I learned enough to satisfy me that General Crook had, in his efforts to bring Chihuahua to terms, been playing too strong a game, and that he had aroused the jealousy of Naiche and Geronimo, who considered themselves the chiefs of all the Chiricahuas, and that they were entitled to more consideration during the conference. The idea of Chihuahua, a sub-chief, receiving more notice during this conference than had been given him had rankled in his breast, and he, as I believed, intended to show General Crook that Chihuahua was not the whole push.

Then also, Chihuahua had surrendered unconditionally and agreed to go wherever he was sent, while Geronimo had insisted that they be allowed to return to Fort Apache and did not wish to accept the general's term of being sent to some isolated post on the Atlantic Coast for two years, they being allowed to take their families with them. However, the general had insisted that those were his terms, and that they might either accept them or take the warpath again.

Geronimo had looked to Chihuahua to back him up in their demands to be allowed to return to Apache, but the latter, knowing all the devilment of which he had been guilty, was only too glad to accept the conditions given him. Thus the conference broke up with a feeling of dissatisfaction among a portion of the hostiles as to the result.

That night pandemonium again reigned in the camp of the Chiricahuas, and the Apache yell could be frequently heard, and an occasional shot was fired.

Later, these shots became more frequent and were directed over the officers' tents and in the direction of the packers' tents, so that my men became nervous. I soon became convinced that all this rumpus was but another big drunk, and possibly with the intention of letting the general know that they, or some of them, were not satisfied, and that they were in an ugly humor.

About 9:00 P.M. Lieutenant Maus came to our camp and said that Captains Roberts and Bourke wanted to see me at their tent. I immediately reported there and found them sitting on the blankets that were spread out on the ground, and they asked me to take a seat with them. I felt before a word was said that, at Lieutenant Maus' instigation, I had been sent for to obtain my views as to the situation.

They asked me if I thought the Chiricahuas would go in to Fort Bowie; if I thought they would start for Silver Springs tomorrow, or will they go to San Bernardino, and generally what I believed was their intentions.

I replied first by asking them a question, and that was: "Did the Chiricahuas promise the general they would go to Bowie, and especially did Geronimo and Naiche make such a promise?" They replied to both that such promises had been made; then I said that I had never known these Indians to break their word with General Crook. I then told them that I did not think they would go as far as Silver Springs, although they might go as far as San Bernardino Creek, but that they would not go into Fort Bowie, although that if they could be taken as far as Silver Springs, they would then go on into Fort Bowie, for then they would have Captain Smith's troop of the Fourth Cavalry behind them.

I then said that they were now in a drunken condition and that the next day they would be as ugly and cross as a bear with a sore head and would not travel far; they will have more mescal tomorrow night, and then they will want to travel a still less distance. If we can get the troops behind them, they will go all right.

We learned the next morning that Naiche had shot his squaw in the leg during the night. Early in the forenoon, Geronimo and all of his band mounted their ponies and rode off yelling and howling like so many devils. They shot at everything in sight and were literally in a drunken frenzy. There is no doubt but what Tribolett sold many a bottle and canteen of mescal that night.

Chihuahua and his band remained in camp, which was another evidence as to how the wind blew and was a sure sign that they intended to keep their word.

About sunrise that morning Lieutenant Maus told me that the general would start back for Fort Bowie as soon as he could have his breakfast. I at first thought that this would be an excellent opportunity for me to have a quiet talk with him, and I therefore told the packers to wait until after we had breakfasted before coming to the mess canvas, but when it came to expressing myself, I thought better of it and said nothing about his going at this time. I had thought that it would have been far better for him to remain and bring in these people with him, and I wanted to tell him so, but I feared he might tell me it was not my business, and so I let the opportunity pass.

I knew that he was well acquainted with the circumstances; that he knew the feeling between the two bands; that they were at loggerheads, and no one there could control them as he could, and no one understood the Indian character better than he did.

However, after finishing his breakfast, he said good-bye and started for Bowie.

--- ◆ ---

"The Geronimo Campaign [Concluded]," *Journal of the United States Cavalry Association* 19, no. 70 (October 1908): 247–62

After the general left, I felt that I should have spoken my mind to him regarding what I believed would be the outcome of his leaving at that time and felt guilty for not having done so. But, as I have stated before, I knew that General Crook understood the Indian character as well as any man living, and although I foresaw the coming troubles with him away, I feared to suggest to him that it was not a proper time for him to leave this difficult job to his subordinates.

Had Captain Bourke told me in the conference in his tent the night before the general left what influences had been brought to bear on Geronimo to induce him to surrender, apart from those that had been offered Chihuahua, as

I learned them afterwards, I could have told him and General Crook that he (Geronimo) would never reach Silver Springs with the command. There had been influences at work night and day among the Chiricahuas, and the real work had been done before the two conferences were held.[23] Geronimo felt that the "hell" that he received from the general should have been put on the shoulders of Chihuahua; while, to make matters worse, Chihuahua had received all the attention from the general down to the interpreters, and this caused him and Naiche to become jealous and envious. As a consequence, both took advantage of the opportunity offered by Tribolett's supply of whiskey and mescal and got gloriously drunk, and the Chiricahuas made the night hideous, as before related.

There is no doubt but that Geronimo made up his mind that night to play a trick on General Crook that he would never forget and to prove that Chihuahua was not the whole push.

Shortly after General Crook left for Fort Bowie, I received orders from Lieutenant Maus to break camp, and soon thereafter we pulled out on the trail for the line. Lieutenant Maus left with Chihuahua's band, and I brought up the rear with the pack train and a few of our scouts.

When about four miles from the Cañon de los Embudos, one of the Chiricahuas came running up to me and said, "John Daisy Nantan (Mule Captain), Geronimo is very drunk; come and see him." I halted the train and followed the Chiricahua to where Geronimo lay on the ground in a drunken stupor. I shook him and tried to rouse him, and finally he rolled over and recognized me. He spoke to me in a mixture of Apache, Spanish, and English, and said, "Nantan, mescal heap no good; mucho sick, give me agua." I gave him a drink of water and finally got him up and on his pony, and then he wanted a drink of whiskey or mescal, which I of course refused to give him. I, however, promised to give him a drink and a good supper when we got to camp and told him he would feel all right then. His eyes were bloodshot and bulging, and generally he was a pitiable spectacle. I left him in care of the Chiricahua who had come for me and told him to bring him on into camp, where I would look him up.

As I had anticipated, the Chiricahuas refused to go any further that day when they reached our old camp at the canyon, and unsaddled there, thereby forcing Lieutenant Maus to encamp there also.

When the noon meal was ready, Lieutenant Maus, Geronimo, Naiche, Chihuahua, and two or three others were invited to it, and I tried to make it pleasant for them, although I could see that there was trouble brewing. I had hustled around and gotten a drink of mescal for Geronimo, as I had promised, and I had hopes that we would be able to get them on to Silver Springs the following day.

The next morning, March 30, we broke camp bright and early, with the Chiricahuas in the lead and I bringing up the rear with the pack train, as usual. About five miles out was Contrabandista Springs, where the man Tribolett had a small hut, from which he supplied beef to the commands and incidentally kept a supply of whiskey, mescal, and tobacco for anyone, white or red, who had money. As the Chiricahuas seemed to have plenty of money, they never lacked for mescal from the day they first arrived at the Cañon de los Embudos, and as was to be expected, it was a continuous drunk from day to day.

About this time, Lieutenant J. B. Erwin, Fourth Cavalry, who was attached to Captain Smith's troop and stationed at Silver Springs, took a detachment of his troop and proceeded to Tribolett's ranch, and there siezed all the mescal and other liquor that he could find and emptied it on the ground. Had this been done earlier, when the hostiles first came to the rendezvous, a world of trouble would have been saved.

As we were following the trail at a good gait, and having made such an early start, everyone was in good spirits, and we had visions that we might finally get the renegades to Fort Bowie. However, we soon saw that the head of the column had halted, and one of the scouts came back and reported that the Chiricahuas were going into camp. This stop there, after we had traveled such a short distance, meant but one thing to me—that the Chiricahuas had gone as far towards Fort Bowie as they intended going.

I rode up to Lieutenant Maus, who told me that the Chiricahuas said they were tired and would go no farther, and that they had gone into camp without any further explanation. He then ordered me to select a camp for the pack train.

Seeing that Geronimo had bivoaucked his band on the rise of ground on the left of the trail, and that Chihuahua and his band had camped on the low ground at the foot of this incline and also on the left of the trail, I chose the ground on the open flat on the right of the trail and facing both of the hostile camps, thus being in a position where we would be free from annoyance and still be able to watch them.

Later, when discussing the situation with Lieutenant Maus, I expressed the opinion that Geronimo would leave camp before morning, but the lieutenant seemed to think otherwise.

Soon after dark, as the lieutenant and several of us were sitting around the packers' campfire, a shot was fired over our heads by someone of the Chiricahuas in Geronimo's camp. Lieutenant Maus asked me what that meant, and I replied that I thought that it was an invitation for us to leave the campfire and go to bed. Soon afterwards a couple of Chiricahuas, one very drunk and the other seemingly sober, came by our fire and made wild gesticulations, at the same time cursing in a mixture of Spanish and Apache. I told our party not to notice them and said it was only another of their bluffs to get us to retire. I then motioned the packers to leave the fire and go to their beds about the cargo, where they usually slept, which they did, leaving the lieutenant and myself at the campfire. A few minutes later another shot was fired from the same direction and probably by the same Chiricahua, who had, I thought, been detailed to drive us away from the fire and to bed.

I then told Lieutenant Maus that in my opinion the hostiles were at that time making their preparations to skip out and that they did not want us prowling around to see what they were doing, and that they would not be certain that we could not until we turned in for the night. I also remarked that there would not be a Chiricahua in camp in the morning, and to prove this I will take the "bell horse" around the point in rear of Geronimo's camp and turn the mules loose to graze there, so that when the hostiles leave their camp they will scare the bell horse as they pass by in the direction of Fronteras. I knew that the bell horse, if frightened, would break for camp, followed by the mules, and that this would awaken me and the packers.

The lieutenant still did not think so and went off to bed, and I soon followed him, but did not sleep. I had my rifle and ammunition by my side, as I rolled myself in my blanket and there waited patiently for what I felt sure was to follow. The night was perfectly clear, and I could see Chihuahua's band wrapped in their blankets, with no a sign of anything moving. At 2:30 A.M., by my watch, I again took a look at Chihuahua's camp, but there was no sign of movement, and I began to think that I might be mistaken, or that at least Chihuahua was not in the plot with Geronimo.

Sometime after 3:00 A.M. I thought I heard the faint tinkle of the bell, and soon there was no doubt of it, as I could hear it coming closer and louder. I at once ran with gun in hand to Lieutenant Maus and told him they were gone. He asked, "What is gone?" When I said, "The Chiricahuas—Geronimo has gone," he replied, "You are crazy; do you not see them over there?" I then said that Chihuahua and his band are there, but Geronimo has gone, and asked him if he did not hear the bell horse coming as fast as he could travel. He still did not believe me, and I asked him to go up on the hill with me and be convinced. By this time the packers were all up, and we went up the incline to where Geronimo's camp had been, only to find that they had skipped for the Sierra Madre.

Upon our return, the lieutenant asked what was to be done then and, upon my advice, went to Chihuahua's camp and asked him and Ka-ya-ten-nae their opinion as to Geronimo's movements. They, having heard the stir and noise in our camp, were getting up and said they would look around and report later. Ka-ya-ten-nae saddled his horse and rode off, and was gone nearly an hour.

In the meantime, the lieutenant had counted Chihuahua's band and found that about eighty, young and old, of his band had remained with him.

While he was doing this, I interviewed Chihuahua, I having known him well when he was a first sergeant of scouts under Lieutenant Maney, and got his opinion regarding the prospects of Geronimo returning after getting over the effects of his spree. He said that he would never return of his own accord.

When Ka-ya-ten-nae returned, he reported that the trail led off toward the Sierra Madre, and that he had followed their trail for some distance in that direction.

After discussing what was the best thing then to be done, Lieutenant Maus decided to send what Chiricahuas there were left on into Fort Bowie under charge of Lieutenant Shipp, sending with him what pack mules we did not need, and that he with the scouts and the remainder of my pack train would

follow Geronimo's trail. I had advised him that it would be absolutely necessary to make some such demonstration in order to satisfy General Crook that
we had done all in our power to bring Geronimo and his party to Fort Bowie.

As soon as possible we pulled out on their trail and followed it in the
direction of the hamlet of Fronteras, striking the Bavispe River about fifteen
miles from our camp. On the other side of this river the trail split, one party,
evidently the old men, women, and children, heading for the Sierra Madre, and
the other took up the river. This latter trail was evidently that of the warriors,
and they were without doubt bent on a raiding expedition to replenish their
stock and supplies, which we found out later was the case.[24]

The scouts, finding the trail divided, told Lieutenant Maus that there was
no further use of following it, and he decided to return to Fort Bowie, which he
did the next day.

While on the return march the next day, April 1, our scouts saw some signals, which upon investigation proved to be made by two of the Chiricahuas,
who, having been too drunk to keep up with the renegades, had laid down and
gone to sleep and had been left behind. On seeing our party they decided to
join us, and did so. They said that if it had not been for the mescal that they
and the others had gotten, that none would have left, and all would have
returned to Fort Bowie.

In my opinion, the primary cause of this outbreak of Geronimo from the
camp was due to the unfortunate manner in which the two conferences were
conducted, in which, in the first, Geronimo was humiliated, and in the second,
Chihuahua was lauded and treated with all the courtesy possible. This aroused
the jealousy of Geronimo and started the antagonism between the two bands.
Geronimo felt that, inasmuch as up to that time Chihuahua's band had committed all the depredations and murders, he was being unjustly discriminated
against, and this, with the easily obtained mescal, started him off on his debauch,
which ended by his leaving Lieutenant Maus's camp on the night of March 31.[25]

We arrived at Fort Bowie on April 3, and Lieutenant Maus reported the
unfortunate circumstances to General Crook. What passed between them I do
not know, but on the following day we learned that the general was to be
relieved by General Miles.

This astonished me greatly (I am writing from the notes made at that time
in a diary that I kept), because I thought there was, or should be, no trouble in
inducing Geronimo to come in after he had fully recovered from the effects of
his drunks, provided that the proper man was sent after him.

There were several officers among those who had been in command of
the scouts in whom the Indians had confidence, to whom Geronimo would
have listened, whose advice he would have followed, and who could have
gone to his camp with perfect safety. I could have named half a dozen such
officers, any one of whom Geronimo would have received, and with whom he
would have gladly returned to Fort Bowie. With the exception of Geronimo,
Naiche, and Ka-ya-ten-nae, all had served from one to three enlistments as

scouts, and these Indian companies had always been under the command of an officer, chosen usually from the cavalry, whom they liked and who had their confidence.

When Captain Crawford was killed, General Crook lost his right-hand man, and the unfortunate trouble with Lieutenant Gatewood regarding the Holbrook post office incident deprived him of his next best man, although there were many other officers whose services were as valuable, except that these two were in close touch with the Chiricahuas for from three to six years and were much beloved by them.

A few days later, while engaged in a game of billiards with General Crook at the officers' club, he spoke of this escape of Geronimo and said he had almost lost confidence in human nature. I then told him that I had been on the point of suggesting to him the morning he took breakfast with me at the Cañon de los Embudos that he ought to remain and come in with the Chiricahuas, and that had he done so all this trouble would have been avoided. He replied that other duties put upon him by the War Department required his immediate presence at Fort Bowie.

A few evenings later this matter of Geronimo's escape and the best means of effecting his return was being discussed in the club room, and while all agreed that it would have been better to have had in some manner two or three troops of cavalry present at the time of the conference, or soon after, but all feared that the approach of cavalry would have alarmed the hostiles and have caused all of them to leave before the troops could arrive. They, of course, were watching every approach to the rendezvous. Upon being appealed to for my opinion, I stated that it was too late to express my ideas as to what should have been done, but the only possible way to have gotten troops there would have been to have sent word to Captain Smith at Silver Springs and have him send a courier to us with information that the Mexican troops were on the way to Geronimo's camp and that he was coming with his troops to protect the hostiles from an attack by them. The fear of Mexican troops being in the vicinity would have induced them to accept the protection of the American soldiers. However, all this was an afterthought.

A few days later General Nelson A. Miles arrived at Fort Bowie and assumed command of the Department of Arizona on April 12, 1886, and soon thereafter active operations against Geronimo were resumed. As in the preceding campaigns, the services of Indian scouts were employed, these being organized into companies commanded by selected officers from the cavalry service.

In these operations against Geronimo, General Miles used the heliograph, by establishing stations on prominent peaks in the zone of operations, these being under the supervision of Lieutenants Dravo and Fuller of the Signal Corps. It was thought that this and the more general use of military forces, in conjunction with the Indian scouts, would bring the campaign to an early conclusion.

On May 1 my pack train and that of Willis Brown,[26] who had been my

Captain Henry Lawton. NELSON A. MILES. *PERSONAL RECOLLECTIONS AND OBSERVATIONS.*

cargador in the previous campaign under Captain Crawford, were selected to carry supplies for the command of Captain H. W. Lawton, Fourth Cavalry.

On May 2 I received orders to proceed with both pack trains to Fort Huachuca, and on arrival there to draw the necessary supplies from the Quartermaster's Department, rations, etc., and make all preparations for an early start upon the arrival of Captain Lawton.

These supplies were divided equally between the two trains, so that each mule had a load of about 250 pounds, and the cargo was made ready for moving at an instant's notice.

On the afternoon of the fourth Captain Lawton and Assistant Surgeon Leonard Wood arrived. I had known Captain Lawton for many years, ever since 1866. He was of athletic build, tall and large of frame; his hair at that time was raven black, and when close cut, as he usually wore it, stood straight up like bristles; his eyes were jet black, and when he was excited, they had a nervous twitch; his nose was rather large and inclined to aquiline; forehead low and narrow; he had a delicate mouth which hid a remarkably fine set of teeth; his ears were large and prominent, and he always wore a mustache, of which he affected great pride. He was always physically aggressive towards enlisted men and civilian employees, sometimes harshly so, but in later years his disposition underwent a radical change in this respect, apparently to me, as his hair changed from a coal black to perfect white, from a rough rudeness to the manners of a Chesterfield. He was always outspoken, even to superiors in rank; strong in his friendships and the reverse to those he disliked. As a quartermaster he had few, if any, superiors in the art of handling field transportation, and he had rendered invaluable service to General Mackenzie throughout his many Indian campaigns in the Southwest ever since the close of the Civil War. He was essentially a soldier and delighted in his profession.

On May 5 Captain Lawton's command, consisting of thirty-five men of Troop B, Fourth Cavalry (Lawton's), twenty men of Company D, Eighth Infantry, Lieutenants Terret and Johnson,[27] twenty Indian scouts[28] under Lieutenant L. Finley, Tenth Cavalry, and Tom Horn as chief of scouts (Horn had served under Captain Crawford and Lieutenant Maus in a similar capacity in the preceding campaign and rendered valuable service); Assistant Surgeon Wood, and the two pack trains of fifty pack mules and fourteen packers each, started from Fort Huachuca, Arizona, ostensibly for the Sierra [Madre], passing down by old Fort Crittenden, Calabasas, and Nogales.

When Geronimo had split up his party by sending the women and children to some stronghold in the mountains, he and the others raided the neighboring hamlets and obtained what mounts they needed, in addition to some beef and cattle, and then joined the others, the entire band consisting of twenty bucks and sixteen women and children.

He naturally expected that General Crook would keep his promise and pursue him until the last one was either captured or killed, and in his stronghold in the mountains awaited developments. Finally, becoming restless and anxious to know what was going on, he made a flying raid to Fort Apache in the latter part of April. There he learned that the troops were on the move, and he again divided his band into two parties, leaving the women and children in some secure and secluded place, and headed for the Patagonia Mountains and the neighboring ranges. This was farther west and in a more thickly settled country than that in which Chihuahua had operated the year before, and he went there probably for two reasons: First, to let the citizens who had been anxious for his scalp know that he remembered their wishes and was willing to give them the opportunity to take it; and second, by confining his operations to the Patagonia, Pinito, Mariquilla, and Canea mountains, he would be able to wear out any mounted troops that should attempt to follow him, particularly as this would secure the safety of the squaw camp in the mountains farther north. After leaving Fort Apache, Geronimo passed south through the Santa Catalina, Colorado, Whetstone, Mustang, Patagonia, and Pinito ranges. In this last range he was engaged in a fight with Captain Lebo's troop of the Tenth Cavalry, where a corporal was badly wounded, and who was rescued while under a galling fire by Lieutenant P. H. Clarke.[29] I had the pleasure of meeting this young and gallant officer before and afterwards.

Again they were engaged with, or rather surprised by, Captain Hatfield's Troop D, Fourth Cavalry, on the fifteenth near the Santa Cruz River, where they lost their ponies and all their camp outfit. However, they in turn pursued Captain Hatfield and recaptured their ponies and camp plunder, with the loss to the troop of one man killed.[30] Many acts of bravery were displayed in this fight by Sergeants Adams, Craig, and packer Bowman in rescuing the wounded man before he died, he having used all the ammunition he had in his belt in defending himself.

After this fight, the Chiricahuas separated, one party going east and north in the direction of Apache, and the other to the northwest in the direction of San Carlos, taking advantage of the mountain ranges in each case. Captain Lawton also separated his command, he with Packmaster Brown going west, and my train going with the infantry under Lieutenants Johnson and Terrett.

We reached Calabasas about June 1, where we were joined by Captain Lawton and Dr. Wood. General Miles and his aide, Lieutenant Dapray,[31] arrived about the same time.[32]

The hostiles, having reached the neighborhood of Apache and San Carlos, turned and headed for the Santa Catalina Mountains, where they were attacked by the Tucson Rangers under Dr. Samaniego. In making their escape, they left a small Mexican boy that they had captured in the hands of the rangers. From there they passed down through the Colorado, Whetstone, Mustang, and Patagonia mountains, and in the latter were surprised by Lieutenant R. D. Walsh, Fourth Cavalry, who captured their ponies and camp outfit. Captain Lawton continued the pursuit with a detachment of cavalry and scouts—about twelve or fourteen of each—into the Azul Mountains, where they turned in a southeasterly direction and headed for their squaw camp, which was located either in the Oputo, Bacadehuachi, or Nacori mountains. After the Chiricahuas left the Azul Mountains, the chase after Geronimo came to an end, and preparations were then made for a campaign into the Sierra Madre. New scouts were enlisted, a fresh detachment of infantry detailed, and a permanent supply camp was established at Oposura in the state of Sonora, with Lieutenant Benson in command, the supplies being hauled to this camp by wagon transportation.

As the Geronimo campaign practically ended with their leaving the Azul Mountains, it may be well to give a brief summary of the events up to this time.

When Geronimo and Naiche broke out from their camp at Fort Apahe on May 16, 1885, they took with them 132 Chiricahua men, women, and children, of whom 40 were bucks, and these 40 led the troops on many a long and weary chase during the years 1885 and 1886. Naiche, the head chief, divided his following into three bands under the sub-chiefs Geronimo, Mangus, and Chihuahua, and they headed for the Sierra Madre in Old Mexico.

There they selected a suitable camp for the women and children, and then proceeded to divert the attention of the troops so as to prevent their discovering the whereabouts of this camp. This they did by leading them, as before related, over the highest mountain ranges in their efforts to wear out the horses and men of the pursuing troops.

Mangus operated in the states of Chihuahua and New Mexico, Chihuahua in the states of Sonora and Arizona, while Naiche and Geronimo guarded the squaw camp. The latter were kept informed of the movements of the troops from time to time.

When the two commands of Major Wirt Davis, operating on the north of the Sierra Madre, and Captain Crawford, on the south, had Geronimo between them, as before stated, Lieutenant Britton Davis captured fifteen of the women and children and old Nana, and about the same time Lieutenant M. W. Day,

Ninth Cavalry, captured about the same number of women and children, a squaw and two children being killed by the scouts under his command. This was the first time the squaw camp had been located, and Geronimo found it necessary to divert the troops from that vicinity. This was done by sending raiding parties under Chihuahua, Josanie, and Mangus by different routes in the direction of Apache and San Carlos. As they had the scouts in their rear, these raiding parties led them from one range to another, over the highest summits, and occasionally stealing what stock they needed, and killing a few miners and taking their supplies of food and ammunition.

At no time during this campaign were the hostiles without communication between their camps and Fort Apache or San Carlos, and were well posted as to the movements of all commands, and they relied on their friends to warn them of approaching danger. It was almost impossible to surprise them, although this was done on a few occasions and their ponies captured, but it was easy for them to travel on foot over the highest mountains, their endurance in this respect being simply marvelous. It was also easy for them to obtain remounts by making a raid on the ranches on either side of the line.

To return to the campaign under General Miles: Soon after the supply camp was established, Captain Lawton, learning of some depredations committed by the hostiles in the vicinity of Tonabava, left Oposura the first week of July with a command consisting of a detachment of scouts and some infantry, the former under Lieutenant Brown, and the latter under Dr. Wood, the latter taking the trail on foot with the scouts and infantry, and at the same time caring for the sick.

I was compelled to return from Oposura to Fort Huachuca for treatment in the hospital for sciatic rheumatism, and where I remained for four or five weeks. I returned to Captain Lawton's camp in company with Lieutenant A. L. Smith, Fourth Cavalry, and Billy Long, a dispatch carrier, his camp then being located about fifteen miles south of Nacori, Captain Crawford's old camp.

Soon after I returned, the captain sent for Tom Horn, chief of scouts, and myself to come to his camp. We found him with a map spread out on his bed on the ground, and he pointed out to me his route since leaving Oposura and then asked our views as to where the hostiles were then located. He and Horn agreed that they were somewhere within forty or fifty miles south of his camp, but I differed with them and said there was nothing in that direction to take them there, as the people were poor, with no cattle, stock, or firearms, and there was no game whatever, not even a jack rabbit. I told him that he would probably next hear of them in the Cumpas Valley, or perhaps farther east, in the vicinity of Granadas or Oputo.[33]

However, Captain Lawton did not think so and made preparations to cross the Haros River, which was high, and a dangerous stream to cross.

As I was still suffering with sciatic rheumatism (I was being treated by Dr. Wood, who gave me morphine to ease the pain), Captain Lawton informed me that he was going to send me back to the supply camp, as it would be

Crossing the Haros River. NELSON A. MILES. *PERSONAL RECOLLECTIONS AND OBSERVATIONS.*

impossible for me to go on, and that he would send me in charge of the infantry that he intended sending back to Oposura. He said that in case I met General Miles, I was to tell him that he (Captain Lawton) did not want any more infantrymen, and told me to say to him that he might as well try to hunt Indians with a brass band.

On the way to Oposura I met Lieutenant Wilder, Fourth Cavalry, who enquired as to the whereabouts of Captain Lawton and the hostiles. I told him the direction Lawton had taken and where I believed the Indians had gone; and while I had not cut any signs, that he had better keep a sharp lookout for them. The following day I met a Mexican courier with dispatches for Captain Lawton, whom I directed where to find him.

On arriving at Benson's camp, I learned that Geronimo had passed down the Cumpas range and had killed some miners,[34] and that he was then at Fronteras trying to make terms with the Mexican officials. I did not think that Geronimo was seriously considering this, as it would mean their extermination, but that he was secretly endeavoring to procure supplies, as well as mescal.

I learned later that Lieutenant Gatewood was then on his way with two friendly Chirichuas to locate Geronimo with a view of inducing him to surrender. Gatewood knew full well his influence with these Indians and did not underestimate his powers when he proposed to bring them in.

The two friendlies made their presence known to Geronimo by signal smokes and, on being answered, entered his camp. On telling them that Gatewood wanted to come in and talk with him, Geronimo went out and met him and asked him why he did not come in with the friendlies. Gatewood replied that he was not certain that Geronimo would receive him, upon which the latter replied that his friends were always welcome in his camp and that it was always safe for them to come.

The Mexican courier that I had met on his way to Captain Lawton had a dispatch informing the captain that Lieutenant Gatewood was in communication with Geronimo and ordering him to proceed to Fronteras and join Gatewood as soon as possible. He (Lawton) immediately proceeded with a few scouts and, riding night and day, joined Gatewood and there met Geronimo.[35] The latter at once asked for supplies, to which request Captain Lawton replied that his pack train would be in soon, when the supplies would be forthcoming. Geronimo then told him that his pack train was lost back in the woods and would not be in for two or three days. Captain Lawton seemed surprised at this, and was more surprised when Geronimo told him every camp he had made and how he was dressed.

The result of the conference of Geronimo and Gatewood and Lawton was that he agreed to move with Lawton's command to Skeleton Canyon, inside our lines, where he would confer with General Miles.

While waiting for General Miles at Skeleton Canyon, Geronimo saw what he thought was an indication of an attempt to surround his camp. He at once notified Captain Lawton that it must stop or he would leave. No further attempt was made to surround him. I mention this fact to show the nervous fear that Geronimo had that some trick would be played on him, and were it not for the fact that Gatewood was present, he would not have remained during the prolonged delay that they waited there for the arrival of General Miles.

The general at last came on September 3, in an ambulance, and after the conference with Geronimo and Naiche, they and a few others were requested to get in the ambulance and ride with the general to Fort Bowie. This they did, and they arrived at Fort Bowie on the evening of September 5. Captain Lawton arrived with the remainder of the Chiricahuas three days later, when all were put on board the cars and sent to Florida.

— ◆ —

"Scouts Good and Bad," *The American Legion Monthly* 5, no. 2 (August 1928): 24–25, 66–70

In the fall of 1885 I arrived at Fort Bowie in charge of a party consisting of two Apache scouts, Jack Wilson, and myself that had been sent into the mountains to recover stolen mules and break up a gang of army stock rustlers. We found the mules and the thieves. We brought the mules back with us, and this procedure met with the pleasure of General Crook, to whom I reported.

About this time Captain Emmet Crawford, Third Cavalry, rode into the post, bound for Fort Apache to engage scouts for an expedition into Mexico against the celebrated Apache warrior Geronimo. Captain Crawford was one of the famous Indian fighters of his day. Returning from Fort Apache with 195 scouts, he organized his expedition along rather novel lines. Geronimo being able to cover one hundred miles to white troops' twenty-five, and to subsist on what troops would refuse to eat, Crawford resolved to take no troops. The peril of the procedure was pointed out, but Emmet Crawford was afraid of nothing on this earth. I frankly felt complimented when he asked me to command one of the two pack trains of the expedition.

With three officers, a surgeon, two chiefs of scouts, the pack trains, and 195 scouts, we crossed the border on December 1, 1885, and entered the trackless mountains of northern Mexico. Inasmuch as everything, our lives included, depended upon the fidelity and success of the scouts, I fell to studying them, which was not difficult, as scouts and packers were always thrown a good deal together on the march. At night, scouts usually gathered about the campfires of the packers. The chief scout (not chief *of* scouts) was a Chiricahua Apache named Noche. The medicine man was a Coyotero Apache named Nah-wah-zhe-tah, or Nosey, as we called him because of his long nose. A band of scouts without a medicine man was inconceivable. He was their spiritual leader and was expected to foretell the future. I knew these Indians to be all right, but there were others I was not so sure of, in particular one Dutchy, as we called him.

I had served with Dutchy on other campaigns and knew him to be a drunkard, a thief, and a murderer. At Fort Cummings, New Mexico, one night he got his skin full of mescal and was running the other scouts around with a butcher knife. I was directed to arrest him. I motioned to Yuma Bill and Rowdy, two scouts I could rely on, and had Yuma Bill approach Dutchy in front and engage his attention while Rowdy and I slipped up from behind and disarmed the renegade. We took him to the guardhouse, where an officer made him carry a load of wood on his back for two hours. It was a punishment very humiliating to an Indian, and I knew Dutchy would wait his chance to get even with the United States Army. When Captain Crawford made Dutchy his body servant, I thought it little better than hugging a rattlesnake and resolved to keep my eyes peeled.

After being out about a month we were two hundred miles below the border, and from signs and actions of the scouts, I became convinced that they knew more about the movements of Geronimo than they were reporting to Captain Crawford. I talked it over with chief of scouts Tom Horn (who, poor fellow, was eventually hanged for murder as a result of a killing I believe to have been accidental). Horn was of my opinion about the scouts. Diplomacy was necessary, however, for there we were, a handful of white men in hostile country, surrounded by 195 Indians on whom we were entirely dependent to get back to civilization. I talked to Corporal Juan, one of the scouts, and being satisfied that my suspicions were correct, I called in Noche, the chief scout, and told him that he had better go to the captain and tell him all he knew. Next morning Noche and the medicine man, Nosey, approached Captain Crawford, followed by a number of scouts. A long powwow followed, Nosey telling the scouts what was expected of them. He made them kiss the medicine bag—a small buckskin sack—and repeat a vow. The performance had the appearance of sincerity, and I thought that we should presently encounter Geronimo.

And sure enough, that afternoon word came that the hostiles were located in camp and sun-drying meat. Crawford decided on a reconnaissance. He told me I must stay behind with the trains but that he would send for me in time to get in on the attack. The captain and I were standing in front of a fire, talking it over, when someone came up from behind and placed one hand in friendly fashion on one of my shoulders and the other on the captain's shoulder. It was Dutchy.

"Mule Captain," he said in Spanish, meaning me, "you know much." Most southern Indians spoke Spanish but not English.

"Yes," said I, "and Dutchy, you are going to stay here with me."

Crawford knew what I was driving at. "No, no," he said. "Dutchy, you come with us." And to me in English, "Oh, he's all right."

"It is to be hoped so, Captain," I observed.

As the night wore on, Nosey made medicine, and a wild and weird performance it was, or at any rate, it struck us that way because of the tenseness of the atmosphere. During the show we were startled by the arrival of two white men, who proved to be Sherriff Stevens of Cochise County, Arizona, and Frank Leslie, a rancher, who had come to arrest Dutchy for murder. Captain Crawford took them out of earshot and explained the delicacy of the situation. He promised to deliver up Dutchy after the campaign, which satisfied the officer. But the scouts suspected something, and I am pretty sure they guessed the truth of what had happened.

Next day Captain Crawford left with practically the entire scout command. I climbed a spur of rock and followed the winding column until it disappeared from view, and returned to camp with a feeling of depression I have never experienced before or since. I understood Crawford's reason for taking Dutchy. He wanted to show the Indians that he did not fear the worst of them. That is one sure way to impress an Indian, but just the same, this time I did not like it.

The next few days of waiting were long ones indeed. One morning I was awakened before dawn by a pull at my blanket. I opened my eyes to behold Corporal Juan, the scout whose duplicity had been detected a week before, bending over me. He had a note from Captain Crawford. It said to break camp, take some supplies, and follow Juan, who would lead me to the main command.

Two days later, at about 11:00 A.M., another scout approached us with a message from Lieutenant Maus. It said that Captain Crawford had been mortally wounded in a fight with Mexican troops, that the command was out of rations, and for God's sake to hurry up. We lightened our loads and pushed on at forced-march speed, and that afternoon met the main body with my unconscious friend, the captain, on a litter. I took charge of the litter and carried it with my train for five days, when Captain Crawford breathed his last without regaining consciousness. So passed the finest soldier and noblest gentleman I ever knew.

Maus told me what had happened. When Geronimo's trail was picked up, Captain Crawford had stretched a corral rope about camp at nights and refused to let any scout outside without permission, so that no unfaithful member of his party might give the hostiles warning of the approach. Finally, Geronimo's camp was located, and Crawford disposed his command for a surprise attack. Despite the greatest precautions, the surprise was lost by the "accidental" firing of a scout's rifle beforehand. Thus Geronimo was warned and the attack failed, the hostiles scattering among the mountains like so many quail, and just as impossible to pursue. Crawford encamped on the ground formerly occupied by Geronimo, and while there a body of Mexican troops, also after Geronimo, turned up and attacked Crawford's camp under the impression that Geronimo was still there.

Crawford's scouts hated the Mexicans and were returning their fire heavily when Crawford rushed out to stop it. The Mexicans naturally kept on firing, and after several attempts to let them know that they were assaulting the wrong people, Crawford, accompanied by Dutchy, went along to a point of vantage. Handing his rifle to Dutchy, he climbed upon a boulder in full view of the Mexicans and, waving a white handkerchief in each hand, shouted, "No tiro, no tiro—Americanos!"

A moment later Dutchy came running up, saying that Captain Crawford had been shot by the Mexicans. The captain was found at the foot of the boulder. He had been shot on the side of the head, and his arm had been broken by the fall from the rock. A search of his person failed to reveal anything but a watch with a broken crystal, although it was known that Crawford carried a large sum of money. Dutchy had robbed his commanding officer. No one else could have done it, and I have always believed that Dutchy, and not the Mexicans, killed Captain Crawford. The nature of the wound and the disappearance of the money were evidence enough for me, irrespective of Dutchy's known character.

Nevertheless, nothing was ever done about it. When we got back to Arizona, the wily Dutchy went hostile before the officers could get him for any of his previous murders. He joined Geronimo as a warrior. After the capture of Geronimo, he was sent as a prisoner of war to Florida, and then to Oklahoma, where I hear that he got into trouble and was killed. If he wasn't, he should have been.[36]

The Difficulties of Indian Warfare

BRITTON DAVIS

Army and Navy Journal 33, no. 13 (October 24, 1885): 242–44

Those who are impatient of what they are disposed to consider the inaction of our troops in Arizona with reference to the Apaches should read the report of Second Lieutenant Britton Davis, of the Third Cavalry, which we publish this week. It not only explains clearly and intelligently the cause of the Indian outbreak, but describes most graphically the difficulty of pursuing and catching a band of nomads who can cover ninety miles in twenty-four hours without rest and then be prepared to push on a hundred miles further if necessary; who pick up fresh mounts as they go along; who encamp in inaccessible points far from wood and water, and when necessary abandon everything and scatter among the mountains on foot, making it difficult or impossible to trail them. Some of the Indians, Lieutenant Davis says, when they left the reservation had excellent field glasses, and with these their lookouts, posted day and night, can watch a large extent of country and start the main body to running again for two or three hundred miles at the sight of any suspicious-looking object, such as dust or smoke.

FORT BOWIE, A.T., Sept. 15, 1885.

The Adjutant-General, Department of Arizona:
 SIR: Regarding the causes of the recent outbreak of the Chiricahua and Warm Spring Indians, and my action in the matter, I have the honor to inform you that as far as I have been able to ascertain from inquiries made at the time and subsequently, the outbreak was not at all premeditated. Among a certain class of Indians there had been more or less dissatisfaction, growing out of their own worthlessness and a determination on their part not to be punished for offenses committed on the reservation. But this feeling was not general by any means, nor in the ordinary course of events would it have led to such a culmination. The leader in this movement of opposition to the exercise of authority over them was a chief known as Mangus, a man who was otherwise one of the best behaved and most industrious Indians under my charge. He was encouraged in his insubordination by his wife, a former Mexican captive who

Apaches watching troops with field glasses. NELSON A. MILES. *PERSONAL RECOLLECTIONS AND OBSERVATIONS.*

knew just enough to make her troublesome. Unable alone to prevent the punishment of his people for their offenses, he set about enlisting the sympathies of others and, in connection with an Indian known as Nadoski,[1] succeeded in so working upon the fears of Geronimo, another chief, that the latter joined him in an attempt which it was determined to make for the purpose of putting an end to all future punishment.

Fearing the consequences of such an act, Geronimo and Mangus moved their camp to the vicinity of a creek known as the Bonita, about eighteen miles from my camp. Their intention seems to have been to secure a place from which they could escape into the surrounding mountains, should their plans not result as they expected. Thursday night[2] before the outbreak, a favorable opportunity presented itself in the shape of a tiswin drink, in which most of the Indians near Turkey Creek were engaged. Among the number implicated were two chiefs known as Naiche and Chihuahua. Knowing that they would be punished for their drunkenness, they readily listened to the proposition made them by Mangus to the effect that all should come to me together the next day, tell me that all were drunk, and as I would be unable to punish them all, all would escape. This plan was carried out, two other chiefs, Loco and Zele,[3] being forced into the combination. Seeing the object of the affair, I declined to take any action and said I would report the matter to General Crook. This report was made Friday morning.

After waiting two days and hearing nothing more about their attempt to resist my authority, their fears of the consequences had so much increased that Saturday night Geronimo and Mangus determined to leave rather than remain and undergo the punishment which their fears pointed out to them. Not being strong enough in point of numbers to make the move alone with their bands, they waited until the next day, Sunday, when, everything being in readiness, they began to move. Three scouts by previous agreement deserted and were to have killed Chatto and myself, but for some reason the attempt was not made. But Mangus and Geronimo went to the other chiefs, telling that we had been killed, the scouts had deserted, and that all of the Indians were going to leave the reservation. The two chiefs previously mentioned, Chihuahua and Naiche, frightened at the part they had previously taken, readily believed what was told them, and gathering up the stock they had immediately around them, they followed Mangus and Geronimo. My action I have previously reported.

Since making that report I have ascertained that when the Indians reached the Mozalton Mountains, troubles arose among them, growing out of the circumstances under which Chihuahua and Naiche were forced off the reservation. Chihuahua and Naiche claimed that Mangus and Geronimo had lied to them and frightened them into leaving, and the night they had this trouble Chihuahua, with his brother and a man known as Atelueitze, set out to kill Geronimo, who was camped some little distance apart from them. Mangus and Geronimo heard of their intentions and started at once with their bands, going south. Naiche was in Mangus' camp at the time, but sent word to his wife and child, who were with Chihuahua, to return at once to the reservation and that he would join them as soon as he could.

The woman and her child started back, but at Eagle Creek they saw scouts, as I was coming out the second time. Being badly frightened, they returned to the mountains and joined Chihuahua again. It was the intention of those with Chihuahua, after Geronimo left, to remain hid in the mountains north of the Gila until the excitement should die out. They had agreed to commit no depredations, and as soon as a favorable opportunity presented itself, they were going to return to the reservation, surrender themselves, explain the circumstances of their leaving, and trust to their subsequent conduct in the mountains to save them from severe punishment. But unfortunately for them, when I reached the point where their trail left Geronimo's, the scouts, not knowing the condition of affairs, took the northern trail, which proved to be that of Chihuahua. Seeing the scouts in pursuit, all their hopes of returning to the reservation were at an end, and they started at once for Mexico. We overtook this same band on June 23, and after the fight I am informed that some of them are supposed to have returned to the reservation or to that vicinity. Subsequent events up to the meeting of our command with that of Lieutenant Day, 9th Cavalry, have been previously reported.

On the eleventh of last month [August] Captain Crawford left Lieutenant Day near Nacori, in Sonora, and proceeded to the place of Day's fight, where we took up the trail of the raiding party of bucks, who had returned to the camp two days before we reached it. The mountains at that point were so abrupt that we experienced great difficulty in crossing them. A detachment of packers and scouts was kept continually ahead of the pack trains for the purpose of making a trail, but even with these precautions, the difficulty of pro-ceeding was so great that several mules were killed and injured each day through rolling down the mountains.

After reaching the summit of the Sonora slope of the Sierra Madre, I was detached and sent forward with a party of scouts under Sieber to follow the trail of the hostiles, who were moving east and traveling rapidly. We took with us six days' rations, which with the aid of horse meat, beef, and game when obtained, lasted us eleven days. Heavy rains fell almost daily, and at times it was next to impossible to keep the trail. The hostiles, on the contrary, had nothing to carry but themselves, and were also driving a number of fresh ani-mals. As soon as their horses would give out they would kill them and mount the fresh stock they were driving. They lived upon the flesh of the horses they killed and upon such wild fruits as they could gather along the route. Fearing that we might run into them at any moment and be discovered before we saw them, it was necessary to keep a few scouts eight or ten miles in advance each day, and our progress was necessarily slow. The country through which we passed was so soft that our mules with even their light loads sank to their knees in the mud, and riding at times was out of the question. Had the Indians caught sight of us, they would have scattered in every direction, and further pursuit for the time being would have been useless.

After leaving the scene of the fight, the hostiles moved nearly due east across the Sierra Madre, a distance of nearly two hundred fifty miles, reckoned from Nacori, on the western slope, to Via de Buenaventura, on the eastern slope. Arriving in the vicinity of Via, the trail turned toward the southeast, avoiding the larger towns and ranches until the town of Santa Clara was reached at a point following the Indian trail, about a hundred miles further to the east.

Arriving in this vicinity, the bucks hid their women and children in an almost inaccessible mountain range and went themselves to raid the town. Returning as soon as possible with fresh horses, they remounted their party and, leaving the mountains, turned directly north. Before reaching Santa Clara they had, by their rapid marching, exhausted and killed their animals until they had only one horse and one mule left. The continued heavy rains had not only kept us wet and spoiled what little food we had, but had otherwise aided the hostiles by so obliterating the trail that it was only by the greatest care and exertion that we could follow at all. For the last day or two before they obtained their fresh stock they had been afoot, and with their two remaining animals had crossed two very rocky chains of mountains. Following them under such circumstances became a very difficult matter, and it was not until they obtained fresh horses from Santa Clara that we were able to proceed with any rapidity at all.

But at this juncture a new difficulty presented itself, for as soon as the Indians got their fresh mounts they doubled their marches, while our pack mules, seven in number, were beginning to feel the effects of the marches they were making. In addition to a distance of more than a thousand miles marched by these mules in the earlier part of the campaign, we had called upon them during the last two weeks to make a march of three hundred fifty miles through a mountainous country, where their food was, as a rule, coarse pine grass with very little strength in it. To attempt to double our marches under such circumstances was likely to prove fatal to our success, but as it subsequently appeared, we had no choice in the matter. The day we turned north we marched forty-five miles to obtain water, the following day thirty miles, and the day after this we were obliged to go fifty miles before we camped. At this end of this last march the water, when obtained, was so strongly alkaline that the following morning three mules gave out and two others grew weak. It was impossible to take them further, but we would have proceeded on foot and trusted to the country for food had we not been met by a Mexican force under Colonel Mesilla, who informed me that two other Mexican forces—one infantry and one cavalry—had cut the trail twenty-four hours in advance of us and would push the Indians across the line on into the Sierra Madre.

At this time we were without food; the country through which we would have to pass was an alkali desert, destitute of game; our shoes were worn out and the Indians partly barefooted, several were sick; and in order to proceed further we would have to abandon our mules. Knowing that it would be impossible to effect anything in that condition, and that I would endanger the lives of my party by attempting to cross the desert country to the north of us, afoot, without food, and with no facilities for carrying water, I thought it best to make for some near point where I could communicate with you. Through the kindness of the manager of the St. Domingo cattle ranch, we obtained sufficient supplies to last us to Fort Bliss, at which point we arrived September 5, having traveled, since starting on the fourteenth of the month previous, a distance of more than five hundred miles.

The actual distance scouted over was largely in excess of this, as we were obliged to send scouts eight or ten miles in advance each day, who returned to camp at night and went on with the main party the next morning, thus going three times over the same ground. When we started on the trail we knew nothing of the country through which we would have to pass. There are no maps of it, and the information obtained from the Indians was necessarily meager. When the hostiles are frightened and running from a pursuing party, they travel so as to leave as little sign as possible, scattering in every direction, and where the ground is favorable, separating entirely to meet again at some point in advance. Where the mountains border a country which is of such a nature that footprints are not easily seen upon it, they will often leave the mountains, scatter, and move as though to cross directly through the open country, but upon getting out two or three miles, they will suddenly change direction, and each one by himself will make his way back to the fastness and meet the others at some place previously agreed upon. Let a heavy rain fall after one of these moves, and the difficulties of trailing them can well be imagined. At times we would find the tracks of a single person or animal for miles before others would join it. They avoid all beaten paths and go from point to point through the country by routes known only to themselves. At times it is impossible to find the trail at all, in which event it is necessary to delay until scouting parties sent out on either flank have managed to cut it again further to the front on more favorable ground.

At one time during the campaign, a band of Indians whom I was following caught sight of the scouts and, with their women and children, in twenty-four hours marched more than ninety miles without rest. Had it been necessary, I believe they could have gone a hundred further with equal ease. It is little trouble for them to obtain all the fresh stock they need, the bucks going eight or ten miles to either side to raid, while the women and children travel rapidly toward whatever point they desire to reach, the bucks joining them on the road with fresh horses. While being pursued they have guards to the front, to the rear, and on either flank, who keep the main body advised of any force seen in the vicinity. When in camp they choose the most inaccessible points they can find, preferably the rocky extremity of some mountain spur, along which they can retreat into the mountains proper in case they are attacked. These camps are often several miles from wood and water, which will be carried up to the camp by the squaws. Guards are put in such positions that they can watch the country for miles around, and upon the first indication of the approach of danger, the camp is alarmed and the race begins again. Even when not being pursued they seldom stop for more than three or four days in any one place. When necessary they abandon all their property, and getting into the mountains afoot, they scatter in every direction, making it extremely difficult, and at times impossible, to trail them. Some of the Indians, when they left the reservation, had excellent field glasses, and with these their lookouts can watch a large extent of country. Lookouts are kept posted day and night, and any suspicious-looking object, such as dust or smoke, is sufficient to send them running again for two or three hundred miles.

It is not so much a question of fighting these Indians as it is of our catching them; they on the one hand being able to catch any abundance of fresh horses, while on the other hand their pursuers are obliged to use the same animals throughout the campaign or, as in the case of the scouts, follow them afoot. On one occasion I marched the scouts fifteen and a half hours, at an average speed of about three and a half miles per hour. But it is impossible to keep this up for any length of time without breaking the scouts down completely. A portion of these Indians left the mountains and raided through northern Chihuahua. In following them it was necessary to make long marches without water, and the water even when obtained is so strongly alkaline that it is almost undrinkable. At one place it became necessary to cross a shallow alkali pond, some four or five miles in width, and as we could not ride through the mud we were obliged to wade, leading the mules. The alkali was so strong in the water that it blistered our feet and legs, some of the Indians becoming so footsore that it was only with great pain that they could travel at all. The scouts behaved well throughout the campaign, and reports charging them with mutiny or insubordination are without foundation.

> Very respectfully, your obedient servant,
> BRITTON DAVIS, Second Lieutenant, Third Cavalry.

Engagement in Guadalupe Canyon

W. B. JETT

Winners of the West 14, no. 9 (August 1937): 3, 5

In April 1885 Troops B and D and others of the Fourth U.S. Cavalry were called to go in search of Geronimo and his band of Apaches who had gone on the warpath. The trail led into Mexico. At that time a soldier in Troop D, I was driving a six-mule team for the government. In July, I think it was, I was left in Guadalupe Canyon to look after horses, mules, provisions, and ammunition left behind by the troops as they went on after their quarry. Seven other soldiers who were on sick report, though up and about, along with a doctor, were also left in camp.

Sometime early in August,[1] a courier came into camp and said there were no Indians in that part of the country. The doctor,[2] however, said he had his doubts about that, and that he was going to leave camp, which he did. An old soldier of nearly thirty years' service, Neihaus, a German, said there was no danger, as the Indians would not attack a soldier camp. One day while we were eating dinner under the one tree in the little open valley, and when the sentry on lookout and watching the animals had left his post and come into camp contrary to orders, we were surprised by a thundering volley from the hills nearby. At the first shot Neihaus, right by my side, was killed by a bullet in his forehead. He fell with a biscuit and a piece of meat in his mouth and did not move again.

The sentry referred to above, and who, being a recruit, had said he wanted to see an Indian fight, immediately ran but was shot down before he could reach the opposite hills. Two others, one of whom had run into his tent and fallen on his knees in prayer until the sergeant in charge of the camp[3] called him out, made for the opposite hills and escaped. This left four of us, who sought some protection behind the wagons and fired for about an hour at the point where the smoke from the guns of the Indians came from behind the rocks on the bluff above our camp.

Twice the sergeant was shot, and then a third time, by my side. At the third shot he said, "Boys, I'm done for." In some way the wagons caught fire, and soon the ammunition would begin to explode, we knew. We four then made across the open land for the opposite hills already referred to. A German whose name I cannot now recall put his arm under the sergeant's arms and helped him across, but as they were climbing the mountain, the sergeant was shot the fourth time and killed in the German's arms. This German soldier afterward received a medal for bravery.

We three, the German, a soldier named [J. L.] Sprinkle, and the writer, fired for some time behind the rocks at the smoke spots across the vale (I should have said we had hardly reached the mountainside when the ammunition in the wagons began to explode with a mighty roar), but we could not see an Indian. We did see, however, by the change in the source of the smoke from their guns that they were gradually surrounding us.

Late in the afternoon we went down the mountain and started up the canyon in the only direction there seemed a way of escape. Sometime that night we came out in a valley, where we found a cattle ranch called Cloverdale, I believe. The cowboys took us in and treated us kindly till, some few days thereafter, part of Captain Lawton's command came and restored us to our comrades. In the meantime Roberts, one of the soldiers who had left when the firing began in the canyon, had also showed up at the ranch.

The night the command came for us I was sent twelve miles to another ranch for the other soldier who had escaped early in the fray. I had to light matches to keep on the trail, I remember, but strange to say, I am not certain that the man I went after came back with me. My recollection is that he did not, and yet I seem to remember someone riding back behind me on my horse.

When the command reached Guadalupe Canyon and found the camp had been burned, and the doctor saw the charred hog bones, they said we had been burned up, as the bones were evidently human bones. Some remarked that they did not know we were so much like hogs. Neihaus and the other dead bodies were still on the ground.

Great surprise was expressed by Indian fighters that seven sick men and one teamster should have been left by the commanding officer in such a death trap as Guadalupe Canyon.[4]

The above is as my memory goes, and that is right excepting where I have expressed doubt. Other details someone else may better recall. I have omitted some amusing things for fear of too much length. I will say, however, that when the firing began I was scared till I saw it seemed I might not be hit, then I was scared that if I was killed the devil would get me, as I was not a Christian. I never knew of but one soldier who professed to be a Christian.

In the Days of Geronimo

HARRY R. WRIGHT[1]

Pearson's Magazine 26 (February 1905): 196–200

Great swales of heat undulated above the stunted mesquite and sagebrush. Miniature cyclones of sand, like gigantic mushrooms, twirled and gyrated —a strange and terrible ballet. And over all the molten sun of Arizona glowed within the rim of the mountains.

It was ten in the morning of August 25, 1885. H Troop of the Fourth United States Cavalry, sixty-five strong, was marching from Guadalupe Canyon to Camp Rucker in the Chiricahua, through the valley of the San Simon.

There were no jests from the men. Silence was in the ranks, save for the squeak of boot to saddle leather, the rattling of rein ring on bit, and the ploof, ploof of the hoofs, as little clouds of alkali dust fluffed up and sprinkled man and horse with the white, acrid powder. Prairie dogs sat up and stared as we passed, and an occasional jack rabbit scurried out of sight. I was riding at the head of the column beside Lieutenant Elliott, for I was detailed as scout. The Indian trailers were trotting ahead. The days were the days of Geronimo.

We had nearly reached the San Simon Cienega, the only water hole within twenty-five miles, when one of the Indians turned and, with a "huh," pointed with his rifle to the sky.

Far away, in the direction of the Chiricahuas, we could see a tiny speck; we glanced around us and descried more—buzzards, grim attendants of all tragedies of the desert. They were converging toward us.

With a "Halt" from the lieutenant, the column came to a stop.

"Wright," he commanded, "detail three men. Go and see what's the matter over there. I will wait for you half an hour, then take the back trail and report to me at Rucker Canyon."

Privates Durr, [J.] Courtney, Linsky, and myself headed due west, the direction where the buzzards were settling. We had not gone far when we picked up the trail of a burro and a man. The little burden bearer of the desert was laden; his deep hoofprints showed that. Already the story was half told. A prospector—for nothing save the quest of gold would bring a lone man out in Arizona when Geronimo was scourging the country.

We followed the trail, and soon the hoarse croaking of the buzzards showed us that we were near the tragedy. We burst through a small clump of mesquite.

Courtney was taken with nausea at the sight, while Linsky drew his six-shooter and nervously cocked and uncocked the hammer. Durr could say nothing but, "My God! My God!" And for myself, I could but curse. We were men who had heard and had seen many things. This is what we saw now:

Tied to a stake, with the ill-smelling, raucous-voiced birds tearing at his flesh, was the semblance of a man. The soles of his feet had been cut off, and the stake driven in the ground over a red-ant hill. He had been wounded in the side, but the ants had finished the work. The buzzards had withdrawn at our approach; and they sat, eyeing us sullenly as we robbed them of their prey.

Indians! And the murder had been most wanton, for the pack, taken from the burro, lay scattered about. Nothing was missing—the pick, shovel, and frying pan; his rations of flour, bacon, and coffee—there was nothing that any Indian wanted among them. We gathered them together and buried them with the poor devil, planting his own pick and shovel on his grave as headstone.

We had found the Indian trail. But it was too old to follow. As we rode back, nothing was said. But when the story was told after joining the command, there were many hungry looks toward the head of the column, where the Indian scouts tramped along.

Stoner, who had twenty years of the bitterness of the service at his tongue's end, told us a story that night in Rucker Canyon!

A man named Mullin of G Troop, Fourth Cavalry, was captured by Victorio, the Apache, in the late seventies. The Indians determined on sport with him. They tied him down with strips of rawhide, staking him out so that he could just move his head. They passed a buckskin thong through an incision in the neck of a rattlesnake. And they staked the snake just beyond striking distance. Men, women, and children had come out of their [wickiups] to enjoy the appalling sequel. Water was slowly poured on the rawhide, which contracted, drawing Mullin near the snake, which, with jaws distended and fangs exposed in fury, was straining to bite on something in the extremity of its pain. Slowly, drop by drop, on the thong that held the snake, the water fell; and unlike the rawhide, the buckskin expanded. Mullin, shrieking, drew toward death. The snake, wild with envenomed rage, slowly drew nearer to its victim. There came a little more water—a little drawing closer of snake and man. Some poison from the eager fangs spurted on his brow; and then—

They were found the next day—the dead soldier and the dead snake, where the Apaches had left them.

The men who listened to Stoner carried that scene into their dreams and awoke with its memory hot within them.

The next morning a detachment was sent to Cottonwood Springs to act as mail carriers between Cloverdale, New Mexico, and Camp Rucker. Incidentally we were to look out for trails. I was still acting as scout. To relieve the monotony, I determined one day to take the trip over to Cloverdale. Some of the men had seen "slow deer"—beef cattle. I had not gone very far when Dick, my horse, gave a snort and shied. You do not jerk a horse for that in the army. You look, instead, for the cause. I found it—a red-hot trail and the Apache flag in evidence. No slow deer that day.

Dick was hooked up with spurs, and we were off on the back trail at a gallop. I had all the men out with my yells before we reached camp; there was no necessity for "Boots and Saddles."

"What's the matter?"

"Never mind. Come on! Hustle!"

We picked up the trail, and it grew hotter every moment. The upturned stones had not even whitened under the sun.

With a yell, we rode for them. We topped the rise to a mesa and saw the Indians scurrying away. They had left the herd with a squaw, and as I ordered a detail away for the chase, four of us determined to have that herd. The squaw was quirting the bunch and trying to stampede them; but we rounded up the ponies and thought to capture the squaw also.

When I tried to get her, she bit me. When Burns charged down on her, she slipped his grasp and whipped out a knife. Two of us dismounted and attacked her, front and rear. She slashed us with her quirt. I felt like killing her. Burns cursed her and said he would fix her.

He recoiled his picket rope. He tried and missed twice. But at last the rope swung around her neck. He took in the slack and made his turns on the pommel of the Whitman saddle; but she had managed to slip the noose down from her neck until it fell under the armpits, just as Burns started off. It was all the difference between life and death. She knew it as well as Burns did. Away she went, dragging on the ground like the tail to a kite before it takes to the air. The prospector came again to our minds. And we thought of Mullin and certain dead men. She was so near her death that I called: "Halt there, Burns! Halt; or, by heaven, I'll shoot!"

"Shoot and be damned!" he called back. "I'll kill this one anyhow."

My horse was the better and I overtook them. Stopping him, I managed to release her. The men were furious at the interruption to their sport. She was nearly dead. Her face was gashed; her arms were full of cuts, and her body was terribly bruised. As she opened her eyes, she spat on us. We took her back to camp. The other men returned after chasing the Indians to the Mexican line. The squaw and ponies were sent to Camp Rucker the next day and the squaw's condition explained as due to a fall. She was returned to the reservation; if she is alive today, there is one Apache murderess who knows that the white man's patience may be tried too far.

In the army the same feelings pervade the breasts of officers and men. The "shavetail" fresh from West Point, who has known nothing of frontier hardship, goes out with a command and roughs it. The first day he is miserable. He misses his military brushes, his pajamas, and other little comforts. The second day he asks Private Smiler for a match. After that, it is easy. The inner man always comes to the level of his environment. It is the responsibility of his position that causes the officer to control himself—and his men.

Lieutenant Smith[2] assumed command of H Troop after Lieutenant Elliott went away on sick leave. We had been ordered to Cloverdale to relieve I Troop, whose horses were exhausted. The second night after reaching camp, "Nosey," one of the Indian scouts, became *loco* from drinking mescal.

He paraded up and down the quarters and called us by pseudonyms not to be overlooked. He was impartial, in that he spared not even the officers.

"Soldiers heap no good!" he yelled. "Officer, big squaw. Come on out! Come out and fight! Me, Nosey, big chief."

And he patted his Springfield rifle to show us what he wanted. It was all we could do to keep from rushing him. Some of the men had made a start, when, "Steady, steady men!" and Lieutenant Smith appeared.

"Nosey," he said, "you go back to tepee. Tomorrow I will see you."

"You ———," said Nosey.

That was enough. The men jumped for him.

"Stand back there, stand back!" shouted the lieutenant, as he swung his Colt .45 around. "Don't touch him, I'll take care of him. Hold hard there. I'll shoot the first man who touches him. Attention! Fall in! Sergeant, call the roll and detail these men for five days' extra police duty."

That was a fine example of the self-control of one man and of the exercise of authority over sixty-five men who were aggravated beyond endurance.

There are three graves in Guadalupe Canyon with sun-bleached piles of stones. This is how they come to be there:

A courier from F Troop brought the news of a trail. As we swung into the saddle, the four "coffee coolers"—men who guard a camp—waved us good-bye. It was only a six hours' chase. The trail split at the Mexican line; and as Captain Lawton—General Lawton (killed in the Philippines) later on—swung the column back after the other trail, it became evident that we were making a loop toward our own camp. The chief of scouts told Lawton something.

"Trot!" came the command; then "Gallop."

That told us. The Indians had made a flying charge back to camp for our supply wagons. There was a chance of life for those fellows of ours if we got there in time.

A horse is down—jump him! One staggers to the side—leave him! The gallop became a charge, for we were nearing the camp.

We rushed down the hill, to the ragged rocks topping the canyon, and saw the smoke from our wagons. The Indians had been there. Dismounting, we scrambled down the rocks and rounded a little bend. Poor old Sergeant Neihaus was propped up against a tree, the scalp ripped off his head, and two or three chunks of bacon gripped tight between his teeth—a gory, grinning satyr of what had been a kindly, lovable man. Moriarty, a recruit, lay on his back with his abdomen slashed open and bunches of hay stuck in the cuts.

Dumb, wild rage seized us and we looked at one another, each man ready to slay his brother.

The crack of a gun came from the hills ahead. In our madness, we thought it strange that we heard no more shots. Halfway up the hill we found the body of another soldier; and at the top, another—Snitzer. He was alive, though unconscious. He had seen us and fired the shot.

"We were eating dinner," he told us later, "when the Indians jumped us. Neihaus and Moriarty went down the first volley. Collins was shot but staggered to his feet. We started up the hill, where we could find some shelter. They got him again, and he fell. I picked him up, and he hung on my back. They got him once more, and as his arms fell from my back, I dropped beside him and let them have a couple of shots myself. All I could see was the smoke from their guns. They soon drove me out. I ran here to the top of the hill. They shot me twice on the way up. That's all I remember, until I saw you fellows down in the canyon."

We buried them, placing cairns of stone over their graves; and there they lie to this day. I was new to the frontier then and was skeptical when told that the squaws had done the work. But afterward, when I saw indisputable evidence that a squaw had run a knife around a man's head and then ripped off all of his skull covering, I knew.

Across Apache Land

MICHAEL M. RICE

The Great Divide 12 (July 1895): 158–60

Having been commissioned by the agent of the Associated Press for Arizona to proceed to the front and join the command in the field, I applied to Brigadier General George Crook, commanding the Department of Arizona, for permission to accompany the troops as news gatherer in the Indian campaign. The necessary credentials having arrived, I started from Clifton to join the 4th Cavalry on the Mexican frontier.

Hearing that General Sheridan was expected to pass through Lordsburg on his way east, I determined to ride over from Gage Station, on the Southern Pacific Railroad, where I was awaiting the arrival of Captain Lee's command of colored troops,[1] who were chasing Geronimo and his band through the Mule Mountains in New Mexico.

Being an ardent admirer of Sheridan, I desired to meet him and, if possible, obtain an interview. In this I was successful. When the train pulled into the depot I was informed that the general and party occupied a special car attached to the end of the train. I approached and inquired for General Sheridan. There were a party of ladies and officers occupying seats on the rear portion of an observation car. When I mentioned the general's name, a clear, penetrating voice from the crowd replied, "I am General Sheridan, what can I do for you?"

Seeing the party from which the reply emanated, I was inclined impulsively to think that someone desired to perpetrate a practical joke at my expense, as the individual addressing me bore no insignia of rank or distinction; on the contrary, he looked more like a man who had escaped the ravages of a cyclone than the commander of the army of the United States.

He was dressed in a rough traveling suit of blue material, his head and part of his face swathed in bandages, and his general appearance conveyed every impression but the poetic one of a conquering hero. One eye was visible, and beneath a decidedly Celtic nose bristled a coarse, gray, stubby mustache; he was short in stature and nervous in movement; but to describe the penetrating power, the inquisitive glance, the snap, fire, and humor that danced alternately in that exposed eye, is beyond the power of an ordinary scribe.

With the alacrity of discernment for which he was celebrated, he saw that I was in a quandary, or at least in doubt to his identity, and with an encouraging smile he extended his hand and, shaking mine, invited me to a seat on the platform.

After ascertaining my name and desires, he referred humorously to his unmilitary appearance, explaining that his condition was the result of a serious railway accident that occurred at Santa Monica, California, some time previous, in which he and Mrs. Sheridan came near losing their lives. He introduced me to Mrs. Sheridan, who was also badly marked about the face; also to members of his staff. He then interrogated me closely as to my knowledge of the disposition of the troops in the field; location of the different companies; distance between water; movements of the Fourth Cavalry, for which he expressed a special fondness; method of equipment and facilities for transportation of supplies; in fact, instead of being the interviewer, he transposed the subject in such a manner that I became the interviewed.[2]

With a field glass he scanned the surrounding horizon [and] discussed the topography of the country within his range of vision, exhibiting a personal familiarity with the region infested by the hostiles. His anxiety expressed for the safety of the isolated settlers in the invaded region was profound. His last words were expressive of his utmost confidence in General Crook's soldierly qualities and ability to subjugate the murderous Apaches.

The interview lasted about thirty minutes, when the autocrat of the train called, "All aboard," and with extreme reluctance I bid adieu to my ideal soldier, the "Hero of Winchester."

I left Lordsburg the following morning to join the Fourth Cavalry, under command of Captain Lawton at Guadalupe Canyon, going by the way of Victoria mining district, in the southwestern part of Grant County, New Mexico. This was the route that Chatto and his band followed a few years previously after his assassination of Judge McComas, his wife, and little son Charlie, one of the most barbarous butcheries in the annals of Apache atrocities.

I went into camp that night at a place notorious as the scene of the most treacherous attack, as well as the most gallant defense, in the history of a country whose records are replete with deeds of desperate daring and undaunted heroism.

Two prospectors named Devine and Ferguson were traveling from Victoria district toward Las Playas. In passing over a divide in the Hachita Mountains late one afternoon, they were waylaid by Chatto and his band of cutthroats, and before they were able to offer resistance or recover from their surprise, a deadly volley was fired into their midst, breaking both of Ferguson's thighs and killing the mules in their tracks, Ferguson tumbling out of the wagon onto the ground.

Hastily making a breastwork of the wagon and dead animals, Devine dragged his crippled companion beneath the improvised barricade and, securing his Winchester, fought desperately against odds of fifteen to one. For hours he kept the red fiends at bay, occasionally laving his companion with water from his canteen, resuscitating him sufficiently to permit the use of his Winchester to good effect.

The cunning Apaches tried every ruse to draw them from cover, but without success. Time and again the wounded Ferguson appealed to Devine to leave him to his fate and save himself, as he believed his wounds were mortal, and the brave fellow did not desire to see his friend and partner sacrifice his life in what he considered a hopeless cause. Death was more preferable to Devine than the abandonment of a wounded and helpless companion, so he continued the desperate encounter until darkness caused the Indians to withdraw from the scene.

Knowing that the attack would be renewed the following morning, and taking advantage of the well-known superstition of the Apaches in regard to night attacks, Devine carried the helpless Ferguson a distance of half a mile up a rocky hillside and, selecting an advantageous position for further defense, constructed a fort of rocks on the exposed side, making a successful attack impossible if the least resistance was shown by the occupant.

Leaving some provisions and what water was left from the siege, with Winchesters and ammunition Devine started on foot to the settlement to procure assistance and a means of conveying his companion to a place where surgical aid could be rendered. Arriving at Victoria in the dead of night, he was not long in enlisting a party of miners, who returned to the scene of the bloody encounter, where they found Ferguson still alive, although suffering the most excruciating pain. With gentle hands, he was removed to a conveyance and conducted to Deming, from whence he was forwarded to the Sisters' Hospital at Albuquerque, where, by careful nursing, he was restored to health, although he never entirely recovered the use of his limbs.

After familiarizing myself with the scene of the above-described encounter, I continued my journey, arriving at Las Playas that evening, where I met a party of men employed by the late United States Senator Hearst[3] constructing houses for the accommodation of the cowboys engaged on the range. My arrival was the first intimation they had of the Apache outbreak.

The next day, in company with a range rider, I reached the old Gray ranch, where a company of the Fourth Cavalry was stationed under command of Captain Hatfield. The following day I arrived at Cloverdale, where Captains Lawton, Hatfield, and Wood[4] concentrated their commands, it being the most practicable point of interception of any marauding parties who might attempt to enter the Sierra Madres from the north or east.

Indian campaigning has its ludicrous as well as its tragic aspect, as the following circumstance doth attest:

Colonel A. E. Head, manager of the great cattle interests of Haggin, Head, and Hearst, arrived from Deming with a party of friends about the time and, being desirous of showing his appreciation of the beneficent services accorded to the firm by the permanent protection of their interests by Uncle Sam's troops, gave an elaborate blowout to the officers of the command; there were hampers of the most costly liquids, an abundance of imported Havanas; the fatted calf was ruthlessly slaughtered, and general good cheer prevailed.

After the impromptu banquet, and while the merits of weed and beverage were being discussed, blood-curdling tales of Indian warfare dilated on by experienced participants, a sudden and alarming commotion occurred, accompanied by the detonation of rifle shots; the heart-chilling war whoop of the Apache resounding in the distance caused the party to break up in disorder.

The erratic Wood jumped for his sabre, yelling, "Apaches, by God!" The order "To arms" came simultaneously from a dozen different throats; the cowboys lounging 'neath the ramada caught the epidemic, and everyone— even the doughty Colonel Head—who could secure a mount volunteered for active service.

In fifteen minutes from the time of the first alarm, the whole command was mounted and the pack train complete in all its details. The ranking officer, Lawton, instructed his subordinates in the plan of campaign, and the army advanced against the enemy.

Captain Hatfield's troop was ordered to take a position on the left; Wood was sent around to the right; and Lawton, with Colonel Head and the volunteers, occupied the center. The command to advance was given, with instructions not to fire unless the hostiles should give battle, and the troops proceeded in the direction of the scene of disorder.

Lieutenant Roach, with a detachment of San Carlos scouts, took the lead and began the ascent of the steep ridge from which the sound of musketry came; Colonel Head, with 250 pounds of avoirdupois on a bareback mule, following close behind; the recorder of the event cautiously seeking a place of observation secure from flying bullets; when attention was attracted to an Indian in all his gorgeousness of war paint standing out prominently on an overhanging cliff, hundreds of feet above, wagging in one hand a red bandanna and in the other a black object indiscernible in the distance. He was frantic in his endeavor to convey the intelligence to the officers below that their exertions were unnecessary. Crying out in his loudest tones, "No hay Chiricahua, no hay Chiricahua, catch em, kitten!" at the same time approaching Lieutenant Roach and laying at his feet a young bear cub that had been shot through the head.

The chagrin of the officers and men can better be imagined than described, as every man in the command candidly anticipated a fight with Geronimo and his band.

The deception was caused by Roach's Indian scouts, who were doing picket duty on the mountain overlooking the camp. The relief detail encountered a bear and two cubs in a cedar thicket, and they were compelled to kill them to save the life of one of their number, hence the war whoops, rifle fusillade, and general commotion.

Captain Lawton and his subordinates felt so digusted over the affair that they exacted a promise of absolute silence in the matter, and one of the most ludicrous incidents of army life has never before been given publicity.

Captain Lawton's headquarters of operations against the Apaches was established in Guadalupe Canyon, at a point near the monument designating the corners of New Mexico, Chihuahua, and Sonora. All supplies were forwarded via San Bernardino ranch.

He had no sooner located and arranged his camp than a courier arrived with the news that the Indians were heading in the direction of Cloverdale and Skeleton Canyon, and with instructions to proceed at once to Cloverdale and Lang's Ranch and intercept them. This was on or about June 1, 1885.

The camp equipage consisted of tents and accoutrements, four large government wagons containing a supply of rations and ammunition, medical supplies, harness, saddles, officers' clothing, forty-five head of mules, and eight cavalry horses.

Leaving the government property in charge of a detail consisting of Sergeant Munich and seven men and Doctor [George] Andrews, the surgeon of Fort Huachuca, with instructions to preserve strict discipline and maintain a regular picket duty, the command proceeded at once to Cloverdale and Lang's Ranch, there to await further orders or arrest the renegades if they attempted to pass through to the Cajon Bonito, the favorite rendezvous of Geronimo in his former raids.

After the departure of the command, the detail remaining in charge of the supply train relaxed their watchfulness and entered into the enjoyment of a good time, card playing and otherwise disposting themselves, even to the extent of absolute disobedience of orders by withdrawing the picket that was to be maintained on an adjacent hill commanding the view of a large radius of the country; the sergeant, whose temerity soon afterward cost him his life, telling the doctor and his men that he did not believe there was an Indian within a hundred miles of the camp and therefore picket duty was unnecessary.

Dr. Andrews became alarmed, and he determined to seek Captain Lawton and report the recklessness of the detachment. Arriving at Cloverdale on the evening of June 5, he made the commanding officer familiar with the state of affairs at the supply camp.

That night I volunteered to proceed to Guadalupe Canyon with a reprimand for the derelict sergeant, and at break of day on the morning of June 6 I started on the journey, a distance of twenty-two miles.

The trip through Guadalupe Canyon is at no time very inviting, and particularly in those days, when the Indians were on the warpath and the desperadoes of both republics made it their stamping ground. Its trail had been baptized in blood, and the phonographic echoes of its precipitous walls are burdened with the whistle of musketry and the dying groans of lawless men in desperate encounters. A feeling of insecurity pervades the lonely traveler, and cold chills penetrate the nerves as he reads the silent record in the mounds that contain all that is mortal of the outlaw and adventurer. A volume would not suffice to contain even a brief transcription of the carnage perpetrated in its rugged fastnesses.

I cautiously felt my way through the canyon till I reached the spring that forms the source of Guadalupe Creek. It rises under an overhanging bluff of sandstone and is protected from the sun's rays at all hours of the day, making the water cool and refreshing. I dismounted and unsaddled, intending to give my animal an hour's rest before proceeding to my destination. In stooping to take a drink from the spring, I was confronted by numerous moccasin tracks, knee and hand prints in the damp soil on the brink of the pool, quite as recent and fresh as my own indentations. Hurriedly resaddling, I lost no time in getting away from the place, and I doubt if Tom O'Shanter's famous ride through glen and bracken was prosecuted with like impetuosity as was mine on that eventful forenoon.

Arriving at the supply camp, I witnessed a scene of utter desolation. Where the tents were pitched and the wagons stood were nothing but charred remnants, warped wagon tires, and volumes of smoke issuing from the debris of smouldering bacon and other semicombustible material. No sign of life except the buzzards hovering over the remains of the dead. The flat of several hundred acres on which the camp stood was denuded by the flames of every vestige of grass and shrub.

At the base of a sycamore tree I found the body of Private Neihaus, shot through the brain. In one hand was tightly grasped a half-eaten biscuit, and between his clenched teeth protruded a slice of bacon; a cup and pannikin lay by his side, showing that he was shot while partaking of his noon meal.

A short distance down the creek lay the body of a young recruit who had arrived that morning from Camp Bowie bearing dispatches for the commanding officer.

The scene and circumstances precluded the possibilities of extended investigation, and I did not undertake to find further evidence of human destruction, so I hastily started back to Cloverdale to report the disaster.

On my way up the canyon my animal added to my anxiety by starting and shying at shadow and substance. The birds that fluttered in every bush intensified my imagination, and every footprint in the trail appeared an index of impending peril. A chipmunk assumed the dimensions of a mature burro, a band of whitetail deer scampering through the brush some distance in advance caused my horse to hesitate in his breakneck speed, and every hirsute tuft on my fevered brow entered into a painful contest of competitive erection, and only after a distinct view of the harmless animals was my mind disabused of the illusion that a bloodthirsty Apache lurked in every depression on the trail.

My ride resolved itself into an actual parody of the famous Sheridan's. While the "hero of Winchester" spurred his horse toward material cohorts of death and disaster, I voicelessly yet strenuously urged my Pegasus to placing material space between myself and a conjured-up legion of painted Apaches.

It is needless to state that I passed the spring without stopping to quench the thirst of myself or animal. About dusk I reached the apex of the divide between Guadalupe and Cloverdale and for the first time breathed the air of temporary security. My spirits revived as I saw the flickering lights of the cow camp and anticipated the kindly reception and congratulations on my safety from the generous-hearted princes of the range. My arrival was antedated some hours by two soldiers—Snitzer and Jett—who escaped the massacre. Then I learned the circumstances attending the destruction of Lawton's supply train.

The attack occurred about noon. The soldiers were caught, some napping, some playing cards in their tents. Cook Neihaus, the first victim of the attack, called all hands to dinner, and simultaneously with the dinner call came the yell of the Indians and a deadly volley fired from the bluff of rocks overlooking the camp. Sergeant Munich and Private Snitzer, a young Swiss, reached their carbines and therefore were able to make some defense. Getting into the hollow square formed by the wagons, they pumped lead into their adversaries until by some means, either from their own fire or that of the Indians, combustible matter in the wagon containing the ammunition became ignited and they were forced to retire from their cover and make a fight in the open ground. The Indians were concealed among the rocks some hundred feet above and had every advantage of security and position. Appreciating the fact that it must be a fight to the death, and thinking that the balance of their comrades were killed, they determined to keep together and if necessary die together. The fire of the hostiles, about thirty in number, was concentrated on the retreating pair, who, with their faces to the foe, poured a desultory fire in the direction of the unseen enemy. Sergeant Munich was shot in the foot and dropped helplessly to the ground. His Swiss companion came to his relief and, raising him, supported him with one arm while both continued the unequal combat. Carrying and dragging his crippled companion up a steep slope in the face of a murderous fire, on reaching the apex of the ridge they sought the shelter of a cedar tree, where the gallant sergeant received his death stroke by a rifle ball through the heart while still in the arms of his loyal comrade.

After performing as sacred a duty as mortal man could for his fellow, Snitzer sought safety beyond the range of the Indian fire and lost no time in placing distance between himself and his merciless foes. Being familiar with the topography of the country, he was soon beyond the danger, and about sundown reached Cloverdale, somewhat exhausted but none the worse from his terrible experience.

Private Jett, being cut off from his arms in the beginning of the fray, escaped up the canyon unseen by the Indians,[5] and another soldier, a young German, got away armed and equipped, deserting his comrades and the army. He was afterward captured, court-martialed, and sent to Alcatraz; while the brave Snitzer was rewarded for his loyalty to friendship and duty by promotion to a sergeantship in the command he so gallantly represented.

With Crawford in Mexico

ROBERT HANNA[1]

The Overland Monthly 8, 2nd ser. (July 1886): 78–83

It was my fortune to accompany the command of Captain Emmet Crawford, who continued the pursuit of [Geronimo's] band into the Sierra Madre of Mexico. After a hard chase after a portion of the hostiles as far as Lake Palomas, in Mexico, the command to which I belonged was ordered to go to Deming and report to Captain Crawford. We found Crawford awaiting us with a train of stock cars, all ready to pull out as soon as some Indian scouts should arrive on the train from the east.

The main body of the hostiles were reported as making their way south, to the west of us, and telegrams reporting their position were coming all day long; but the train from the east was late, and we did not get away till afternoon. It soon discharged its motley load of Indian scouts, whose appearance bore evidence of the long, hard chase they had just concluded; for they had been following the hostiles from the north and were put in cars in the Rio Grande Valley to endeavor to head them off to the west of Deming before they got to the railroad. We were soon loaded and off, and after dark disembarked at Separ, having heard nothing from the hostiles since leaving Deming.

The darkness was intense, and unloading the animals on an open freight platform difficult in the extreme. The cries of the scouts, the trampling of loose animals, and the efforts of the men to find their belongings in the darkness created an indescribable confusion; while the resemblance to pandemonium was, if anything, increased by the little fires the scouts had lighted, which illuminated the somber darkness in places and showed the savage faces and almost naked forms of the Indian scouts gathered around them.

It was midnight before the tired men got to rest, and at daybreak the camp was astir, and we were soon marching away over the gray-looking plain stretching off to the southwest. Crawford had received telegrams that the hostiles had crossed the railroad to the south of us, and we were going southwest to find the trail. We learned afterwards that the hostiles had gone off to the west, and thus we missed seeing their trail till long afterward.

We continued to the southwest to Skeleton Canyon, where we were joined

Chatto. JOHN G. BOURKE. *ON THE BORDER WITH CROOK.*

by the Chiricahua scouts under Chatto, and our transportation increased by another pack train. Chatto was a chief of the same tribe as the hostiles, the Chiricahuas, and it was said that he was desirous of killing Geronimo and the other chiefs of the hostile band in order to become head chief, and that we were indebted to this ambition for the company of himself and braves on our expedition against his brethren.

In the course of interviews with Crawford, Chatto said that he knew just where the hostiles intended to rendezvous in Mexico; and it was finally determined to proceed directly to the spot instead of wasting time in following trails, which is necessarily a slow process. We went to Lang's Ranch, on the Mexican line, the next day, and on the following day went through the San Luis pass and turned south along the eastern base of the Sierra Madre and around the Mexican line. To the west of us were the mountains, and off to the east stretched the great Janos plain, and to the south could be seen the blue outlines of high mountains in Mexico. The scouts could be seen outlined against the sky as they crossed the ridges of the foothills ahead of us, while behind us followed the long line of cavalry, followed in turn by the white, pack-covered mules, each train led by its bell horse with his tinkling bell.

Our command consisted of nearly a hundred Indian scouts and a troop of cavalry, and for transportation we had two pack trains of fifty pack mules each, and a full complement of packers with each train. The scouts went ahead of the rest of the command and, with the exception of a few who had captured horses or mules in a previous encounter with the hostiles, were all afoot. Where the country would admit of it, they would cover nearly a mile of country between

Better Homes and Gardens®

2014

July

S	M	T	W	T	F	S
		1	2	3	4	5
6	7	8	9	10	11	12
13	14	15	16	17	18	19
20	21	22	23	24	25	26
27	28	29	30	31		

August

S	M	T	W	T	F	S
					1	2
3	4	5	6	7	8	9
10	11	12	13	14	15	16
17	18	19	20	21	22	23
24	25	26	27	28	29	30
31						

September

S	M	T	W	T	F	S
	1	2	3	4	5	6
7	8	9	10	11	12	13
14	15	16	17	18	19	20
21	22	23	24	25	26	27
28	29	30				

October

S	M	T	W	T	F	S
			1	2	3	4
5	6	7	8	9	10	11
12	13	14	15	16	17	18
19	20	21	22	23	24	25
26	27	28	29	30	31	

November

S	M	T	W	T	F	S
						1
2	3	4	5	6	7	8
9	10	11	12	13	14	15
16	17	18	19	20	21	22
23	24	25	26	27	28	29
30						

December

S	M	T	W	T	F	S
	1	2	3	4	5	6
7	8	9	10	11	12	13
14	15	16	17	18	19	20
21	22	23	24	25	26	27
28	29	30	31			

Better Homes and Gardens.

2014

January

S	M	T	W	T	F	S
			1	2	3	4
5	6	7	8	9	10	11
12	13	14	15	16	17	18
19	20	21	22	23	24	25
26	27	28	29	30	31	

February

S	M	T	W	T	F	S
						1
2	3	4	5	6	7	8
9	10	11	12	13	14	15
16	17	18	19	20	21	22
23	24	25	26	27	28	

March

S	M	T	W	T	F	S
						1
2	3	4	5	6	7	8
9	10	11	12	13	14	15
16	17	18	19	20	21	22
23	24	25	26	27	28	29
30	31					

April

S	M	T	W	T	F	S
		1	2	3	4	5
6	7	8	9	10	11	12
13	14	15	16	17	18	19
20	21	22	23	24	25	26
27	28	29	30			

May

S	M	T	W	T	F	S
				1	2	3
4	5	6	7	8	9	10
11	12	13	14	15	16	17
18	19	20	21	22	23	24
25	26	27	28	29	30	31

June

S	M	T	W	T	F	S
1	2	3	4	5	6	7
8	9	10	11	12	13	14
15	16	17	18	19	20	21
22	23	24	25	26	27	28
29	30					

their flanks. There was no attempt at any regular order of march; each scout would follow his own inclination, all keeping the same general direction. As a rule, they would get quite a long distance ahead of the cavalry and pack trains by 10:00 A.M. or 11:00 A.M.; they would then sit down under trees and rest and smoke awhile, and as we would come in sight, would move on, always keeping ahead of the cavalry with apparent ease, although on foot. Mountains or hills seemed to have no terrors for them, and they would generally go over a mountain, no matter how steep, if it would shorten the distance.

Finding no water in the foothills, we turned off to the east toward a rugged-looking mountain that stood out in the plain, called the Sierra en Medio or Middle Mountain. Here, a few years ago, the troops had a fight with the hostiles. A rough, rocky hill, somewhat detached from the main mountain, with an occasional skeleton of a horse or a man about it, and the rocks spattered with lead, told the tale.

The horses and mules were turned out to graze, and we went into camp. Our animals got no feed except what they would pick up, and they were always grazed all night under charge of a guard. We used no tents, so were spared the necessity of putting them up. The usual rule was, when there happened to be any trees, to spread our blankets in the shade, and after a wash in the one tin washbasin that sufficed for all the headquarters, lie around until the cook should announce dinner.

The officers messed with the packers and were about equally divided between the two trains. The tin plates and cups would be laid out on a *manta*, or pack cover, on the ground, and we would squat around, Indian fashion. Our cook, who rejoiced in the name of "Nibs," and who looked more like a cowboy than a cook, would yell, "Chuck!" and everyone would then be expected to come to dinner. Everyone helped himself, but it was not considered good form to put one's foot on the table in order to reach things unless absolutely necessary. Our fare was but little better than the ordinary soldier's ration, and it was always safe to say that for dinner, breakfast, and supper it would consist of bacon, bread, beans, and coffee. Our dinner over, it grew cooler as the sun went down, and after a smoke nearly everyone turned in to sleep, so as to be up by daybreak the next morning for another long day's march. After the Sierra en Medio, we went back to the main range to the west, and after two days' travel in the mountains, through a beautiful wooded country covered with live oaks, we camped at an old abandoned ranch on the trail across the Sierra Madre, leading from Janos, in Chihuahua, to Bavispe, in the state of Sonora.

Chatto had been having frequent interviews with Captain Crawford, which were carried on through the medium of two interpreters, one Spanish, the other Apache. The Apache rejoiced in the name of "Mickey Free," and it was said that he was not an Indian, but the son of an Irishman and a Mexican woman, and had been a captive among the Apaches all his life. Mickey certainly had a Milesian cast of countenance, although in every other respect he seemed a thorough Indian. His knowledge of Spanish did not include any use of tenses, so that it was extremely difficult to tell whether he meant the present, future, or past, in his translations from Apache into Spanish. We, however, learned enough to know that Chatto was exceedingly averse to going through any of the Mexican towns, on account, as we thought, of his depredations when formerly in Mexico; so the next day we traveled on the Bavispe trail until we were about halfway down the western slope of the mountain, then turned to the south to avoid going into Bavispe.

In the evening we brought up in a deep canyon in front of a mescal distillery, where we were obliged to halt and camp. The distillery was well supplied with Mexican firewater, and before morning we were in the company of nearly a hundred drunken savages. It was not a pleasant feeling to know that we were in a foreign country, and that a not overly friendly one, with a small force, in the company of such utterly irresponsible beings; moreover, some of our savage allies had been raiding in this very country only a short time before and might be tempted to try it again.

Our march the next day led down a valley by the side of a stream grown up with immense cane brakes, and about 10:00 A.M. we came out of the valley in front of the town of Bavispe, which our Apache friends were so anxious to avoid the day before. Bavispe is a little Mexican town, built in the usual Mexican style, with a plaza in the center, in which is a church of apparently considerable antiquity. The town is situated on the river of the same name, which here runs nearly due north along the western base of the Sierra Madre. It is a clear-running mountain stream, and there is considerable land under cultivation in the vicinity of the towns in the valley.

We observed that all over this country there seems to be no attempt to occupy ranches at any distance from the towns, although the abandoned ranches all over the country indicate that at one time it was not so, and that insecurity of life and property at any distance from the towns has caused this state of affairs. The Apaches have made their homes in the Sierra Madre and literally devastated the surrounding country.

The Mexicans in the towns we passed recognized Captain Chatto and asked after Captain Geronimo, not as yet knowing that that noble chieftain was among them with blood in his eye. Our information on that subject created a visible coolness towards Captain Chatto and his followers. That brave, and in fact the majority of our braves, were very tired indeed, between Mexican whiskey inside and the Mexican sun outside, so we camped on the river opposite the town of Bacerac, a village much resembling Bavispe. The male inhabitants of these towns seemed to be largely in the minority, and we were unable to account for it until told that the majority of them had gone off to the Yaqui war then going on.

We kept traveling south until we reached the Tesorababi Creek, where General Crook camped in 1883 before going into the Sierra Madre; and then the Indians pointed out to us the dim outlines of a mountain far to the southwest, where they said the hostiles were to rendezvous. The Indians called it the

"Klee," or "Horse" Mountain, but we afterwards learned the Mexicans called it the Sierra del Tigre. Our march from here led over the roughest country I have ever seen; although the Mexicans called the trail the *camino real,* and it was used as a highway between towns, it was all but impracticable for animals. We walked and led our half-starved horses, for since leaving the eastern slope of the Sierra Madre grass was but scarce and poor, and they had nothing else to live on.

Down into interminable canyons, thousands of feet, under a broiling sun, we toiled, only to find when we got to the bottom [that] we had to climb up another place on the other side just as bad. The canyons seemed to be the bottoms of immense craters in some places, and had it been cool enough to have appreciated the beauties of nature, I do not doubt we should have admired the grand views that often burst upon us; but it was too hot for anything except a rest, and we could not take a rest then.

The Indians had been making "medicine" and singing their "medicine" songs every night since we started. After they had had supper and had all smoked their cigarettes, they would start in to sing a monotonous chant, in which all joined; and they would keep it up till the small hours, no matter how hard the day's march had been. We were all lying around in our blankets one night, when camped in the bottom of one of the craterlike canyons, when we were honored by a visit from Uklenny, the principal medicine man, accompanied by most of the scouts. The gloomy canyon was in darkness except an occasional campfire, and the guttural tones of Uklenny as he told his story made an evident impression on all his hearers. He said he had come to tell us that he had made medicine, and the medicine was good; that we should have a fight in three days and someone would be killed; but if Captain Crawford would kill a white cow and let them eat it, we should catch the Chiricahuas. The singular part of it was that the next day, a part of his story came true.

After a long, hot march of nearly forty miles, a great deal of which was on foot, having crossed the Batipito River and gone into camp at the foot of the Sierra del Tigre, word was brought in that one of the scouts had been killed and another wounded by Mexicans, while lagging behind the column. This created the greatest excitement among the scouts, and many of us feared that if they attempted reprisals on the Mexicans, as they threatened, we should have a poor chance with our little command ever to get out of Mexico. We shortly after received a letter from the presidente of Huasavas, a small town on the river south of us. He enclosed a letter from an American, explaining the circumstances. The Americans had come over a hill suddenly and, seeing the scouts, thought they were hostiles and fired upon them. This was explained to the Indians, and apparently they were satisfied, but they neither lagged nor straggled after that.

The letter from the presidente of Huasavas also contained the information that the hostiles had left the Sierra del Tigre, where we were then camped, and had been seen near the village of Oputo, north of us. They had evidently gone to these mountains as Chatto said they would. We sent out and buried the dead scout, and brought in the wounded one, and the next morning started for Oputa.

We camped about three miles above Oputa, and had it not been for the kindness of the people of that town, our animals would have fared badly, as there was no grass in the country. They allowed us to turn the animals into their stubble fields and showed in every way a very kindly feeling. The singing of the scouts had grown so tiresome that we got them out of hearing by placing them on the opposite side of the river from us. The river was broad and shallow at our camp, and on each side there was a large growth of cottonwoods, under which we were camped.

After some scouting in the vicinity, the scouts announced that they had located the camp of the hostiles; so that evening a part of the command was detailed to go on foot at night, with a view to surrounding the camp and surprising them. Each man carried one hundred rounds of ammunition and three days' food. Just as the moon rose over the distant peaks of the Sierra Madre, they silently stole out of camp. The moon shone brightly on the broad rim, and the cottonwood trees threw both camps into a dark shadow, beneath which it would be difficult to imagine a command like ours was concealed. The silence was only broken by the croaking of the frogs, and the scene had certainly little in keeping with the object of the little command then going out. The party that went out traveled about twenty miles and the next morning surprised a band of hostiles under Chihuahua and captured eleven women and children. They made but little fight, but fled as fast as they could, leaving one dead upon the ground, all their camp equipage, and horses. We had one scout seriously wounded. So although Crawford did not kill the white cow, as Uklenny desired, we did catch the hostiles.

The women and children were a miserable-looking lot and showed in their appearance that their flight from the reservation had been no pleasure excursion to them. Among the captives were the squaw and children of Chihuahua. The next day I was ordered to take the prisoners and wounded, and an empty pack train, with an escort of ten cavalrymen, to the nearest camp in the United States.

We had to travel through a country totally unknown to me and had for guide a scout named "Dutchy," a brother of Chihuahua, who was sent in because he had declined to go out and fight his brother. Among our prisoners was a woman shot through the hips, and we had no way to carry her but on a horse. She suffered horribly and had to be taken off frequently to rest. The groans of the wounded and the cries of the children, some of whom were wounded, made our little column rather a melancholy procession.

We had received a caution from Captain Crawford to keep a good lookout, as he was somewhat afraid the hostiles would attempt to recapture their families, which, with our small party, and taking into consideration that we had Chihuahua's family with us, seemed not unlikely. Uklenny, the medicine man, and another scout accompanied us. I suspect Uklenny's success in his prophecies had made him such a reputation he was going into the reservation to retire on his laurels.

We traveled silently over the rugged and barren foothills of the Sierra del Tigre and only made a short march the first day on account of the difficulty in getting the wounded along. We camped the first night at the bottom of a deep canyon, in which were some immense trees that looked like mahogany. The Mexicans had been getting out logs of this wood, hewing them, and hauling them to the river.

The next day we crossed a large trail of Indians. Uklenny and the scouts declared that this had been made the day before and expressed great fear that we should be attacked the next morning. After arrival in camp, the scouts built themselves a little fort of rocks, put in their canteens and a bucket filled with water, placed the prisoners around the outside, and prepared to stand a siege. We thought they ought to know what they were about, [and] so made the best disposition we could of the little party for an attack. Everyone was ordered to be up at 3:00 A.M. so as to be ready at daybreak, the usual hour for an Indian attack.

We were not molested, however, and the next morning continued our march along the summit of the Sierra del Tigre, through a beautiful country. The hills were covered with live oaks, and in the canyons there were great numbers of immense cabbage palms, fifty and sixty feet high. Ledges cropped out across the hills, and there was every evidence of valuable mineral. The trail was an old smuggler's trail and but little traveled, but the small wooden crosses and piles of stones beside them, marking the graves, indicated that it had not always been as peaceful as it looked then.

We finally crossed the Sierra del Tigre and came out into a broad valley, and two days after camped near the town of Fronteras, where we were the objects of great curiosity and visited by almost the entire population. After several days of marching over an interesting country, we arrived at Fort Bowie, Arizona, to learn that we had been reported massacred by the Indians, our prisoners recaptured, and that a party had been sent after us.

After assisting in putting Dutchy into irons in the guardhouse for mutiny, and turning over our prisoners to the commanding officer of the post, I rested a few days and went back to the Mexican line with other scouts going into Mexico, and began anew my wanderings over the dusty plains and rugged mountains of Arizona and New Mexico. I did not return to Crawford's command and never again saw him. A few months later his tragic death at the hands of the Mexicans put an end to an honorable and useful life and deprived us of the services of a conscientious officer and a just commander.

Captain Crawford's Last Expedition

WILLIAM E. SHIPP[1]

Journal of the United States Cavalry Association 5, no. 19
(December 1892): 343–61

In the United States Army Register for 1887 we find the following entry: "Died—Captain Emmet Crawford, Third Cavalry, January 18, 1886, near Nacori, Mexico, of wounds received January 11, 1886, in an attack made on his command of Indian scouts by a force of Mexicans."

The circumstances attending his death were so sad and so peculiar, and the character of Captain Crawford was so elevated and noble, that the story of his last expedition possesses a mournful interest for those acquainted with it.

It was the lot of the writer to be a member of this expedition and to be thrown into intimate association with him, and so to learn to know and to love him; to witness his fall and death; and finally to see his remains buried in the land of strangers—of those who had killed him while he was trying to help them. It is the fact of having had these opportunities, together with the desire to pay a tribute to the memory of one so worthy to be classed among our heroes, that furnishes the reason for writing this account.

What is generally known as Geronimo's outbreak led to the circumstances which resulted in the death of Captain Crawford, and it will therefore be necessary to begin our story by a brief account of that outbreak.

In May 1885 a large portion of the Chiricahua and Warm Springs Apaches, then united as one tribe, without cause left their reservation at Fort Apache, Arizona. Naiche was their hereditary chief and, being a man of ability in addition, was the real leader; the son of old Cochise, who was for many years the terror of the Southwest, Naiche was worthy of his father. Geronimo was the medicine man and orator of the tribe. He was not a great warrior; but, like Sitting Bull in the North, his influence was powerful among his people. A man of diabolical appearance and with a character to correspond, he always appealed to the bad side of the Indian nature; and they, like too many people in this world, generally listened to him in preference to better men. By some chance Geronimo was always credited by the whites with being at the head of the renegades; this error is of so little importance that, for the sake of convenience, we will adopt it.

The Indians at once entered upon a career of murder and pillage, embracing in their zone of operations large portions of Arizona and New Mexico in the United States, and Chihuahua and Sonora in Old Mexico. The theater of war was so rough and barren that it was with great difficulty that they were followed at all by the troops. Fitted by nature and by long experience for such warfare, and finding plenty of food by stealing cattle and horses, they laughed at their pursuers and continued to spread desolation and terror wherever they chose to go. The broken-down horses and the ragged and worn-out soldiers showed the work the troops had been doing—work discouraging and doubly hard on account of the almost total lack of success.

Seeing that the efforts of the regulars were fruitless, General Crook, the department commander, turned to a plan which had long been a favorite with him: the employment of Indian scouts to subdue their own people. The hostiles, or "broncos" as they were generally called, had made their headquarters in the great Sierra Madre range in Mexico, where they had a safe base for operating both in our country and in Mexican territory. A treaty was now made in Washington which allowed our troops to cross the border, but it had the great drawback of not allowing us to establish any supply camps in Mexico.

Under General Crook's plan two expeditions were organized, composed mainly of scouts and commanded by Captain Wirt Davis, Fourth Cavalry, and Captain Emmet Crawford, Third Cavalry. The latter had been recalled for this duty from Texas, where he had just gone with his regiment. He had entered the army after the war from the volunteer service and had since been almost continuously in active service on the frontier, taking part in most of our great Indian wars and making for himself a reputation for bravery and devotion to duty not surpassed by that of any officer of the army. Though he had distinguished himself in the northern campaigns against the Sioux and others, yet it is probable that his service in Arizona had been still more valuable. In 1883 he had commanded the scouts in General Crook's expedition into Mexico, the first expedition ever organized for a campaign against Indians in that country.

Returning from this duty, he was placed in police charge of the San Carlos reservation, where he had entire control of the Indians lately on the warpath and where he also kept order among the other turbulent elements. Constantly opposed by employees of the Interior Department and other interested parties, his final overthrow of his enemies and the exposure of their frauds led to a lasting change in the administration of affairs on the reservation; a change for which the people of Arizona have yet cause to be thankful. Captain Crawford had a thorough knowledge of Indian (especially Apache) character, and he knew personally a great number of the men of this tribe. This knowledge, together with his high character, gave him great influence with them. They knew from experience that they could believe him and trust him; he was kind to them, yet never allowed familiarity; his pure life, his devotion to duty, and his fearlessness in the discharge of it won their respect. Hence he was peculiarly fitted to command them when they took service under the government.

The two expeditions sent into Mexico were as successful as could have been expected, each capturing a number of squaws and children and breaking up the camps which had formed the homes of the broncos. The wearing-out process seemed to furnish the only hope of subduing them; this process, however, promised to be long and somewhat tedious.

In the fall the commands were brought in and thoroughly reorganized. It had been necessary to send out the first expeditions rather hastily; now time was taken to more carefully select the scouts and to more thoroughly equip the commands. The commanders remained the same, but some changes were made among the other officers. Captain Crawford chose the White Mountain Apaches and friendly Chiricahuas as his scouts because they were mountain Indians and were less civilized than the other tribes, and therefore, in his opinion, better fitted for the work to be done. The Chiricahuas were part of the tribe then on the warpath and had themselves been at peace only about two years. No soldiers were to be taken. The peculiar material selected was believed to be the best adapted to the task of following Geronimo's people into their retreats in the terrific fastnesses of the Sierra Madre, where it was hoped to surprise them and compel their surrender. Surprise was absolutely necessary to success; once aware of the proximity of the foes, the hostiles would scatter and render it impossible to follow them. Indians of other tribes and soldiers were not believed to possess the skill and endurance necessary to surprise the vigilant Chiricahuas; Captain Crawford in his previous expedition had found the soldiers he had with him a burden.

The great risk taken in trusting so largely to relatives of the hostiles seemed justifiable, as they alone knew the haunts and habits of the enemy. Many gloomy predictions were made about their treachery, but the many eager offers of service by the young officers in the department showed that they at least were not daunted by the prospect. The selections made were First Lieutenant M. P. Maus, First Infantry, and Second Lieutenant W. E. Shipp, Tenth Cavalry, to command scout companies; Second Lieutenant S. L. Faison, First Infantry, to be adjutant, quartermaster, and commissary; Dr. T. B. Davis, U.S. Army, to be surgeon. One hundred scouts were enlisted at Fort Apache and started for Mexico on November 18, 1885. But before we follow the command on its march, it will be necessary to take a look at its organization and personnel.

Two white chiefs of scouts assisted the officers, their principal duty being the daily issue of rations—daily because the scouts would always eat up at once whatever was given to them. One of these men, Horn, also interpreted from Spanish into English. Concepcion, an old Mexican who had been a captive, was Apache interpreter. The two interpreters were necessary because no one could be found to interpret directly from Apache. The interpreters were used only in important talks, as the scouts and their officers understood each other well enough for ordinary purposes. Noche, a Chiricahua, was the sergeant major and performed the duties of leading guide and scout. His superior for these duties never existed. The other conspicuous scouts who were always selected for difficult service were Cooney, Cuso, Dutchy, Wassil, Kat-e-kahn, and Chi-kiz-in, among the Chiricahuas; Naw-wah-zhe-tah, Good-e-na-ha, Loco, and Josh, among the White Mountains. Some of these deserve our notice. Cooney and Cuso were two short, big-chested men with almost unlimited powers of endurance; in their savage way they were as honest and loyal as men could be and were splendid scouts. Dutchy was a known murderer, brutal and mean, but in many respects a valuable scout.

Our captain's treatment of Dutchy well illustrates his methods with Indians. During the previous summer this man had mutinied and had been sent to Fort Bowie, where he was put in irons. Though he was undoubtedly guilty, Captain Crawford took him again as a scout but refused to give him the chevrons he demanded. He, however, selected him as his body servant and trusted implicitly this man who had not long before threatened his life. The result was the establishment of a complete ascendency over Dutchy and increased respect on the part of the others, as they saw how little he feared this dangerous man.

Wassil was an old man, a fine scout, and the best hunter of all. His claim to fame rests, however, on his escape from the train conveying him to Florida in September 1886 and his return from Independence, Missouri, to Arizona. His long journey through an unknown country, part of it thickly settled, shows what an Indian can do towards finding his way. He is now (1891) a renegade in the mountains, has committed several murders, and seems safe from capture.

Nah-wah-zhe-tah, or Nosey, as he was irreverently but appropriately called, was a great medicine man—which means that he was a doctor, preacher, conjurer, and prophet, all in one. Dressed in an old alpaca coat, ornamented with a pair of shoulder straps and a pair of cavalry officer's trousers much too long for his short legs, his first appearance was hardly in keeping with his solemn character and functions. Though undoubtedly a humbug, yet his influence was exercised for good and rendered the task of governing the wild scouts much easier. Poor old Nosey is now in jail for killing his own chief, the result of too much tiswin, the Apache intoxicant.

The scouts were not burdened with much clothing—the soldier's blouse, a pair of cotton drawers and a waist cloth, moccasins, and a red headband constituted the usual costume. Their picturesqueness and, above all, their efficiency were not spoiled by attempts to make them look like regulars. In these men were apparent the results of heredity and long training. Small and unable to compete with white men in any athletic sports, yet they made us feel like babies when it came to mountain work. The Chiricahuas especially were a never-ending source of wonder. Their knowledge of country; their powers of observation and deduction; their watchfulness, endurance, and ability to take care of themselves under all circumstances made them seem at times like superior beings from another world. No wonder our soldiers could not catch people like these. If our little army of twenty-five thousand men were composed of such men and animated by the proper spirit, it would be unconquerable by the best army now existing in Europe.

The command exercised over the scouts depended mainly upon the moral influence of the officers. Eager as they seemed to be to do their duty, care was taken to avoid trying to force them into ways foreign to their nature and training. They fully understood their work, and except to exercise a general control and supervision over them, no attempt was made to interfere. The temptation to be unduly meddlesome was, however, not strong, for most of the scouts had been on the warpath, which meant that many white men had been killed by them. They were, however, treated with perfect confidence, and soon little thought was given to their former bloody records.

Their methods of camping and marching were in conformity with the character of these troops. They cooked their own food without the necessity of supervision, and on going into camp, they always voluntarily took such precautions as circumstances made necessary. They were ready to start by sunrise, or sooner, and when not in a dangerous neighborhood, much liberty was allowed them, so that they scattered on foot in hunting parties; at the same time, they were sure to find signs of the hostiles if the latter were anywhere in the neighborhood. The officers and chiefs of scouts, on mules or on foot, accompanied the scouts to see that no depredations were committed. This free life had many charms, despite the hardships often accompanying it. All supplies and baggage were carried on the pack mules, these being divided into three big trains, under Daly, Hayes, and Rover, forty-five packs to each train. The aparejo was, of course, the pack saddle used; each mule, when in good condition, could carry comfortably about 250 pounds. Each train was complete in itself, with its "boss packer," its cargador (the man who arranged the loads and kept everything in repair), its blacksmith, its cooks, and its bell horse. Seven other men belonged to a train, but no matter what a man's position was—boss or cook—he was expected to help pack. Most of the mules were seasoned to mountain work, and the packers were old hands, many of them having spent the best years of their lives in the government service. There was very little room for improvement in these trains; if the government could always count on service as efficient as that rendered by the packers in this campaign, there would be no cause for complaint. The trains have now all been broken up, many of the mules sold, and most of the packers discharged without reward or recognition. It is a pity that these schools for the difficult art of packing no longer exist. Someday, perhaps even in a civilized war, there may be cause to regret it.

From the starting point at Fort Apache the command went to Fort Bowie, Arizona—General Crook's field headquarters—where it was inspected by General Sheridan. After a few words of encouragement from him and from General Crook, we started on a night march to the Dragoon Mountains, Arizona, as a band of hostiles had been reported in that neighborhood. After a week's scouting, no trail being found, we crossed the Mexican line into Sonora on December 6, heading toward Fronteras. From there we went south to the mining town of Nacozari, and then, leaving all roads, struck into big mountains on the west slope of the Sierra Madre, where there was plenty of hard work. An abundance of deer made the fare good, however, and compensated us for other hardships.

Emerging from the mountains, we found ourselves in the valley of the Bavispe, a tributary of the Yaqui, and camped at the town of Huasabas, where groves of orange and lemon trees showed the tropical nature of the country. The fruit helped at the Christmas dinners, which otherwise would have been almost wholly made up from Uncle Sam's army ration. The valley of the Bavispe was fertile, but the inhabitants did not appreciate the advantages Nature had given them; they were a miserable people, living in mud huts almost bare of furniture and wanting in every comfort. Wheeled vehicles were unknown; the burro did the freighting for the country. The Apaches had long been a terror, but the Mexicans seemed to regard them as a natural evil not to be gotten rid of by any effort on their part. There were no doctors among them, and during our stay they availed themselves of the services of our kindhearted surgeon, who was never idle, receiving, however, as fees only a few oranges or a cheese, sometimes a welcome bottle of mescal.

Huasabas was the scene of our first serious trouble with the Mexicans. One of the scouts, who was drunk but unarmed, was so badly shot in the face by a soldier that he had to be sent back home. At such times the exertions of the officers alone prevented bloody fights; their duties were dangerous and not at all pleasant.

There were plenty of rumors of outrages still farther south, so we crossed the mountains in that direction and came to Bacadehuachi, a tiny town for such a name. Here, hid away in these wilds, was a crumbling mission, one of those monuments to the wonderful old priests who ages ago braved hardships and dangers to plant their religion among the Indians; sometimes accomplishing much, their zeal too often brought their lives to an end in torture. The priests of that day must have been experts at solving the labor question to have gotten out of the ancestors of the lazy people we saw the work necessary to build this big brick church with its bells, its towers, and its wings.

The Apaches had left their mark all through the country we were now traversing. The abandoned and ruined ranches, and occasionally a deserted village; the way in which the people spoke; the dismal stories they told, and the scars they showed; and the general desolation which prevailed in this fertile and well-watered though rough country all bore witness to the curse these Indians were. Nacori, the next village, was surrounded by a wall to protect the inhabitants, and the little fields hugging the town showed that they did not dare to go far from it.

Our hardest work was now at hand; the country was getting rougher still, and there was no doubt that the hostiles were not far away. The surplus rations were stored in Nacori, and Lieutenant Faison was sent to Lang's Ranch, New Mexico, with two pack trains for more. Taking Daly's train, Captain Crawford, marching at night, went into camp about twenty miles to the south of Nacori and sent out a small party on foot to explore. This party having returned without seeing any signs, it was decided to leave the pack train in camp with a small guard and to strike out on foot for the rough country near the forks of the Yaqui, where the Mexicans had reported Geronimo's headquarters to be located. Safe in this retreat, where they had never yet been followed, the Indians had been sending out small parties to kill and to steal. Twelve days' rations and one blanket for each officer and scout were to be packed on a few of the best mules, the three packers accompanying them being the only men allowed to ride. When the scouts found that we were to walk with them, they begged hard to be allowed to go alone, as they felt certain that the white men could not keep up. But the captain would not submit to such an arrangement, and they reluctantly gave up.

Before starting, there was a big medicine dance, at which old Nah-wah-zhe-tah for the first time unrolled the sacred buckskin which he had worn over his shoulder since he had left Fort Apache. The ceremonies were impressive, even to the white men. So thoroughly in earnest were the Indians that the solemn dances and marching, the kneeling before the sacred buckskin as it was presented to be kissed, and the old medicine man's blessing of the arms seemed not meaningless to us as we looked on in silence. With Noche and a picked band equally divided between the Chiricahuas and White Mountains leading, we started out on January 3, 1886, and camped that night on the Haros River, a large tributary of the Yaqui. On this and the following marches the advance guard marched far ahead, thoroughly reconnoitering the country; immediately preceding the main body were a few good scouts; Captain Crawford always led the main body and allowed none of the scouts in it to get in front of him. Fording the river in the morning, we were toiling up and down the steep hills beyond when, about six miles from the river, a small trail of Indians was struck and, soon after, the trail of a big band traveling east. Many tracks of ponies and cattle showed how successfully they had been marauding. From some slight sign the scouts declared that Naiche was with the band, which meant that Geronimo was there also. Cautiously as we had been advancing before, it was now necessary to be still more careful, for we were on the trail of Indians whose vigilance never relaxed, even here where they had never been followed. The extreme caution of these Indians was shown by the location of their camps, which were always high up on some well-guarded point, whence all the approaches could be watched. It mattered not to the bucks who selected them how many miles the poor squaws had to carry wood and water. The way the trail ran, concealed as it ascended the hill and exposed to view as it descended, was another evidence that they did not intend to be caught napping. This necessitated many a weary detour, as their watchful rear guard might at any time discover us if we followed the downhill trail.

In the hope that the Indians would establish a permament camp, we hustled on, thinking it possible that the scouts, as expert as they, might be able to surprise them. From the time we started on this foot scout, the hardships had been great. The country was so rough that it seemed Nature must have made a special effort in that direction. Wearing moccasins whose thin soles allowed the feet to feel every stone of the millions that lay in the path, we had to keep up with our Indians, who had been climbing mountains since they were babies and whose ancestors had for ages been mountaineers. The days were fairly warm, but the high altitude made the nights bitterly cold. Without shelter and limited to one blanket each, and with no fires allowed, sleep was almost impossible to all except the scouts, who slept in long rows, with one's head at his neighbor's feet, and seemed tolerably comfortable. We could not start till the advance scouts had thoroughly reconnoitered the country, so that it was always late in the day when we broke camp. The marches did not end till late at night, when camp, cheerless as it was, was at least better than the endless climbing of mountains or falling over rocks. Often we had to follow some canyon in which lay immovable boulders made slippery by the water which had once flowed over them. Going through them in the dark, it seemed as if we would surely break our necks or dash out our brains, so often did we fall.

Deer were plentiful, but none could be killed for fear of betraying our presence. The blouses were turned so as to expose the gray lining, which was less conspicuous than the blue side, and all prominent marks about the person were discarded. When it was necessary to make fires for cooking, the scouts took charge; in the daytime small smokeless fires were made from very dry wood; at night the fires were hid away in some gully or depression so that they could not be seen a few yards away. In crossing ridges, care was taken never to expose the body against the skyline. Whether in camp or on the march, the scouts exercised a constant watchfulness, and no precaution that could possibly be taken was ever neglected. Long habit had made these things come naturally to them. Watching the scouts, one could not help thinking how hopeless was the attempt to catch people like them with men trained and equipped in the manner of our own soldiers. The Apache seems to see everything and to know everything when in the field; no matter how dim a trail may be, it may be made by a few moccasined feet passing over rocks, he follows it by sight as easily as the good hound follows his prey by scent. Soldiers, I mean officers as well, nearly always scorn the precautions that Indians never neglect. Many a time the pursuer has found himself only too glad to escape from the little band he had started out to destroy. We made but few miles a day, so many halts had to be made to reconnoiter, the country was so rough and night marching so difficult. Cattle from which only a few pounds of meat had been cut were often found lying on the road. On the sixth the remains of a number were found, the meat having been carried off, and no more tracks were seen. On the seventh the trail crossed the Haros, and we found ourselves in that terrible country between the Haros and the Satochi so appropriately called by the Mexicans "Espina del Diablo," or Backbone of the Devil.

On January 9 the start was made about noon, and we had already made a good day's march when, at dusk, Noche reported that the hostile camp had been located. Fearing that we would be discovered if we delayed, it was decided to march all night and attack at daylight. The mules were far to the rear and had to be left behind; so with empty stomachs, we began this toilsome march that was to test the strength of the scouts no less than that of the white men. The doctor remained with the packs, as did the old interpreter, Concepcion, who was worn out and unable to keep up. His absence was afterward a source of much trouble. During all this dark night we climbed steep mountains covered with loose stones, or struggled through gloomy canyons, following our Chiricahua guides, who seemed perfectly at home. Sometimes we almost despaired and felt like succumbing to the fatigue that nearly overpowered us, but at such moments the thought of what dawn should bring buoyed us up and revived our drooping spirits.

At length, just before daylight, we drew near the high rocky point where the camp was said to be, and the command was divided so as, if possible, to surround it. After some delay we crept forward, scarcely breathing as we moved; and to some of us there came strange sensations, as in the dark still night we thought of the isolation of our position, for in this wild and unknown region we were led on by allies who had often proved how crafty and bloodthirsty they could be. But success seemed almost assured, and exultation was taking the place of these feelings, when some burros in the herd of the hostiles began braying and aroused the camp to a sense of its danger. Some of the "broncos" running out to try and carry off their stock were fired upon by the scouts, who then rushed into the rocks nearby and opened a lively fusillade, accompanying it with their shrill cries of defiance. Answering shots came from the camp, close at hand in a cluster of large rocks, that we afterward saw formed a stronghold capable of defense by a very few men. The behavior of the scouts at this juncture was very disappointing. A rush into the camp would have ensured the capture of the squaws and children at least, probably after a bloody fight. But they scattered through the rocks and, deaf to all appeals, allowed themselves to be held in check by the fire of the hostiles, who finally escaped in the darkness, leaving behind all their stock, provisions, and blankets. The officers could do nothing, for the Apaches always fight in their own way, and instead of following one who tries to lead them to a charge, they look upon him as a fool and unworthy of confidence. In this case it was impossible for us to tell friend from foes; every time I myself attempted to shoot I was stopped because I was about to shoot a scout; at last, in desperation, I fired two shots at some figure dimly seen. Who he was I never knew, for I missed him.

In this affair one bronco was slightly wounded. We suffered no casualties whatever. Soldiers in the place of the scouts would have behaved better, but then, a sufficient number of soldiers could never have been gotten so close without being discovered. Daylight before the end of the skirmish might have changed matters somewhat, but when there was light enough to see, the band had all escaped and were scattered through the mountains, and the scouts, worn out by eighteen hours' continuous marching, were no longer able to fol-

low. It would have been useless to do so anyway, for once aware of our presence, there would have been no chance of catching the hostiles until they had
again settled down.

From what I saw of the Chiricahua scouts on this occasion, and subsequently when we had talks with the Indians, I am satisfied that though they
fired a good many shots, yet they had little desire to kill, in spite of their wish
to see the war ended by the surrender of the renegades. These men worked too
hard and were too faithful under temptation to give any reason to suspect them
of treachery. But it does not seem unreasonable to believe that they did not
strongly desire the death of people belonging to their own tribe. They had not
only been their friends, but some were relatives. Moreover, in their eyes the
hostiles had committed no crime, for they themselves had likewise been on the
warpath. They wanted peace, but not at the expense of much bloodshed. The
White Mountain scouts were too much afraid of their Chiricahua brethren to
oppose them, so they have not been considered in the above statement. It was
one of the many difficulties of General Crook's task that at that time there
seemed to be no one but these Chiricahua scouts who could follow the hostiles
to their retreats in this unknown region.

Disappointment at the result of the fight was, however, soon forgotten in
the search for food. Supplies were not lacking, but the white men, exhausted
by their long march without food, found little to tempt them in the lean horse-
meat without salt and the roasted heads of mescal which lay around the abandoned camp. The meat, toasted on ramrods, was about as satisfactory as pieces
of gunny sack, while the sweetness of the mescal soon produced nausea. The
exhaustion of the command was shown by the way the men threw themselves
anywhere on the ground to sleep. Some scouts were sent back to bring up the
party with the pack mules, but they went to sleep on the road, and nothing was
heard of the train.

In the afternoon an old squaw came in with a message saying that Naiche
and Geronimo wanted to have a talk outside the camp. From what she told
him, Captain Crawford believed that they were ready to surrender; the correct-
ness of his belief was shown by statements made by these chiefs to an officer
eight months later, when on their way to surrender to General Miles. The
absence of the interpreter, however, compelled a delay, and the meeting was
appointed for the next morning. The squaw reported that her people were without food, begged some for herself, and departed, leaving us very hopeful for
the morrow. Having now nothing to fear from the hostiles and being worn out,
the scouts relaxed their usual vigilance, and all lay down to sleep by the side of
the big fires, which had been built to keep off the bitter cold of the night,
which caused much suffering. All the white men and most of the scouts were
without blankets or covering of any kind.

A heavy fog made the morning of January 11 very obscure, and just as it
was getting light enough to see, the Indians shouted out that the Mexicans
were coming. Lieutenant Maus, chief of scouts Horn, and I, who were awake

at the time, ran forward to prevent any trouble, at the same time calling out who we were. But shots from the advancing party drove us into the rocks, where the scouts had taken refuge. Some of them had commenced returning the fire, but this was soon stopped.

Our camp lay on the left bank of the Haros River, which was in sight and was about fifty miles southwest of Nacori. The ridge on which it was located fell off abruptly to the riverside in a high rocky bluff, along the edge of which ran a line of big rocks; outside of these rocks was an open space containing a few scrubby trees. We had nearly all been sleeping in this open space, but the firing caused it to be speedily vacated. In the dim light we could not tell who our assailants were, but an idea soon began to prevail that they were Major Davis's scouts who had taken us for hostiles. The thought of being killed by our own friends was agonizing, and we loudly called out the names of the officers on duty with Davis's battalion. In a few minutes the firing ceased, and the voices of Mexicans were heard crying out. Horn answered in Spanish, and a small party appeared in the open space near us. It had now grown light, and the white men showed themselves while Horn called out to the leader of the band, then about twenty-five yards from us. The scouts still lay hidden in the rocks; they did not trust the Mexicans.

Captain Crawford had been asleep when the first alarm was given, and it was not thought necessary to stop and wake him. When the firing began he, like the rest, ran into the rocks. He now appeared, standing on a high rock, conspicuous above every other object. It is impossible to tell how he viewed the situation, though he must have known that in so exposing himself he ran a great risk, no matter under what circumstances the attack had been made. Thinking no doubt, that by exposing himself to full view in his uniform, he might save us from being again attacked, he did not hesitate, but climbed the rock and stood waving a white handkerchief in token of peace. In a moment a single shot rang out, followed by a volley. Crawford fell, struck, the scouts said, by the single shot. The Indians returned the fire, and for several minutes there was a hot fight. Horn was wounded by the leader of the Mexicans, who was dropped dead where he stood by a Chiricahua named Bender, who lay at our feet.

The command had fallen to Lieutenant Maus, the next in rank, who had to choose between continuing the fight or terminating it as soon as possible by acting strictly on the defensive. The latter course involved two considerations. The first was that if the Mexicans believed us to be hostile Indians, we could defend ourselves until we could make them understand who we were. On the other hand, if they really knew us, we could demonstrate to them our ability to defend ourselves and show them how useless it was to keep up the fight. There were many good reasons why the offensive should not be taken, the principal one being the doubt that then existed as to whether we were being attacked by mistake or not. The first attack seemed to be due to a mistake. During the progress of the second, there were no means of determining whether the mistake still existed or not. As one looks back at any affair, things have a different

Marion P. Maus. NELSON A. MILES. *PERSONAL RECOLLECTIONS AND OBSERVATIONS.*

appearance to him, and he wonders why he did not see them in their true light at first. In this case many incidents tended to show that the Mexicans were not acting in good faith. But at the time little thought was given to that, for we were under fire, and the situation was so unexpected and puzzling that every point was not given due weight; in fact, outside of one's individual experience, very little was known. Afterward, when the different stories were put together and the ground looked over, calm reflection made us believe that the second attack was no mistake. It was not until nearly two days after the fight that the treacherous capture of Lieutenant Maus and the interpreter Concepcion removed all doubt.

The situation was such, however, that had we then certainly known that we were being intentionally attacked, there would have been little choice about our course. The Mexicans were evidently much superior in numbers—two to one, it turned out. They occupied a line of hills from three to five hundred yards distant that commanded the ground between us and afforded them a very strong position. At this time we were so far down in Mexico that it afterward took three weeks' marching to get us back to the border. The Mexicans were in their own country, and our only dependence was on the scouts, who were so hated, both as Apaches and also as American soldiers, that there would have been difficulty in securing reinforcements against them unless some amicable arrangement was made. We were entirely without rations and almost without ammunition; to have tried to fight our way out of Mexico would have meant that the command would have had to scatter and make its way home as best it could. This would have made it necessary to abandon our wounded and probably all the pack trains that were scattered through the mountains on their way to us. Had we not made peace there could have been little doubt that the Chiricahua scouts would have joined the hostiles, who were then in sight across the river looking on.

During the fight a hurried conversation was held between Lieutenant Maus and myself, in which these points were touched upon. We did not feel sure of the meaning of the conduct of the Mexicans; we had not given up the hope that the hostiles would surrender after all, and we did not wish to abandon the attempt to bring them in. So much had been sacrificed that we felt it our duty to continue the effort, especially as there still remained a hope of success. These reasons have been given fully because there has been some criticism on the conduct of the command in this affair among both army people and civilians, who seem to think that all we had to do was to attack the Mexicans in their position and avenge Crawford's death. Their judgment has been hasty and unjust. They have not put themselves in the place of officers suddenly called upon to face a situation unparalleled in the history of the army, in which there lay no alternative between the course adopted and ruin, and which would have involved the betrayal of the trust reposed in those officers had they tried, with the knowledge they then possessed, to assume the role of avengers.

Our course determined upon, there still remained the task of conducting the defense, at the same time controlling the fire of the scouts and continuing the calls to the Mexicans to stop firing. The party that had advanced so near us was soon disposed of, but the main body kept up a heavy fire from the hills, and several attempts were made to flank us, which were, however, frustrated by the scouts. We were strongly posted among the rocks, but the position was entirely open in rear and would have been untenable had the Mexicans succeeded in getting a party on that side. The shots finally became less frequent, we could plainly hear their voices as they called to each other, and their failure to answer us began to be very suspicious. Finally they replied, and when the firing ceased, Lieutenant Maus and Horn went out to meet a party halfway. An understanding being reached, quiet was restored, and we looked after our wounded. Captain Crawford's case was seen to be hopeless; his wonderful vitality alone prevented his instant death. On examination, one arm was found to be broken near the shoulder, the result of his fall from the rock. One scout was found to be badly wounded through both legs. Two others had slight wounds. Horn was suffering from an ugly flesh wound in the left arm. We had been very uneasy about the party with the mules, but they arrived soon after the close of the fight, bringing rations and other supplies. They had been on the way to us when the firing began and were then close to the Mexican position. The packers and scouts refusing to proceed, they had taken refuge behind a hill and fortunately had not been discovered.

Parties of Mexicans came over to carry off their dead, four of whom lay in our camp, their major and a lieutenant being among them. It is not known how many more were killed. The scouts always claimed at least seven in all. Five men were known to be badly wounded, as Dr. Davis dressed their wounds; some of them he thought would probably die.

Looking over the ground and hearing the different stories, we saw that there was little cause to believe that the Mexicans thought we were hostile Indians when they shot Crawford. The man who fired the fatal shot was just twenty-eight paces distant; the captain had a brown beard and wore his uniform, so that he looked altogether unlike an Indian. The experiences of Lieutenant Maus, chiefs of scouts Horn and Harrison, and of hospital steward Nemeck likewise confirmed us in our belief. But all lingering doubts were dispelled by the conduct of the Mexicans on the twelfth, when they treacherously captured Lieutenant Maus and Concepcion and compelled them to ransom themselves with six mules. That plunder was their object in attacking us is certain. They saw only a few white men, and the fire of the scouts was so weak at first that they had no reason to believe us a large party.

Our assailants were not regular troops, but were a body raised in the state of Chihuahua to fight the Indians. They had been seventeen days on the road and had with them no animals except a few burros. Their rations and blankets were carried on their persons. They were a hard-looking set; dressed in cotton clothing and wearing moccasins, some of them rawhide sandals, they had little appearance of being soldiers, but at the same time they seemed well suited to following Indians in a rough country. A temporary and perhaps irresponsible organization, they would, if successful in killing us, have had little trouble in evading all responsibility for their acts. The locality of their crimes would have made the detection of the perpetrators almost impossible. Their version, as published in official reports, shows that they would not have been wanting in excuses. They sturdily claimed that we were in league with the hostiles; that they had been following our trail for days; and that the mules (all marked U.S.) taken as ransom had been stolen by the Indians from Mexicans. With regard to their following us, it is only necessary to say that their trail, which we saw, came directly from the east, while ours came from the west; they had never followed our trail at all, but had been guided to us by the light of our fires.

It has been said that the hostiles were spectators during our fight with the Mexicans. How they must have enjoyed it! As their enemies were engaged in deadly strife before their eyes, it must have seemed that Providence was looking out for them, and no doubt crafty old Geronimo took advantage of the situation to work upon their superstitious feelings and to encourage them to follow still further their bloody career. It must strike us too that it was a strange mischance that caused these two commands to meet at this particular time and in a country perhaps never before traversed by similar parties. Different as they were, either might have done good work but for the presence of the other.

The experiences of the expedition after the fall of Crawford were strange and interesting; but we will not attempt to tell of them, for the story is long and complicated. We cannot, however, lose sight of it for a few days longer, though nothing except a brief and incomplete outline of events will be attempted. The camp was moved a few miles on January 13, and no more was seen of the Mexicans. Negotiations with Geronimo were reopened, which

The death of Captain Crawford. NELSON A. MILES. *PERSONAL RECOLLECTIONS AND OBSERVATIONS.*

resulted in the surrender of a part of his band and the promise of the remainder to meet General Crook on the border, which they did in March. For many reasons the command was obliged to return to the United States, and its march was continued till the supply camp at Lang's Ranch, New Mexico, on the boundary line, was reached on February 1. Orders were given by General Crook for a similar withdrawal of Major Davis's battalion from Mexico, and for a time operations were suspended.

The transportation of our wounded was a serious trouble. Incessant rains not only increased the discomforts already existing and caused much actual suffering on account of the lack of shelter and clothing, but it also made the rough country almost impassable. The litters, composed of canvas stretched between bundles of canes, had to be carried by hand; the canes were so pliable that the litters were clumsy affairs, requiring eight men to carry one of them. Then the moccasins went to pieces in the wet and left many of us barefoot in this stony region. In a few days, however, Daly's train met us and brought us more comforts. A new litter was then made for the captain, and as pine poles were now available, they were substituted for the canes, and one end of the litter fastened to a mule; on account of the rough trail, the other end was carried by hand. The badly wounded scout was rigged upon a mule and caused but little more trouble.

A week went by without any sign of consciousness or of suffering on the part of Captain Crawford, who, gradually growing weaker, on January 18 passed away so quietly that the end was not perceptible to those watching by his side. Four days later his body was deposited in the dreary little burying ground at Nacori; the hope that this was only a temporary resting place was soon realized by the action of General Crook in sending a suitable party to bring his body back to the United States. He was finally buried at the home of his brother at Kearney, Nebraska, where a monument erected by his brother officers now marks his grave.

The killing of Captain Crawford gave rise to much feeling against Mexico and some talk of war upon that country. The matter was taken up by the State Department but was finally dropped without action by our government. The reasons for this course were doubtless good, but it is much to be regretted that they have never been made public; for there is a belief that our country has allowed one of its best officers to be murdered while doing his duty and has failed to take steps to punish his assassins.

The attack of the Mexicans not only caused the death of a valuable officer, but it also prolonged the resistance of the hostiles for eight months. There is little doubt that they would have surrendered in January but for this affair; it was September before they finally did so. In his report General Crook says, "There is reason to believe that had he (Crawford) lived, he would have received the unconditional surrender of Geronimo's and Naiche's bands"; and again, "He was thoroughly known to all the Indians and had their confidence. It is believed that he was the only white man besides myself who could have induced the hostiles to surrender." When we reflect that after January probably more than a hundred people were killed by these Indians, and when we also consider the incalculable losses in property, both to the government and to private parties, and remember that during all these months no one was safe in a region containing hundreds of square miles, we can realize that the importance of that little fight is not to be measured in the number of slain.

It would be well if all of us could keep in our minds the memory of this devoted and chivalrous soldier, whose whole life was one long sacrifice, and whose death was the direct result of his efforts to save others. Such characters are not common. Let us try to remember this one as our ideal of what a true man should be. Though we may never be called upon to face difficulties of the kind that confronted him, yet the elements of character that enabled him to overcome them and to win the love and respect of all who knew him will tell in all walks of life; and though such men sometimes fall, yet the name they leave behind them is worth far more than the greatest success.

Apache Campaign Notes—1886

JAMES S. PETTIT[1]

Journal of the Military Service Institution of the United States
7 (September 1886): 331–38

Since May 17, 1885, the territories of Arizona and New Mexico have been raided by bands of hostile Apaches. Many citizens have been murdered and much stock stolen. To the old settlers the terrible atrocities committed by these red demons are not new, as Cochise, Victorio, Juh, Nana, and Geronimo have in years past broken from their reservations and, defying the troops, have murdered, robbed, and mutilated the miners and settlers who ventured unprotected in this region.

After hard campaigns, with much loss of life and at great expense to the government, they have in turn been either killed or forced back to their reservations, to nurse their sullen discontent and to cunningly lay by arms and ammunition until another opportunity should offer to satisfy their wild craving for the blood of the whites.

At the conference between General Crook and the hostiles in March of this year, neither Geronimo nor Chihuahua could give any reasonable excuses for taking to the warpath, which leaves us to infer that such a course must have been due to their bestial savage natures and an inborn love of strife and bloodshed. It will be impossible to give any detailed account of the operations in the thirteen months we have been at war with these savages; suffice it to say that the Fourth, Sixth, Tenth, and part of the Second and Eighth regiments of cavalry, with parts of the First, Eighth, Tenth, and Thirteenth infantry regiments, and two hundred Indian scouts (or nearly one-sixth of the entire army of the United States), have been in the field continuously since the summer of 1885, and at this writing (June 15) we seem farther from the goal than ever. To say that nearly one-sixth of our army has been pursuing between fifty and one hundred Apaches for over a year and accomplished nothing, while it may be true literally, is in the greatness of the task before them no discredit either to the courage or zeal of the troops.

Those who have never traveled through this region, with its high mountain ranges, deep rocky canyons, and wide sandy plains, will fail to comprehend the trials, hardships, and annoyances which the troops are constantly required to undergo.

Information untrustworthy and misleading. OUTING MAGAZINE, JANUARY 1887.

Fifteen miles on a New York turnpike is only a delightful drive, but over "malpais" rocks and through stony gorges devoid of water, it is a hard six hours' march and very fatiguing, especially to the horses, which perhaps traveled forty or fifty miles the day previous without grain food and but scanty grass and poor water. The very smallness of the band of hostiles is greatly in their favor, as they have but little impedimenta and leave an ill-defined trail. When closely pressed by the troops they scatter like coveys of quail, and skulking through canyons or along the very highest ridges, they meet again at some prearranged spot on the mountains. The country from the Apache reservation to the heart of Sonora is as familiar to them as Madison Square to an old New Yorker. While they prefer to travel mounted, they can readily travel seventy-five to one hundred miles in twenty-four hours on foot. Again, the information given to the troops by citizens is often untrustworthy and misleading. In June 1885 some companies of the Tenth Cavalry were drawn into a march of many miles by a gambler who "stood in" with the telegraph operator at a little town; a message was sent to the commanding officer to the effect that the Indians had killed several men near the place and were in the mountains nearby. Upon arriving at the town it was learned that the telegram was a hoax to entice the soldiers, who had just been paid, into the neighborhood in order that this "professional" might win their money. I have heard other officers tell of similar experiences. Such things are not encouraged by good citizens. These are a few of the many difficulties and discouragements which continually surround our troops. There are other difficulties incident to our service.

The supply of horses is totally inadequate to the demands of such severe work. Cavalry troops, which are allowed sixty-five men by law, are compelled to go into the field with from thirty-five to forty-five men all told. In action, from one-third to one-fourth of this number must be employed in holding the horses and pack animals, so that a troop commander can inflict but little punishment on the hostiles when he strikes their camp, and may be considered as having done very well if he has simply held his ground. Again, there is a scarcity of officers, the heavy list of absentees, sick, and on the detached service leaves but one officer with each of the troops; on the skirmish line, and with the stock to care for, there is ample work for the three officers of a troop.

Our officers are zealous and ambitious, and our men willing and courageous. It is only a question of time; the result is certain. Many times in the history of the world have small, determined bodies of men defied great nations, as did the pirates of the Mediterranean the great Roman Empire, but all have met the same fate, and let us hope that in the end there may not be a single Chiricahua left in Arizona to perpetuate the memories of these bloody tragedies, or to incite other tribes to the butchery of the citizens who bring their lives and fortunes to swell the growth and prosperity of our great West.

The little sketch on page 333 [of the original article] gives a fair idea of the country our troops are operating in.[2] From foreground to background is about forty miles, a very long day's march, over a hilly, rocky trail. The mountains in rear are not far from the spot at which the conference was held in March of this year.

Our camps at times present picturesque and warlike scenes, with the troops of cavalry coming and going, companies of scouts lying around, and the great pack trains coming in for supplies or rest.

As darkness comes on, the fire in the scouts' camp grows into greater brilliancy, and the thumping of a rude drum on the hands of a medicine man calls the braves to the dance. The medicine man is "master of ceremonies." The dancers form a circle around the fire, and at the tapping of the drum the circle moves round and round as long as the drum is heard, all joining in the weird chanting. The devil's dance is well worth seeing. Stripped of all clothing, save a bandage around the loins, and with the head tied up in a dark cloth, and a long wooden sword in each hand, they leap and roll and go through wonderful muscular contortions for hours at a time. In common with our circuses, they have a clown, who is made white by covering him with flour. He carries a firebrand in his hand, and his efforts were ludicrous imitations of the movements of the dancers. The scouts seem to prefer their own medicine men when seriously ill and believe the weird singing and praying around the couch is more effective than the medicines dealt out by our camp "sawbones."

They have many peculiar customs and idea, but they have already been given to the public in a most entertaining volume by an officer well known in army circles and of great experience.[3]

The death of the gallant Crawford, who was so foully murdered, was the most unfortunate episode of the entire campaign. Unfortunate for the service at large, for it lost one of its bravest, noblest officers. Unfortunate for the campaign, for it occurred just as he had apparently accomplished the task of bringing the hostiles to terms. The Indians are naturally suspicious, but Captain

Crawford having been their agent for some years, they knew him well and would have given him their confidence, and it is thought would have surrendered to him. After he was killed they would talk to no one but General Crook.

Shot down in broad daylight, in the uniform of the United States and after two of his party who spoke Spanish well had repeatedly called out that they were friends. The taking of that precious life must and ever will be termed murder by all who are conversant with the facts, and these facts will not soon be forgotten by officers of our army.

The unconditional surrender of Geronimo could scarcely be called a surrender, as is implied in military parlance. He did not give up either his arms, horses, ammunition, or money, and he was at the time well supplied. Nor was he at any time under physical restraint, but was free to go and come almost at will. He undoubtedly promised to come in in his own way, but he and the twenty braves left before they reached the United States.

A brute called a man started a grog shop just inside of the Mexican line and for some days before the conference sold mescal whiskey and ammunition to the hostiles, until his place was sacked by order of the commanding officer. He was a citizen of Arizona, and that he still lives is ample proof of the respect our officers have for law, even on Mexican soil.

The following questions have been discussed freely around the campfires, and from a purely military point of view the conclusions were generally agreed on:

First—Are Indian scouts of great practical value when operating by themselves, unsupported by regular troops? The records and the opinions of experienced officers seem to be largely in favor of a negative answer.

Second—Are Indian scouts loyal and energetic when employed against their own people? Nature seems to answer this question at once and decidedly, and the weight of opinion seems to coincide with her. The records at least do not show many cases in which scouts have inflicted serious punishment on their hostile brothers, cousins, etc. This may be due to the fact that as a rule they are very poor marksmen. Fortunately also, the hostiles are not crack shots, for had they been skilled marksmen, at least two commands in the past years would have been well nigh massacred.

This Apache war will go into history as another instance of what a few determined, active, cunning savages can do when assisted by the vagaries of nature so freely spread over this country. And what odds! Fifty to one hundred against four thousand, and although the end is certain, "it is not yet."

On the Trail of Geronimo

NELSON A. MILES[1]

Cosmopolitan 51 (June 1911): 249–62

In July 1885 I was assigned by the president to the command of the Department of the Missouri, but before reaching there I was directed to report to Lieutenant General Sheridan, commanding the military division at Chicago, and accompany him to the Indian Territory, where a serious Indian war was threatened. The Indians' land in that territory had been leased to white men owning large herds of cattle, presumably for the benefit of the Indians. The system afforded the Indians a very small revenue, but the disadvantage to them was far in excess of any benefit they derived. While General Sheridan investigated the complaints of the Indians, I devoted my attention to the military forces, as one-fourth of the army had been concentrated and placed under my command. After days of earnest effort, we succeeded in avoiding an Indian war. The Indians were pacified by our assurance that their rights would be respected, their property protected, and their country would not be ruthlessly overrun. General Sheridan recommended that the cattle leases be discontinued and the vast herds removed from the territory. This was approved and so ordered by President Cleveland.

I could not long remain in that most agreeable department. The Indian wars in Arizona and New Mexico had been for years attracting public attention. The history of the conflict between the Indians and the white race in that remote country would carry us back through the centuries to the first occupation of that region by the Spaniards, fifty years before the Pilgrims landed at Plymouth Rock. The Apaches believed themselves to be the first and superior man. They excelled in activity, cunning, endurance, and cruelty. They recognized no authority nor force superior to their own will. Led by Mangas Coloradas, Cochise, Victorio, and later by Geronimo, Naiche, Chatto, and Mangus, they kept that whole country in a state of terror. General Crook had for years been trying to subjugate them and bring them under control, and finally, on April 1, 1886, he asked to be relieved from command of that department. On April 2 I was, by President Cleveland, assigned to the command. It seemed a very undesirable duty and a most difficult undertaking. Under a mil-

Major General Nelson A. Miles. NELSON A. MILES. *PERSONAL RECOLLECTIONS AND OBSERVATIONS.*

itary rule at that time, I had just been deprived of my personal staff officers and was obliged to go to Arizona alone. I knew but few of the officers or troops serving in that department and less of the topography of the country. I had, however, followed the history of those Indian hostilities and traced the movements of the Indians on the military maps.

On arriving at Fort Bowie, Arizona, I assumed the command of the department and divided the country up into districts of observation, making the post commanders responsible for keeping their districts clear of hostile Indians.

Having completed these arrangements, I looked for a suitable command to take up the pursuit of the Indians south of the Mexican border. At Fort Huachuca I found the commander for such a force, Captain H. W. Lawton of the Fourth Cavalry, who as a young officer had rendered distinguished services in the Civil War and the most excellent services in Indian campaigns on the frontier in Texas, Arizona, and New Mexico—a resolute, brave officer, active and ambitious. He was a giant in stature, and a man of great energy and endurance. He was afterward the most distinguished general in Cuba and the Philippines, where he was killed. At that time he was the ideal leader of a body of active brave men. I detailed Lieutenants Johnston, Finley, Benson, Brown, Walsh, and Smith, all young and efficient officers, to report to Lawton. I selected for his command one hundred of the best soldiers that could be found, all excellent riflemen, and a small number of scouts, guides, and friendly Indian trailers. I also detailed for this force Assistant Surgeon Leonard Wood, a young athlete fresh from Harvard Medical College, and directed him to accompany the troop.

The commands so organized awaited the developments of the Indians, as it was not known at that time in what district they were located. I did not expect to overcome or capture them in a single encounter, but adopted the same methods used to capture bands of wild horses years ago on the plains of Texas—constantly pursuing them, putting in fresh relays, and finally wearing them down. This method, though it took five months to accomplish, proved successful. The Indians soon disclosed their position by making a raid from Mexico into the southwest corner of Arizona. They were then pursued by troops under Captain Lebo, Lieutenants Powhatan H. Clarke, H. C. Benson, Captain C. A. P. Hatfield, and Lieutenants Brown, Walsh, and Brett; the latter made one march in that arid country of twenty-four hours without camping and eighteen hours without water.

In the encounters with the troops, the Indians were always defeated, but made good their escape. They could not, however, throw the commands off their trail, but were constantly pursued in New Mexico, Arizona, and northern Mexico. Captain Lawton's command finally took up the trail and followed them down into Old Mexico, to the Yaqui River country, some two hundred miles south of the boundary. By perseverance and tenacity, Lawton's command followed the Apaches for three months over the roughest mountain country on the continent, the Indians trying by every possible device to throw the command off their trail. They frequently abandoned their horses and crossed the mountains, jumping from rock to rock, yet the sharp-eyed Indian scouts with Lawton would pick up their trail where it was impossible for white men to discover any trace of their movements.

Being constantly pursued by the different detachments and commands for five months, they were worn down and in condition to surrender. After the fight with the troops under Captain Hatfield, I found one of their wounded warriors, who had made his way back to the Apache agency.[2] He reported the hostiles in an exhausted condition when he left them. I sent him, under charge of Lieutenant Gatewood, to the hostile camp with a demand for their surrender. In the meantime, Captain Lawton had also opened communication with them through the efforts of Lieutenants Wilder and Finley. Geronimo sent word to Lawton that he would surrender to the highest authority. This was communicated to me, and I answered that if he sent an assurance that he was acting in good faith I would go down to meet him near the Mexican border. He sent his brother to Fort Bowie, Arizona as an earnest of his honest intentions, and for eleven days his camp marched north near the troops of Captain Lawton. I went down to Skeleton Canyon, near the Mexican line, and there met Captain Lawton's command with the Indians camped a short distance away. Geronimo came to me to ask what disposition would be made of him in case he surrendered. He said that if they were all to be killed, he might just as well die fighting. He prayed only that we would spare his life and those of his people.

He was told that he must surrender as a prisoner of war and accept what disposition the government deemed best to make of him and his followers;

that we did not kill our prisoners; that their future would depend upon the orders of the president at Washington. He was informed that I had directed Colonel Wade[3] to move all the Indians at the Apache agency in northern Arizona out of the territory; that he and his people would be removed; that Indian depredations and atrocities must end forever in that country. He was in no position to dictate terms. I explained to him the folly of contending against the military with all its advantages of communication and transportation. While watching a corporal use the heliograph and flash a message in a few seconds by the sun's rays a day's journey for his horse, he was struck with awe and amazement. He sent an Indian runner to Naiche, who remained out in the mountains, to tell him he was in the presence of a power he could not understand and that Naiche was to come in and come quick. He afterward stated that he had seen these flashes on the mountain peaks but thought they were spirits and not men. They then formally surrendered and placed themselves entirely under our control.

The day following I took Geronimo and Naiche and four other of the principal men, with the escort of a troop of cavalry, and made a march of sixty-five miles to Fort Bowie, Captain Lawton following three days later with the rest of the Indians. A small band under Mangus that remained out was pursued for weeks by Lieutenant C. E. Johnston and finally captured by troops under Captain Charles L. Cooper. Thus the country was cleared from the devastating and terrifying presence of the Apaches.

There has seldom appeared a more ruthless marauder than Geronimo. He had the most determined face and piercing eye that I have ever seen. Naiche was the hereditary chief of the Apaches, a tall, slender young warrior, whose dignity and grace of movement would become any prince.

The Apache Campaign of 1885–1886

CLARENCE CHRISMAN, CORPORAL, COMPANY F,
THIRTEENTH U.S. INFANTRY

Winners of the West 4, nos. 4–8 (March–July 1927)

On September 22, 1885, three companies of the Thirteenth U.S. Infantry, D, F, and H, and the regimental band assembled in front of their quarters at Fort Wingate, Mexico. The band was at the farther end of the row of quarters, and as it struck up an air and came marching by, the three companies fell in behind in their turn and were off to the time of a lively quickstep amid the cheers of the women and children and the remaining soldiers of the garrison.

Little did we dream at that time that we were entering upon what would prove to be the longest, most exciting, and most arduous campaign that the white man ever carried on against his perpetual foe—the red man. Yet this turned out to be the case, for this campaign, from start to finish, lasted well over a year—almost two. And before it was over, two great Indian War generals were in command of it, and under these generals were thousands of the best soldiers of Uncle Sam's army, which is to say, the best soldiers the world ever saw.

And that such soldiers were needed goes without saying, for they had to march hundreds of miles over hot and desolate sandy plains, almost utterly devoid of vegetation and water, and across ranges of mountains that seemed to pierce the very sky itself, often in midwinter, through almost impenetrable drifts of snow and sheets of ice. And always with death hovering over, for no one knew at what moment he would fall the victim of an ambuscade, perhaps sent to his eternal rest by the noiseless arrow of his foe.

And soon after the band had turned to one side and made its way back to its quarters, our real work began. For just back of Fort Wingate rises the range of the Zuni Mountains, and we found ourselves marching on the upgrade almost from the moment of leaving the fort. And I must say we were all rather soft at that time. For a while there was some joking and talking, but soon it ceased, and the only sounds to be heard were the creaking of the wagon wheels of the supply train, the cracking of an occasional whip, and the shuffle of our feet as we toiled wearily up this steep incline. The day was hot, and the sun caught us fairly on that side of the mountain, and by the time we had reached

540

a level place on the top of that immense plateau, it seemed as though we had traveled a thousand miles.

After a short rest the march was resumed, everyone being cheered by the thought that we would soon be on the downgrade on the other side of the mountain, and that would be easier. So it was, in a way, for we could have easily rolled down. But that would not have been very dignified. So we marched like the true soldiers we were, but every step on that steep declivity, weighed as we were with rifles and ammunition, seemed to drive our knee joints right up into our hips. But everything comes to an end, and finally we reached our first camp.

On the particular campaign about which I am writing, I carried with me a little leather-backed notebook, about four by six, and in this precious little volume I have a record of every march and every camp we made that memorable campaign. And besides, as I was handy with a pencil, I made sketches of many of the camps and of scenes in the vicinity. It is doubtful if this had ever been done before on an Indian campaign, and at that time I had no idea in the world that many years later I would be consulting this little book for data concerning our trip.

On the first page I had entered, "Camp 1, on the Nutri, September 22, 1885." And under this heading, in part, appears the following: "Left Wingate about 11:00 A.M., marched to the beautiful valley of the Nutri, and went into camp at 5:30 P.M. Our camp is beautifully situated at the foot of a high, rocky bluff, and nearby is a running stream of clear, cold spring water. This is what is called Nutri River, but it is nothing more than a babbling, rippling brook. I am on guard tonight, and it is 1:40 A.M. I am writing this by the light of our campfire, assisted by a full, bright moon. The coyotes are giving a serenade while I write, and their distant howl and grating yelp lend a dreariness to the lonely hour."

Although I made no entry of some of the incidents of our first camp, I remember distinctly how the fellows yanked off their shoes, good old heavy regulation government brogans, and began doctoring blisters and sore spots, and that night how we gathered around the campfires, some laughing, some singing, and some, especially the recruits (we had a bunch of raw ones with us), casting furtive glances at the dark woods surrounding us and up at the towering bluff, as though expecting any moment to hear the crack of firearms and the war whoop of hostile Indians. But most of us gave no thought to such things, and we grouped about the fires, exposing ourselves as openly and brazenly as though there were no Indians within a thousand miles. Once a rookie voiced aloud his thought, "I wonder if we will get to fight any Indians?" Sergeant Maguire, happening to overhear him, said, "Don't worry, my bucko, you'll get plenty of fighting before this thing is over; and if you'll take my advice, you'll write to your best girl and your mamma this very night, and tell them good-bye, while you have a chance." Down in our hearts, we older soldiers wished only that he was right.

Everything in this world goes by contrast. Sometimes you conclude you are having it pretty hard unless you happen to think of a time when you had it much harder. Up in those mountains it gets exceedingly cold at night, even in midsummer, and while I was on guard I could hear fellows turning and groaning as they tried to keep warm under a blanket or two, and not a soft spot on which to rest their weary bones. But the rocks of New Mexico are not noted for being soft. I couldn't help but think, listening to the occasional growl of some poor rookie, about the time, some nine months previously, in the dead of winter, with snow and ice piled around me, I had made camp with several other soldiers in that identical spot. We were then on an expedition from Fort Wingate to Fort Craig, New Mexico, and had followed the backbone of the Rockies, through snow and ice, all the way.

Finally, some of the rookies could stand it no longer, and out they piled and joined me at the campfire. One of them had a small photo at which he gazed intently, and by the firelight I caught a glimpse of a tear bedimming his eye. "Your sweetheart, Buddy?" says I. "Sweetheart, hell," says he. "That's my mother."

Let us go back a little in time and see what this campaign was about. Although Geronimo was not a regular Apache chief, being more of a medicine man, he had a great influence over the members of his tribe—the Chiricahua Apaches—and over a period of some ten or twelve years had frequently led bands of these Indians on raids through Arizona, New Mexico, and Old Mexico. One of his favorite tricks was to dash into Old Mexico, murder Mexicans right and left, stampede herds of their horses and other stock, and drive these up into Arizona. These exploits were both amusing and profitable to the Indians, but to those who were raided, and who lived to tell the tale, they were anything but funny.

In May 1885, having no doubt run out of supplies and feeling that it was about time to replenish the larder, Geronimo and several other so-called chiefs of the tribe organized another band of malcontents, several hundred in all, counting the squaws and papooses, and leaving the reservation behind, again headed south towards the land of plenty.

Thus began the historic Apache campaign of 1885–1886, which was not brought to a close until September 4, 1886, when the hostiles surrendered to General Nelson A. Miles at Skeleton Canyon, not for from Fronteras, Old Mexico. Geronimo and all his followers were then placed on a train and taken to Florida.

During the period of the entire campaign over two hundred citizens, ranchmen, miners, prospectors, women, and children were murdered in cold blood by these Indians. Very few soldiers were killed or even injured; their engagements with the hostiles were few and far between and usually took place only when the Indians had everything in their favor or were forced to give combat. The truth of the matter is that the hostiles kept as far away from Uncle Sam's men as possible. They did not want to fight us—they knew better.

So the campaign of 1885–1886 developed into a marching campaign, and I have no doubt that in this respect it was the greatest campaign of all time. General Miles had superseded General Crook in April 1886, and he immedi-

An incident of the march. CENTURY MAGAZINE, MARCH 1891.

ately started all available troops in hot pursuit of the hostiles, sometimes selecting for exceptionally long marches only such men as had been proved by experience to have the necessary stamina and courage to endure such an ordeal. Here is what the general himself telegraphed to the War Department September 6, 1886, concerning the troops and their marches: "Too much credit cannot be given to the troops for their courage, fortitude, and tireless endurance. Those gratifying results of the campaign, fraught with extreme hardships and difficulties, are due to their most laborious and dangerous service. The Indians have been pursued over two thousand miles in the heart of Arizona and Mexico, through the most rugged mountain regions. Captain Lawton's command alone has followed the hostiles over sixteen hundred miles, over mountains from two to ten thousand feet high, and through canyons where every boulder was a fortress."

Most vivid of all in my memory are those long, grueling marches, often with no water and sometimes with mighty little to eat—marches that exacted the last ounce of a man's strength, where literally a man had to do or die. For to be left behind on some of those vast stretches of burning sand would have meant certain death; a slow, lingering, horrible death, with the sun flaming above you like a ball of molten brass; and perhaps a few buzzards winging their indolent way across your field of vision, waiting, waiting, patiently waiting.

Taking into consideration the topography and extent of the territory covered, the extreme climatic conditions, the number of troops engaged, the length of actual service in the field, and distances marched, the campaign of which I am writing should go down in history as one of the great epics of the ages. Surely no human beings ever rendered a greater service to humanity and civilization than the boys in blue who followed their leaders so faithfully through the trying years of 1885–1886 over the sunbaked plains and icy mountains of the Southwest.

The Regular army soldiers of the '80s were wonderful men, and those of this and other campaigns against the wily Apache excelled in their ability to make long and arduous marches and to take care of themselves in the most inhospitable and dangerous surroundings. One cause of their excellence was no doubt due to the fact that for several years prior to the campaign there had been numerous desertions, a sort of weeding-out process, and those that remained were men who could stand the gaff, men of blood and iron.

Immediately upon taking charge of the campaign, General Miles ordered out all available troops and dispersed them in such a way as to form a veritable ring of steel around the hostiles. The territory assigned to the companies of the Thirteenth Infantry was the northeast segment of this circle, the southwestern part of New Mexico, the birthplace and former habitat of the notorious Geronimo.

In guarding this section, our companies were shunted back and forth like the shuttle of a sewing machine. Upon consulting my diary, I find that we marched close to one thousand miles and made some fifty-six camps, sometimes camping at the same place five or six different times. Thus we became pretty well acquainted with the territory covered and became quite expert in the matter of making and breaking camp. When word would come that the hostiles were headed in our direction, detachments consisting of a noncom and five or six men would be sent out to protect the ranches in the vicinity. And there they would be welcomed with open arms and shown every courtesy. At most of these ranches the men would be given at least one meal a day, dinner usually, and surely the cooks must have enjoyed seeing them eat, for never were good meals more appreciated.

Along in the spring of 1886 Geronimo headed for his old stamping grounds, the Mogollon Mountains. If Geronimo had concluded to go a little farther north, instead of turning back to Old Mexico, the prophecy of Sergeant Maguire might have been fulfilled, and there would have been plenty of fighting for us. But I assure my readers that had he and his followers shown any signs of wanting to start something, they would have met with a warm reception. For by this time we were thoroughly hardened field soldiers, and almost every man was either a marksman or sharpshooter. I am pretty sure that I myself was about the worst shot in the company, as I had never become even a marksman, but even at that I don't think Geronimo would have cared to have me draw a bead on him. Besides shooting at targets, we had by this time had much experience in shooting at moving targets, such as deer and antelope. And those old Springfield rifles, with their long, bottle-necked .45-caliber cartridges, could certainly send a ball a-whizzing. And it was good-bye to anything it happened to hit. Each man carried a web belt of fifty of those death dealers, and although we scarcely feared a night attack, we nevertheless, when in the immediate vicinity of the hostiles, slept with these belts encircling our waists, and the good old trusty Long Tom snuggling beside us at the edge of our blankets.

When Geronimo and his followers surrendered at Skeleton Canyon in September 1886 and allowed themselves to be bundled on a train and hustled out of the territory, the curtain fell on the most picturesque and stupendous drama that was ever enacted on the American continent.

And it is a drama that never can be duplicated. The sky-piercing icy mountains, the sun-scorched plains, the rugged rocks and burning sands are still there, and no doubt the men and equipment of the soldiers could be duplicated, but the important actors of the drama, the merciless Apaches, have degenerated to such an extent that they no longer could enact the roles played by their ancestors. Nor would present conditions permit this, even though they were competent to play the part. For the march of what we call civilization has swept aside all necessity and incentive for the heroic adventures of the 1880s. Thus we may well believe that the past is truly dead, and at the present time there are very few living who participated in the stirring events of the Indian campaigns of that period. Only by mere chance, perhaps one in a thousand, did I myself manage to survive, and am alive at present to write about that colorful and glorious past. And as I bring my narrative to a close, I want you to have as good a mental picture as I can sketch for you of our homecoming.

On September 16, 1886, we arrived, three companies of us, on the western slope of the Zuni Mountains, overlooking Fort Wingate. About 150 of us in all, and the only way you could detect that we were Regular army soldiers was by examining our arms and equipment. Aside from that, I must say that we looked more like tramps than soldiers. We went out dressed in blue flannel shirts and trousers, with regulation campaign hats, boots, or shoes. We returned almost literally covered with buckskin, scarcely a patch of blue to be seen, and had on all sorts of hats, boots, or shoes, or what was left of them. Keeping ourselves well shod had been one of our greatest difficulties. One thing we had in plenty, and that was whiskers, for it had been anything but easy to keep well shaved under such conditions. And sunburned—don't mention it. We were as dark as Mexicans.

As we sat there on that sun-baked mountainside, travel-weary and glum, looking down at the roofs of the fort, our features suddenly relaxed into a broad smile as we caught a glimpse of the glittering instruments of the band and knew that they were coming out to meet us. And this they did, marching toward us playing a welcome air, and oh how sweet that music sounded! For a long, drab year no such sounds had fallen upon our ears.

The command was given to fall in, and down the side of the mountain we went with a brisker and more cheerful step than for many a day. And as the band played "Johnny Comes Marching Home," we swung along to the handkerchief waving and the cheering of the "stay-at-homes." Once again we were in front of the familiar quarters; the band had passed on. The command "Break ranks, March," rang out, and the memorable Apache Campaign of 1885–1886 was at an end.

On Campaign in Sonora

LEONARD WOOD

Report of Assistant Surgeon Leonard Wood, U.S. Army, Fort Bowie, A. T., September 8, 1886, to Brigadier General N. A. Miles, U.S.A., Albuquerque, New Mexico, n.p., n.d.

FORT BOWIE, A.T., SEPTEMBER 8, 1886

To Brigadier General N. A. Miles, U.S.A., Albuquerque, N.M.

SIR: I have the honor to forward the following report relating to the recent expedition in Sonora against the hostile Apaches.

This command was organized to operate against hostile Apaches in Sonora, and it was in that state that most of its work was done.

Sonora is a rough, mountainous country, presenting obstacles of a most serious nature to any command operating in the states. Taken as a whole it is a continuous mass of mountains of the most rugged and broken character. Range follows range with hardly an excuse for a valley, unless the narrow canyons be so considered.

The Apaches are thoroughly acquainted with this country and naturally select the rougher sections of it in avoiding troops, as their thorough knowledge of it and their long training in mountain work render it less difficult to them than to the troops, equipped and dressed as are our soldiers.

This section of the country is thinly populated, in fact, in many portions devoid of inhabitants. It produces nothing save a few wild fruits, cactus, and more or less game. Troops operating in these sections are dependent for all supplies on pack trains, no other means of transportation being practicable. Such is the roughness in some portions that even these cannot pass through. Water is scanty and often of poor quality. Grass almost wanting during the dry season. The heat is intense, often reaching 120 degrees Fahrenheit. There is hardly a valley which is not malarial. Other sections of the country are a little smoother, and now and then one finds a small town.

These small towns are curious affairs and are often built inside a walled enclosure, with walls eight or nine feet high and several feet thick. Inside this, one finds clustered numerous one-story adobe houses and scores of partly naked children, and adults with little superfluous clothing. These little walled towns are indications of the fear and dread which the Mexicans have of the

Leonard Wood. NELSON A. MILES. *PERSONAL RECOLLECTIONS AND OBSERVATIONS.*

Apaches, and each has its history of sacks and repulses by them. Leading into and out of these little towns are trails, seldom or never a wagon road, pack trails furnishing the means of ingress and egress to some of even the larger towns, and nearly all these smaller ones, save in the northern and southeastern portions of the state. The people of the eastern and northern portions are, as a rule, uneducated and mostly of Indian or mixed descent—poor and shiftless—producing just enough to live on, which, by the way, is wonderfully small.

Years and years of defeat and disaster at the hands of the Apaches seem to have taught them little, and one finds them poorly armed and ready victims to the hostiles.

The object of the command was to capture or destroy a band of forty Apaches who up to that time had successfully eluded all pursuit and done an immense amount of injury, both in Sonora and Arizona.

Thoroughly acquainted with the country, capable of great exertion, stimulated by the fear of death, their capture became an affair of the greatest difficulty. Mountaineers from infancy, they found little difficulty in passing through the roughest country. The cactus and various roots furnished food. Water or its equivalent was also furnished by the former plant. Rats, mice, rabbits, and deer contributing to the meat rations, also the horse, when forced as far as he could carry his rider, was killed, and as much meat taken as could be carried along. Now and then a raid into one of the more thickly settled portions resulted in a supply of flour and other luxuries. When worst came to worst they were capable of going for a couple of days without food or water.

They are excellent walkers and make great distances on foot. Their muscular development is excellent, especially that of the foot, leg, and thigh. Lung power remarkable. In short, they are a tough, hardy, well-developed race of men, fighting in a country where everything was in their favor, and against a regular organization. Their raiding parties were continually obtaining fresh

Lawton's pursuit of Geronimo. NELSON A. MILES. *PERSONAL RECOLLECTIONS AND OBSERVATIONS.*

mounts, while the command in pursuit had to get along with the same mounts or on foot.

Opposed to these was a command composed of infantry, cavalry, and Indian scouts, depending for their supplies upon large, well-equipped pack trains, bringing supplies in most cases several hundred miles.

During the early days of the expedition a good deal of work was done by the cavalry (B Troop, Fourth Cavalry) in southern Arizona and northern Sonora. Now and then forage could be obtained, and the command remained in fair condition and did excellent work, but on reaching the rough, mountainous country of eastern Sonora, with little grass and water, it went rapidly to pieces and was sent into camp at Oposura to recuperate. Cavalry cannot serve for any length of time in the rougher portions of Sonora, that is, to do any real work; want of grass and water, and especially mountain climbing, rapidly use up the horses, and the selection of camps with regard to grass and water often causes a good deal of extra work and trouble. The infantry did most excellent work from first to last, marching for a greater portion of the time with the scouts, and were the only portion of the command, excepting the scouts, which could do anything in the rough country along the Haros and Yaqui rivers. In this region cavalry could have done nothing, for there is hardly any grass and very little water, except in the rivers. This section of the country has been regarded as impassable, and it is nearly so.

During the latter part of June and July it was my good fortune to command the infantry. During this time we were constantly on the trail about these rivers and eventually jumped the hostiles' camp, capturing everything except the hostiles. In the detachment of companies D and K, Eighth United States Infantry, were men who had served in India and South Africa, and in their opinion this was by far the hardest and roughest service they had ever seen. Some idea of the heat may be gained by these facts: Men could not bear their hands on the iron work of their guns or on rocks. Pack trains had to be stopped after five or six miles on account of animals being overheated and played out. The temperature and roughness of the country combined made marching work of the most severe nature. I kept one man in the rear of the line with led animals to bring along any men who were overcome by heat and fatigue. These infantrymen were supposed to be selected on account of their fitness for the work, but even then only about one-third proved fit for the duty, and many were sent back.

The men who stood the work best, as a matter of course, were the younger and more resolute ones, mostly under thirty-five years of age. The detachment did splendidly and deserves great credit. Men for this work should be carefully selected and, in addition to physical fitness, possess determination and energy. The Indian scouts were very efficient and hard workers and were constantly in the advance, always willing and ready, and physically the equals of the hostiles, but of course lacking the incentive which urged the latter on. Compared with troops, I should say that, on the whole, while they are physically equal if not superior, how they would compare with a picked body of soldiers, and it is with such they should be compared, for they (the Indians) represent the survival of the fittest, is a question, but I think the comparison would be favorable. There is no doubt in my mind but that picked soldiers, with a month or so of mountain work, will march with scouts on ordinary, if not all, occasions. The greatest good feeling existed between our scouts and soldiers, and I can say from my own experience that they are obedient and kind to their officers. Making a trip with scouts alone has always been a very pleasant experience.

The uniform is totally unfit for Sonora, or along our southern border, and troops on expeditions where hard work is to be done have got to have something lighter and cooler. Of course, men can work under great disadvantages, but the wisdom of putting them in such a position is not evident. A cavalry soldier with his heavy clothing and clumsy boots is unable to do more than a portion of the work he can do properly dressed.

In the first place, he is carrying about twice the weight of clothing required. If, instead of the heavy woolen clothing, something of the nature of stable or fatigue clothing were issued, and with this a pair of shoes with light uppers coming up to the ankle and having a medium thick Scotch sole with a few hob nails around the edge, and in place of the heavy overcoat a rubber poncho, they would then be in a fair shape for as much work as could be expected.

As it is, a man is to all intents and purposes a sweat box, and a subject for chafes, etc. Aside from this, it puts him at a great disadvantage when opposed to an enemy lightly and properly dressed. Infantry on this expedition marched in drawers and undershirts and found that they were much more comfortable, and could do more work, and do it with much less exertion. I do not remember seeing a pair of blue pants put on after once wearing the lighter article mentioned above.

As an indication of what was preferred to walk in, a number of the men paid as high as six dollars per pair of moccasins. The sewed shoes are totally unfit for field service (at least all we had were), and they were the cause of much suffering, wearing out usually in six or seven days, and in some cases on the second. The stitching seems to have been very poorly done, resulting in the sole falling off after a short time. The uppers appeared to be of good quality. The old brass-screwed shoe turned out to be a little better but is nothing like it should be. If a soldier were on hard duty in a rough country and was forced to wear the sewed shoe, I think his pay would be about enough to keep him shod. The shoe which gave the best results was a shoe similar to the Mexican shoe but made of American leather. This stitching is done with sinew and passes only partway through one sole, simply picking up a portion of the upper surface, and is not exposed. The upper is made of light American leather, and the sole of an ordinary piece of sole leather. All the tools required are an awl and a knife. It stands water well, is as light as a moccasin, very comfortable, and will outwear the ordinary shoe. As to its cost, it would be far below that of the present shoe. All the officers and men who wore this shoe were much pleased and preferred it to any other.

The ration as commonly issued is enough to keep a man alive, but he cannot do a great deal of hard work on it in this climate, or sustain long continued fatigue, simply because he gets no meat and, as a rule, poor bread. I say no meat; perhaps I should say very little. This, however, would be a very liberal estimate.

Bacon, half cooked and almost entirely fat, is hardly attractive even to a hungry man when served in a temperature of 115 degrees, and although it will sustain life, it will not keep men in good condition.

It is safe to say that over fifty percent of the bacon issued on this trip has not been eaten, and had it not been for the issue of canned beef, breakfast bacon, rice, etc., few of the men would have stood the trip. In a cold country, bacon may be eaten and be of great service, but in a climate such as Arizona or Sonora, it falls far short of representing what should be the meat ration. Few workmen would live contentedly on fat bacon, bread, and coffee for several months, doing during this time hard work, yet troops are sent out and expected to do the hardest kind of work on this ration. The extra ration in the form of corned beef, rice, etc., was of the greatest service.

If corned beef in cans could be issued, also rice, cornmeal, and oatmeal in place of a portion of the flour, the men would get a change now and then. All the articles mentioned are highly nutritious, easily transported, and can be cooked in various ways and, I am sure, would be of great value in the field. In the post the extras make the present ration ample.

The health of the command has been fair, taking into consideration the fact that they were serving in an unhealthy country, and for a portion of the time during the rainy season, and were frequently drenched. Many of the marches during the rainy season were in canyons, in which were running streams which were constantly crossed and recrossed. The principal complaints were diarrhea and malarial troubles. Many men were sent back, not on account of any particular disease, but because they were worn out. One sergeant died of cerebral hemorrhage, and a number of men acquired varicose veins and inflamed joints due to excessive climbing. Every opportunity was taken to give them fresh meat and vegetables, but these were not often obtained. Those who were sick bore their ills without complaint and expressed regret at being sent back.

> Very respectfully,
> Your obedient servant,
> LEONARD WOOD,
> First Lieutenant and Assistant Surgeon, U.S. Army

The Geronimo Campaign

HARRY C. BENSON[1]

Army and Navy Journal (July 3, 1909): 1240–41

On April 30, 1886, I was at Fort Bowie, having just mustered out a company of Indian scouts which I had commanded during the expedition undertaken by Major Wirt Davis and later commanded by Captain J. H. Dorst, both of the Fourth Cavalry. On this date I received a telegram to proceed to Huachuca to accompany the Lawton expedition. I reached Fort Huachuca on the evening of May 1, and on arrival learned that the information had been received that the hostiles had the previous day attacked a ranch near Calabooses, killing some people, and had carried off a sister-in-law of a man named Peck. As Captain Lawton's expedition was not ready to proceed as a whole, I was directed to take a portion of it (Troop B of the Fourth Cavalry) and proceed by forced marches over the border and take possession of the trail, in order that that portion of the treaty with Mexico, which required that the troops in pursuit should follow on the trail, be complied with.

I arrived late on the second day at Nogales. About an hour after I arrived in this town, a soldier of Captain Lebo's command of the Tenth Cavalry rode in with his horse nearly exhausted and reported that Captain Lebo had had a fight with the Indians and that but a few of the soldiers had been able to escape. I immediately telegraphed to General Miles, stating that there was no question, of course, that Captain Lebo had had a fight, but that the soldier's report of the fight was undoubtedly untrue, and asked instructions.

I was directed to proceed at once to where Captain Lebo was to take up the trail that night. I left at 11:00 P.M. that same day and reached Captain Lebo's camp in the Pinito Mountains about noon of the fourth. Captain Lebo had had a very stiff fight with the Indians the previous day, in which he had had one man killed and one man wounded, and in which fight Lieutenant P. H. Clarke justly won a medal of honor. Captain Lebo's command was without rations and was much exhausted, as it had been relentlessly pursuing the Indians for several days and had finally overtaken them. As the trail was to be turned over to Captain Lawton on his arrival, and Captain Lebo was without rations, he told me that I could have the trail as well then as later. I had been

552

joined on the second at Nogales by five Indian scouts who had been sent out by rail. Of these five, but one could speak English, and I had previously known him as a convict at Alcatraz Island, where he was serving a fifteen-year sentence for mutiny in the Cibicue campaign.

I took up the trail on the morning of the fifth, and as the Indians expected immediate pursuit, they selected the worst possible country to travel over. During this day I lost three of my sixteen mules over the side of the mountain, as we were often obliged to slide down slopes composed of rock only, and there was not sufficient footing at the bottom to enable the animals to recover their balance, and they pitched over the cliffs. After following the trail for some six or seven hours, the Indian scouts became greatly excited and declined to follow the trail. I allowed four of them to drop to the rear, but compelled "Chimney," the one who could speak English, to proceed with myself and three soldiers as advance guard, the troop following about one hundred yards behind. About an hour later, Chimney suddenly dashed over the side of the mountain, the rocks and underbrush preventing my getting a shot at him—and deserted, turning up some four or five days later at Fort Huachuca. This left me without any interpreter for the other scouts, but I succeeded in forcing one of the others to keep the trail. We did not reach water until 7:30 P.M., and it was with great difficulty that we succeeded in getting down the side of the mountain to water then, as the Indians had set fire to the country over which they had passed, and we had to pass through fierce forest fires to reach the water. I followed this trail for the next three days over exceedingly stiff country, and then sent out couriers to connect with Captain Lawton, and his command reached my camp on the evening of May 9.

Troop B of the Fourth Cavalry started on this expedition on May 2 and remained with it until the end, so that besides the three officers—that is, Captain Lawton, Doctor Wood, and Lieutenant Benson—there were at least forty enlisted men who were with the command from start to finish.

On May 16, when Captain Lawton was much discouraged and had come to the conclusion that the Indians were not in that vicinity, Lieutenant R. A. Brown of the Fourth Cavalry arrived in camp, having been following the Indians all day, and had succeeded in capturing from them five horses, three saddles, their entire camping outfit, and a complete Winchester reloading outfit. He had been obliged to leave the trail for water and so came upon us. The next morning Lieutenant Brown put Captain Lawton's command on the trail. Later in the day we came up with Captain Hatfield's command.

Captain Hatfield had run upon the Indians early on the morning of the fourteenth and had captured their entire equipment, consisting of twenty ponies loaded with plunder, their riding ponies—in fact, their entire equipment. Later on this day, as Captain Hatfield's command was watering in a very narrow and rocky gorge within three miles of a Mexican town (the command had had no water since 4:00 A.M.), the Indians suddenly opened upon him, they having been able, due to the nature of the country, to slip in between his flankers and in rear of his advance guard. A stiff fight resulted in which two soldiers were killed and three wounded. The following day (the eighteenth) we left Captain Hatfield and Lieutenant Brown and proceeded due west, and continued on the trail for the next four days, when it was lost near Calabasas on the twenty-second.

May 19 was the only day during the entire campaign when rations did not reach the command. On this date the pack train and the infantry did not come into camp, and I went back to look for them. It developed that the officer in command of infantry had become intoxicated, had taken his command and the pack train and proceeded to Nogales, where I found them at 11:00 P.M. that night. I took a portion of the pack train and hurried back to Captain Lawton and the cavalry, having ridden ninety miles in nineteen hours. The infantry officer was put in arrest, charges preferred against him, and he committed suicide.

From May 22 until June 5 Captain Lawton's command, as a command, did not follow the Indians. Lieutenant Walsh—who had joined on May 20—and myself made several scouts from Calabasas. On June 4, as it had been concluded that the expedition could do no more as the trail had been lost, we were ordered to return to Fort Huachuca. The infantry had already returned, not from being worn out, but as their services were not then needed, the First Infantry under Captain Tisdall[2] being then in camp at Calabasas and doing the scouting from that point. As Captain Lawton was absent in Nogales, the rest of the command did not go, but remained at Calabasas awaiting his return. Before he returned, Lieutenant Walsh on June 6 took Troop B out on the trail toward Harshaw Mine and soon struck the hostiles, had a fight, and captured ten ponies and a cooking outfit.

Captain Lawton went out to join Lieutenant Walsh the evening of the seventh, and on the eleventh Doctor Wood and I started to join him with rations and the remainder of the command. On the twelfth instant I was ordered to Huachuca to conduct a fresh command to Captain Lawton. This command consisted of—first, a detachment of Indian scouts under Lieutenant R. A. Brown, Fourth Cavalry; second, nineteen men selected from four companies of the Eighth Infantry. The detachment was made up as follows: Two men, Company C, First Infantry; six men, Company D, Eighth Infantry; eleven men, Company K, Eighth Infantry, (no officer was available for accompanying this command, so that the detachment was in charge of a noncommissioned officer); third, a wagon train and a pack train.

I left Huachuca with this command on June 18 and proceeded via San Pedro, Miller's Ranch, etc., toward Oposura, and crossed through that country with the first wheel transportation that had ever passed over it. At Bacuachi I left the wagon train and infantry and cut across the mountains to Arispe with Lieutenant Brown and his scouts and the pack animals. On the twenty-fifth we joined Captain Lawton about twenty miles below Chinoquipa. From this point Lieutenant Finley returned with his scouts, and Lieutenant Brown, with his scouts, became a part of the Lawton command. On June 27 I crossed the mountains, accompanied only by a guide, and late that night reached the infantry and wagons at Cumpas. On June 29 Captain Lawton reached Cumpas and went into camp, where he remained until July 6. On July 6 he started on his march to the Yaqui River, striking the Indian trail some distance below Nacori. It was on this date—that is, July 6—that Doctor Wood took charge of the infantry detachment and looked out for it during the next three or four weeks, marched in the wake of the Indian scouts, who were commanded by Lieutenant Brown. This detachment never got into a fight, and after the dispersal of the Indians on the Yaqui River, the command returned to Fronteras on information furnished by couriers and by myself that the Indians had proceeded northward on the other side of the mountains, up Sonora River, and had crossed over near Carroll's ranch, where on August 10 they had a severe fight with six ranchmen, in which the brave O'Brien and Hatcher (two miners) were killed. It was in this fight that Naiche had his arm shattered.

The statement "Lawton wore out three companies of soldiers in making the capture, and when each company was exhausted he ordered it back to the barracks and got another" is not true in any particular. Troop B of the Fourth Cavalry started on this expedition on May and remained with the expedition until its close. The company of infantry that left with Captain Lawton on May 5 and took up the trail on May 10 ceased work with the command after May 22.

The detachment of Indian scouts under Lieutenant Finley of the Tenth Cavalry, who started on May 5, left the command on June 26, as the term of enlistments of the Indian scouts expired on June 30. The Indian scouts under Lieutenant Brown, who left Huachuca on June 18, remained with the command until the end of the campaign in August. No troops or scouts became exhausted, and none were relieved for this reason.

Troop B of the Fourth Cavalry did most of their work on foot, leading their horses behind them, and they remained with the command from start to finish and had very much the hardest work, but they never became exhausted nor were ordered back.

There were always officers with the command. The only detachment that had no officer with it was the infantry detachment which joined Captain Lawton's command on July 5. Lieutenant Smith of the Fourth Cavalry joined the command on July 22 and remained with it until the end. Lieutenant Walsh, who had joined the command on May 20, left it August 15 to convey some sick soldiers and Indian scouts back to Huachuca and rejoined before the surrender.

Due credit has never been given to Lieutenant Wilder (now lieutenant colonel and inspector general) for the part he played in securing the surrender of Geronimo. It was he who learned at Fronteras, about the middle of August, that the Indians were attempting to make conditions with the Mexicans. He had a conference with the woman who was the go-between and advised her to tell Geronimo not to attempt to deal with the Mexicans, but to make terms with General Miles, and Lieutenant Wilder furnished General Miles with the information which enabled him to bring Captain Lawton to this part of the country and also to throw many different commands into this part.[3]

These statements, except so far as they relate to Lieutenant Wilder, are not matters of memory with me, but are taken from a diary which I kept at the time and wrote down the events on the date on which they occurred.

While it is never necessary to tell a lie, it is not always wise to tell *all* the truth, consequently many facts connected with the campaign will probably never be known. But this much is certain: first, that Lawton and Wood were not the only men who endured the whole campaign; second, water was not scarce, nor did the command ever travel where there was no shade nor grass visible; third, that the command was never without supplies; fourth, that no company of soldiers ever became exhausted and were ordered back to barracks for this reason; fifth, that no portion of Captain Lawton's command, except Troop B of the Fourth Cavalry, ever had a fight with the Indians during the entire campaign, and at this fight Doctor Wood was not present; sixth, that Doctor Wood never saw a hostile Indian from the time he started until Geronimo came into Captain Lawton's camp to talk surrender, and that he never heard a shot fired at any hostile Indians; seventh, that the nominal command of a few soldiers of infantry—traveling over a country for a few weeks in the wake of a detachment of Indian scouts commanded by an officer who had, while in command of a troop of cavalry not connected with the Lawton command, run onto the hostiles, and who with his detachment discovered the camp of the hostiles on the Yaqui River, when he was ten miles in advance of Captain Lawton, Doctor Wood, and the infantry detachment (the hostiles had abandoned the camp unseen by even the Indian scouts, so that not a shot was fired even by the scouts at any hostiles); and though no fight was had during these few weeks by this infantry detachment, nor a shot fired by them—secured for the person in nominal command, a reputation (entirely outside the army) for command and for capacity in Indian fighting, and also a medal of honor.[4]

Trailing Geronimo by Heliograph

WILLIAM W. NEIFERT[1]

Winners of the West 12, no. 11 (October 1935): 1, 4

E arly in April [1886], General Nelson A. Miles was ordered to Arizona and with as little delay as possible proceeded to Fort Bowie, assuming command of the department on April 12, 1886. He had in previous Indian campaigns made efficient use of the heliograph and soon after taking command of this section decided to make prominent use of the Signal Service. He so notified the chief signal officer, who promised to furnish twelve men with appliances for making such service useful and effective. Miles directed that signal detachments be placed upon the highest peaks and prominent lookouts to discover the movements of Indians and to transmit messages between headquarters and the troops on the march or in camp. Six men were to be selected by competitive examinations in the use of the telegraph apparatus from the two classes of young men then undergoing the regular course at the Signal Corps school of instruction at Fort Myer, Virginia.

Notwithstanding the dangerous character of the prospective service, nearly every member at the school was anxious to be one of the squad to start for field service in Arizona. The result of the examination was eagerly watched, and the following winners were ordered to prepare for the journey: Charles C. Capwell, Henry Goucher, William W. Neifert (the writer), William A. Whitney, and James I. Wildmeyer, while Richard O'Dowd was subsequently selected and followed. In those days privates did not ride in Pullman cars, and there was no Y.M. representative at the station to give us a supply of fresh fruit and chewing gum. The outstanding bright spot was a check signed by "Wells Willard, Captain and C.S." in the amount of $9.00 for commutation of rations, six days, at $1.50 per day.

We started from the old B. & O. Washington depot on June 12, and six days' railroad travel brought us to Bowie Station, on the Southern Pacific, during the forenoon of the eighteenth. On the surrounding prairie we found a lively scene with much noise and loud profanity from the troops, packers, mechanics, with all their horses, mules, and all sorts of impedimenta, making up supply trains for the various military posts in the section. The stage agent got out a special coach to take our party to Fort Bowie, while the hazardous undertaking upon which we had embarked became more and more apparent, though we were "game" as we were in quest of laurels growing along Indian trails.

The driver, of course, saw that we were "Tenderfeet, Oh! so Tender," and some of the blood-curdling yarns that he related for our benefit added to our gloom. He particularly emphasized his remarks as we were passing the post cemetery that nestled on the mountainside in the canyon a short distance below the post. Pointing out that at least half of the headstones gave a single line, "Unknown, killed by Apache Indians."

We reported at headquarters and were at once turned over to Lieutenant A.M. Fuller, Second Cavalry, the signal officer for the districts of Bowie and Huachuca, for general instruction and station assignments. We remained for several days, when we separated for specially designated permanent stations in the line of communication that had just been established. In this arrangement Fort Bowie was Station Number One, and Bowie Peak (or sometimes called "Helen's Dome") was Number Two. The writer was ordered to station number eight, on Mount Baldy, in the Santa Rita Mountains. This station was reported to be one of the hardest of the system, not altogether because of the great amount of signaling, but because of its elevation above sea level (approximately seven thousand feet) and the arduous climb several times each day from our camp in the canyon to the station on the peak. Six other Signal Corps men selected from western-city weather stations were already in the field, though mostly in the New Mexico District, under Lieutenant Dravo, Sixth Cavalry.[2]

My start for Mount Baldy was made without delay, going on the first lap of the journey to Fort Huachuca, where I was to pick up Private Bluste of Troop K, Fourth Cavalry, who had been detailed as an extra signalist.

Here I was also to receive my "weapon of war," grub, and further details as to the duty on the mountain station. Lieutenant Fuller had been at the mountain during the previous week, setting up the posts for the signaling apparatus, arranging camping details, etc. He was accompanied by Corporal Crowley of Troop K, Fourth Cavalry (who had been a telegrapher in his native Ireland prior to coming to America), and three men of the Eighth Infantry. In the chain Fort Huachuca was Number Seven, where Private Von Herrmann, Signal Corps, was already on duty. Anticipating my arrival, he was on hand to greet me when the mail stage rolled in from the railroad. He was an old frontiersman, so besides instructions in the work before us, he was in a position to assist me in other ways.

To reach Mount Baldy we went by train to Crittenden, where a troop of the Tenth Cavalry was encamped. The commandant, Captain Keyes,[3] had been instructed to furnish an escort, mounts, and pack train to take us to the station, with our food, clothing, and camp equipment. In addition, he furnished three men from his force for our camp guard, cooks, etc. The detail was Corporal Scott, Privates Belden and Johnston. The guide to lead us was Mike Grace, an old-timer, reputed to be a member of the prominent New York family of the name.

We started early the next morning on the twenty-mile trip—especially long to a tenderfoot unaccustomed to horseback riding. We went up and up over a trail that at many points was hard to follow, and as we ascended, breathing became more difficult, requiring frequent stops for rest. We cleared the summit late in the afternoon and settled down to its occupation. After a meal, the escort and pack train started their return trip, taking with them the three infantrymen, who were to go to another site.

We at once began our actual work, both on the station routine and making the camp as comfortable as possible. We made "dugouts" between the rocks that furnished protection against attack and used Sibley tents for coverings—roofs, so to speak. We were above the timber line, the crest being entirely of rocks, while at the camp there were a few straggling pine trees and some bunches of tough mountain grass. Otherwise it was rock, and nothing but rocks, in which abounded chameleons, a few squirrels, some small birds, and short, stubby rattlesnakes. For our water we went to a spring a short distance from the camp down into Josephine Canyon. We used the mule, Balaam by name, with an aparejo for bringing it to camp over a circuitous trail of more than a mile. We also used the mule as transportation to make weekly trips to Crittenden for mail and such few supplies that we would bring in the saddlebags.

From the peak in that clear atmosphere we had an interesting view that covered many miles, even beyond the international border. Nogales, fifty miles away, was plainly visible, and away to the eastward one could see a surprisingly long distance.

The heliographer, or "sun telegraph," as it was often spoken of on the frontier, is an instrument for signaling by sunlight reflected from a mirror. Metallic mirrors were originally used, but in service they were hard to keep bright and hard to replace if broken in the field. Consequently, glass mirrors were adopted, and much successful work was accomplished by using this method of signaling in the armies of different nations, and at that time it was the most valuable instrument for field signaling. We used two five-inch mirrors, mounted on heavy wooden posts that were firmly set between the rocks. Vertical and horizontal tangent screws are attached to the mirrors by which they can be turned to face any desired direction and keep the mirrors in correct position with the sun's movement. As the flash increases about forty-five times to a mile, it could be read with the naked eye for at least fifty miles.

Equipped with a powerful telescope and field glass, we made frequent observations of the surrounding country so that any moving body of troops, or other men, as well as any unusual smoke or dust, might be detected and at once reported by flashing to headquarters. Troops in the field carried portable heliograph sets that were operated by specially trained and detailed soldiers, by this means communicating through the mountain stations with headquarters.

From our station we worked occasionally with Nogales, fifty miles, and regularly with Fort Huachuca, thirty-seven miles distant. Then troops located at Calabasas and Tubac required some attention, and in addition a station, Number Eighteen, was later established at Crittenden, with an infantryman named Lovejoy in charge.

We alternated in the weekly trips to Crittenden, going down usually on a Saturday and returning on Sunday. This gave each one an opportunity to procure several "square" meals at a dining room table. Furthermore, there was usually a Mexican baile each Saturday evening. These were nice dances with plenty of refreshments, though the ladies did not smoke; each man was required to "park his personal artillery" during the dancing.

Considering the situation, we lived well. "Joe" Johnston was an excellent cook and furnished well-balanced menus. We had a goodly supply of dried fruit and some vegetables, besides the regular ration of flour, bacon, and other staples, all from the Huachuca commissary, and occasionally some game that our hunting parties brought in from the lower levels.

For the regular daily station work but two men were required, so by this arrangement each operator could take advantage of every third day for rest or recreation. On such days we usually made hunting trips, in which I selected Scott for my associate. He joined the army shortly after the Civil War, and he had the faculty of imparting the knowledge gained by his long service. He frequently related experiences of the early service in western Arkansas and eastern Indian Territory. We did not encounter any of the hostiles during the summer, though we had evidence that some parties crossed from one valley to the other over the "hogback" below our camp. We managed to keep well occupied—yet it was a long and tedious season, relieved by an occasional Crittenden journey or by scouting trips on the days that we were not on regular station duty.

The department commander carried on a vigorous campaign, and the troops gave the Indians no rest, pursuing them for nearly 2,000 miles, from New Mexico to Arizona, then in Old Mexico, and thence back into New Mexico again, over the most sterile districts of the Rocky and Sierra Madre mountains, beneath the burning heat of summer, until worn down and discouraged they found no peace in either country and were finally glad to lay down their arms and ask for mercy from the gallant officers and men who, despite every hardship, had achieved the success their endurance and fortitude so richly deserved.

When General Miles on the evening of September 3 met the troops with the renegades at the mouth of Skeleton Canyon—a fitting spot for the closing event of this extensive manhunt—Geronimo noticed the heliograph apparatus. Interested in the sun telegraph, he asked the general to explain just how it worked. He was amazed when the operator on Bowie Peak threw a strong flash on the party while the surrender parley was in progress. He was astonished when told that each mountaintop was equipped with a similar instrument, and the men were constantly on the lookout for him.

On the evening of September 4 the Indians surrendered as agreed, and early the next morning the general started for Fort Bowie, taking with him Geronimo, Naiche, and four other Indians. The same day, the troops started for the post with the main part of the Indians, and by making slow marches reached there several days later. The condition of their stock and their clothing showed that they had been relentlessly pursued, and the signal stations on the mountaintops played an important part at beating the Indian at his own game, and in his own stronghold, with everything in his own favor.

About the end of September we were ordered to close the station and report to Colonel Forsyth at Fort Huachuca. The order from district headquarters prescribing this movement was the first official intimation that we had received of the close of the campaign, although we were not unprepared for it, having heard of the occurrences at Skeleton Canyon. The guard was at once ordered in by Captain Keyes, though the three operators remained several days longer to salvage the property. Our rations were practically exhausted, though we had some flour and water was plentiful. We killed and ate some squirrels and the small birds that we had fed all summer, until finally we waved "adios" to Mount Baldy and started on our last trek down the mountain and to civilization. Crowley and myself went by rail to Fort Huachuca, and Bluste rode Balaam back to the post.

At Station Number Eight we handled many hundreds of messages containing many thousands of words, and in a final personal communication, Lieutenant Fuller wrote, "I was perfectly satisfied with your work and considered that you had one of the hardest stations on the line, on account of the cold weather (owing to its altitude) and the difficult ascent to the station from the camp each morning."

In his report on the campaign, General Miles made the following reference to the system: "It was the most interesting and valuable heliograph system that has ever been established. These officers (Lieutenants Fuller and Dravo) and the intelligent men under them have made good use of the modern scientific appliance and are entitled to much credit for their important work."

Awaiting assignments to permanent Signal Service stations, Von Herrmann, Whitney, and Neifert were at Fort Huachuca for several weeks, enjoying a real rest after their arduous summer's work. On the day for final good-byes, Whitney started for Pensacola, Florida; Von Herrmann for La Crosse, Wisconsin; and Neifert for Fort Reno, Indian Territory.

A Theatrical Campaign

JAMES R. CAFFEY

Omaha *Bee*,[1] September 29 and October 10, 1886

C AMP GRANT, Ariz., Sept. 18 [Correspondence of the *Bee*]—For ten days past Geronimo, General Miles, Captain Lawton, and the "captured" Chiricahuas have been the all-absorbing topics of discussion in this territory, alike among the civilian inhabitants and the army. The Apache campaign is supposed to have ended, and from the reports which I read in the eastern papers, its parting volley has enveloped General Miles in a halo of glory. If the correspondents who have been so liberally stuffed with bogus information are to be believed, poor Geronimo, worn out and weary with the "relentless pursuit" of Miles's regulars, "surrendered" on the field of battle and threw himself on the mercy of his captors, to be dealt with as they saw fit. Parties who know the actual state of affairs, especially officers who have taken part in the campaign, make no attempt to conceal their disgust at the nonsensical reports with which the eastern papers have been flooded for the sole object of concealing the true state of affairs. The facts are bound to come out officially. Let me present them as they are and as they will be proved to be before many days have passed.

Geronimo's surrender to General Crook in May and his subsequent escape are well remembered. It was followed by General Miles's arrival in the territory. Miles came to this country of mountains and canyons fresh from a command which had to deal with a different class of Indians. Entirely inexperienced in Apache warfare, he made his first mistake in his loud boasts of what he proposed to do "by reversing Crook's methods." According to his fuglemen the Indian scouts were to be abandoned as untrustworthy, the regular cavalry were to do the pursuing, and the Apaches were to be worn out by a relentless pursuit into "unconditional surrender" or annihilation in the field. The papers were loaded with statements of the organization of his campaign, of the additional troops called for, the enrollment of frontier legions, the equipment of a corps to signal the trail of the savages, and the tremendous efforts which were to be made to close the war with dispatch. There was an enormous amount of buncombe, all for public effect, a large display of wasted energy, several useless

562

campaigns without results, and finally a surrender of the Apaches on their own terms.

I had the pleasure yesterday of talking with an officer recently in the field about the close of the campaign and send you his statement, given to me with no idea of its publication.[2] He said:

There has been so much claptrap and misrepresentation in regard to Geronimo's "unconditional" surrender that it is difficult for one to talk about it without showing some little feeling of disgust. I cannot be accused of prejudice, because I am not personally acquainted with either General Miles or Lawton, the two heroes of the hour. I do not desire to detract one iota from the credit and glory fairly won by either of them or by any other soldier. But I happen to know the facts of Geronimo's surrender and departure, and of all the proceedings before those events, and if there is not a boomerang in store for somebody, I shall be greatly surprised. I fail to understand why the army should be placed in a false light when the truth must certainly come out in time. The dispatches sent out have been carefully worded to connect the "coming in" of the hostiles with the operations of Lawton's command and have conveyed the impression that the hostiles were cornered and surrendered unconditionally. Nothing could be farther from the truth.

About two months ago Second Lieutenant Brown, in Captain Lawton's command, with a detachment, ran upon a hostile camp down in Sonora and got a few horses and some camp baggage. There was nothing remarkable in this, as it is something the troops have done a number of times since the hostiles went out nearly two years ago. But to read the dispatches printed and furnished through Miles's literary bureau one would have thought that the achievement was stupendous. As a matter of fact, resultless as it was, this was the only time that Lawton's command ever struck the Indians. He marched a great deal, worked hard and persistently like everyone else has who has had anything to do with field service here, but he didn't bring in Geronimo, because he was not yet ready to admit that the Apaches could not be captured and would not surrender except upon their own terms. Lawton did not do the service of the command of Davis and Crawford last year. Still, the effort has been made to identify him wholly with all that has been attained out here when, and mark my words, he never had a fight, never drew blood, and never captured an Indian. For these reasons there was no opportunity afforded Miles or Lawton for the valorous achievement and gallantry with which the country is being dosed.

It finally began to dawn upon Miles that if anything was to be done, it could only be accomplished by a return to General Crook's old and well-tried methods. The discarded Indian scouts were taken up, and the officers in charge were given to understand that the Apaches must be brought in on any terms, but brought in without delay. Accordingly, Lieutenant Gatewood, with two Chiricahua scouts, set out on the mission of finding Geronimo and treating with him for his surrender. He had no difficulty in finding them on this basis, I assure you. Geronimo had been anxious to treat ever since he got over the scare with Crook and his family were sent by that general to Florida. Lieutenant Gatewood had a talk with the Indians and persuaded them that it would be quite safe for them to come in to the neighborhood of Lawton's commands. Geronimo and Naiche positively refused to surrender to Captain Lawton for reasons well known to army officers.[3] They would do nothing more than agree to a conference with General Miles, and upon the urgent representations of Lawton that the Indians would certainly skip out unless the general came down, Miles posted off as hastily as possible to hold the conference. Meantime, Geronimo informed Lawton that if Miles wanted to see him, he could be found at Skeleton Canyon, and at that point several days later the conference was held. There the treaty or bargain was made. The conference opened by Miles handing Geronimo a cigar. The Indians were clearly and definitely given to understand that they would be sent to Florida to join their people there and that their lives were in no danger. They were urged to follow General Miles back to Bowie, not as prisoners of war, but as parties to an agreement made on terms to suit themselves. Geronimo frankly admitted that he would have come in anytime during the past twenty weeks on these conditions, but that the bloodthirsty talk of Miles had led him to believe that he would be butchered if caught. He said he was anxious to see his wives and children, and that his people felt as he did. Everybody familiar with these Indians has known all along that this was the easiest and most practicable method of getting them in. It was precisely the policy of Crook, only it was easier for Miles than Crook, because the latter band had every inducement to join their relatives and friends. And this was the famous "unconditional surrender," a surrender on Geronimo's own terms, made in his own camp, when he was free to do as he pleased and had Miles and his officers at his mercy.

After the conference was ended, Geronimo, Naiche, and five others rode into Bowie at once in company with Miles himself. Lawton followed with the remainder of the Indians, the Apaches marching along with him under no restraint whatever, just as they came up from San Bernardino before.

And now for a little piece of information. At a camp about nine miles from Bowie, Lawton camped overnight. In the morning, when the Indians were rounding up their ponies preparatory to marching, seven of them—three bucks, three squaws, and a boy—skipped out. This was not known for some time afterwards, and the cavalry, I am told, have been out after them ever since. On the night of the thirteenth citizens came in and reported that these Indians had stolen twelve of their horses on the previous night near Camp Emmet Crawford and had killed a number of cattle. The troops and scouts are still in pursuit. This has been carefully suppressed, because it will not hitch well with that story of unconditional surrender.

General Miles has acted like a theatrical manager in the whole business. Everything possible has been done to make Geronimo's surrender look like a personal triumph. When Captain Lawton arrived at Fort Bowie the Fourth Cavalry band, which had been sent for the purpose, discoursed thrilling martial music. The Indians were placed under no restraint, although I notice in the newspaper reports that they were in irons in the guardhouse. They were treated with marked consideration in every respect and paraded themselves around as if they owned the post. Geronimo, as big as a lord, togged out in store clothes and a new hat, strutted to and fro, the hero of the hour. One day General Miles had pickets put out around the post, but it was to eject citizens and to keep them from annoying the Indians. Three troops of cavalry marched down to Bowie station with the Indians, the band playing them out of the post. They have gone east to their friends and families; gone where they have been anxious to go ever since Crook broke the back of the outbreak by exiling nine-tenths of the band, and where they would have been sent months before if General Miles had not been more anxious to pose before the public than to wind up the campaign.

Let me summarize. General Miles failed miserably until he adopted every one of Crook's methods, scouts and all. Geronimo surrendered to Gatewood and on his own terms. Since poor Crawford's death, not an Apache has been killed, wounded, or captured, and Geronimo would still be skipping about in the mountains of Sonora unless Miles had surrendered his much-vaunted policy and yielded to the Apache's demands.

FORT GRANT, Arizona, October 2, 1886 [Correspondence of the *Bee*]— In my last I gave you the true inwardness of the Apache campaign and the inside history of Geronimo's surrender to Miles or, as the army men have called it, Miles's surrender to Geronimo. The story is now, as I predicted it would be, public property. No one here pretends, not even General Miles himself, that Geronimo was captured or gave himself up until he had exacted his own terms from the army officers who took him in charge. General Miles's report shows just what I said it must show, that his famous campaign had absolutely nothing to do with the Apaches' capture. Young Gatewood took two of Crook's old scouts and went to hunt Geronimo, found him of course, promised him his life and a free pass to Florida, and brought him in without any more trouble than Crook would have had if the War Department hadn't forbidden him to make terms with the wily Apache. This is the long and short of the case. General Miles feels that he has blundered but feels worse to see the clouds of glory, which he imagined were wreathing in halo over his head, disappearing under the sharp criticism which he is receiving for sailing under false colors.

Army officers through the territory are greatly disgusted over the inglorious close of the Apache campaign. They have obeyed orders without questioning, as was their duty, although they knew from experience which Miles did not have that the style of campaigning at first adopted would be without results. And now, after all the hardship, the claptrap and nonsense about "heliographs" and frontier scouts, they have seen the campaign closed just as Crook offered the War Department to close it before ever Miles came down with his boasts and braggadocio, and on methods which Crook was forbidden to employ because the War Department wished to make "an example" of the hostiles. As the truth comes out that there was no need of any campaign at all, that Crawford virtually closed the war months ago, and that Geronimo has been playing squat tag with the troops and waiting his chance to surrender on terms of his own making, the army officers, worn out and tired with their senseless work, are not slow about speaking out their minds privately about the whole business.

Lawton has received a great deal of undeserved credit for Geronimo's surrender. He had nothing whatever to do with it. Lieutenant Gatewood with two scouts begged Geronimo to come in and promised him immunity from danger and secured the return of the whole Chiricahua cavalcade. It is said here that Gatewood was highly incensed over the way in which his strategic move was suppressed for Lawton's benefit and threatened to "blow." General Miles was equal to the emergency and smoothed matters over by making Gatewood aide-de-camp the other day and assigning Captain Lawton to the acting inspector generalship. The announcement of the appointments has probably reached you by this time. General Miles's friends here are boasting that General Crook is out of favor with the administration. I do not know how that is, but he certainly is not out of favor with the army officers of Arizona, if we except a certain disgruntled colonel who will never recover from the shock he received when General Crook frankly gave him the reasons for not placing him in an important command for which he was unfitted.[4]

Escorting Chihuahua's Band to Florida[1]

JOHN P. GARDNER[2]

National Tribune, September 27, 1923

L ate in December 1885 Company E, Eighth U.S., was stationed at Fort Halleck, Nevada. While eating dinner one day our captain, E. B. Savage,[3] received a message ordering us to Arizona immediately. In less than thirty minutes we were on our way to the railroad station, fifteen miles away, through twelve inches of snow. We were under light marching order, with one blanket and overcoat, haversack, canteen, gun, and belt.

We arrived at Bowie Station, Arizona, in the heart of the San Simon desert, New Year's Day. The ground was frozen and a few inches of snow covered the desert. The north winds and sand storms were fierce. We were supplied with A-tents, two men to a tent, and slept on the ground. We stayed there with other troops until April 5 [1886], and by that time twenty-seven of the thirty-two men were down with lumbago, pleurisy, rheumatics, etc.

About that time they brought in a bunch of Indians to be transported to St. Augustine, Florida, and the officers drew straws to determine who the lucky company should be to escort the Indians. Our captain won, and the next day we were on our way to Florida with two coaches full of Indians—old bucks, squaws, and papooses—seventy-six in all. We not only didn't lose any, we arrived with seventy-seven; there had been a new arrival en route.[4]

It took us six days to make the trip. We were obliged to stop often to feed them. They would not eat canned stuff and hardtack such as was issued to us, so we would telegraph ahead to have beef at the depot for them. Then we took them out and formed a chain guard around them while they cooked a "Mulligan."[5] Every town so honored took a holiday to see the performance. Upon arrival at New Orleans the people were wild—most of them had never seen an Indian. We were a sight, too, with our dirty redwood jumpers and overalls and unshaven faces. They treated us jumpers royally, though, and our money was no good—they simply would not let us spend a cent and told us to be sure and stop over a day when we returned, which we did, and they showed us the time of our young lives. The town was wide open to us and everything free—they wined and dined us to the queen's taste.

When we arrived at Jacksonville the crowd was there to receive us and almost swamped the ferry that took us across the river. The Indians were disappointed, as General Crook had told them that they were going to Washington to see the "White Chief." Among the warriors was Chief Chihuahua and old Chief Nana, rawboned and six feet, three inches tall, dressed in a dirty linen duster, straw hat, and breechclout. We arrived back at Bowie on April 21, just fourteen days in making the round trip.

Resume of Operations against Apache Indians, 1882 to 1886

GEORGE CROOK

Headquarters, Department of the Platte, Omaha, Nebraska,
December 27, 1886

The Adjutant General, U.S. Army, Washington, D.C.

SIR: As the Chiricahua Apache campaign has ended with the surrender of Geronimo, Mangas, Naiche, and Chihuahua, with their followers, and as the official reports connected therewith have been submitted and published, in view of my long service in connection with the troubles of which these Indians were the cause, I deem it proper to submit the following resume of operations in Arizona for the information of the War Department, to be published and then placed on file as a part of the history of our Indian troubles in that territory.

An experience obtained in eight years of service in Arizona enables me to speak with a certain authority on this question and justifies the forwarding of this paper on a subject which, during the past year, has attracted no small degree of public attention and interest.

Upon assuming command of the Department of Arizona in 1882, a careful and thorough investigation revealed the existence of anything but a satisfactory state of affairs. The Indians generally were sullen and distrustful of all white men; many were on the verge of war, and some were in open hostilities. There was a general feeling of uneasiness among the whites, and the business interests of the territory were paralyzed by the uncertainties of the situation.

Since my departure from the territory in 1875, its property interests had largely increased in value, and these interests, and the lives of citizens engaged in peaceful pursuits, demanded protection.

Such being the condition of affairs, it was therefore required of any line of policy adopted that it be directed to the attainment of three main objects: the maintenance of control over the Indians remaining on the reservations, the protection of life and property of citizens, and the subjugation of the hostiles.

The first of these objects would undoubtedly be attained, in the most permanent and satisfactory way, could the Indians themselves be brought up to a degree of civilization sufficient to render them harmless to settlers, self-sustaining, and subordinate to authority. To raise and elevate the condition of the Indian himself was the object to which my first attention was directed.

Fortunately, I was able to command the respect and confidence of the Indians then on the reservation, and who had been under my control in 1871–1875. It was essential not only that this confidence in me should be retained, but to produce the best and most lasting results, that it should also be extended to the whites generally.

As a first step to this end, the following order was published to the troops of the department:

HEADQUARTERS, DEPARTMENT OF ARIZONA,
WHIPPLE BARRACKS, PRESCOTT, A.T., October 3, 1882.

GENERAL ORDERS, No. 43

The commanding general, after making a thorough and exhaustive examination among the Indians of the eastern and southern part of this territory, regrets to say that he finds among them a general feeling of distrust and want of confidence in the whites—especially the soldiery; and also that much dissatisfaction, dangerous to the peace of the country, exists among them.

Officers and soldiers serving in this department are reminded that one of the fundamental principles of the military character is justice to all—Indians as well as white men—and that a disregard of this principle is likely to bring about hostilities and cause the death of the very persons whom they are sent here to protect.

In all their dealings with the Indians, officers must be careful not only to observe the strictest fidelity, but to make no promises not in their power to carry out; all grievances arising within their jurisdictions should be redressed, so that an accumulation of them may not cause an outbreak. Grievances, however petty, if permitted to accumulate, will be like embers that smolder and eventually break into flame.

When officers are applied to for the employment of force against Indians, they should thoroughly satisfy themselves of the necessity for the application and of the legality of compliance therewith, in order that they may not, through the inexperience of others or through their own hastiness, allow the troops under them to become the instruments of oppression.

There must be no division of responsibility in this matter; each officer will be held to a strict accountability that his actions have been fully authorized by law and justice, and that Indians evincing a desire to enter upon a career of peace shall have no cause for complaint through hasty or injudicious acts of the military.

BY ORDER OF BRIGADIER GENERAL CROOK:
[Signed] J. P. MARTIN, Ass't Adjutant General.

But this alone would do little; the Indians themselves had to be reached, and authority established over them, before they could in any way be controlled or their condition advanced beyond the primitive savagery in which they existed.

Some of the leaders of the different bands were interviewed and were, by various means, induced to exert their influence for the maintenance of order. These Indians the more readily yielded to control because of their previous acquaintance with me in 1871–75, when I had subjugated and placed over five thousand of them on the reservation. But the Chiricahua and War Springs Apaches, during my former administration in Arizona, had been excepted from my control and had escaped the punishment due them for their outrages. The Chiricahuas had been given a reservation south of the present line of the Southern Pacific railway, on the orders of Mexico. I was prohibited from interfering in any manner with their management and was not able even to learn the terms upon which this reservation was given to them.

The reservation of the Warm Springs Apaches was in New Mexico at the Ojo Caliente and therefore outside the limits of my command. Subsequently, some members of these bands were induced to remove to the White Mountain reservation, but prior to my reassignment to the command in 1882, they had all left it and were located in the Sierra Madre in Mexico, where their presence was a constant menace to the people living within the territory subject to their depredations, which extended on both sides of the international boundary. While these Indians remained off the reservations, life and property within those exposed limits would be unsafe, and it was determined to effect their return.

The raid of Chatto in March 1883 enabled me, without violation of treaty stipulations, to follow this band to the Chiricahua strongholds in the Sierra Madre.

The details of this expedition were fully set forth in my annual report for 1883 and need not be repeated here. It is sufficient to state that it resulted in the surrender of the renegades—not only those who had at any time lived on the reservation, but also those who, when their bands had been moved from the Warm Spring and Chiricahua reservations to the White Mountain reserve, had escaped to the Sierra Madre. In compliance with the surrender then made, over 600 souls, 120 being men and boys capable of bearing arms, were brought to the reservation, their status being nominally that of prisoners of war. At this time the Chiricahuas were the wildest and fiercest Indians on the continent; savage and brutal by instinct, they hesitated no more at taking human life, when excited by passion, than in killing a rabbit. For more than two centuries they had been a thorn in the flesh of the Spaniards, and although during this time almost constant warfare had been carried on, all efforts to conquer these tigers of the human race by force of arms had been fruitless.

For centuries the Apaches had been subjected to hardships and privations, which began with their birth and ended only with their lives. The mountain country in which they lived furnished all that was necessary for their existence. The advance of a people to even the simplest form of civilization is marked by the creation of artificial necessities. The Apache was independent of these, and his contact with the whites led him to adopt only their weapons. They resented anything like an attempt to regulate their conduct, or in any way to interfere with their mode of life.

The problem presented was to bring under control, reduce to subordination, and civilize, so far as was possible, these Indians, to whose restive natures restraint of any kind was unknown. In accepting their surrender, I was deeply sensible of the responsibility which I assumed, but I believed then, and believe now, that in no other way could I hope to put an end to the constant raids to which Arizona and New Mexico had, for generations, been subjected by these Indians. Their regeneration could be a work only of time and of the most patient watchfulness and care.

They were placed under the charge of officers in whose ability and discretion I reposed great confidence. Confidential Indians were employed as secret-service scouts and kept constantly in the camps of the savages to observe their every movement, to listen to their conversation and report their demeanor. Indians of their own tribe were selected, preferably the most influential and energetic of their number, who were enlisted and paid as scouts, and every effort was made to gain their confidence and secure their cooperation. By this means, the several bands were disintegrated, divisions created among them and, by degrees, a following obtained that was interested in repressing disorder. This step gained, it became possible to go further and, by exercising the greatest discretion, to punish offenders. Whenever it was practicable, this was caused to be done by the Indians themselves, and in this way several of the prominent young "bucks" were arrested while fomenting discontent, tried by Indian juries, by them sentenced and severely punished. Disorders repressed in this way not only accustomed them to a certain degree of self-government, but were most invaluable in cultivating a spirit of subordination among them. By these and other methods, too numerous to describe here and which have been set forth more in detail in my annual and other reports for 1883–84–85, these wild and reckless spirits were brought under control and were gradually set at work farming, in which labor was performed not only by the women, but also by the men. This too was accomplished without violent shock to the prejudices and without exciting their suspicions.

It is impossible to eliminate the discouraging effect of the obstacles against which it was necessary to contend in following out these methods to a finally successful issue: the unfriendly criticism of the territorial press; the more or less open and always covert opposition of the Indian Department, up to the time of the outbreak in 1885; the undisguised hostility of the numerous rings [and] contractors and speculators, whose success depended upon their ability to defraud the Indians; all these adverse elements had to be overcome, and against such odds, success would have been impossible except for the zealous cooperation of such men as Captain Crawford, Lieutenant Gatewood, Lieutenant Britton Davis, and others associated with them in the management of Indian affairs on the White Mountain reservation. These officers constantly carried their lives in their hands; the service in which they were engaged was one of the greatest possible delicacy and danger, where the slightest indiscretion would have proved fatal to them. But it seemed, in my judgment, the only way in which the Indians could be reached and taught that subordination to authority which is an essential requisite to any degree of advancement, however slight, toward a state of civilization. For this reason I allowed officers, the value of whose lives was inestimable, to engage in the most dangerous duty that ever falls to the lot of soldiers to perform.

The method indicated above had been applied with success to the management of the other Apaches, who, it should be remembered, were in 1871 in all respects as brutally savage as these Chiricahuas were in 1883, and there was every reason to believe that the same means which had proved so effective with the former would produce equally good results with the latter, and they did, in fact. For the first time in their history, they were placed under restraint and taught subordination, while at the same time they made rapid progress toward self-government and complete self-support. For more than two years Arizona and New Mexico enjoyed a respite from Indian troubles, during which period not an outrage or depredation of any kind was committed in the United States by an Apache Indian. This was the first time, within the memory of man, that there were no Apache Indians on the warpath. During this period the question of the management of the Chiricahuas was practically settled. I had gained their confidence to such an extent that I am firmly convinced that, had I known of the occurrences reported in Lieutenant Davis's telegram of May 15, 1885, which I did not see until months afterwards, the outbreak of Mangus and Geronimo a few days later would not have occurred. As it was, though nearly all the prominent chiefs except Chatto were among the renegades, less than one-third of the fighting strength left the reservation. Over 80 men and 350 women and children still remained on their farms. Although the hard and conscientious work expended upon these Chiricahuas did not prevent a portion of them leaving the reservation, it enabled me to select with certainty of faithful service 50 of those remaining for enlistment as scouts. I should have enlisted more, except for the reason that I wished the rest to remain to protect the women and children from hostile raids. These Indians were selected as scouts, in preference to those belonging to other bands of Apaches, for the reasons that they were thoroughly familiar with the country in which they would be required to operate; they were superior as soldiers to any other Indians and fully up to the standard of the renegades.

It is not my purpose in this paper to present the details of operations against the hostile Chiricahuas, as they have already been fully discussed in my annual reports for 1885 and 1886, to which attention is invited. As, however, the surrender of the renegades to me in March 1886 has been made the subject of much discussion in the public press and indeed has, in some quarters, been curiously misrepresented, it is deemed proper to insert, in full, the following correspondence relating thereto:

HEADQUARTERS DEPARTMENT OF ARIZONA,
In the Field, Fort Bowie, A.T., September 17, 1885.

The Adjutant General, Division of the Pacific.

Sir: It has been my intention to turn over to the civil authorities any hostile bucks captured for trial under the provisions of Section Nine of the Act of Congress, approved 3 March 1885, with reference to jurisdiction of the courts over certain offenses committed by Indians. But upon consultation with several prominent lawyers on the subject, I am assured that it will be impossible to secure conviction in the civil courts, owing to the impossibility of obtaining evidence against individual Indians, and that the same difficulty will be experienced in obtaining proof should the Indians be indicted for conspiracy. Unless aided by a stroke of good fortune, it will take years to kill all these hostiles, situated as they are, and so long as any of them remain out in the mountains, life and property will be unsafe within their reach and it will be impossible to prevent their depredations.

It is desirable to have them surrender, and this they will not do if they think they are to be killed or, what they believe is worse, turned over to the civil authorities.

It is believed they could be induced to surrender after a little more hammering, if they are assured that their lives would not be forfeited and that they would simply be transported. Please give decision by telegraph.

It is important that this matter should not gain publicity so as to get to the ears of the Indians.

Yours respectfully,

Your obedient servant,
(Sgd.) GEORGE CROOK,
Brigadier General, Commanding.

In reply to this letter, the following telegram was received October 8, 1885:

HEADQUARTERS DIVISION PACIFIC,
Presidio, San Francisco, California, October 8, 1885.

General Crook, Fort Bowie, A.T.

The following dispatch is repeated for your information and action. Please acknowledge receipt.

BY ORDER OF MAJOR GENERAL POPE:
(Sgd.) TAYLOR, Aide-de-camp.

Referring to General Crook's application, dated September 17, inquiring whether promise can be made to hostile Chiricahuas that their lives shall not be forfeited if they surrender, the secretary of war approves a recommendation of the lieutenant general that General Crook be authorized to secure the surrender of the Chiricahuas now at large upon terms of their being held as prisoners of war, but it must be understood that any negotiation looking to their surrender must include all hostile Chiricahuas, and that as soon as the surrender is made that they at once be sent under suitable guard for confinement at Fort Marion, Fla. Please so inform General Crook by telegraph and direct him to acknowledge receipt. No publicity must be given as to the intentions of the government in this matter beyond what is absolutely necessary in communicating with the Indians.

(Sgd.) R. C. Drum, Adjutant General.

After the receipt of information of Crawford's fight, his subsequent death, and the request of the hostiles for a personal interview with me, the following dispatch was received:

HEADQUARTERS ARMY OF THE UNITED STATES,
Washington, D.C., February 1, 1886.

General George Crook, Fort Bowie, Arizona.

I had a consultation with the president last Thursday afternoon on the subject of Lieutenant Maus's dispatch. He fully understands the instructions under which you can act, transmitted to you September 30, 1885, but desires me to notify you to make no promises at all to the hostiles unless it is necessary to secure their surrender.

(Sgd.) P. H. SHERIDAN, Lieutenant General.

In compliance with the authority contained in the above communications, I proceeded to the point where the Indians were in camp and on March 25, 1886, had my first interview with them. I found the hostiles, though tired of the constant hounding of the campaign, in superb physical condition, armed to the teeth, and with an abundance of ammunition. In manner they were suspicious and at the same time independent and self-reliant. After my first interview I telegraphed the lieutenant general as follows:

CAMP EL CAÑON DE LOS EMBUDOS,
Twenty miles S.E. San Bernardino, Mexico, March 26, 1886,
Via Fort Bowie, Arizona, March 28, 1886.

Lieutenant General P. H. Sheridan, Washington, D.C.

I met the hostiles yesterday at Lt. Maus' camp, they being located about five hundred yards distant. I found them very independent and as fierce as so many tigers—knowing what pitiless brutes they are themselves, they mistrust everyone else. After my talk with them it seemed as if it would be impossible to get any hold on them except on condition that they be allowed to return to the reservation on their old status. Today things look more favorable.

(Sgd.) GEORGE CROOK, Brigadier General.

That evening spies managed to get among them, and in this way their feelings, both toward each other and toward their pursuers, were ascertained. On information gained in this way it was possible to shape a policy. Though it is believed that all the hostiles had implicit confidence in me, I preferred to work on individuals and selected Chihuahua and Naiche, who were the most influential leaders of the renegades, and concentrated my efforts upon them. From the scouts were selected trustworthy Indians of their own tribe, who were carefully instructed and sent to talk with these chiefs, who finally agreed to surrender on terms the most favorable I could hope to exact. This at once divided the hostiles into two parties and broke up the band. The fact that this had been effected through the personal efforts of their own people had an effect not only of a peculiarly demoralizing nature upon the hostiles, but also upon all others of the tribe, and rendered their subsequent management anywhere an easy matter. Before this, merely to have hinted at the possibility of their removal from their old haunts would simply have stampeded the whole tribe to the mountains.

These results may be traced directly to the work that had been done among these Indians during the two years they had been on the reservation and were followed on the next day by the surrender of the whole body of hostiles, which fact was communicated to the lieutenant general in the following telegram:

CAMP EL CAÑON DE LOS EMBUDOS, MEXICO
March 27, 1886, via Fort Bowie, Arizona, March 29, 1886.

Lieutenant General P. H. Sheridan, U.S.A., Washington, D.C.

Confidential

In a conference with Geronimo and other Chiricahuas, I told them that they must decide at once upon unconditional surrender or fight it out. That in the latter event hostilities should be commenced at once and the last one of them killed if it took fifty years. I told them to reflect on what they were to do before giving me their answer. The only propositions they would entertain were these three. That they should be sent east for not exceeding two years, taking with them such of their families as so desired, leaving at Apache, Nana, who is seventy years old and superannuated; or that they should all return to the reservation on their old status; or else return to the warpath with all its attendant horrors. As I had to act at once, I have today accepted their surrender upon the first proposition.

Ka-ya-ten-nae, the young chief who less than two years ago was the worst Chiricahua of the whole lot, is now perfectly subdued. He is thoroughly reconstructed, has rendered me valuable assistance, and will be of great service in helping to control these Indians in the future. His stay at Alcatraz has worked a complete reformation in his character. I have not a doubt that similar treatment will produce results with the whole band, and by the end of that time the excitement will have died away. Mangus, with thirteen Chiricahuas, six[1] of whom are bucks, is not with the other Chiricahuas. He separated from them in August last and has since held no communication with them. He has committed no depredations. As it would be likely to take a year to find him in the immense range of mountains to the south, I think it inadvisable to attempt any search at this time, especially as he will undoubtedly give himself up as soon as he hears what the others have done.[2]

I start for Bowie tomorrow morning, to reach there next night. I respectfully request to be informed whether or not my action has been approved and also that full instructions meet me at that point. The Chiricahuas start for Bowie tomorrow with the Apache scouts under Lieut. Maus.

(Sgd.) GEORGE CROOK, Brigadier General.

There is not the slightest doubt that their surrender was made in good faith. The fact that Geronimo and Naiche, having been filled with fiery mescal and alarmed by the lies of a designing man,[3] stampeded on the route to Fort Bowie with a party of their following was an unfortunate but not irreparable accident. The men sent to Fort Marion were among the bravest and ablest of the renegades; the old chief Nana, despite his age, was the acknowledged brains of the band; Chihuahua and Josanie[4] were their most influential leaders; while among the prisoners were two wives and three children of Geronimo, the family of Naiche, and also relatives, or some members of the families of all that remained out.

It was only necessary to communicate with the renegades, which, with the aid of the scouts, would have been a matter of but little difficulty when they had recovered from their fright and had time to consider the position in which they were placed, and the trouble would, in all probability, have been settled without further bloodshed. This course would have been adopted, but my relief from the command of the department prevented such action being taken.

The voluntary return of two of the Indians who had stampeded on this occasion is a very significant fact when considered with reference to this line of policy.

The following telegraphic correspondence shows clearly all remaining facts connected with the surrender of the hostiles:

HEADQUARTERS DEPARTMENT OF ARIZONA
In the Field, Fort Bowie, A.T., March 30, 1886.

Lieutenant General P. H. Sheridan, Washington, D.C.

A courier just in from Lieutenant Maus reports that during the night Geronimo and Naiche, with twenty men and thirteen women, left his camp, taking no stock. He states that there was no apparent cause for their leaving. Two dispatches received from him this morning reported everything going on well and the Chiricahuas in good spirits. Chihuahua and twelve men remained behind. Lieut. Maus, with his scouts, except enough to take the other prisoners to Bowie, have gone in pursuit.

(Sgd.) GEORGE CROOK, Brigadier General.

HEADQUARTERS ARMY OF THE UNITED STATES
Washington, D.C. March 31, 1886

General George Crook, Fort Bowie, Arizona.

Your dispatch of yesterday received. It has occasioned great disappointment. It seems strange that Geronimo and party could have escaped without the knowledge of the scouts.

(Sgd.) P. H. SHERIDAN, Lieutenant General.

HEADQUARTERS DEPARTMENT OF ARIZONA,
In the field, Fort Bowie, A.T., March 31, 1886.

Lieutenant General P. H. Sheridan, Washington, D.C.

Your dispatch of the 31st. received. There can be no question that the scouts were thoroughly loyal and would have prevented the hostiles leaving, had it been possible. When they left their camp, they scattered over the country so as to make surprise impossible, and they located their camp with this in view, nor would they all remain in camp at one time. They kept more or less full of mescal. They had so tamed down since we first met them that some of the most prominent were hunting their ponies unarmed the evening of the night they left.

(Sgd.) GEORGE CROOK, Brigadier General.

HEADQUARTERS ARMY OF UNITED STATES,
Washington, D.C., March 31, 1886.

General George Crook, Fort Bowie, Arizona.

You have not acknowledged receipt of my telegram of March 30, conveying instructions of the president. Inform me at once of this and telegraph me any further information you may have of the escape of the hostiles and the prospects of their recapture.

(Sgd.) P. H. SHERIDAN, Lieutenant General.

HEADQUARTERS DEPARTMENT OF ARIZONA,
In the Field, Fort Bowie, A.T., March 31, 1886.

Lieut. General P. H. Sheridan, Washington, D.C.

In reply to your dispatch of March 30, to enable you to clearly understand [the] situation, it should be remembered that the hostiles had an agreement with Lieutenant Maus that they were to be met by me twenty-five miles below the line, that no regular troops were to be present. While I was very averse to such an agreement, I had to abide by it, as it had already been entered into. We found them in camp on a rocky hill about five hundred yards from Lieut. Maus, in such a position that a thousand men could not have surrounded them with any possibility of catching them. They were able, upon the approach of any enemy being signaled, to scatter and escape through dozens of ravines and canyons which would shelter them from pursuit until they reached the higher ranges in the vicinity. They were armed to the teeth, having the most improved guns and all the ammunition they could carry. The clothing and other supplies lost in the fight with Crawford had been replaced by new blankets and shirts obtained in Mexico. Lieutenant Maus, with Apache scouts, was camped at the nearest point the hostiles would agree to his approaching. Even had I been disposed to betray the confidence they placed in me, it would have been simply an impossibility to get white troops to that point either by day or by night without their knowledge, and had I attempted to do this, the whole band would have stampeded back to the mountains. So suspicious were they that never more than from five to eight of the men came into our camp at one time, and to have attempted the arrest of those would have stampeded the others to the mountains. Even after the march to Bowie began, we were compelled to allow them to scatter. They would not march in a body, and had any efforts been made to keep them together they would have broken for the mountains. My only hope was to get their confidence on the march through Ka-ya-ten-nae and other confidential Indians and finally put them on the cars; and until this was done it was impossible even to disarm them.

(Sgd.) GEORGE CROOK, Brigadier General, Commanding.

———————

HEADQUARTERS DEPARTMENT OF ARIZONA,
In the Field, Fort Bowie, A.T., March 31, 1886.

Lieutenant General P. H. Sheridan, Washington, D.C.

Your dispatch of the thirtieth conveying instructions of the president was received this A.M. and answered as soon as possible. To inform the Indians that the terms on which they surrendered are disapproved would, in my judgment, not only make it impossible for me to negotiate with them, but result in their scattering to the mountains, and I can't at present see any way to prevent it. There is nothing further to report with reference to the escape of the hostile, nor is it probable I shall be able to give any positive information until the second or third proximo when I can interview the Indians now en route. Lieutenant Maus has eighty scouts and can perhaps remain out a week before he will be obliged to return. While it is possible he may succeed in getting the hostiles to return it is extremely doubtful.

(Sgd.) GEORGE CROOK, Brigadier General, Commanding.

———————

Telegram received 2:11 P.M.
Washington, D.C., April 1, 1886.

General George Crook, Fort Bowie, Arizona.

Your dispatch of March 31 received. I do not see what you can do now except to concentrate your troops at the best points and give protection to the people. Geronimo will undoubtedly enter upon other raids of murder and robbery and, as the offensive campaign against him with scouts has failed, would it not be best to take up defensive and give protection to the people and business interests of Arizona and New Mexico. The infantry might be stationed by companies on certain points requiring protection and the cavalry patrol between them. You have in your department forty-six companies of infantry and forty companies of cavalry and ought to be able to do a good deal with such a force. Please send me a statement of what you contemplate for the future.

(Sgd.) P. H. SHERIDAN, Lieutenant General.

———————

HEADQUARTERS DEPARTMENT OF ARIZONA,
In the Field, Fort Bowie, A.T., April 1, 1886.

Lieutenant General P. H. Sheridan, Washington, D.C.

Your dispatch of today received. It has been my aim throughout present operations to afford the greatest amount of protection to life and property interests, and troops have been stationed accordingly. Troops cannot protect property beyond a radius of one-half mile from their camp. If offensive movements against the Indians are not resumed, they may remain quietly in the mountains for an indefinite time without crossing the line, and yet their very presence there will be a constant menace and require the troops in this department to be at all times in position to repel sudden raids; and so long as any remain out, they will form a nucleus for disaffected Indians from the different agencies in Arizona and New Mexico to join. That the operations of the scouts in Mexico have not proved as successful as was hoped is due to the enormous difficulties they have been compelled to encounter from the nature of the Indians they have been hunting and the character of the country in which they have operated, and of which persons not thoroughly conversant with both can have no conception. I believe that the plan upon which I have conducted operations is the one most likely to prove successful in the end. It may be, however, that I am too much wedded to my own views in this matter, and as I have spent nearly eight years of the hardest work of my life in this department, I respectfully request that I may now be relieved from its command.

(Sgd.) GEORGE CROOK, Brigadier General.

HEADQUARTERS DEPARTMENT OF ARIZONA,
In the Field, Fort Bowie, A.T., April 2, 1886.
Confidential.

Lieutenant General P. H. Sheridan, Washington, D.C.

The hostiles who did not leave with Geronimo arrived today, about eighty. I haven't ascertained the exact number. Some of the worst of the band are among them. In my judgment they should be sent away at once, as the effect on those still out would be much better than to confine them. After they get to their destination, if they can be shown that their future will be better by remaining than to return, I think there will be but little difficulty in obtaining their consent to remain indefinitely. When sent off a guard should accompany them.

(Sgd.) GEORGE CROOK, Brigadier General.

HEADQUARTERS DEPARTMENT OF ARIZONA,
In the Field, Fort Bowie, A.T., April 2, 1886.

Lieutenant General P. H. Sheridan, Washington, D.C.

In an interview with the hostiles today after they arrived, I learned that bad liquor was at the bottom of the party with Geronimo and Naiche leaving. They are of the opinion that Lieutenant Maus stands but little chance of coming up with them.

(Sgd.) GEORGE CROOK, Brigadier General.

Telegram received 2:40 P.M.
Washington, D.C., April 3, 1886.

General George Crook, Fort Bowie, Arizona.

Your telegram of April 2 received. Under authority from the secretary of war, you will as soon as practicable arrange for the transportation and subsistence of the Chiricahua prisoners now in your possession at Fort Bowie and send them to Fort Marion, Saint Augustine, Florida, where they will be turned over to the C.O. Saint Francis Barracks as prisoners under the terms directed by the president in my telegram of March 30. Send with them, under suitable officers, a sufficient guard to insure their safety.

(Sgd.) P. H. SHERIDAN, Lieutenant General, Commanding.

HEADQUARTERS DEPARTMENT OF ARIZONA,
In the Field, Fort Bowie, A.T., April 4, 1886.

Lieutenant General P. H. Sheridan, Washington, D.C.

Two men of the hostiles who left with Geronimo are here, having joined Lieutenant Maus sixteen miles from this post yesterday and come in with him. They say that they were sleeping together on the night of the stampede and heard the others leaving and went themselves because they thought something wrong. After they got out and it became light, they made up their minds that there was no reason for leaving. They saw Lieutenant Maus with his scouts following the trail made by the hostiles; after hiding in the mountains for a day they concluded to return. They report that there are several others with Geronimo who are very tired of the life they have been living. Upon investigation it appears that a man named Tribolett, who has been selling the Indians large quantities of bad liquor, is at the bottom of all this trouble. Lieutenant Maus followed the trail of the renegades for two days until it broke up and scattered in the mountains west of Fronteras and until he became satisfied that further pursuit would be useless.

(Sgd.) GEORGE CROOK, Brigadier General.

HEADQUARTERS DEPARTMENT OF ARIZONA,
In the Field, Fort Bowie, A.T., April 4, 1886.
Confidential.

Lieutenant General P. H. Sheridan, Washington, D.C.

Your dispatch of April 3 designating Fort Marion as the place of confinement for the hostiles received. Arrangements are being made for their transportation, and they will be sent as soon as possible. I shall not inform them that the president has disapproved the terms upon which I accepted their surrender, for the reason that I can communicate nothing to them through interpreter without everyone knowing what is said, and if the fact was known, it would absolutely prevent the return of any others, and unless this war is ended by the surrender of the hostiles, it is likely to last for years. The fewer the number that remain out, the more difficulty there will be in catching them.

(Sgd.) GEORGE CROOK, Brigadier General.

Telegram received 4:15 P.M.
Washington, D.C., April 5, 1886.

General George Crook, Fort Bowie, Arizona.

Your telegram of April 4 received. Your action is approved. It is the desire of the president that the prisoners be sent off without delay. Please inform me when they will be started and the number of men, women, and children.

(Sgd.) P. H. SHERIDAN, Lieutenant General.

Telegram received 7:30 P.M.
Washington, D.C., April 5, 1886.

General George Crook, Fort Bowie, Arizona.

The present terms not having been agreed to here and Geronimo having broken every condition of the surrender, the Indians now in custody are to be held as prisoners and sent to Fort Marion without reference to previous communications and without in any way consulting their wishes in the matter. This is in addition to my telegram of today.

(Sgd.) P. H. SHERIDAN, Lieutenant General.

HEADQUARTERS DEPARTMENT OF ARIZONA,
In the Field, Fort Bowie, A.T., April 7, 1886.

Lieutenant General P. H. Sheridan, Washington, D.C.

The Chiricahua prisoners numbering fifteen men, among them Chihuahua, Nana, and Josanie, thirty-three women, and twenty-nine children, left Bowie Station about 4:00 P.M. today under charge of Lieutenant Richards, Fourth Cavalry,[5] escorted by a company of the Eighth Infantry. Among the men were five of the boldest and ablest of the renegades, and three of them were in the raiding party which did so much killing in November and December. To avoid any possible trouble by reason of their stopping at stated times at stations en route, they were sent by special train as far as San Antonio.

(Sgd.) GEORGE CROOK, Brigadier General.

On April 11, in obedience to the orders of the War Department, dated April 2, 1886, I turned over the command of the department to General Miles.

The policy pursued by me in the operations mentioned above has been criticized as one "of operating almost exclusively with Indian scouts." I am unwilling that such a summary should be placed on official record without a protest, lest by my silence I should seem to acquiesce in the justice of a criticism which would seem to imply that the Regular troops at my disposal were not used at all, or were used to little advantage.

A further criticism is implied in the suggestion of the lieutenant general that the troops be used defensively for the protection of life and property. The hostiles were in Mexico; it was therefore necessary, [in order] to secure this protection, to prevent, if possible, their recrossing the line. To attain this end, troops were stationed in detachments along the frontier. To each detachment was assigned five Indian scouts to watch the front and detect the approach of the hostiles. These troops were stationed at every point where it was thought possible for the hostiles to pass. Every trail, every water hole from Patagonia Mountains to the Rio Grande was thus guarded. The troops were under the strictest orders constantly to patrol this line, each detachment having a particular section of country to its special charge.

In addition to this, a second line was similarly established in rear of the first, both to act as a reserve and to prevent the passing of any hostiles who might elude the vigilance of the first line. Behind this again were stationed troops on the railroad who might be sent to any desired point on the whole front, forming thus a third line.

The posts of Forts Thomas, Grant, and Bayard, with troops stationed at various points on the Gila at Ash Springs, in the Mogollon Mountains, and other places, formed in reality a fourth line.

The approach of the hostiles toward any point on the border was telegraphed to all threatened points and the citizens warned in advance. In no case did the hostiles succeed in passing the first line of troops without detection and pursuit. All troops, wherever stationed, had orders to pursue vigorously and as long as possible any hostiles who might come within striking distance. In spite, however, of all the efforts of the troops, the hostiles did pass these lines, and the pursuits that followed, though they were persistent, indefatigable, and untiring, and frequently successful in capturing the Indians' stock, resulted in no other loss to the enemy. Troops never worked harder or [more] deserved success, but during the entire sixteen months of these operations, not a single man, woman, or child of the hostiles was killed or captured by the troops of the Regular army.

It cannot be maintained that the failure of the troops to accomplish more than they did was due to lack of opportunity, owing to the disposition made of them. The movements of the hostiles gave ample opportunities to the troops, and they did not fail to take advantage of them. They did all that could justly be demanded of any troops.

It will be seen that persistent and constant use was made of the Regular troops; that they were not employed in service for which they were not fitted should certainly not be a reason for an implied censure. For the zeal and energy displayed by them, and for the privations and hardships uncomplainingly endured in pursuing these Indians, too much praise cannot be given them.

But a mere passive defense would not alone suffice to protect citizens or property; as long as the Indians remained at large, there could be no safety. A few of these Chiricahuas, with the ability they had of traveling with almost marvelous rapidity over great distances, could have kept the territories of Arizona and New Mexico in a state of constant terror. The raid of eleven of these Indians through these territories in 1885 sufficiently indicates this.[6] The smallness of their number only rendered their escape easier and their movements more difficult to detect. Protection must therefore be sought not only in defensive measures, which could not prevent the passage of the Indians across a line of over a thousand miles in length and at best could only detect their passage within a short time after it had been effected, but the hostiles must be subjugated and placed under control. Therefore, in addition to the measures above described, two commands consisting each of a picked troop of cavalry and one hundred Indian scouts were organized to follow the hostiles south of the border. They were reduced to the minimum of impediments consistent with the nature of the arduous duty assigned to them, which was to follow the hostiles wherever they went, strike them wherever they were found, and pursue them incessantly until they were killed, captured, or until they should sue for peace. In this service the cavalry, picked though it was, proved to be really an impediment to successful operations and was subsequently relieved on the recommendation of the officers in command of these expeditions.

To these mixed commands of picked cavalry and Indian scouts was specially entrusted the task of subjugating the hostiles.

The use of these scouts in this way has been made the subject of adverse criticism, and I desire here to express my convictions with regard to it. Nearly eight years of my life have been spent in Arizona, and much of that time in actual hostilities with Apache Indians. I am, therefore, entitled to speak from the knowledge gained through experience, and I cannot too strongly assert that there has never been any success against these Indians unless Indian scouts were used either as auxiliaries or independent of other support. Regular troops have always failed on our side of the boundary line, and any apparent success in Mexican operations has been attained by the grossest treachery, the effect of which has been to make the Indians, if possible, even more suspicious and savage than before and to infuriate them to fresh outrages.

I assert, moreover, without reserve or qualification of any nature, that these Chiricahua scouts under Chiefs Chatto, Noche, and others, did most excellent service and were of more value in hunting down and compelling the surrender of the renegades than all other troops engaged in operations against them combined. The reports circulated to the effect that they were disloyal and unwilling to fight the renegades are absolutely false. It has been said that the hostiles obtained ammunition, supplies, assistance, and reinforcements from the scouts and from those who remained on the reservation; this statement, in whatever form repeated, is entirely incorrect.

During the whole of the sixteen months following the departure of the renegades up to their final surrender, they did not receive an addition of a single Apache from the reservation. It is true that the hostiles at several different times obtained cartridges from the bodies of scouts and soldiers whom they had killed; and in other instances considerable amounts in camps which they attacked, as for instance in Guadalupe Canyon in June 1885, when they killed three men belonging to a detachment of Captain Lawton's command and captured probably two or three thousand rounds of fixed ammunition; and in another instance, when Naiche and other Indians attacked Captain Hatfield's troops in May 1886.

It has been alleged that while the Chiricahua scouts could be depended upon to use their best efforts "to capture or induce the surrender of the hostiles, they had no wish to kill their kindred."

It may well be questioned whether it be the policy of the government simply and absolutely to kill a number of Indians or to restore peace and secure the safety of its citizens. The instructions given to me plainly and specifically authorized me to secure the surrender of the hostiles, without conditions if possible, with conditions if necessary. It was not until my successor assumed command that orders were given "looking to the destruction or capture of the hostiles," simply.

But the facts do not support the theory that the scouts would not kill the hostiles. On the contrary, during the entire course of the operations against them, from May 1885 to the surrender to General Miles of the party under Naiche and Geronimo in September 1886, the only hostiles killed or captured were in encounters with the scouts alone, except two men, one of whom was killed by a White Mountain Indian near Fort Apache and the other by an American near Fronteras in Mexico, in March 1886. During the entire campaign, from first to last, without any exception, every successful encounter with the hostiles was due exclusively to the exertions of Indian scouts, and it is the unanimous testimony of officers commanding scout companies that the Chiricahuas were the most subordinate, energetic, untiring, and by odds the most efficient of their command. The use of Indian scouts was indeed a feature of my policy in dealing with the renegade Apaches, and one which my own experience in former campaigns in Nevada, Idaho, California, Oregon, Washington, Arizona, and in the Sioux troubles in 1876 and '77, as well as that of soldiers the world over, afford convincing proof that it is a feature of great value, and that results are obtained by the use of these auxiliaries that cannot be obtained in any other way. As a military principle, it is not the part of wisdom to neglect an auxiliary force which has proved always useful and at times indispensable. In the military service universally, men have been, so far as possible, assigned to the work they are best qualified to perform. The Chiricahua Apache, both by nature and education, is beyond cavil better qualified than anyone else for the warfare which for years past has been carried on in the mountains of Arizona and Mexico. The use of Indian scouts is therefore dictated by the soundest principle of military policy.

In his annual report for 1886 the lieutenant general says that he thinks that these scouts "were faithful as far as to try to capture or induce the surrender of the hostiles." On this ground alone the employment of these scouts would be amply justified. In the same report it is also stated that but for the unfortunate assassination of Captain Crawford by Mexican troops, he would "have terminated the cruel and bloody atrocities which continued thereafter for many months." It is necessary to add to this statement that Captain Crawford's command consisted of Indian scouts only.

Not only as an efficient fighting force were these scouts valuable. Their employment in communicating with the hostiles, who could never have been reached without their aid, and their services in bringing about the disintegration and surrender of the hostile bands, were of very great value. Without the use of scouts, the surrender of the Chiricahuas in 1883 would have been impossible. Without them, the surrender of the whole body of the hostiles in March 1886 could not have taken place. Although in this last case some of them escaped after the surrender, it should not be overlooked that as its result, and in accordance with its terms, some seventy-seven of the renegades were sent to Florida, leaving but thirty-three men, women, and children in the band under Naiche and Geronimo.[7]

And finally, the surrender to my successor of this party was accomplished solely by the use not only of scouts, but of Chiricahua scouts. The report of the lieutenant general allows the inference to be made that this was due to a departure from the methods employed by me and resulted from the use exclusively of Regular troops. The fact is that after an experience of months, absolutely without gaining one step, during which time troops, horses, and pack trains had been worked beyond the limits of endurance and citizens, Mexicans, and friendly Indians of other tribes had been employed in vain, Lieutenant Gatewood, with the aid of two Chiricahua Apaches, obtained the surrender. In other words, the campaign was closed only by a return to the methods which constituted the distinctive feature of the policy adopted and followed by me.

It is difficult to arrive at the true conditions accepted by the Indians in this surrender, and the question is of little importance, so far as this discussion goes. One fact, however, is certain, the efforts of the troops in the field had little or nothing to do with it.

The difficulties and cost, both in life and money, of protracted Indian wars are too well known to need discussion. They have ever been out of all proportion to the results obtained. The Seminole War, lasting through eight years of constant warfare, cost thousands of lives and between twenty or thirty millions of dollars.[8]

"The power of the army aided by deception, fraud, and perfidy was tried in vain," but the Seminoles were never conquered by force of arms, and peace was at last obtained with the inauguration of a different policy. The confidence of one of their most powerful chiefs was gained by an act of simple justice, and by means of negotiations carried on through this chief a portion of them were induced to surrender, with the understanding that they should be moved beyond the Mississippi. The first Indians sent west induced a disposition on the part of those who remained to follow. The wedge had been inserted, and time alone was required to drive it home.

There are many parallel points in the Seminole and Apache wars, among which may be distinguished the difficulty of operating presented by the natural features of the country.

In both cases it was almost impossible to get within striking distance of the hostiles. It was the ability on the part of the Indians to evade their pursuers which prolonged the Seminole War, and the Apaches possessed the same advantage, although in a very much greater degree. In the Seminole War, the force of arms and fighting accomplished little more than the destruction of the

Indian villages and their contents and the capture of women and children. After many years of costly war, negotiation succeeded where arms had failed. The same is true of the Apache campaign, except that from the first the utility of negotiation, through and by means of the Indians themselves, was recognized. As in the Seminole, so in the Apache War, the surrendered Indians were sent to a distant part of the country. In one case as in the other, the ties of friendship and love for kindred, wives, and children were the strong incentives which induced the Indians who remained out to surrender.

PART SIX

The End of
the Apache Wars

The Apache Problem

GEORGE CROOK[1]

Journal of the Military Service Institution of the United States
7 (September 1886): 257–69

Any article which treats of the present mode of warfare of the American Indians must necessarily be incomplete without a glance backward at their history. It is important at first to show the conditions which existed at the time the first European settlers established themselves on this continent.

The Indians who occupied the Atlantic Coast of America were all in a greater or lesser degree sedentary; they all lived in villages or collections of huts; all cultivated the soil and raised maize and possibly other vegetables and were experts in the chase. The almost trackless forests which then covered the eastern slope of the Appalachian range were their hunting grounds. Their arms were exclusively of their own manufacture; bows and arrows, the war club, and the lance, their implements equally of warfare and the chase. As with all other peoples they have been quick to profit by such improvements in weapons of offense as have come to their notice. It is an axiom in the military science that troops with superior weapons can always overcome mere numerical superiority.

These Indians recognized at once the inferiority of their bows and arrows to the firearms of the European colonist, and for this reason, if no other, as a rule were almost uniformly friendly in their first intercourse with the white settlers, and it was not until they became convinced that their country would soon be overrun by the new race that they ventured, as a last resort, to engage in hostilities. These early wars were bloody but of short duration. The ever pressing forward of the white men made it necessary that the red man should be driven back. One tribe was beaten, often annihilated, and at once their lands were taken and occupied by the victors, and again and again the operation was repeated. Each year found the frontier advanced, and the Indians, or the remnant which remained, as a rule became vagabonds and lingered among the white settlers. They learned easily the vices of the white man but not his virtues.

That, in brief, is the history of the Indian race east of the Mississippi. Their lands were arable, and the constantly increasing tide of settlers occupied them with irresistible force. Several attempts were made by means of formidable confederacies to stem the tide, but though great loss of life was often inflicted on the colonists, the result was inevitable; civilization always conquers barbarism, and it is a sad commentary on civilization to think that a few scattered remnants are all that now remains of the Indian race who peopled the vast territory east of the Missouri 250 years ago.

The red race, driven from the fertile forest and prairie country which, until within a few years, has been deemed the only region suitable for agriculture, found for many years a secure roaming place west of the Missouri. Their lands were not coveted because their capabilities for cultivation of the cereals were not understood. The forced movement westward, however, had its natural effect upon the Indians. Those dispossessed of their hunting grounds east of the great river either drove the Indians still farther toward the occident or were in the clash of tribes annihilated, or in some instances assimilated with the stronger band. The Sioux, under their various names, were unquestionably the strongest of all the tribes between the Mississippi and the Missouri; and when it became necessary for them to cross the Missouri, we find that the tribes occupying the valleys of the Platte and of the tributary streams farther to the north suffered from their incursions, until but fragments remain of the powerful tribes, such as the Omahas, the Poncas, the Mandans, Arickarees, etc., who had lived, perhaps for centuries, on the lands which were now needed by their enemies the Sioux. It is probable up to this time [that] the Sioux were sedentary Indians and, in common with most of the tribes east of the Missouri, raised corn and some kinds of vegetables; but when dispossessed of their homes they became pure nomads and lived almost exclusively on flesh. The buffaloes which roamed in immense herds over the whole of the region they had seized furnished them food, and their skins, shelter.

From this time forward until the discovery of gold in California, their only intercourse with the dominant race was with trappers and traders, with which they lived on friendly terms; the occasional conflicts of detached bands with trapping parties of whites were probably due more to the jealousy of rival trading companies than to any hostility of the Indians against the white intruders.

Their habits of warfare continued practically the same; the treeless plains offering no inducement to settled homes; they followed the buffalo in its migration; they did not attempt to build defensive works, and their warlike operations were always offensive. They depended on sudden surprises, and if their attack failed, as a rule they disappeared as rapidly as they assembled. Their weapons, though they steadily and perseveringly sought to obtain firearms and did obtain many, though of inferior quality, mainly remained such as they could manufacture themselves. The stone or obsidian arrowhead and lance point gave place to those made of iron, but they were still conscious of their inferiority in this respect to the white man.

The rush overland to California following the discovery of gold, while it undoubtedly led to much bloodshed, did not materially change the friendly relations between the Indians of the Great Plains and the whites, and it was not until the tide of immigration following the building of the transcontinental rail-road began to press them from their hunting grounds, and the rapidly dimin-ishing numbers of buffalo endangered their food supply, that they again concluded to measure their strength with the invaders. Their vast superiority in numbers for a time succeeded in setting at defiance the power of the govern-ment, and a treaty was made with them, setting aside a reservation for their use stretching from the Missouri to the Rocky Mountains and causing the aban-donment of several military posts.

In the meantime the invention of breech-loading firearms has made a momentous change in the whole system of military operations, and while it added for a time uncalculated strength to troops, in the course of a few years to a still greater degree added to the difficulties encountered in savage warfare. The muzzle-loading firearms were scarcely more to be feared in the hands of Indians than the bow and arrow, since they could not be used to advantage on horseback. But when the Indians began to get breech-loading arms and the fixed ammunition, their tactics and whole system of warfare were changed. Instead of attacks like a whirlwind upon detached parties, they changed their methods and in secure retreats awaited onsets. From an offensive warfare exclusively, they adopted a system of offensive-defensive operations. The result was manifested in the fight on the Little Big Horn, in which General Custer was killed and the greater portion of his command of Regular soldiers annihilated. The advantages resulting to the Indians of the Great Plains from the possession of the new arms and ammunition were lessened by the fact that they had large herds which, owing to the physical condition of the country, could be followed and captured, leaving them on foot; being essentially mounted Indians, they were at the mercy of their pursuers when dismounted. Then, too, the intense cold of northern winters compelled the Indians to go into camps for shelter, and these camps could be located and attacked by troops, as instanced by the surprise of the Piegans in Montana, the Sioux under Crazy Horse in Dakota, and the Cheyennes under Roman Nose in Wyoming.

But though all these various conditions and the successful attacks upon them must have convinced the Indians of the ultimate superiority of the white man, there was no disposition shown to abandon the struggle, and it became apparent to thinking soldiers that other means must be sought to secure the pacification of the formidable tribes, such as the Sioux, Cheyennes, and Ara-pahoes. This end was attained by enlisting Indians as soldiers, or rather, to be more precise, as scouts. Large numbers were armed and organized under intel-ligent, active, and brave officers. The Indians, finding that their own people were being used against them, gave up the fight, as they knew that the result was inevitable, and today the whole of those powerful tribes are quiet and will probably remain so unless driven again upon the warpath by the greed of the white man. The danger from this source may be instanced from the threatening demeanor of the Cheyennes and Arapahoes during the past summer, the outbreak of which tribes was probably prevented by the wise and skillful adjustment of their grievances.

The mode of warfare of the Indians occupying the western slope of the Rocky Mountains is in many respects as dissimilar from that of their brothers living on the plains to the east of the continental divide as in the physical character of the country in which they live. In a paper of this nature it is hardly necessary to consider the fish-eating Indians of the Columbia, as their numbers and present condition practically preclude the possibility of their ever becoming a source of trouble to the government, so far as warlike operations are concerned, and the limits of this article will not admit even a passing reference to the Bannocks, Shoshones, and their southern cousins, the Utes, the more especially as the prominent characteristics of the mountain Indians, as compared with the Indians of the Plains, are exhibited in a greater degree in the Apaches, who are today the representative Indians of America, so far as ferocity, courage, cunning, and skill in savage warfare are concerned.

The country these Indians occupy, and which in event of hostilities is subject to their raids, consists of the territories of Arizona and New Mexico, northwestern Texas, and the states of Chihuahua and Sonora in Mexico. At times their raids have been extended to the states of Durango and Sinoloa, and as far to the west as the Pacific Ocean.

It is the roughest portion of the continent, and it is impossible for persons not acquainted with it from personal inspection to form any correct idea of its rugged mountains and arid plains. The character of these Indians is such as might be expected under such surroundings. The constant struggle with adverse conditions, with hunger, with exposure to extremes of heat and cold, and to danger of every kind kills in infancy the weak and sickly children; only the strong, perfectly developed child survives. Consequently, the adult Apache is the embodiment of physical endurance—lean, well proportioned, medium-sized, with sinews like steel; insensible to hunger, fatigue, or physical pains, the Apache warrior resembles as little the well-fed Indians of the eastern reservations as does the hungry wolf the sleek house dog.

Greatly as the invention of breech-loading arms and fixed ammunition has changed the nature of war with all Indian tribes, with the Apaches it has added to the difficulties to be contended against and overcome to an almost incredible extent. Each individual represents, in his own personality, the effect of generations of warfare and bloodshed. His own nature differs but little from the wolf or coyote, and from his earliest infancy he has been accustomed to defend himself against enemies as cruel and revengeful as his own nature. They are no longer our inferiors in equipment. Their weapons of even ten years ago have given place to the best arms of the best makers. Like the coyote, he is perfectly at home anywhere in the immense country over which he roams, and which affords him all the sustenance he requires. Even in his rapid flights he gets a rabbit here or a rat there, and this, with the wild roots and the mescal, gives him all the food he needs. It is, therefore, unnecessary for him to carry provi-

An ambuscade. HARPER'S NEW MONTHLY MAGAZINE, APRIL 1890.

sions. They have no property which they cannot carry on their backs in their most rapid marches; nor have they, when on the warpath, any settled habitations of any kind, and their temporary resting places are chosen with the instinct resulting from the experience of generations.

The Apache can endure fatigue and fasting and can live without water for periods that would kill the hardiest mountaineer. Everything he has ever received from the white man is a luxury which he can do without, as he has done from time immemorial.

From these preliminaries an idea can be formed of the labors and dangers to be encountered in fighting the Apaches, and yet it is only by actual experience that these difficulties can be appreciated. In fighting them we must of necessity be the pursuers, and unless we can surprise them by sudden and unexpected attack, the advantage is all in their favor. In Indian combats it must be remembered that you rarely see an Indian; you see the puff of smoke and hear the whiz of his bullets, but the Indian is thoroughly hidden in the rocks, and even his exact hiding place can only be conjectured. The soldier, on the contrary, must expose himself, and exposure is fatal. A dozen Indians in the rocks can withstand the onset of a battalion of soldiers, and though they can be driven from their position at the cost of many lives in the attacking party, it only results in their attaining another position equally as strong as the first, or in their scattering like quail in the rocks, to appear at some point miles away, in front, on either flank, or in the rear, as may seem to them desirable.

The Apaches only fight with Regulars when they choose and when the advantages are all on their side. If pursued to their rocky strongholds, they send their families to some other point beyond the immediate reach of danger, while the bucks absolutely without impediments swarm your column, avoid or attack as their interests dictate, dispute every foot of your advance, harass your rear, and surround you on all sides. Under such conditions Regular troops are as helpless as a whale attacked by a school of swordfish. The tendency of military drill and discipline is to make the individual soldier a machine, dependent upon the officer in command for its movement and action, and upon cohesion with its fellow machines for its efficiency. His individuality is completely lost in his organization, and he therefore cannot compete on equal terms with an enemy whose individuality under all circumstances is perfect. In operating against them, the only hope of success lies in using their own methods, and with the above facts in view, it must be evident that to successfully operate against them, a partial tribal disintegration must take place, and that a portion of the tribe must be arrayed against the other. Acting upon this principle was due the success attending operations against them in 1872 and 1873, which resulted in placing over five thousand of them on the White Mountain reservation. The application of the same methods settled the Sioux troubles in 1876–1877.

In this connection it may not be amiss to describe the measures which I first employed in making this valuable auxiliary force useful in Indian campaigns. The first difficulty was in overcoming the prejudices of army officers to commands of this character and securing men properly qualified for such duty. The officers secured, I selected Indians for enlistment. There are negative characters among Indians as among white men, and the nearer an Indian approaches to the savage state, the more likely he will prove valuable as a soldier. I therefore selected, preferably, the wildest that I could get. They were organized in companies of conventional size. To give the scouts confidence, positive orders were given that they should only be used to discover the locations of the hostile rancherias, and when discovered, such dispositions should be made that under no circumstances should any of the scouts be injured in the fight. Within a short period the scouts became so encouraged that their efficiency was greatly improved, and at times they suffered severe loss without demoralization.

In organizing Indian scouts, too much attention cannot be given to the selection of the officers who are to command. The American Indian cares very little about our idea of rank. Efficiency, and efficiency only, is what he looks for in the man who is to lead him on the warpath. Their leaders necessarily have to be of the best physique, in robust health, capable of enduring great fatigue, of undisputed courage, of great patience, good judgment, and discretion. The commanders of Indian scouts have therefore, as a rule, been selected from the younger officers, whose health is still unimpaired and whose ambition is a guiding motive, rather than from officers of more experience, upon whose vigor and energy the effects of long service have begun to tell.

The scouts are not mounted. The Apache is a foot Indian, capable of making from forty to sixty miles a day in this rough, mountainous country. Horses would be useless, as it would be impossible to keep them in remounts on such service. Supplies cannot be carried, except by pack trains. The organization and management of these is a matter to which too much care and thought cannot be given.

No opinion can be more fallacious or dangerous than the idea which seemed to have obtained with some officers that the pack train is merely a secondary consideration, something which can be beaten and hammered along the trail "by the labor troops." An efficient pack train is, next to Indian scouts, an important adjunct in this warfare. To detail soldiers to manage it entails upon them extra labor of the severest kind and duties of which some of them at least must be ignorant. As a consequence, the animals suffer and become sore and worn out. An experience of more than thirty years convinces me that a pack train can only be efficient when composed of mules expressly selected and used solely for that purpose. The packers should be civilians, hired and paid liberally as such.

In further explanation of the method of Apache warfare, I cannot do better than refer to an incident of the present operations against the Chiricahua Indians. Early in November a party of eleven hostile Chiricahuas crossed the border and went up into New Mexico.[2] At that time every point along the line which afforded sufficient water for a troop of cavalry was guarded, and the country between was constantly patrolled. The Chiricahuas, finding that their water holes were guarded, changed their usual tactics and, avoiding them, made their passage in the most difficult point of the mountains. They are not dependent upon the water holes for water but can go one hundred miles without halting, carrying such water as they need for themselves in the entrails of cattle or horses killed by the way, and abandoning such animals they ride when these drop, exhausted by thirst or fatigue.

The soldiers in pursuit have each but one horse. When any of their horses or pack mules give out from any cause, the command is not only weakened by such loss, but extra work is imposed upon the poor beasts which are still able to stagger on their feet.

The Chiricahuas secured a remount at ranches on their route and at the end of a march of one hundred miles were possibly in possession of fresher and better animals than when they started. They push across the valleys by night and remain hidden by day in the rocky places and high points of the mountains, from which they can watch the surrounding country, note the approach of pursuers, and lie in ambush for them or scatter like coyotes, to come together again at a place known only to themselves. No human wisdom or foresight can predict exactly where that is to be; it may be in the original direction of their line of march, on one or both flanks, or they may whip around [and] appear far in the rear of their pursuers.

To follow them, only one thing can be done—the trail must be stuck to and never lost, if possible. The Apaches may retard pursuit or baffle it completely in either one of the ways indicated, and it has happened during the present campaign that our faithful Apache scouts have slowly and patiently led the troops for twenty miles over rocky stretches, where a white man could not detect the faintest indication of a trail until, upon reaching more favorable ground, the unerring sagacity of the scouts was attested.

The country contains many rough places where a dozen men, armed as the Chiricahuas are with breech-loading guns, could hold a brigade in check. In approaching these the commander of a detachment of troops has to choose between taking the precautions necessary to guard against the surprise and probable destruction of his men, which will make his own progress slow and give the hostiles so much greater advantage in time and distance, or he must assume the risk, with all its consequences. When night comes the command must halt and wait for the coming of dawn to enable it to resume the pursuit; in the meantime, the raiders have put miles between them and the soldiers.

This was the state of the case with the band of raiders here spoken of, as explained above. They succeeded in eluding our troops and passing the line; but word of their incoming was telegraphed to all points, and detachments were pushed out to intercept or follow them. Troops in front were placed in ambush at every available point which it was thought possibly might be in the line of route. Every conceivable effort was made and artifice employed which an experience of a generation of Indian wars could suggest. They were very closely pursued, but having no impediments of any kind, they dashed through comparatively well-settled districts, murdering and plundering with grim impartiality citizens, soldiers, and friendly Indians. Their very feebleness of numbers made them all the more dangerous, as it rendered it so much the more difficult for people to know they were in any particular vicinity, until they had surrounded a ranch or ambushed some unwary traveler.

The pursuit was never relaxed, and at all times parties were on the trail or moving to intercept them. But, although the party was so closely followed that twice they were compelled to abandon their horses and plunder and take to the rocks on foot, and in their next flight left no more trail than so many birds, they finally crossed back into Mexico with no loss that can be positively stated, beyond one of their numbers killed by the friendly Apaches near Fort Apache.[3]

For months the statement has been industriously disseminated by interested parties that the Apache scouts were untrustworthy, that they had mutinied, and everything of that kind. But in none of these reports is there a spark of truth. The Apache scouts, for this class of warfare, are as worthy of trust as any soldiers in the world, and in all the experience I have had with them, they have proved themselves energetic, reliable, truthful, and honest.

It has now, no doubt, been made sufficiently clear how and why the savages of the rocky, barren mountains of the Pacific Coast region have been such a thorn in the side of civilization; that while their fellows of the Atlantic Coast and Missouri valley were no doubt vastly richer, yet these very riches placed them at a disadvantage, as they had to move slowly to protect their herds, which always left great trails, easily followed, and in the winter their camp had to have some permanency to keep horses and families from freezing to death and were, therefore, located on the bank of some stream which would afford shelter and food for their animals.

The Apache has had the climate even in his favor and has never been obliged to go into camp on account of the severity of the seasons. He has absolutely no impediments of any kind, having no baggage that he cannot pack about on his back and no horses so dear to him that he would not rather eat them than not; no enemy so alert that signal smokes will not announce his coming the moment he approaches the mountains. After that the Apaches fight or not as they please; but if they fight, it is always on ground of their own choosing and with every point in their favor.

Such were the Apaches, and such the condition of their country when first I assumed command of Arizona in 1871. With many misgivings I set about the attempt of reducing them to peace and quiet. At first the task seemed hopeless. The Apaches were cut up in small bands, each independent of its neighbors and united only in slender bonds of language, and of hatred and contempt of the whites.

It was necessary for me to go from band to band, from man to man, in the hope of being able to distinguish the good from the bad, the reclaimable from the depraved and treacherous.

I saw that the keynote of the problem lay in my success or failure to win to my side the boldest, most daring, most savage of all the young chiefs. These men are the high-mettled horses of the herd, the born leaders who, if once curbed and broken, help in the management of the negative spirits in all communities.

The Apaches had such a deep-seated distrust of all Americans that four points of policy at once obtruded themselves. First, to make them no promises that could not be fulfilled. Second, to tell them the exact truth at all times. Third, to keep them at labor and to find remuneration for that labor. Fourth, to be patient, to be just, and to fear not.

The greatest of these was the question of compensated labor. No sermon on the dignity of labor could prove so eloquent an appeal to the dormant better nature of the Apaches as the disclosure of the fact that one hundred pounds of hay was worth $1.00 at the quartermaster's corral. To show him that the labor of his squaws and children was worth money was soon followed by the teaching that more money could be made if he added his labor to theirs. At large posts like Camp Apache there is a steady demand for every pound of hay the Apaches can put in, but there is also a cry for fuel for the troops and grain for the horses. We are taking the Apache by the hand and quietly teaching him the use of the axe and the plow. He is receiving his first money earned by the honest sweat of his brow. What shall he do with it? "Put it into cattle; they graze on your hillsides and grow in value while you sleep."

The Apache is becoming a property owner. It is property won by his own toil, and he thrills at once with the pride of acquisition and the anxiety of possession. He is changing both inside and out; exteriorly, he is dressed in the white man's garb, wholly or in part; he hasn't so much time for gaudy ornamentation and indulges less in beads, feathers, and paint. Mentally, he is counting the probable value of his steers and interested in knowing how much of his corn crop the quartermaster may want next month.

He is receiving his education. Education is progress. Progress and vagabondage cannot exist in the same village. The Apache who owns ten or a dozen cows becomes a man of power; his opinions are heard with respect, and his decisions sought in the disputes of his neighbors. He sees that he has gained an influence greater than that of warriors or medicine men, and it is gratifying to know that his prosperity, instead of exciting envy, has encouraged emulation.

In this sketch I have tried to make clear the guiding principles by which the Apaches have been pursued in war and handled in peace; in both I can truthfully claim some experience, and with equal truth I can assert that the greed and rapacity of the vultures who fatten on Indian wars have been a greater obstruction in the path of civilization than the ferocity of the wildest savages who have fought them.

Man is at all times the creature of his surroundings. Place in the cultivated circles of the older states, no matter what may be his color or race, his nature becomes softened and refined, the angles are rounded, his manner and language become gentle and polished. Place him on the desert or the mountaintop, force him to struggle with the elements, to contend for existence with the wild animals which surround him, and he degenerates rapidly into an equality with these animals. Like them, he develops keenness of vision, sharpness of hearing, stealthiness of tread. He learns to bear without complaint hunger, thirst, fatigue. Excessive heat is familiar to him and extorts no more complaint than does the excessive cold which follows it. To cross over steep, rocky mountains, to swim swift rivers, are incidents merely in a career which is a never-ceasing struggle for the preservation of the dubious boon of life. It is in such a struggle that we should look for the survival of the fittest, and it is in just such a struggle we find it—acuteness of sense, perfect physical condition, absolute knowledge of locality, almost absolute ability to preserve oneself from danger, let it come from what source it may.

We have before us the tiger of the human species. To no tribe in America can these remarks apply with more force than to the Apaches of Arizona. To see them as they first appeared to the white man—half clad, half fed, covered with vermin, with no semblance of property beyond the rude arms with which they doggedly waged war against unpitying nature—it was easy to believe, and many Americans did believe, that nothing could be more easily affected than their extermination or subjection. It has taken the expenditure of countless treasure and blood to demonstrated that these naked Indians were the most thoroughly individualized soldiers on the globe; that each was an army in himself, waiting for orders from no superiors—thoroughly confident in his own judgment and never at a loss to know when to attack or when to retreat.

The Apache can be compared most aptly to the wild animal he fittingly calls his cousin—the coyote. The civilized settlements are his sheepfolds, and even supposing that a toilsome campaign results in destroying forty out of a band of fifty, the survivors are as much to be dreaded as ever, until the very last one can be run down, killed, or got under control and taught to labor for his bread.

In one brief sentence I may embody the idea that man is more or less savage according to the certainty with which his food may be obtained and that, all things being equal, the difficulty of subjecting any given race or people will be in the inverse ration of its food supply. Those tribes which have the largest accumulations of food and clothing will in nearly every case fight desperately for the preservation of their villages; but those villages once destroyed, their power is broken, and they soon sue for peace.

But where man raises no harvests, dries no fish, preserves no meat, lives simply from hand to mouth, the trouble in effecting his capture becomes immeasurably greater, and after he has been provided with improved breechloaders, he is transformed into a foe of the most dangerous character within human knowledge.

The Indian Question in Arizona

ROBERT K. EVANS[1]

The Atlantic Monthly 58 (August 1886): 167–76

In the last five years, the raiding parties of the Apaches in southern Arizona have been so active and constant in their work of murder and pillage that there has been no security for either life or property outside of the few towns. In that time more than one thousand citizens have been murdered, with all the accompanying barbarities of savage warfare, and an immense amount of property has been stolen or destroyed. Meanwhile, all industries in this region—trade, grazing, mining, and agriculture—have suffered partial or total paralysis. The government seems powerless to protect its citizens or to maintain its peace and dignity against these outrages.

The press has been loud in its comments on the subject, but these do not usually go beyond the statement of the murders and depredations which have been committed, with an occasional aspersion on the efficiency of the Regular army. They do not attempt to trace the causes of the evil, or to suggest a remedy for it, further than to express the simple opinion that the army should catch and kill the Indians who may chance at the time to be on the warpath.

The parties engaged in this bloody tragedy, which is being perpetually enacted, may be divided into four general classes: the Indian, the frontiersman, the army, and the government.

The Indian is no exception to the general law of cause and effect. That he is a murderer and a bandit can surprise no one who will reflect on what has been his treatment for the last twenty years.

In 1871, in order to open certain parts of Arizona to civilized occupation, about eight thousand Indians were placed on the San Carlos reservation, a region one hundred miles square. The agency is situated on the Gila River, in a low, hot, dirty, unhealthful spot. Some of the tribes now forced to dwell there were mountain Indians. In their native haunts they enjoyed one of the most delightful climates in the world. At San Carlos they endure one of the most abominable. There they suffer from long and extreme heat, bad water, fever and ague, and ophthalmia. They must appear at the agency on the weekly ration day. If they stay away, they get no rations. In going through the camps of the Chiricahuas and Warm Springs, I have been struck by the misery of their condition. It is these mountain Indians who have caused the most serious trouble. So far as I know, no successful effort has ever been made to instruct or assist them in agriculture. The government feeds them, and the agents have not, as a rule, considered it the policy of their craft to make the Indians self-supporting. The game in that locality is nearly exhausted, so his occupation as a hunter is gone. There he exists, in a hot, sandy camp, on the banks of a low, sickly stream, without amusement, without hope, with no incentive to any good or useful labor.

But he has one agreeable relaxation from his wretched imprisonment on the reservation, that of raiding the surrounding ranches. These raids are to him the most delightful diversion conceivable. The pleasure of killing and plundering, with the very slight risk of capture and punishment, renders this the ideal pastime in the Indian's estimation.

Let us imagine a few young bucks, utterly tired of their dreary camp life on the Gila. They talk over their position and organize a raiding party. They easily supply themselves with arms and ammunition, which most frontier tradesmen will sell them in any quantity. They tell their chiefs that they are going out; or if he chance to disapprove of such expeditions, they say that they are going on a hunt to the northern part of the reservation, about Camp Apache and Mount Ord. Then, having determined the first ranch to be attacked, they quietly leave their camp and move by easy marches on the doomed family. They reach the place. One or two creep forward and carefully reconnoiter. All the party assume their positions in the rocks or grass and patiently wait until they can take the family at the greatest disadvantage. For, though devoted to the sport of killing others, the Apaches are very much opposed to taking the slightest chances against their own lives. The looked-for opportunity arrives, and they spring from their concealment. They kill every human being about the place, unless they can manage, with perfect safety to themselves, to capture some of the ranchmen alive, in which case they will have the opportunity of enjoying an Indian's favorite amusement—that of watching a white man die by slow degrees under the most inhuman tortures which savage ingenuity can invent. This entertainment completed, they help themselves to whatever pleases their fancy in the house and then set it on fire. Finally, they collect all the horses and, mounting the best, drive the others before them.

The ball is now open. They will move with great rapidity and will promptly agree on the destruction of another ranch, one hundred miles or more distant. Away they go, now galloping, now trotting, and subsiding into a walk only when the trail is very steep and rough. During this rapid march, they show great skill in keeping the loose horses ahead of them on the trail. An Indian can ride a tired horse from ten to twenty miles farther than can a white man. When a horse is entirely exhausted, his rider calmly dismounts and proceeds to kill him, usually by stabbing him many times with a long knife. It is very seldom that he will waste a precious cartridge on such an occasion, but under no circumstances will he leave a living horse behind him.

Now, if the party be in the humor for a meal, they build a small fire, cut slices from the dead horse, cook them a little, and eat their fill. Thus in the stolen horse is combined both the means of transportation and the commissary. In this, the Indian possesses a vast advantage over his soldier pursuer, who must ride one horse through an entire campaign, and whose rations and spare ammunition must be carried with him on pack mules. In this way the raiding party can easily cover one hundred miles in twenty-four hours, while a company of cavalry, with its indispensable pack train, can with difficulty accomplish more than thirty in that rough, roadless country.

With the second ranch, the program of the first is repeated. The Indians murder the inhabitants, plunder and burn the house, and drive off the horses.

After this, the party may be seized with a desire to witness the effect of their escapade on the neighboring military posts. If so, they climb to some commanding elevation on Mount Graham, or about Helen's Dome.[2] From this vantage ground they can survey the surrounding country for a long distance, and their practiced eye can easily detect, by the clouds of dust in the valleys, the approach of a column of troops twenty or thirty miles away. If they can see several of these columns on the march, they enjoy all the delights of a successful practical joker, for they are confident of their own safety and have the satisfaction of knowing that they have put into the field several hundred troops.

If their appetite for murder and plunder is still unsatisfied, they may go into Old Mexico and continue their tactics of rapid transit, ambuscade, and pillage. But it is probable that they will now be content with the results of the expedition. They will break up the loose organization of the party and, traveling singly by night, individually make their retreat to the camp on the Gila.

The return of an Indian from such an expedition is a proud day in his life. He is a hero, he is a rich man. He has several good horses and money, clothes, arms, and ammunition. He enjoys the approval of the old men of his tribe, the envy of the young ones who stayed in camp, and the boundless admiration of all the squaws. On the next ration day, he presents himself at the agency and calmly resumes the enjoyment of the bounties of the government. If he has been missed—which is not probable—and is asked to give an account of himself, he says that he has been hunting on the reservation, or that he has been looking for some ponies which had strayed away from his camp. Every Indian in his tribe would sooner die than utter a syllable to throw a ray of light on the case.

Here you have the picture of the Apache, his home life, and his amusements. He is born a warrior and a robber. Before the white man became his neighbor and his prey, he exercised his bloody proclivities on the surrounding Indian tribes. There is no law to punish him, even could his crimes find him out, for he is a citizen or subject of a nation with whom our government has entertained treaty relations, and the acknowledgment of the treaty-making power has always been held to be the most complete admission of the autonomy of a people. He is supposed to live under the restraints of tribal law. But what is the tribal law? The Apache code will occupy but a few lines. Here it is:

Theft committed in the tribe is punished promptly and often severely.

Murder in the tribe is a personal affair, to be settled by the payment of an indemnity or by retaliation.

All crimes successfully committed against persons and property of individuals outside of the tribe are commendable achievements. The Chiricahua, for instance, who kills and robs a white man, or an Indian of another tribe, is looked upon by his people very much as we regard a hunter who kills a deer, eats his flesh, and takes his skin—merely as a successful sportsman.

There, among the people of Arizona, dwelling about their ranches, their farms, and their mines, our government quarters, feeds, and looses this outlaw, who is swift as the eagle, cruel as the hungry wolf, and who, "Fierce in a tyrannous freedom, knows but the law of his moods."

The frontiersman who settles in Arizona or New Mexico belongs to one of two classes. Either he is a poor man, who goes West to conquer a home from the vast and unoccupied public domain; or he is a rich man, taking his capital to new fields, where it will be more remunerative than in the already crowded industries of the East. In either case, if he succeeds in creating tax-paying property from what was formerly unproductive waste, he is a public servant and benefactor. He has accepted the invitation of the government to make his home on the public domain. He has complied with all the forms of law. He is putting forth his labor, his enterprise, his capital to increase the national wealth, and the government is under the most sacred obligation to exhaust all its wisdom and power to ensure him perfect security for life and property. That the richest and most numerous civilized nation under the sun is unable to afford its citizens absolute protection from the murderous incursions of a few hundred savages is a proposition too absurd to deserve a moment's consideration.

When the frontiersman year after year sees his neighbors, his friends, his relations fall an easy prey to the unrestrained Apaches, and when he sees no laws enacted, no adequate means devised, to protect them, he has a right to consider that the government has utterly failed in its obligations to him. Not only has it failed to protect him, but it has actually placed his enemy in a city of refuge in easy striking distance of his home and family, and is further responsible for a system which enables that enemy to prey upon him with almost complete immunity from punishment.

In May 1882 I followed the trail of an Apache war party from near San Carlos to San Simon, New Mexico, and counted forty-two men, women, and children murdered in mere savage caprice and, when time and opportunity permitted, murdered with accompanying barbarities which curdle the blood and sicken the heart.

It is clearly the imperative and immediate duty of Congress to devise some effectual means of protecting the frontier citizens and restraining the Indians. In default of an Indian code vigorously enforced, the Apache in his present condition must be exterminated. Let every man judge for himself which horn of the dilemma is humanity and which is barbarism.

The army represents the strong arm of the government for controlling the Indian and protecting the frontiersman. How inadequate are the means to the end is conclusively shown by the fact that on the warpath, the relative speed of the Indian and the soldier is three to one. This is no aspersion on the efficiency of our cavalry. They are ready and willing to do all that brave men can do, but the task imposed upon them is simply impossible. I do not believe that there is a body of cavalry in the world that can keep in sight of a raiding party of Apaches after they have plundered a few ranches and provided themselves with several spare horses to the man.

The treatment of the army by the government in Indian affairs is both discouraging and unjust. Let us assume for the moment that the various Indian tribes are really nations, possessing treaty power—the power to declare war and to make peace. One of these nations makes war on the United States. Both powers put their forces into the field. The Indians utterly disregard all the laws of civilized warfare. There is no such thing as an exchange of prisoners. If a wounded soldier falls into their hands, he is invariably put to death after being subjected to the most cruel and savage tortures which it is possible to invent— and the originality and ingenuity of the Indian in this respect is vast and varied. In short, they fight under the black flag.

Now, one of the most firmly established rules of international law is that known as the *lex talionis*, the law of retaliation. This principle, applied to the treatment of prisoners, demands that they be treated with like consideration by both contending parties. If your enemy murders his prisoners, as a simple act of self-defense you are bound to retaliate by putting to death an equal number of your prisoners. To fail to do this is not only encouraging him in his atrocities, but it is an injustice to the men whom you send to fight him.

The Indian invariably makes a rigorous application of this law in his wars with other tribes, and he fully appreciates the great advantage which he possesses over an enemy who persistently declines to apply it to his own protection. I have talked with several Apaches on the subject, and they have expressed surprise, not unmixed with contempt, at our policy of nonretaliation.

Now let us look at the position of the soldier in his relations with the hostile Indian.

Every officer of the army, before he receives his commission, is supposed to be instructed in international law and the laws of war. He makes the acquaintance of the lex talionis and reads General Orders No. 100 of 1863, being the rules for the government of the armies of the United States in the field, compiled by Francis Lieber, LL.D., a manual still in force with us, and which is considered so able a treatise on the subject that it has been translated and adopted by nearly every civilized nation. Note the following extracts from General Orders No. 100:

Article 27. The law of war can no more wholly dispense with retaliation than can the law of nations, of which it is a branch. Yet civilized nations regard retaliation as the sternest feature of war. A reckless enemy often leaves his opponent no other means of securing himself against the repetition of barbarous outrage.

Article 59. All prisoners of war are liable to the infliction of retaliatory measures.

Article 62. All troops of the enemy, known or discovered to give no quarter in general or to any portion of the army, receive none.

After learning his lesson from books, the young officer passes his examination, receives his appointment, and is assigned to a regiment in the West. Let us suppose that in the course of time, he is ordered to take part in an expedition against hostile Indians. In following the trail of the war party, he sees burned ranches and the mutilated corpses of men, women, and children. During the campaign there is a brush with the enemy. The advance guard comes upon them strongly posted among the rocks. A skirmish line is deployed, and their position attacked. During the encounter several soldiers are wounded, and that part of the line, being hotly pressed, gives way before reinforcements can come up. The Indians rush down and carry off the wounded men. Meanwhile, the whole command has come up and been deployed for action. The Indians beat a hasty retreat, and night stops the pursuit.

The next day the young lieutenant comes upon the remains of the captured men. They have been staked out upon their backs, and hundreds of small pieces of wood, sharpened at one end, have been stuck into their flesh. The bits of wood have then been lighted and allowed to burn until they have extinguished themselves in the victims' blood. The charred bodies are buried, and the command moves on.

At last, after hundreds of miles of marching, some of the Indians are captured. They are brought into camp and turned over to the commanding officer.

Now, thinks the young officer, if ever there was an occasion that justified the prompt application of the lex talionis, and Articles 27, 59, and 62 of General Orders No. 100, it is here. In breathless interest he approaches the commanding officer, who sends for the officer of the day, who comes up and salutes. The commander says, "Sir, you will take charge of these prisoners and place over them a strong guard in the center of the camp. First, you will take every precaution to prevent their escape; second, you will see that none of the guides, scouts, or frontiersmen with the command approach within one hundred paces of them, for some of these men have had friends and relations killed by these very Indians, and I fear that the sight of the murderers of their people may so inflame their grief and resentment that they will attempt to kill them while in my keeping. This I am determined to prevent. You will notify the command that any person offering violence to the prisoners will be promptly and severely punished. That is all, sir."

The young officer is immensely surprised at these instructions. He had expected to bear the order for the execution of the prisoners. He had even gone so far as to make surmises on the probability of his having command of the firing party. But when he hears careful directions given for their safe preservation, his astonishment is so great that he even ventures to interrogate his commanding officer on the subject.

"Sir," he says, "will not these prisoners be either hanged or shot, in retaliation for the atrocities which they have committed on citizens and prisoners?"

The commanding officer turns and regards in silence his interrogator for some seconds, while his surprise at the question and the earnest manner of him who puts it gives way to an appreciation of the fact that this is the youngest lieutenant in the regiment; that it is his first campaign; that he is fresh from theories, books, and orders; that he knows little of the practical methods of handling the Indian question on the frontier; and that he does not yet appreciate the difference that often exists between the national statutes and the national practice. Then he says, gravely and kindly, "Young man, I would rather go through a dozen Indian fights than kill one of those prisoners."

"But, sir," says the lieutenant, "of what force, then, are the lex talionis, and Articles . . ."

"I know all that," interrupts the commanding officer. "They are in the books, but the sentiment of the East will not stand it. If I should retaliate on these prisoners, I should expect to be ignominiously relieved from my command and perhaps never get another. I should in all probability be either court-martialed or investigated by a committee of Congress. The eastern press would denounce me as an assassin and a monster of cruelty. I am now a major, after twenty-five years of hard service in the late war and on the frontier. In a short time I expect my promotion as lieutenant colonel. But if I followed your very just and natural suggestions I should be so reviled by the press that my confirmation by the Senate would probably be contested and defeated, and my career would be blasted in the profession to which I have devoted my life. An officer must regard the dominant prejudices of the day as well as the laws of war and general orders. We serve in the people's army, and we must be careful of their feelings. I might tell you more than one incident in the lives of officers whom I have known, who have acted in the manner indicated by the international code and the orders you quote with just such a result—an interrupted career, popular indignation, obloquy."

After vouchsafing this explanation, the older officer turns away, leaving the lieutenant to reflect on the intricacies of the profession of arms and the complicated nature of the Indian problem, both of which he had considered as very simple and entirely mastered by himself, when he joined his regiment six months ago.

The main body of the hostiles soon dissolves into small parties, which, scattering in the mountains, leave behind such slight trails that pursuit is impracticable. The command of soldiers then breaks up, and the various companies return to their garrisons. Our young officer watches with interest the fate of the prisoners. They are sent to the nearest post, where they are kept under guard, each receiving the daily ration of a soldier. Finally, they are formally turned over to their agent. Just what he does with them is a mystery. Probably he administers a severe lecture. Possibly he grants them pardon and absolution. At all events, they are soon at liberty on the reservation, enjoying the pleasures of camp life and government rations, and receiving the same treatment as the Indians who have spent the summer peacefully at home.

Perhaps some readers will say that this is merely a romance. But every incident in my hypothetical case has been repeatedly true in the lives of many officers now in the service. Indeed, most of it is my own experience in the campaign against the Bannocks in 1878.

The experience of the civilized world shows conclusively that in extreme cases capital punishment is a just, necessary, and eventually a humane expedient. It acts as a protection to the good and as a restraint upon the bad members of society. On the same principle, any reflecting person will appreciate how terribly our system of dealing with our wild Indians is in need of an act of Congress, or an order from the president or secretary of war, reviving and enforcing the law of retaliation in Indian wars. Such an order would have a civilizing and humanizing effect upon the Indian himself, for it would deprive him of a great temptation to indulge his savage proclivities for torturing and murdering his prisoners—the knowledge that he can do so with impunity. It is also nothing more than an act of simple justice and humanity towards our army, in its struggles with a barbarous foe, to allow it to protect itself against his nameless atrocities by taking advantage of this natural and fundamental law.

In reflecting on that lawless and bloody chaos known as our Indian policy, now existing over a large portion of our frontier, the unprejudiced observer will be struck with the fact that the government and the nation owe themselves, the Indian, and humanity a solemn debt—a debt until now almost entirely unpaid. If public sentiment has now brought sufficient pressure to bear to cause the government to really desire to abandon its long-continued practice of applying ineffectual means to solve a great problem, then it must promptly and vigorously do two things:

First, enact an Indian code, establish Indian courts, and enforce their judgments by a machinery of law especially adapted to the peculiar circumstances of the case.

Second, give the Indians land in severalty and encourage them to become self-supporting, independent farmers. If, after allowing them a fair trial, they will not work, then punish them under the Indian code as vagrants having no visible means of support.

The condition as regards laws and morals on the San Carlos reservation I can best illustrate by two incidents.

The Apaches make from fermented corn a liquor called by them *tizwin*. By a judicious use of this, after from one to two days' fasting, they can get very drunk. Tizwin is to them what whiskey is to the white man. One Sunday in

August 1882, a report was brought into Fort Apache that there was a tizwin party and fight in progress among some Indians in camp across the river from the fort. The commanding officer,[3] fearing that some of the Indian scouts belonging to the post, and hence temporarily under his jurisdiction, might be involved, ordered that the combatants should be brought to him. The guard found, lying around a blanket, strewn with cards and red and white beans, one Indian alive and unhurt, another dead, with a ball through his heart, and two more rapidly bleeding to death from several deep cuts which they had mutually dealt each other. These were the remains of an Apache tizwin and card party.

The living man was brought to the commanding officer, who asked him if he had killed a man in the camp across the river. The Indian answered that he had. The commanding officer then asked if he did not know that he had committed a great crime and that he was a bad Indian, to which he laughingly replied, "No, no. I not a bad Indian. I play cards with boy. He lose. He lose more. He no money—he no pay—he no good. So I kill him. That's all right."

The commanding officer, perceiving that the Indian was too drunk to be safely set at liberty, ordered him to be confined in the guardhouse. The next morning, after he was perfectly sober, he was released and ordered to leave the post. The commanding officer had no right to keep him in the guardhouse after he ceased to be a dangerous person by reason of his intoxication. Had he been sent to the agent at Carlos, still there would have been no law under which to proceed against him. Or had the agent delivered him over to his chief, to be punished according to tribal law, the chief would have considered a murder over cards as a purely personal matter and have taken no notice of it. So much for tribal government among the Apaches.

Again, I know an Indian named Chatto,[4] who deliberately killed his own father and received as the price of this most unnatural crime ten cartridges. Both the Indian and the crime are well known in Arizona. But there is no law to reach such cases. Perhaps Chatto's chief considered the laborer worthy of his hire. And so the matter ended in Apache ethics.

When we know the recklessness with which Indians kill each other, can we wonder at the levity with which they sometimes kill white men?

I quote the facts concerning the major crime of murder. The same deplorable state of affairs exists in regard to lesser crimes and misdemeanors. In view of this, no humane and just man can deny the immediate necessity of putting them under the restraint and protection of a code of laws. This code should be administered by a judge appointed by the president, for they are not sufficiently advanced to appreciate the jury system.

The next step is to do away with the ration system and make the Indian self-supporting. The practice of issuing rations, though seemingly charitable and humane, is in the end demoralizing and degrading to the last degree. To be self-supporting under the conditions of our civilization, he must be a farmer. To be a farmer, he must have land; to feel any security in the permanence of his condition or any hearty interest in his work, the land must belong to him.

To this it may be objected that he is not sufficiently advanced to have land in severalty. This is true. But if we wait for him to advance by nature's slow process from the condition of huntsman to that of the husbandman, he will be exterminated long before he is ready for his land.

In looking to the ultimate settlement of the Indian question, it is practically useless to set aside a reservation for a tribe. Such acts are merely temporary. We know, and the Indian knows, that the government has been, and probably will continue to be, powerless to ensure any tribe in the peaceful possession of a reservation after white settlers have once determined to take it for farms. But if the titles were in severalty, instead of tribal, as now, and could not be conveyed within the period of ninety-nine years, it is possible that each Indian might then be able to hold enough land on which to earn his living.

Look at the history of the Delawares, at peace with us since Braddock's defeat in 1755, many of them our allies in the Revolution. Yet they have been pushed across the country from Pittsburgh to the Indian Territory and, in their retreat, have had five separate reservations "solemnly secured to them forever."

Many of the Indians at San Carlos are anxious to become independent by farming. But to raise anything on their land, irrigating ditches are necessary, and to construct an irrigating ditch requires much labor and some slight knowledge of engineering. An officer who once acted as agent for a short time told me a pathetic story of a tribe—I think the Chiricahuas—who have furnished so many murders of late. They went to work, under a medicine man as engineer, to make a ditch to irrigate some land upon which to raise corn and vegetables. They worked hard for several weeks, but when their work was done, the water did not flow into the head of their ditch by three feet. Their engineer's calculations were at fault, and their labor was lost. It is probable that their disappointment at the failure of their laudable endeavor resulted in several raids on neighboring ranches. If the government gives these Indians land and encourages farming, it should also construct the irrigating ditches for them. The saving in rations would in a short time more than pay for the ditches.

So much for the peaceable Indian with his laws and his lands.

Now for a method of dealing with bad Indians.

The code which I contemplate would punish major crimes—murder, rape, arson—with death, and lesser offenses with fine and imprisonment. Leaving the limits of the reservation would for a long time have to be regarded as a serious misdemeanor. The public safety in the West imperatively demands this restriction, at least in regard to the Apaches. To make the system practicable, it would be well to introduce a feature of the French law. In France, in all prosecutions for offenses except those punishable with death or imprisonment, it is not necessary that the offender be present at his trial. He is indicted and notified that on a certain day he will be tried for a certain offense. If he sees fit to flee the country, the trial proceeds without him. The witnesses are called and testify, the case is thoroughly investigated, and finally the sentence is duly pronounced and recorded. This may strike the American mind very unfavorably;

yet if France, one of the foremost civilized nations, adopts this method of procedure in her courts, we may certainly afford to use it, at least for a time, in enforcing the laws with our criminal Indians. The judge must have ample powers to employ posses to enforce the sentences of his court; otherwise, the law will promptly fall into contempt. There is nothing which seems more despicable to the Indian than weakness or failure in any endeavor.

The law thus equipped is ready to deal with offending Apaches. When an Indian has been tried and convicted, if he is not present to receive his sentence, the judge should have authority to send in pursuit of him several posses from tribes other than that of the criminal. In cases where the sentence is death, they will be authorized to deliver the culprit dead or alive at the agency. In other cases, he must be brought in alive and no undue severity used in his arrest. It will be left to the discretion of the judge to determine in what extreme cases to employ the expedient of trial in the absence of the prisoner. The posse, consisting of five or six Indians, who capture the absconding criminal should be paid $1,000. This would be about a just remuneration. Some statistician has worked out the problem and asserts that every Indian killed on the warpath, with our present methods, costs the government $100,000, not counting the lives of citizens and soldiers constantly lost. If these figures are correct, here is a murderer brought to justice, society avenged, and the law vindicated at a saving to the government of $99,000.

This solution of the problem makes the Indian a person before the law, which at present he is not, any more than is the buffalo or the wolf. It gives him a code to protect and restrain him. It gives him land and a home, and makes it possible for him to become the independent, self-supporting, productive, and useful rear guard of our civilization.

In the Apache Country

WILL C. BARNES

The Overland Monthly N.S. 9 (February 1887): 172–80

Situated almost in the center of the territory of Arizona lies the White Mountain, or San Carlos, Indian reservation. Nearly square in form, measuring about sixty-five miles either way, it manages to cover the garden spots in the territory. On the south it touches the fertile Gila valley and includes that of the San Carlos River. On the north the two forks of the White River flow westerly until, uniting, they form the Black, which at its junction with Cedar Creek, a little tributary from the north, forms the Salt River. Flowing into these White and Black rivers are numerous clear mountain streams with broad fertile valleys, which are farmed by the various bands of Apaches who live about them.

In the country lying along the San Carlos and Gila rivers one finds the typical Arizona climate: hot sultry summers with frequent sandstorms and the merest touch of winter. Ice seldom forms, and houseflies are almost as bad in January as in July. The northern portion, being from two to four thousand feet higher and very mountainous, presents an entirely different climate. The summers are not extremely warm and have cool nights, and the winters are quite rigorous, with considerable snow. Let us spend a few weeks looking over this land of the Apache and see what it and he are like. We are at Camp Thomas, a frontier military post located on the Gila, just off the reservation line. Three troops of cavalry and one company of infantry uphold the honor of the stars and stripes here and do their share in protecting the settlers along the valley from the raids of the Apaches.

Our "outfit," as everything of the kind is called in this country, consists of two diminutive pack mules and a Mexican packer to look after them. Mules and packer are hired for the trip. For ourselves, we have each bought a stout little cow pony, an animal that will travel forty or sixty miles a day, find his dinner at night on the prairie, and turn up ready for the next morning as fresh as ever.

We get an early start from the post for San Carlos, the main agency, some thirty-five miles west of Thomas. Our little pack train, loaded with our camp outfit and bedding, driven by the swarthy packer, trots behind us. Each of the party carries a Winchester, slung cowboy fashion under the left leg, and a six-shooter with belt full of cartridges around the waist.

The road to San Carlos is sandy, dusty, and dry. Huge freight teams, prairie schooners, are met and passed—some carrying ore and supplies to and from the mining camp at Globe, west of San Carlos, and others laden with agency supplies. It is a veritable desert of sagebrush and sand. The only trees are those along the rivers—cottonwoods, the "plainsmen's friends." Occasionally huge jack rabbits go flying across the road, every few rods squatting and cocking their great ears; then, dropping down, away they go with long, easy jumps that make the fleetest hounds simply green with envy. In the distance, the white tails of a band of antelope attract the eye and tempt the rifle, but they are too far for a shot.

About fifteen miles from Thomas we ford the Gila and enter the reservation. A little farther down the river is the sub-agency, where the Chiricahua Apaches were kept for some time and a futile attempt made to get them to farm. But a Granger life didn't suit them, and one day they killed all the agency employees they could find handy and lit out for their haunts in Sonora, where a few of them yet evade capture.[1]

As we draw near the agency, the Indians begin to appear. We pass them along the road, whole families going in for ration day. Ahead rides the old buck on his pony, with his long rifle slung across the saddle in front of him. A bright piece of red flannel around his head serves for a hat; a cheap calico shirt gathered under his cartridge belt at the waist, together with the breechclout and a pair of moccasins, complete his costume. His cheeks are smeared with vermilion, and black wavy lines are drawn over his nose and across his chin. His squaw comes behind with a baby slung in its basket to the horn of her saddle and a child sitting behind her. From each side of the pony hang enormous wicker baskets, fancifully painted and decorated with little tin bangles. The squaw has a bright calico skirt to match, with fancy moccasins. She rides astride like her lord and like him unceasingly belabors the ribs of the long-suffering pony with her heels. Following her comes a patient, slow-moving burro, ridden by two boys about ten or eleven years of age, each dressed in a complete suit of nothing, from head to foot, excepting the usual breechclout about the waist. Besides the boys, the burro carries a pair of long saddlebags hanging nearly to the ground on both sides. These and the baskets on the pony are for the rations to be drawn on the morrow.

Such family parties grow more and more frequent as we near San Carlos, which is today the general rallying point for all the Indians down on this end of the reservation.

San Carlos Agency lies on the river of the same name. The buildings, fences, and corrals all are of the usual material—adobe—and grouped together in the form of a hollow square for purposes of defense. They consist of quarters for the agent and agency employees, guardhouse, military telegraph office, store and issue houses, and corrals for agency stock. Two trading stores and a large schoolhouse stand at a little distance from the main buildings.

We are kindly received by the agent, who shows us around the place, through huge storehouses full of flour, sugar, coffee, and all the component portions of the ration that is served out every ten days to the Indians, not forgetting the bales of bright calico, white sheeting for covering their huts, red flannel shawls, cheap jewelry, hand mirrors, beads, and the thousand and one little fancy things that are distributed among them as annuity goods. Back of the agent's office is a well-stocked magazine whose walls are covered with Winchester and Remington carbines, Colt's revolvers, and belts of ammunition, with which to arm the agency employees in case of trouble.

We are told that in round numbers there are about five thousand Apaches upon this reservation, and that they have actually increased in population during the past ten years. (The writer believes this due more to a better and more thorough census than to an actual increase in population.) The agent explains to us that while they are one family of Apaches in name, they are divided into a dozen different tribes, each speaking a different language and generally living apart from each other, every tribe by itself. The principal tribes are the Sierra Blancas (White Mountains), the Tontos, the Coyoteros, the Apache-Mojaves, the Apache-Yumas, the Mescaleros, the Chiricahua Apaches, and the Warm Springs Apaches. The last tribe is but a handful, the best part of them having fallen in the war under old Victorio; over one hundred were killed in a single fight in the fall of '82.[2]

After dark the countless campfires scattered everywhere around the agency make the scene a gay one indeed. The children especially are having a grand frolic. They seem to be everywhere, scores of them, running and jumping and making a noise and clatter that reminds one of a country school at recess. And the dogs—big dogs, little dogs, lean dogs, fat dogs; dogs of every color, size, shape, and breed; dogs with three legs, with only one eye, with ears cut off, and ears split (showing the school in which the youngsters are raised, for most of such work is due to the innate deviltry of the Apache boy).

Later on the fires go out, and around the agency things grow quiet. As we spread our blankets for our bed, we hear from down the river the dull boom of a drum—a steady "tum tum," which, we are told, comes from some dance the Indians are holding. The Apaches are devoted to such things, for besides their war dances they hold squaw dances, corn dances, and several others of a religious nature, and such gathering as the present always sees some of them.

Everybody is astir early the next morning. The Indians having previously been furnished with ration tickets, one for each, no matter whether it be a gray-haired buck or a two-day-old baby, range themselves along the main building and, passing from window to window, are rapidly supplied with rations. At one window flour, at the next sugar, the next coffee, and so on. Each squaw—for they do such work, their lords merely looking on outside the line—is obliged to furnish something to carry her stuff away in, and generally deer skins are used, although some of them manage to appear with flour sacks.

The flour is poured into the center of a deer skin, and the hide gathered together; a string is tied around it, and on top of that goes the sugar; and so on. Salt, coffee, and such smaller things are tied up in a corner of her waist or skirt; and on emerging from the line, a squaw frequently has the major portion of her clothing used up in such ways. It gives her an odd appearance but has one advantage—she can't, like her civilized sister, lay it down on the counter and forget it, or leave it in the streetcar on her way home.

The beef they draw at another place, where it is chopped off to them by the butchers in huge chunks. Sometimes they turn the animal over to the Indians and let them butcher it themselves. A scene then follows. One steer is let out at a time, and a dozen Indians ride at it with yells and shouts and shoot it down. Sometimes a steer will have twenty balls in him before dropping. This seems a rather questionable way to keep up their love of blood and killing—to say nothing of improving their marksmanship.

And such a noisy, busy scene! Whatever may be the characteristics of other tribes of Indians, the Apaches are lively and talkative. The men, as a rule, have good full voices, and those of the squaws are most musical, albeit a trifle high-pitched. They love to blarney, as an Irishman would say, and a constant stream of chaff and shrieks of laughter is kept up as they pass along the row of windows. Everything is laughed at. One poor old thing, in tying up the sugar in her dress, loses the ends and away it goes to the ground amid perfect torrents of laughter and fun. No one offers to help her as she scrapes it carefully up, but she good-naturedly joins in the general laughter and hastens to regain her place in the line. To all this din add the dogs, boys, and ponies, and you almost have a pandemonium—burros braying, colts calling to their mothers, lost to them in the crowd, and the ponies themselves fighting and stamping at the flies.

Leaning against wagons and buildings are dozens of little baskets with baby Apaches sucking their fists therein. The baskets are of the regular Indian style, and the poor babies are strapped and laced into them tight and snug, nothing showing but the round chubby face and two tiny fists. Some squaws hang their baskets to the saddle horn, because if they are left standing on the ground, the dogs go round and lick the babies' faces, much to the little ones' discomfort. One rather frisky pony with a baby on the horn of his saddle wanders from the bunch and is immediately surrounded by a crowd of dogs. Their barking starts him to trot, and with a shriek, the mother rushes from her place in the line to catch him. But the pony doesn't want to be caught, and from a trot turns to a run, and away he goes—the basket, flapping on his side, only making him run the harder. No one seems to be sorry for the poor baby, whose yells are drowned in the general burst of laughter that goes up. Finally, the strap that holds the basket breaks—down comes poor baby, thump, to the ground, face down, and the pony, after running a few more rods, is caught by a boy, while the distracted mother picks up her unfortunate infant and, immediately unlacing the deerskin cover, takes it out to assure herself it is sound in body after its rather risky ride and fall.

And thus it goes all day long. It is a curious crowd to study. Such a variety of faces, costumes, and colors. Moving along the crowd are several cavalry officers, their bright yellow facings making their uniforms conspicuous even in this place. They are here from Camp Thomas to oversee the issues on behalf of the War Department, which is now partially responsible for the management of the Apaches.

Leaving San Carlos, we retrace our road as far as the subagency, where, turning to the north, we take the trail for Camp Apache, some ninety miles from the agency.

Every foot of the trail now is a rise. Toiling up Green's Hill[3] to the top of the Gila Mountains, we passed along the trail the graves of two prospectors killed by the Indians in a raid in 1882. At the top of the hill we get a grand view. Arizona mountains generally are smooth and destitute of timber, and those to the south are especially so. The Gila lies below us some three thousand feet, yet only twelve miles away. The green fringe of cottonwoods along its banks mark its course for miles and miles. Off to the southeast Mount Graham, lone and beautiful, stands guard over the broad San Simon plains. A little to the right of it you can see the Santa Catalinas near Tucson and distant from us nearly one hundred miles.

Across a broad valley, covered everywhere with a most splendid growth of wild oats—a perfect paradise for a cattle ranch—and we camp at the foot of Rocky Canyon. Well named it is too, for a rougher, rockier place could hardly be imagined. The military road running for some eight miles through and up its sides is cut for three miles almost entirely out of solid rock.

In the canyons and valleys around here, wild potatoes are found in considerable quantities. They are the genuine *Solanum tuberosum*, as scientific men have determined, but how they came to be growing wild here seems to bother them.

Working up the trail the next morning, we meet at a little spring a party of Apaches, gathering and putting up mescal. Mescal is the root of the century plant, the American aloe, which grows around here very plentifully. The sides of the canyon are fairly bright with its beautiful crimson blossoms. The stalks rise straight and clean for ten feet; then a few branches put out, and in June they blossom. The root is like a large artichoke. The Apaches bake it on bits of red-hot stones and put up great quantities of it, for it keeps almost any length of time. The mescal whiskey, the universal drink in Mexico, is also a product of the century-plant root. One branch of the Apache nation, the Mescaleros, are so called because mescal is their staple food.

One cannot help noticing the great variety of cacti along these hillsides. The most prominent, of course, are the saguaros, or great cacti. They rise, some of them, as high as fifty feet straight and clean. Some have two or three branches from the main stock like huge arms, but most have only the stiff, straight trunks, generally from twelve to eighteen inches thick, covered from top to bottom with sharp needles from two to three inches long. Another curious variety is one that grows a bunch of straight, dry sticks, like a dozen fish poles set in the ground together. Not a leaf, blossom, or sign of life is on them at this season of the year—unless we mention the long needles or spines with which each pole is plentifully supplied. There is certainly life in them, if you happen to let one strike your leg as it hangs along the trail.

Then there are a hundred different shapes of the niggerhead cactus, a round green ball, sometimes two or three in a bunch, from the size of a baseball up to that of a bushel basket. The little fellows of this variety are regular traps for the careless, and many a weary traveler has thrown himself down on a grassy spot, only to find that the cactus was there before him and ready for business.

There are also many varieties of the yucca or, as it is more generally called, the bayonet plant, whose leaves make excellent paper and whose roots the Indians and Mexicans use for soap; it makes a lather equal to the finest soap.

Almost at the top of the canyon can be seen a little stone fort, erected some years ago by a Lieutenant Fisher of the Fifth Cavalry, who with three or four men was cornered here by a band of Apaches.[4] They hastily built this little circular breastwork of stones, from behind which they fought until help came. The soldiers named it Fort Fisher, and the name will probably always remain.

At the summit we are some thirty miles from the Gila and about four thousand feet above it. The trail now winds along through a heavy pine forest for some twenty miles. The military telegraph line, which is about the only piece of civilization that Apaches can boast of, runs along the trail, strung mainly on the trees. The Indians give great trouble to the government by pulling down this line. They throw a lariat over the wire and pull it from the supports, and then hammer it in two between rocks, frequently dragging it away off the trail. Sometimes they tie the wire across the trail from tree to tree at such a height as will sweep a horseman from his seat. The writer experienced the trick once, and several others have been victims to this peculiar style of Apache humor. Once the line was cut and the break hunted after for over two weeks. Over and over again did the repairmen go over the line but without finding the break. Finally, however, after the point had been located by testing, a careful hunt discovered the wire cut close to an insulator in a big oak tree and tied to the bracket with a piece of rawhide, the leaves and branches hiding the thong very carefully.

At Black River the trail goes down fully two thousand feet to the water. What a climb it is too, in this high, thin air, and from one top to the other seems scarcely a stone's throw, yet a long hour is used in going down and up.

Down in the bottom of the canyon lies a sample of Interior Department management. It is a gristmill with turbine wheel all complete—or rather it was once. Years ago, when the nearest railway was at least one thousand miles from here, some bright Indian agent conceived the idea of setting up a mill for the Indians to grind their grain. Black River, with its swift, strong current, offered a fine site, and so this mill was hauled over the desert and up the mountain at a cost that must have about equaled its weight in dollars and deposited here. At that time a fair-sized coffee mill would have ground all the grain the whole nation raised.

At the top of the hill, as we are resting after our long steep climb, the call of an old turkey gobbler is heard near, answered by the "chirp, chirp" of his flock; and almost before we can get our guns from the saddle, a flock of fifteen or twenty wild turkeys, led by a majestic gobbler, come feeding down the hillside, wholly unconscious of our presence. Two fall at the first shot, and three more are killed on the wing as they sail, in their long peculiar flight, clear across the canyon into the thick pines on the opposite side. Surely there is no nobler game than the wild turkey.

A few miles from this we pass by the roadside seven graves, three soldiers and four citizens, killed by Apaches in September 1881. They were in a wagon, and the Indians shot down their horses, forcing them to leave it and take to the trees. After they were killed, the wagon was burned. The iron work still lies there, a mournful relic. A mile or two further on we pass another grave, that of a courier with dispatches who was killed the next day after the seven.

Fort Apache lies in a beautiful valley at the junction of the two forks of the White River—a rushing, rollicking trout stream of the purest water. The valley is completely circled by mountains, whose sides are thickly clothed with pine, cedar, and juniper. It is generally open but dotted here and there with clumps of cedar or pine. Everywhere, all over the valley, are the rude huts or camps of the Indians. These around here are the White Mountain Apaches. They are independent of the agent and of government aid, according to the agreement when the reservation was laid out. They dreaded to go to San Carlos and so agreed never to ask aid from the government, in return for which the government lets them live here in their own wild mountains. They are looked after and kept in order by the commanding officer of the post. The government also buys their corn from them and also all the hay for the post, some two thousand tons yearly; and this, together with the fine hunting, gives them a very fair living. They certainly are self-supporting in the fullest sense of the word. They farm all along both forks of the White River and of all the streams in this vicinity. The government occasionally helps them in digging their irri-gating ditches where they find rock and blasting becomes necessary.

Haying season is their harvest, and the vicinity of the hay corrals and scales offers a most animated spectacle. They pack the hay in every way—on their backs, on ponies, and on burros. The hay is cut, generally, with sickles or knives and often with the heavy Mexican hoe. Enough is gathered to make a bundle of sixty to seventy-five pounds, which is bound with the tough fibers of the yucca. Four or five of these bundles are tied on the burro's back; and with another on her own back, and ofttimes a baby on top of it, the squaw drives her burro in to the post, where the hay is weighed and a check given her for the number of pounds, which is paid upon presentation at the post quartermaster's office. As high as two hundred pounds is often brought in on a squaw's back, and a burro will be loaded with three or four hundred more.

With two or three hundred squaws talking, laughing, and shouting around the scales, each trying to get her load weighed first and always accusing the weigher of cheating, the scene is a novel one. The cry of cheating is generally raised because they are up to such tricks themselves. Huge stones, green logs, and all sorts of articles are found in their bundles to make them weigh more. As each bundle is weighed, a man standing beside the scales takes it off, cuts the binding, and opens it to prevent this cheating; and oh, what a shout goes up when someone is caught! Her bundle is confiscated, and she sneaks off amid the jeers and jokes of all the rest, a sadder and wiser Apache.

Fort Apache is built like all frontier military posts—simply a place for housing and feeding the troops. The large parade with the stars and stripes in the center is faced at one end by the hospital, a large, handsome adobe building, and the other end by the different offices and guardhouse. On each side stand the quarters; on the north the officers,' on the south the men's. The buildings are of all kinds—stone, adobe, log, and timber.

Although Apache is the most isolated post in the territory, it is the most coveted by army people for a station, its fine climate, beautiful surroundings, and splendid hunting and fishing being more than an offset to its isolation.

Few people have a fair conception of the amount of work the United States army performs on the frontier. The general idea is that both officers and men do nothing from one year's end to the other but drink, gamble, and sleep, wear fine clothes, and have a general good time. The man who enters the United States Army, the cavalry branch especially, will find that he works as hard as any day laborer who ever lived, and often harder. Almost the entire work of improvement falls on the troops, and this, with constant field service, escorts, and scouting, keeps them continually on the go.

Apache boasts a steam sawmill and a fine system of waterworks, water being forced from the river to a high hill back of the post, and from a reservoir there down to and all over the garrison.

A two days' trip takes us westward into the edge of the wonderful, picturesque Tonto Basin on Cibicue Creek, where, on that fatal day in August 1881, the Indian scouts turned on the troops under General E. A. Carr of the Sixth Cavalry and killed Captain Hentig—as brave an officer and noble man as ever drew a saber—and six men. Their bodies were all removed to the post afterwards, and only the rough headboards made from ration boxes, with the names burned in with red-hot irons lying about, mark the spot where the battle took place.

These valleys here are perfect garden spots. The Indians raise wonderful crops of corn, melons, and beans.

Coming back to Apache, we see the place on the trail as it turned around a mountain where, on the night of the Cibicue fight, as the command was retreating back to the post, a pack mule laden with ammunition lost its footing and rolled down the cliff a full one thousand feet. Of course, in the darkness and confusion, nothing could be done, and the Indians, following up the command, found it the next morning and doubtless used some of the cartridges in the attack on the fort the day after.

A detour of a few miles takes us to a salt spring which is really the head of the famous Salt Creek. The spring is some twenty feet wide, and on all sides the pure white salt is piled up in layers a foot thick. A large stream runs from the spring into Cedar Creek, turning the pure creek water into a regular ocean brine. A few miles below, the Salt River proper is formed; but if any of those numerous persons who have gone up Salt River have reached its head, they certainly should be in the vicinity of this spring.

We return to the post just in time to see three troops of cavalry preparing to take the field in response to a telegram announcing a hostile raid to the southeast. What a busy scene! Orderlies flying around, horses being saddled, ammunition distributed, rations packed up, and everything in apparent confusion—and yet a confusion with a system, for in less than three hours from the first order, the command is drawn up on the parade for inspection.

Everything looks meant for service. Two-thirds of the men wear large white sombreros; buckskin pants and shirts are frequent; hardly an officer wears anything to show his rank, the saber being only for garrison use; each officer now carries a carbine and revolver like the men, for Indians must be fought almost man to man, and in such places every shot counts.

The men are drawn up in a long line. At the right are a dozen Indian scouts squatting around, each armed with a long rifle. They are invaluable as scouts, trailers, and couriers, and always on foot. In their midst stands the guide and interpreter, a tall, weather-beaten man, a typical frontiersman who has been on such duty for years and years.

Back of all, the packers vainly try to keep the pack train of about fifty mules in some sort of order. Each mule has had his load slightly cinched and lashed on, and the consequent squeezing they are undergoing makes them uneasy and vicious. One would hardly think there could be bedding, rations, and supplies for such a number of men in so small a space, but then, no feather beds are taken, and an army field ration isn't so very bulky.

Every mule is given his load—usually not over two hundred pounds, except in emergencies. It is divided as nearly as possible into two equal packs and is lashed onto the large aparejo—a peculiar style of Spanish pack rig—by the famous diamond hitch. It is wonderful how rapidly a well-trained crew will pack up a lot of stuff, and still more wonderful is the stuff that can be packed. In fact, there is hardly anything, however clumsy or awkward to handle, that a pack train cannot carry, providing, of course, it comes within the limit of weight. The writer has seen everything from a cookstove and Saratoga trunk to a bedstead, sent over to the pack corral, and nothing ever came back; although I remember that the mule with the bedstead ran against a tree with the long side pieces, going down a steep trail, and rolled some five or six hundred feet, alighting on his back in a creek below. When the lashings were cut the mule rolled over, struggled to his feet, and began to drink, as if such things were of everyday occurrence in his family. As an Irish orderly remarked: "Well, bedad, if that mule didn't save his bacon, his bacon surely saved him."

The packers are generally Mexicans and always citizens, being employed by the quartermaster's department. They are paid from $50 per month and rations for common packers, up to $125 a month for the packmaster; but I will venture the statement that a packer in an army train comes about as near earning his $50 every month as any living mortal, for harder and more disagreeable work cannot be imagined, especially in cold or wet weather.

Having been inspected, the command moves off, the scouts in the lead, the surgeon and commanding officer next, and by twos or in single file, as the trail permits, the rest of the command. Following them comes the pack train, led by an old bell mare, and the rear is brought up by the rear guard of about eight men.

And here we bid adieu to fair Apache land. The news of the outbreak brings our trip to a close. It will not be safe, we are told, to travel over the reservation, and although we are longing for a hunt up in the high mountains where the elk are, we do not consider it worth risking our scalps for; and instead of returning by way of Camp Thomas, over what is now a hostile country, we leave the post and strike northward toward the Atlantic and Pacific road, some one hundred miles distant.

Our trip is an uneventful and pleasant one. We spend a day in Snowflake, a Mormon settlement in the midst of green fields—a regular oasis in the desert—where we are tempted to stay and study these people in their homes. At Holbrook, a thriving little town on the railroad, we feel ourselves once more in civilization, or at least on its outskirts. This is a cow town, the wild and woolly cowboy being here found in all his glory. Thousands of cattle are ranging over the country near here, and nothing but cows, brands, ranches, and stock is talked of.

We sell our saddle ponies, settle up with our Mexican packer, who goes back alone, and as we give him a hearty handshake on leaving, we say to him, "Adios, amigo."

Geronimo and His Warriors in Captivity

WALTER REED[1]

The Illustrated American 3 (August 16, 1890): 231–35

Ten years ago the remnant of the Chiricahua and Warm Spring Apache Indians, numbering some eight hundred souls, driven from their reservations by the encroachment of the whites, had established their home deep in the fastnesses of the Sierra Madre in Old Mexico. From this well-nigh inaccessible hiding place bands of mounted warriors, armed with the most modern weapons, descended from time to time like a pestilence upon the states of Chihuahua and Sonora, Mexico, spreading terror and dismay in the hearts of the settlers and always leaving behind them the ruined homes and mangled bodies of their unfortunate victims. So well conceived and rapidly executed were these raids that before troops could be put into the field by either government, the damage was done, and the wily Apache, laden with plunder and decorated with scalps, was beating a hasty retreat over ground thoroughly familiar to him.

These war parties had become so frequent and so disastrous in their results to property and lives that the late General George Crook, U.S.A., then in command of the Department of Arizona, determined to organize a final expedition and, when once upon the trail of the Indians, to follow them, if necessary, even to the city of Mexico. This scouting party, well rationed and equipped, with trusted Indian scouts as guides, was led by General Crook in person across the Mexican border in the spring of 1883. If this matchless Indian fighter had already won the sobriquet of "Gray Fox" from the Apaches, the result of his campaign must have left no doubt in the minds of these Indians as to his cunning and shrewdness. Two months later Geronimo and his warriors, returning from a successful raid in Old Mexico, flushed with victory and enriched with booty and captive women, were filled with consternation to find that during their absence, American soldiers had entered their hitherto inaccessible canyons and were between them and their home.

Leaving his captives to care for themselves as best they could, the great Apache war chief and his young men rushed pell-mell through canyon and over divide, only to find "Gray Fox" sitting in quiet possession of his camp of women and children and perfectly willing to accommodate him either with

On the way to Florida. NELSON A. MILES. *PERSONAL RECOLLECTIONS AND OBSERVATIONS.*

battle or powwow. Geronimo wisely surrendered and, following his captor across the Mexican border, was placed upon a reservation in Arizona, there to learn the arts of peace. As time went by, some of the more restless spirits, including Geronimo, Naiche, and others, finding agriculture rather irksome and longing to exchange the sandy plains of Arizona for the lofty heights and grassy slopes of the Sierra Madre, concluded to decamp for their old home. This they did in 1885, inducing about 130 men, women, and children to accompany them. Another expedition, commanded by the lamented Captain Emmet Crawford, Third Cavalry, was successful in recapturing these Indians in the spring of 1886, although its complete success was greatly marred by the death of Crawford and the subsequent escape, through treachery, of Naiche and some of the worst element. The remaining captives, numbering about one hundred, were sent to Fort Marion, Florida, for imprisonment. Disgusted with Apache treachery, General Crook was at his own request relieved in the spring of 1886, and Major General Nelson Miles, U.S.A., succeeded to the command of the Department of Arizona.

By untiring energy in the field, this officer soon had Geronimo and his renegades once more corralled and then promptly settled, by a brilliant coup, the Apache problem which Crook had labored so faithfully to accomplish. No sooner were the hostiles well in hand than they found themselves going toward the rising sun, bag and baggage, as fast as steam could carry them—Geronimo, with sixteen men, including the principal chiefs, going to Fort Pickens, Florida, and the balance of the Apaches to join their relatives at Fort Marion, St. Augustine, Florida. For this decisive blow General Miles will always be held in grateful remembrance by the people of two territories.

May 1, 1887, found the captives at Mount Vernon, Alabama, whither they had been sent on the ground, of health. Here they were afterward joined by Geronimo and his small band from Fort Pickens. The arrival of the great war chief, upon whom the Apaches had so implicitly relied in their war against the whites, was an event of importance. One would have supposed that the whole Indian camp would have turned out to greet the incoming train. On the contrary, not an Indian appeared, and when the veteran of a hundred fights led his little band up the hill to the northern gate of the barrack wall and reached a spot where he could survey the camp, not a living soul was in sight.

Leaving his small party seated upon their baggage, the stern old chief advanced some paces, paused, and calmly surveyed the scene. No sound broke the stillness save the melancholy sighing of the pines. This camp of 350 souls seemed instinctively to realize that they were again under the burning gaze of their great warrior and priest. What thoughts passed through the warrior's mind as he beheld all that remained of his once powerful tribe transported from their native mountains to the pine lands of Alabama, we can only imagine. While he gazed intently, a woman was seen to emerge from a distant tent and to advance with slow step and bowed head. Geronimo appeared to take no notice of her approach. Nearer she came, hesitated, and then, womanly feeling getting the mastery, hurried to the old chief, threw her arms about his neck, and wept as if her heart would break. During this trying ordeal, not a muscle of the grim old warrior's face relaxed, nor did he show by any outward sign of recognition that his only daughter was twining her arms about him. Perhaps the recollections of his people's wrongs came flocking in to steel his heart against the softening influences of the moment.

The Indian prisoners now gathered at Mount Vernon numbered 390: 80 warriors, 180 women, and 130 children. As many of them were sick and the health of all debilitated from close confinement at Fort Marion, Florida, the officer in charge directed his first efforts toward securing a more liberal ration and better clothing. His application was favorably considered by the secretary of war, who ordered that the United States Army ration should be issued to adults and a half ration to all under twelve years of age. When later their health had been somewhat recuperated, it was thought best to teach the Apache that a part of his bread, at least, should be earned by the sweat of his brow.

The first call for a working party of twenty men met with strong opposition on the part of all the warriors. To have obligingly killed a few enemies of the commanding officer would have been a pleasant pastime for these braves, but to shoulder spade and pick and delve into the earth was too degrading to be entertained! Whereupon the chiefs put their heads together and soon found, as they supposed, a happy solution to the difficulty. With every mark of wounded dignity, they bade the interpreter say that if the officer desired laborers, they would be most happy to supply not only twenty but forty *women* and to recommend them as good and faithful workers. When made to understand that men and not women were wanted, they only yielded in the presence of physical force. Thus the Apache warrior unwillingly took his first step toward civilization and found it, as his white brother had found it before him, the most difficult and painful.

Thereafter no trouble was experienced, nor could more faithful laborers be desired. From pick and shovel to hammer and saw was an easy step, and although these tools were awkwardly handled at first, and many a painful contusion of finger and thumb sustained, the Apaches kept bravely at their work and, under proper guidance, had within a few months cut the timber, hewed the logs, ripped out the material for roofing, and erected 150 good cabins. Any mechanical idea presented to them was quickly grasped. Yet it must not be forgotten that so simple a thing as rolling a wheelbarrow was to the Apache a difficult task. There seemed to be a lack of proper muscular coordination, and in spite of his efforts, over would go the load, to the intense amusement of his companions; for, notwithstanding his savage nature, the Apache has a wonderful appreciation of the ludicrous and can give and take a joke with perfect good humor.

During the building of the village the Indians were required to keep their camp clean, and as an aid to personal cleanliness, washtubs and washboards were liberally distributed. In the absence of clotheslines the squaws adopted the rather novel method of drying their clothes by putting them on and promenading in sunlight until the moisture had evaporated. These clinging garments served to bring out perfectly the Apache female "form divine," which, in breadth of shoulders and hips, is simply amazing. This physical development is due to the heavy burdens to which they are subjected from childhood. The female is the beast of burden among all Indian tribes.

In October 1888, through the instrumentality of the Boston Citizenship Committee, a school was begun, the War Department erecting the schoolhouse and the committee furnishing the teachers. The Indians, however, having in mind the recent transfer to Carlisle, Pennsylvania, of 106 of their brightest boys and girls, were very suspicious of the department's intentions, and not till General O. O. Howard's visit the following spring and assurance that this school was not a stepping stone to Carlisle did they freely consent to send their children. Then even Geronimo lent his presence and acted as a kind of head usher. From that time the school has been in a flourishing condition, both children and adults making good progress in reading, writing, and arithmetic. It may be questioned whether in taking their children to Carlisle the government was right, although the purpose was a most laudable one. If the Apaches have any redeeming characteristic it is love for their children. Their grief over this compulsory separation has been genuine and unabating; and when death has claimed one of their absent children, their intense manifestation of sorrow has touched the hearts of all. It would seem far better to imitate the Boston committee, so that they can see with their own eyes the improvement from day to day and derive both encouragement and benefit therefrom, rather than advance their children so far in ideas of civilization, at some point, that upon their return they are ashamed of even their own fathers and mothers.

The limits of this article permit only a bare reference to the beliefs and social customs of the Apaches. The belief in a Good and Bad Spirit is well fixed, and it is astonishing to see with what fantastic figures they bedeck the legs, arms, and body of the sick in order to drive away the devil. They must also believe that his Satanic majesty's ears are very sensitive to sounds, for nothing seems to keep him so well at a distance as the beating of the "tom-tom."

In referring to the dead the Apache always points upward. The medicine man, too, before beginning his song to the Good Spirit, rinses his mouth with pure water, thus indicating the belief that "what cometh from within defileth the man." In the absence of remedies, the medicine men and women are agreed that nothing is so conducive to the recovery of the patient as a good kneading of the abdomen. So that one of the everyday sights of the camp is a half-grown daughter or son dancing, not too tenderly, upon the stomach of his parental ancestor. It is hardly necessary to add that the Apache, like his igno-rant white brother, violates every rule of hygiene and hence is subject to many ailments. The sick are always carefully, if not gently, attended by relatives, and when death comes, as come it does very often, they consider it a duty to con-tribute some of their household goods, wearing apparel, and valuable articles to enable the dead one to make a good appearance in the next world.

A man can have as many wives as he feels able to support, and hence the family tie is not very strong. Incompatability of temper or neglect to serve her lord's supper in good form may lead to the lady being ejected from the cabin. When thus discarded, she is quite at liberty to listen to the soft proposals of another swain. Virtue occupies a high place among these Indians, since the loss of virtue was formerly promptly followed by the loss of the woman's nose! To the honor of the Apache women, be it said that only three of their number bear this indelible mark upon their faces. Further, when it is remem-bered that a man is not allowed to speak or even look at his mother-in-law under any circumstance, who will say that the Indian is altogether behind the Caucasian in civilization?

A Hot Trail

POWHATAN H. CLARKE[1]

Cosmopolitan 17, no. 10 (October 1894): 706–16

One evening in March,[2] as I was finishing a most pleasant dinner at Fort Thomas, Arizona, my host and hostess, having just returned from a long leave in the East, were telling me of the splendid time they had been having, and my mind was far off in the gaily lit theaters and ballrooms, when the commanding officer was announced. After a few remarks to the hostess, he nonchalantly turned to me and, with an odd smile, said that I might as well hurry up with my coffee, as the Apaches had killed a man a few miles from the post and he had ordered a detachment out for me, which would start in ten minutes. Little time did I have to dream over receptions, pretty faces, and music, for in another minute I was sitting on that old familiar McClellan saddle, watching the men file out from the stable. A quick inspection for cartridges, horseshoes, canteens, the blacksmith's kit, etc.; "mount," "form rank," "fours right," "this way," "right by twos," "trot," and quicker than you can read it, we are off in our route column.

There is something noiseless, practical, quick about the working of an American cavalry outfit; a youngster may love to howl those long useless commands of our cavalry tactics when he first joins, to show the men that he has a powerful voice; but after a few "trips," and perhaps after noticing an ironical expression or two about the face of an old sergeant who has "raised" several generations of youngsters, he finds a few movements, a signal for them with the hand, and the least noise possible get him in and out of camp most speedily.

After pulling back once or twice to see that all the men were sitting up and "closed" and that the gait was steady, not making any of the horses gallop, I gave my black his place at the head of the column, settling down to a good eight-mile trot, musing over the strange contrasts in life, and mentally cursing the Indians for depriving me of a most charming evening.

Five miles out we met a train of immense freight wagons, bringing copper from the mines at Globe, north of the San Carlos Agency. They were driving like artillery in retreat, whips, profanity, and fear dragging the great, creaking

Arrival of a courier. CENTURY MAGAZINE, MARCH 1891.

schooners along in clouds of invisible, choking dust. One of the soldiers called to them that they were out rather late. No information could be gotten for them. One old fellow asked to go back, as he was a friend of the freighter supposed to have been killed. As soon as he had unhooked his saddle horse we struck out again. I noticed with quiet delight that neither he nor my cowboy guide relished the steady trot. These frontiersmen always travel at the walk or gallop, and not having yet acquired the effeminate method of posting, nor being practiced in the military seat, they enjoy our trot about as much as we enjoy their bucking ponies.

If you have the patience to read anything written by a cavalry officer, you must have the patience to allow him to air his hobbies, and one of the greatest is the love for long stirrups and the close trot. I have seen the short stirrup used in the European cavalry, and upon once seeing the men try to mount on quiet horses, I wasted no more thought on the short stirrup. Of course, there is a theory about agile, active cavalrymen vaulting into the saddle, but after a few days' hard field work and sleeping in the rain, there are few men who don't need the stirrup to get up into the saddle, especially with its pack on. As for posting, the short stirrup is certainly easier on the man until he gets accustomed to the close seat. It is said to be easier on the horse, but that will never be proved until the horse says so himself. At any rate, it won't do for the soldier. He must have his heels low and his leg swinging as freely as possible to enable him to use his spurs; above all, he must have a seat that will keep him with his horse till the horse falls flat. Riderless horses are not what we want when we strike an enemy at the end of a charge. After many years and the trying of many saddles, I am convinced that we have the best saddle and seat for cavalry in the world.

To return to the Thomas-San Carlos road that we were pulverizing so mercilessly as we glided along past the tall cottonwood trees down by the river, then through long, dark lanes of mesquite, until, turning the bend round a long promontory of black granite, we caught sight of a smoldering fire half a mile away in the middle of the road. Suddenly, with a snort, my horse shied, the others following suit, and across the wagon track lay a body. So many false reports come to us about Indian depredations that we are generally quite skeptical, and even when taking the body to the light of the fire, I was not sure the man had not fallen from his wagon and been run over. But the discovery of two small bullet holes, and so truly placed, soon convinced us that we had a trail to take.[3]

There is not much time to be wasted in these matters. The old freighter refusing to take the body on his horse back to Thomas, we wrapped it in the wagon sheet and swung it up into a tree to prevent the coyotes from disfiguring it. It was a weird sight about the fire of the poor fellow's burning wagons—the frightened horses, the old graybeard freighter examining the body of his unfortunate friend, who a few hours before, in the bright sunshine, swinging his cracking whip and gaily urging on his horses to camp, had met him on the road, sending messages to his people at the quiet, pretty village of Leighton.

There had been a good deal of uneasiness felt concerning some of the Apaches, and it was impossible to imagine how many of them had been implicated in this murder and, consequently, on the warpath. The telegraph wire being cut at about 7:00 P.M., my orders were to go through to San Carlos and mend the wire en route, getting all information possible. The river bottom varies from one to two miles in width, covered with the fields of the Indians, while their numerous villages of hemispherical wicker wickiups line the edge of the tableland, rising abruptly from the bottom and gradually sloping back to the high distant mountains.

From one village to another we went, but not a living thing could be found in any of them. I began to think that the whole race had taken the warpath. The night was bitterly cold; in crossing the river several times, from one village to the other, our horses went up to the saddles in the swift, cold stream, which did not add any comfort to the chilly sensation one has when examining another man's camp in the dark, and not by any means assured of his sentiments. At last we found some squaws, who, before being asked any questions, volunteered the information that they knew absolutely nothing about anything; so, getting disgusted, I hurried up to the old sub-agency, eighteen miles from Thomas, where the stage line has a relay and feeding station, with a white man to guard it. Here I most fully expected to find the man dead and the relay gone, but to my surprise and joy, the clear, well-known voice of my good-natured, jolly friend, with whom I had taken many a pleasant lunch on my trips to Carlos, challenged me. With him I found one of the men of the Interior Department in charge of one of the camps I had passed, but neither of them could tell me any more than that a man had been killed and that the news had been taken to San Carlos. Being assured of the latter, I determined to save my horses the remaining eighteen miles, to take the trail in the morning, and at once gave orders to feed.

The men made a great fire and, in their habitual jolly way, began to laugh, telling stories while trying to dry themselves and thaw out. An hour had thus gone by, when the heavy trot of a cavalry detachment silenced everyone; all eyes were turned toward Carlos.

Soon into the great fire-lit circle came Lieutenant Watson and a number of Apache scouts on steaming ponies, followed by a detachment of the Fourth Cavalry. After the usual salutation of "How in the devil did you get here?" had been satisfactorily answered on both sides, Watson determined that we would go to the scene of the murder at daybreak; so, stretching himself out on the floor of the station, with a sack of barley for a pillow and a blanket for cover, set me the good example of going fast asleep. I soon followed him. He had been sent out with even less delay than I had and appeared in a new undress uniform, with a high white collar and tie of the most faultless style, exactly as he had left dinner at San Carlos, except that he had drawn a pair of long woolen stockings over his trousers and wore a pair of canvas walking shoes, a most quaint but practical scouting dress, though the collar and cuffs were a source of intense amusement during the trip. His trust in his scouts was proved by his carrying no arms.

Day was just breaking as we finished a cup of coffee and attempted to swallow some pasty biscuit and oily bacon. The first morning on a scout, before good, hard toil has made the system greedy for anything, is not pleasant, and one longs for the white cloth and a neat breakfast at the mess.

Soon in the saddle, we took the road back toward Thomas, the scouts, their black hair streaming, galloping in front with the officers in many and bright colored costumes, with light, easy seat, swaying gracefully to every motion of their ponies, as active and wiry as themselves. At times, one or two would drop back and scrape up an acquaintance with the men, selecting those who seemed to be best supplied with tobacco, then dart forward to the front.

One cannot imagine the beauty of a morning in Arizona until he sees every stage of the picture as it is brought to light. Coming out of the dark wearisome night on a strong, spirited horse, the motion and glorious sunlight dispel the chill and gloom, the very dust hangs sparkling in the air, and from green thickets the motionless columns of smoke stand, as by enchantment, while the vision seems to reach to infinity, catching the sharp outline of rugged ranges scores of miles away. A magic stillness holds the vast scene spellbound. To those who have grown to love the great solitude, a feeling of independence, of strength, of joy possesses the soul: the man feels more the master of destiny than when face to face with his greatest monuments or most powerful machinery.

As we passed the camps we found the Indians all returned, and hurrying toward the one nearest the place where the freighter had been killed, we found the chief, meditatively watching his old wife toasting coffee on the top of a condemned oil can, while a younger favorite sat beside him making her toilet by the aid of a small, round mirror framed in beaded buckskin. After an absence of all ceremonial salutation and the rolling of inevitable cigarettes, the old gentleman told us, in a quiet, dignified way, that only five Indians were concerned in the murder, that they had been against the government for some time and, having got drunk, had killed the freighter to get his horses and provisions and had probably joined the Kid.

"The Kid," at one time first sergeant of scouts at San Carlos—who had passed his course at the Carlisle school—had felt obliged to kill another chief. On being ordered into arrest, he had mutinied with some of his scouts, shot the lionhearted old chief of scouts, Sieber, and almost killed Captain Pierce, whom every Indian looked upon as his best friend. He was run down by the Indian scouts under Lieutenant Johnson,[4] tried by court-martial, sentenced to twenty years, and turned over to the civil jury at the end of one. When on his way to the Yuma penitentiary, he and his companion overpowered the sheriff and his deputy,[5] killed them, and were seen no more, except by the many unfortunates whose souls his bullets have relieved from care and the other Indians who from time to time have fed him and fought with him. To the citizen, he is a terror; to the soldier, a myth; and to his brother Indians, a hero with a charmed life, perfect attainments, and a glorious record. The fact that he is still at large only shows how much faith the government has in the power of the lonely ranchmen, struggling in desolate places to make a home for manly citizens, to defend himself against an enemy more cunning and implacable than wildest fancy can picture.

No long-departed mother could show less interest in her children than is sometimes shown in these sturdy people, who, rather than be crushed under the leveling foot of civilization, throw themselves into the desert like those ancestors of whom we are so proud, and in the face of every hardship and danger, rear families of strong, hardy, free-minded, typical Americans.

When one has lived among these peoples, known their trials, shared their hospitality, he is more capable of judging the right and wrong than is the philanthropic and sentimental student in whose brain a cup of tea generates harrowing pictures of oppression of the Indian. If the Indian is ill-treated, punish those who are responsible, correct the abuse. He has a right to live; we owe it to him to civilize and protect him. He is manly and brave, loyal to a degree as a soldier; but this is no reason why our own people should be left to his mercy when he has been hounded into mutiny.

A few minutes' examination of the tracks by the scouts, to fix them in their minds, then time to raise the telegraph wire, and we are off. I looked hopefully back toward Thomas for the dust of the pack mules, coming with luxurious bacon, flour, and coffee, but not a grain of dust seemed to rise, and in fact, the train never overtook us. Up along the narrow path we rode, the scouts barely watching the trail, as the broncos had taken no pains to conceal their tracks and seemed to have meant good, fast, fair play. As we neared the wall, a narrow gorge opened in the solid rock, then, clattering along through a pillared passageway, we came to the foot of the great Gila range, and then rang out the old, heartless, dreary command that deadens the spirit of the American cavalryman and has made his feats the marvel of the European—"Dismount!"

If I could but paint the picture for you, or half describe the feeling as an Apache chaser, after a few months' rest, finds himself at the foot of the first jagged, peaked, rocky, gravelly, slippery trail, covered with sticking Spanish bayonet and cactus and barred by bushes that seem to take a catlike delight in clutching, with barbed thorns, every bone and joint. The recruit may look upon hundreds of feet and encourage himself with the idea that far above, where the leading scout is, whose pony seems as large as a rat terrier, the mountaintop exists, and that he will find a grassy slide down on the other side, into a valley with flowing streams; but alas, each step upward brings to his no longer admiring gaze terrace piled upon terrace.

At last you see that your men can do no more. Many are old companions of many a trail, and their black faces have cheered you as you have watched them about the campfire when, homesick and discouraged, you were fresh from the Point. You know that when they look serious and drawn, they are tired—real tired. You motion the halt and close up. Your own blood is surging through your head, you taste blood in your throat, your knees tremble as you stand, but there is no chance for rest yet, for some of your new men *think* they can't "close up," and you must go down, far back on the trail, and persuade them that they can. They can't be left; you can't wait; and your persuasions usually succeed, although at times you hardly have the heart to punish the poor fellows when you know how you feel yourself. This is only the beginning, and many a life may hang on your success.

At noon, far up in the mountains, we found overhanging a trail a breastwork of stone, semicircular, filled with soft grass where the broncos had slept for an hour or two, waiting for the moon; a wicked little fortress from which their rifles could sweep the ascending divide for two thousand yards, the first challenge from our enemy. At about 3:00 P.M. we began to climb down, sliding, falling, expecting at every step to have a frightened horse come tumbling down on top. It is under such conditions that one knows what it means to be "weak in the knees."

Toward sunset we are beside a wild, beautiful brook, under great oak trees; all about roll grassy hillocks that we must take advantage of for our hungry horses. How grateful the poor brutes seem as the saddles are thrown down and the men rub their steaming backs. The herd guard reports, get its instructions; a few seconds more, free from all tether, the ponies and horses are rolling and grazing in the grass. It is all they will get to eat; perhaps tomorrow they will not even have grass.

Nothing wakes up weary, listless troopers like getting into camp; there is music in every sound, from the clicking of the blacksmith's hammer, tightening shoes, to the low, melodious simmering of smoking fires. Scowls and deep curses become smiles and jests. Not long does it take to get the simple meal prepared; then, as you stretch out on your blankets with your head on the saddle, the stars come out, the dancing fires throw fantastic shadows about through the dark wood, a deep, serene feeling of rest coming over you that pays for this and many more days of toil.

It soon turns bitter cold; for once the sun is behind the mountains, a sudden chill comes over the light, fine air; from being bathed in perspiration by exertion, you are chilled to the marrow.

Breakfast is all ready, it is 5:30 A.M. It takes some courage to dip your nose into the icy stream. At 6:00 A.M. we file out, wondering where dinner would come from, hoping that some luckless cow would stray across our path. At noon the trail crossed the San Carlos-Apache road. Our lame horses and sick men were sent on it, with a most urgent request for something to eat. While getting them ready, an old Mexican came along on a burro, without any arms or food, with a gourd tied to his saddle for a canteen, a look in his eye that trusted Providence alone, but that with trust unlimited. We asked him about the broncos as a matter of form, and as a matter of form received the imperturbable "Quien sabe."

There is a quaintness about "Quien sabe" that makes me envy the Mexican. You hear it a million times; it sounds new, it has new tones about its low, drawling accents that you have never yet appreciated; nor does the same Mexican ever use it twice in the same way.

The Mexican has not many belongings. He usually has a large, expensive hat, and by standing up when it rains, he keeps dry. He always has a cigarette, generally a burro; but his greatest possession is "Quien sabe." He gives it to you when you ask for your way, the price of his horse, if he is married. He has been known to send hale and hearty criminal lawyers to a drunkard's grave with that eternal imperturbable "Quien sabe"; if he loves you, he will add "yo no se," and you feel very grateful.

That day we moved over the tableland, each mile bringing us to a great chasm with vertical sides, and from encouragement I had to pass to threats to get some of the weaker men along. Fasting is weakening under any circumstances, but to full-grown men in the saddle and on foot, ten long, hard hours in that crisp, light atmosphere, it is killing. At sunset we can follow no longer; we must get some beef tomorrow or give up. The cook finds that he has enough beans to give everyone a few spoonfuls, but it takes beans an eternity to cook, up in that altitude; it is not until 10:00 P.M. that we get them. Fortunately, there is grass for the horses.

Early next morning we are out, consoling ourselves that if we have no breakfast, at any rate we don't have to wait for the cook to pack up. Fortunately, the trail runs along foothills, through a pass. For twenty miles we have a square trot, halting once to water the horses and tighten the cinches. The trail leads to the Salt River, and we at last commence to see signs of cattle. But at

1:00 P.M. even Watson gives in and determines to leave the trail to get provisions from a mining camp a few miles from where we are.

Eight miles brings us to an abandoned camp, where we find one old man; from him we get one hundred pounds of flour. Two miles below him we find grass and water, beside which a fat yearling is meditating peacefully upon us. A bullet, some knives, a very small fire, and still less time finds us meditating on the yearling. Never was a meal more welcome than that half-cooked beef. I was beginning to get dizzy, and the very air at times seemed black. Some scouts sent along the trail soon came in with the welcome news that it was still clear and that the broncos still had the same two horses.

This made the third day at about forty miles; our horses began to look gaunt. That evening a courier came from San Carlos, overtaking us with a dispatch informing us that a train of mules with provisions would be sent to this very mining camp.

As we pulled out of camp, leaving a scout to guide the train when it should come, a tall black sergeant of "I" Troop rode in, reporting to Watson that the train had arrived. An old veteran, that sergeant, who had fought in the war and been in the Tenth since its first day's existence in 1867. All night had he ridden, but he sat in his saddle as if on review—sinewy and straight, the model of the noncommissioned officer. At any rate, we felt that we would have some coffee that evening.

After winding about, up and down, until again we lost all feeling, we came to a great precipice and far down caught the first sight of Salt River, swollen by melting snow, roaring and surging through gorge and over cataract. Along the river bottom, which we finally reached, ran the trail in the sand made the day before. We seemed to be gaining, and our fugitives can evidently not get across that torrent. Hope begins to come, when suddenly the sand strip ends against a promontory of rock, around whose foot the angry stream is tearing, and there lie the two horses, while an overturned stone or broken cactus is all that is left of the trail, going up from ledge to ledge on the face of the precipice.

To me this was despair, and I should have given up, for how could even an Apache follow, from rock to rock, a trail that has no trace nor visible sign? But Watson knows his scouts, and they know a man who has never given up until fresh horses or rain have turned perseverance into folly. Quickly deciding, he orders the scouts to go out on foot, while we toil back up and down over country tortured by volcanic fire, cut by torrent until it seems like a storm-swept sea, held rigid by enchantment; red, glaring, barren, and desolate, with no sign of life, no motion but the roaring of the thundering river. Again at sunset we halted, having kept within a few miles of the scouts, camping on our own trail where we had been at 11:00 A.M.

Early in the morning we are again struggling along, trying to keep near the Indians. Some of the men seem jaded and almost unable to keep up, and we are fearfully annoyed by the riderless ponies of the scouts. The latter can be seen climbing and groping up and along of rock like creeping lizards. Soon a turn in the river throws it across our path. Far down, where it widens out, giving room for several acres of land, can be seen a hut and horses. I felt sure that here would end our expedition—another victim, a gun, and fresh horses, and as we say, "Adios broncos."

One hour brings us to the valley. We have cut the river below and ahead of our scouts. We find the house cannot be reached, and we are quenching the everlasting thirst with the cold water, when suddenly, far up and behind, comes a shot echoing above the sound of the river, then another, then a fusillade. It startles us for a second, and we think of our ambushed scouts. We can't tell how many renegades may have been joined since the horses were abandoned.

Few orders, as usual. Watson in the lead. "Come on, men," and this time it is no "dismount." Up the mountain till the horses can no longer get a foothold, and jumping down, leaving the trembling beasts, a few men are cut off to guard and gather them. These men, who thought they could not go two miles more, go tearing, springing from rock to rock. The carbines click in a dry, businesslike way as the cartridges are put in. Yet far up is a scout, calling us to come on, gesticulating wildly. Again that awful feeling of utter exhaustion comes; the lungs seem ready to split. We can't go on; a few seconds for breath. Another shot urges us up. At last the summit; and then we find Rowdy, the scout sergeant, showing to Watson where the broncos lie under cover.

The surprise was from our side. The plucky Yuma, far ahead of his men, saw the hostiles as they glided far down along the river's edge on the concave side of the bend, in the arena of a great natural amphitheater. He sent some men running along the ridge, but thousands of feet over them, and the luckless renegades were suddenly checked by a ball striking in front of them. Turning, they get one from the opposite direction. They are caught at their own game and at once take to the rocks, from which they return the fire of the scouts, the latter keeping at a good long range, thoroughly willing to wait for the soldiers to pull the rattlesnake out of the bushes. So steep are the sides of this amphitheater that we can only get down at a few places, and so vast is it that we cannot tell just at what part of its base are the hostiles, and the pleasant duty of locating them is one that has no element of fun.

There is a seriousness, a calm chill, about looking for a live Indian with a gun down in one of these great canyons that carries anything but enthusiasm with it, and as we came out, four of us, along an open stretch of sand, waiting for that first puff of white smoke, I for one would have been entirely willing to have joined the trappists and have left all military fame to the scouts.

Far up on the rock the puff came, at 150 paces, with it that cutting sound of a close-aimed bullet, followed by several more, while the canyon rang with the echoing and reechoing shots, as the soldiers and scouts above us turned themselves loose on the puffs of smoke. We fell in the sand at once, but one glance showed there was no approach along that target range. The Indians, sheltered by overhanging rock, had all of their energy to devote to us, while far on one flank our men mistook us for the broncos and began to drop shots into the river near us. We soon came to the conclusion that a huge rock behind us was the very place we had come so far to find.

Knowing now where the cover was, we climbed back and up, and on reaching Rowdy were treated by him to a long oration on fighting and courage in general, and how he was most anxious to come into a hand-to-hand struggle with any number of broncos. Rowdy himself has a fine record for courageous service to the United States, but I noticed here, as is always the case, that in a hot place the Apache likes the soldier to have the glory of the lead. He is not a coward by any means; he takes desperate chances in his way; but his ideas of future happiness are not well defined. He is thoroughly satisfied with physical existence, and he thinks that a man who deliberately stands up and lets another man shoot at him must have sad chapters in previous portions of his diary or acute insanity; he really pities him.

The precipices are not escalated as rapidly as the pen writes it. When we began our descent on the broncos, it was about 3:00 P.M. Feeling sure of success, there was no need of sacrificing life until the final moment came; and one becomes also a little *fin de siecle* by associating long with the Apaches. From rock to rock we jumped, but not a shot could we get. They were called upon to surrender but informed us that they were tired of life and intended to plant as many of us in the Salt River canyon as they could. Looking over a rock, seventy feet below, an Indian was seen lying flat. A shot fired at him proved that he had already been hit. After five years and many a chase, this was the first really quiet hostile Indian I had ever seen, and I took delight in it. When you know that within a few yards of you lie men watching you step by step, following you with the open ends of steel tubes and craving for time enough to send pieces of lead into you, you take indescribable joy in finding that one of these brothers has been laid aside.

It is wonderful how little you see or hear of an Apache renegade; look as you may, close up to him, search with your glass, the jet black hair and copper skin blend with rock and bush, stretched lizardlike behind them. His rifle sights cover his enemy until he thinks his shot is sure. Fortunately for us, he is nervous, nor has he enough practice to make him always deadly when excited by the presence of scouts and soldiers; but many a corpse picked up in the roadway and trails, or by the very door of ranches, shows how perfect he is in ambush and surprise. You have but to see him gliding, springing, crawling upon most watchful game to make you marvel at the superhuman suppleness and strength of those steel-like muscles sheathed in bronze and guided by sight and cunning beyond all races of other human beings.

Suddenly, from a bush to the left of the group in which Watson is standing, comes a startling shot, and here I see true Apache courage, for without dodging too late, when the bullet had passed, a young scout by him sends a bullet into the very smoke, like the counterblow of a boxer. Then down they all go and fire from over the edge of the platform, until "Cease firing!" is ordered, as a yell of agony tells that no more danger lies in that bush.

The scouts called to the wounded Indian and used him to induce the others to come out; but these evidently thought they could stand us off until dusk and then take a plunge into the river. It was impossible to get a place from which a shot could be aimed, though one of the sergeants, an excellent shot, by firing against a rock almost in front of their cave, thereby splattered lead and splintered rock in their faces. At last a few of us got within fifty feet of them, on the very edge of the river, in a clump of bushes and boulders, only a narrow sandy strip between us. But as the shadows begin to fall, it seems rough to send men, in cold blood, into a hole like that, for some must be left, and so far we have not had one of these true, plucky fellows hit.

The order is about to be given for a rush, when the wounded Indian calls to his companions, telling what is going on. He then tells us they are afraid we will kill them if they give in. At once one of the men drops his pistol and stands out unarmed and tells them to come out. It seems for a second to fail; he is about to spring back when an old man steps out, ashy with fear, followed by the last two—such moments make life worth living.[6]

Surprising is it how quickly, from hatred for an armed enemy, the civilized man turns to pity for a prisoner who has shown nerve. Never shall I forget, as I reached the wounded Indian—the leader—a handsome young chap, hearing him call my name and recognizing him as a former scout of the first detachment I had been given several years before.

Some of the scouts were much disappointed when they found that we really did not intend to kill the broncos, especially not the wounded one, in whom they could see no earthly use. The practical Rowdy at once searched for concealed knives, telling the men to take the cartridges out of their revolvers, to prevent the prisoners from grabbing them in a fit of despair. Scouts and broncos soon departed with some of the men, to reach the horses and pack train before dark.

With the wounded Indian, twelve of us worked for several hours to get but halfway out of the canyon, three on each side and six others pulling these six up. At 10:00 P.M. we could do no more, having had nothing to eat since daybreak. We were too weak and determined to wait till a pack mule should arrive at the summit, in the meantime resting. Everything seemed on end; a fire we made licked the rock, as if trying to hold on, while we braced ourselves against the bushes. The Indian suffered frightfully and asked me to shoot him. One of the men said: "Mister, we's all pow'ful sorry about you, but damned glad 't ain't one of us." And so was I glad that it was not one of my good men.

As I woke up from a half hour's doze, all was black, the fire out, my Indian quiet. Touching him, he was cold, and I was glad that a man was dead. The men sprang up, happy to be relieved from that suffering mass. Soon again we begin to descend, letting ourselves down by bushes and the sides of crevices, having often to climb back from the edge of some brink, all black and bottomless beneath; an hour and a half more, it seemed like ten, when suddenly the bright, blazing campfires burst upon us. As we stood over them, the day seemed like a dream, but the glitter of the carbine barrel of a statue-like scout standing over two prostrate forms sent a thrill of reality to the very heart.

Next morning we passed near the hut of the day before. The old ranchman seemed to be rather glad that we arrived ahead of the broncos.

Thirty-six miles on level cow trails and a road. What a luxury is a road! What a relief to ride in the cavalry, after pulling your horse up and down for days! Why not send infantry? It has been done. The bronco then takes to broad, white, waterless stretches between the mountain ranges. Next day, sitting in calm seclusion on a high peak, under the shade of a cedar, he rolls a cigarette and takes a good long nap while Johnnie comes marching on at three miles an hour. Poor Johnnie; he gets more wheelbarrow and less training than his brother who has horses to groom.

Reaching the mining town of Globe, we are given a royal welcome, meet many old acquaintances, the hospitable citizens give the command a ball, and we get up next morning, sorry to leave. Twenty-eight miles more, and we are at the agency again. Near it lies the great cantonment of San Carlos, the dreariest place of exile on this continent, and where no officer or man should be allowed to remain longer than six months. White, hot, arid, treeless, grassless, desolate, swept for hours each day by clouds of parching dust. Here I left Watson, and I will never cease to thank Providence for putting me under him on that chase. Five hours' trot brings us to Thomas, every man and horse sound and hearty, except two sent back the second day and a lead horse lost on the day of the capture. A merry day it was for old K Troop as it welcomed back its comrades.[7]

Scouting in Arizona, 1890

JAMES W. WATSON[1]

Journal of the United States Cavalry Association 10, no. 37
(June 1897): 128–35

In March 1890 a Mormon freighter was murdered by Apache Indians on the road between San Carlos and Fort Thomas, in Arizona. Detachments were sent out from these posts to apprehend the murderers. After riding most of the night, the two detachments met about sunrise[2] near the scene of the murder. The detachment from Fort Thomas was under Lieutenant Clarke of the Tenth Cavalry, with Tenth Cavalry soldiers of his own troop; and the one from San Carlos was under Lieutenant Watson of the same regiment and consisted of Indian scouts and Fourth Cavalry soldiers.

Clarke was a typical cavalry officer—an expert rider who could do anything with a horse, energetic, dashing, bold to the point of utter recklessness, and fond of field service. Chief among the scouts and most faithful of them all, and one of the ablest and pluckiest, was Rowdy, then a sergeant. He was young in years—only about twenty-eight then—but old in Indian wars and loved campaigning and fighting and killing even better than he loved whiskey. He was very much loved and also feared by his brother scouts and had great influence over them. Among the Fourth Cavalrymen was Sergeant Daniels, a Texan, who had been a cowboy. A braver, cooler, and more genuine cavalryman than Sergeant Daniels never rode a horse.

The trail of the murderers was soon found, taken up, and followed by the united forces. The murderers had taken with them the two large horses of the dead freighter, and their large tracks aided the scouts very much in following the trail, which led up the bare, rugged sides of the Gila range of mountains. Sunset found us about fifty miles on the trail, which was going in a northwestern direction.

The day's work had given us some important information.

We found from the trail there were five of the murderers; we found also that the murder was not one of those sporadic ones so common then among the Apaches, resulting from a tizwin drunk, but it was simply the first act of a regular outbreak. The party was a regular war party, who had renounced their allegiance to all constituted authority and gone on the warpath. The freighter happened to be the first white man they had run across so far, and they had simply killed him on general principles and in accordance with the code of the warpath. It was supposed, when we left our posts, to be merely the result of a tizwin drunk and that we would find the murderers somewhere about their camps. For this reason, we had only one day's rations with us. But our information put a new aspect on affairs. We were now on the beginning of a trail that would probably lead all over Arizona and New Mexico and into Old Mexico. We had only half rations for the next day. The question of rations, however, did not cut much of a figure as we would most likely get near some military post and could send in. In the meantime, there were plenty of cattle in the valleys and deer in the mountains, and the trail would no doubt lead into some ranch where the hostiles would go to get fresh horses.

The prospects of a spring campaign were viewed with pleasure. Clarke was overjoyed to get in the field again. The soldiers were delighted to get out of drill and fatigue duty. After supper the scouts lit their cigarettes and, gathering around their campfire, discussed the situation. Rowdy, on such occasions, was a most interesting and entertaining talker to his brother scouts, as would be shown by their faces, now grave and fierce, now convulsed with laughter. On this occasion he told them how it was most likely we would get down into Mexico and how we would probably have a fight with the Mexicans, who had put him in jail once in Captain Crawford's time. The scouts were much interested, for they all had old scores to settle with the Mexicans. The abundance of mescal (Mexican whiskey) down there and the ease in getting it was no doubt another attraction Mexico had for them. Indeed, Mexico had a peculiar fascination for all scouts and many cavalrymen. There was something to appeal to all temperaments and dispositions down there. It was a foreign country, full of novel and interesting sights for an American. There was mescal in abundance. There were all kinds of gambling games, and scouts were great gamblers. There was always a first-class show for a fight with the Mexican irregular troops. So the prospects of a long ride over Arizona and New Mexico and probably into Old Mexico were hailed with delight, and the fact of having no rations in no way dampened the feeling of exultation.

A scout or a cavalryman of the Plains is never more at home than on the wide prairies or in the rough mountains of that country. It is his element, his home. He is very likely to get lost or "rattled" in a large city and perhaps not find his way back to his hotel at night, but he will never get lost or rattled on plain or mountain. As long as his horse and carbine are in good condition, he feels at ease under all circumstances. The boundless, pathless plain and the rough and ragged mountains, peak after peak and range after range—it is all his love and special domain; and the young cavalry officer with a good command of trusty Indian scouts, or scouts and soldiers, and a roving commission over this vast country feels that he is monarch of all he surveys.

At daylight next morning[3] we were in the saddle and trotting along the trail. It was plainly making for the rough country in the Sierra Ancha mountains. Towards noon one or two recruits, who in some way got in the detail, began to play out. They were utilized to send into San Carlos, then about thirty miles distant, for rations. By figuring on the time it would take them to get in and where the trail would take us by that time, and then figuring again on where the trail would take us the next day and the time it would take to get rations out—a kind of indeterminate equation, to speak mathematically—it was possible to fix on a place where rations could be sent to meet us without our having to wait for them. We knew the country well and could figure very closely on the way the trail would have to go. It took us within two miles of the place designated, which we reached a little before sunset next day; the rations, however, had not arrived. Here we got our first meal of the day, having killed a beef and having obtained about half rations of coffee and salt from a ranchman who lived near. Just as we were pulling out, about sunrise next morning, Sergeant Cheatham of the Tenth Cavalry, with a small detachment, emerged from a little side canyon and fell in in our rear with the much desired rations just in the nick of time, not even a halt being made. He had left San Carlos at 11:00 P.M. the night before and had made a night march to this point of forty-five miles. The last half of this was over a mountain trail, a hard road to travel at night. The old fellow looked very tired and worn as he rode up, but his indomitable nerve and pluck carried him on forty-five miles more this day—a continuous ride of ninety miles from 11:00 P.M. to sunset next day.

The country this day was of the roughest description. The trail led up and down rocky mountain ridges not far from perpendicular, where it was extremely difficult to lead the horses—for we had to lead them nearly all day—and the poor animals would become rattled and seemed to gaze with piteous and pleading eyes at their leaders, as if imploring not to be forced over such a fearful country. It was a day that tested hearts and lungs to the uttermost, and if anyone had been along with a weak heart or lungs that day he would surely have succumbed.

In the afternoon we got down to the bottom of Salt River Canyon, which here presents the striking and awe-inspiring features of the Grand Canyon of the Colorado. The hostiles had here got into a place so rough they could not use their horses anymore and in accordance with the customs of the warpath had killed the poor animals that had carried them so far. From here on the trail was on foot, which made it much more difficult to follow. For several hours it was lost entirely. The scouts became disheartened and discouraged and would sit down or lie down and rest instead of looking for the trail. Appeal had to be made to their sensibilities. Rowdy was fond of notoriety, and he was told how all the papers would talk of him if we captured the hostiles; how he would be praised for his good work, even in Washington; how all the people in Arizona would know of him and thank him; and last but not least, of the large reward in money the scouts would get if the murderers were caught. The appeal had the desired effect, and they went to work again with a will, getting down on

A reconnaissance. CENTURY MAGAZINE, JULY 1891.

their "all fours" and working along like so many foxhounds. At last, after three or four hours of slow, patient work, the trail was picked up on the banks of the river, in the sand, and we slept on it again that night down in the somber depths of the Salt River Canyon.

At dawn next day[4] Rowdy, with the best trailers among the scouts, took up the trail on foot, for after the hostiles got on foot, horses could follow it no longer. Indeed, few soldiers or white men could go where the scouts had to go. The remainder of the detachment, with all the animals, had to work their way around as best as they could to where the canyon opened out, about fifteen miles below. This point was reached about 1:00 P.M., and the scouts, whom we had not seen since they left in the morning, had not yet arrived. They were somewhere in the rough country behind us that we had gone around. We were watering our horses in the river, when suddenly the distant echoes of a rifle shot were heard in the mountains behind us, then another, and another. It meant the scouts had come up with the hostiles. Next was seen the dim outline of a human figure on top of a high ridge a mile or so distant, waving his arms. It did not take long to get to the top of the ridge. After a short dash over brush and boulders, the horses were left at the foot of the ridge, and everyone clambered on foot up the steep and rocky sides. Sergeant Daniels was the first man on top. The waving figure was Rowdy. He was already in fighting costume; that is, entirely naked except his breechclout. The other scouts hurriedly got themselves in the same savage but warlike dress, taking off even their moccasins, so their feet would have firmer hold on the rocks, and tying their long hair back behind their heads to keep their eyesight always clear.

Dispositions were soon made for the approaching fight. The result was to put the hostiles' position in the center of an equilateral triangle and a group of about seven soldiers or scouts at each vertex. So arranged, the fire from each group into the hostiles would pass between the other two groups. If the hostiles should make a break to get out, they would have to pass between two groups and be exposed to their fire as well as the fire from the third group. The hostiles were hidden away in a clump of rocks and bushes about one hundred yards from each group. There was no possibility of their escape. The main problem was to get all of them without losing any of our men, all of whom were securely sheltered behind rocks. The far-reaching voice of a scout was used to call down to the hostiles, telling them they could see for themselves there was no possibility of escape, and if any of them wished to surrender they would be allowed to do so. The leader called back, "If you want us, come down and get us," and added some uncomplimentary remarks about the agent.

The order was given to "commence firing," and very soon three converging showers of bullets were pouring into the hostile position. The hostiles immediately returned the fire, and at first their puffs of smoke came with vigor and rapidity, but soon slackened down and came only at intervals. The whole field of action was filled with whizzing and zipping bullets, which, hitting the rocks, would glance off in all directions. The "whiz" of the bullets was more sharply distinct than the report of the carbines. No one was in sight. Only the puffs of smoke showed where the firing came from. The hot fire of the three groups was raising a cloud of dust, leaves, and broken fragments of rock about the hostile position; the mountains and hills around reverberated with the rapid reports of the carbines; and the whole valley became filled with the smoke and every variety of "whiz" from the flying bullets. A French general said of the charge of the Light Brigade at Balaklava, "It is magnificent, but it is not war." So all this smoke and din and whizzing of bullets was a very fine sight and magnificent too, on a small scale, but neither was it war, because it was not bringing us any results in the shape of dead hostiles. The fire that would break out from them now and then showed they were still as much alive as ever. It was necessary to draw the lines closer around them. Two of the groups united and worked up under cover of the rocks or any kind of shelter to within fifty yards of the hostile position. We were fighting Apaches, and we fought them according to their own tactics. Their cardinal principle is "Kill as many of your enemies as you can, but don't be such a fool as to get killed yourself." All we could see were the puffs of smoke from their position. So all they could see of us were puffs of smoke; and we had the great advantage of being able to move around, while they could not.

Our new position did not help us much. The closest scrutiny did not reveal the least glimpse of a hostile. After some random firing from this position, a small party of about ten scouts and soldiers, including Clarke and Rowdy, taking advantage of all cover, made a rush which took them right among the rocks of the hostile position. Here was a large rock, or boulder, approximately the size of a freight boxcar, but of a rough and irregular shape. We were on one side of this rock, and the hostiles were on the other and not more than forty feet distant.

Clarke, who was always ahead in dangerous places, was the first to clamber up this rock and peep over on the other side. After looking around for some time he got a glimpse of a patch of red skin. Two shots fired at this patch of red skin did not cause any kind of movement, from which it was concluded the hostile was already dead. And so it was found afterwards. A bullet had entered his right eye and gone through his head. He had been killed by one of the hundreds of bullets in the act of firing, no doubt, as was indicated by the position of his rifle.

Rowdy, who had got on top of the large rock, discovered another patch of red skin, which he made out to be an arm. He fired at this, and in return, three bullets spattered against the rock close to his head. Rowdy peeped over again, and this time he made out the left side of the same hostile. He aimed with great deliberation, and the shot brought several bullets in return, but soon groans were heard from the wounded hostile. Rowdy, as he squirted a mouthful of tobacco juice over the rock, remarked, "I guess I got that feller that time."

But the wounded Apache was game. He was discovered again through the foliage and rocks; this time a small part of his leg showed just above the knee. Another bullet struck him, about six inches above the knee, shattering the bones of his leg. The nervy fellow, wounded to death as he was, roused up enough strength to send back several bullets in rapid succession, which spattered against the rock near our heads. The last bullet had, however, given him his mortal wound and ended the fight. He called up to us that he could not fight anymore and said he had told the others to surrender, as their cause was hopeless. He was chief of the band. The others soon came out of their hiding places and surrendered. One was wounded in the arm. One was found dead, as previously mentioned. The chief, a handsome young fellow, was shot in the left arm, had two ribs broken on his left side—Rowdy's two shots—and the bones of his right thigh were shattered into fragments. We tried to carry him back to camp—an extremely difficult undertaking over such rough country, and it was then about dusk. Rowdy, who was always very practical in all matters, remarked, "I don't think we'll ever get that feller up that hill; I think we better kill him." The poor fellow was suffering the most intense agony and begged us to kill him. Even in these supreme moments he would break out now and then into snatches of an old Apache war song. We did all we could for him, but to no purpose. Death soon put an end to his sufferings. None of the hostiles escaped. Our success was complete and was owing mainly to the good work of the scouts in trailing and, above all, to the bulldog tenacity and faithfulness of Rowdy. None of us were injured, which was due to the fact that we used the hostiles' own tactics against them.

Rowdy got everything that was promised him that fearfully tiresome day down in Salt River Canyon. He got a medal from Congress. He and the other scouts got the reward from the governor of Arizona. He made hosts of friends in Arizona. And what pleased him probably more than anything else, he got his name in every paper in Arizona and New Mexico. Rowdy was an original and interesting character. He had some virtues of a high order and many vices. He was unswervingly faithful to his friends and terribly faithless to all others. He would kill a wounded prisoner to save the trouble of getting him to camp but would cry like a child on saying good-bye to a friend.

NOTES

Introduction

1. C. L. Sonnichsen, editor, *Geronimo and the End of the Apache Wars* (Tuscon: Arizona History Society, 1987), 49; Dan L. Thrapp, *The Conquest of Apacheria* (Norman: University of Oklahoma Press, 1967), viii. Thrapp's is the best single work on the Apache wars. The finest works from the Apache perspective are Eve Ball's *In the Days of Victorio* (Tucson: University of Arizona Press, 1970) and *Indeh, An Apache Odyssey* (Provo: Brigham University Press, 1980). Her two most prominent informants, Daklugie, son of Juh, and James Kaywaykla, grandnephew of Nana, both disputed the "White Eyes'" broad classification of the Eastern and Southern bands as Chiricahuas, saying that only the bands of Cochise and Chihuahua were true Chiricahuas. Ball, *In the Days*, 43, and *Indeh*, 22.
2. Quoted in Gordon C. Baldwin, *The Warrior Apaches* (Tucson: Dale Stuart King, 1965), 32.
3. Ball, *Indeh*, 26–27.
4. Ball, *In the Days*, 28.
5. Ralph H. Ogle, *Federal Control of the Western Apache* (Albuquerque: University of New Mexico Press, 1970), 215.
6. Thrapp, *Conquest of Apacheria*, 367.

PART ONE: RAIDS AND REPRISALS IN APACHERIA, 1865–72

William F. M. Arny: Indians in New Mexico

1. An ardent abolitionist and former chairman of the Kansas committee of the Republican Party, William F. M. Arny (1813–81) was appointed agent to the Utes and Jicarilla Apaches of northern New Mexico in 1860. In 1862 he was appointed territorial secretary for New Mexico, a position he held until 1867.

Edward Palmer: A Great Slaughter of Apaches

1. Apparently the post surgeon at Camp Lincoln.
2. Hiram S. Washburn (1820–89), a surveyor and miner whom the territorial governor had commissioned in the summer of 1865 to raise men for the Arizona Volunteers.
3. Renamed Camp Verde on November 23, 1868.
4. The volunteers did good work until a lack of pay and supplies, as well as sickness and desertions, forced their disbandment in the autumn of 1868.

John C. Cremony: The Apache Race

1. John C. Cremony (d. 1879) got his first taste of frontier life in the Mexican War as a second lieutenant in the 1st Massachusetts Infantry. During the Civil War he served as a captain with the 2nd California Cavalry, taking part in the Battle of Apache Pass in 1862. Cremony was mustered out as a major a year later. He returned to San Francisco, where he wrote articles for *The Overland Monthly*. In 1868 Cremony published *Life among the Apaches*, an account of his exploits with the Bartlett Boundary Survey after the Mexican War. His article "The Apache Race" appeared in *The Overland Monthly* later that year.

2. As it appeared in *The Overland Monthly*, "The Apache Race" contained several introductory paragraphs unrelated to the Apaches; these have been dropped from the text presented here.
3. The Navajo and Apache languages are similar, but not identical; the Navajo are usually regarded as a separate tribe. The Lipan Apaches dwelled on the plains of western Texas.
4. A *jicora* (not jicara) is a cup fashioned from a gourd.
5. "Journey of the Dead Man," a desolate stretch of New Mexico also called the *Jornada de Muerte*, or "Journey of Death."
6. It is evident that Cremony included in his numerical estimate the Navajos and Eastern Apache peoples; most contemporaneous observers placed the number of Western Apaches and Chiricahuas at closer to six thousand. Ogle, *Federal Control*, xvii.

Camillo C. C. Carr: The Days of the Empire—Arizona, 1868–1869

1. Camillo C. C. Carr (1842–1914) enlisted in the 1st U.S. Cavalry in 1862. Carr was promoted to captain for his successful scout against Big Rump. He became editor of the *Cavalry Journal* in 1890 and retired a brigadier general in 1906.
2. Maj. Gen. Irvin McDowell (1818–85) commanded the Department of California from 1864 to 1868.
3. George B. Sanford (1842–1908). Breveted lieutenant colonel for gallantry during the Civil War, Sanford served widely on the postwar frontier. He retired as colonel of the 6th Cavalry in 1892.
4. Carr stumbles on both the Latin and Spanish names; they are the *Carnegiea gigantea*, or saguaro cactus.
5. The people Carr describes in such fantastic terms were early Pueblo Indians.
6. The palo verde is unsuitable for fuel, not because it will not burn, but because it burns too rapidly and leaves no coals.
7. According to an 1860 census, the white population of Arizona County, New Mexico (as the territory was then known), was 2,421. By 1866 the non-Indian population had climbed to 7,200.
8. Capt. Clarence E. Bennett (1833–1902) of the 6th U.S. Cavalry. A member of the West Point class of 1855, Bennett rose to the rank of lieutenant colonel of the 1st California Volunteer Cavalry during the Civil War.
9. Probably Lt. Frederick E. Camp of the 32nd U.S. Infantry.
10. The scout lasted from September 27 until October 6, 1868. Lieutenant Thomas Ewing of the Arizona Volunteers guided the scout with a Maricopa, and not a Pima, Indian as trailer. Five officers and ninety-one enlisted men participated in the scout.
11. Carr errs on two counts. Delshay, or "Red Ant" (c. 1838–74), was either a Tonto or Yavapai chief. Carr also mistook Wa-poo-eta, or "Big Rump" (d. 1869), another Yavapai chieftain and an inveterate raider, for Delshay. Wa-poo-eta claimed the loyalty of 748 people, while Delshay's band numbered only 200—too few for the several hundred Apaches Carr says came into Fort McDowell. Both Delshay and Wa-poo-eta remained bitter foes of the whites until their death.
12. Maj. Gen. Henry W. Halleck (1815–72) commanded the Military Division of the Pacific from 1865–69.
13. Bvt. Maj. Gen. George Crook assumed command of the Department of Arizona on June 4, 1871.
14. Literally, "bad country."
15. Carr returned to Arizona in November 1871 to participate in Crook's Tonto Basin Campaign, the results of which he lauds in this article.

James Deine: An Incident of the Hualapais War

1. Charles Spencer (1840–86) drifted into the Arizona Territory during the Civil War. He bore the Hualapais no grudge for his brush with death. "I do not blame the Indians so much as people think I ought," he later wrote. "It was wartime for them, and their men, women, and children had been killed by the whites, so why not retaliate?" Spencer remained in the Hualapais' country, mining for ore and marrying a Hualapai woman. He attained great influence in the tribe and organized Hualapai scouts for the army. A violent, hard-drinking man withal, he was killed in a drunken brawl with a business partner in November 1886. Leo W. Banks, "Charley Spencer's Final Battle," *Arizona Highways* 75, no. 11 (November 1999): 10–13.
2. Lt. Levi H. Robinson (1840–74) of the 14th U.S. Infantry.
3. Maj. William R. Price (1838–81) of the 8th U.S. Cavalry.
4. Scherum was one of three principal Walapai chiefs, the others being Wauba-Yuba and Walapais-Charley.

John Green: Interesting Scout among White Mountain Apaches

1. John Green (1825–1908) of the 1st U.S. Cavalry later won the Medal of Honor for service during the Modoc War. He retired a lieutenant colonel in 1889.
2. Not found with the copy I examined.
3. A board of survey later found Gallager responsible for the lost mules and supplies.
4. Corydon E. Cooley (1836–1917) later married two daughters of the White Mountain chief Pedro and became a prosperous rancher.
5. Henry W. Dodd (1839–86), later a successful scout.
6. Green misunderstood Miguel's Apache name; it was Esh-ke-iba. Miguel (d. 1874) proved a fast friend of the whites.
7. Bvt. Maj. Gen. George W. Getty (1819–1901).
8. Probably a reference to Carrizo Creek.
9. Ditches.
10. Green later received authorization to build his post, establishing Camp Apache in May 1870.
11. The Natanes Mountains, also known as the Natanes Plateau, located on the western part of the San Carlos reservation.
12. A reference to the Santa Catalina, or Catalina, Mountains.
13. Eureka Springs is located fifteen miles west of Fort Grant.
14. Aravaipa Creek rises near Eureka Springs and flows southwest into the San Pedro River.
15. On April 29, 1869, Green led elements of three troops of the 1st U.S. Cavalry and detachments from the 14th and 32nd U.S. Infantry regiments on an attack against an Apache rancheria at Turnbull Mountain.

E. Andrews: Military Surgery among the Apache Indians

1. E. Andrews was professor of surgery at the Chicago Medical College at the time he wrote.
2. A probable reference to an engagement between troops D and K of the 3rd U.S. Cavalry and renegade Mescalero Apaches at Sierra Diablo, New Mexico, on October 18, 1867, in which Indian casualties were reported at between twenty-five and thirty killed and wounded.

Mary W. Adams: An Arizona Adventure: An Incident of Army Life on the Frontier

1. Mary Wildman Adams (d. 1917) was the wife of Lt. John Quincy Adams (1843–1919) of the 1st U.S. Cavalry. Married to Lieutenant Adams on December 17, 1867, she joined her husband in Arizona in late 1868. Their first child was born at Fort Bowie the following year.
2. Adams mistakenly gives the year as 1870; her husband's company left Arizona for Oregon in February 1871.
3. A reference to Reuben F. Bernard (1834–1903) of the 1st U.S. Cavalry, his wife, Alice Frank Bernard, and their two-year-old son, Harry (a daughter, Victoria, who had been born prematurely on October 27, 1868, died in March 1869). A former enlisted man, Bernard had been promoted through the ranks for gallantry during the Civil War.
4. Gerald Russell (1832–1905) of the 3rd U.S. Cavalry. Hereafter, I have replaced the first initial of last names—the manner in which Adams identifies people—with their complete last names.
5. Henriette McElroy Russell (d. 1892).
6. A short range some twenty-five miles northwest of Tucson.

"Gashuntz": On the March to Fort Yuma

1. Troop K, 1st. U.S. Cavalry, apparently trailed Captain Bernard and his party, whose march is described in the preceding article, by several days. Troop K was en route to a new duty station at Fort Halleck, Nevada. Unlike Bernard's group, the troopers encountered no hostiles.
2. A reference to sunrise.
3. Now a national monument, Casa Grande is one of the finest examples extant of pueblos constructed during the classic period of Hohokam culture in the Southwest (c. 1300–1450 A.D.).

William S. Oury: Historical Truth: The So-called "Camp Grant Massacre" of 1871

1. A former Texas Ranger, William S. Oury (1817–87) was a veteran of the Texas War for Independence, the Mexican War, and campaigns against the Comanches. He settled in Arizona in 1856 and was the first mayor of Tucson; from 1873 to 1877 he was sheriff of Pima County.
2. There were two other Tucson residents chosen to call on Stoneman: Charles S. Mowry and D. A. Bennett. Oury and his associates visited Stoneman in late March 1871.
3. Pierson W. Dooner published the *Weekly Arizonian* until competition from the weekly *Arizona Citizen* compelled him to close shop and leave Tucson the very day of the Camp Grant massacre.
4. Leslie B. Wooster, killed March 20, 1871.
5. William Cook, killed when the Hughes ranch at Crittenden was "jumped" on March 18.
6. This occurred on March 10.
7. Jesus Maria Elias, member of a once wealthy family of ranchers whose properties near Tubac had been wiped out by the Apaches.
8. Francisco Galerita (d. 1879), chief of the Papagoes.
9. Oury neglected to mention that all but 8 of his 144 victims were women and children—raped, clubbed to death, hacked to pieces, or brained by rocks.
10. John Montgomery (1830–1924) owned Tombstone's OK Corral.
11. The Apaches seldom took scalps.

Andrew H. Cargill: The Camp Grant Massacre

1. John M. Ross (d. 1884) of the 21st U.S. Infantry.
2. Alexander O. Brodie (1849–1918) of the 21st U.S. Cavalry, later lieutenant colonel of the Rough Riders in the Spanish-American War and a territorial governor of Arizona.
3. Cargill erred; General Stoneman, rather than Crook, was then in command of the Department of Arizona.
4. Merejildo Grijalva (1842–1916), of Opata or Mexican parentage, had been captured by Cochise at age ten. He later became one of the leading guides and scouts in the Southwest.
5. This occurred in early February 1871.
6. Eskiminzin (1828–95) was head chief of the Aravaipa Apaches. After bolting briefly from the San Carlos reservation in 1873, he took up farming and became steadfast in his desire for peace.
7. Delshay was not among those who came in with Eskiminzin; the two who accompanied Eskiminzin were Santos and Little Captain. Don Schellie, *Vast Domain of Blood: The Story of the Camp Grant Massacre* (Los Angeles: Westernlore Press, 1968), 84–85.
8. A wild exaggeration on someone's part; Eskiminzin commanded the loyalty of just over three hundred Indians.
9. Estimates of the dead vary. The post surgeon at Camp Grant, Dr. Conant B. Briesly, said he saw 21 bodies but added that Apache survivors told him 85 had been killed; Miles L. Wood, the beef contractor for Camp Grant, counted 138 dead. Whitman himself reported 125 killed. Thrapp, *Conquest of Apacheria*, 90.
10. Vincent Colyer later recorded that Eskiminzin had lost two wives and five children.
11. A former California Forty-niner and Union soldier, Converse W. C. Rowell took office on July 1, 1869, as the United States district attorney for the territory of Arizona.
12. Henry R. Mizner (1827–1915) emerged from the Civil War a brevet brigadier general of volunteers. As major of the 12th U.S. Infantry, he commanded Camp Lowell until August 1872.
13. Granville H. Oury died in 1891, while a delegate to Congress.
14. Tucson businessman Hiram Stevens (d. 1893) had been elected chairman of the town's committee of public safety, formed to deal with the Indian problem.
15. Sidney R. De Long (1828–1914) worked for a mercantile and freighting firm in Tucson at the time of the Camp Grant massacre. He was elected mayor of Tucson in 1872. From 1905 until his death, De Long was secretary of the Arizona Pioneers Historical Society.

Sylvester Mowry: The Arizona Indians

1. Sylvester Mowry (1833–71) settled in the fledgling Arizona Territory after resigning his commission as an army lieutenant in 1858. He became a successful mining entrepreneur and land promoter. Arrested as a Southern sympathizer during the Civil War, Mowry was not permitted to return to Arizona until the war ended.
2. Howard B. Cushing (1838–71) enlisted in a volunteer artillery battery during the Civil War, ending the conflict as a second lieutenant in the 4th U.S. Artillery. Two of his brothers attained reknown during the war: Lt. William Cushing, of the Navy, for sinking the Confederate ram *Albemarle* with a torpedo, and Lt. Alonzo Cushing of the army, who died at Gettysburg, commanding his regular Artillery battery. Howard was transferred to the 3rd U.S. Cavalry in 1867. He carved out a reputation as a daring and resourceful Indian fighter in Arizona.

3. Cushing was killed on May 5, 1871, ambushed during a scout in the Whetstone Mountains. Dan Thrapp doubts that Cochise participated in the affair, believing Juh to have been the Apache war leader in that action. Thrapp, *Conquest of Apacheria*, 77.

4. Here Mowry confuses Cochise with Eskiminzin.

Charles B. Genung: Indians and Indigo

1. Charles B. Genung (1839–1916) was one of Arizona's most prominent pioneers. Poor health led Genung to strike out for Arizona in 1863, where he helped extract gold at the famed Vulture Mine near La Paz. Genung gained prominence fighting Indians during the Civil War years, and in July 1867 George W. Dent, brother-in-law to Ulysses S. Grant and the superintendent of Indian affairs for the Arizona Territory, made Genung agent for the Yavapais and Mohave Apaches of the Colorado River Indian Reservation. In later years, Genung built a wagon road across west-central Arizona, staked numerous mining claims, served as a justice of the peace, a postmaster, a constable, and a deputy sheriff in Yavapai County.

2. Edward F. Bowers, later an unsuccessful candidate for sheriff of Agua Fria County.

3. The dead herder was John Gantt, a Civil War veteran.

4. A noted Arizona character, Thomas G. Roddick (c. 1837–79) was a good Indian fighter, competent scout, hard drinker, and successful miner.

5. John B. Townsend (1835–73) served briefly in the Confederate army before drifting into Arizona in 1863. The notoriety he gained killing Indians won him a scouting job on Crook's Tonto Basin Campaign. In late September 1872 Townsend took fifteen scalps while on a scout, which led Crook to dismiss him.

6. Their guide was José de Leon, considered by many to be the best guide in Arizona.

7. Detachments from Troops A, E, and G of the 3rd U.S. Cavalry under Charles Morton (1846–1914), a future general.

8. It was Genung, in fact, who named the mountain "Ox Yoke." Barnes, *Arizona Place Names*, 213.

9. Polles Mesa.

10. The fight occurred on June 8, 1871.

11. The base of the Mazatzal Mountains.

12. The valley of Tonto Creek.

13. Genung is correct, and the running fight there on June 9, 1871, was named for the creek. For the two days of fighting, Lieutenant Morton recorded fifty-six Indians killed and eight wounded, with no losses to his or Townsend's command.

14. Camp Reno had been abandoned in March 1870.

15. He was a Greek named Philip Tedro, who had converted to Islam and taken the name Hadj Ali. His southwestern acquaintances corrupted his adopted name to Hi Jolly.

16. Nathan A. M. Dudley (1825–1910) of the 3rd U.S. Cavalry.

17. Townsend was killed on September 16, 1873, at Dripping Springs, sixteen miles south of the present Mayer, Arizona.

18. June 17, 1871.

19. The inscription on the stock read, "Presented to J. B. Townsend by the citizens of Prescott, June 1871, Honor to the Brave!"

Frank K. Upham: Incidents of Regular Army Life in Time of Peace

1. Frank K. Upham (1841–1899) served as a lieutenant in the 7th California Infantry during the Civil War; afterward, he was commissioned a second lieutenant in the 1st U.S. Cavalry. He retired a captain in 1892, became acting governor of the Vol-

unteer Soldiers' Home in Los Angeles, and was killed by the accidental discharge of a weapon in 1899.

2. On April 1, 1871, Upham married Sarah Elvira Camp at Dixon, Illinois, and brought her west.

3. Camp Apache.

4. The Uphams' first child, Frank, was born in September 1872.

[William D. Fuller]: An Evening with the Apaches

1. William D. Fuller (d. 1886) was a graduate of the West Point class of 1861. He commanded Company B, 21st U.S. Infantry, at Camp Apache until June 1872, when he was placed under arrest for reasons not made public, and he resigned his commission before the matter came to trial. Internal evidence suggests Fuller to be the author of this article.

2. Miguel (d. 1874) was in fact a Cibicue Apache chief.

3. The dance Fuller describes was ceremonial in nature, with the masked dancers impersonating the mountain spirits, or *gaun*, of White Mountain Apache mythology. The gaun were held to have power over humans, either for good or evil, depending on how one approached them. Gordon C. Baldwin, *The Warrior Apaches* (Tucson: Dale Stuard King, 1965), 106. As Miguel was a Cibicue Apache chief, and the gaun dance was of the White Mountain Apaches, Fuller's article suggests the two bands interacted both socially and in ceremonial matters on the Camp Apache reservation.

4. For another description of the gaun dance, see James S. Pettit's "Apache Campaign Notes—1886," in part 5 of this volume.

[Guy V. Henry]: Cavalry Life in Arizona

1. These anonymous recollections of cavalry service in Arizona in 1871–72 undoubtedly were written by an officer of Troop D, 3rd U.S. Cavalry. Only two officers, Capt. Guy V. Henry and Lt. William H. Andrews, accompanied the troop to Arizona. Judging from their contents, it would seem Henry authored the letters.

   Guy V. Henry (1839–99) graduated with the West Point Class of 1861 and rose to the volunteer rank of colonel in the Civil War, earning a Medal of Honor for gallantry at Cold Harbor. Henry accompanied Crook north on the Big Horn campaign of 1876, taking a bullet in the face at the Battle of the Rosebud. A major general of volunteers during the War with Spain, he was military of governor of Puerto Rico from December 1898 to May 1899.

2. Edwin H. Shelton (d. 1880), West Point Class of 1870.

3. Bernard G. Semig (c. 1841–83), a Hungarian immigrant.

4. Anson Mills (1834–1924) rose to the rank of colonel, serving with distinction during the Big Horn and Yellowstone expeditions of 1876. Mills became a millionaire after the army adopted for general use a cartridge belt he had patented.

5. A reference to John Townsend.

6. Henry had attended the Artillery School at Fort Monroe, Virginia, from 1867 to 1869.

7. A reference to the Townsend expedition.

8. In the Tonto Basin.

9. Probably a reference to French Joe Canyon in the Whetstone Mountains.

10. William J. Ross (1846–1907) resigned his commission and settled in Arizona in October 1875.

11. Frank Stanwood (1842–72) was a popular and able officer who died of tuberculosis at his father's home in Massachusetts.

12. William W. Robinson (1846–1917) served in the Nez Perce expedition of 1877

and the fight at Wounded Knee in 1890. He was retired for age as a brigadier general in 1910.

13. Charles Meinhold (1827–77) was a German immigrant who earned two brevets for gallantry during the Civil War.

14. Thomas L. Brent (c. 1845–84) was retired for disability after his horse stumbled and fell on him; he died blind and nearly paralyzed.

15. What Henry does not say is that Moore shied away from a chance at ambushing Cochise in Sulphur Springs Valley. "We thus lost one of the prettiest chances of giving the enemy a severe blow," wrote Crook angrily, because Moore "lacked one of the most essential qualities of a soldier—courage." Thrapp, *Conquest of Apacheria*, 98–99.

16. Not found. In late August 1867 Captain Henry led a scout composed of three companies of the Third Cavalry, Mexican scouts, and a company of newly enlisted Indian scouts from Camp Apache to Camp McDowell. His Indian scouts proved invaluable, enabling his cavalry to locate and defeat the hostiles in several engagements.

17. Vincent Colyer and his delegation.

Azor H. Nickerson: An Apache Raid, and a Long Distance Ride

1. Azor H. Nickerson (1837–1910) emerged from the Civil War a brevet major for gallantry at Antietam and at Gettysburg, where he sustained a chest wound so severe, recalled Gen. George Crook, that he "was left for dead and his recovery regarded as almost a miracle. He has now [1871] a hole in his chest which you can nearly stick your fist in, and at times suffers terribly from this wound. Notwithstanding all this, his ambition and zeal to do his duty has been so great, that he has been constantly on duty ever since the war." Nickerson served on Crook's staff for ten years, until his promotion to major on June 15, 1878. He retired four years later. Dan L. Thrapp, *Encyclopedia of Frontier Biography*, 4 vols. (Spokane: Arthur H. Clark Company, 1990–94), 3:1054.

2. May 22, 1872.

3. Archie McIntosh (1834–1902), the son of a Scotsman and a Chippewa woman.

4. Nickerson may have heard this from John Cremony, who claimed that Apaches were able to drive sheep faster than cattle. Arranging the sheep in a parallelogram, with the strongest animals on the edges, "in this manner the Apaches will run a flock of twenty-thousand sheep fifty to seventy miles in one day," wrote Cremony. Cremony, *Life among the Apaches*, 115.

5. Lt. William H. Boyle (1836–1919) of the 21st U.S. Infantry (major of volunteers during the Civil War) and Lt. Max Wesendorff (1836–1906) of the 1st U.S. Cavalry.

[George Crook]: General Howard's Mission

1. George Crook (1829–90), West Point class of 1852, saw wide service in the Pacific Northwest before the Civil War. He emerged from the war a major general of volunteers. Returning to the Northwest, he defeated the Northern Paiute Indians in several sharp skirmishes before being given command of the Department of Arizona in June 1871.

Although not attributed to Crook, this letter to the *Army and Navy Journal* bears every evidence of having been written by him, or perhaps for him by his aide-de-camp, John G. Bourke.

Like the anonymous correspondent cited as the source, Crook had fifteen years' experience fighting Indians. He habitually made use of the press to raise objections to policy or to trumpet his own successes, or had Bourke write such

articles for him. Crook objected to Howard's peace mission as absurdly inappropriate in view of continued Apache depredations. In April 1872, at the time the letter appeared in the *Journal*, Crook would have had urgent cause to criticize Howard's intentions openly—but anonymously, as he was required officially to cooperate with Howard. Howard, Crook said in his memoirs, was then trying to win officers of Crook's command over to his way of thinking by offering as an inducement easy duty in the East. Martin F. Schmitt, editor, *General George Crook, His Autobiography* (Norman: University of Oklahoma Press, 1960), 168–70.
2. A derisive reference to the Quakers.

[Oliver O. Howard, et al.]: General Howard's Treaties

1. Oliver O. Howard (1830–1909) rose to army command during the Civil War. Deeply religious, he was commissioner of the Freedman's Bureau from 1865 to 1872. Howard served in the Nez Perce campaign and commanded the Military Division of the Pacific.
2. In July 1872 Howard traveled first to New Mexico, then to Arizona to Cochise's mountain stronghold to seek peace with the Chiricahua chief. Cochise agreed to move onto a reservation in the Dragoon Mountains of southeastern Arizona; their accord was never set down in writing.
3. Santo had some time before yielded leadership of the Aravaipas to his son-in-law, Eskiminzin.
4. Oscar Hutton, a well-known guide and sometime Apache hunter.
5. Concepcion, an interpreter.
6. Crook said Howard had induced those residents of Tucson who had adopted Apache children taken in the Camp Grant Massacre to bring them to the council under the promise that if the children had no living parents, he would not turn them over to the Indians. Eskiminzin conceded them to be orphans but insisted on their return. Howard agreed, at which point, said Crook, "Judge McCaffrey got up in the presence of all and denounced Howard as being a liar and a brute." Martin F. Schmitt, ed., *Crook*, 172.
7. Several concluding paragraphs treating of subsequent conversations between Howard and the peaceable Pimas have been omitted from the text presented here.

A. P. K. Safford: Something about Cochise

1. Anson P. K. Safford (1828–91) served two terms as governor of the Arizona Territory, from 1869 to 1877. Safford advocated aggressive action against hostiles but dealt justly with peaceful bands. In 1870 he persuaded the War Department to make Arizona a separate military department, then engineered the removal of department commander George Stoneman in favor of George Crook.
2. Cochise (c.1805–74) ranked among the first order of Apache chieftains, with an influence that extended far beyond his Chokonen band of Chiricahuas.
3. The boy was seized along the Sonoita River, in Arizona, twelve miles west of Fort Buchanan, where Bascom was posted. He grew up to become the Indian scout and interpreter Mickey Free.
4. The incident at Bascom's tent occurred on February 4, 1861. Cochise was innocent; raiding Pinal Apaches had taken the boy.
5. The unfortunate station keeper was James F. Wallace, who was not dragged to his death that day, but rather killed along with three other Americans several days later. It may not have been Bascom, but rather a superior officer, 1st. Lt. Isaiah N. Moore, who ordered the hangings of the Chiricahaus in retaliation for the murder of Wallace and the other hostages Cochise had taken. For a thorough treatment of

the Bascom affair and its aftermath, see Edwin R. Sweeney, *Cochise: Chiricahua Apache Chief* (Norman: University of Oklahoma Press, 1991), 142–65.

6. Thomas J. Jeffords (1832–1914) was a well-traveled frontiersman, having driven stages and mined for gold in Colorado before coming to the Southwest.

Frederick G. Hughes: The Military and Cochise

1. Frederick G. Hughes (1837–1911) was a prominent Arizona pioneer who served in the Arizona Territory during the Civil War. Mustered out in 1866, Hughes settled in New Mexico until his friend, Indian agent Thomas J. Jeffords, asked him to work for him on the newly created Cochise reserve. Hughes later clerked for the Pima County board of supervisors and was an officer of the Arizona Pioneer Historical Society. For burning down the Tucson Courthouse to cover up peculations and gambling away historical society funds, Hughes served a short prison term.

2. Nick M. Rogers (1847–76).

3. A reference to the Nednhi, or Southern Chiricahuas.

4. This occurred in February 1873.

5. Most sources attribute Cochise's death to stomach cancer.

6. Taza (1843–76) was the eldest son of Cochise. Eskinya (1820–76) was both a medicine man and a famed raider.

7. Rogers and his assistant, Orizoba O. Spence, were killed after plying Eskinya's band with rotgut whiskey.

8. John P. Clum (1851–1932), later proprietor of the famous *Tombstone Epitaph* and mayor of the town.

9. Col. August V. Kautz (1828–95) commanded the Department of Arizona from 1875 to 1878.

10. Maj. Curwen B. McClellan of the 6th U.S. Cavalry.

11. Lt. Austin Henely (1848–78) of the 6th U S. Cavalry.

12. Capt. Frederick D. Ogilby (d. 1877) of the 8th U.S. Infantry.

PART TWO: CROOK'S TONTO BASIN CAMPAIGN AND AFTER, 1872–77

John G. Bourke: Crook's Campaign in '72

1. John G. Bourke (1846–96) enlisted in the Union army at age sixteen, winning a Medal of Honor at the Battle of Stones River. After the Civil War he attended West Point and was commissioned in the 3rd U.S. Cavalry. Bourke joined General Crook's staff when the latter took command of the Department of Arizona and served with him for the better part of the next fifteen years. A dedicated ethnologist, meticulous observer, and superb writer, Bourke published widely on the Indians with whom he came into contact. Notable among his ethnological writings are *The Medicine Men of the Apache* and *The Snake Dance of the Moquis*. He authored several invaluable historical works, the most noteworthy of which is the classic *On the Border with Crook*. Bourke also kept a remarkably full diary, 124 volumes of which are preserved in the United States Military Academy Library.

2. While a member of Crook's staff, Bourke often gave interviews or fed stories to the press favorable to his commander. Although sometimes an apologist for Crook, Bourke spoke truthfully and with a conviction based on close and meticulous observation.

The latter portion of Bourke's remarks pertain to the Sierra Madre Campaign of 1883, which had been concluded less than two months before Bourke's inter-

view with the *Inter-Ocean*, and for which Crook had come under attack in some quarters for seemingly lenient terms accorded the surrendered Chiricahua.
3. Chalipun was an Apache Mojave chief who controlled over two thousand of the hostile Tonto Basin Indians.

Anonymous: Early Days in Arizona with the Fifth U.S. Cavalry

1. The article was signed simply "An Old Non Com of the Fifth U.S. Cavalry."
2. The author makes the common error of referring to the Indian inhabitants of the Mazatzal and Pinal Mountains and the Salt River region as Apache. They were in fact Yavapais, a Yuman tribe linguistically unrelated to the Apache.
3. William H. Brown (1840–75) of the 5th U.S. Cavalry. An excellent combat officer, Brown also went on several special missions for General Crook of a more diplomatic nature, including a visit to Cochise to learn the terms of his treaty with General Howard.
4. Earl D. Thomas (1847–1921) of the 5th U.S. Cavalry became an aide to department commander August V. Kautz in March 1875, serving in that capacity until Kautz was relieved in March 1878. Thomas went on to serve in the Department of the Platte and retired a brigadier general in 1911.
5. December 28, 1872.
6. William J. Ross.
7. Francis Cahill (1846–77), an Irish immigrant and former enlisted man who joined on as a blacksmith with the 5th Cavalry. On August 17, 1877, after a quarrel near Fort Grant, he became the first shooting victim of Henry Antrim, the future Billy the Kid.
8. The first official report of the fight reported fifty-seven warriors killed; the number of women and children who perished was not reported. Brown brought away eighteen prisoners.

John G. Bourke: The Salt River Cave Fight

1. Salt River.
2. Bourke errs in labeling his enemy Apaches. They were Yavapais, a Yuman tribe linguistically unrelated to the Apaches.
3. George M. Randall (1841–1918) of the 23rd U.S. Infantry. Generally regarded as the finest infantry captain then serving in the territory, Randall was also a superb administrator of reservation Indians, who regarded him with respect and affection. Randall served in the Spanish-American War and later commanded the Department of Luzon in the Philippines. He retired a major general in 1905.
4. "Buy a lot" and "May."
5. Joseph Felmer (1830–1904) was a Prussian immigrant who served as an officer with the 1st California Cavalry during the Civil War. After the war he married an Apache woman, took up ranching in Arizona, and scouted for the army.

John G. Bourke: A Conference with Cochise

1. Although occupied principally with the ongoing Tonto Basin operations, General Crook kept a weather eye on Cochise and the Chiricahuas. To ensure their intentions remained peaceable, on January 5, 1873, he sent Captain Brown with six troops of the 5th U.S. Cavalry to visit Cochise. Thomas Jeffords, the agent for Cochise's band and an intimate friend of the chief, acted as interpreter for their conference.

   Brown and Cochise met on February 3. Neither was in good health. Brown had been ill for most of the expedition; Cochise was slowly dying of cancer. The following year Brown was detailed to purchase horses in California, then went on a year's sick leave. Apparently despondent over the June 3, 1875, marriage of Lt. General Philip H. Sheridan to Irene Rucker, whom he purportedly loved, Brown committed suicide the day after the wedding.

As in all matters he recorded, Bourke took pains to transcribe accurately the conference between Major Brown and Cochise. The delay occasioned as Jeffords translated gave Bourke the chance to capture the discussion nearly verbatim.

2. Bourke refers to Captain Brown by his brevet rank of major.

Wesley Merritt: Incidents of Indian Campaigning in Arizona

1. Wesley Merritt (1834–1910) was a successful Indian-fighting general who saw wide service on the Northern Plains. He retired a major general in 1900. The material presented here is excerpted from an article by Merritt entitled "Three Indian Campaigns."

2. Although Merritt does not name his informant, from the context it may be presumed to have been Capt. George M. Randall.

3. George F. Price, *Across the Continent with the Fifth Cavalry* (New York: D. Van Nostrand, 1883), 192.

4. George Crook.

5. Crook's program of "tagging" male Apaches began in earnest in the spring of 1873, after the surrender of Chalipun.

6. The account that follows appears to relate to Lt. Walter S. Schuyler's arrest of the notorious Tonto renegade Delshay in August 1873. Schuyler had with him at least eight soldiers and, probably, the veteran chief of scouts Al Sieber. Dan L. Thrapp, *Al Sieber, Chief of Scouts* (Norman: University of Oklahoma Press, 1964): 120–24.

7. Mojave Charley.

8. On May 27, 1873, Chunz and Chan-deisi, a discharged scout belonging to Cochinay's band, shot and killed Lt. Jacob Almy at the San Carlos agency.

9. Lt. Charles H. Watts (1849–1917) of the 5th U.S. Cavalry led the detachment.

10. The agency had been moved to San Carlos before Almy's death.

11. This occurred at the end of January 1874.

12. Captain Randall led this expedition, which grew to include White Mountain scouts and elements of six troops of the 5th Cavalry. Archie McIntosh served as guide.

13. One group of fifty renegades raided as far north as Tempe, where they tortured and killed a family of six.

14. A reference to Captain Randall.

15. March 7, 1874.

16. The *Chronological List* shows hostile losses to have been twelve killed and twenty-five captured; there were no federal losses.

17. Many of the bands had in fact returned to the agency and thrown themselves on the mercy of General Crook. Said General Crook of his terms: "I refused to accept their surrender, but told them I could not harm them, as they had thrown themselves on my mercy, but I would drive them all back into the mountains, where I could kill them all, that they had lied to me once, and I didn't know but what they were lying to me now. They begged to be allowed to remain, making all kinds of promises for the future. I finally compromised by letting them stay, provided they would bring in the heads of certain of the chiefs who were ringleaders, which they agreed to." Schmitt, *Crook Autobiography*, 181.

Charles King: On Campaign in Arizona

1. Charles King (1844–1933) graduated from the West Point Class of 1868. During the Civil War, the sixteen-year-old King enlisted as a volunteer mounted orderly to his father, Brig. Gen. Rufus King, formerly publisher of the *Milwaukee Sentinel*. The younger King declined a brevet promotion for the fight at Diamond Butte, Arizona. After recovering from his wound at Sunset Pass, King participated with Crook's command in the Sioux War of 1876. Retired for disability in June 1879, King returned to Milwaukee and began writing of his Indian War experiences for the *Milwaukee Sentinel*. His articles on the Sioux War formed the basis of his highly regarded book *Campaigning with Crook* (New York: Harper and Brothers, 1890). King became a prolific writer of war novels and pursued a second military career as adjutant general of the Wisconsin National Guard and a brigadier general of volunteers during the War with Spain.

2. A reference to Camp Verde, located on the east bank of the Verde River, one mile north of its juncture with Beaver Creek.

3. Capt. John M. Hamilton (1839–98), later killed at Santiago, Cuba, during the Spanish-American War.

4. Charles H. Heyl (1849–1926) of the 23rd U.S. Infantry.

5. 1st. Sgt. Rudolf Stauffer and Cpl. (not Sgt.) Leonard Winser. Stauffer had won the Medal of Honor for service during the 1872 Tonto Basin campaign.

6. A reference to skirmishes on the summit of Stauffer's Butte on May 24 and at Black Mesa on June 3, 1874. Indian losses in the two engagements totaled nineteen killed.

7. The Apache-Mojaves and Apache-Yumas were not separate tribes, as many contemporaneous writers assume, nor were they Apaches, but rather were bands of the Yavapais differentiated on the basis of habitual abode. The Yavapais themselves recognized three groups among their tribe: the Western, Northeastern, and Southeastern, all of whom spoke a Yuman language of similar dialect, with but slight differences in vocabulary. The term Apache-Mojave may be applied to the Northeastern and Southeastern Yavapais; the term Apache-Yuma to the Western Yavapais. William T. Corbusier, *Verde to San Carlos* (Tucson: Dale Stuart King, 1968), 13–14.

8. Mogollon Mountains.

9. Black Mesa.

10. Cpl. Alexander Garner of K Troop.

11. Capt. (and Bvt. Col.) Julius W. Mason (1835–82) of the 5th U.S. Cavalry.

12. George O. Eaton (1848–1930) of the 5th U.S. Cavalry.

13. Named for Brig. Gen. George Stoneman.

14. Known as "The Rim of the [Tonto] Basin," or "The Mogollon Rim," it stretched east from Camp Verde to intersect the road from Holbrook to Camp Apache.

15. Sgt. Bernard Taylor and Pvt. Frank Biffar, both of Troop A, 5th Cavalry.

16. More commonly known as Chavez Pass, located some fourteen miles from Sunset Pass.

17. King was the only member of his detachment struck in the engagement at Sunset Pass; one hostile Indian was killed. King had been struck in the right arm while scouting ahead with Sergeant Taylor. But for Taylor, who carried him down the mountain, and Lieutenant Eaton, who raced up with the command to scatter the attackers, King would have been killed. As it was, he permanently lost much of the use of his right arm. Sadly, Sergeant Taylor died of lung congestion on April 15, 1875, before being presented the Medal of Honor his conduct at Sunset Pass had earned him.

L. Y. Loring: Report on [the] Coyotero Apaches

1. Leonard Y. Loring (1844–1903) was commissioned in 1867 and served in the Arizona Territory from 1874 to 1877. He had been at Camp Apache six months when he wrote his report on the White Mountain Apaches.
2. Over time a confusing multiplicity of names has been applied to the groups and bands of the Western and Chiricahua Apaches. The five groups and twenty bands that constituted the Western Apache division often were collectively labeled Coyoteros. During the final decades of the nineteenth century the name was commonly given to those of the White Mountain group who lived south of the Black River. The White Mountain Group more correctly is divided into two bands, the Eastern and Western White Mountain Apaches, whose prereservation lands stretched from the White to the Pinaleno Mountains. It was the Eastern White Mountain band that had congregated around Camp Apache at the time Loring wrote; the Western White Mountain band had removed to Dewey Flats, along the Gila River. For a discussion of Western Apache groups and bands, see Grenville Goodwin, *The Social Organization of the Western Apache* (Chicago: University of Chicago Press, 1942), 1–62.
3. Esh-kel-dah-silah (fl. c. 1850–75), among the most respected chiefs in White Mountain Apache history, was generally well disposed toward Americans.
4. Polone was killed in an intratribal fight in 1880.
5. The chief and medicine man whose teachings were to spark the Cibicue Creek affair in 1881.

E. C. Kemble: Victorio and His Young Men

1. E. C. Kemble was an inspector with the Bureau of Indian Affairs.
2. An Eastern Chiricahua, Victorio (c. 1825–80) was among the greatest of Apache warrior chiefs.
3. The reservation at Tularosa, New Mexico, was abandoned in July 1874.
4. Kemble here is referring to himself.
5. The agent was John M. Shaw of Socorro, New Mexico.
6. In his report, Hatch said they reached Ojo Caliente on April 20.
7. Apparently, family members of Chiricahua raiders belonging to the bands of Skinya and Pionsenay who had murdered the proprietor of a stagecoach station, M. N. Rogers, and his assistant, A. O. Spence, near the Chiricahua reservation in early April. Most of the raiders themselves took up refuge in the Dragoon Mountains.
8. A probable reference to an incident in April 1856, when a military detachment under Bvt. Lt. Col. Daniel T. Chandler fired upon a group of peaceful Mimbres who had assembled to meet with their agent.
9. Agent Shaw was permitted to submit his resignation, which he did on June 19, 1876.

PART THREE: UPRISINGS AND UNREST, 1878–83

Charles B. Gatewood: Campaigning against Victorio in 1879

1. Charles B. Gatewood (1853–96) of the 6th U.S. Cavalry. From the time of his arrival in Arizona in February 1878 until January 1885, he was almost continuously in the field against hostile Apaches or managing troublesome reservation bands. Having played an instrumental part in the final surrender of Geronimo, Gatewood served from October 1886 to September 1890 as an aide to Gen. Nelson A. Miles. He died of cancer before his promotion to captain.

2. Nana (c. 1800–96) was an important Mimbres leader but neither a chief nor a sub-chief. He escaped death with Victorio at Tres Castillos in Mexico because his band was on a raid. In 1881 the elderly Nana led a handful of warriors on one of the most successful of all Apache raids, covering more than one thousand miles in southwestern New Mexico and southern Arizona, fighting a dozen skirmishes with American troops, and capturing hundreds of horses and mules, before vanishing into the Sierra Madre.

3. Gatewood never saw Victorio in person, and his description of the chief varies sharply with that of agents, army officers, and others who knew him at the time. They all agreed he was yet vigorous, able, and the true chief of the Mimbres. Gatewood may have mistaken Victorio for Nana, who was aged, though still vigorous. Dan L. Thrapp, *Victorio and the Mimbres Apaches* (Norman: University of Oklahoma Press, 1974), 364n.

4. Victorio had not yet, as many officers then supposed, crossed into Mexico.

5. At Animas Creek, September 18, 1879.

6. Augustus P. Blocksom (1854–1931) of the 6th U.S. Cavalry. Wounded at San Juan Hill in the Spanish-American War, he retired a brigadier general in 1918.

7. Albert P. Morrow (1842–1911) ended his career as colonel of the 3rd U.S. Cavalry in 1891.

8. Morrow entered the field with a force numbering 6 officers, 36 scouts, and 191 enlisted men.

9. On September 29, 1879.

10. W. T. Jones and six members of his Mesilla volunteers were ambushed near Lloyd's ranch, three miles southwest of abandoned Fort Cummings, on October 13, 1879.

11. George A. Purington (1838–96).

12. Byron Dawson, then a first lieutenant.

13. Charles H. Campbell (1845–1915) was allowed to resign in 1881 in lieu of standing court-martial on charges arising from drunkenness on duty.

14. On October 27, 1879.

15. Robert T. Emmet, Matthias W. Day, Leighton Finley, and Charles Schaeffer.

John Conline: The Campaign of 1880 against Victorio

1. John Conline (1844–1916) of the West Point Class of 1870 was breveted captain for gallantry during the fight at Hembrillo Canyon on April 7, 1880. Retired for disability as a major in 1891, he served as police commissioner of Detroit from 1896 to 1900.

2. Curwen B. McLellan (1829–98) of the 10th U.S. Cavalry.

3. Seven troopers later died of their wounds.

William R. Price: A Scout among the Havasupai and Hualapais Indians

1. William R. Price (1838–1881) of the 8th U.S. Cavalry. A highly regarded cavalry officer who had won brevets to the grade of brigadier general of volunteers during the Civil War, Price had been serving in Arizona since 1867, when he played a lead role in ending the Hualapais War. At the time of the scout of which he here reports, Price was slowly dying of diabetes. Not long after the scout, he was sent east on sick leave, and he died at his sister's home in Germantown, Pennsylvania, on December 30, 1881.

2. Coues (1842–99) resigned from the army in November 1881 and went on to become a prominent ornithologist and historian.

3. About twenty-five miles northwest of Tucson.

4. Also known as Kerlin's Wells.

5. F. C. Kerlin.
6. Cataract Canyon begins about twenty miles northeast of Williams, Arizona, and runs northwest into the Grand Canyon.
7. Located on the southern extreme of the Hualapai reservation.
8. Any of several types of large American salamanders.
9. Hualapai Charley.
10. Under the upper rim of the Grand Canyon.
11. Pine nuts also were a staple of the Hualapai diet, which made Pine Springs, with its abundant growth of yellow pine, an attractive element of the proposed reservation.
12. Price's recommendations were accepted and in 1883 became the basis for the Hualapai reservation.
13. A stage station on the Fort Mohave–Prescott road.

John F. Finerty: On Campaign after Cibicue Creek

1. The *Chicago Times* sent veteran war correspondent John F. Finerty (1846–1908) to Arizona to get at the truth of the Cibicue Creek affair and to cover what was expected to be a brutal retaliatory campaign. Finerty had earned the respect of General Crook and his officers for his conduct under fire during the Battle of the Rosebud in the 1876 Sioux campaign. From that assignment came his highly regarded book, *Warpath and Bivouac*.
2. Finerty's dispatches appeared in the *Chicago Times* out of chronological order; I have reordered them in their proper sequence. The correct first installment, given below, appeared on September 18, 1881, as "Arid Arizona."
3. The dispatches that follow appeared in the October 4, 1881, issue of the *Chicago Times* as part of an article entitled "Fierce Foes."
4. A probable reference to Rock House Canyon.
5. Sanchez assumed the chieftainship of Diablo's band of Cibicue Apaches after the latter was killed in an intratribal fight.
6. The murders occurred on August 31, 1881.
7. Peter Moran joined Bourke as field illustrator for the captain's ethnological work among the Hopi Indians.
8. The slain man was Johnny Cowden, an elderly employee of ranch owner John Phipps.
9. The dispatch that follows appeared in the September 20, 1881, issue of the *Chicago Times* as "Taking the Trail."
10. "Today" being September 18, 1881.
11. Four civilians and three soldiers were killed, all on August 31, 1881.
12. Carr was mistaken. As Thomas Cruse observed, Christianity had a confused but indelible influence on the mystic Noch-ay-del-klinne's thinking. Sent to Santa Fe as a young man to attend school, he "absorbed but hardly understood the elements of the Christian religion," said Cruse. "He was particularly impressed by the story of the Resurrection." Thomas Cruse, *Apache Days and After* (Caldwell, ID: Caxton, 1941), 93–94.
13. John Y. Blake (c. 1856–1907), later commander of the Irish Brigade during the Boer War.
14. Both of Company G, 6th U.S. Cavalry.
15. The dispatches that follow appeared in the October 4, 1881, *Chicago Times* article "Fierce Foes."
16. Pvt. William Miller.
17. John Byrnes.
18. Finerty was mistaken; Sanchez had surrendered to Tiffany, asking only that if tried, he be given legal counsel and accorded a fair trial.

19. Louis Craig (1851–1904) of the 6th U.S. Cavalry.
20. Charles G. Gordon (1837–98), who had succeeded to company command upon the death of Captain Hentig at Cibicue Creek.
21. Pvt. John Sullivan of D Troop, 6th U.S. Cavalry.
22. Pvt. J. F. Foran of E Troop, 6th U.S. Cavalry.
23. General Willcox had ordered the arrest of Chiefs George and Bonito on September 23, 1881.
24. A reference to an operation against Victorio in December 1880 by Mexican general Geronimo Trevino that succeeded only in driving the Apaches across the frontier into New Mexico.
25. The next dispatch appeared October 14, 1881, as "Apache Actions."
26. Juh's band of Chiricahuas committed the murders.
27. Apparently a reference to an indecisive brush with Juh's Chiricahuas near Cedar Springs on October 2, 1881.
28. The next dispatch appeared in the October 5, 1881, issue of the *Chicago Times* as "The Red Men's Rising."
29. On October 2, 1881, Juh's band killed six freighters and plundered their wagons near Cedar Springs, then murdered a lone settler on the road from Fort Grant. Later that day they killed four soldiers sent from Fort Grant to repair the telegraph line. Pursuing cavalry battled the Chiricahuas until nightfall.
30. Ranald S. Mackenzie (1840–89), one of the most talented and successful commanders to emerge during the Indian Wars.
31. The next dispatch appeared on October 7, 1881, as part of the article "Wary Warriors."
32. The dispatch that follows appeared on October 11, 1881, as part of the article "Vengeful Vagabonds."
33. James H. Cook (1857–1942), noted cowboy and scout.
34. The next dispatch ran in the October 21, 1881, issue of the *Chicago Times* as "Apache Atrocities."
35. M. G. Samaniego of Tucson.
36. John N. Glass (1853–1892) of the 6th U.S. Cavalry.
37. Point of Mountain was a stage station on the southeastern base of the Galiuro Mountains, a few miles northwest of Willcox.

Thomas Cruse: From Hembrillo Canyon to Chevelon's Fork

1. Thomas Cruse (1857–1943) of the 6th U.S. Cavalry. Cruse was awarded the Medal of Honor for his conduct at Big Dry Wash. He retired a brigadier general in 1918.
2. William Shunk.
3. May H. Stacey (1837–80) of the 12th U.S. Infantry.
4. The three-day fight at Hembrillo Canyon left one officer and seven enlisted men wounded; Indian losses, apart from a dead warrior Cruse saw after the fight, were not known.
5. Lt. Charles W. Taylor of the 9th U.S. Cavalry.
6. In the *Chronological List*, 72, Indian losses are given as ten killed.
7. Benjamin H. Grierson (1826–1911), a citizen soldier who rose to the rank of brigadier general of volunteers during the Civil War. After the war, he commanded the 10th U.S. Cavalry and was a strong advocate of black soldiers. He retired a brigadier general in 1890.
8. Lt. Leighton Finley (1856–94) of the 10th U.S. Cavalry.
9. Sgt. John F. McDonald, Troop E, 6th U.S. Cavalry.
10. George L. Converse (1857–1946) of the 3rd U.S. Cavalry.

11. George H. Morgan (1855–1932) of the 6th U.S. Cavalry.
12. Indian losses are reported in the *Chronological List*, 76, as sixteen killed.
13. A reference to a group of local roughnecks who falsely claimed ownership of horses and ponies the Indians had stolen.

Will C. Barnes: The Apaches' Last Stand in Arizona: The Battle of Big Dry Wash

1. Will C. Barnes (1858–1936) enlisted in the Signal Corps in 1879 and, while serving at Fort Apache, earned the Medal of Honor for climbing a high, hostile-infested ridge near the post to watch for the return of Colonel Carr's Cibicue expedition. After his discharge, Barnes went on to become a prosperous rancher and an inspector for the U.S. Forest Service. He also wrote a number of works about early Arizona.
2. The leader of this band of Cibicue Creek insurgents was Na-ti-o-tish, who had escaped arrest the night before Juh and Naiche broke out, in September 1881.
3. Albert D. Sterling (1835–82).
4. That which follows is Cruse's account of the fight.
5. A rank he attained in 1901.
6. Daniel Conn, a "wisp of a Boston Irishman" with a thick brogue who, after twenty years' service, had landed the normally soft job of ration sergeant. The Apache scouts nicknamed him "Coche Sergeant," or "Hog Sergeant," as pork was a standard field ration. Thrapp, *Al Sieber*, 253–54.
7. John T. Horan, then a corporal.
8. Joseph McLernon.
9. Lt. Col. George W. Schofield of the 6th U.S. Cavalry.
10. Barnes neglected to include among this number Al Sieber's small company of Indian scouts.
11. Tom Horn, *Life of Tom Horn, A Vindication* (Louthan, Co.: N.p., 1904).

William A. Rafferty: Rafferty's Trail

1. William A. Rafferty (1842–1902) of the 6th U S. Cavalry. He saw action at the battles of Santiago and San Juan during the Spanish American War and, as colonel of the 5th U.S. Cavalry, commanded the District of Mayaguez, Puerto Rico.
2. The Chiricahua band of Loco, which had left their subagency near San Carlos reluctantly in early April 1882 under pressure from raiding parties of Chatto, Chihuahua, and Naiche.
3. With Tupper's command as chief of scouts and guide was Al Sieber.
4. Anson Mills.
5. The commands of Rafferty and Tupper climbed five thousand feet in crossing the Peloncillo Mountains along this trail.
6. Francis J. A. Darr (1859–1918) of the 12th U.S. Infantry.
7. The Sierra Enmedio, which scout Tom Horn called "a very rough, small mountain in the middle of the Janos plains." Thrapp, *Sieber*, 229.
8. The fight opened prematurely when Loco's unsuspecting son and three Apache women wandered toward Lieutenant Darr and his concealed scouts, looking for mescal that Loco's band had hidden among the rocks. When they came within twenty-five yards of the scouts, Darr gave the signal to open fire.
9. Lt. Col. George A. Forsyth (1837–1915) had a command, huge by Apache campaigning standards—of some four hundred cavalrymen—most from his own regiment, the 4th U.S. Cavalry, with a few companies of the 6th Cavalry and fifty scouts. Forsyth recorded his exploits in Mexico in an article entitled "An Apache

Raid," *Harper's Weekly* 43 (January 14, 1899): 43–46, which was reprinted in his *Thrilling Days in Army Life* (New York: Harper's, 1900).

10. Col. Lorenzo Garcia, one of Mexico's most successful Indian fighters, and his 6th Mexican Infantry.

Al Sieber: Military and Indians

1. Albert Sieber (1844–1907) was one of the greatest of all frontier army scouts. A German immigrant, he enlisted in the 1st Minnesota Infantry and was badly wounded at Gettysburg. After the war he went west, settling near Prescott, Arizona, as a ranch foreman and manager. When General Crook arrived in the territory in 1871, he signed Sieber on, first as a packer and shortly thereafter as chief of scouts. From 1872 until his wounding during the Apache Kid outbreak in 1887, Sieber participated in nearly every major campaign of the Apache Wars. Thrapp characterized him as "highly intelligent, honest, intrepid, loyal, and worthy of the many encomiums from army officers for whom he had worked." Thrapp, *Encyclopedia*, 3:1307.

2. The article was represented as being a letter from Al Sieber dated Fort McDowell, May 17, 1882, to the Prescott *Weekly Courier*, which was run by his friend John H. Marion (1835–1891). Thrapp believes that Marion either heavily edited or at least assisted Sieber in composing the letter. He nonetheless considers it reliable. Thrapp, *Sieber*, 225.

3. Forsyth had five troops of cavalry with him.

4. The fight began in Doubtful Canyon and concluded in Horseshoe Canyon, by which name it is usually known.

5. A short-lived silver camp that later became a rustlers' retreat.

6. Charles G. Gordon (1837–1898) served as an enlisted member of the 2nd California Cavalry during the Civil War. After the war he was commissioned a second lieutenant in the 6th U.S. Cavalry. He was retired for disability in 1887.

7. It was after 10:00 P.M. at night when Sieber spotted Loco's camp.

8. Some accounts say three women accompanied Loco's son.

9. Timothy A. Touey (1852–1887) of the West Point Class of 1875 served in the Southwest until his death, at age thirty-five, from "exhaustion due to chronic disease."

10. The soldier's name was Goodrich.

11. Thrapp, *Sieber*, 227, identifies the man as Rohner.

12. Of Sieber's critique, Thrapp writes, "Al Sieber's analysis of the campaign, warmly worded as it was, though undeniably authoritative, probably expressed accurately the feeling of many of the bold and fiery frontiersmen." Thrapp, *Sieber*, 242.

Alchisay, et al.: The Apache Story of the Cibicue

1. Bourke's minutes of the meetings were also contained in General Crook's official report of his talks with the reservation Indians. See Bureau of Indian Affairs, Letters Received 1882, No. 19337, National Archives, Washington, D.C.

2. Alchisay (c. 1853–1928), White Mountain Apache chief and scout. He won the Medal of Honor for service in the 1872–73 Tonto Basin campaign. Alchisay later became a prominent stockman and made several trips to Washington, D.C., in his later years, visiting with Presidents Theodore Roosevelt and Warren G. Harding.

3. Agent J. C. Tiffany.

4. Pedro (c. 1835–85), White Mountain Apache chief, two of whose daughters married Corydon E. Cooley. Pedro was a constant friend of the Americans.

5. Gracias Severiano (c. 1841–post-1883) was a Mexican whom the White Mountain Apaches had captured as a child and raised.

6. By most accounts, Indian and white, Charles Hurrle was a disreputable figure. A German immigrant, he came to Arizona as a private in the 6th U.S. Cavalry. How he learned the Apache language is unclear, but upon his discharge in May 1881 he took up with a notorious Apache prostitute named Hannah. Charles Collins considers him a prime instigator of the Cibicue troubles, and Dan Thrapp doubts his proficiency in the Apache language. Collins, *Apache Nightmare: The Battle of Cibicue Creek* (Norman: University of Oklahoma Press, 1999), 227; Thrapp, *Crook and the Sirra Madre*, 20–22.

7. Melville A. Cochran (1836–1904) of the 12th U.S. Infantry.

8. Corydon E. Cooley.

9. The Apache version of how the fight commenced is markedly different from that of the white officers involved, who later testified under oath that the scouts opened fired first, having arrayed themselves in a firing line, such that their volley was clearly premeditated.

10. Another name for the Battle of the Big Dry Wash, or Chevelon's Fork.

11. Bourke does not indicate who spoke these words.

12. Capitan Chiquitito, an Aravaipa chief who lost many of his people in the Camp Grant masssacre but remained friendly to the Americans.

13. Sanchez, a Cibicue Apache chief who had been closely associated with Noch-ay-del-klinne.

14. Nodeski was a friendly chief who remained loyal during the Cibicue unrest and had tried to negotiate the surrender of the hostiles afterward, only to be frightened away by agency police.

15. Literally, "fat son of a whore."

Murat Masterson: General Crook's Return

1. Masterson was the editor of the Prescott *Arizona Democrat*; presumably it was he who interviewed Crook.

2. Charles P. Eagan (1841–1919) was an Irish immigrant who served as chief of subsistence for the Department of Arizona. Crook's predecessor, Brig. Gen. August V. Kautz, was initially taken with Eagan's conversational charm, until he found Eagan's "extreme views and interference with other peoples' business" had made the captain unpopular with his brother officers. In November 1877 a court-martial convicted Eagan of gambling, an activity regulations forbade for a disbursing officer. Eagan's career suffered little, however, and he retired in 1900, a brigadier general and commissary general of subsistence.

James H. Toole: Agent Tiffany Torn to Tatters

1. Philip P. Wilcox.

2. Such was the opinion of the *Star*'s editor, Louis C. Hughes (1842–1915). His praise for the jury's work is worthy of serious consideration when assessing the culpability of Agent Tiffany and his cohorts. A veteran of the Civil War, Hughes was a reformist of sterling credentials. Before coming to Arizona, Hughes had agitated in Pennsylvania for an eight-hour workday. He practiced law in Tucson and established the *Arizona Star* in 1877. Hughes served two terms as district attorney, was elected territorial attorney general, and served one term as governor. Among his reformist activities in Arizona were opposition to gambling and traffic in liquor, and the advocacy of women's suffrage.

John G. Bourke had this to say about the verdict of the grand jury: "A frontier jury never yet has said a word in favor of a red man unless the reasons were fully patent to the ordinary comprehension. The report of a United States grand jury is about as strong a document as is usually to be found in the dusty archives of courts." Bourke, *On the Border with Crook* (New York: Charles Scribners' Sons, 1891), 439–40.

Frederick Lloyd: A Profile of the San Carlos Agency

1. Despite his self-professed limitations, Doctor Lloyd produced what one bibliographer correctly termed an "exceedingly interesting (although sometimes erroneous) report." Colin Storm, *A Catalogue of the Everett D. Graff Collection of Western Americana* (Chicago: University of Chicago Press, 1968), 638.

   Where Lloyd generally erred was in his categorization of the various Apache groups and bands, mistakes common both then and now. Indeed, as explained in my introduction, there yet is no consensus as to precisely which Apache bands constituted a given group or nation. It is generally accepted, however, that the White Mountain and Coyotero were bands of the San Carlos group, and that the Tontos constituted two distinct groups: the Northern and Southern Tontos. All the "tribes" then at the San Carlos agency, however, shared characteristics commonly associated with the Western Apache.

2. The Apaches also buried their dead in the ground.

3. Lloyd seems to have overstated the prevalence of plural marriages; most other observers suggested the practice was confined largely to wealthy chiefs or subchiefs. Also, women were permitted to divorce with practically the same ease as men.

Anton Mazzanovich: Life in Arizona Army Posts during the 1880's

1. Anton Mazzanovich (1860–1934) emigrated from Austria in 1868. Joining the army at nine years of age in 1870, he was assigned to the band of the 21st U.S. Infantry and discharged in 1873. He enlisted again in 1881 and was assigned to Troop M of the 6th U.S. Cavalry. In later life Mazzanovich acted in Hollywood Westerns and worked on Broadway stage productions.

2. Mazzanovich is referring to Frank P. Cahill, the army blacksmith at Fort Grant, whom Billy the Kid killed in August 1877.

3. George A. Gordon (1833–78) of the West Point Class of 1854 emerged from the Civil War a brevet lieutenant colonel of volunteers. He was the post commander of Camp Grant at the time of which Mazzanovich writes.

4. Headquarters ranch for the Norton and Stewart Cattle Company, about sixteen miles from Camp Grant on the road to Camp Thomas.

5. Anton Mazzanovich, *Trailing Geronimo* (Los Angeles: Stanley J. Wilson, 1926).

6. Joseph B. Girard (1846–1918) served intermittently as a field and post surgeon in Arizona between 1872 and 1888. He retired a colonel in 1910.

7. Mazzanovich was honorably discharged on July 10, 1882, for disability.

8. Thomas H. Barry (1855–1919) of the West Point Class of 1877.

PART FOUR: THE SIERRA MADRE CAMPAIGN AND AFTER, 1883–85

John G. Bourke: With Crook in the Sierra Madre

1. The account of the Sierra Madre campaign Bourke took down in his diary formed the basis of three articles in *Outing* magazine (August–October 1885). These were reprinted as *An Apache Campaign in the Sierra Madre* (New York: Charles Scribner's Sons, 1886). The occasional digressions into the syntax and grammar of the Apache language that Bourke made in his diary have been omitted from the text presented here, as have his periodic discussions of clan affiliations of individual Apaches.

2. James Biddle (1832–1910) of the 6th U.S. Cavalry.
3. Although assigned to the expedition as General Crook's orderly, Harmer spent a good deal of his time assisting Bourke in his field studies. An accomplished artist, Harmer drew the illustrations for Bourke's first book, *The Snake Dance of the Moquis of Arizona.*
4. Sacaton is a coarse perennial grass used for making hay in alkaline regions.
5. Gustave J. Fieberger (1858–1939) of the Corps of Army Engineers.
6. A reference to Pah-na-yo-tishn (c. 1853–1933), a Cibicue Apache better known to the army as "Peaches."
7. Acting Assistant Surgeon George Andrews.
8. Adna R. Chaffee (1842–1914) of the 6th U.S. Cavalry. Beginning his military career as an enlisted man in the Civil War, Chaffee rose to become a lieutenant general and chief of staff of the U.S. Army in 1904.
9. A. Franklin Randall (1854–1916) was a newspaperman and photographer. He accompanied General Crook's Sierra Madre expedition as a correspondent for the El Paso *Times.* Randall photographed widely in California and northern Mexico; an album of his work is at the Huntington Library and Art Gallery, San Marino, California.
10. The chief packer of one of Crook's pack trains.
11. Col. (not Gen.) Lorenzo Garcia of the Mexican Army.
12. They further protested that Crook could not hope to whip the Chiricahuas so long as Randall retained the bird; Crook ordered it released at once. Bourke, *Apache Campaign,* 74.
13. A metate is a large bowl commonly used to grind corn.
14. Juh (c. 1825–83) was a noted war leader of the Chiricahuas.
15. Geronimo (c. 1823–1909) was not a chief, but rather a medicine man and war leader of the Bedonkohe band of Chiricahuas.
16. Emmet Crawford (1844–85) of the 3rd U.S. Cavalry was one of Crook's most trusted and competent officers.
17. The fight in question took place on April 25. It had begun when Col. Lorenzo Garcia, with eighty-six federal troops and fifty guardsmen, pursued a band of Chiricahuas into the Sierra Madre. Locating the hostiles after a five-day search, Garcia split his command into two columns and attacked. Garcia falsely claimed to have routed the Apaches; he lost four dead and seven wounded in the encounter.
18. Irrigation ditches.
19. Bonito was a White Mountain Apache chief.
20. Hamilton C. McComas (1830–83) was a locally prominent attorney and chairman of the board of commissioners of Grant County, New Mexico. On March 28, 1883, he and his wife were murdered by Chiricahua raiders as they rode their buckboard from Silver City to Leitendorf Springs. The Apaches abducted five-year-old Charlie McComas, whose fate was never certainly ascertained.
21. Bourke later noted in his journal that the photo album did not belong to the McComas family.
22. Chatto (1854–1934) was a Chiricahua war leader who later became a loyal scout.
23. Chihuahua (1822–1901), a Chiricahua subchief.
24. A swamp or marsh.
25. Neither Loco nor his families had gone north. However, twenty members of Loco's family had returned to San Carlos before Crook reached the Sierra Madre.
26. A reference to General Crook.
27. On May 24, 1883, Crook and his colorful column of soldiers, scouts, packers, and surrendered Chiricahuas began the return march to the United States, effectively ending the Sierra Madre campaign.

U. S. Grant, et al.: Where is Crook?

1. When General Crook vanished into the Sierra Madre, wild speculation followed him. Frontier newspapers spread rumors of his death at the hands of Chiricahuas. Headlines bewailed a massacre as bloody and certain as the Little Big Horn, some speculating that Crook's Apache scouts had betrayed him. As the following articles show, neither the American nor the Mexican high command were any better informed.
2. Brig. Gen. Ramon Raguero, Mexican Army commander in Chihuahua (the El Paso *Times* correspondent misspelled his name as Regaro).
3. Chihuahua was the true leader of the raiding party described here.
4. False rumors spread by the Mexican Army in Sonora and Chihuahua.

William Forsyth: A Diary of the Sierra Madre Campaign

1. Dan Thrapp in *The Conquest of Apacheria*, 283, speculates that the author of the diary, which appeared anonymously in the Tucson *Arizona Daily Star*, was Lieutenant Forsyth (1856–1933) of the 6th U.S. Cavalry; I find no cause to dispute Thrapp's surmise.

George Crook: Apache Affairs: An Interview with General George Crook

1. General Crook was interviewed on July 7, 1883, in Washington D.C. by a correspondent of the New York *Herald*. Crook had been ordered to the capital to confer with the commissioner of Indian affairs and the secretaries of war and the interior as to the management and disposition of the Apaches humbled in the Sierra Madre campaign. The conference yielded a memorandum giving Crook the authority over reservation Indians he had long sought. Captured Apaches were to be placed on the San Carlos reservation under the exclusive control of the War Department, to be fed, cared for, and policed by that department.

   Reticent in the company of his troops and fellow officers, Crook warmed in the presence of journalists, knowing the importance of a good press. His interview with the *Herald* gave Crook his first opportunity to explain publicly how he intended to use his new authority over the Apaches and to discuss the Sierra Madre expedition.
2. Oakland, Maryland, the home of his wife's family.

Charles P. Elliott: An Indian Reservation under General George Crook

1. Charles P. Elliott (1860–1943) of the West Point Class of 1882. In 1899 he took part in an exploring expedition in Alaska and later served as superintendent of construction at West Point. Elliott retired a major in 1918.
2. As it originally appeared in *Military Affairs*, Elliott's article included a lengthy introduction by Brig. Gen. Charles D. Roberts. Roberts's introduction simply provided an overview of Apache campaigns up to 1884; it is omitted here. A footnote to the article said that Elliott's manuscript bore internal evidence of having been written about 1901.
3. Fort Apache was sixty miles north of San Carlos.
4. Hampton M. Roach (1857–1923) had been promoted from the ranks.
5. Stewart Mott (1862–87) of the 10th Cavalry, a graduate of the West Point Class of 1886. He was stabbed repeatedly on March 10, 1887, by the son of an Apache whom he had placed in the guardhouse, and died the following day.

G. Gordon Adam: Resolution Adopted at Meeting of Residents of Cochise County, Arizona regarding Outbreak of Indians from San Carlos Reservation

1. A former New York City assistant defense attorney, William Herring (d. 1912) was the manager of the Neptune Mining Company near Hereford, Arizona. He also was the Earp brothers' attorney before being named attorney general of the territory.
2. Newspaperman Charles D. Reppy (1846–1914?) was publisher of the *Tombstone Epitaph* and later a member of the territorial legislature.
3. William H. Stilwell was district court judge, First Judicial District, Cochise County.
4. John V. Vickers (d. 1912) was president of the huge Chiricahua Cattle Company and, as such, one of the richest men in Cochise County.

PART FIVE: CHASING GERONIMO, 1885–86

Charles P. Elliot: The Geronimo Campaign, 1885–1886

1. Francis C. Pierce of the 1st U.S. Infantry.
2. Mangus (1846–1901), a Mimbres Apache, was the son of Mangas Coloradas and the brother-in-law of Cochise.
3. Robert D. "Rosie" Walsh (1860–1928) of the 4th U.S. Cavalry, a brigadier general during the First World War.
4. The affair at Guadalupe Canyon occurred on June 8, 1885.
5. The action occurred on June 23, 1885. According to the *Chronological List*, one hostile was killed and fifteen captured; none were reported wounded.
6. Lt. Guy E. Huse (1852–93) resigned his commission in September 1886 to avoid a court-martial on charges of absence without leave and indebtedness.
7. Samuel L. Faison (1860–1940) went on to an illustrious career, gaining fame as a brigadier general in the First World War.
8. The engagement occurred on August 7, 1885. Five hostile Indians were killed and fifteen captured; no members of Wirt's command were lost. *Chronological List*, 77.
9. John W. Martin (1850–1903), whom General Crook called "an exceedingly energetic and deserving officer," served intermittently in Arizona until February 1887, when ill health compelled his early retirement.
10. Charles D. Viele (1841–1916) served in Arizona until 1889. He commanded the 1st U.S. Cavalry at the Battle of San Juan in the Spanish American War and rose to brigadier general on the retired list.

Henry W. Daly: The Geronimo Campaign

1. Henry W. Daly (1850–1931) was born in Ireland but made his way to the American West in 1865, at the age of fifteen. He became a civilian packer for the army in the early 1880s. After the Geronimo campaign he went north, packing for the army during the Wounded Knee operation. He became the first chief packer of the Quartermaster Department, served ably in the Spanish-American War, wrote numerous manuals on pack transportation, and taught the subject at West Point. He retired a major in 1920.

  Daly wrote several versions of his experiences during the Geronimo campaign. The first, and by far the fullest, entitled "The Geronimo Campaign," appeared in the July and October 1908 issues of the *Journal of the United States Cavalry Association* (*JUSCA*). These articles were reprinted in the *Arizona Historical Review* in 1930. In an article for the *American Legion Monthly* in August 1928, entitled

"Scouts Good and Bad," Daly related his belief that the Apache scout Dutchy, rather than Mexicans, had murdered Captain Crawford. A third rendition of Daly's experiences on the campaign, entitled "The Capture of Geronimo," appeared posthumously in the December 1933 issue of *Winners of the West*.

I have supplemented Daly's *JUSCA* articles with excerpts from "Scouts Good and Bad" and "The Capture of Geronimo" to present the fullest possible rendition of Daly's experiences.

2. Geronimo was then sixty years old.
3. One scout was wounded in the fray. The jumped rancheria belonged to Chihuahua.
4. Daly is mistaken; Nana was not captured in this encounter.
5. Otho Budd (1841–1928).
6. Mickey Free also accompanied them.
7. Elliott himself said he had only eight scouts.
8. Daly is the only participant in the expedition to have claimed that Crawford's command crossed the Sierra Madre. In view of Britton Davis's categorical assertions to the contrary, Thrapp dismisses Daly's account. Davis, *Truth about Geronimo*, 183–88; Thrapp, *Sieber*, 309. On the other hand, Davis was not then with the main body, nor did he ever rejoin it, so he may be mistaken.
9. The account that follows of Crawford and Daly effecting the release of Elliott would seem to be fiction, as neither Davis nor Elliott mentions Crawford being anywhere near them at the time the Mexicans released Elliott and his scouts. Thrapp also discounts Daly's version. Thrapp, *Sieber*, 309.
10. A clash between the 6th Mexican Infantry of Col. Lorenzo Garcia and Loco's band in May 1882.
11. William L. Carpenter (1844–98) of the 9th U.S. Infantry, a first lieutenant at the time of which Daly wrote.
12. Apparently Daly had cut the trail of a party of twenty Chiricahuas who had recrossed the international border to do some raiding in Arizona and New Mexico. Thrapp, *Conquest of Apacheria*, 332.
13. Troop G, commanded by Capt. William A. Thompson (1844–1908).
14. Thrapp doubts Daly's implication that Crook relieved Davis and Sieber after their interview with him, "because the *emeute* was in no way Davis's fault, as Crook would have discovered, and Sieber was retained as chief of scouts in the field for several more months." Thrapp, *Sieber*, 312–13.
15. Frank P. Bennett (1852–post-1925) was a well-respected scout who began his frontier service in the Indian Territory in the early 1870s.
16. Mexican casualties included the officer in command, Maj. Mauricio Corredor, 1st Lt. Juan de la Cruz, and two privates killed.
17. Maus marched into the Mexican camp on January 12, the morning after the skirmish in which Crawford was mortally wounded.
18. January 12, 1886.
19. Literally, "bad country."
20. Tribollett eventually met a deserved end. Arrested near Fronteras several years later for planning a stage holdup, he was arrested and then shot "while trying to escape."
21. Charles M. Strauss.
22. As previously noted, the leader of the raid was not Chihuahua but his brother.
23. Here Daly is referring to the presence of Ka-ya-ten-nae and Alchisay, whom Crook had sent into the enemy camp to split up the hostile factions and induce Nachez and Chihuahua to surrender; Crook had little hope from the start that Geronimo would give up.
24. On April 27, 1886, Naiche and Geronimo led a raid across the border into the Santa Cruz Valley of southernmost Arizona.

25. Daly is incorrect as to the date; Geronimo bolted on the night of March 29, 1886.
26. In his diary of the campaign, Leonard Wood called the man William Brown. Jack C. Lane, editor, *Chasing Geronimo, The Journal of Leonard Wood, May–September 1886* (Albuquerque: University of New Mexico Press, 1970): 26.
27. Colville P. Terrett (1852–1913) arrived on May 29, after Henry Johnson, Jr. (1856–86), was dismissed from the command for drunkenness. Johnson resigned his commission on July 2, probably to avoid a court-martial, and died a month later.
28. Wood says thirty.
29. This fight occurred on May 5, 1886.
30. Two men—Hatfield's blacksmith and cook—were killed, and two sergeants wounded.
31. John A. Dapray.
32. Miles and Dapray arrived by train on June 7.
33. This conference presumably occurred in late July.
34. Naiche was wounded in this fight.
35. Lawton reached Fronteras on August 22, by Wood's account, in order to prod Gatewood, who was seriously ill, out of town to find Geronimo. Lawton himself first spoke with Geronimo on August 27. Lane, *Chasing Geronimo*, 99–104.
36. Dutchy never made it to Oklahoma, being killed in 1892 at Mount Vernon Barracks, Alabama.

Britton Davis: The Difficulties of Indian Warfare

1. In *The Truth about Geronimo* (New Haven: Yale University Press, 1929), Davis spells his name as Nadiskay and identifies him as a Coyotero malcontent married to a Chiricahua.
2. May 14, 1885.
3. Zele was a Chiricahua subchief who was satisfied with reservation life and who refused to break out with Geronimo. Zele also had opposed Ka-ya-ten-nae during that Indian's renegade days.

W. B. Jett: Engagement in Guadalupe Canyon

1. Jett's recollection of dates is faulty, because the engagement at Guadalupe Canyon occurred on June 8, 1885.
2. Doctor George Andrews, post surgeon at Fort Huachucua.
3. The sergeant's name was Munich.
4. The attackers consisted of some twenty-five to thirty warriors of Chihuahua's band of Chiricahuas. Besides killing three cavalrymen, they destroyed three wagonloads of supplies and made off with several thousand rounds of ammunition.

Harry R. Wright: In the Days of Geronimo

1. Harry R. Wright of the 4th U.S. Cavalry was detailed as a scout on Capt. Emmet Crawford's expedition against the Chiricahua in the summer of 1885. His immediate commander was Lt. Charles P. Elliott.
2. Allen Smith (1849–1927) was a captain at the time of which Wright wrote; he retired a brigadier general in 1905 after seeing action in the Philippines.

Michael M. Rice: Across Apache Land

1. Part of a squadron under Maj. Frederick Van Vliet, formed of Troops D, E, H, and K of the 10th U.S. Cavalry and sent out from Fort Grant in search of the hostiles.
2. Crook informed Sheridan of the breakout of Naiche and Geronimo from the San Carlos reservation by telegram on May 19, 1885, while Sheridan's train was en route east. Crook had not reported the breakout earlier for lack of "definite infor-

mation." Crook to Sheridan, May 19, 1885, George Crook Letter Book, Rutherford B. Hayes Presidential Center, Fremont, Ohio.

3. George Hearst (1820–91), senator from California and the father of William Randolph Hearst.

4. Abram E. Wood (c. 1845–94) of the West Point Class of 1872.

5. For a very different account of Jett's actions, see his "Engagement in Guadalupe Canyon," also in part 5 of this volume.

Robert Hanna: With Crawford in Mexico

1. Robert Hanna (1848–1908) of the 6th U.S. Cavalry graduated with the West Point Class of 1872. He saw extensive service in Arizona, first with the 6th Cavalry and later as a commander of Indian scouts. Promoted to captain in 1888, he participated in the Pine Ridge campaign in the Dakotas in 1890–91. Hanna retired because of disability on February 24, 1891.

William E. Shipp: Captain Crawford's Last Expedition

1. William E. Shipp (1861–98) of the 10th U.S. Cavalry graduated with the West Point Class of 1883. He fell in the charge up San Juan Hill on July 1, 1898.

James S. Pettit: Apache Campaign Notes—1886

1. James S. Pettit (1856–1906) of the 1st U.S. Infantry commanded a supply camp at Lang's Ranch, Arizona, from June 1885 until August 1886, when his regiment left Arizona. He taught military science at West Point and at Yale University; he also served as colonel of the 4th U.S. Volunteer Infantry during the Spanish-American War.

2. The sketch by Pettit that appeared with the original article showed a view west from the San Bernardino River toward Cañon de los Embudos.

3. A probable reference to works of John G. Bourke.

Nelson A. Miles: On the Trail of Geronimo

1. Nelson A. Miles (1839–1925), a volunteer officer who was four times wounded during the Civil War and emerged from the conflict a major general of volunteers. Appointed colonel of the 5th U.S. Infantry in 1869, he saw service in the Red River War of 1874 and captured Chief Joseph of the Nez Perce in 1877. An unpleasant self-promoter of inordinate ambition, Miles became commander in chief of the army in 1895.

   As it appeared in *Cosmopolitan*, Miles's article contained an account of both the Geronimo campaign and the chase of the Nez Perce; only that portion pertaining to Geronimo is reproduced here.

2. A skirmish between Troop D, 4th U.S. Cavalry, and hostile Chiricahuas on May 15, 1886, in the Pinto Mountains of Mexico. Two enlisted men were killed and two wounded in the affair; oddly, given Miles's comment about the wounded renegade, the *Chronological List*, 78, shows no Indian casualties in the encounter.

3. James F. Wade (1843–1921) commanded the post of Fort Huachuca until his promotion to colonel of the 5th U.S. Cavalry in April 1887. As a major general in the Regular army, he commanded the Division of the Philippines in 1903.

Harry C. Benson: The Geronimo Campaign

1. Harry C. Benson (1857–1924) of the 4th U.S. Cavalry, a Phi Beta Kappa graduate of Kenyon College. He taught mathematics at the U.S. Military Academy from 1887 to 1891 and in 1908 became superintendent of Yosemite National Park.

   Benson's article appeared as a letter to the editor of *Army and Navy Journal*, dated May 17, 1909, from Fort Yellowstone, Wyoming. He did not write from memory, but consulted a diary he had kept during the campaign.

2. William N. Tisdall (1834–99) of the 1st U.S. Infantry.

3. In General Field Order No. 12, dated October 7, 1886, General Miles said, "After a most rigorous campaign of three months, in which [the Apaches] had been pursued more than 2,000 miles, an opportunity occurred for Lieutenant W. E. Wilder, Fourth Cavalry, then with a command near Fronteras, Mexico, to notify them to surrender."

4. Of Wood's service during the campaign, General Miles, in General Field Order No. 12, said, "He not only fulfilled the duties of his profession, in his skillful attention to disabled officers and soldiers, but at times performed satisfactorily the duties of a line officer, and during the whole extraordinary march by his example of physical endurance greatly encouraged others." In the same document, Miles also noted that "Benson's ride of ninety miles in nineteen hours and Dr. Wood's skill and remarkable marches with a detachment of infantry are worthy of mention." Lane, *Chasing Geronimo*, 29, 124.

William W. Neifert: Trailing Geronimo by Heliograph

1. During the Geronimo campaign, William W. Neifert served as a private in the fledgling Army Signal Service; at the time he wrote the article, he was a major in the Signal Reserve and a retired Weather Bureau meteorologist.

2. Edward E. Dravo (1853–1932) served in the Southwest until 1893; later he was acting chief commissary officer for the China Relief Expedition of 1900.

3. Alexander Keyes (1846–1909) rose from the ranks during the Civil War to earn a Regular army commission; he retired a major in 1896.

James R. Caffey: A Theatrical Campaign

1. The *Omaha Bee* was a newspaper friendly to General Crook.

2. I have been unable to identify Caffee's informant. Any number of junior officers—including Gatewood himself, Lieutenant Brown, and Lt. Thomas J. Clay—had ample cause to complain about Miles, who favored Lawton and Leonard Wood above all others.

3. Lawton was known for his mercurial and abusive temperament and tendency toward heavy drinking; indeed, there is good evidence that he was drunk at times during the campaign. Knowing how badly they themselves behaved when drunk, Naiche and Geronimo were understandably loath to put themselves under the protection of one similarly inclined. For more on Lawton's drinking, see Lane, *Chasing Geronimo*, 136–37.

4. Again, I am unable to identify this officer.

John P. Gardner: Escorting Chihuahua's Band to Florida

1. Condensed from an article that originally appeared under the rather misleading title of "Geronimo's Last Stand."

2. Gardner was an enlisted member of Company E, 8th U.S. Infantry, at the time of which he wrote.

3. Egbert B. Savage (1843–1927), who received a direct commission after enlisted service in the Civil War; he retired a lieutenant colonel in 1899.

4. General Crook reported that seventy-seven Chiricahua prisoners (fifteen men, thirty-three women, and twenty-nine children) left Bowie Station at 4:00 P.M. on April 7, 1886. George Crook to P. H. Sheridan, April 7, 1886, Lyman M. V. Kennon Papers, Duke University, Durham, North Carolina. A birth along the way would have brought the total to seventy-eight.

5. A stew made of beef and vegetables.

George Crook: Resume of Operations against Apache Indians, 1882 to 1886

1. Crook said in a footnote to the *Resume* that "there were but three men with Mangus, as was ascertained subsequent to the time of writing of this telegram."
2. Crook guessed correctly; Mangus surrendered in October 1886 and was sent to Fort Marion, Florida.
3. Robert Tribolett.
4. Josanie, or Ulzana (1821–1909), brother of Chihuahua, was a noted raider.
5. James R. Richards (1854–1914).
6. In early November 1885 fewer than a dozen warriors under Josanie slipped across the border from Mexico and created havoc in New Mexico. They slaughtered twenty reservation Apaches who refused to take the warpath with them and a dozen or more white civilians before returning to Mexico in late December. Scores of cavalry troops had tried vainly to catch Josanie's band north of the border.
7. In a footnote to the *Resume*, Crook said, "Mangus and his party, eleven in number, had separated from the others soon after leaving the reservation and had taken no part, so far as can be learned, in any of the outrages committed by the renegades."
8. A reference to the Second Seminole War, 1835–42.

PART SIX: THE END OF THE APACHE WARS

George Crook: The Apache Problem

1. John G. Bourke may have ghostwritten Crook's essay. For a discussion of Bourke's activities at the time, see Joseph C. Porter, *Paper Medicine Man: John Gregory Bourke and His American West* (Norman: University of Oklahoma Press, 1986), 208–9.
2. The leader of this small band of Chiricahuas was Josanie.
3. The slain Chiricahua was named Azariquelch.

Robert K. Evans: The Indian Question in Arizona

1. Robert K. Evans (1852–1926) graduated with the West Point Class of 1875. As an officer in the 12th U.S. Infantry, he took part in the Nez Perce expedition of 1877 and the Bannock campaign of 1878, and was assigned to Arizona in September 1878. He served four years in the territory before being transferred east. His intellectual gifts, quite apparent from his *Atlantic Monthly* article, landed him assignments teaching military law at the Infantry and Cavalry School and as military attaché in Berlin. Evans won a Silver Star for gallantry at the Battle of El Caney in the Spanish-American War. He commanded the Department of the Philippines in 1917 and retired a brigadier general, having been awarded the Distinguished Service Medal for a career of exceptionally meritorious service.
2. An elevation of 4,956 feet near the Chiricahua Mountains, in Apache Pass.
3. Col. Eugene A. Carr.
4. A probable reference to Dutchy, whose father had slain a white man. At the behest of an Indian agent, who told Dutchy it was necessary for the salvation of his and his father's soul, Dutchy supposedly killed his father. As Dutchy was part of Chatto's party during the Sierra Madre campaign, Evans may have confused the two.

Will C. Barnes: In the Apache Country

1. A probable reference to a June 1886 affray in which five renegade scouts and five other Chiricahuas shot and wounded Al Sieber and escaped from the reservation.
2. A reference to the Tres Castillos fight.

3. Better known as Green's Peak, a 10,115-foot elevation named for Col. John Green, 1st U.S. Cavalry, who commanded at Camp Apache in 1873.

4. Barnes evidently is mistaken; no Lieutenant Fisher appears on the rolls of the 5th Cavalry during its Arizona service, nor is there a record of such a fight in the *Chronological List.*

Walter Reed: Geronimo and His Warriors in Captivity

1. Walter Reed (1851–1902) earned his medical degree at the University of Virginia in 1869. Commissioned an assistant surgeon in the army in June 1875, Reed was sent to Arizona, where he served first at Fort Lowell and later at Fort Apache. In 1887 he was assigned to Mount Vernon Barracks, Alabama, where the surrendered Chiricahuas were held prisoners of war. Named curator of the Army Medical Museum in 1893, Reed achieved lasting fame for his yellow fever work in Cuba during the Spanish-American War.

Powhatan H. Clarke: A Hot Trail

1. Powhatan H. Clarke (1862–93) of the 10th U.S. Cavalry won the Medal of Honor for having rescued a wounded trooper during a fight in the Pinito Mountains of Sonora on May 3, 1886. While stationed at Fort Custer, Montana, Clarke drowned when he struck his head on a rock after diving into the flooding Little Big Horn River to rescue a soldier.

2. March 2, 1890.

3. The dead freighter was named Fred Herbert.

4. 1st Lt. Carter P. Johnson.

5. While escorting the Apache Kid and four other renegades to the territorial prison at Yuma on November 2, 1889, Sheriff Glenn Reynolds (1853–89) was shot and killed, and the stage driver, Eugene Middleton, wounded. Deputy William H. Holmes died of a heart attack during the fray. Contrary to Clarke's assertion, the Apache Kid not only did not fire on the white men, but he also prevented his companions from finishing off the wounded Middleton.

6. In May 1890 the surrendered Indians were tried and convicted of murder. El-chus-choose was sentenced to hang, In-dees-doo-day was sentenced to life imprisonment, and Nas-good to fifteen years in prison.

7. On March 15, 1890, members of the local Grand Army of the Republic headquarters tendered Watson and Clarke a written letter of thanks "for the promptness with which they captured the Indians who committed the crime of murder of the freighter." Jess G. Hayes, *Apache Vengeance: The True Story of the Apache Kid* (Albuquerque: University of New Mexico Press, 1954), 136.

James W. Watson: Scouting in Arizona, 1890

1. James W. Watson (1854–1920) of the 10th U.S. Cavalry. He took part in the Santiago campaign of the Spanish-American War. Watson retired a major in 1906 and returned to Cuba to live in 1914.

2. March 8, 1890.

3. March 9, 1890.

4. March 11, 1890.

INDEX

Author's Note: In preparing the index for *Eyewitnesses to the Indian Wars, 1865–1890: The Struggle for Apacheria*, I have deviated a bit from standard indexing practice. As indexed items (names, places, concepts, etc.) generally appear frequently in the same article—sometimes on every page—I have cited only their first appearance in an article.

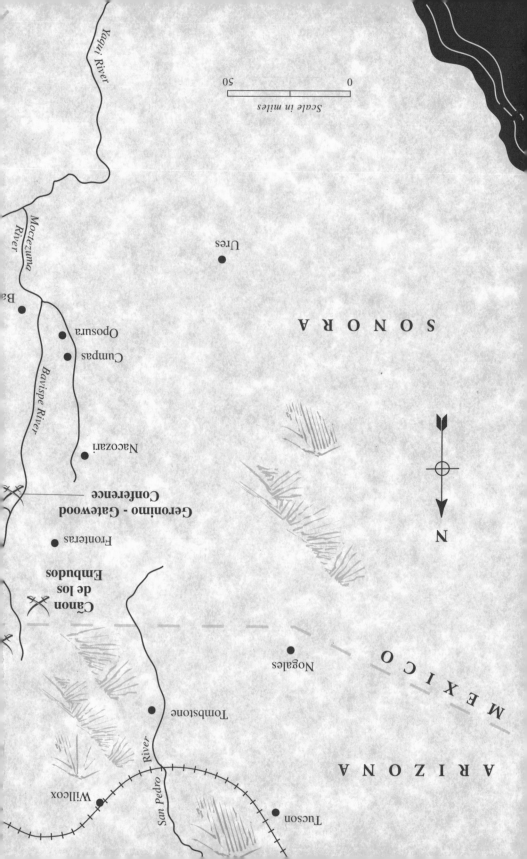